Critical Philosophy of Race

PHILOSOPHY OF RACE

Series Editors
Linda Martín Alcoff, Hunter College and the Graduate Center CUNY
Chike Jeffers, Dalhousie University

Socially Undocumented: Identity and Immigration Justice
Amy Reed-Sandoval

Reconsidering Reparations
Olúfẹ́mi O. Táíwò

Unruly Women: Race, Neocolonialism, and the Hijab
Falguni A. Sheth

Critical Philosophy of Race: Essays
Robert Bernasconi

Critical Philosophy of Race

Essays

ROBERT BERNASCONI

OXFORD
UNIVERSITY PRESS

Oxford University Press is a department of the University of Oxford. It furthers
the University's objective of excellence in research, scholarship, and education
by publishing worldwide. Oxford is a registered trade mark of Oxford University
Press in the UK and certain other countries.

Published in the United States of America by Oxford University Press
198 Madison Avenue, New York, NY 10016, United States of America.

© Oxford University Press 2023

All rights reserved. No part of this publication may be reproduced, stored in
a retrieval system, or transmitted, in any form or by any means, without the
prior permission in writing of Oxford University Press, or as expressly permitted
by law, by license, or under terms agreed with the appropriate reproduction
rights organization. Inquiries concerning reproduction outside the scope of the
above should be sent to the Rights Department, Oxford University Press, at the
address above.

You must not circulate this work in any other form
and you must impose this same condition on any acquirer.

Library of Congress Cataloging-in-Publication Data
Names: Bernasconi, Robert, author.
Title: Critical philosophy of race: essays / Robert Bernasconi.
Description: New York, NY: Oxford University Press, [2023] |
Series: Philosophy of race | Includes bibliographical references and index.
Identifiers: LCCN 2022029994 (print) | LCCN 2022029995 (ebook) |
ISBN 9780197587973 (paperback) | ISBN 9780197587966 (hardback) |
ISBN 9780197587997 (epub) | ISBN 9780197588000
Subjects: LCSH: Race—Philosophy. | Critical race theory.
Classification: LCC HT1521 .B44 2023 (print) | LCC HT1521 (ebook) |
DDC 305.8001—dc23/eng/20220707
LC record available at https://lccn.loc.gov/2022029994
LC ebook record available at https://lccn.loc.gov/2022029995

DOI: 10.1093/oso/9780197587966.001.0001

1 3 5 7 9 8 6 4 2

Paperback printed by Marquis, Canada
Hardback printed by Bridgeport National Bindery, Inc., United States of America

To the Muses

Contents

Foreword by Linda Martín Alcoff	ix
Acknowledgments	xvii
Note on Sources	xix
Introduction	1

I. WHAT IS CRITICAL PHILOSOPHY OF RACE IN THE CONTINENTAL TRADITION?

1. Critical Philosophy of Race	21

II. THE CONSTRUCTION OF RACE

2. Racialization and the Construction of Religions	33
3. The Philosophy of Race in the Nineteenth Century	51
4. Racial Science in the Nineteenth Century	76
5. The Policing of Race Mixing: The Place of Biopower within the History of Racisms	87
6. Crossed Lines in the Racialization Process: Race as a Border Concept	103

III. BLACK PHILOSOPHERS SPEAK OUT

7. Ottobah Cugoano's Place in the History of Political Philosophy: Slavery and the Philosophical Canon	123
8. A Haitian in Paris: Anténor Firmin as a Philosopher against Racism	142
9. "Our Duty to Conserve": W. E. B. Du Bois's Philosophy of History in Context	157

viii CONTENTS

10. Frantz Fanon and Psychopathology: The Progressive
Infrastructure of *Black Skin, White Masks* 176

11. Frantz Fanon's Engagement with Phenomenology: Unlocking
the Temporal Architecture of *Black Skin, White Masks* 186

IV. THE CONSTRUCTION OF THE CONCEPT OF RACISM

12. Nature, Culture, and Race 205

13. A Most Dangerous Error: The Boasian Myth of a
Knock-Down Argument against Racism 220

14. Making Nietzsche's Thought Groan: The History of
Racisms and Foucault's Genealogy of Nietzschean
Genealogy in *"Society Must Be Defended"* 235

15. Existentialism against Colonialism: Sartre, Fanon,
and the Place of Lived Experience 251

Notes 263
Bibliography 325
Index 361

Foreword

Robert Bernasconi is internationally recognized as one of the founders of the new field of study called the critical philosophy of race. Yet the papers he has written in this area over the last several decades are scattered far and wide in journals and books across the (primarily) English-speaking world. For some years now, many have been pressing him to collect his papers on the topic of race in book form; finally, this wish comes to fruition with this volume and its companion, second volume.

These collections will provide a comprehensive and systematic overview of Bernasconi's scholarship on race, enhancing our general understanding of the origin of the concept in modern European philosophy and the new sciences. This collection will also contribute to our understanding of the ongoing ways in which European ideas about race were contested by Africana philosophers from the beginning. Reading European thinkers alongside Africana thinkers helps to open up the question of how to define racism, and how the twentieth-century formulations of racism emerged historically. Together, these papers reveal the contributions that a specifically continental philosophical approach can make to our efforts to understand the influence of racist ideas on the development of the modern West.

The subfield that Bernasconi has helped to inaugurate, which is now called the critical philosophy of race (CPR), follows in the wake of critical race theory in taking a critical approach to the concept of race, that is, to its validity as a means of characterizing human difference. CPR urges us to denaturalize the concept of race and instead take a historicist approach. As a concept, "race" has meant different things at different times and has no single "correct" meaning but multiple iterations operating to produce varied effects in the context of specific social structures but always within the overarching development of European and U.S. empire building. In sum, the project of CPR is not one of establishing the final truth about race so much as to see how varied ideas about race emerged and multiplied and how these ideas played a role in retaining the power of racism in modern, liberal, ostensibly democratic societies.

Bernasconi's contributions are distinguished by their attentiveness to interpretive methodologies that can show why, and how, the major writings of modern European philosophy need to be read in the fullness of their historical and intellectual context as transnational colonial empires emerged and systems of race-based slavery became institutionalized. The aim of this critical approach to the tradition of modern philosophy is not to establish that it has no positive content that remains useful and relevant, or that we can now simply forego its study. Rather, the point is to argue that the judgment of modern philosophy's contributions cannot be made in a substantive and persuasive way until we interpret these texts without ignoring those claims, passages, and theoretical arguments that helped to justify the formation of racist nation-states. This interpretive work will then be able to help in assessing the seeds of racism, as well as its contributing elements.

The essays collected in this volume open up the question of how to define racism well beyond the sphere of individual intention or affect, to which it is still too often consigned. To be sure, the lived experience of racialization in individual lives has also been fruitfully described and debated, as Bernasconi details here. And yet the focus on lived experience by thinkers such as Franz Fanon is embedded within a phenomenological tradition that seeks a social, non-naturalist approach to the ways in which we inhabit our bodies and our communities and navigate our relations with others *differently*. If we center human experience, we can actually discern the way it is socially constituted.

Thus, Bernasconi's own approach makes use of the rich resources in the broad continental European philosophical tradition to dissect the problem of race, as will be outlined herein. Adding to these resources are the writings by a number of colonized subjects who began to engage in varied ways with the ideas of racial empire but whose work has been until recently neglected in canonical histories of philosophy. These were contemporaneous writings, and by placing them in conversation with the conventional canon, Bernasconi deftly challenges the idea that the modern European theorists were simply men of their time, and thus that their racism should be excused on these grounds. Or perhaps we should affirm, he suggests, that they *were* men *of their time*, and then insist that we read their work in the full context of their historical period in which competing ideas about racial groups were being elaborated and circulated.

Racism became an interlocking system of ideas in early European modernity, and only later became hardened into ideology and grounded in biological claims, Bernasconi argues. In his work on the English philosopher John

Locke, he shows that we can trace a form of proto-racism against slaves that was manifest prior to fully formed concepts of race. The scientific formulation of shared inherent physiological features that were causally determinant over a variety of behavioral and intellectual capacities emerged antecedently to explain and organize racist dispositions and judgments already in place. Hence, Bernasconi dates the emergence of biological concepts of race differently than others: not as the necessary genesis of racism, but as its offshoot. The important implication here is that at least some analytic approaches to the history of race and racism are guilty of a kind of idealism, in the sense of making concepts primary, such as the concept of biological race. The history of racism can be tracked beyond the emergence of biological ideas about racial differences between human beings.

In the remainder of this Foreword, I want to briefly describe five important interventions that Bernasconi's work has made in the developing scholarship on race in philosophy as well as the broader field of social theory in general.

First, Bernasconi's historical scholarship and original interpretations have helped to show that the ideas and arguments of major figures as well as emerging disciplines such as religion and anthropology must be interpreted with race as an important theme. He has contributed his own archival research to trace the contemporaneous discussions that can establish different and more complete analyses of key texts, by showing their interlocutors, critics, and other relevant writings not usually discussed in philosophy (some that, indeed, have been all but unknown to philosophers until recently, such as the work of Anténor Firmin, and the interesting history of the classic phenomenologists' discussions about race, including Husserl, Schutz, Stein, and Sartre). Bernasconi has more than a dozen papers on Kant and Hegel, each offering new historical information and analysis; these will be collected in Volume Two. Thus, for the first time, in one location, readers will be able to view the comprehensive considerations Bernasconi brings out in regard to the interpretation of Kant's ideas about cosmopolitanism and Hegel's conception of freedom. This work of historical scholarship showcases his approach to philosophical historiography in general, which leads to the next point.

The second intervention Bernasconi has developed is to show that the eclipse of race in the modern canon is the result of methodological choices. While the egregious and undeniable racism, and sexism, of many central figures in the European canon is no longer disputable or so easily dismissable as "obviously" irrelevant to their central claims, new methodological strategies

xii FOREWORD

have emerged that reduce the significance of the racism in the existing canon, and thus the necessity for seriously engaging with it. Bernasconi argues that present-day defenders make use of three primary strategies: compartmentalization, decontextualization, and creative reconstructionism. Together these operate to deflect historical contextualization, as if unnecessary, and to mitigate the importance of reinterpreting the major texts.

Compartmentalization allows interpreters to set aside the evidence of racist ideas and commitments in a philosophers' writings, separating certain passages as having no bearing on what are taken to be the essential features of the theory. Decontextualization allows the process of interpreting texts to proceed without any understanding of the contemporaneous intellectual environment, and especially the alternatives and contestations that were at the time being discussed and debated, thus allowing readers to believe that the views expressed by canonical philosophers were more widely accepted than in fact may have been the case. The third strategy is perhaps the strongest and most innovative. Creative reconstructionists argue that the value of a figure's ideas and theories are most fairly judged by determining what can be most constructively (and creatively) fashioned out of their writings, or sections of their writings. This method allows interpreters to leave behind any limitations in the textual arguments themselves, or contravening evidence of the author's actual views, in order to imagine an anti-racist vision based on a racist philosopher's ideas.

Bernasconi argues that these three strategies hobble our capacity to analyze this period of writings not only historically but also, and more importantly, philosophically. Compartmentalization is a bad practice to inculcate in our students, since it teaches them that we can take any text and discern the full complexity of its meaning by only attending to the pretty parts. The method of decontextualization cannot but fail to explain the development of intellectual ideas, which are always to some extent social and communal, developed in relationship with existing and competing ideas as well as with practices, institutions, and communities structured in part by their immersion within overall economic and cultural systems. And creative reconstruction licenses apologetics, in which we might continue to hail slave owners as the founders of democratic theory. A complex, nonreductive, and nuanced account of the contributions of a given text or philosopher requires that we contextualize their writings and strive to understand the whole, after which we can assess what may continue to be useful and true. Together these three methods adversely affect interpretive practices and political understanding as well as an appreciation of the historical developments of ideas. Thus, they have not served the profession, trained students well, or helped broader audiences grasp the truly complicated legacy of modern ethics and political philosophy and how precisely these require improvement.

The third intervention Bernasconi's work offers to the critical philosophy of race is to stress that there are multiple and varied and sometimes contradictory problematizations of race and racism rather than a singular coherent problematic, or one that can be organized via a singular topic of concern, such as the validity of the biological concept of race or the debate over the criteria for determining if an individual is racist. The controversies over the defining criterion of an individual's racism—cognition or affect, for example—so rife in analytic philosophy's work on race are interestingly absent in continental philosophy's discussions, where there is more of a focus on structures and systemic conditions, both material and discursive. Thus here we have not simply a difference in problems philosophers choose to work on but the effect of different framing assumptions on how problems are formulated.

Bernasconi argues that the focus on the emerging biological concept of race, and whether a biological definition can be updated and refashioned in light of new work in population genetics, assumes the possibility of distinguishing nature from culture. In other words, most of the current debates on the scientific validity of race assumes that we can lift the idea of race out of its social and historical context in order to assess its validity as a natural kind, that we can separate the "nature" of race from its constitution within social and cultural systems. Thus, the question of whether or not there is a "referent" for the concept of race in the natural world, or one that can be suitably fashioned with however many qualifications, needs critical investigation itself.

Formulating the question of race as a traditional metaphysical question allows theorists to sidestep questions of power in the formation of language and ideas. What is the larger project of inquiry within which a concept of race would be inserted if it was found to be scientifically kosher, so to speak? What institutional practices might be unleashed by validating a scientific understanding of racial categories? If there *is* a central problematic in regard to race, that should obviously be the problematic of racism, but separating the scientific or metaphysical approach to the concept of race from the question of its ethical and political effects assumes we can debate race without

xiv FOREWORD

concern for the way in which racism may be affecting standards of adequacy and approaches to interpretation as well as influencing the formation of empirical data.

Separating out the question of a scientific approach to race also assumes certain framing assumptions about the way that language and concept formation work that Bernasconi, as a phenomenologist, does not share. As he explains in this volume, Alfred Schutz argued that racism operates in the domain of social experience, feeling, and perception, producing predictable and quantifiable findings, such as fear, for example, but not ones that should be taken as natural occurrences or universal human tendencies. In Chapter 1, Bernasconi explains Schutz's phenomenological approach in this way:

> . . . what one sees is not a body with certain characteristics on the basis of which one subsequently infers that a person has such-and-such characteristics. What one sees is a style in the form of a *Gestalt*.

In contrast, the presumed separability of nature from culture has generated questions about the "natural" human response to visible differences, providing more of an alibi than a useful explanation for racism.

The fourth significant intervention follows from this critique of naturalistic tendencies in the philosophy of race. In the chapters that follow, Bernasconi provides a powerful synopsis of what the phenomenological method has to offer in the way of explaining how racialization operates. If the third intervention is to displace the way in which certain singular problematics in the philosophy of race have been centered and represented as the most basic, a phenomenological approach urges a localized and contextualized understanding of the concepts and problematics of race, racism, and racialization. Centralizing the focus on lived experience requires attention to specific locations and time periods, and this counsels a decentralized set of philosophical problematics.

Rather than pursuing natural conditions imagined as existing prior to cultural meaning systems, the idea is to seek to understand experience in its full complexity, involving somatic, affective, hermeneutic, and perceptual dimensions in conversation within specific cultural locations. He explains and critically assesses the contributions made toward this by various figures, such as Edmund Hussel, Edith Stein, Alfred Schutz, Jean-Paul Sartre, Simone de Beauvoir, and Frantz Fanon, as well as more contemporary philosophers, noting their differences and disagreements. His analysis offers especially significant interpretations and assessments of Sartre and the evolution of his thinking about racial identities in relation to his concepts of the situation and the practico-inert. He also assesses Sartre's engagement with Fanon, as well as their differences, in regard to the general characterization of racial identity, oppression, objectification, and vulnerability. Thus, while advocating broadly for the strength of the ability of the phenomenological tradition to help us understand race, Bernasconi also traces its evolution, limitations, and internal variation.

Finally, Bernasconi makes a fifth intervention in helping to bring to the fore the writings of Africana philosophers in the broad diaspora. Here we have included a paper on the political philosophy of Ottobah Cugoano in which Bernasconi offers an interpretation of the specific way in which Cugoano took up the critique of slavery, and how his arguments remain relevant today in debates over evolutionary social change, the responsibility of bystanders, and the practice of an insurrectionary ethics. Readers will also find in this volume his interpretive analysis of the work on Anténor Firmin, W. E. B. Du Bois, and two chapters on Fanon, demonstrating their original arguments on such topics as the meaning of citizenship and mixed-race identities and also retrieving the intellectual context of their arguments to provide new interpretations. As Bernasconi helps to show, the canon of modern political philosophy needs, at the very least, an expansion.

Together these five interventions spell change for the way in which modern European philosophy should be interpreted, judged, and taught in the future. But the overall contributions that Bernasconi's scholarship provides go well beyond the reassessment of the history of philosophy to help us understand the nature of racism itself, and to avoid certain popular and easy solutions sometimes put forward, such as the simple extension of liberal ideas to all, or the idea that pointing out the inadequacy of biological essentialism will change the way we interact with, judge, and understand one another.

When I was a young student at Florida State University in the 1970s, sitting in philosophy classes, political philosophers did not explore the problem of racism, even in courses on Marxism. Metaphysics courses stayed on the topic of parts and wholes and personal identity, without raising questions about social kinds. Epistemology courses were obsessed with the sort of false beliefs caused by painted wooden signs made to fool passersby into thinking they were seeing barns. Even my phenomenology courses at the time ignored the contributions of Fanon or the lived experience of racialized and gendered social identities. This was the era of Black Power, yet there was no mention of Black, or Brown, power mentioned in my philosophy classrooms.[1]

Today, few departments can get away with such an effective erasure of one of the main forms of injustice in our time. We should not overplay how much progress we have achieved, but the work of the critical philosophy of race has opened up for debate the frameworks by which we approach the history of philosophy, philosophical historiography, social ontology, epistemic norms of justification, even the aesthetic dimensions of racism. The work of Robert Bernasconi has played a pivotal role in this transformation. Dogged in his attention to scholarly detail and archival sources, he has spent decades speaking on Locke and Kant and Hegel's racism, on Fanon and Sartre's contributions and debates, bringing tattered first editions to history of philosophy panels at the American Philosophical Association meetings to demonstrate the authors' real views written in their own handwriting in the margins. This tall, rather awkward Englishman has enlightened so many audiences around the world with his historical erudition that this area of study can no longer remain marginal. Here, finally, we have his own contributions more easily available for all.

Linda Martín Alcoff

---

1. The one exception was all the courses I took with Donald Hodges, where political philosophy engaged with anti-colonial and anti-imperial movements around the world. Hodges made philosophy relevant to the most vital questions of social movements and social change.

Acknowledgments

This book was put together during the COVID-19 pandemic. This context gave me ample opportunity to think about the many people who have helped me along the way. I have run through their names many times in my head. But I have finally decided not to make a public record of them all lest it looks as if the book begins with a Litany of the Saints, although I like the analogy.

Speaking in general terms, my deepest debts are, as always, to my friends. Friendship implies trust, and it is only under conditions of trust that one can risk thinking freely with other people, share half-baked ideas, be corrected without becoming defensive, change one's mind, learn, and grow. I have been privileged to enjoy the friendship of many people who are not academically inclined and who think I am somewhat eccentric because I never go anywhere without a book or a pile or papers, even when out late at night listening to live music. Their willingness to put all suspicion to one side and talk openly and honestly with me about their lives, their experiences, and their aspirations has been a gift all the more welcome because I believe that they had no idea how much it meant to me.

I also have deep debts to my teachers, to my students, to my colleagues both in Memphis and at Penn State, and to many fellow critical philosophers of race. Most of these essays began as conference presentations: in my view my best thinking happens when I am writing with a specific audience in mind. And usually at the last minute, in the plane, in bed the night before, or even in a car on the way to the venue. I thank those who had sufficient faith in me to issue those invitations to come and speak. Without those invitations, these essays would not exist.

However, some people who helped me turn these published essays into book chapters must be named. First, I thank Linda Alcoff. Others have tried to persuade me to collect some of my essays on racism into a book, but they were not as relentless as Linda. Without her, there would have been no book. I thank her, and also Jenny Bryant, for being my audience for the Introduction and for showing me how to improve it. I also thank LaVerne Maginnis, who prepared the manuscript for publication and who is responsible for the index. There would, I suppose, still have been a book without her, but it would have appeared at least two or three years late in a process that would have taken many more years than that off my life. She also deserves everyone's thanks for spotting a number of errors that she found in the manuscript and that I had missed. Finally, I thank Christina Chew, my partner of many years. As I said at the beginning, the book was put together while the COVID-19 pandemic was raging around us and we were both staying home in Memphis, still my happy place even when I cannot go outside. Christina has always supported my dedication to a life dominated by teaching and reading, but during these months she had more occasion than ever to complain about me spending all day and most of the evening in my library. But she did not complain at all, and she still accepts me as I am and does so, as always, very graciously.

This book is dedicated to my muses. I still aspire one day to write something worthy of them.

Note on Sources

I am grateful to the publishers listed below for giving me permission to reprint the following essays. Astute readers will notice a few minor corrections, stylistic or otherwise, but I have for the most part resisted the temptation to rewrite them.

1. "Critical Philosophy of Race." In *The Routledge Companion to Phenomenology*, ed. Sebastian Luft and Søren Overgaard, 551–62. New York: Routledge, 2012. © 2012. Reproduced by permission of Taylor and Francis Group.

2. "Racialization and the Construction of Religions." In *A Cultural History of Race in the Reformation and Enlightenment*, Bloomsbury, ed. Nicholas Hudson, 2021. Reprinted with the permission of Bloomsbury Academic, an imprint of Bloomsbury Publishing Plc.

3. "The Philosophy of Race in the Nineteenth Century." In *The Routledge Companion to Nineteenth Century Philosophy*, ed. Dean Moyar, 498–521. London: Routledge, 2010. © 2010. Reproduced by permission of Taylor and Francis Group.

4. "Racial Science." In *A Companion to the History of American Science*, ed. Georgina M. Montgomery and Mark A. Largent, 502–11. Oxford: Wiley Blackwell, 2016. With the permission of Wiley.

5. "The Policing of Race Mixing: The Place of Biopower within the History of Racisms." *Bioethical Inquiry* 7 (2010): 205–16. Republished with the permission of Springer Nature.

6. "Crossed Lines in the Racialization Process: Race as a Border Concept." *Research in Phenomenology* 42, no. 2 (2012): 206–28. With the permission of Brill Publishers.

7. "Ottobah Cugoano's Place in the History of Political Philosophy: Slavery and the Philosophical Canon." In *Debating African Philosophy: Perspectives on Identity, Decolonial Ethics and Comparative Philosophy*, ed. George Hull, 25–42. New York: Routledge, 2019. © 2019. Reproduced by permission of Taylor and Francis Group.

NOTE ON SOURCES

8. "A Haitian in Paris: Anténor Firmin as a Philosopher against Racism." *Patterns of Prejudice* 42, nos. 4/5 (2008): 365–83. Reprinted by permission of the publisher (Taylor & Francis Ltd., http://www.tandfonline.com).

9. "'Our Duty to Conserve': W. E. B. Du Bois's Philosophy of History in Context" was originally published in *South Atlantic Quarterly* 108, no. 3: 519–40. © 2009, Duke University Press. All rights reserved. Republished by permission of the copyright holder. www.dukeupress.edu

10. "Frantz Fanon and Psychopathology: The Progressive Infrastructure of *Black Skin, White Masks*." In *Race, Rage, and Resistance: Philosophy, Psychology, and the Perils of Individualism*, ed. David M. Goodman, Eric R. Severson, and Heather Macdonald, 34–45. New York: Routledge, 2019. © 2019. Reproduced by permission of Taylor and Francis Group.

11. "Frantz Fanon's Engagement with Phenomenology: Unlocking the Temporal Architecture of *Black Skin, White Masks*." *Research in Phenomenology* 50, no. 3 (2020): 386–406. With the permission of Brill Publishers.

12. *Nature, Culture, and Race.* Södertörn Lecture 5, 11–46. Stockholm: Södertörn University, 2010. © Robert Bernasconi.

13. "A Most Dangerous Error: The Boasian Myth of a Knock-down Argument against Racism." *Angelaki* 24, no. 2 (2019): 92–103. © 2019. Reproduced by permission of Taylor and Francis Group.

14. "Making Nietzsche's Thought Groan: The History of Racisms and Foucault's Genealogy of Nietzschean Genealogy in '*Society Must Be Defended*.'" *Research in Phenomenology* 47, no. 2 (2017): 153–74. With the permission of Brill Publishers.

15. "Existentialism against Colonialism: Sartre, Fanon, and the Place of Lived Experience." In *Sartre and the International Impact of Existentialism*, ed. Alfred Betschart and Juliane Werner, 327–42. Palgrave Macmillan, 2020. With the permission of Springer Nature.

Introduction

The critical philosophy of race puts philosophy to work in the fight against racism. One challenge that it faces is that racism is not and never has been static. Throughout modern history it has frequently changed its form and the language in which it is expressed. This is especially true today when racism is often at pains to stay hidden. There is still no shortage of unapologetic racists, but most people who are called out for their racism are quick to reject the accusation, even in instances when the denial is implausible. This raises a number of philosophical issues. For example, who gets to decide if an utterance or an action is racist, and to what extent is any such decision conditional on knowledge of the person's intentions? The courts face related questions when deciding if some act should be considered a hate crime. These issues are much discussed in the literature, but there are a whole range of philosophical problems that have proved more recalcitrant. It is now widely recognized outside philosophy that racism is not confined to the beliefs, feelings, or actions of individuals. Terms like "institutional racism," "structural racism," and "systemic racism" are frequently heard. One might have anticipated that these concepts would have provoked an intense philosophical debate. In fact, philosophers have so far done relatively little to clarify them. In the course of this Introduction, as a prelude to describing the individual chapters, I will provide a brief and tentative sketch of how institutional, structural, and systemic racism can usefully be distinguished from each other and from individual racism. These are not discrete forms of racism; they are intertwined. But they serve as different frames through which to view racism, and each of them is best addressed at a different level, using the approach best suited to it. Investigating structural racism using a philosophical method that was developed to investigate individuals is liable to fall short because in the process society is reduced to an aggregate of individuals and disappears as such. Once the debate about the different levels of racism begins in earnest in philosophy, it will quickly become a debate among rival methodologies. There is a great deal at stake in which methodology one adopts.

Critical Philosophy of Race. Robert Bernasconi, Oxford University Press. © Oxford University Press 2023.
DOI: 10.1093/oso/9780197587966.003.0001

2 CRITICAL PHILOSOPHY OF RACE

The task of making the operation of systemic racism in particular both visible and intelligible to skeptics is no easy matter. The idea of systemic racism is not only philosophically challenging but also politically challenging. It runs counter to both the dominant ways of thinking about society, especially in the United States, and the deeply embedded vested interests committed to keeping systemic racism concealed. What is at stake in the difference between those who confine racism to individual racists and those who take a broader view can be illustrated by examining the current debate about the long history of police violence directed against Blacks. That people of color in the United States are treated with a level of violence and disrespect that is markedly different from the way White people are treated is, because of the availability of extensive video evidence, now incontestable. But there are still many White people who are reluctant to view this evidence as anything more than an indication that "rogue cops" are more prevalent than had previously been recognized. For them, honest police officers can still be relied upon to root out the "rotten apples" who abuse the privileges and trust that most White people habitually accord the police. But if one listens to the testimony of people of color, especially those living in poverty under conditions of de facto segregation, they will tell you that they are seen by the police as threatening targets to law and order even when they are not under suspicion of having committed any specific offence.

Over and beyond the prejudices of individual police officers, we are now at a point when any encounter between a police officer and a person of color is overdetermined from the start. Both parties start from a position of fear, and this quickly leads to a heightened level of aggressivity. It seems that the police in the United States are not trained in techniques that would de-escalate the now inherent tension in such situations, at least not to the level that one sees in many other countries. This lack of training contributes to the culture of policing. There are other factors, too: some police forces lack diversity; some police officers are not as familiar with the neighborhoods as they would be if they were from there or if they lived there; there is the code of silence; and there is pressure on Black officers to behave in the way that the White officers alongside them behave in certain situations. These factors and others like them generate what we might call institutional racism in policing. But there are also structural factors that arise from the constraints placed on the budgets of individual police forces and the effectiveness of the external controls to which they are subject that derive in part from external expectations of how a specific neighborhood should be policed, expectations that may well differ depending on the race, class position, and gender of those involved. These elements are better classified as structural racism. They parallel the structural racism that is clearly visible in the distribution of educational resources across the United States whereby many cities have much less to spend per child than neighboring counties with a more affluent tax base and newer buildings. The correlations between structural racism in policing and education can be extended to other areas, too, such as health outcomes. These correlations call for a more synoptic view. To see the way they are connected, often because of a long history that goes back at least to legalized segregation but often much longer, one would need a different kind of inquiry altogether. The label "systemic racism" seems an appropriate name to describe what this synoptic view aims at. One often sees the term "systemic racism" used in the face of overwhelming statistical evidence of unequal outcomes for the different races. Numerical analyses can provide strong prima facie evidence of systemic racism, but they do not in and of themselves offer a diagnosis. They bring visibility and attention, but they do not render intelligible the various forces operative across the different spheres that produce these effects. I propose reserving the term "systemic racism" for those cases when what is being investigated is not an aggregate of separate events, but rather the forces that connect these events and lead to them being endlessly repeated, albeit sometimes in different ways and under different circumstances.

The statistical evidence is crucial because without it these outcomes of systemic racism can become so normalized as to be almost invisible everyday occurrences: they are hidden in plain sight. However, they become visible in moments when the veneer of stability is broken. These moments of breakdown occur when, for example, the response of the police is so incommensurate with the situation that they were facing, or when a jury returns a verdict that is so contrary to the evidence which was presented to them that they still possess a shock value in a society which has become almost immune to shock. These kinds of cases can be investigated on an individual, an institutional, and a structural level. But they can also be investigated on a systemic level in which case one is looking for what produces them and what guides the response, or lack of response, to them. To fail to engage these events at the systemic level as reflections of the society at large is a form of complicity. This is especially true in the case of policing insofar as the police act in the name of all the members of society, but wherever public services are not equitably distributed, leading to communities of color suffering disproportionately from poor health, reduced life expectancy, and cross-generational poverty, there is

4 CRITICAL PHILOSOPHY OF RACE

not only evidence of structural racism but questions to be asked about systemic racism, questions that the society at large should be raising on its own account.

Reliance on statistics contributes to the tendency to see society as an aggregate of abstract individuals, but that is not inevitable. The development in the nineteenth century of the notion of society as an organism, in part a consequence of the *Polizeiwissenschaft* (study of public policy) of the eighteenth century, also relied heavily on statistics. However, within both frameworks the concrete individual, the individual as a relational agent who can be understood only in terms of their context, is eclipsed in favor of abstraction. The price paid by such accounts can be measured by the difference that is felt when an individual human face is put on a problem. Concrete individuals must be integrated into the account of systemic racism, not least because without them there is always the threat that people will think the very scale of the problem relieves them from responsibility, the obligation to respond to suffering whether one caused it or not. It can legitimately be argued that terms like "systemic racism" are so broad that what is being opposed readily collapses into a vague and unproductive indeterminacy. Counterposing such an account with individual testimonies is something of an antidote to this. They are especially valuable if they go beyond descriptions of individual encounters with racists to give a record of what it is like to live in a society in which one is consistently devalued.

If systemic racism is to mean more than the widespread prevalence of acts with outcomes where one race or another suffers disproportionately, then as a first step one has to look beyond the study of the present to recognize the genesis of the societal structures operating in any given society. The forces at work, both material and ideological, are most visible in the transformations that take place. Critical philosophy of race remains a blunt instrument unless it is fully informed by the study of history. The essays included in this volume were in large part selected out of a desire to illustrate and advocate for what might be called a historical turn in critical philosophy of race. This is not to say that historical study has been absent from critical philosophy of race hitherto. There have indeed been some fine examples of its use, some of which are referenced in the chapters that follow. But all too often historical references in mainstream critical philosophy of race rely on received narratives in spite of the fact that one major part of the struggle against racism is to interrogate those narratives by examining the historical record afresh.[1] Interrogating these narratives and the interests they serve, even when at first sight they appear benign and progressive, is a task not only for the historian but also for the philosopher as genealogist. This means that the critical philosopher of race must embrace a vast array of approaches and draw on multiple sources. Studying the history of ideas and concepts is certainly indispensable, but it is only one of the areas to be investigated. Critical race theory, critical philosophy of race's older cousin, has shown that laws and court cases are a valuable resource for identifying a society's priorities and the categories that they intend to deploy in the service of those priorities. But critical philosophy of race attempts to take a broader view and ultimately a global one. Given that the claim behind the idea of systemic racism is that almost no part of society is untouched by racism and that it is rooted in the material conditions and institutions of the world order, the net must be cast wide.

That, too, would be only a beginning. Any attempt to separate structural racism as such from the other forms of structural oppression, such as those based on gender, class, sexual orientation, and religion, that are deployed within any given material system is artificial and distortive. A study that isolated racism from other forms of oppression would ultimately fail to be systemic in the operative sense. What is today called intersectionality gestures in that direction. Race is simply one lens, albeit a historically powerful one, through which to approach systems and structures. No one should need persuading that racism functions very differently for different members of a society depending on their gender, class, sexual orientation, religion, and so on. If one tries to sort the data at one time in terms of one social category and at another time in terms of a different such category, on each occasion one is sacrificing the concrete to the abstract until such time as they are brought together in an account of the operation of the system on concrete individuals as members of multiple groupings. Individuals do not disappear from an account of systemic racism. Indeed, it is only by understanding individuals in terms of the social forces that determine their lives and their struggles and the obstacles they face that the philosopher can hope to make visible and intelligible what for those individuals is simply their concrete experience. The critical philosopher of race is thus faced with the challenge of trying to gain an ever more synoptic view, while at the same time not losing sight of concrete lived experience.

Addressing this methodological challenge is especially urgent when the alliances that might establish forms of solidarity among the oppressed are disrupted by a too heavy reliance on abstract categories. It is a familiar enough philosophical problem: how do we put together what analysis has

6 CRITICAL PHILOSOPHY OF RACE

unavoidably taken apart through a process of abstraction? But here it has a strong political edge. This can be illustrated by focusing on chattel slavery. We rightly see it as a racialized system, with various structural dimensions— economic, legal, social, and so on—but even in the middle of the nineteenth century, when race functioned not just as a lens through which the slaves were seen and discounted, but as the core of what was understood to give legitimacy to slavery, the slaveholders were at pains to divide the slaves from each other in an effort to frustrate any attempt they might make to unify by identifying with one another. The slaves were divided not only by age, religion, sex, and language but also by how long they had been in servitude and by whether they worked in the field or in the house. Then as now, analytic categories were deployed as a weapon in an effort to conceal from the oppressed their shared interest in addressing the operation of the system.

Countless historians of the United States have shown how the new institutions, laws, penal orders, ways of organizing the labor force, and, of course, racist theories that marked the final third of the nineteenth century were in large measure efforts to keep intact as much as possible of what had seemingly just been dissolved with the emancipation of the slaves. As often happens, these efforts to keep everything the same only succeeded in bringing about conditions very different from what they intended. So, for example, in an effort to restore the supply of cheap labor that had been lost with the abolition of slavery, some emancipated Blacks were re-enslaved through the convict-lease system. But this slavery by another name led to the invention of new "crimes" to satisfy the demand of labor and set the United States on the path that led to the development of the so-called prison-industrial complex in a country with a vastly higher incarceration rate than any other. But it was not only alleged "crimes" that were being policed; with segregation every aspect of social relations came under scrutiny. Investigating these continuities and discontinuities is crucial to rendering intelligible the world we now inhabit and addressing its injustices. All of this is obvious to the many descendants of slaves who understand very well that their existence is still structured by the legacy of slavery. Nor does one need in fact to be descended from slaves to be viewed through a lens that is distorted by the conditions that slavery produced and the ideas that were introduced to justify slavery. And yet all too often when philosophers approach racism they take cases in isolation and abstract racism from the history that produces and sustains it. This tendency is visible in the debates about whether racism was fundamentally a belief or an emotion to the neglect of institutional, structural, and systemic racism. I have on occasion also adopted the proposal of those historians who suggest that one should speak of racism in the plural: one should speak not of racism, but of racisms. This seems right, but the study of how the different racisms relate to one another, how new forms arise and from where, how at one time and in one place one form is more prominent than at others, and how these different racisms reflect different concepts of race is still in its infancy.

The various chapters of this book address that task in various ways. They show, for example, how under certain material conditions the racist theories built around the nineteenth-century idea of the historical destiny of the White race shifted in favor of theories whose central idea was biological determinism. They also document how race mixing, which was promoted by some biologists in the early nineteenth century, came to be seen as a danger to the health of society. It is tempting to believe that the dominant class of the dominant race in any given society will simply draw on the racist ideas that best serve its interests at any given time. Under slavery, slave owners could rape their slaves and at the same time believe they were increasing the value of their "stock." After 1865 maintaining the alleged purity of the White race was seen as fundamental to maintaining what was already being called White supremacy.[2] But whereas in some contexts it may not have mattered which racial theory was in the ascendancy at any given time (as the explorer Georg Forster made clear when in 1786 he asked Kant if the thought that Blacks are our brothers has ever anywhere, even once, caused the raised whip of the slave driver to be lowered),[3] it was not always a matter of indifference, as demonstrated by the example of how those of mixed race were viewed. If critical philosophy of race is to engage in the task of rendering intelligible the material conditions that perpetuate systemic racism, then the complex ways in which ideas and material conditions shape each other must be explored.

Researching the different racisms, while a far from pleasant occupation, is indispensable to countering them. In the chapters that follow readers will find examples of anti-racism fighting yesterday's racism and strawman racism. If anti-racism is to become equal to the mobility and inventiveness that one finds in racism, then it needs to be more agile, more creative, and equipped with a richer and historically informed understanding of how racism operates. One way in which anti-racism has recently become more agile has been demonstrated in discussions of White privilege. It has been successful in persuading those White people willing to listen that being identified as White has served them in everyday interactions in ways that

8　CRITICAL PHILOSOPHY OF RACE

they may not have recognized at the time. But there is a form of privilege that should be central to the discussion and has another dimension to it. It concerns how self-identifying as White serves as a source of meaning, in much the same way that self-identifying as American or English or French can serve as a source of meaning because of the narrative with which the identity is associated. Indeed, given the way that historically national identities, especially in Europe, were considered racial identities, the two cannot easily be separated. But one must understand that if one embraces a racial or national narrative with pride, one is also implicated in a history that one might wish to disown if one examined it honestly. One cannot have it both ways. Just as a person might rejoice in the values and accomplishments that are associated with a given identity, so they must take responsibility for the crimes that were performed by those with whom they share that identity, especially when those crimes were committed under the name of that identity. Responsibility here does not mean accountability. In neither case did one bring these things about oneself, but just as we are all responsible for human suffering in the sense that one is called to respond to it, additional obligations to rectify harms done in the past accompany ownership of an identity. An early version of this argument can be found in Ottobah Cugoano's 1787 work *Thoughts and Sentiments on the Evil and Wicked Traffic of the Slavery and Commerce of the Human Species*, which is discussed in Chapter 7. But the argument is refined if we recognize the work done by one's chosen identities in giving one's life meaning. This belongs to what the phenomenologist calls lived experience. The lived experience of the White and the meaning Whites attach to being White is still underscrutinized by philosophers in comparison with the attention they give to the lived experience of the Black. And yet it is central to what is at stake in the current culture war that is being fought over what, how, and ultimately whose history is taught in schools and universities.

Every critical philosopher of race is faced in their work with the task of selecting the methods that best serve them in their investigations of the various forms of racism. The narrow approaches to racism that one often finds in the philosophical literature seem unequal to the challenge. This is perhaps not surprising. For example, the dominant forms of moral philosophy tend to operate with isolated examples, and this approach has often carried over into the discussion of racism. There are contexts in which the skill set cultivated by analytic philosophers is at a premium. For example, in formulating laws it is often necessary to supply tightly drawn definitions that can be applied

INTRODUCTION 9

with clarity. But where the lived experience of being racialized is at issue, where conceptualizing systemic racism in nonreductive terms is considered urgent, and where the anti-racist recognizes racism as a moving target, then phenomenology, dialectics, and genealogy are respectively best equipped to handle what is at stake. Critical philosophy of race is at a crossroads. It is not enough to say that if one is an analytic philosopher, then one will address it in one way, but if one is a continental philosopher, one will approach it in another way, as if the decision were neutral. The approach one adopts must be determined not by one's training but by the subject matter to be addressed.

It is now time to say in more detail how the various chapters of this book are supposed to contribute to critical philosophy of race as I have been presenting it here. Although I received my initial philosophical training in England beginning in 1969 at a time and place when analytic philosophy was perhaps even more dominant than it is today, I had the good fortune to be at the University of Sussex, where my enthusiasm for continental philosophy was tolerated and, most importantly, at times even encouraged. My approach to critical philosophy of race with its emphasis on lived experience, on material systems, and on history, reflects this philosophical formation, and these factors are presented as a small part of the case that continental philosophy is well suited to the task of exposing various forms of racism that have developed over time and contribute to systemic racism.

That is why I selected as the first chapter in the book the essay "Critical Philosophy of Race." It was originally written as a survey article for a handbook on phenomenology. It makes no pretense to cover the whole field of critical philosophy of race. For that, one would be better advised to look elsewhere, for example, to Charles Mills's rich essay under the same title.[4] But I have chosen to include my essay on this topic here because it introduces the three thinkers whose work has been most important for my own understanding of how continental philosophy can contribute to the critical philosophy of race: Jean-Paul Sartre, especially the later Sartre, Frantz Fanon, and Michel Foucault. I remain convinced that they still have a great deal to offer, notwithstanding their clear limitations. But the continental philosopher must also take responsibility for the striking faults found in other representatives of the phenomenological tradition referenced in that essay, most notably Martin Heidegger, Oskar Becker, and Ludwig Ferdinand Clauss. One major task of the critical philosophy of race is to examine the racism within philosophy and the way the racism of historical philosophers can be perpetuated by insufficient attention to their deficiencies.

10   CRITICAL PHILOSOPHY OF RACE

The next five chapters focus on changes in the concept of race and how these changes can be shown to be related to racist practices and institutions. If race is a social construct, which is a belief most theorists endorse, then it would seem to follow that one should attend to the social forces and the interests attached to the specific concept of race operating at any given time. They will not always be the same. I began the research that culminated in the second chapter at a time when it was widely being suggested that Islamophobia cannot be a form of racism because Islam is a religion, not a race.[5] A study of primary documents from the seventeenth century governing the regulation of slaves, together with a study of the debates about the purity of blood statutes dating back to the fifteenth century, which many scholars saw as a major source of modern racism, persuaded me that the intuition that gives the separation of religion and race a kind of self-evidence is the product of a history that was worth documenting as a guide against anachronistic readings of the past. I also hoped that in doing so I could give some insight into the early history of what we think of as racial divisions before the concept of race became attached to a biological notion of heredity. If the focus on the racism of individuals is one way in which our understanding of racism has been curtailed, the fixation on the racism that is tied to a belief in the validity of race as a biological category is another.

"The Philosophy of Race in the Nineteenth Century" was written in part to show that, even with the introduction of heredity and what might be called a proto-biological notion of race in the late eighteenth century, that conception of race did not immediately take over to the exclusion of other conceptions. I sketch here briefly my arguments, found elsewhere in more detail, that the first strong advocate of a science of race in which race was determined by permanent hereditary characteristics was Immanuel Kant. But the main point of this essay is to indicate how varied the approaches to race were in the nineteenth century and to argue that, at least until the work of Charles Darwin began to have a major impact, the philosophy of history, rather than the philosophy of biology, was the dominant force in racial thinking. Here Hegel's impact was crucial.[6]

The brief fourth chapter, "Racial Science in the Nineteenth Century," was written for *A Companion to the History of American Science*, a fact which explains its focus on the United States, albeit some of the other essays in this volume can legitimately be criticized for the lack of any such excuse. This essay is included here as preparation for the following chapter, "The Policing of Race Mixing," where I put to work Foucault's account of how

INTRODUCTION 11

systems of power came to be integrated with systems of knowledge (what he calls "knowledge-power"). Drawing on Foucault's genealogical account, I identify the new form of biopolitical or medicalizing racism that emerged in the late nineteenth century around the fear of race mixing. As Chapter 2 documents, a fear of race mixing can be traced back to the purity of blood statutes of fifteenth-century Spain, albeit the concern there was with Jews and Muslims mixing with Christians. Furthermore, in Virginia in April 1691 "An act suppressing outlying Slaves" quickly moved from legalizing the killing of runaway "negroes, mulattoes and other slave or slaves" to legislating the "prevention of that abominable mixture and spurious issue" that would arise from the "intermarrying" of "negroes, mulattoes, and Indians" with "English, or other white women."[7] But taken together, Chapters 4 and 5 show how something new emerges in the mid-nineteenth century when, with the polemics of Josiah C. Nott of Alabama, race mixing came to be seen as a strictly medical threat to the races involved: it was understood to lead to a shorter life span and possible sterility. Whereas the spread of biological racism narrowly construed cannot be separated from the attempt to justify a system of slavery that was already in place, or a colonial system that was expanding its reach, the medicalizing racism that took hold at the end of the nineteenth century quickly took structural forms, the consequences of which are with us to this day: for example, it is still present in the housing segregation that places many poor Black people in an unhealthy environment and denies them the quality of education that is often given to White people in the same town or city. The strict biologically based racial essentialism that took shape in the first part of the nineteenth century was important because it did not allow for exceptions. It rigidified the racial hierarchy, but it did so according to gradations: people of mixed race were placed between Blacks and Whites. By contrast, the medicalizing racism that sought to outlaw so-called miscegenation was fixated on people of mixed race as a threat to the whole of society, especially when they were able to "pass."

In Chapter 6, "Crossed Lines in the Racialization Process," I document how Nott's arguments, suitably refashioned for the new circumstances, radically altered the way people thought about racial differences and gave rise to laws and institutions designed to regulate what one can legitimately call an apartheid system. Its unprecedentedly severe biological population policies subsequently went on to influence Nazi population policies. During the long period when the slavery system structured Southern society, there was, what seems to us today, a strange arbitrariness about determining the borderline that determined who was White and who was Black. The legislatures of the different states at different times applied different fractions of Black parentage as a way to rule that someone was Black, even though they might not look it. This procedure also meant that someone's racial identity, at least in legal terms, could be changed overnight without their even being aware of it. That is to say, the boundary line that divided the races was far from clear and was constantly being re-legislated. These shifts in racial definition were not made on the basis of new biological knowledge, but, as best as we can gather, were refinements of the efforts of legislators to maintain social control given the ever-present threat of slave revolts. But, after Reconstruction, science, specifically the rediscovery of Mendel's laws of inheritance, when combined with the pseudoscience built around the idea of miscegenation as a biological threat, meant that laws to protect White racial purity were put in place. When in 1691 Virginia passed the Act Suppressing Outlying Slaves, provisions designed to keep Blacks and Whites from having children together were included. The same intent lay behind Virginia's Racial Integrity Act of 1924, but the state of Virginia now considered it a primary duty to identify those people as Black who might not look Black because it was thought that one drop might be enough to contaminate the biological line. To be sure, the support for this and similar provisions that structured daily life throughout the country was not simply about the new statistically based science of eugenics. For most people, it was once again about social control and preserving privilege, but this should not conceal from us the difference between thinking about race in this way compared with the more fluid system that had proved sufficient under slavery until the middle of the nineteenth century when the slave lobby doubled down on racial justifications of slavery. The system of chattel slavery, after 1830, was under attack as never before. It produced new biological justifications that, with changes in biological theories, made possible the medicalizing racial system that ultimately replaced the slavery system. In both cases the focus of attention was less on the clear cases, but whereas under the slavery system the focus was on where to draw the line that separated the races, the focus in medicalizing racism was on those who seemed capable of crossing the racial line without anybody noticing. The imposition of a rigid racial biopolitics on top of the previous more fluid framework that preceded it led to incoherencies and anomalies that still feed people's intuitions about race. To challenge those intuitions, for example, those surrounding so-called colorism, one must know the history. Medicalizing racism in its late nineteenth-century incarnation may no longer be with us as a theory, but its legacy lives on.

The five chapters that constitute the third section focus on the contributions of four Black philosophers to our understanding of race and racism. The first of these philosophers, Ottobah Cugoano, a former slave, issued what was perhaps the strongest attack on slavery up to that time. Some of his arguments are still relevant today, such as his argument about the responsibility of those who are complicit with racism. It is a travesty that he is almost totally ignored by historians of philosophy today. Indeed, these same historians tend to ignore the whole debate about slavery. Almost no textbook on the history of moral philosophy and of political philosophy in the modern period does much more than mention it, if that. One might be excused for thinking that this is because the canonical philosophers of the time had nothing to say about slavery, but, as I demonstrate in this chapter, that is simply not true. What is true is that, when judged against their contemporaries, the canonical philosophers were, at best, too concerned to avoid controversy and, at worst, were on the wrong side from the best of their contemporaries. It is hard to draw any conclusion other than that historians of philosophy have ignored slavery because the reputation of a number of canonical philosophers as models of moral thinking would suffer if the issue were broached, as is already beginning to happen with Locke and Kant. Philosophers who identify as Lockean or Kantian are trading under a brand name that is compromised, much as those who invest in being White, English, or North American do so. The acceptance of any of these identities at the very least brings additional responsibilities.

Anténor Firmin from Haiti was another Black philosopher who has been unjustly neglected. Just as reading Cugoano shows what it was possible to think and say in 1787, reading Firmin shows what it was possible to think and say in 1885 against Gobineau, but, more particularly, against the French anthropologists who had adopted many of the prejudices and arguments of the Southern school of polygenesis promoted by Nott, even though when they were initially proposed few Southerners had been moved by them. Neither Cugoano nor Firmin attracted a broad audience in their own time, but they are of immense assistance in helping to limit the range of what the "child of his time" defense can excuse with regard to any given moment in history. To be sure, there are also clear limitations to their views when judged against our own predilections. But that is not the point. The point is to learn while developing our historical sensibilities.

14   CRITICAL PHILOSOPHY OF RACE

By contrast with them, nobody today can say that W. E. B. Du Bois is neglected. His 1897 essay "The Conservation of Races" was the center of attention in the 1980s, at a time when what subsequently came to be called critical philosophy of race was gaining traction, and it remains there. But it was initially treated in a way that was anachronistic. His definition of race as "a vast family of human beings, generally of common blood and language, always of common history, traditions and impulses, who are both voluntarily and involuntarily striving together for the accomplishment of certain more or less vividly conceived ideals of life," initially was the main focus.[8] This is because readers were focusing on the question of whether the concept of race, as a biological concept, should be preserved or not. There was a widespread assumption that Du Bois was trying to displace biology in a novel way, and this led to the further question as to whether or not his proposal was legitimate. In Chapter 9, " 'Our Duty to Conserve,' " I show that Du Bois's definition of race was in keeping with the nineteenth-century dominance of the historical conception of race. Some people today might find it hard to think of race outside of what we think of as biological heredity, but clearly that was not the case for Du Bois or many of his contemporaries. What Du Bois was asking was whether African Americans had a distinct mission as a race or if "self-obliteration" was all they had to look forward to. He was not asking whether they should embrace nonracialism, as if that was an option in a country that was in the process of being transformed by the *Plessy v. Ferguson* decision of the Supreme Court. In other essays written around the same time, Du Bois and other members of the American Negro Academy directly challenged the medicalizing racism that maintained that Black people, understood as a largely mixed-race population, were, as Nott had prophesied, facing extinction. Being seen as an existential threat to the nation led Du Bois to raise the existential question: "What, after all, am I?" He was calling for African Americans to make an existential decision that recognized the new circumstances into which they had been placed. His answer lay in their cultivating their own "race ideal." Just as Cugoano gives us an alternative perspective on late eighteenth-century slavery, and Firmin gives us an alternative perspective on late nineteenth-century polygenesis, Du Bois's "The Conservation of Races" is a response to medicalizing racism that allows us to see it from a different perspective.

I have written a great deal about Fanon, arguably too much, but I find his work inexhaustible. The two essays that take their place here as Chapters 10 and 11 are interventions in the current debates surrounding how to read

Fanon. "Franz Fanon and Psychopathology" is an attempt to shift the focus from Chapter 5 of *Black Skin, White Masks* to Chapter 6 and, in a sense, "Franz Fanon's Engagement with Phenomenology" is an attempt to shift the focus from Chapter 6 to his concluding chapter. Both the essays included here are concerned with the progressive structure of Fanon's first book, which is rarely discussed. They are also concerned to mine his sources, which are all too often neglected. I see this as an issue of respect. One does not, in my view, do Fanon any service if one ignores what he read and what he points to in his footnotes: as with any major philosopher, one way of honoring them is to read what they read and to see what they did with those texts. One main casualty of the attempt to read Fanon in isolation is a failure to appreciate the complexity of his relation to Aimé Cesaire.[9] Another has its source in what I see as a misguided desire to downplay Sartre's importance for Fanon on the grounds that to do otherwise might seem in some way to diminish him. But Fanon is no more in Sartre's shadow than Hegel is in Kant's. Fanon had some devastating criticisms of Sartre early on: most notably there is the line "Jean-Paul Sartre had forgotten that the Negro suffers in his body quite differently from the white man."[10] But they arguably grow closer together as they come to share the same priority: the attack on colonialism. To be sure, some people today want to read Fanon in relation to other philosophers, such as Deleuze. There is nothing wrong with that. It can give rise to creative readings. But attention to the historical record throws, at least in this case, significant light on some of the philosophical issues that Fanon explores, including his account of how one can be released from the danger of becoming a prisoner of the past, a danger that can be enhanced by refusing to go beyond the lived experience of racism. This relates to the various levels at which his account of racism is conducted and that includes extensive reference to the way what he called "cultural imposition" is embedded in the structures of a society. Cultural imposition refers to the way we are brought up in a culture that to a large extent determines what we see and fail to see, especially if we are not alert to this dimension of existence. This concept retains its relevance and is important for understanding cultural racism.

Whereas the second section of *Critical Philosophy of Race: Essays* was in large part motivated to counter the tendency to exaggerate the role of biology in defining what is meant by race, the fourth and final section begins by tackling head-on how an exclusive focus on the biological concept of race came to form the dominant strategy for undermining racism after the Second World War. In Chapter 12, "Nature, Culture, and Race," I look at the attack on the

16 CRITICAL PHILOSOPHY OF RACE

biological concept of race in the context of the UNESCO Statement on Race of 1950. In particular, I highlight the distinction between nature and culture on which the argument relies. If race is confined to nature and is the preserve of the biologists, then it is up to the biologists alone to decide whether there are any races and, if so, what they are and what characteristics each race might possess. Those who are not biologists are told that they have to follow what the scientists tell them and adapt their speech accordingly. I demonstrated in the second section how science had lent its authority to certain forms of racism. It was good that the scientists now wanted to try to undo what science had done. But scientific racism arrived somewhat late on the scene and, while it influenced some of the ways societies came to organize themselves, this was only one form of racism among others.

I extend my attack on the narrowness of the UNESCO strategy in Chapter 13, "A Most Dangerous Error." The strategy had its origins in the attempt by the Boasian school of anthropology during the 1930s to dismiss the anti-Semitism of National Socialism on the grounds that the Jews did not qualify as a race. But the target was still defined too narrowly and in such a way that many Nazis would not have felt impacted by it. Much later the argument was extended to deny that there were any biological races, but throughout this process the Boasian approach met only limited opposition: many racists, including the Southern segregationists and the architects of apartheid, did not think of the racist systems that they advocated to be founded on biology.[11] For the most part the colonizing nations also felt untouched by this argument because they no longer thought of colonialism as at root based on biology, although it is undeniable that at an earlier time a number advocates of colonialism were unstinting in their appeals to biology and there were some that still did so. The UNESCO strategy is a perfect illustration of an anti-racist strategy defining its target so narrowly that it is easy to evade: one need only deny the existence of biological races to exonerate oneself from all charges of racism. The strategy also suffered from the defect of fighting yesterday's racism. The Boasians lacked a rigorous account of racism or its history. It held racists to account for being in the wrong, but not so much on account of their complicity with a racist system, but because they had not yet caught up with what biologists were saying about race. If one only considers as racism those cases where people are discriminated against on the grounds of what belongs to their nature, in the sense of that which is permanent or biologically inheritable, then discrimination against someone on account of their culture is not racism. It was to fill the gap that UNESCO had left behind that Fanon in 1956 coined the term "cultural racism."[12] In this chapter I also juxtapose the Boasian approach to the approach one finds in Oliver Cromwell Cox, in Fanon, in Sartre, and in *Black Power* by Stokely Carmichael and Charles V. Hamilton, according to which racism is a morally corrupting material system rather than a system of false ideas. As Sartre wrote in the *Critique*, "racism is a passive constitution in things before being an ideology."[13]

In the penultimate chapter I return to Foucault. It perhaps fits less well into the overall arch of the essays I selected for this volume, but just as the chapters on Fanon provide an occasion for thinking about the role of lived experience in discussions of racism, "Making Nietzsche's Thought Groan" provides a context for illustrating and thinking about genealogy as a philosophical method. In particular, it illustrates a way of thinking reflexively about the self-critical aspect of a genealogy of racism. Foucault's *"Society Must Be Defended"* has been justly criticized because its genealogy of racism is too limited. But there are redeeming features. One point of this chapter is to show how in *"Society Must Be Defended"* Foucault seems to implicate himself in the very structures that he was attacking and in a way that avoids the self-aggrandizement that seems to accompany both those people who seem to think that accusing someone else of racism automatically exonerates them from the same charge and those other people who seek to deflect any charge of racism by admitting to it a little too openly and too readily.

With the final chapter the book turns directly to the idea of systemic racism that underlies so much of what went before. Sartre in *Search for a Method* highlighted how certain forms of thought have the effect of rendering certain aspects of existence invisible to the point where it seems that this is what they are designed to do. Whether by design or not, a rigid commitment to analysis, abstraction, and ahistorical thought has this same effect when it comes to systemic racism. The fluidity of racism that has been demonstrated in the previous chapters calls for an equally fluid response, even if thought cannot renounce passing through an analytic stage. The purpose of this chapter is to show the dialectic at work in Fanon's *The Wretched of the Earth*, where he demonstrates how colonialism becomes intelligible as a system through praxis. The late Fanon and the late Sartre retain the original impulse of existential phenomenology, which is to aim at the concrete. More specifically, they are directed toward those who, no longer trapped by the past, struggle for independence and a concrete improvement in their existence.[14] It is this that rescues the account of systemic racism from being so

18   CRITICAL PHILOSOPHY OF RACE

broad as to be indeterminate, as does the significance Sartre gives to a specific understanding of lived experience that emerges in his late writings and interviews and that he combines with a historical genetic approach that aims to render the present intelligible. The late Sartre and the late Fanon provide only a sketch of how one might approach the system without losing sight of the concrete, but they give at least some indication of how one might meet one of the more serious methodological challenges with which the critical philosopher of race is faced when addressing systemic racism.

Writing the essays in this volume has been a voyage of discovery. Writing this Introduction has helped me to see more clearly what I was doing when I wrote the first of them. Now that these essays are no longer isolated but have been brought together as chapters, I hope that the Introduction will help to guide the reader through them in my various efforts to free up our sense of what race is and of what constitutes racism. To be sure, I cannot claim to have done more than sketch an approach to systemic racism, but I present this book as an invitation, a guide to a possible path critical philosophy of race might take, if it is to meet the challenge of rendering systemic racism more visible and more intelligible. I concede that I have fallen short when it comes to the ambition of critical philosophy of race to be global, but, if it happens at all, that is work that only multiple scholars and activists drawn from all over the world will be able to perform.

I.

WHAT IS CRITICAL PHILOSOPHY OF RACE IN THE CONTINENTAL TRADITION?

1

Critical Philosophy of Race

The Task and Early History of Critical Philosophy of Race

Critical philosophy of race consists in the philosophical examination of issues raised by the concept of race and by the persistence of various forms of racism across the world. It is philosophical not only in employing a wide variety of methods and tools (including interdisciplinary sources) to clarify and scrutinize the understanding of race and racism but also in its engagement with traditional philosophical questions and in its readiness to engage critically some of the traditional answers. In this way it intersects with issues in ethics, sociopolitical philosophy, epistemology, metaphysics, philosophy of science, and the history of philosophy.

Critical philosophy of race calls itself "critical" not only because it investigates and attacks racisms wherever they may be found but also in recognition of the pioneering work done both by critical race theory within legal studies, which is a forerunner of work in this area, and by critical theory (the Frankfurt school). Although there is some overlap between critical race theory and critical philosophy of race, the former, at least as it developed initially, tended to offer only a partial picture.[1] Critical race theory highlighted the important ways in which laws shaped the way race was constructed, but for the most part without giving sufficient weight to the role also played by science in legitimating racial thinking. It also tended to focus on the legal framework established in the North American context, whereas critical philosophy of race is committed to a global perspective.

In this chapter I take "phenomenology" in its narrow academic sense, although I have included some references to broader developments within so-called continental philosophy. However, critical philosophy of race, like feminist philosophy, is one of those areas of philosophy where the boundaries between analytic, continental, and pragmatist approaches are fluid. Indeed, critical philosophy of race and feminist philosophy at their best often work closely together. Today this is called "intersectionality," but it is not new,

Critical Philosophy of Race. Robert Bernasconi, Oxford University Press. © Oxford University Press 2023.
DOI: 10.1093/oso/9780197587966.003.0002

22   CRITICAL PHILOSOPHY OF RACE

and the intersection of race, class, and gender is already demonstrated by Anna Julia Cooper in her *A Voice from the South* (1892).

The term "critical philosophy of race" emerged only in the twenty-first century after the study of race theory within philosophy had already gained an institutional presence in the United States, largely through the cumulative work of a small number of Black philosophers who bucked the post–Second World War trend to keep the discussion of race out of philosophy. In doing so, these Black philosophers were able to draw, in addition to Cooper, on a distinguished prehistory. That includes Henry Highland Garnet's *The Past and the Present Condition, and the Destiny, of the Colored Race* (1848), Frederick Douglass's "The Claims of the Negro Ethnologically Considered" from July 1854, Martin Delany's *Principia of Ethnology: The Origins of Races and Color* (1879), and Edward Blyden's *Christianity, Islam and the Negro Race* (1887). Anténor Firmin's *The Equality of the Human Races* can usefully be understood as the founding text of critical philosophy of race, even though when it was published in 1885 it seems to have been largely overlooked outside Haiti. It merits this status because of the depth with which the concept of race is engaged explicitly.[2] Firmin's text is paradigmatic for one of the central tasks of critical philosophy of race: a philosophically informed critical engagement with contemporary racism (see Chapter 8).

The two philosophical texts that have preoccupied critical philosophers of race in the twenty-first century more than any others are W. E. B. Du Bois's "The Conservation of Races" and Frantz Fanon's *Black Skin, White Masks*. Although Du Bois's essay has at its center the existential dilemma, "Am I an American or am I a Negro? Can I be both?,"[3] it has tended to attract more attention from philosophers working in the analytic and pragmatist traditions than from phenomenologists (see Chapter 9). Fanon's *Black Skin, White Masks* draws heavily on psychotherapy, but first and foremost it is a work of existential phenomenology (see Chapter 11). The prominence that phenomenology enjoys today within critical philosophy of race has much to do with the compelling and indispensable nature of the phenomenological accounts of the lived experience of racism presented by Frantz Fanon in the immediate aftermath of the Second World War.[4]

The difference between the phenomenological and analytic scientific approaches to race goes somewhat deeper than a mere difference of emphasis, because of the dominance of naturalism within analytic philosophy. The analytic reading of Du Bois tended to read him through the grid of the distinction, enshrined in the 1950 UNESCO Statement on Race, between biology and anthropology (corresponding to the distinction between nature and culture), according to which the concept of race is assigned to biology. Because race had been abandoned by most serious biologists, argument could be made that the concept should be abandoned altogether. Du Bois's statement that race "perhaps" transcends scientific definition but is known to the historian and sociologist was rejected as disingenuous on the grounds that all definitions of race are understood to be parasitic on biology.[5] Furthermore, because racism was itself seen from this perspective as parasitic on the concept of race, racism came to be approached less as a moral failure than an epistemological error. It is striking that when Appiah came subsequently to revise his position and rehabilitate a notion of race, he in part drew on Sartre to do so.[6] Nevertheless, one should not see in this a coming together of the analytic and phenomenological approaches. Phenomenology has always rejected the consensus that the starting point for the consideration of race should be that relatively late form of the distinction between nature and culture that led to a divorce between physical anthropology and cultural anthropology in the second quarter of the twentieth century (see Chapters 12 and 13).

Early Phenomenological Racial Theories

For the phenomenologist, the distinction between nature and culture is considered artificial and not originary: the distinction has no place in immediate experience. Critical scrutiny of the distinction between nature and culture has played a prominent role in the history of the phenomenological method, even though Husserl at times seemed to appeal to it. Indeed, in the context of one of his relatively rare references to race, Husserl located in the surrounding world "first of all, things as mere nature, and then all concrete cultural formations as things of a higher level."[7] However, he immediately conceded that the distinction between mere nature and a spirit that is alien to it rested on an abstraction and was not an appropriate basis for subsequent investigation. "In the natural life of the Ego we do not always—indeed not even predominantly—consider the world in a naturalistic way, as if we were doing physics and zoology."[8] In other words, the distinction between nature and culture lacks phenomenological warrant at a fundamental level.

The implications of Husserlian phenomenology for the theorization of race were most clearly drawn by one of his students, Ludwig Ferdinand

24 CRITICAL PHILOSOPHY OF RACE

Clauss.[9] Clauss believed that the phenomenological method supplied the tools with which to develop a concept of race that left the natural sciences behind. His theories are not salvageable as they stand, but he does indicate where one might look for resources to combat the biologization of race, just as he himself was critical of some of the leading Nazi racial theorists like Fritz Lenz for seeing race in predominantly biological terms. Clauss's approach had advantages, too, in avoiding certain forms of racism. There was no attempt on his part to construct a hierarchy of races on the basis of racial data. He dismissed all such attempts caustically: "That the Nordic race is gifted in relating to its own culture is as obvious as the truth that everybody speaks their own language best."[10]

Race belonged to the soul, but in keeping with Husserl's position in the second volume of *Ideas*, the soul was not understood as external to the body but interwoven with it.[11] According to Clauss, what one sees is not a body with certain characteristics on the basis of which one subsequently infers that a person has such-and-such characteristics. What one sees is a style in the form of a *Gestalt*. To be sure, Clauss acknowledged that sometimes the body does not correspond to the soul, but even though he did not conclude that this refuted the idea of style, it did leave him to some rather bizarre statements. For example, when acknowledging that the body does not always express the soul in a unified way, he commented: "We often find in black hair and thin stature at the same time a blonde and slim soul, that is, a soul to which—if we may put it so, belongs according to its style a blonde and slim body."[12] It perhaps helps to know that Clauss was less interested in classification than in understanding. For this reason Clauss spent four years living among the Bedouins adopting their style in order to better understand them. Eric Voegelin praised Clauss's racial theories in 1933,[13] but Clauss's reputation was severely tainted during the 1930s by his association with the Nazis.

Whereas race was for Clauss a style, Edith Stein retained the then-conventional idea of race as a type which can, insofar as it forms a geographic unit, shape itself into a people by becoming active as a culturally creative personality.[14] This culture could extend beyond the race but had its foundation there. For Max Scheler and, following him, Alfred Schutz, race was a material factor (*Realfaktor*) alongside political power relationships and conditions of economic production.[15] Schutz was especially clear about the implications of the phenomenological approach to racism on the basis of locating race within the prior realm of social experience. Prejudices are elements of the interpretation of the social world for the fight against racism: "it makes little sense to tell the Negrophobe in the South that in terms of biological science there is no such thing as a Negro race."[16]

Subsequent Phenomenological Racial Theories

Contemporary philosophers who draw on the work of Jean-Paul Sartre and Maurice Merleau-Ponty have found significantly richer resources for developing a phenomenology of race than did the generation who drew directly from Husserl. Whereas all phenomenologists share the conviction that one does not arrive at race by isolating a natural component from what is cultural or artificial, the second generation introduced a new set of concepts which could be used to articulate this insight and shape it into an existential account of what it means to live in a racialized society. Already in *Being and Nothingness* Sartre modified the notion of facticity to present race as a facticity. Fanon also adopted this formulation.[17] But it did not mean to either of them that one has to accept one's race as it is given to one. To say that race is a facticity is not to reduce it to the status of a mere fact. It is what Sartre calls an "unrealizable," which is to say it is never simply given but is always to be renegotiated.[18] In his *Critique of Dialectical Reason* Sartre enriched his analysis to show how past oppressions are embedded in the material conditions of facticity. Race comes to be seen, like class, as "the crystallized practice of previous generations"; it is a matrix, a milieu, a sort of passive weight, and is not reducible to beliefs about biology.[19] To explain the reality of race while still seeing it as socially constructed, people often refer to the reality of money, which is also socially constructed. But one should recognize that Sartre did not think of money or race as an invention of the mind but rather as "a petrification of action," to which he also gave the name "the practico-inert."[20]

In recent years a number of authors have revived the project of a phenomenology of race, in the sense of an investigation of how one sees race, drawing on Merleau-Ponty's account of the habitual body. Most prominently, Linda Martín Alcoff in "The Phenomenology of Racial Embodiment" showed how meanings can be located on the racialized body. Alcoff suggested that "critical phenomenological description" has the potential to open a space within which the perceptual habits of racialization might be challenged.[21] The attempt to understand what one sees when one sees someone as raced has another side: the lived experience of racism. The two should not be separated because no account of the racialization process—what one sees when one

26 CRITICAL PHILOSOPHY OF RACE

sees race—should be accompanied by an understanding of how being seen in that light might be experienced.

The Lived Experience of Racism

Some of the early philosophers of the negritude movement, beginning with Paulette Nardal, gave accounts of the experience of coming to an awareness of race that might in retrospect be called phenomenological.[22] Du Bois's account of double consciousness in *Souls of Black Folk* can also be understood as phenomenological.[23] However, the now canonical text for the phenomenological account of the experience of racism is Frantz Fanon's "The Lived Experience of the Black," an essay from 1951 republished the following year as the fifth chapter of *Black Skin, White Masks*. Fanon had moved to Lyons in 1946, where he attended Maurice Merleau-Ponty's lectures, and it was probably from him that he learned of the concept of *l'expérience vécue*.[24] Fanon presented his description of the lived experience of racism as a modification of Sartre's account of the objectifying gaze. Sartre had written that the anti-Semite makes the Jew.[25] Although Sartre's formulation has been rightly criticized for ignoring Jewish history, a point he himself subsequently conceded, Fanon readily adopted it: "it is the racist who creates the inferiorised."[26] Through Fanon, the phenomenology of the gaze has inspired a number of African American philosophers.[27] Sartre's notion of bad faith has also been incorporated into accounts of racism by, for example, Simone de Beauvoir, Robert Birt, and Lewis Gordon, who argued that "Black people have the misfortune of being situated in the *what* mode of being."[28] Other accounts of the phenomenology of the lived experience of the raced body have drawn on Merleau-Ponty. Of particular interest is novelist Charles Johnson's "style paper" in phenomenology originally written in 1975 for the PhD program in philosophy at SUNY at Stony Brook. Merleau-Ponty has also inspired phenomenological descriptions from the perspectives of Asian Americans, including Emily Lee.[29]

Although Fanon presented his account of anti-Black racism as a modification of Sartre's *Anti-Semite and Jew*, he also provided a critical reading of Sartre's "Black Orpheus" that culminated in the judgment that "Jean-Paul Sartre forgets that the black man suffers in his body quite differently from the white man."[30] Although Sartre's commitment to the cause of anti-racism cannot be underestimated,[31] Fanon showed Whites that when it comes to giving an account of the lived experience of racism, there is a need for them to say less and listen more, a perspective also promoted by another existential philosopher, Richard Wright.[32] That different groups have different perspectives, such that something that might seem obvious to one is far from obvious to another, is a fundamental phenomenological perspective that was shown at length with regard to the differences between White American and African American perspectives at the time of *Brown v. Board of Education* by Alfred Schutz.[33] This has also been the basis for phenomenological criticisms of White feminism from the standpoint of women of color.[34]

Even though Sartre and Fanon did more than anybody else to inspire the accounts of the lived experience of racism that are so prominent in recent discussions within critical philosophy of race, their major accomplishment was to highlight how racism is not simply about what is said, thought, or felt about people of another race, but about material conditions and power structures.[35] In keeping with this insight, Sartre, in the context of a critique of Albert Memmi's phenomenological account of racism as a relation produced by the colonial *situation* which unites colonizer and colonized,[36] Sartre proposed seeing racism in terms of colonialism as a *system*.[37] Given Sartre's belief that race is a petrifaction of action rather than simply a set of doctrines or personal prejudices, it is natural that he would develop an understanding of racism as "a passive constitution of things."[38] In *The Wretched of the Earth* Fanon similarly modified his earlier conviction that the colonizer makes the colonized, by adding that the colonizer "derives his validity, i.e. his wealth, from the colonial system."[39] It was to counter the power of this system that Fanon endorsed the idea of an "anti-racist racism" which Sartre had already introduced in "Black Orpheus."[40] In other words, one can legitimately organize around race to counter racism. Indeed, given that the colonial system gains much of its power from its success in reducing the oppressed group to a series of individuals who each find that following their personal interests set them against one another, this can be crucial. In Sartre's example, when anti-Semitism is rampant and Jews are accused of getting the best jobs, it is the case "for every Jewish doctor or teacher or banker, every other banker, doctor or teacher will constitute him as dispensable (and conversely)."[41] That is why Fanon gave such a positive role to violence: he saw it as necessary to move from seriality to solidarity.[42] Nevertheless, in the course of doing so, he recognized that the struggle would often be played out in terms of nation rather than race, or at least not in terms of race as the colonizers had theorized it.[43]

28 CRITICAL PHILOSOPHY OF RACE

The Genealogy of Racism and Racial Theory

With Heidegger's *Being and Time*, phenomenology turned to hermeneutics so as to acknowledge the mediating role played by language and supplement what might otherwise be a naïve reliance on mere description, by locating the terms of that description within a history of concepts. In the case of a term like "race," an even more broadly conceived history, a critical genealogy that takes into account the material conditions and the interests that shaped it, is necessary. Lucius Outlaw has shown that this is a more complicated task than is often imagined.[44] The concept of racism also must be scrutinized. It is a relatively recent concept that was shaped in the 1930s largely to describe Nazi racial policies, especially those directed against Jews, and needs modification to describe other forms of racially based oppression. It was not formulated to describe, for example, the kind of racisms that the Allied Powers were exercising in their colonies.

Historical sensitivity is also necessary to address the question of whether one can legitimately call "racism" those forms of oppression that predate the concept of "race" as such, but that are directed against a group that subsequently came to be identified as a race. The phenomenologist is not as likely as some to be impressed by the argument that racism is discriminating against someone because of their race and so depends on the existence of a racial theory. Indeed, a strong case can be made for saying that, for example in the case of the development of a racialized form of slavery, it was the decisions made in the early years to treat African slaves differently from other slaves that led to the development of the concept of race. Along these lines Sartre in an essay from the late 1940s shows how systems of oppression attempt to legitimate their operation and establish the good conscience of the oppressor.[45]

It is characteristic of the phenomenological tradition that it is directed less toward the scrutiny of arguments than it is toward understanding. Histories that bring a richer understanding of the subject matter deserve to be called philosophical. Voegelin's *The History of the Race Idea*, Lukács's *The Destruction of Reason*, Hannah Arendt's *The Origins of Totalitarianism*, and Michel Foucault's *Society Must Be Defended* fit this description. They show that anti-Semitism and racism must be approached historically. However, there are dangers for the phenomenologist here.

These dangers are on display in Arendt's *The Origins of Totalitarianism*. She dates racism to the late nineteenth century and sees it as a by-product of imperialism rather than of slavery. There are certain phenomenological components to Arendt's study. She attempted to explain the attitude of Europeans to Africans by offering this description: "What made them [Africans] different from other human beings was not at all the color of their skin but the fact that they behaved like a part of nature, that they treated nature as their undisputed master, that they had not created a human world, a human reality."[46] Even if this was intended merely as a description of how Africans appeared to Europeans, which is questionable, Arendt's uncritical repetition of it renders it problematic.[47] However, it seems that Arendt employs this phenomenology as a kind of excuse which emerges when she compares the European exploitation of Africans to that of Asians: "there could be no excuse and no humanly comprehensible reason for treating Indians and Chinese as though they were not human beings. In a certain sense, it is only here that the real crime began, because here everyone ought to have known what he was doing."[48] One can clearly see here the dangers of a phenomenological approach if it is not combined with a critical interrogation of what appears.[49]

Although Foucault, like Arendt, restricted racism to a period beginning in the second half of the nineteenth century, his notion of bio-power has proved productive for ongoing attempts to write this history and has contributed to seeing racism in a different light. It should be noted in this context that Foucault's account at very least resembles some of Heidegger's account of the workings of technology as he developed it in the 1940s. Most of that material was not available until after Foucault's death, so even if Foucault was directly indebted to Heidegger's "Overcoming Metaphysics" and "The Question Concerning Technology," Foucault himself fully deserves the credit for developing these ideas. Nevertheless, it is not always recognized that one prominent model for Heidegger's understanding of technology was his observations about how eugenics had reduced the human being to being stock (*Bestand*).[50] The basis for this observation was Heidegger's recognition that "race" was not something given by nature but something made. Falguni Sheth's observations about relating race to technology using Heidegger's account of the latter find their basis in Heidegger's own diagnosis of modernity.[51]

Knowledge of the history of race thinking shows that a number of ideas that we think of as new or even transgressive, in fact, have a long history. For example, the notion of hybridity or of mixed race does not deconstruct inherited notions of race but has from the time of Kant tended to sustain

30   CRITICAL PHILOSOPHY OF RACE

them (see Chapter 5). Furthermore, the idea that the human races are natural or given, which was fundamental to the assignment of race to biology, was not the dominant idea historically. Race was understood as produced, so that racial purity was not something to be maintained but, to the extent that it was possible at all, something to be produced by breeding programs. Indeed, this was expressly stated by Houston Stewart Chamberlain, one of the forerunners of Nazi ideology.[52]

Racism within Phenomenology

Another main task of critical philosophy of race is to examine the Western philosophical canon not only in an attempt to identify resources that might help clarify and combat racism but also to identify the ways in which a number of the major representatives of that tradition have contributed to racism. So far the focus has tended to fall on such figures as Locke, Kant, Hegel, and, of course, Heidegger, and studies of them attempt to determine the extent to which their philosophy is contaminated by such associations. Heidegger's support for National Socialism is well known, and there is also evidence that, in spite of the number of Jewish students who followed his lectures, he was fearful of Jews having a prominent role in German philosophy. Nevertheless, during the 1930s he was attacked for not having a racial theory by Oskar Becker, another of Husserl's former assistants who was a more ardent Nazi than Heidegger.[53] Even Emmanuel Levinas, who from early in the 1930s developed his philosophy in large part to combat the racism of the Nazis, was unable to avoid importing a certain racism into his own thinking.[54] The history of racism within philosophy generally and within phenomenology in particular, and the apparent ease with which even the best intentioned can succumb to racism, provides no cause for self-satisfaction or consolation. It does make clear why critical philosophy of race as an investigation into racism has a central role to play in the future of philosophy.

II.

THE CONSTRUCTION OF RACE

2

Racialization and the Construction of Religions

True Religion, False Religions

That races and religions belong to very different orders seems obvious today, at least in the West. That was not the case during the period from the mid-sixteenth century to the mid-eighteenth century. We tend to think of racial and religious identities as radically distinct from each other. During the course of the twentieth century, race was assigned to nature: racial characteristics were not only thought of as inherited and constant, but they were also confined exclusively to the realm of biology in such a way that the biologists could in time renounce the concept of race and proceed to tell everyone else that they should do the same.[1] By contrast, religion has come to be thought of as both cultural and a matter of choice: as a result, it is believed that one can always change one's religion or refuse religion altogether. But the distinction between nature and culture is not to be found in the earlier period, at least not in anything like the way it is understood today. Indeed, there was as yet no biological conception of heredity to which one could appeal in order to give an explanation of the inheritance of physical characteristics.[2] There was only a clear sense of constancy across generations that extended to include customs and even one's religion. Like begat like. As one English Puritan minister, Reverend Thomas Blake, expressed it: "the child of a *Turke* is a *Turke*, the child of a *Pagan* is a *Pagan*, the child of a *Jew* is a *Jew*, the Child of a *Christian* is a *Christian*."[3] One's race and one's religion were in many ways as permanent or as temporary as each other. More to the point, they were so intertwined, or—from a twentieth-century perspective—so conflated, that it is only in certain contexts that one can clearly see the seeds of their subsequent separation.

One indication of the proximity between these two terms can be found in the fact that the Spanish word *raza*, which we would translate as "race," after having initially been used to differentiate breeds of animals and lineages

Critical Philosophy of Race. Robert Bernasconi, Oxford University Press. © Oxford University Press 2023.
DOI: 10.1093/oso/9780197587966.003.0003

34   CRITICAL PHILOSOPHY OF RACE

of nobles, was increasingly used in the sixteenth century to differentiate between religions: it came to refer to "descent from Jews, Muslims, and eventually other religious categories."[4] But at this time, while the word "race" could be use to describe the heritage of non-Christians, Christianity was not thought of as a race. By contrast, Christianity was a religion. Indeed, among Christians it alone had the full right to have that word said of it, because it was the true religion. So when in 1613 Samuel Purchas gave his account of the religions to be found in Asia, Africa, and America, he nevertheless prefaced it with the acknowledgment that "the true Religion can be but one, and that which God himselfe teacheth, as the onely true way to himselfe; all other religions being but strayings from him, whereby men wander in the darke, and in labyrinthine errour."[5] There was the true religion, and outside of it there were only false religions.

What was meant by the phrase "true religion" was disputed still at the end of the eighteenth century. Nicolas-Sylvestre Bergier, Archbishop of Paris and a strong opponent of Deism, in his three-volume work on *Théologie* had one entry on religion, which was largely a polemic against atheism and the idea of natural religion,[6] and another on false religion.[7] However, when in 1795 Immanuel Kant insisted that "there can be only one single *religion* holding for all human beings and in all times," he was not saying the same as Bergier.[8] Bergier followed revelation, whereas Kant believed that religion was based on reason and that all appeals to revelation compromised religion: "a church sacrifices the most important mark of its truth, namely the legitimate claim to universality, whenever it bases itself upon a faith of revelation."[9] What looked like multiple religions were simply "historically different *creeds*," and the phrase "religious differences" was to Kant as odd an expression as "different *morals*."[10] However, when around 1600 such people as Purchas hesitantly began to pluralize religion, they included beliefs but were primarily thinking of what Richard Hooker called its "effects," the customs and practices that defined a people even more definitively than did their physical appearance, whether they be Christians, "heathens, Turks, and infidels."[11] If one understands religion in that sense, then one can indeed say that at this time "religious classifications were taken more seriously than civil or racial ones,"[12] albeit one would need to be clear that insofar as one can attribute an idea of race to that period, it, too, would have more to do with how people thought and acted than what they looked like. As another scholar has observed: "Renaissance geographers and readers considered mental characteristics to be even more fundamental for classifying humans than physical ones."[13]

In presenting a genealogy of the way the current distinction between race and religion was shaped during the period from the mid-sixteenth century to the mid-eighteenth century, this chapter will focus, first, on the use of the term "religion" by Europeans to characterize the customs of various peoples. The chief context in which this took place was in the reports of missionaries and the attempts by the reading public to make sense of, and to a certain extent resist, the diversity to which they were thereby introduced. I will next turn to the seventeenth- and early eighteenth-century controversies surrounding the missions, and specifically the Chinese Rites controversy, to illustrate some of these same issues in a concrete case, before turning to some of the attempts made in the early eighteenth century to survey all the religions of the world. I will then look at the way the term *race* began to emerge in Europe during this period as one of a number of terms used when differentiating peoples on the basis of both their appearance and their customs. Broad divisions within humanity were beginning to be drawn, but there was as yet no attempt to make these into a comprehensive system. Finally, I will examine the laws governing slavery and blood purity to show that the contexts in which race and religion came to be most clearly separated were organized around the possibility of conversion. It was a context that pitted the missionaries against the colonizers, a fact which helps to explain the fervor with which the questions were debated.

The Religion of Gentiles

From the early sixteenth century onward, the reading public in Europe was drawn to travel writings and the reports of missionaries about peoples whose customs and practices were vastly different from those of the Christians, Jews, and Muslims with whom they were already somewhat familiar. At the same time scholars were investigating classical texts for knowledge of the ancient customs and religions of peoples who had apparently disappeared from the world and who were thought by many, especially in the late sixteenth and early seventeenth centuries, to have been in possession of a superior form of knowledge. Jean Bodin in his *Methodus ad facilem historiarum cognitionem* (*Method for the Easy Comprehension of History*), first published in 1566, provided an extensive account of the origins and histories of peoples that anticipated later general histories of the races. He dismissed those "historians who attack the superstition, impiety, magic, infamous lusts, and cruelties of the Greeks, Egyptians, Arabs, and Chaldeans, yet omit the qualities which are praiseworthy," adding that it was from them that "letters, useful arts, virtues, training, philosophy, religion, and lastly *humanitas* itself flowed upon earth as from a fountain."[14] The philosophy of progress that denigrated earlier times as primitive had not yet taken over.

It was by no means inevitable that the flood of information that became available in this period about the customs and practices of ancient and distant peoples would be processed in terms of specifically *religious* practices. However, one consideration that helps to explain why it proved so compelling to writers at that time to impose the category of religion on those customs and practices was expressed with particular clarity by Edward Herbert of Cherbury in his *De religione gentilium* (*On the Religion of Gentiles*), published posthumously in 1663. He was concerned with the long-standing problem of whether eternal salvation was in principle attainable for all members of the human race, a problem that had become more acute with the recognition that the world was larger and more varied than had previously been realized. Instead of condemning pagans, he called for more consideration for their souls.[15] The basis he gave for this tolerance was his claim that behind the errors and superstitions of the pagan religions lay a common core that included belief in a Supreme God, who is owed worship and who rewards virtue and piety, while punishing their absence if one fails to repent. This core of gentile religion could be understood as a kind of natural religion implanted by God by a kind of original revelation. Scholars in Europe scrutinized the writings of travelers and missionaries looking for evidence of monotheism and even of the idea of the trinity to the extent that they might be found lurking among the superstitions and idolatry. There were thus four religions—Christian, Jewish, Muslim, and Gentile—just as later, for example in Kant, there would be four races: White, Negro, Hun, and Hindu.[16]

The idea that everyone, or at least every people, was religious by nature was attractive because it showed how God had given to all nations the means by which they could bring themselves closer to Him. As Pierre Charron, the Catholic theologian and follower of Montaigne, observed, the multiplicity of religions was "dismal and deplorable (*effrayable*)," but some consolation could be found by locating the "general Point in common" in most, if not all, of them.[17] David Hume launched a frontal attack on this approach in *A Natural History of Religions* when in the middle of the eighteenth century he rejected both the assumption that religion was "an original instinct" and the assumption that religious sentiments are everywhere the same.[18] However, even before that, the claim that everybody is religious by nature and therefore everybody could access the truths of religion through reason was being turned against Christian authors. These claims could easily be subverted into the deist argument that the superstition and idolatry evident in gentile religions also pervaded Christianity. Some Protestant authors made precisely this complaint against Roman Catholicism, but it could also be turned back against them. Charles Blount defined religion as "Sacrifices, Rites, Ceremonies, pretended Revelations and the like."[19] If the superstitions could not be divorced from religion, or if the superstitions constituted religion, then, as Blount sought to demonstrate through discussions of the Egyptians, Etruscans, Druids, Turks, Mexicans, and Japanese, there was arguably no place for religion at all. In response, Christian authors highlighted the beliefs that the Gentiles lacked and that made it all the more necessary for missionaries to convert them so as to secure their salvation.[20]

Missionaries in China and India

In the seventeenth century the question of what constituted a religion was debated in the context of the Chinese Rites controversy. It was a test case of how European Christians should view the customs of peoples that were very different from their own. Matteo Ricci, who had arrived in China in 1582 and was in 1597 appointed Major Superior of the Jesuits there, directed his fellow Jesuits to respect Chinese customs when converting them. On his view it was unnecessary for the followers of Confucius to abandon such practices as ancestor worship as a prerequisite of conversion to Christianity: that would only be necessary if ancestor worship amounted to a religion. This approach was challenged especially by the Dominicans, and the conflict between the two parties was only finally resolved in 1939 when Pope Pius XII issued the decree *Plane Compertum Est*, which acknowledged Confucianism as a philosophy rather than a religion.[21] The terms of the debate were set in 1687 when Philippe Couplet published *Confucius Sinarum Philosophus sive Scientia Sinesis (Confucius, Philosopher of the Chinese, or Chinese Wisdom).*[22] The volume consisted of translations of some Confucian classics together with a long introduction that sought to show that, insofar as the teachings of Confucius amounted to a philosophy, those teachings did not amount to

38   CRITICAL PHILOSOPHY OF RACE

a challenge to Christianity's claim to be the true religion. However, because that might suggest that Confucius was an atheist, the Jesuits argued that Confucius had anticipated the "true religion." Proof of this could be found in the moral virtues, the rules for good life, and the fair government of the nation.[23] Some Jesuits even suggested that Confucius could be considered a saint who had a premonition of the coming of Jesus.[24]

That the Chinese Rites controversy helped to shape the concept of religion for the following century is suggested by the fact that the same dispute was repeated when some Pietists attacked Christian Wolff's 1721 lecture "Practical Philosophy of the Chinese." Wolff claimed that the rationality of his own ethics was confirmed by its similarity to the ethics of the Chinese. The argument relied on the premise that the Chinese had arrived at their conception of virtue through reason, not religion. Wolff primarily understood "religion" to be a matter of the way in which one honored God through external observances.[25] But in his treatment of the Chinese he had not taken the same precautions that the Jesuits had taken to avoid the conclusion that Confucius was an atheist. And if Confucius was an atheist, then by implication Wolff was at very least complicit with atheism. When, in the wake of the controversy that the lecture had provoked and that had led to his expulsion from the University of Halle, he finally published his lecture in 1726, it was accompanied by copious notes in which he sought to defend himself. He broke with the growing tendency to seek to ascribe a religious instinct to everyone by arguing that having no religion was better than having a false religion. He could sustain this argument only by insisting that having no religion did not amount to atheism. Confucius was not an atheist because to be an atheist one had to deny God and the Chinese did not have a clear idea of God. At the same time Wolff announced his dedication to the teachings of Christ,[26] as well as his reverence for the theologians.[27] Although for a while Chinese morality and Chinese statecraft retained a high status, in trying to save himself, Wolff had made the study of Chinese philosophy a risky undertaking so that Wolffian historians of philosophy did little to promote it.

The Pietists in Halle were motivated in their opposition to Wolff in large part because of their missionary activity in East Asia.[28] But, within the context of the conviction that everyone has a religion by nature, such that God had provided everyone with some access to some truths of religion, albeit not the true religion, the activities and impact of the missionaries were increasingly under scrutiny. Protestants used the writings of Bartolomé de Las Casas to highlight the cruelty of the Spanish in the Americas and their subordination of religion to trade and the "insatiable Covetousness" of the colonizers.[29] Matthew Tindal, in *Christianity as Old as the Creation*, not only allowed that "God at all Times, has given Mankind sufficient Means of knowing what he requires of them,"[30] but also presented natural religion as more reliable than revealed religion.[31] Revealed religion was open to distortion by the clergy and led to persecutions, inquisitions, crusades, and massacres, as he demonstrated by reference to the behavior of missionaries in the East and West Indies.[32]

The foremost of the Protestant missionaries, Bartholomäus Ziegenbalg, meticulously recorded the criticisms of the Christian religion made by Tamil Brahmins. They objected that the funeral rites of the Christians were inadequate. In addition, they ate cows, lacked cleanliness, and used alcohol. "The law of the Christians abstractedly consider'd in itself, 'tis a holy Law, but is not accompany'd with good Works."[33] In other words, the debate between the two parties seems to have been about customs and practices rather than doctrine, even though Ziegenbalg insisted on faith in Christ as a prerequisite for salvation:[34] "whether they be White or Black Men, Heathen or Christians, they must believe in Christ, and repent heartily of all their Sins."[35] At one point he suggested that they had no religion as they had no law,[36] but he elsewhere attributed a religion to them.[37] Indeed, he used the words "religion" and "sect" interchangeably and with some flexibility, so that one cannot attribute to him the orientalist construction of Hinduism as a single religion.[38] He acknowledged that the heathens of Malabar knew from the light of nature that there is a God and did not need to be taught that by Christians: "they would consider it an act of the greatest atheism if they should hear that there are some people in the world who believe that there is no god from whom everything comes and who is to sustain and to rule everything." But this led him to reflect that "such atheism is even found among the Christians and especially among some learned people."[39] The fact that, even in the early eighteenth century, a Protestant missionary writing in 1713 would use the word "Christian," instead of the word "European" or "White," to describe an atheist is an indication of how at that time what to our ears is clearly a religious identity served in places where we would think a racial identity would have been more appropriate.

The hierarchical sense of superiority that came to be attached to whiteness derived in part from the superiority that was attached to being Christian. One can see this in the writings of François Bernier, who spent some twelve years in India in the middle of the seventeenth century. His account of his efforts

40   CRITICAL PHILOSOPHY OF RACE

to convert people in India included a telling anecdote. Having observed the bathing practices in India that had to be performed in running water, he told his Brahmin interlocutors that such behavior would not be advisable in the cold climate from which he came because it would put one's life in danger. He explained that this was proof that their law could not have had a divine origin but must have had a human invention. In response, they told him that they would not call Christianity a false religion because it might indeed be good for Europeans. They explained that God had not intended their religion to be for everyone, but for them alone, and for that reason they could not receive foreigners into their religion.[40] This story has a sequel. Over a century later Kant took Bernier and his story at face value when, in his lectures on anthropology in 1791–1792, he seems to have relied on a memory of Bernier's anecdote to dismiss the Indians for their failure to follow the maxim that one should "think from the standpoint of everyone else," by which he understood adopting a universal standpoint.[41] Kant could not acknowledge a religion that did not seek to be universal. But if a religion can be considered the true religion only to the extent that it asserts its universality, then that commits its adherents to missionary activity and the promotion of conversion and assimilation.

From Religion to Religions

The Jesuits had a reason to promote the idea that there was something called a Confucian school (*Schola Confuciana*),[42] but the terms "Confucianism," "Taoism," "Buddhism," and "Hinduism," at least in English, were largely a product of the nineteenth century, and, with the exception of "Buddhism," none of them were common until the twentieth century.[43] To be sure, the impact of giving them names should not be overstated. It is sometimes said that Hinduism is an imaginary entity invented by Christian missionaries so they could attack it as a false religion,[44] but they were already doing that long before certain practices were given that name. When in 1631 Johannes De Laet, one of the founding directors of the Dutch West Indies Company, compiled from a variety of sources a discussion of that part of the world, Hindus (*Hindoi*) were the inhabitants of Hindustan, rather than the name for the adherents of a religion. Indeed, in his chapter on "The Character, Customs, Institutions and Superstitions of the Inhabitants," he used the word *religion* only once and then it might well have been to refer to the Muslims in India,

RACIALIZATION AND THE CONSTRUCTION OF RELIGIONS   41

rather than to the rest of the population whom he called simply Gentiles.[45] Something similar can be seen in Bernier's 1667 account of "the superstitions, strange customs and Doctrines of the Indous or Gentiles of Hindustan." It is not clear how much direct contact he had with the inhabitants outside of a small privileged circle, but in this account he referred only once to "religion" as such, and he did so in the context of the indecent and extravagant dancing of the women.[46] In fact, the word *Indous* appears only in the title of the letter suggesting that, as will be shown later, characterizing and categorizing peoples as such was not his interest, any more than the category of religion was. In the seventeenth century, natural historians were beginning the task of making inventories and catalogues, but the age of classification, the age of Linnaeus, had not yet come to fruition.

Surveys of religion from the mid-seventeenth century to the mid-eighteenth century were more concerned with establishing both the superiority of Christianity and the unity or commonality of the religion of the gentiles than with multiplying religions on the basis of the different customs and practices they displayed. This can be seen in Alexander Ross's *Pansebeia, or, a View of All Religions in the World: With the Several Church-Governments, from the Creation, to These Times* from 1653. When it came to the religion of the ancient Europeans, his strategy was to assimilate their religion to that found in other parts of the world: "the same Paganism was professed among them, that was in the other parts of the world, and which is yet professed in Lapland, Finland, and some parts of Norway, *Lituania, and Samagotia.*"[47] Ross was well aware that there would be those who would object that "seeing the world is pestered with too many Religions, it were better their names and Tenets were obliterated then [*sic*] published."[48] This shows the suspicion under which such surveys of religion were held at this time. Ross's response was to attack heathenism while supporting the idea of natural religion.

This was still the case with Thomas Broughton's *Bibliotheca Historico-sacra*, which consisted of some 1,100 pages published in two volumes between 1737 and 1739, with subsequent editions appearing under the title *An Historical Dictionary of All Religions from the Creation of the World to This Present Time*. There is a brief discussion of "Brachmins or Bramins," who were described as "a sect of Indian philosophers," but the word "Hinduism" does not appear.[49] And somewhat unusually, albeit in a discussion that lasted barely a page, there was an entry on Budsdo that described the religion of "Budsdoism" whose followers were Budsdoists and whose founder was Budha.[50] Broughton retained the framework of only four grand religions—Jewish, Christian,

42   CRITICAL PHILOSOPHY OF RACE

Mahommedan, and pagan—and remained attached to the idea that there could be only one true religion and that the others were "falsely so called" and "consequently takes in superstition."[51]

Hannah Adams is sometimes credited with being, in 1784, the first of the major classifiers to break with the division of religions into true and false. However, as late as 1817, in *A Dictionary of All Religions and Religious Denominations*, which was the fourth version of her ever more expansive account of the religions of the world, she was still organizing religions, other than the Jews, Christians, and Mahometans, geographically by countries and their inhabitants. These were the so-called pagan or heathen religions. So there was an entry on the great variety of sects of "the Hindoo religionists," but in her mind "the Hindoos" were first and foremost the original inhabitants of Hindoostan.[52] There was no separate entry on the Buddha or on Buddhism, although there was one on "Birmans," who were the worshippers of "Boodh" in the Birman country of India, and one on Budso, a form of pagan worship in Japan whose author was the Buddha.[53] With Adams the process of differentiating religions was underway, but there was still no attempt even in her exhaustive surveys to give to each religion encountered a specific name for the purpose of classification. One commentator has suggested that "the early modern taxonomic system does not identify *religions* as such—that is, its aim apparently is not to sort out the plurality of 'belief systems' as we understand the term today; instead, it recognizes and categorizes different 'nations,' or in our terms, different 'peoples.'"[54] In support of this claim, one can still find as late as the fourth edition of Adams's *Dictionary* entries on the Chinese, the Japanese, and on Negroes.

If there is a book that transcends the limits on display in Ross and Broughton, it is Jean-Frédéric Bernard's *The Ceremonies and Religious Customs of the Various Nations of the Known World*. It began publication in 1727 and was celebrated not least because of the quality of the illustrations supplied by Bernard Picart.[55] These volumes included extracts from important studies of Jews, Roman Catholics, Greeks, and Protestants (expanded to include Anglicans, Puritans, Quakers, Pre-Adamites, and so on), as well as Mahometism. There were also two volumes devoted to the "Ceremonies of the Idolatrous Nations" that addressed the Americans, East Indians, Banians, Chinese, Japanese, Persians, Laplanders, and Africans, among others, highlighting the particular customs of each of them. In a General Preface to the whole work, which was not included in the English translation, Bernard, intentionally echoing Charron, wrote of "the extraordinary practices that men have put to work in the service of God," and in keeping with the general tendency of the time, remarked that "they agree on many things, have the same principles and foundations in the spirit of a good part of mankind, and generally accord with the same thesis, hold the same progress and walk together, except for the characters of revelation that even methodological libertines have been forced to recognize in some religions."[56] In the introductory "Dissertation on Religious Worship," which was also not included in the English translation, he gave an explanation of "the origin of the extraordinary ceremonies, multiple extravagant devotions, and the infinite number of formulae used in prayer."[57] Although he acknowledged that these would seem bizarre to anybody who had not previously heard about them, they arose from the same impulse: all human beings ask God for the same things. The similarity of their needs lies behind the similarity of their prayers, but over time humanity became perverted and lost the true idea of divinity. As a result, superstition was added to worship.

It has been argued that the book marked a significant step toward religious tolerance and cultural relativism, but even if Bernard and Picart were not as judgmental as some of their contemporaries and so can be given some credit for that in the long run,[58] this salutary impact was by no means immediate. Although Bernard's emphasis was on treating differences as superficial, it was inevitable that the differences would attract attention, something that Picart's engravings did not fail to highlight. Nor should one underestimate Bernard's hostility toward what he saw as the idolatrous character of Roman Catholicism. In this he was like John Toland with whose views Bernard expressed some sympathy.[59] Toland was another of those thinkers who used the practices of the heathens to expose absurdities in the Christian churches of his age. Whether it be music, feasts, incense, pilgrimages, or sacrifices, "almost every Point of those superstitious and idolatrous Religions are by these or grosser Circumstances reviv'd by many Christians in our Western Part of the Word [sic], and by all the Oriental Sects."[60] But if one is looking in the mid-eighteenth century for the new conception of religion that will come to dominate for the next two hundred years, one could do no better than turn to Johann Christian Edelmann, who promoted what he called "the equal validity of the religions (*Gleichgültigkeit der Religionen*)" and separated beliefs from religion because beliefs differentiated people from each other.[61]

Race and Monogenesis

Just as the tendency in the West was to see differing customs and practices through the lens of a conception of natural religion that supported monotheism, so the biblical commitment to monogenesis meant there was also a tendency to want to see the unity of the human species behind the visible differences. To be sure, there were exceptions. In the seventeenth century Isaac de La Peyrère engaged in a debate about the origins of Indigenous Americans.[62] It led him, in the light of the limited time span allowed by biblical history, compared to the longer time frame that the Chaldeans, Egyptians, and Chinese ascribed to their histories, to advocate an early form of polygenesis.[63] Some planters appealed to polygenesis to justify slavery,[64] as did Edward Long in the eighteenth century.[65] However, the main impetus toward polygenesis in the second half of the eighteenth century was the recognition that characteristics such as skin color and hair texture were more permanent than had previously been recognized.

Prior to that, environmental theories dominated. These were deployed to explain differences in customs and forms of worship as well as physical differences. We have seen how Bernier explained what to him were the strange bathing customs of the Gentiles of Hindustan by the need to cope with the extreme heat in India. The Earl of Shaftesbury in his account of Egypt had similarly pointed to environmental factors, specifically floods and meteors, when trying to explain what he called "the natural Causes of Superstition" that created conditions "of which their Priesthood cou'd make good Advantages."[66] The best-known example of an environmental account was set out by Montesquieu in *The Spirit of the Laws* in 1748. Montesquieu believed that the climate not only impacted the laws of people but also was reflected in their religions. So, for example, in considering how the legislators of China "made their religion, philosophy, and laws all practical," he understood that it was because they opposed the vices favored by the climate.[67]

It was widely thought, even in the middle of the eighteenth century, that skin color and other distinctive physical aspects change as a result of variations in climate and diet, even if it took a few generations for such changes to occur. Indeed, Buffon in 1749 in the third volume of his *Histoire naturelle* insisted in his essay on human varieties that if a colony of Africans were brought North after eight, ten, or twelve generations they would be less black than their ancestors and perhaps as white as the local inhabitants.[68] Given his conviction that these visible markers changed over time, he sometimes appealed to dispositions, manners, and customs to establish that varieties that looked alike, such as the Chinese and the Tartars, were different.[69] Buffon also singled out those races or peoples that he believed had no religion, such as the Laplanders, Tartars, and Tongusians. So, for example, the Laplanders "have no idea of religion, nor of a Supreme Being. They are mostly idolaters and they are all very superstitious."[70] When Buffon returned to the question of human varieties in 1777, he again emphasized their superstitions, but with the added observation that even those Laplanders who converted to Christianity persisted with their idols.[71] A lack of (true) religion was in this context seen as evidence of inferiority.

Buffon's chapter on human varieties contributed to the long process by which "race" eventually, at some time in the mid-nineteenth century, became the decisive word for the discussion of human differences. Prior to that, the term "variety," which Buffon also favored, seemed more likely to serve in its place, given the preference that Johann Friedrich Blumenbach and James Cowles Prichard also showed for this word. However, in this same chapter Buffon deployed the word "race" albeit he left it undefined, and indeed for much of the essay he deployed "species" as a synonym for it. Only in the final paragraph did he declare that humankind is not composed of essentially different species and that there was originally only one human species, which, having spread itself out across the surface of the earth, subsequently underwent changes under the influence of climate, differences of nutrition, the manner of existence, epidemic diseases, and from mixing.[72]

It was Kant who in 1775 offered the first definition of race to signal radical, even permanent, diversity, without compromising the idea of humanity as a single species against the proponents of polygenesis. Races were understood to be subspecies that "persistently preserve themselves in all transplanting (transpositions to other regions) over prolonged generations among themselves and which also always beget half-breed young in the mixing with other variations of the same phylum."[73] With this definition he succeeded in reconciling monogenesis with an account of hereditary differences similar to that promoted by the polygenists. Beyond any impact that the environment might have, the differences between races were permanent and could be changed only by race mixing.[74] Buffon's descriptive *histoire naturelle* was in this way transformed by Kant into a natural history that was teleological. The way was opened to a progressive history where what previously had been seen as inferiority was transformed into a permanent condition of primitivity. There

46 CRITICAL PHILOSOPHY OF RACE

could be races outside history altogether, as there had earlier been peoples without religion.

But, before being a historical category, as it was in the nineteenth century, even more than a biological category, "race" was a geographical category. Bernier seems to have been the first to use the word as part of an attempt to give an exhaustive list of the different varieties of people in the world. He did not clearly distinguish "race" from "species," a distinction that would not be made with any clarity until the 1770s. That he used the two words as synonyms is clear from the title of his 1684 essay, "A New Division of the Earth According to the Different Species or Races of Men."[75] But the title also makes clear that his own interest was not primarily in dividing the peoples of the earth into groups, but in redrawing geographical boundaries. For this reason he did not even bother to name the different races or species, although they seem to correspond roughly to what would later be called the White, Black, Mongol, and Lapp races with the possibility that Indigenous Americans and Hottentots would constitute additional races. Strikingly, he understood many of the inhabitants of Asia to belong to the same group as the Europeans, which suggests that in his eyes the gulf that separated him from the inhabitants of India was, to use terms that were only then beginning to take on their modern meaning, not a racial division but a religious one. But it should be remembered that religions were also seen geographically. According to Thomas Browne, there was "a Geography of Religions as well as Lands, and every Clime distinguished not only by their Laws and Limits, but circumscribed by their Doctrines and Rules of Faith."[76]

The Conversion of Slaves

The dominant interest in the case of the missionaries was conversion and thus a form of religious assimilation, but the maintenance and future prosperity of the existing order were dependent on maintaining existing differences, even after conversion. To illustrate the significance of conversion in the genealogy of the distinction between race and religion, I will examine, first, the introduction of laws in the North American colonies that determined that African slaves would still be slaves even after baptism and then, in the following section, the purity of blood statutes in Spain in the fifteenth and sixteenth centuries and their subsequent transfer to Spanish America. Within histories of racism these laws are sometimes presented one-sidedly in terms of race

RACIALIZATION AND THE CONSTRUCTION OF RELIGIONS   47

replacing religion as the decisive category, a move from a world governed by religious differences to one governed by racial differences, but this is to suppose that religion and race were already by then established and separate categories of classification. Rather, what is most striking is how in these two instruments the interweaving of what became race and religion is clearly visible.

At the beginning of the seventeenth century there was a convention that Christians would not enslave their fellow Christians,[77] but it was put under pressure in the colonial context because the missionaries believed it was their duty to convert the slaves in order to save their souls. The resistance of the slave owners to this proposal was documented by Richard Ligon, who described how a slave called Sambo, who desired to be a Christian, was refused that possibility because his master judged that "being once a Christian, he could no more account him a Slave."[78] By contrast, some religious leaders saw slavery as a path to baptism. Richard Baxter, who was a relatively lone voice in the seventeenth century to announce in print a principled opposition to the enslavement of Africans, insisted on Christian baptism as the only legitimate basis for the practice: "Make it your chief end in buying and using slaves, to win them to Christ, and save their souls."[79] The eventual solution to the quandary was to introduce laws that allowed for the baptism of slaves without a change in status so long as the slaves were Black. The most egregious example of such a law can be found in "The Fundamental Constitutions of Carolina," first promulgated in 1669. It read: "Every Freeman of Carolina shall have absolute power and authority over his Negro slaves, of what opinion or Religion so ever."[80] The phrase "of what opinion or Religion so ever" shows an uncertainty as to whether the practices and superstitions of Africans should be seen as a religion or not; the phrase "absolute power and authority" meant that African slaves were under a perpetual death sentence. Notwithstanding the fact that there were also free Blacks in the colonies, it was because they were of African descent that these slaves were treated differently from other slaves or from indentured servants, but the colonists themselves were not yet ready to embrace a fully racialized identity for themselves. They preferred to think of themselves primarily as Christians.

This can be seen in the strained vocabulary of the colonists, as emerges in an analysis of legal documents. Within the Barbados Assembly, up until 1690 the term "Christian" still dominated, and it was only later that the term "White" took over.[81] A similar process can be seen in the Acts of the Virginia Assembly. Initially the term "Christian" was juxtaposed with the

48 CRITICAL PHILOSOPHY OF RACE

term "Negro." If the word "Christian" was not used, "Englishman" served as a synonym, as can be seen in a 1662 Act that ordered that the child of an Englishman and Negro woman would be a slave if the woman was a slave.[82] But when "An Act Concerning Servants and Slaves" was passed in October 1705, in part to reaffirm with a few minor exceptions the principle that all servants who were not Christians in their native country "shall be accounted and be slaves, and as such be here bought and sold notwithstanding a conversion to Christianity afterwards," the language quickly became convoluted.[83] So, for example, the Act read in part that "no negros, mullatos, or Indians, although Christians, or Jews, Moors, Mahamotans or other infidels" could purchase "any christian white servant, nor any other, except of their own complexion."[84] The final phrase not only makes use of a racial label alongside a religious one, but it is accompanied by an explicit reference to skin color. Furthermore, in another place in the same Act, the term "Christian" is also accompanied by the qualification "not being negro, mulatto or Indian," when it would seem that it might have been easier to write simply "White."[85] This illustrates the extent to which the Virginian colonists were still committed to thinking of themselves as Christians first and only secondarily as White. One can say that "Anglo-Virginians created whiteness during the seventeenth century and redefined Christianity as a religion of white people,"[86] so long as this is not taken to mean that there was already then a shift from a system of discrimination based on religion to one based on race. It is closer to the truth to say that, at least from a twenty-first-century perspective there is still in this context, among others, a "conflation of religion and race."[87] It seems that the Virginians did not mean to create anything new with this law, but, if so, then in spite of themselves they had taken a step toward racialization by trying to retain a not yet fully racialized order under circumstances that had changed as a result of the decision to promote the baptism of slaves.

The Conversion of Indigenous Americans

The purity of blood statutes (*estatutos de limpieza de sangre*) were formulated by various towns and organizations in Spain beginning with Toledo in 1449, although it was not until the middle of the sixteenth century that they had the support of the Spanish king, by which time they had been extended to apply not only to Jewish converts to Christianity but also to Muslim converts.[88] The statutes barred all such converts together with their descendants from

RACIALIZATION AND THE CONSTRUCTION OF RELIGIONS 49

certain secular offices, guilds, monasteries, and other religious organizations, as well as from marriage with the so-called old Christians (*Cristianos viejos*) or Christians by nature (*Cristianos de natura*). It seems that the initial motivation for these statutes was doubt about the sincerity of those who claimed to have been converted, but the fact that they led to an industry dedicated to the construction of genealogies supports the claim that soon "purity of blood came to overshadow purity of faith."[89] Nevertheless, one should beware of projecting a biological racism onto this discourse. Fifteenth-century ideas of heredity and race are distant from twentieth-century biology or even from eighteenth-century natural history: Jewishness was not understood as being inherited on a strictly biological basis. It was transmitted like an infection or a form of pollution. For example, it was believed that people "of the purest lineage (*de limpiissima generacion*)" developed "perverse inclinations" because they had been fed the milk of Jewish wet nurses.[90]

When in the seventeenth century the purity of blood statutes were imported by the Spanish into their American colonies, their application gave rise to controversy. Ildephonsi Perez de Lara Toletani insisted that the same principles that had been used to exclude Jews and Muslims or Moors (*Maures*) in Spain should be applied to Indigenous Americans and Blacks (*Æthiopes*) to produce similar effects.[91] This view was challenged by Juan Escobar del Corro, who argued that the Indigenous Americans and Blacks were a different case from the Jews and Muslims. On his account, "purity of blood had its source in the main from gentile people who, after having received in baptism our true Catholic faith of Christ the Lord, observed it constantly and intrepidly without ever departing from it."[92] He recognized that the families of the old Christians must themselves have converted to Christianity at one time and that the conversion of the Indigenous Americans could be understood on this model. In other words, their conversion was more like the conversion of the Confucians from heathenism than a conversion from Judaism or Islam. In his defense of colonialism, *Politica Indiana*, Juan de Solórzano Pereira sided with Escobar del Corro against Perez de Lara Toletani.[93] The meeting of the Supreme Council of the Inquisition, held some time toward the end of the seventeenth century, followed his assessment.[94] By the late eighteenth century, contemporary documents show that for Spanish American Creoles ascription of blood purity was confined to those who were "known, held, and commonly reputed to be white persons, Old Christians of the nobility, clean of all bad blood and without any mixture of commoner, Jew, Moor, mulatto, or converso in any degree, no matter how remote."[95] And

50 CRITICAL PHILOSOPHY OF RACE

yet for those of mixed race who did not qualify in this way, one could at the end of the eighteenth-century petition, and if approved, buy a certification of whiteness.[96]

The same welcome and the same opportunities were not shown to the Black population of Spanish America, whether free or slave, pure or mixed. However, as with so much else, the picture was not uniform. So, for example, the University of Mexico and the University of Lima were both founded in 1551, but whereas the former stipulated from the beginning that Negroes, mulattos, and former slaves could not receive degrees, the latter did not show any concern about this issue until after 1750 and then primarily because the number of mulatto graduates in medicine was perceived as threatening the livelihood of White doctors.[97] It was only in 1774 that the Inquisition specifically added Black ancestry to its categories of impurity, but it seems that this delay occurred because up until then the Inquisition had found ways to discriminate against people of African descent without a formal policy for doing so.[98]

Conclusion

"Religion" is as much of a social construction as "race" is. Both terms are, especially when applied to the sixteenth and seventeenth centuries, distorting lenses, and their meanings at the end of the sixteenth century were very different from what they would be two centuries later. In Europe around 1600, if the term "race" was used at all, it implied a plurality of races, whereas religion was most properly used in the singular. Christians believed themselves in possession of the (true) religion; it was the others who might share a race. Two centuries later everyone had a race and, except in the case of atheists or people at the very bottom of the hierarchically organized racial ladder, everybody had a religion. Furthermore, the accounts of both races and religions in their plurality were being increasingly turned into a taxonomy, even if, as yet, there was no science of religion and no racial science as such. What constituted a race or a religion in 1760 was still vague, but through the effects of race mixing and conversion, which brought a fluidity to the categories used to designate races and religions, it was thought necessary for the purpose of establishing social control to legislate the proper usage of both terms and, more decisively, the boundaries that determined to which race and which religion everyone belonged.

3

The Philosophy of Race in the Nineteenth Century

The Task of a Philosophical History of Race

The nineteenth century was the age when the concept of race came of age. In mid-century, Benjamin Disraeli, who would become Prime Minister of Britain in 1868, could write: "All is race. In the structure, the decay, and the development of the various families of man, the vicissitudes of history find their main solution."[1] This was not an isolated claim. It was a view shared by others, such as Robert Knox, an anatomist who had also studied the transcendental philosophy of Immanuel Kant and the *Naturphilosophie* of Lorenz Oken, and who wrote "Race is everything: literature, science, art—in a word, civilization, depends on it."[2]

Any account of the history of the concept of race needs to be broad. A critical philosophy of race cannot confine its historical component to listing what the canonical philosophers have had to say about race: their contributions can only be assessed if they are seen in their context, that is to say, as interventions in ongoing scientific debates and responses—or failures to respond—to the social movements of the day: such as calls for the abolition of slavery, the pursuit of Empire, and demands for segregation.

Another reason why any such study cannot limit itself to those who are now regarded as canonical philosophers is that the boundary line between philosophers and scientists was a great deal less clear in the nineteenth century than it became later. The nineteenth century was a time of growing specialization in philosophy as a result of the birth of a number of new disciplines such as biology, ethnology, anthropology, and sociology, all of which made race central to the definition of their task. However, because these disciplines were not as isolated from each other, and especially from philosophy, as they tend to be today, they cannot be altogether omitted even from a brief account.

Critical Philosophy of Race. Robert Bernasconi, Oxford University Press. © Oxford University Press 2023.
DOI: 10.1093/oso/9780197587966.003.0004

52 CRITICAL PHILOSOPHY OF RACE

The history of race thinking in the nineteenth century is a great deal
more complex than is usually recognized, and what is needed today is an
account that offers a richer sense of that complexity than can be found in
the caricatures of that thinking upon which philosophers today often rely
when they contrast their own views with those of the past. I will organize
my remarks around four issues with which philosophers were deeply involved, leaving aside many other questions that a broader survey of racial
issues would need to address. The four are as follows: first, the debate between monogenesis and polygenesis as the source of the scientific concept
of race; second, the place of race mixing in the philosophy of history; third,
the role of Lamarckianism in inhibiting a full-blooded debate between racial
essentialists and racial environmentalists; and, finally, eugenics both in its relation to Darwinism and in its introduction of the distinction between nature
and nurture.

The Introduction of the Scientific Concept of Race as a
Response to Polygenesis

At the beginning of the nineteenth century, there was little clarity about
what the simple-sounding word "race" meant. There was no intimation that
this would become the preferred term dividing humanity into usually four
or six varieties according to certain inherited characteristics, both physical
and mental. Even when the term "race" usually referred to these few main
races, it was also often used as a synonym for "people." For example, when
Herder's *Ideas* was translated into English at the beginning of the century,
Volk was sometimes translated as "race," even though Herder in that text
explicitly rejected the term "race" (*Rasse*), which he associated with Kant.[3]
The term "race" continued to be used throughout the nineteenth century to
refer to "peoples," like the English, the French, or the Italians. Because of the
ambiguity of the term, I will, when it seems important, specify whether I am
talking about the designated few main races, on the one hand, or the subsidiary or secondary races, on the other hand, but it should be remembered
that this was not a firm division for most of these theorists. Much depended
on the context: in the United States the focus tended to fall on a few main
races, whereas the imperial project led Europeans, particularly in the final
years of the nineteenth century, to highlight differences between the subsidiary races.

THE PHILOSOPHY OF RACE IN THE NINETEENTH CENTURY   53

The passion for classification among natural historians in the seventeenth and eighteenth centuries meant that they wanted to record and find a place for all human varieties. The attention of Northern European scientists in particular was fixed initially on gypsies and Laplanders, although in England the Irish were often singled out, too. Native Americans also long presented a problem because the apparent geographical isolation of the continent made it unclear how it came to be populated. In the same period, Africans were subjected to investigation because of their color. All skin colors had to be explained, but the frameworks that had been devised had the consequence that black skin was understood to present special problems: for example, those who believed that skin color was simply a consequence of the heat of the sun or lack of it had to contend with the fact that it was virtually impossible to find instances where black skin was eradicated.[4] The burgeoning debate over chattel slavery toward the end of the eighteenth century provided another reason why the focus of natural historians fell increasingly on Africans, but the information reaching Europe was supplied by partisan observers who had already taken sides in the debate. The ease with which, in the same period, Indians and Chinese were lumped together in the same main racial category, in spite of the lack of any obvious resemblance between them, is an indication of the fact that the primary focus of European scientists fell elsewhere. Africans were believed to be on the margins of humanity and, for that reason, at the center of all discussions of race.

François Bernier in 1684 seems to have been the first to use the word "race" to refer to a few main human varieties, but Immanuel Kant was the first to single out the term and give it a precise sense.[5] In 1775, Kant defined races as subspecies that "persistently preserve themselves in all transplantings (transpositions to other regions) over prolonged generations among themselves and which also always beget half-breed young in the mixing with other variations of the same phylum."[6] Racial characteristics derived in equal measure from both parents and were confined to those that were "unfailingly hereditary."[7] If those two conditions were not met, the differences formed "varieties."

Kant had insisted on the word "race" as part of his attempt to respond to the challenge posed by what would later be called "polygenesis," the idea that human beings did not descend from a single pair, as the Bible maintained, but were the result of several local creations. Isaac de La Peyrère had promoted polygenesis in the middle of the seventeenth century in an effort to defend the authority of the Bible from the challenge presented by the fact that the

54   CRITICAL PHILOSOPHY OF RACE

Chinese, Chaldeans, and Egyptians recorded a longer history than could be found in the Bible.[8] These peoples then must have been created before Adam and Eve, who were not therefore the original parents of all human beings but only of the Jews.[9] However, by separating the Jews from the rest of humanity in this way La Peyrère did not think of himself as demeaning them: they were in his eyes God's people.[10] By contrast, when some planters in the West Indies adopted a form of pre-Adamism it was to diminish the humanity of those they had enslaved. But, more often, they appealed to the so-called curse of Ham, as one observer recalled, to "infer their Negro's Brutality; justifie their reduction of them under Bondage; disable them from all Rights and Claims, even to Religion itself."[11] Indeed, in the eighteenth century some planters were said to have claimed that "*Negroes* are Creatures destitute of Souls, to be ranked among Brute Beasts," although Francis Brokesby, who is one of the main sources for this, seems to have understood their views through the lens of Henry Dodwell's argument, which originally had been applied to explain why virtuous pagans were precluded from immortality: they, too, lacked souls.[12]

In the middle of the eighteenth century, a strong form of what we today would call environmentalism seemed the only way to reconcile monogenesis, as the Bible maintained, with the limited time frame the Bible seemed to allow for the history of humanity. As late as 1766, Buffon thought that what would later be called racial characteristics, such as skin color, were largely a product of the environment and that as one moved from one climate to another those characteristics would completely change, perhaps in as little as ten generations.[13] However, because the evidence increasingly seemed to suggest the permanence of racial characteristics, Henry Home, also known as Lord Kames, led a revival of polygenesis, which also found favor among those who wanted to cast doubt on the Bible, like Voltaire.[14]

Kant resisted polygenesis by appealing to Buffon's role of species identification, according to which only members of the same species could propagate fertile offspring across successive generations. This established the unity of the human species, but in the process he had conceded to the polygenists the essential point that there were unfailingly hereditary characteristics within the human family, while denying their claims about the origins of those permanent characteristics. To be sure, his explanation of how he could combine these two positions was somewhat artificial. Kant posited the existence of four seeds or germs (*Keime*) that were allegedly present in the first human beings and that corresponded to the four main races that he identified. Initially, these were the White race, the Negro race, the Hunnish race, and the Hindu race, albeit within two years he had substituted the American race for the Hunnish race.[15] The actualization of these seeds, together with the corresponding racial characteristics, depended on the climate and other environmental conditions that human beings encountered as they spread throughout the world. As one set of racial characteristics developed, the possibility of realizing the other characteristics disappeared.[16] Race mixing and the possibility that a certain group in these early migrations might move from a warm climate to a cold climate before the germ had been fully actualized explained the existence of intermediary forms.

Kant went far beyond natural description, which is what occupied most of his contemporaries. He acknowledged that he was engaging in speculation, but he believed that this was forced on him, given the limitations of knowledge of the past at that time. Somewhat misleadingly, he borrowed the phrase "natural history," which some of his contemporaries had already used to refer to what he called "natural description," in order to differentiate the kind of inquiry he was engaged in from what they were doing. However, he increasingly recognized that many scientists were also going beyond simple description in their work: he saw this, for example, in Johann Friedrich Blumenbach's account of a formative drive (*Bildungstrieb*).[17] In marked contrast with Kant, Blumenbach believed that the divisions that could be drawn among the human varieties were somewhat arbitrary and formed a continuum. He labeled them the Caucasian, Mongolian, Ethiopian, American, and Malay.[18] When he used the term "race" in earlier works, it was as a synonym for "variety," which was his preferred term.[19] However, in 1797, Blumenbach adopted Kant's distinction between "race" and "variety," as well as his claim that when two races mate, their offspring is a half-breed that shares equally in the racial characteristics of both parents.[20]

Blumenbach cited Kant as if he was a scientific authority. Skin color was Kant's primary example of an inherited characteristic that borrowed equally from both parents, and surprisingly, Blumenbach in 1795 accepted this claim from Kant, even though he had dismissed the reliability of skin color as an indicator some years earlier and even though Georg Forster, who had traveled with Captain Cook, had earlier made the point that Kant knew little on this topic at first hand.[21] The boundary line between philosophers and scientists was not yet fixed, and this remained the case until at least the middle of the nineteenth century. Franz Theodor Waitz, professor of philosophy at the University of Marburg, presents a clear example of a philosopher who

56   CRITICAL PHILOSOPHY OF RACE

devoted a significant portion of his energies to the study of race, in addition to his innovative work on pedagogics and psychology. In his multivolume *Anthropologie der Naturvölker*, the first volume of which was translated into English, he not only showed a remarkable knowledge of the ethnological data, but in his defense of the unity of humankind he exercised all of his philosophical skills in a field where rigorous argumentation was often lacking.[22]

One of the most prominent advocates of monogenesis and a strong opponent of Lord Kames was the American, Samuel Stanhope Smith. In 1787, while professor of moral philosophy at Princeton, he published *An Essay on the Causes of the Variety of Complexion and Figure in the Human Species*. In line with the speculations of another North American, John Mitchell, more than half a century earlier, but asserted more decisively, he supplemented the account of the impact of climate with a recognition of the role of the "state of society" in modifying the influence of climate.[23] He published a heavily revised and expanded edition of his book in 1810 while president of the College. It incorporated some of the insights of Blumenbach into his defense of monogenesis, and he thus did more than anyone before him to integrate North American ideas of race with those in Northern Europe.[24]

The impact of the Kantian formulation of race on subsequent thinking is evident from a thinker like James Cowles Prichard, who was perhaps the leading racial scientist in Europe in the first half of the nineteenth century. Prichard often gave credit to Blumenbach, but, unlike Blumenbach and like Kant, Prichard established the unity of species by reference to hybridity, defined race in terms of hereditary permanent characteristics, and, when pressed on the issue of how races with permanent characteristics arose from an original pair, he resorted to the Kantian language of germs and predispositions. However, he made this last point only in the second edition of his *Researches into the Physical History of Mankind*.[25] Like most monogenists, his preferred way of negotiating the problem was by choosing to ignore it, beyond general statements of the kind found in Samuel Stanhope Smith about how racial characteristics are transformed as a race becomes more civilized.[26]

The significance of Kant's essays on race is more evident in the German context. In 1799, at the beginning of his *First Outline of a System of the Philosophy of Nature*, Friedrich Schelling embraced the notion of race, understood, following Christoph Girtanner, in terms of the action of Blumenbach's *Bildungstrieb* on the Kantian seeds, which then give rise to inherited characteristics.[27] Indeed, Schelling seems to have seen how Kant's attempt to justify

THE PHILOSOPHY OF RACE IN THE NINETEENTH CENTURY   57

his doctrine of races led him to develop the account of teleological judgment that he presented in *Critique of the Power of Judgment*, and which was the inspiration for Schelling's own philosophy of nature. Nevertheless, Schelling's further discussions of race reflected the significant changes in racial thinking that took place in the first half of the nineteenth century. In 1842, while still favoring monogenesis, he proposed that Europeans no longer be thought of as constituting a race: he restricted the term only to those parts of humanity that he considered "degraded."[28] And before his death, in 1854, when he was still working on the philosophy of mythology, he can be found drawing on Georges Cuvier's *Discours sur les révolutions du globe* and Samuel Morton's *Crania Americana*, both of which were representative of the increasingly polygenist tendencies in natural history.[29] This led Schelling to taunt his readers with a possible "scientific justification of slavery and of the slave trade" on the grounds that it was only through contact with Europeans that Africans could be elevated.[30]

Polygenists in general had little use for the term "race," given that, strictly speaking, they recognized many species rather than many races, a point Prichard had made earlier.[31] However, by this time the term "race" had a life of its own and was not easily eradicated, even as polygenesis came to dominate, first in France, then in North America, and finally, more generally. Already in 1864 Alfred Russel Wallace used Darwin's theory of natural selection to declare the debate between monogenists and polygenists to be an irrelevancy, because one could believe both that man was once a homogenous race, and that man only became man, strictly speaking, when the higher faculties developed. There was thus a sense in which both monogenesis and polygenesis could be true, but this argument was not widely accepted.[32]

Race Mixing and the Philosophy of History

In the 1820s, Georg Wilhelm Friedrich Hegel dismissed the debate between monogenesis and polygenesis as one that lay outside philosophy.[33] At first sight, race did not have the same philosophical significance for Hegel that it had for Kant, but he still accepted from natural history the thesis that races are permanent and have different characteristics.[34] He can be found, for example, arguing that the Americans constituted a proper race.[35] However, Hegel's major significance for the history of race thinking was the way in which he incorporated race into his philosophy of world history. As he announced in

58   CRITICAL PHILOSOPHY OF RACE

his 1830/1831 lecture course, history proper was the history of the Caucasian race.[36] At the same time he excluded Africa proper—more precisely, sub-Saharan Africa—from history.[37] To help make his case, he deliberately distorted his sources to produce a wicked caricature of Africans.[38] Somewhat puzzlingly, given what he had said about the exclusion of Africa, sub-Saharan Africans do make an appearance in world history in such a way as to make world history's transition to Greece necessary. This took place in Egypt and was associated with the fact that the attempted fusion of the African element with the Oriental burst out in the form of "monstrous productions."[39] It was only with the introduction into Egypt of the Caucasians, initially in the form of the Persians, and then the Greeks, that history could progress further.[40]

Hegel's view of non-European peoples as either excluded from history or largely static had a major impact on subsequent nineteenth-century theorists, including Karl Marx. Less attention has been given to the impact of Hegel's views on the role within history of race mixing. Although he believed that race mixing led to the downfall of Egypt, his history includes a number of examples where mixing within the Caucasian race contributed to fruitful transformations. But, particularly in his 1830/1831 lecture course he celebrated purity when he turned to "Germany proper," that is to say, Germany without the portions colonized by the Romans.[41]

By the middle of the nineteenth century, the Northern European obsession with race mixing had been turned into a law of history based in biology. Northern Europeans had previously objected to race mixing on theological, social, or personal grounds: it was against God's plan, disrupted the clear divisions between "types" of people, and offended the brute racism of those who found the very idea repulsive. However, strictly biological objections to race mixing became widespread only in the early 1840s. There were only a few who anticipated this idea, such as Friedrich Ludwig Jahn, sometimes called the father of gymnastics. He was a strong advocate of German racial purity and in 1810 in his *Deutsches Volksthum* he issued a warning: "Hybrid animals have no genuine power of reproduction, and mixed peoples have as little capacity for their own national survival."[42]

As long as one focused on the view that the human varieties were permanent—it did not matter whether they had been formed monogenetically by germs or polygenetically by direct creation—racial inequality would serve as the ultimate reference point of historical explanation. But within the context of the philosophy of history, the focus shifted to explaining change: races and peoples arose in history and then declined

THE PHILOSOPHY OF RACE IN THE NINETEENTH CENTURY   59

or disappeared. In the late eighteenth century, the supposed decline, disappearance, or even static character of certain races led Kant to ask why the Tahitians exist.[43] It seemed that the disappearance of races deemed inferior was necessary for progress. But in the nineteenth century the approach was more proactive. The extermination of races who were not considered useful was a strong temptation, and the argument was that if they stood in the way of progress and they were going to disappear anyway, one was merely hastening the inevitable.[44]

It was in the context of the writing of history that the focus shifted decisively from a largely static portrayal of races to an account which highlighted the fashioning or making of races. To be sure, the experience of animal breeders had already been applied haphazardly by slave owners seeking to improve their "stock" and satisfy their sexual desires at the same time. But for the nineteenth-century philosophers of history who denied that any pure races existed, except perhaps among the Jews or in isolated parts of the world, the picture was more dynamic. Racial purity was viewed not so much as something to be preserved as something to be produced by breeding out variation.

The injection of a specifically biological notion of race into the writing of history in an effort to explain its development seems to have been the contribution of the Saint-Simonians. The biological notion employed was that of William Frédéric Edwards, who in 1829 argued that when neighboring races mix, as had happened in France, the differences were preserved. It was mixing between the main races alone that produced a hybrid that shared the racial characteristics of the parent races equally.[45] Two more Saint-Simonians, Victor Courtet de l'Isle and Gustave d'Eichthal, incorporated this insight into a program that advocated race mixing.[46] In 1835, Wolfgang Menzel called for a universal mixing of the colored and White races in order to secure the victory of Christianity and civilization. He believed that after a time race mixing leads to the production of a new race with its own purity, and in this vein he proposed that the mixing of Whites and Blacks would lead after eight generations to a totally White population.[47] In a somewhat different idiom, but with a somewhat similar conclusion, Gustav Klemm, director of the library at Dresden, maintained that the blending of the originally separate active and passive races promoted the fulfillment of the aim of nature and the completion of humankind in the blossoming of culture.[48] Prichard also argued, albeit more soberly, that race mixing was as advantageous among human beings as it was among animals.[49]

60 CRITICAL PHILOSOPHY OF RACE

The biological argument against the efficacy of race mixing was put by Honoré Jacquinot,[50] and especially Josiah Nott. In 1843, Nott published a short essay in the *American Journal of the Medical Sciences* whose title said everything: "The Mulatto a Hybrid—Probable Extermination of the Two Races If Whites and Blacks Are Allowed to Intermarry."[51] Foucault traced the introduction of biopolitics to eighteenth-century *Polizeiwissenschaft*, and although it already had a racial application at that time—for example, Johann Frank in his *System of Complete Medical Police* advocated the mixing of races on health grounds and explained the weakness of American Indians on their lack of opportunity to mix[52]—Nott took it in the reverse direction and to another level. Nott, a physician based in Mobile, Alabama, was looking for ways to defend what was euphemistically called "the Southern way of life." By coediting with George Gliddon *The Types of Mankind*, an enormously successful volume dedicated to the memory of Samuel George Morton, whose cranial studies were widely respected, and by soliciting for this volume a contribution from Louis Agassiz of Harvard University, Nott found a way to give his own research a high level of respectability it did not deserve.[53] Paul Broca, founder of the Société d'Anthropologie de Paris, frequently cited Nott. Georges Pouchet had the work of Nott and his collaborators in mind when he wrote, "At present France and England walk entirely in the scientific path opened by the American school."[54] Nott's claim was that mixed-race populations were more susceptible to diseases, including decreased fertility. The result was that hybridity—at least in the case of mulattos, the mix of Blacks and Whites—came to be considered a medical condition that should be prevented: the health of society called for measures to prevent it.

The suspicion that those of mixed race were less vital than other people contributed to the rejection of monogenesis, precisely because its defense, as in Buffon and Kant, had been based on fertility across the races. Nott succeeded in persuading many of the leading scientists in Europe that, because the offspring of Blacks and Whites were supposedly shorter-lived and less fertile, they must constitute two different species. Although there was a much more open response to race mixing in South America than North America, and even some idealism, as in the case of Simón Bolívar,[55] by the final quarter of the century attitudes had changed. Even Brazil's cultural elite had been persuaded by the North American school of polygenists that miscegenation was a disease.[56]

Racial amalgamation would never entirely disappear as a proposed solution to alleged racial inequality, but, after Nott, it was less likely to be promoted

THE PHILOSOPHY OF RACE IN THE NINETEENTH CENTURY   61

on biological grounds than it had been with, for example, d'Eichthal and Prichard. Long after Darwinism had rendered Nott's advocacy of polygenesis virtually irrelevant, the impact of Nott's promotion of racial purity on biological grounds would persist. However, most theorists acknowledged that, insofar as races were made, not given, then racial purity itself was to be created, as one might develop a new breed. This dynamic conception left a constant uncertainty about when a race in this sense was constituted. Did the label "White" embrace a number of such races? There were numerous controversies over whether the people of a given nation were made up of a single race, a mixture, or more than one distinct race.

Like Menzel, Count Arthur de Gobineau believed that race mixing was the key to history. In Gobineau's *Essai sur l'inégalité des races humaines*, published between 1853 and 1855, his thesis statement went far beyond the assertion of a static racial hierarchy: "that the racial question overshadows all other problems of history, that it holds the key to them all, and that the inequality of the races from whose fusion a people is formed is enough to explain the whole course of its destiny."[57] He believed that race mixing had been essential for the development of civilization. Artistic genius, for example, arose only as a result of mixing between the White and Black races.[58] Civilization had reached its zenith in his own time and the history of humanity was moving into its second half, a period of "waning and inevitable decline" as a result of race mixing leading to "total amalgamation."[59] Gobineau posited a law of revulsion, which led all races to be repelled by the prospect of race mixing, but he immediately supplemented it with a law of attraction that led the conquering races to disregard the first law and instead seek to mix.[60] This observation, with its suggestion that in the North American context the desire White slave owners felt for their Black female slaves was unreciprocated, was clearly too much for some Southerners to bear. When Nott promoted Gobineau's racial theories in the United States, this idea was omitted from the translation.[61]

Gobineau's impact was strongest not in his own time but in the 1920s and 1930s. When a second posthumous edition of the *Essay* was published in 1884, it needed a subvention from Richard Wagner's circle in Bayreuth. By the time Gobineau appeared in German translations, between 1897 and 1900, his theories were eclipsed by those of Houston Stewart Chamberlain, a member of the Bayreuth Circle, whose books, *Foundations of the Nineteenth Century* and *Immanuel Kant*, were at the time more highly regarded than Gobineau's.

62   CRITICAL PHILOSOPHY OF RACE

In 1850, Knox, a strong opponent of race mixing, had already proclaimed race war a reality.[62] By the end of the nineteenth century the idea had become an obsession among intellectuals, and Chamberlain was one of its main exponents. He feared the Russians and the "busy soulless yellow race," but above all he feared "the millions of the blacks poverty-stricken in intellect, bestially inclined, who are even now arming for the war of races in which there will be no quarter given."[63] He saw the alternative as follows: "our human society must either enter upon the most brutal barbarism which ever prevailed, the barbarism of artificially civilised superstitious races, hostile to nature, debilitated, intellectually poverty-stricken,—as dreamless as so many cattle, or it must, boldly conscious of its aims, prepare for a further step and climb a new stage, a markedly higher stage, of culture."[64] Chamberlain declared that Kant had shown the way to the second path, but he believed that the Aryan race could pursue that path only by leaving the other races behind. The Aryans should try to progress on their own, as the Jews had done.

Chamberlain was not troubled by those who cast doubt on the existence of an Aryan race.[65] An Aryan race could be made: "Race is not an original phenomenon, it is produced; physiologically by characteristic mixture of blood, followed by in-breeding [*Inzucht*]; psychically by the influence which long-lasting historical and geographical conditions exercise upon that special, specific, physiological foundation."[66] He believed that prohibiting race mixing should be a matter of social policy. He even cited Benjamin Disraeli's celebration of the racial purity of the Jews and turned it around to present them as threatening the preeminence of the Germans, who were less pure racially. Whereas Disraeli had thought of the Jews as belonging to the Caucasian race, Chamberlain shared the growing conviction that the Jews were a separate race.[67]

The process by which the Jews became a race is not easy to determine, in part because of the ambiguity in the source literature between main and subsidiary races. As we have seen, La Peyrère already isolated the Jews in midseventeenth century by arguing that they were the result of a distinct creation. Indeed, the purity of blood statutes in Spain in 1492 had already indicated that inheritance could surpass religion in importance,[68] and this language of purity was exported by the Spanish into colonial Mexico, where it was applied to give Indians, as well as the Spanish-Indian mestizaje, a special status almost equal to that of the Spanish, in contrast to anyone of African descent, with only very few exceptions.[69] But the racialization of the Jews is probably best thought of as having been accomplished in the nineteenth century.

THE PHILOSOPHY OF RACE IN THE NINETEENTH CENTURY   63

Already in 1816, Jakob Fries, while professor of philosophy at Heidelberg, wrote a virulent attack on the Jews and identified them as "a race," but it is not entirely clear what he meant by this.[70] Even Ernest Renan, who seems to have done as much as anyone to establish the Jews as the Semitic race par excellence and the Semitic race as distinct from the Indo-European race, thought that they could not be distinguished on a physiological basis but only on the basis of their language, literature, and religion.[71] Renan had a major influence on Moses Hess, an early figure in Zionist thought, who, in 1862, was among the first to present the Jewish race as one of the primary races of humankind, unchanging in spite of changes of climate.[72] Nevertheless, as late as 1880, Hermann Cohen proposed assimilation as an answer to the racial issue and in terms that suggest that this included for him becoming physically more German.[73]

Race mixing proved a decisive issue. In 1843, Bruno Bauer wrote an essay on the Jewish Problem, to which Marx responded. He returned to the theme in 1863 when he dramatically differentiated the Jews and Germans, denying that a true mixture was possible on the grounds that a Jew cannot be Germanized, whereas a German can take on certain Jewish qualities.[74] This turned the Jews into a remarkable exception because, at least up until 1853, Bauer had insisted that only race mixing would supply the intellectual and moral elasticity that would give a people the force needed for world domination.[75] Concern about Germans mixing with Jews became even more pronounced in the writings of Eugen Dühring. Dühring acknowledged that healthy neighboring races could produce healthy offspring, but he did not put the Jews and the Germans together in that category. Indeed, he considered the "Judaisation [*Verjudung*] of the blood of modern peoples" to be a great evil.[76]

Concerns about race mixing within the White community in the United States about the effects of race mixing on the Black community came to a head in the 1890s and gave rise to one of the classic texts of the critical philosophy of race, W. E. B. Du Bois's "The Conservation of Races." The context was the publication of Frederick Hoffman's *Race Traits and Tendencies of the American Negro*. Hoffman, a leading statistician, updated Nott's argument that people of mixed Black and White ancestry had less vitality than people of either pure Black or pure White ancestry. He drew the further conclusion that, given that most of those who were designated African American were mixed, they were destined for extinction, although he did allow that there might be a reprieve if they changed their moral nature.[77] Both Kelly

64   CRITICAL PHILOSOPHY OF RACE

Miller[78] and W. E. B. Du Bois responded in 1897 at the inaugural meeting of the American Negro Academy, although on that occasion Du Bois did not mention Hoffman by name.

Some philosophers today have tried to impose their question of whether "race" is a legitimate concept onto W. E. B. Du Bois's "The Conservation of Races," but this is anachronistic.[79] There were certainly questions about the usefulness of the term "race" within biology at that time, but the complaint was that the multiple uses of the word had left it with a scientific utility that matched its social usefulness and not that there was nothing in the world to which it corresponded. Du Bois was not concerned about whether the word should be maintained, but rather whether the races themselves should conserve their identity. It was his answer to segregation since, by 1897, Whites had blocked the path of assimilation, and the argument of Frederick Douglass was that, because many African Americans were already mixed and could neither be expatriated nor annihilated, they should look forward to being absorbed through further race mixing.[80] The context establishes that Du Bois was not defending a narrowly scientific concept of race, but arguing for race loyalty, and doing so in the context of the philosophy of history.

Du Bois, Miller, and Hoffman all embraced social Darwinism in some form or another, and that meant that survival was meant literally, as when Du Bois asked his fellow African Americans: "Have we in America a distinct mission as a race—a distinct sphere of action and an opportunity for race development, or is self-obliteration the highest end to which Negro blood dare aspire?"[81] It is this that gives the essay its almost existential feel as when Du Bois asks "What, after all, am I? Am I an American or am I a Negro? Can I be both? . . . Does my black blood place upon me any more obligation to assert my nationality than German, or Irish or Italian blood would?"[82] The fact that Du Bois wrote of conservation rather than preservation, suggests that he was not averse also to applying physical principles to philosophy and history, as Herbert Spencer and Walter Bagehot had done.

Whereas Alexander Crummell and Edward William Blyden had preached the duty to preserve the Black race on theological grounds,[83] Du Bois presented the same claim in the language of the philosophy of history. It is in terms of the philosophy of history, with its heavy reliance on the concept of race, that his contribution (including his so-called definition of race) can best be understood. To be sure, Du Bois's philosophy of history employed arguments that relied heavily on references to Providence, as did those of Kant and Hegel. For Du Bois "the duty of the American Negro descent, as a

THE PHILOSOPHY OF RACE IN THE NINETEENTH CENTURY   65

body, to maintain their identity" was addressed not in terms of racial purity, but race ideals, and once those ideals had been incorporated within history, then and only then would "the ideal of human brotherhood" become possible.[84] Strong echoes of both Herder and Hegel have been found in Du Bois's essay, even though these two German philosophers are usually understood as occupying opposing positions within the philosophy of history. Herder explicitly rejected Kant's model of Europe giving law to the other continents and proposed in its place a kind of latent multiculturalism according to which each people had its own model and that all these forms contributed to whole framework of humanity.[85] By contrast, Hegel believed that each people was assigned its own time in which to take the central place in world history, but that not every race was capable of raising itself up to form peoples or nations and thus be candidates for playing such a role.[86] It was on this basis that he confined history proper to the Caucasian race and excluded the African race from history altogether. Du Bois lifted that restriction and, by discounting the once-widespread view that Egypt was African, and by overlooking the fate of American Indians, Eskimos, and South Sea Islanders, who seemed not to have a moment in history,[87] Du Bois held out the prospect that the time of the Black race still lay in the future (see Chapter 8).

Eighteenth-Century Environmentalism and Nineteenth-Century Lamarckianism

In 1809 in *Philosophie zoologique* Jean-Baptiste Lamarck challenged Buffon's rule, which in any case Buffon himself had already put into question by questioning the sterility of the offspring of a horse and an ass.[88] Lamarck argued that hybridization across species led through time to the formation of new races and then through time to new species.[89] He did not exempt humanity from this process.[90] This would be important for theorizing the human races, but its impact was completely overshadowed by Lamarck's doctrine of the inheritance of acquired characteristics, according to which an organism's environment (*circonstances*) imposed needs upon it in response to which it developed characteristics that were then passed on to its offspring.[91] This, too, was not an altogether new idea, but he had generalized it, and his name came to be attached to it. Because it is the environment that is credited with making the changes that subsequently became permanent, some commentators call this a form of "environmentalism,"[92] but it is very different

66 CRITICAL PHILOSOPHY OF RACE

from what was thought of as environmentalism in the eighteenth century, which was understood to operate more quickly and was usually thought of as reversible. In the eighteenth century, environmentalism, understood as the attempt to refer the existence of races to climate and nutrition, was an idea that had failed because it did not explain the kind of issues that led Kant to posit races, such as why, after a time, races seemed to stop changing or changed only minimally. Environmentalism became a viable explanation of the human races again only as the time frame allowed for human evolution became massively extended, but this new environmentalism was a very different kind of theory. Meanwhile, so long as it held sway, Lamarckianism excluded any straightforward application of the nature-culture distinction to the topic of race, and this is why nineteenth-century discussions of race do not readily conform to the categories that philosophers have tended to employ at least since the end of the Second World War.

I have already indicated that what we today call "racial essentialism," at least in its core sense, was not as widespread in the nineteenth century as is often thought. Some commentators have been tempted to cast John Stuart Mill as one of its early opponents, but there is a danger that this reading may distort the terms in which he saw the debate. It is perhaps better to use Mill to show how the framework which determined how race was viewed in the middle of the nineteenth century was very different from what it is today, and that is why I shall give it more attention than perhaps it deserves in its own right. Mill's contemporaries observed that he was relatively silent on the question of race, and they attributed this to his focus on the individual.[93] Mill wrote at the time of the triumph of organism epitomized by Carl Carus's essay on Goethe.[94] The separation of body and mind, which had already been challenged in the eighteenth century by such thinkers as Charles Bonnet and Herder, seemed less and less relevant in this context. But it should be remembered that whereas what Mill called "national character" could change, it was still consistent with what many, if not most, of his contemporaries would have called "race," in one of its many senses.

Mill's main public statement on the question of race was made in response to Thomas Carlyle in a debate that was conducted in mid-century in the pages of *Fraser's Magazine*. The controversy is often presented as pitting Carlyle's crude racial determinism against Mill's enlightened environmentalism, but this would be anachronistic and overdetermined. Mill attributed to Carlyle the view that there was "an original difference of nature" between the races,[95] but when he caught Carlyle describing "the Negro" as born to be the servant

THE PHILOSOPHY OF RACE IN THE NINETEENTH CENTURY   67

of Whites, Mill refused to hold Carlyle to it, saying only that the latter did not know what he was saying.[96] Mill did not rule out the possibility of some form of essentialism; he simply dismissed the evidence available at that time as insufficient to prove it. Furthermore, he knew that Carlyle's essay was not a theoretical piece but an intervention within the ongoing debate about British policy toward the West Indies. Indeed, Carlyle described it on its first publication as "an occasional discourse." He was less interested in addressing the question of the nature of the different races than promoting his "gospel of work," and it was for this reason that he presented Blacks as having been happy and indolent under slavery, whereas, since emancipation, they had become hard-pressed and beleaguered. Because Mill observed that two trees from the same stock may grow to different sizes because of differences of climate,[97] commentators, even in the late nineteenth century, attributed to him a form of environmentalism,[98] but the application of that label to Mill was a projection made possible by a shift in the intellectual horizon. In fact, although Mill believed that many of his contemporaries exaggerated the importance of race, he himself did not deny "the great influence of Race in the production of national character" and used it, for example, to explain the similarities between the French and Irish in spite of their different histories and social circumstances.[99]

Mill was inclined to highlight education more than either race or environment. In a letter he wrote to Charles Dupont-White in 1860, he explained that in place of the indelible differences of nature, "the influence of both education and of the social and political milieu" should be highlighted.[100] Initially he had supported d'Eichthal's proposals for uniting or fusing Europeans and Orientals[101] and Whites and Blacks[102] on the grounds that their characteristics were complementary. As time went on his thinking took a somewhat different direction. In "The Subjection of Women," he proposed that education and cultivation should be the main means for "correcting . . . the infirmities incident" to the temperament of women or races. However, it seems that, at least on this occasion, he was talking about the fact that some European races, such as the French, the Greeks, and the Italians, were "excitable" and yet still capable of excellence and did not have a broader view in mind.[103] In "On Liberty" Mill had described despotism as a legitimate mode of government in dealing with barbarians, provided it was directed toward their improvement in such a way that the means employed were both appropriate to the end and effective in bringing it about.[104] This is what makes Mill's response to Charles Dilke's book *Greater Britain* so disappointing. Mill complained to the author

68 CRITICAL PHILOSOPHY OF RACE

about his tendency to reduce the sources of national character to race and climate "as if whatever does not come from race must come from climate, and whatever does not come from climate must come from race."[105] But he said nothing about Dilke's celebration of the Saxon as "the only extirpating race on earth."[106] It is shocking to find that Mill could let such comments pass unchecked. Nor is this an isolated case of Mill turning a blind eye: in 1831, he judged that "The conduct of the United States towards the Indian tribes has been throughout, not only just, but noble."[107]

A generation later, Henry Sidgwick also exhibited attitudes that it is virtually impossible for us to avoid thinking of as racist.[108] He granted that drastic and permanent segregation would be appropriate, if "the social amalgamation of two races would be debasing to the superior race," but like Mill, he allowed that additional evidence might lead him to modify his view. He simply doubted that that had yet been shown and he thus favored only temporary separation as a transitional measure toward complete social amalgamation of "the inferior race" with the colonizing race.[109] This is not the place to try to differentiate the various forms of imperialism that philosophers sought to justify in the final years of the nineteenth century, but mention should be made of the fact that Carl Peters, one of the most vicious imperialists of his generation, wrote a work of philosophy that was heavily influenced by both Schopenhauer and Darwin.[110]

Because Herbert Spencer in his synthetic philosophy linked biological evolution to sociocultural evolution, in such a way that moral intuitions were understood to be biologically inheritable, he can be seen as a representative of Lamarckianism. Spencer's short essay on "Personal Beauty," which was intended for a popular audience, was a defense of the proposition that beauty of character is related to facial beauty. It began with a statement of how transitory forms produce permanent forms, but instead of leading to a discussion of how facial characteristics might in this way reflect personal character, Spencer immediately introduced the phenomenon of hereditary transmission together with the recognition that changes in functions lead to changes in forms. In this way progressive civilization can be correlated with the remaking of features, including changes in the facial angle of the kind that Petrus Camper had studied with regard to the races at the end of the previous century. Even more interesting for our purposes is the way in which Spencer in the second part of his essay addressed the anomalies and exceptions to this general rule. Spencer observed that when pure races mix with those that are already mixed, the features of the unmixed race tend to predominate. And

THE PHILOSOPHY OF RACE IN THE NINETEENTH CENTURY   69

yet, Spencer noted, all civilized races at least are of mixed origin. The point of these observations was to establish a framework in which exceptions to the law that "all forms of feature are related to forms of mind" could be seen as contingencies that would over time disappear, just as hybrids would "dwindle away in a few generations."[111]

One final feature of Spencer's brief discussion merits attention, his observation that when two pure races mix the result is "not a homogeneous mean between the two constitutions, but a seemingly irregular combination of characteristics of the one with characteristics of the other."[112] This of itself was not new, although it contravened Kant's original claim that racial characteristics were those that derived equally from both parents. However, it led Spencer to the further point that certain traits might disappear for a few generations only to reappear, even if only for a single generation. It is remarkable, albeit not untypical, that Spencer would draw attention to this fact in what was in many ways a popular essay, because it was a phenomenon for which the dominant biology of the day did not yet have a ready explanation.

Darwinism, Eugenics, and the Miscegenation Debate

So far as the topic of the human races is concerned, Charles Darwin is less important for what he wrote than for what others made of his writings. The full title of his 1859 book—*On the Origin of Species by Means of Natural Selection, or the Preservation of Favored Races in the Struggle for Life*—already indicated the direction in which others would take his thought, but he himself decided not to address racial issues there on the grounds that the book was already controversial enough. By the time he decided to address these questions in *The Descent of Man*, which appeared in 1871, his opinions were no longer on the cutting edge. In this later book he largely restricted himself to a cautious review of the literature on race without adding much that was new. For example, he questioned the findings of Nott and Broca about the relative sterility of the mixed races, but he did so by relying mainly on the findings of John Bachman, a clergyman from Charleston, South Carolina, who had been Nott's most vociferous opponent in the 1850s.

What one does not see so clearly in Darwin himself, but which is manifest in his contemporaries, is how the effort to come to terms with Darwin's theories intensified philosophical interest in racial theories. In Germany, Fritz Schultze argued that Kant was a forerunner of Darwin and called for

70 CRITICAL PHILOSOPHY OF RACE

greater interest in Kant's essays on race, a call that was answered by Johannes Unold.[113] Meanwhile, Ernst Haeckel, the foremost Darwinian in Germany, who had already showered praise of Kant's *Critique of Teleological Judgement* in his *The History of Creation* in 1868, took the opportunity of revisions to successive editions of the same book to expand on his importance as a forerunner of Darwin.[114] In France, Georges Pouchet issued a second edition of his *The Plurality of the Human Race*, and among the changes was a new paragraph which made clear that evolution had become a genuine philosophic topic: "philosophy commences where science ends, and it belongs to it to give us an explanation of the matter." It was a question not just of the past, but of the future: "The genius of man has no bounds, who can say to what it may reach? who knows whether, like a new Prometheus, a creator in his turn, he may not one day breathe life into some new species, which will suddenly appear from his laboratories?"[115] Perhaps because he was not persuaded that geology had yet resolved enough of the questions to leave the field open to the philosopher, he turned to studying the history of science and published a study of Aristotle's *De generatione animalium*.[116]

Clémence Royer, as the first French translator of Darwin's *Origin of Species*, supplied a long introduction that insisted that Darwin's theory of natural selection showed that the superior races would supplant the inferior races. In her view, Darwin had shown the equality of races to be a dangerous and impossible idea.[117] Royer's use of Darwin to advocate racial inequality is of particular interest because it provoked a strong response from Anténor Firmin, a Haitian member of the Société d'Anthropologie de Paris. Frederick Douglass had already addressed racial ethnology in 1854, but Firmin's *The Equality of the Human Races* was not only at that time the most detailed response by a Black thinker to White racial theories, but it is a philosophical statement of some significance in its own right. Firmin aligned himself with the positivist philosophy of Auguste Comte, sharing the latter's celebration of progress and perfectibility, and its conviction that racial differences were less salient than usually thought. But Firmin drew the implications of a belief in human progress for racial equality more clearly than anyone, including Comte himself. Whereas Comte called for "intimate cooperation" between the races, while still giving the leadership role to the Whites,[118] Firmin, while acknowledging the special role accorded to the advanced nations at any given time, believed every race had a historical role to play. In this respect, his work resembled the account found later in W. E. B. Du Bois's "The Conservation of Races," albeit Firmin seems to have believed in civilization as "common destiny."[119]

THE PHILOSOPHY OF RACE IN THE NINETEENTH CENTURY   71

Firmin was aware of the widespread conviction among Europeans that the "inferior races" were destined to die out and that for the sake of human progress exterminating them could sometimes be tolerated. For example, Alfred Russel Wallace already in 1864 argued that the law of "*the preservation of favoured races in the struggle of our life*" led to "the inevitable extinction of all those low and mentally undeveloped populations with which Europeans come in contact."[120] With the displacement of the lower races by the more intellectual and moral races, there would be continuing improvement until "the world is again inhabited by a single homogeneous race."[121] That Wallace sought to reconcile Darwinism with a belief in the equality of the human races is historically significant. Firmin attempted to arrive at the same result but by emphasizing the influence of the environment, rather than natural selection, in the development of the human races.

Firmin's belief in the equality of the human races was a belief in the idea that under the right conditions all the races could attain the same high levels of virtue and intellectual development.[122] When that happens, "there will be no question of race, for the word implies a biological and natural fatality which has no correlation with the degree of ability observable among the different human communities spread around the globe."[123] For him the only destiny was human perfectibility, which was why an exclusive focus on the accomplishments of the White race was misleading. His attempt to redress this imbalance led him to celebrate the contribution of Blacks to the history of civilization.[124]

Because discussions of evolution were concerned with how nature contributed to the making of races, it was inevitable that they would recognize that, once evolution had become conscious, human beings might dictate to nature at least in part the subsequent course of evolution, thus leading to eugenics. In *The Origin of Species*, Darwin relied heavily on the evidence that the scientist would amass from the experience of animal breeding, and it is hardly surprising that this led to a heightened focus on the breeding of human races.

The term "eugenics" was coined by Francis Galton, Darwin's cousin, in 1883. By "eugenics" Galton meant the science of improving stock, both in the sense of "judicious mating" and taking "cognisance of all influences that tend in however remote a degree to give to the more suitable races or strains of blood a better chance of prevailing speedily over the less suitable than they otherwise would have had."[125] Although Galton was arguably more interested in class than race, he made a significant contribution to the understanding of

72 CRITICAL PHILOSOPHY OF RACE

race through his challenge to the notion of the inheritance of acquired characteristics, both physical and mental. With Galton race comes to be identified with nature and opposed to nurture. Galton defined the terms in this way: "Nature is all that a man brings with himself into the world; nurture is every influence from without that affects him after his birth."[126] The former includes the latent faculties of growth of body and mind; the latter includes "the environment in which the growth takes place, by which natural tendencies may be strengthened or thwarted, or wholly new ones implanted."[127] The equation of race with nature prepared the way for the resolution that would emerge towards the middle of the twentieth century, in which anthropology would confine itself to culture, leaving race to biology, in the knowledge that biology had already renounced the concept as too imprecise to be useful.[128]

Friedrich Nietzsche owned—and read—Galton's *Inquiries into Human Faculty and Its Development*, and at certain points there are clear resemblances in their positions,[129] although Nietzsche tended to understand "breeding" indeterminately in both its moral as well as its biological sense, whereas Galton emphasized simple inheritance. Nietzsche seems not to have read Darwin at first hand and, not surprisingly, his polemic against Darwinism is marked by a number of misunderstandings, although it should be added that Darwin was at that time also misunderstood by many who had read him. Nevertheless, these misunderstandings are nothing compared with the widespread confusion about Nietzsche's ideas of race. There is still a tendency on the part of some commentators to describe Nietzsche's remarks on race as original or transgressive, whereas greater familiarity with the historical context challenges that perception.[130] For example, when Nietzsche referred to the Jews as "the strongest, most tenacious and purest race now living in Europe" and only four sentences later acknowledged that none of the European nations were yet a race because they were still in a state of becoming, this was not a unique perspective, but reminiscent of ideas we have already seen in Disraeli.[131] Similarly, when Nietzsche described the German people as composed of "the most monstrous mixing and blending of races, perhaps even with a preponderance of the pre-Aryan element,"[132] he was merely taking sides in an ongoing debate in anthropology, not engaging in a novel deconstruction of racial concepts. Indeed, at one point he referred to Rudolf Virchow's study of the races of Germany that established this.[133]

Earlier, in 1878, Nietzsche had foreseen the destruction of European nations as a result of commerce and industry, and he believed that this would

THE PHILOSOPHY OF RACE IN THE NINETEENTH CENTURY   73

lead through crossbreeding to a European mixed race. In spite of his complaint that the youthful stock-exchange Jews were "perhaps the most repulsive invention of the whole human species," Nietzsche thought Jews would be "just as usable and desirable an ingredient" of this European mixed race as "the remains of any other nation."[134] It was against this background that Nietzsche in an attack on anti-Semitism, proposed, in response to the desire of many Jews to be absorbed and assimilated into Europe, that they marry into the families of the "more strongly delineated types of new Germanism," the Prussian officers of noble rank.[135] These comments are an important corrective to the misuse subsequently made of his writings by the Nazis. However, his proposal that Jews marry into some of the best German families was far from being the transgressive gesture some commentators like to imagine it to be. Bismarck famously proposed bringing together Christian stallions of German upbringing with Jewish mares.[136]

For Nietzsche race was fundamentally about inheritance: "it is not in the least possible that a human being might *not* have the qualities and preferences of his parents and ancestors in his body." This led him in the same place to describe education and culture as the art of deception "about our descent, the inherited rabble in our bodies and souls."[137] One can see here the impact on Nietzsche of the racial histories of the mid-nineteenth century. So in *On the Genealogy of Morality* he not only took Negroes as representatives of prehistoric man, but he also speculated that physiological inhibition might be traced back to such factors as the crossing of very different races and classes and the migration of races to climates for which they were not suited.[138] His belief that values are passed through the bloodline is reflected in his claim in *Beyond Good and Evil* that when races that had long been separated mix, the resulting hybrids are indecisive and lack a sense of balance. He applied this analysis to offer a diagnosis of contemporary Europe in terms of its "radical class mixing and *consequently* race mixing."[139] Nevertheless, he shared with many of his contemporaries the idea that races are not given but made. That is why he insisted that "There is in all likelihood no such thing as pure races but only races that have become pure."[140] Presenting himself as a philosopher of the future and contrasting himself with the English biologists, Nietzsche insisted that the focus should not be the persistence of a race or even the enhancement of its power to adapt to a certain climate: the task was to produce "a stronger type."[141] For example, when in 1888 in *Twilight of the Idols* he proposed that doctors were morally obliged to suppress degenerate life so as to promote ascending life,[142] he was rehearsing the criticism of Darwin by

74   CRITICAL PHILOSOPHY OF RACE

contemporaries like W. H. Rolph, which was not about preserving what already existed, but creating or enhancing what was yet to be attained.[143]

Conclusion

Today philosophers tend to view race in terms of its opposition to culture, an opposition that can readily be related to other familiar conceptual pairs: nature and history; what is inherited and what is acquired; body and mind; blood and spirit; and, in institutional terms, biology and anthropology. This approach may be popular among philosophers today, but historians are liable to judge it to be anachronistic for understanding the history of the concept of race, not only because the relation of biology and anthropology was very different then, but also because of the dominance within nineteenth-century science of the Lamarckian idea of the inheritance of acquired characteristics. It is no easy matter to separate the biological and cultural conceptions of race in the nineteenth century, and well into the twentieth century scientists found it hard to distinguish the influence of physical inheritance from the impact of environment.[144]

But this is not the only way in which readings of nineteenth-century philosophers of race tend to be anachronistic. We too easily forget that for most of the nineteenth century, races tended not to be thought of as given by nature but as made by human intervention, largely through the policing of race mixing. Galton placed race on the side of nature, but in a sense he could only do so because his whole project was concerned with the influence that human beings themselves exercised on the formation of races through race mixing and emigration.[145] The races were therefore even on this model a product of culture, including a culture either prohibiting or promoting race mixing, and it was this possibility that the African American philosopher Alain Locke explored in 1924 with his notion of "culture-heredity."[146]

Throughout the nineteenth century the idea of race was fundamentally always about race mixing. At the beginning of the century the possibility of race mixing established the unity of the human species. In mid-century, with the dominance of polygenesis, that was placed in doubt, and as a result races were also regarded as species, but in such a way that they could but should not mix. The medicalization of race mixing, particularly when it was united with social Darwinism, led to segregation and apartheid, as well as laws against miscegenation and some of the uglier aspects of eugenics. But this was far from the end of the story. In spite of doubts about the scientific usefulness of the concept of race in the face of the complexity of the phenomena it was called upon to describe, race science was at its most prolific and self-confident during the first two decades of the twentieth century, particularly in Germany. It was a question of making the races conform to an ideal of purity that had come to be associated with strength, survival, and victory over other races.

The rediscovery of Gregor Mendel's theory of inheritance at the beginning of the twentieth century provided a fuller explanation of the problem of regressive traits that had already been observed, for example, by Spencer. The half-breed or blending theory proposed by Kant, which had long been under strain, finally had to be abandoned. This gave rise to a new account of race, according to which an inheritable variation, the so-called Mendelian trait, once introduced, cannot be bred out of a given population and can only be eliminated by the death of those who carried it. In the United States this led to increased anxiety about passing and thus to the one-drop rule, which became law in some states in the late 1920s but was already socially in effect a decade earlier. In Germany it led to a massive sterilization program which eventually gave way to a policy of extermination. Already in 1905, William Bateson, who would become recognized as one of the leading authorities on Mendelism, saw the writing on the wall. He posed the question: "What will happen when civilized society thoroughly grasps what heredity means?" His answer was that "in some country, at some time, not, perhaps, far distant, that power will be applied to control the composition of a nation."[147] The roots of that disaster were firmly planted in the nineteenth century, and to this day it is shocking how few were the voices that were raised in an effort to halt what was coming. The study of the history of race thinking not only helps us understand our current intellectual problems by exposing their genealogy but also calls for greater scrutiny of current ideas on the topic and a suspicion of quick conceptual fixes.

4

Racial Science in the Nineteenth Century

Slavery and Survival

In 1864, the French philosopher and anthropologist Georges Pouchet wrote that "at present France and England walk entirely in the scientific path opened by the American school."[1] He was referring to the work of Louis Agassiz, Samuel George Morton, and Josiah Nott, and their promotion of polygenesis, the theory that the different races had different origins. Nevertheless, only six years earlier, in an earlier edition of the same book, Pouchet had written: "in France and in England the old ideas are still dominant."[2] A similar shift in the status of polygenesis had been noticed twenty years earlier in the United States. In 1842, *The United States Magazine and Democratic Review* had affirmed without question the unity of the human race as a single species, but only eight years later an anonymous reviewer of W. F. Van Amringe's mammoth *Theories of the Natural History of Man* in the same journal declared that "Few or none now seriously adhere to the theory of the unity of races."[3] Even allowing for some exaggeration on the part of these reports, and the fact that it neglects dissenting voices,[4] the question inevitably arises as to how the American school of polygenesis came to hold such dominance, first at home and then internationally.

The international success of American polygenism is easier to explain than its domestic success. American natural historians had long been able to claim a firsthand knowledge of racial diversity that most of their European colleagues often lacked.[5] They were also more deeply invested in racial issues. Anténor Firmin, a Haitian who was a member of the Société d'Anthropologie de Paris and so knew the French scene at first hand, speculated that the American school of polygenesis was motivated by a desire to maintain slavery at all costs, whereas French scientists were drawn to advocate polygenesis because they wanted to separate science from religion and were suspicious that in previous generations many scientists had argued for monogenesis more on biblical than scientific grounds.[6]

Critical Philosophy of Race. Robert Bernasconi, Oxford University Press. © Oxford University Press 2023.
DOI: 10.1093/oso/9780197587966.003.0005

RACIAL SCIENCE IN THE NINETEENTH CENTURY   77

Although it is tempting to see the defense of slavery as the driving force behind American polygenism—and this seems to have been the case for Josiah Nott—neither Agassiz nor Morton fits this model. Indeed, it is hard to find references in Morton's writings to the political problems of the day.[7] Most authors stayed well away from the issue in their scientific writings, addressing it only in other contexts. There was a strong tendency for polygenists to favor slavery, in large part because they were likely to think of the racial characteristics of the so-called inferior races as permanent, but there was no straightforward correlation between what a given scientist believed about the unity of the human races and whether that same scientist supported slavery. So both Rev. John Bachman of Charleston, the foremost champion of monogenesis in the United State in mid-century, and James Cabell, professor of comparative anatomy at the University of Virginia, argued at length against Agassiz and Nott in favor of the unity of humanity, but they still defended slavery. Beginning in the mid-1830s, those scientific writings were culled by advocates on both sides of the debate on abolition, but what was perhaps the first sustained appeal to science to support slavery was an import. In 1837, Guenebault published in translation selections from the second edition of Julien-Joseph Virey's *History of Mankind*. Virey was a polygenist who supported slavery and by choosing to extract passages from Virey's book that favored both causes, Guenebault was making an intervention in the debate. To be sure, the arguments for slavery that Guenebault found there were not new, but it was clearly meant for them to have a greater weight simply because their author was a renowned scientist.[8] In short, slavery as an institution determined what American natural historians saw of Blacks, but by and large its defense did not drive their research.

Nevertheless, although biblical quotations generally carried more weight than scientific citations during the debate on slavery, the fact that both sides were increasingly ready to appeal to the authority of science reflects the growing prestige of science, however crude. Slavery had not been challenged in the United States at the end of the eighteenth century to the degree that it had been in Britain and France, but racial science was at that time in its infancy and so played a smaller role in the debates. Science was a latecomer to the debate about the status of Negroes and Native Americans. Nobody felt the need to appeal to it before alleging that both of these races were inferior. Indeed, the dominant sense of race in Europe in the nineteenth century would be better described as historical rather than biological; that is to say, it was based on the history of nations. It should be remembered that

78　CRITICAL PHILOSOPHY OF RACE

anthropology was still in its infancy, and it would be anachronistic to impose on that time the strict division between cultural and physical anthropology that would become a product of the twentieth century. But it was the politicians, not the scientists, who had the most to say about the meaning of racial identities. The legal definitions of who counted as White, Black, or Native American were frequently changing so that racial identification was usually more about the borderline between races than about racial essences.

The scientific issue that natural historians could not avoid was not slavery, but survival. The population decline of the Native Americans meant that there was a need to find a justification for the genocidal policies directed against them. The survival of African Americans was also debated, although at first it might have been no more than a variation on Thomas Jefferson's fantasy that there might at some indeterminate future time be a way of removing all Blacks "to other parts of the world."[9] In 1854, Frederick Douglass was responding to such ideas when in "The Claims of the Negro, Ethnologically Considered" he declared that African Americans could not be colonized or exterminated and that they would not die out: "His tawny brother, the Indian, dies, under the flashing glance of the Anglo Saxon. *Not* so the negro; civilization cannot kill him."[10] Some even tried to defend slavery as a means to save African Americans from their potential destruction. Cabell suggested that "the actual bondage of the blacks in America was not intended, in the merciful and wise providence of God, as the only means of extricating them from their otherwise inevitable 'destiny'": it was a way of "bringing them under the tutelage of a superior race without danger of becoming 'extinct before' such higher race."[11]

Miscegenation and Sexual Repugnance

At the beginning of the nineteenth century, American natural historians were very much on the margins of the racial discourse that had been begun in the previous century by Buffon, Kant, and Blumenbach, but on one central issue Americans could speak with greater authority. It was the question of adaptation, the impact of moving from one environment to another. Three contributions stand out when one looks back on the early years of race science in North America. First, John Mitchell wrote a groundbreaking essay on skin color in 1744 that concluded with a defense of the unity of the human species based on the idea that skin color in North America was a consequence of whatever was "most suitable for the Preservation of Health, and the Ease and Convenience of Mankind in these Climes, and Ways of Living."[12] Second, William Charles Wells, who at the end of his life lived in England but was originally from Charleston and who has been seen as a forerunner of Charles Darwin, wrote an essay in which he argued that accidental varieties of man that were well suited to combat disease in a given location would prosper there and that this could be used to explain the black skin and "woolly hair" of Negroes.[13]

Finally, there was Samuel Stanhope Smith, who was professor of moral philosophy of the College of New Jersey, which would soon become Princeton College. He was the most influential of the three. In 1787, Smith published a defense of the idea of the unity of human species against Henry Home, Lord Kames, who had argued that the different races were "fitted by nature for different climates" as could be seen from the fact that in Charlestown [sic] Europeans "die so fast that they have not time to degenerate."[14] Although the thought that each race somehow belonged in its own place was revived in 1850 by the Scot Robert Knox,[15] it was not one designed to appeal to the colonists. Smith found an answer in the idea that "nature has given such pliancy to the human constitution as to enable it to adapt itself to every clime."[16] However, Smith went beyond attempts to explain human diversity in terms of the effects of climate by adding a second instrument that he called "the state of society." He did not recoil from the conclusion that the descendants of "Anglo-Americans" who stayed long enough in North America would take on the same skin color as "Native Indians," but with the important proviso that this would happen only if they shared a similar "savage state" with them.[17] The case of Africans transported to North America proved more difficult to accommodate to the theory. Smith conceded that there was no evidence of their skin color lightening in North America, but he insisted that other physiological features of domestic slaves were in the process of being transformed to grow closer to those of their masters, whereas those of field slaves were not, thereby confirming the importance of the state of society as a factor in their adaptation.[18] In 1810, Smith, who was by now president of Princeton, issued a heavily revised and expanded version of the book that took account both of criticisms and, more importantly for Smith's standing, of European authors like Blumenbach, whom he had ignored in the first edition. While repeating his assertion that the black complexion of "American negroes" was not growing lighter, he now claimed that it was highly probable "that time will efface the black complexion in them."[19]

80   CRITICAL PHILOSOPHY OF RACE

Smith's argument seemed to point to the possibility that in the distant future the distinction between the races based on their alleged inequality would disappear. This refutes the widespread idea that in this time period a strong racial essentialism was universal. Throughout the century there were always a few, like Firmin, who held Smith's view.[20] Others, like Frederick Douglass, thought the dissolution of the races and the formation of a new race could be accomplished by race mixing: "My strongest conviction as to the future of the negro therefore is, that he will not be expatriated nor annihilated, nor will he forever remain a separate and distinct race from the people around him, but that he will be absorbed, assimilated, and will only appear finally . . . in the features of a blended race."[21] By contrast, polygenesis clearly lent itself to a form of essentialism insofar as one of the more persuasive arguments in its favor was the idea that racial differences appeared to be permanent.

Charles Caldwell, a physician who went on to play a major role in establishing Kentucky as a center for medical education, was among the first to challenge in detail the evidence Smith used to support his environmentalist account of race. For example, Caldwell disputed Smith's observation that the features of domestic slaves were more agreeable than those of field slaves because of their proximity to the families for whom they worked. It was not a result of performing their duties that certain Negroes had "become active, handsome, and pleasing domestics"; rather, they had been selected to serve as domestic slaves because they were "previously agreeable both in feature and figure."[22] In 1830 and again in an expanded version in 1852, Caldwell moved beyond Smith to take on English ethnologist James Cowles Prichard, the foremost advocate of monogenesis as a scientific, rather than biblical, truth.[23]

In 1839, Samuel George Morton came to Caldwell's assistance by using the evidence of his unsurpassed collection of skulls to show that neither Caucasians nor Negroes had changed in three thousand years. Relying on the widespread belief that it was not much more than four thousand years since the Creation, he concluded that there was not enough time for the Caucasian and Negro races to arise from a single origin given their differences.[24] A similar argument was developed by Peter A. Browne, who used samples of human hair from Egyptian mummies to confirm the permanence of racial characteristics in arguing against the environmentalists with their claims about the power of adaption.[25] If the races were unchanged over three thousand years or so, then the argument could also be made that the hierarchy

RACIAL SCIENCE IN THE NINETEENTH CENTURY 81

that saw the White race at the top might be permanent, especially if the prevailing view that the ancient Egyptians were Black could be toppled.

When the scientific concept of "race" was formulated in the eighteenth century, Buffon's rule for species identification, according to which two animals that can produce fertile offspring by procreating together belong to the same species, was in place and secured a scientific basis for monogenesis. Nevertheless, the number of possible counterexamples was mounting; as a result, in 1847, Morton challenged Buffon's rule as offering "no proof of the unity of the human species."[26] He was thus able to embrace "the doctrine of *primeval diversities* among men—an original adaptation of the several races to those varied circumstances of climate and locality, which, while congenial to the one are destructive to the other."[27]

After Morton's death in 1851, Josiah Nott and George Gliddon prepared a volume dedicated to his memory, *The Types of Mankind*. Part of its success was due to the inclusion of an essay by Louis Agassiz of Harvard University in which he declared with greater clarity than hitherto that "what are called human races, down to their specialization as nations, are distinct primordial forms of the type of man."[28] Since his arrival in the United States from Switzerland in 1846, Agassiz had established a reputation as the foremost scientist in the country, and while it is something of a surprise that Agassiz so readily allowed himself to be used in this way by these two polemicists who wore their extra-scientific agenda on their sleeves, the fact that he did so enhanced their cause immeasurably.

Nott, a medical doctor in Mobile, Alabama, looked for arguments for polygenesis wherever he could find them and, unlike most of the figures involved, he was open about the stakes as he saw them. So, in an essay that addresses the question of the race of the Egyptians, he announced: "I must show that the Caucasian or White and the Negro races were distinct at a very remote date, and that the Egyptians were Caucasians. Unless this point can be established the contest must be abandoned."[29] Nott did not on that occasion specify the "contest," but his audience would have known that he meant the perpetuation of the Southern way of life. Whether he was writing about the Jews, the ancient Egyptians, or the latest discoveries of Morton, his motivation was the same. One essay that proved especially influential was "The Mulatto a Hybrid—Probable Extermination of the Two Races If the Whites and Blacks Are Allowed to Intermarry." First published in 1843, but with the main conclusion widely circulated in *The Types of Mankind*,[30] it was largely based on some dubious statistics and implausible observations, but the thesis

82   CRITICAL PHILOSOPHY OF RACE

announced in the title found a ready audience. He would elsewhere report the standard arguments against race mixing, such as, for example, that "the superior races ought to be kept free from all adulterations, otherwise they will retrograde, instead of advancing, in civilization."[31] Even Bachman suggested that in the United States "the admixture of a superior race with an inferior . . . in almost every case results in degradation and crime."[32] But in "The Mulatto a Hybrid," Nott was one of the first to argue for racial purity on biological grounds. Until then, according to the highest authority, race mixing improved the stock.[33] Nott's basic idea was that to be mixed race was to be susceptible to chronic diseases and infertility to the point where it amounted to a disease in its own right.[34] Agassiz gave support to Nott on this point from beyond the grave when his wife published a selection of his letters. He was quite specific that the very existence in the United States of "the half-breeds" was "only transient, and that all legislation with reference to them should be regulated with this view,"[35] but at the same time he departed from the widespread view that all inferior races would disappear when confronted by a superior race. The "pure black" must be considered as permanent an inhabitant of North America as the White race.[36] It was a mistake to be guided by the disappearance of the "American Indians" because that arose from their "peculiar character."[37] The new racism did not necessarily reject the idea of superior and inferior races, but the hybrid was now at the bottom of the hierarchy.

Nott's challenge to Buffon's rule may have been a great deal less insightful than Morton's, but its impact was far-reaching. Count Oscar Reichenbach offered a modified version of Nott's argument, albeit without acknowledgment.[38] Paul Broca, who as founder of the Société d'Anthropologie de Paris and author of numerous important works, can genuinely be described as an eminent scientist, called Nott "one of the most eminent anthropologists in America" and quoted at length the conclusions of his 1843 article, as Jean Boudin, a French physician, had done earlier.[39] Broca extended Nott's argument to include the impact of immigration when he described how even though the Anglo-Saxons were still dominant in the United States, the influx of many other races raised the prospect that it might soon be inhabited by a hybrid race "containing the germ of future sterility."[40]

Buffon's rule was in trouble even before Nott and Morton attacked it. Prichard had tried to uphold it by reducing it to a natural sexual repugnance between individuals of different kinds. This is what stopped wild animals from mixing across species, thereby creating "a scene of confusion."[41]

RACIAL SCIENCE IN THE NINETEENTH CENTURY   83

Repugnance was nature's mechanism for avoiding hybridity, and yet Prichard conceded that this mechanism could be circumvented when animals were no longer under natural conditions but had been domesticated. In his response to Prichard, Caldwell called into doubt Prichard's claims about repugnance,[42] but Morton saw a way to turn this alleged sexual repugnance against monogenesis by using it as evidence of nature's intent.[43] If the mutual repugnance that existed between Europeans and Africans had "only been partially overcome by centuries of proximity, and, above all other means, by the moral degradation consequent to the state of slavery," then this was further evidence in favor of polygenesis.[44]

The idea of such a natural repugnance for sex across the racial divide gained traction in spite of successive generations of White masters raping their Black slaves. In his monumental essay on inequality between the human races, Joseph Arthur de Gobineau added a new twist. In addition to a law of repulsion "from the crossing of blood," he posited a law of attraction that the White races felt for the other races.[45] Indeed, it was by acting on this sexual attraction that civilization arose.[46] Whereas Guenebault had not hesitated to include in his translation Virey's remarks that once their antipathy and disgust for Negresses had worn off, European men suffered from "a violent and almost morbid fascination" with them on account of their "great lasciviousness,"[47] when Nott arranged for parts of Gobineau's book to be translated for an American audience, Gobineau's observations about the White man's attraction for women of other races were omitted.[48] Combined with Nott's conviction about "the probable ultimate infertility of human hybrids of the mulatto type," the "aversion to hybridity" was nature's way of stopping the two races from "destroying one another by amalgamation."[49] Suitably cultivated, this aversion could be employed to support efforts to "exclude blacks and mulattoes from all political privileges."[50] To defenders of the Southern way of life, aversion to racial amalgamation and the dire effects that followed from it when it did take place were providential. Louisa S. McCord of South Carolina in the context of a review of Knox's *The Races of Men* declared extermination or slavery to be the destiny of the darker races as ordained by God "who, for his own purposes, and in his impenetrable wisdom, has so formed the weaker race that they dwindle and die out by contact with the stronger; has so formed the stronger that they instinctively repel the thought of amalgamation with the weaker; has so formed both, that amalgamation leads to extinction."[51] But the idea of such a repugnance was not restricted to the polygenists. In 1850, Rev. Thomas Smyth, confirming Morton's claim that

84 CRITICAL PHILOSOPHY OF RACE

it was mutual, argued that it supported the idea of the equality and thus of the unity of the human races.[52]

Race mixing between Whites and Native Americans was viewed differently. Roswell Haskins quoted Caldwell as arguing that Native Americans, whom he regarded as a branch of the Mongolian race, came close in cerebral development and general character to the degree of "white blood" they possessed. Mixing with Whites was their only hope for survival: "The only efficient scheme to civilize the Indians, is to *cross the breed*. Attempt any other and *you will extinguish the race*.[53] That was also Nott's view about Native Americans: "the full blood Indian" faced extermination with the approach of civilization and "whatever improvement exists in their condition is attributable to a mixture of races."[54] But the growing consensus was that neither mixing, nor anything else, could help the Native American[55] with the result that "in a few generations more the last of these Red men will be numbered among the dead."[56] Although Henry Morgan in his important study of the Iroquois complained about the treatment they had received and insisted on their potential for "civilization,"[57] the long-standing view was that every "savage" stood in the way of "the perspective into futurity" by occupying the land that could be occupied by "five hundred of rational animals": "the extinction of his race, and the progress of the arts which give rise to his distressing apprehensions, are for the increase of mankind, and for the promotion of the world's glory and happiness."[58]

Eugenics and Biopolitics

At the end of the nineteenth century, American scientists of race would again be on the margins. The decline of the American school had a double cause. The most important was the publication of Charles Darwin's *On the Origin of Species* in 1859. Polygenesis derived its strength and its purpose from the idea that the races were fixed, but that was no longer sustainable within an evolutionary perspective, even though a certain polygenesis still survived, as did a certain racial essentialism.[59] The debate between monogenists and polygenists continued, but it was no longer the "grand problem" Nott had declared it to be.[60] Nevertheless, the question of the possible extinction of so-called inferior races gained in intensity, and now the authority of science seemed to blend with divine authority, as when Herbert Spencer in a book on ethics announced: "if it be said that as the Hebrews thought themselves warranted in seizing the lands God promised to them, and in some cases exterminating the inhabitants, so we, to fulfill the 'manifest intention of Providence,' dispossess inferior races whenever we want their territories; it may be replied that we do not kill many more than seems needful, and tolerate the existence of those who submit."[61] It is easy to forget how callous some of the preeminent minds of the time were.

At the same time, the biopolitical racism that Nott had introduced declared that nature punished those individuals and races that did not follow its dictates. However, the scant or nonexistent evidence was now being argued with a greater pretense at rigor. The 1860 census was presented as confirming Nott's claims. The extinction of slavery would lead to increased "admixture," and thus it would impair "the colored race" without improving it morally. It could follow the same path as Native Americans and was "doomed to comparatively rapid absorption or extinction."[62] In the 1890s, Frederick Hoffman, a statistician with the Providential Insurance Company, declared the Negro in America "a vanishing race": "The Indian is on the verge of extinction, many tribes having entirely disappeared; and the African will surely follow him, for every race has suffered extinction wherever the Anglo-Saxon has permanently settled."[63] This essay and Hoffman's subsequent publications provoked Du Bois to write his classic essay "The Conservation of Races," a work which confirms that race in the nineteenth century was as much a historical as a scientific category.[64]

The new biopolitical racism was most visible in eugenics. The heyday of eugenics in the United States was the first four decades of the twentieth century, but it was already prepared for in the nineteenth. Gideon Lincecum, a Texas naturalist, was among the first proponents in the United States of sterilization as a way of improving the population, when in 1849 he advocated the castration of criminals in place of execution: "The laws of hereditary transmission cannot be overruled."[65] Some proposed castration as the solution to the perceived problem of the sexual crimes of "negroes."[66] Nevertheless, Whites in the United States were sufficiently confident in the boundaries that had been established by Jim Crow legislation: the expectation was that race mixing would end, especially given the tendency of the states to define the White race ever more narrowly in the direction of racial purity, which was now equated with health. Once the barriers separating the races were established, the focus of eugenics was on identifying the obstacles to improving the White race. In a groundbreaking study, Robert Dugdale drew attention to increased instances of degeneracy among Whites—a study that drew

86 CRITICAL PHILOSOPHY OF RACE

praise from both Francis Galton, the founder of eugenics, and Spencer, who favored the operation of the "survival of the fittest" over charity.[67] Dugdale examined degeneracy across seven generations of a family to which he gave the name "the Jukes" and argued that although environment contributed to the problem, the "tendency of heredity is to produce an environment which perpetuates that heredity."[68]

In the early part of the twentieth century, the center of racial science, which had moved to France, shifted back to Germany, where Eugen Fischer became the first to apply Mendelian laws of inheritance to study the effects of race mixing. He concluded that the Boers and Hottentots should not mix further.[69] In time the Germans turned to such Americans as Harry H. Laughlin and Charles Davenport, both of them strong advocates of eugenics as well as strict immigration controls. However, increasingly the influence of Franz Boas and his students came to be felt. His insistence on a distinction between nature and culture led to a division between physical anthropology and cultural anthropology, which in turn led to a separation of physical characteristics from mental characteristics. Race became the preserve of biologists. Eventually this movement led to the UNESCO Statement on Race of 1950 written under the leadership of one of Boas's students, Ashley Montagu. When in the aftermath of the Holocaust the world walked again on the scientific path opened by American scientists, it was to deny the salience of the scientific concept of race.

5

The Policing of Race Mixing

The Place of Biopower within the History of Racisms

In this chapter, I investigate a largely untold era in the history of race thinking in Europe and North America: in the second half of the nineteenth century, there was an often-overlooked shift whereby the hierarchical form of racial essentialism that was used to justify a race-based system of slavery, especially in mid-century, was joined, and in certain contexts displaced, by a medicalizing racism that helped to shape race relations through its call for segregation, apartheid, and eugenics, leading eventually—although I will not be able to touch on it in this brief account—to sterilization programs and the Holocaust.[1] In the course of constructing this account, I will take up the question of whether Michel Foucault's notion of biopower is a valuable tool for those engaged in the task of clarifying the history of racism. Foucault's account of biopower has received a great deal of attention, but because what he actually has to say about race tends to be vague and radically incomplete, many students of the history of racial thinking have understandably been critical of his contribution.[2] For example, the account of the Holocaust in terms of biopower is incomplete and needs to be supplemented.[3] I will argue that in spite of the flaws in Foucault's account, there is still a great deal to be learned from his identification of this biologizing, or, as I prefer to say, medicalizing racism.[4]

Foucault himself indicated that there was a transition from an historical discourse on race to a biological one, but, perhaps because he wanted to insist on the continuity between these two discourses, he offered little assistance in identifying when or how this transition took place. Nevertheless, it is necessary to do so if we are both to isolate those elements of the history of race thinking that contributed most to the violence committed in the name of race in the twentieth century and to clarify the nature and genealogy of the racisms that still persist. Most accounts of racism do not do enough to differentiate the different forms of racism, reducing it to a belief in the essential inequality of the human races. But there are many racisms. They include

Critical Philosophy of Race. Robert Bernasconi, Oxford University Press. © Oxford University Press 2023.
DOI: 10.1093/oso/9780197587966.003.0006

88   CRITICAL PHILOSOPHY OF RACE

systemic, essentialist, xenophobic, environmentalist, gradualist (in terms of the alleged spread of civilization), and medicalizing racism. It is important to be aware of all these different forms and their different targets, both because they often coexist and also because attempts to combat one form of racism can reinforce another. It is here that Foucault's notion of biopower makes a contribution: it helps to identify one of those racisms and in this way contributes to bringing the history of racisms into focus, albeit I do not believe one can adopt Foucault's notion without major modifications, the most important of which is to highlight the role played by a fear of race mixing that was authorized by medical discourse. It is surprising that Foucault did not pay this form of racism more attention, as it not only could be accommodated by his account, but it also helps clarify one prominent form of twentieth-century racism with its emphasis on isolation and segregation.

Slavery and Sovereign Power

When Foucault introduced the notion of biopower to the general public in 1976 in the first volume of *The History of Sexuality*, he referenced race. He explained there that he coined the term "biopower" to refer to "what brought life into the realm of politics as an object of explicit calculation" where what was at stake was not the life of the individual but of large units of population such as races, nations, or even the species as a whole.[5] Foucault was well aware that he had, with this perspective, established the resources with which to write a chapter in the history of racism. Early in the contemporary lecture course, not published in French until 1997, "*Society Must Be Defended,*" he announced his ambition "to trace the full development of a biological-social racism."[6] He distinguished "racism in its modern, 'biologizing,' statist form"[7] from "racism in the traditional sense of the term,"[8] which he elsewhere called "ethnic racism."[9] But biologizing racism was not, for him, just one chapter among others in the history of racism. In "*Society Must Be Defended,*" Foucault wrote that it is only when the state adopts a biological and medical concept of race that one finds what one can properly call racism.[10] Highlighting the transformation that the notion of degeneration allegedly underwent in Morel's *Traité des dégénerescences physiques, intellectuelles et morales de l'espèce humaine,*[11] Foucault presented biologizing racism as covering all forms of degeneration, including alcoholism, even while he restricted it historically to the period that began only in the second half of the nineteenth century.[12] In "*Society Must Be Defended*," he even suggested that the term "racism" should be reserved for a period that began even later, at the end of the nineteenth century.[13]

This has the unfortunate but telling consequence that in one of his rare remarks about colonization, after acknowledging that racism first develops with "colonizing genocide," he proceeded to locate it in the second half of the nineteenth century,[14] as if all forms of colonization prior to that time were free of racism and the desire to exterminate indigenous populations. The omission of race-based slavery from his account of racism is arbitrary and misleading. Nevertheless, I believe that Foucault was right to mark the difference between medicalizing racism and the racisms that preceded it. However, to do so persuasively, one needs to locate it within that broader history of racism in the traditional sense of the term that Foucault chose not to write.

Foucault's discussion of racism is only one part of his overriding argument that a fundamental shift took place when the sovereign's power to take life or let live was complemented—and to a certain extend displaced—by biopower, which was announced by the attribution to the state of a new right: the right to intervene so as to make life or let die.[15] Among the ways in which this new right of the state to "let die" manifested itself was through genocide and the discourse of eugenics and racial hygiene, where it is a question of eliminating biological threats to the population.[16] If it seems strange at first that genocide takes place under the rubric "make live or let die" rather than "take life or let live," this is because genocide tends to hide behind nature's purposes as understood by the social Darwinists: nature, working through history, will extinguish the weak, and because of this, one can, as it were, hasten the process or give it a helping hand.[17]

On Foucault's account, the shift from sovereign power to biopower was preceded in the seventeenth century by a modification within the exercise of sovereign power: the Roman idea of sovereignty, which located in the father of the Roman family, who had the right to "dispose" of the life of his children and slaves, was by this time restricted to the political sovereign's power to employ the death penalty in self-defense.[18] However, Foucault, showing little or no interest in the transformations brought about by the Atlantic slave trade, made no mention of the transfer of a form of sovereign power to slave owners in the Americas. The standard seventeenth-century justification of slavery appealed to the Roman idea that one could legitimately enslave not only prisoners caught in a just war, and those who assisted them, but also

90   CRITICAL PHILOSOPHY OF RACE

their children born in slavery.[19] To be sure, there were people at that time who were well aware that all too often no care was taken to ensure that the African slaves had been taken under the appropriate conditions, which meant that the new practice of slavery did not fit the justification employed to sustain it. But because this practice was not—with very few exceptions—challenged in its early years from within those nations that expected to benefit from it, there was no need for a detailed defense of all aspects of its operation. This meant that there was no need for a sophisticated racial doctrine at this time upon which to base slavery. There was some talk among the planters in the West Indies of Preadamism, a form of what would later be called polygenesis,[20] but it was not until later that explicit racial doctrines were called upon to legitimize the system. At least officially, people were enslaved not because they were Africans but because they were prisoners of war or the offspring of prisoners of war. As late as 1815 Thomas Jefferson explained to a correspondent that one could be enslaved following the condition of the mother (*partus sequitur ventrum*) and yet have so much White parentage that on being emancipated one would be counted "a free *white* man, and a citizen of the United States to all intents and purposes."[21] Nevertheless, even though there were slaves in the Americas who, were they to be freed, would not be Black by the laws of the state in which they were enslaved, there can be no doubt that the number of slaves and even the conditions under which they were transported and held would have been different had not most of them been categorized as "Negroes."

The question that exercised John Locke's contemporaries was not whether slavery itself was legitimate, but whether Africans could continue to be enslaved legitimately after they had been baptized as Christians.[22] This was addressed by the Lords Proprietors of Carolina, of which Locke was Secretary, when in 1669 they declared in Article 101 of "The Fundamental Constitutions of Carolina" that "Every freeman of Carolina shall have absolute power and Authority over his Negro slaves, of what opinion or Religion so ever."[23] This article granted an exception to the convention that Christians could not enslave their fellow Christians on condition that the latter were Africans. At the same time the article placed Negro slaves under a death sentence. This condition was the ultimate source of the sovereignty that the slave owner had over his slaves, even though by the end of the seventeenth century there were in most areas laws in place restricting the exercise of that right, not least because they were the source of the wealth of a given colony as well as of their owner. The fact that Locke in *Two Treatises of Government* denied that slavery was a hereditary condition has led some to try to present Locke as critical of the form of slavery being developed in the Americas, but what needs to be explained is why he felt obliged to offer any justification of slavery, given the fact that the primary purpose of the book was to argue for the freedom of the English from the alleged absolute power of the monarch and why in that book he also went beyond Grotius and Pufendorf, in giving to slave owners a right to kill slaves.[24] It is first in Locke that we find an account of how the sovereign power that is usually the prerogative of the sovereign might legitimately be shared with the slave owner.[25]

The Case against Race Mixing

Biopower is entirely different from this kind of sovereign power, and the racisms associated with each are also different. Foucault did not attempt to chart the transition between them, but in writing the genealogy of biopower he follows the French tendency to highlight the racial discourse of Henri de Boulainvilliers and its transformation across the historical narratives of the Thierry brothers, Augustin and Amédie, into "the theory of races in the historico-biological sense."[26] To insist on this radical shift and locate it where he did, he needed to ignore the specifically racial discourse directed against "Negroes" and others toward the end of the eighteenth century. One of the main points of the present chapter—which is not dependent on whether or not one believes in radical breaks in history—is to indicate the steps taken behind Foucault's back, as it were, that lead from the historical accounts of the Thierry brothers early in the nineteenth century, to William-Frédéric Edwards and in particular Victor Courtet de l'Isle, and ties his account of biopower to a history of racism that he largely ignored. This is the point called for by Foucault's account, but never identified by him, where the historical discourse on race comes to be joined with and, to a certain extent, displaced by a medicalizing discourse on race.

One of Foucault's major contributions to this task is that he identified in eighteenth-century accounts of populations the emergence of a discourse which monitored birth and death rates, life expectancy, state of health, and so on: "this was the first time that a society had affirmed, in a constant way, that its future and its fortune were tied not only to the number and the uprightness of its citizens, to their marriage rules and family organization, but to the manner in which each individual made use of his [or her] sex."[27] It was

92   CRITICAL PHILOSOPHY OF RACE

then that "sex became a 'police' matter" in the sense of "an ordered maximization of collective and individual forces."[28] Foucault's use of the term "police" might sound like an exaggerated metaphor, but in fact it is historically precise. During the eighteenth century, the French began to use the term "police" to refer to the ordering or governing of a city. The word was quickly adopted in England and particularly in Prussia, where a number of chairs in *Polizeiwissenschaft* were established. Foucault references two of the holders of these professorships: Heinrich Gottlob von Justi and Johann Peter Frank.[29]

I will focus here on Frank, who is the better known, at least in the English-speaking world.[30] In a footnote to the second page of his magnum opus, *A System of Complete Medical Police*, Frank explained that "The Task of the Medical Police is to make liberal use of the possibilities of nature and its energy in such a way that from every given couple of persons of both sexes, and under the supervision of good laws, the best, healthiest and most desirable fruits will be obtained."[31] Frank advocated the regulation of marriages so that they would work together with nature to maximize the production of a healthy population (*Bevölkerung*) and minimize the transmission of hereditary diseases. For example, to improve both the physical and moral health of the human race he proposed that each couple before marriage should be obliged to swear an oath "that they, as far as they could and had to know, do not suffer from any grave, infectious, or hereditary disease, whereby the intentions of the married state would be frustrated and the country cheated in its expectations and only miserable and sickly fruits be produced."[32]

When sex became a police matter, so did race, but not merely in the sense of both being regulated, but also because it was thought that by controlling sexuality the potential of a race could be maximized. In proposing a renewed regulating or policing of sexuality, *Polizeiwissenschaft* understood itself not just as a more concerted effort to intervene in nature to maintain the health of a population through breeding, but as directed by specifically medical concerns. This population was already on occasion identified as a race. So, for example, Frank explained the weakness of Native Americans as a result of their failure to mix with other races.[33] On other occasions, as we shall see, a population might consist of two or more races, a fact that gave rise to a specific range of problems.

From its introduction as a scientific concept by Frank's contemporary, Immanuel Kant, the idea of race was organized around the possibility of race mixing. Kant's groundbreaking attempt in 1775 to reconcile the existence of permanent inheritable characteristics such as skin color with a belief in the unity of the human species was based on Buffon's rule about the fertility of sexual unions over time.[34] Furthermore, Kant believed that, just as only successful mating established the unity of any given species, so only an examination of the offspring of two purportedly different races would reveal whether they were indeed different races and which of their characteristics were specifically racial. Racial characteristics were permanent characteristics that the offspring shared in equal measure from both parents. Kant had some trouble specifying physical characteristics, other than skin color, but he included moral and intellectual characteristics, too. Differences that were not inheritable in equal measure from both parents were not racial but varietal.[35]

On Kant's account, race mixing led to a certain uniformity in the senses that the two races were brought closer together, but he argued further that if different varieties, such as nations, mingled, the result was, by contrast, more variety.[36] These ideas soon became widespread and found support in France in the 1820s. When Augustin Thierry denied that race mixing eradicated the very different characteristics of two distinct races, he was thinking not of what Kant called "races" but of the nations that constituted France.[37] The same distinction was made by Edwards in 1829: he confirmed from a biological point of view that when neighboring races—that is to say, Kantian varieties—mix, their characteristics are preserved, whereas when very different races mix, the result is a hybrid that shares the racial characteristics of the parent races equally.[38] The Saint-Simonians took up these ideas and developed them into a political program: Courtet de l'Isle in 1828 and, in the following year, d'Eichthal both advocated race mixing between Blacks and Whites.[39] In this they were following James Cowles Prichard, who had already argued that the breeding of animals had shown that mixing breeds might improve a stock.[40] He relied in part on Félix von Azara's report that the mixed Hispanic population found in South America was superior in height, beauty, and even the whiteness of their skin to the Spanish of Europe.[41]

This promotion of race mixing reversed a tendency among northern Europeans, including the mature Kant, to be against race mixing.[42] This tendency was not confined to them, as is clear from the purity of blood statutes in Spain in 1492 and similar edicts in Mexico in the sixteenth century.[43] In North America there were from early on frequent references to racial identities in the context of attempts to police sexuality. In some cases opposition to race mixing was expressed on theological grounds as frustrating God's providential plan. The very existence of different races was evidence that nature or providential design intended them to persist: race mixing was regarded

94   CRITICAL PHILOSOPHY OF RACE

as unnatural or against nature. But it did not have any bad effects other than that of blurring the boundary lines between the races and so interfering with a system of social stratification that was easy to maintain by virtue of its sheer visibility.[44] However, in 1810, Friedrich Ludwig Jahn transformed the argument claiming in his *Deutsches Volksthum* that race mixing had disastrous physical and moral consequences.[45] Nevertheless, this view had few adherents until the middle of the nineteenth century,[46] because it relied on a widely disputed theoretically grounded idea of race.

That race mixing contaminated nations and could possibly lead to their downfall was claimed by Robert Knox in 1850 when he insisted, with specific reference to race mixing, that "race is everything: literature, science, art, in a word civilization depends on it."[47] A similar argument was made four years later by Count Arthur de Gobineau, who popularized the biologization of the philosophy of history, which we already saw in Edwards and Courtet de l'Isle. In the nineteenth century, theoretical racism was always a historical discourse as much as a biological discourse insofar as there was at that time no clear distinction between nature and culture. However much race was seen as a neutral powerful force, it was also recognized that historical races are not given, and are always to be made and remade.

Gobineau insisted that "the racial question (*la question ethnique*) overshadows all other problems of history, that it holds the key to them all, and that the inequality of the races from whose fusion a people is formed is enough to explain the whole course of its destiny."[48] However, what underlay the belief in the explanatory power of race was a belief not so much in the hierarchy of races as in the impact of race mixing, although it should not be forgotten that Gobineau believed that race mixing had not always been negative in history[49] and was only in his time beginning to lead to decadence.[50]

Degeneration

Although the contributions of Knox and Gobineau are well known, the decisive step in the biologization of the case against race mixing predates their contributions. On October 12, 1842, the prestigious *Boston Medical and Surgical Journal* published an anonymous letter under the title "Vital Statistics of Negroes and Mulattoes." If one wanted an answer to the question, as Foucault himself apparently did not, of when race thinking first came under the sway of biopower, this would seem to be a better place to locate it than with Frank. On the basis of anecdotes and a few select statistics, the anonymous author of "Vital Statistics of Negroes and Mulattoes," who chose for himself the most inappropriate name of "The Philanthropist," argued that hybridity was a medical condition that should be treated as such. There had long been a debate about the physiological effects of race mixing, but this brief letter seems to have been one of the first times that anyone suggested that if those of mixed race were more likely to suffer certain diseases, then it should be considered a disease in its own right and prevented, just as we try to prevent other diseases. This is what lay behind the fear associated with what would twenty years later begin to be called "miscegenation."[51]

The point was not lost on Josiah Nott, a doctor from Mobile, Alabama, who would become known internationally for his promotion of polygenesis, the theory that the races did not share the same origin. Nott was writing to defend the values and institutions of slavery. He quickly published in the *American Journal of the Medical Sciences* an essay that quoted extensively from the anonymous article in the *Boston Medical and Surgical Journal*. Nott's own thesis was clearly stated in his title: "The Mulatto a Hybrid: Probable Extermination of the Two Races If the Whites and Blacks Are Allowed to Intermarry." Whereas Buffon's rule had claimed that the mixing of different species would lead directly to sterility, Nott effectively modified this claim: it would have that effect only in the long run. However, the social impact of such ideas was anything but vague, leading to the proactive project of racial hygiene or eugenics as an attempt to cleanse or decontaminate the social body. With the medicalization of race mixing under the label "degeneration," the policing of race mixing would be pursued with an entirely new urgency: the health of society depended on it, and the health of society must be defended. This necessitated a strong measure of medical control. Dr. Samuel Cartwright is famous for his identification of drapetomania, "the disease causing Negroes to run away." But he also diagnosed what he called "dysaesthesia Aethiopica," which corresponded to what others called "rascality," for which the only known treatment was "government in everything."[52]

Nott found a ready audience, not just in the southern United States but also among the scientific elite in France with Paul Broca and Georges Pouchet. It was to Nott and authors such as Samuel George Morton and Louis Agassiz—who were included in the extraordinarily popular collection *Types of Mankind* (1854)—that Pouchet was referring when in 1858 in *De la pluralité des races humaines,* he wrote: "At present France and England walk entirely in the scientific path opened by the American school."[53] Through the

96 CRITICAL PHILOSOPHY OF RACE

work of the French scientists and the adoption of their ideas more broadly, and long after Darwinism had made the debate between monogenesis and polygenesis largely irrelevant, the promotion of racial purity on the biological grounds of fear of extermination would persist. One sees the spread of these ideas into Germany in, for example, Ludwig Gumplowicz, who added an appendix to the second edition of his *Der Rassenkampf: Soziologische Untersuchungen* that made the point that racial contact would, after conflict, lead to race mixing and thus to stagnation.

Foucault's focus on Morel rather than Nott perhaps reflected a French bias. It is true that they had different concerns, but insofar as Foucault highlighted "degeneration" as "a way of isolating, covering and cutting out a zone of social danger while simultaneously giving it a pathological status as illness,"[54] he might as well have been talking about Nott's view of hybridity. To be sure, Philippe Buchez, a friend of Morel, can be cited in support of Foucault's contention that Morel broadened the notion of degeneration beyond race, even if race in the traditional sense remained central to Morel's case.[55] But the sense of degeneration found in Morel is entirely consistent with that found in contemporary discussions of race mixing, as is apparent from his characterization of half-castes in India as either sterile or with only weak, wretched, and depraved offspring.[56] Morel believed that the so-called inferior races could in appropriate circumstances "assimilate to the general progress of the human spirit," whereas the degenerate were susceptible of only "relative amelioration."[57] This meant that the degenerate were the new site of permanent racial difference. To the extent that those of mixed race were degenerate in this new sense—whereby the Greenlanders, Eskimos, and Lapps, who were all considered degenerate varieties in Buffon's day, were not—then to be of mixed race was to belong to the inferior race par excellence.

As an English reviewer of Morel's book explained, describing the mixture of the Spanish and Portuguese conquerors with the indigenous people, "The conquered races have well-nigh disappeared; whilst the conquerors have greatly degenerated, and their mixture with the aborigines has produced a degraded race, which presents no element of perfectibility in the future."[58] Morel distinguished two forms of hereditary transmission, one that allowed for rapid regression to the previous type—as when animals or humans having been domesticated return to their wild state—and another that did not, which according to Morel, was the case with the degenerate.[59] But for Morel this meant that nature was doing the work of policing degeneration: "the existence of degenerate beings is necessarily limited and, wonderful to say, it is not always necessary that they arrive at the final degree of degradation, because they are struck by sterililty and consequently become incapable of transmitting the type of their degeneration."[60] There was nothing inevitable about degeneration, but it could be avoided only if society squarely faced the dangers of the terrible cataclysm that would otherwise be awaiting it.[61] For the late nineteenth century this racism was natural, and it was not so much society but nature that regulated race mixing by favoring racial purity. One simply had to be more attentive to nature's precepts. It was because race mixing was policed by nature that the individual states judged themselves authorized to be more interventional in their support of it.

The fact that Nott feared the effects of some forms of race mixing did not mean that he believed that the present races were pure. Although Foucault at one point described the role of the state as being "the protector of . . . the purity of the race,"[62] it would be more accurate to say that the state took as its task the creation of racial purity,[63] because it was widely recognized that there were no pure races—at least not in the civilized world. One sees this already, for example, both in Josiah Nott's edited collection *Types of Mankind or Ethnological Researches* and in Gobineau's *The Inequality of Human Races*, and scientists insisted on it increasingly as the century wore on. Nevertheless, contemporaries already saw problems with Nott's view which could not account for the population growth in those parts of South America where miscegenation was widely acknowledged and practiced more openly than in the United States. Nott's efforts to do so were absurd. He suggested that problems of infertility arose only when northern Europeans mixed with Blacks. Southern Europeans faced no such problems as they already had a long history of racial mixing and were the product of both Caucasians and Blacks. But he offered no explanation of why this had not led the southern Europeans into infertility. Perhaps for this reason some of Nott's contemporaries highlighted the alleged inefficiencies of South American countries rather than their alleged problems with infertility.

Nott wrote initially to defend slavery, but some of his biological arguments were readily adapted to promote the social practice of separating the races, which was deemed necessary for the very survival of the nation, or, more precisely the homogeneous part of it: because of the long history of Whites raping Black slaves combined with laws allowing small fractions of African heritage to be enough to determine someone as Black, Blacks—and to a certain extent other so-called non-White races—were mixed and thus understood to be threatened by this biological law. A good indication of how

98 CRITICAL PHILOSOPHY OF RACE

real Nott thought the dangers were can be found in a short essay he contributed to James De Bow's *The Industrial Resources, Statistics, etc. of the United States*, where he warned against offering slave owners insurance on their Black slaves.[64] The same conclusion—that it was commercially unsound to offer Blacks insurance—was drawn in 1896 in the new context of segregation by Frederick Hoffman in his *Race Traits and Tendencies of the American Negro*. He argued that statistics demonstrated that, because most Blacks in the United States were of mixed race, the American Negro was, like the American Indian, in danger of extinction. Racial stratification enabled Hoffman to identify the problem as a Black problem, even though he understood it was not: "Intercourse with the white race must absolutely cease and race purity must be insisted upon in marriage as well as outside it."[65] The initial injunction was phrased in such a way as to be clearly addressed to Blacks. But without saying so directly, it is clear from the second half of the sentence that he knew that White men had been—and continued to be—to blame. W. E. B. Du Bois's "The Conservation of Races" was in part a response to Hoffman, which is an indication of the importance of his *Race Traits and Tendencies of the American Negro* (see Chapter 9).

There were still people who saw race mixing as the solution instead of the problem. "Racial amalgamation" would never disappear entirely as a proposal to correct inequality or as an inevitability, which is how one finds it in, for example, Frederick Douglass,[66] but such ideas increasingly came to appear to contemporaries as absurdly idealistic in the face of the biological case against race mixing. There was a noticeable shift from a racism based on racial hierarchy that ordered the individual races in terms of proximity to whiteness, to a racial hierarchy that privileged racial purity over those of mixed race.

If one studies the literature on race of the Southern United States from the Civil War period and just after, in such journals as *De Bow's Review*, one finds not only a concern about protecting Southern womanhood but also a discourse designed to cultivate the repugnance White men were supposed to feel in the face of Black women. For example, W. W. Wright highlighted an alleged revulsion to the idea of race mixing which he called an "aversion to hybridity."[67] On this account it was supposedly in the first instance nature, rather than society, that regulated sexual selection, just as nature allegedly punished those who went against its dictates. Gobineau, it should never be forgotten, believed that the White race alone desired race mixing, while the other races were repulsed by it. Needless to say, that idea was downplayed in the translation of the *Essay* that Nott organized.[68] But the more common idea among Whites of the time was that for the purpose of discouraging race mixing, nature had given White men an instinctual repugnance for Black women that needed to be cultivated. To be attracted to someone of another race was to go against nature's voice allegedly inscribed in us. The idea was not entirely new. One can find it voiced, for example, in the eighteenth century by Georg Forster as evidence for polygenesis,[69] but it was now understood to be critical for survival. In this way racism in the form of a visceral reaction across race and sex was not only normalized but also understood to be vital for a society's survival. One might link this with Foucault's understanding of eugenics as "a technology of the instincts" in which "the problem of heredity, racial purification, and the correction of the human intellectual system by purification of the race" come together.[70]

Population Policies

The function of racist discourse and segregated institutions in the United States at that time was increasingly to separate the population that had become mixed from that which was understood to be homogeneous, so as to preserve what was understood to be White racial purity. Nevertheless, generations of race mixing meant that there was a real danger that one might be mixed and yet not even be aware of it. The increasing focus in the early twentieth century on degrees of racial purity arose because biology changed the standards of what was meant by racial purity as a result of a transformation in the understanding of heredity. It is true that the courts had long ceased to rely on appearance to determine racial identity, but legal statutes that relied on fractions to do the job meant that a White identity could be restored to a family that had lost it by careful breeding selection. That legal avenue began to be removed in parts of the South when in 1910 the State of Tennessee, by defining the word "negro" in such a way as to include "mulattoes, mestizos, and their descendants having any blood of the African race in their veins," embraced what would come to be known as the "one-drop rule."[71] Virginia took a more decisive step in 1924 with its An Act to Preserve Racial Integrity, which entrusted the Virginia Bureau of Vital Statistics under Walter Asby Plecker with the authority to police the state's laws against interracial marriages using the definition of a White person as someone "with no trace whatsoever of any blood other than Caucasian."[72] People had long

100 CRITICAL PHILOSOPHY OF RACE

known that a person's appearance did not always match the racial identity society wanted to impose on them, primarily for social reasons, but by the early twentieth century it was clear: races were made, not given, and because nature could not always be relied upon to show someone's racial identity to the degree that was necessary to safeguard a race against the danger that followed from race mixing, society had to take over from nature as a matter of strict self-defense. And the Mendelian laws of inheritance had made that task appear a great deal more difficult.

Nott's notion that race mixing led to a decline in fertility was not refuted scientifically until Eugen Fischer published his study *Die Rehobother Bastards und das Bastardierungsproblem beim Menschen* in 1913. Furthermore, Fischer, relying on a more traditional account of the hierarchy of races for his basic framework, affirmed the idea of social Darwinists that mixed-race populations were liable to be annihilated in the struggle for existence. Furthermore, Fischer in this book claimed to be the first to apply Mendelian theories of inheritance to human races in a sustained way, and so there is a shift of paradigms here.[73] We too often forget that even though race was scientifically—at least since Kant—tied to ideas of heredity, it was not until Francis Galton and the rediscovery of Mendel that biologists had at their disposal a viable account of heredity. Kant's idea that the offspring of parents of two different races shared equally in the racial characteristics of both parents had long been rejected, but the Mendelian laws of inheritance equipped Fischer with a scientific account of regressive traits. Regressive traits are variations that once introduced cannot be bred out: two apparently White parents might well have a visibly Black child if there had been race mixing in the past of one of the parents. The idea of making a specifically pure race by breeding thus seemed to be excluded. Fischer argued that a new inheritable variation, once introduced, could always recur and could only be eliminated by the death of everyone who carried the so-called Mendelian trait.[74]

If in the early decades of the twentieth century, fears of race mixing finally gave rise to the one-drop rule in the legal definition of the Negro in certain parts of the United States, it was in large measure because Mendelism had shown the difficulties of simply breeding out earlier race mixtures along the lines proposed by earlier theorists. Hence, the heightened anxiety over "passing." The great fear for Whites was the Black who could pass for White, just as the great fear of Nazis was of German Jews "contaminating" the Aryan race. Concern about passing transforms anti-Black racism from being directed against a visible and often distant Other into suspicion of those within one's circle who look like oneself. From this perspective people of mixed racial heritage came to represent a kind of biological timebomb that could be ignited through one's offspring. One did not know for sure who was the carrier of an alien race, and to the extent that one did not know all the details of one's own racial heritage, White people in particular might even come to suspect their own identity. This gives a personal dimension to Foucault's description of state racism as "a racism a society directs against itself to defend itself," the internal racism of "permanent purification."[75] Nor did it help that it was widely believed that mixed-race populations tended to be susceptible to self-hatred and indecisiveness.[76]

Social Darwinism provided the perfect soil in which such ideas of threats to survival might grow. In a book review published on October 14, 1905, William Bateson, who would before long be recognized as one of the leading authorities on Mendelism, posed the question: "What will happen when civilized society thoroughly grasps what heredity means?"[77] His answer was: "One thing is certain: mankind will begin to interfere; perhaps not in England, but in some country more ready to break with the past and eager for 'national efficiency'.... The science of heredity will soon provide power on a stupendous scale; and in some country, at some time, not, perhaps, far distant, that power will be applied to control the composition of a nation."[78] One should recall this warning when one learns that in Eugen Fischer's inaugural address as rector of the University of Berlin he praised the Nazis' racial policy in these terms: "This intervention can only be characterized as a biological population policy, biological in this context signifying the safeguarding by the state of our hereditary endowment and our race, as opposed to the unharnessed processes of heredity, selection, and elimination."[79] To be sure, by this time Fischer was insisting that the endowments of a race were more important than racial purity, but this did not stop him from participating in a policing of race mixing that originated in themes he had seemingly previously renounced.

In this chapter I have argued that the scientifically based racial essentialism highlighted by most accounts of racism emerged only after the institutions of inherited chattel slavery had already been shaped. Racial essentialism was deployed to defend the institution of slavery after the fact and served to strengthen and prolong the institution, but it did not create it. Nevertheless, it was the medicalizing racism that opposed race mixing that shaped the institutions of segregation and apartheid, as well as various aspects of the sterilization and other eugenic programs that marked the first half of the twentieth century. Foucault's tendency to highlight medicalizing racism at the expense of racial essentialism means that he is not always a reliable guide to the distinction between them. One can, in any case, make the distinction without appealing to Foucault's term "biopower," but it is a term that usefully summarizes what is meant when one talks about racisms beyond essentials: it recalls that there is a tendency today to misconstrue the role racial purity played in earlier discussions. The fear that race mixing would contaminate the health of a population was a different kind of racism from that which shaped slavery, and different again from the essentializing racism that was subsequently introduced to defend it. These and other forms of racism sometimes come together in the same text, but they call for very different kinds of society and nothing is to be gained from confusing them. To combat each of them effectively also calls for very different measures, which is why so much is gained from differentiating them, as I have attempted to do here.

6

Crossed Lines in the Racialization Process

Race as a Border Concept

The Fluidity of Racial Terms

We see race. Or, more precisely, when we see someone, we tend to racialize them according to a given set of racial terms, most of the time without thinking about it. We understand and apply the prevalent racial categories on the basis of both the immediate and the historical context. But we do not think enough about the way these categories, both the terms themselves and the ways in which they are understood, are constantly shifting or being replaced by new categories. As they do so, the racial identities themselves change, and it is among these fluid racial identities that one finds the racial borderlands. For the most part, the academic discussion of racial terms among philosophers still tends to focus more on an alleged core sense than on its borders. In this essay I approach race as a border concept and show that doing so can throw light on the racialization process, that is to say, the practice of seeing people in terms of race.

One great merit of the phenomenological contribution to the critical philosophy of race, as can be clearly seen in the work of Jean-Paul Sartre and Frantz Fanon but also, more recently, in the work of Linda Martín Alcoff, is the focus it places on the process of racialization.[1] Nevertheless, the phenomenological account of racialization is still in its infancy insofar as it has not yet fully taken account of the new view of the fluidity of racial categories proposed by historians. Just as Husserlian phenomenology gave birth to a phenomenological hermeneutics, so the phenomenology of racialization needs to be supplemented and refined by what one might call a hermeneutics of racialization which addresses the terms in which we see and interpret racial difference. To combat racism, we must understand its history, not least because as one comes to know that history one learns how much the past still controls the present. Only a richer understanding of how past racisms have operated and, above all, reinvented themselves in response to attempts

Critical Philosophy of Race. Robert Bernasconi, Oxford University Press. © Oxford University Press 2023.
DOI: 10.1093/oso/9780197587966.003.0007

104   CRITICAL PHILOSOPHY OF RACE

to challenge them prepares us to be truly effective in the fight against current racisms. Because a phenomenological approach to race is equipped to accommodate a hermeneutical approach to race, in the sense of a historically informed study of how race is understood and lived existentially in different times and places, it also helps free us from taking the rigid view of race to which an undue reliance on science has led us, whether that science is legitimating the use of racial categories or denouncing it (see Chapters 12 and 13). I will begin by offering some observations about the history of racialization, to disturb some of the reigning assumptions that govern current discussions of race, especially among philosophers.

First, recognition of the fluidity of racial terms provides an unexpected insight into how racism functions. As Ann Laura Stoler has argued, "racisms gain their strategic force, not from the fixity of their essentialisms, but from the internal malleability assigned to the changing features of racial essence."[2] For example, in the United States racial identities frequently shifted and were often left ambiguous until some form of court action called for a decision. These decisions, made by juries or judges, show clearly that the formal framework provided by science and the law did not always capture the intuitions of ordinary people. Ordinary but empowered people, such as jury members, were willing on occasion to go against the legal and scientific discourses of the time by relying on their own sense of someone's race. In the context of her study of such cases, Ariela Gross observed that "the margins of a category create the core."[3] The uncertainty within the system of racial classification of where to draw the lines dividing the races is at the heart of what Gross calls "the borderlands of race." This was especially true of societies which had laws regulating contact between the races as well as different laws for different races. It was even more likely to be the case at those times when the racial categories being employed were shifting in meaning. Apart from the uncertainly this introduced, it also opened the door to people contesting their assignment to one or another category. Gross wrote: "people revealed what race meant for them only when they needed to adjudicate its boundaries. And in drawing these boundaries, they were re-creating race."[4] In the United States today, we can readily accommodate and be comfortable with the fact that we might be unsure of someone's race. At other times and in other places, race laws made such uncertainties less easy to live with. And yet we should not underestimate the level of uncertainty that might be sustained even before anyone had heard of postracialism. For example, it would sometimes happen that a witness in a trial would testify that they were unsure whether they were White or "Colored."[5]

Second, philosophers tend to promote the idea that racism is essentialist because it allows them to think that they can wave a philosophical wand in order to eradicate racism, but it needs to be understood that racial essentialism is far less dominant in the history of racism than is often thought. Formulations that sound essentialist at first sight were certainly widespread in the past and, of course, can still be heard today, but when the proponents of such ideas allow for numerous exceptions, this shows that the alleged racial essentialism was not theoretically grounded even at a minimal level. Racial essentialism, strictly understood, was largely a late invention, relatively rare at least until the mid-nineteenth century. It was a desperate response to the challenge to justify racist practices, like slavery, that had ceased to make sense even in their own terms.[6] Polygenesis, especially in its North American version as presented by Josiah Nott and Samuel George Morton, was seen as a way of grounding a dogmatic racial essentialism, and in this form it spread to Europe, especially France.[7] This contrasted sharply with the view proposed by Johann Friedrich Blumenbach, who is frequently called the father of racial science. Writing toward the end of the eighteenth century, he saw the different human varieties or races as forming a continuum: "no variety exists, whether of color, countenance, or stature, etc., so singular as not to be connected with others of the same kind by such an imperceptible transition, that it is very clear that they are all related, or only differ from each other in degree."[8] In Blumenbach's view there were no racial essences but a spectrum of varieties, and insofar as one wanted to bundle these varieties into four or five major divisions, one had to accept that where one drew the boundary lines was "very arbitrary."[9] Assigning people to race was an especially important task in the early twentieth century for the U.S. courts as they attempted to apply immigration laws, but the earlier paradigm was not lost sight of entirely. In the case of Takao Ozawa, a Japanese immigrant who filed for naturalization in 1914, not only Blumenbach's divisions but also his belief in the way the varieties ran into each other was cited in his brief to the Supreme Court.[10]

Third, we are today encouraged to see past systems of racial classification as part of a general tendency within modern science to identify natural divisions, but it was widely understood throughout much of the nineteenth century that races were not given by nature; they were made and were constantly being remade. This was thought to happen when, as a result of the impact of the environment, an organism changed in ways that became heritable, following what in Lamarckianism was called the inheritance of acquired characteristics.[11] But it also took place through racial crossings and by the accompanying decisions made about how to understand the results of such amalgamations. Furthermore, it was widely believed that when lines of descent were crossed they could give rise to a new race. At one time there was even some thought of the creation of an American race. In 1885, Clarence King, a White American who chose to live part of his life as an African American, in *The North American Review* imagined a time "when the composite elements of American populations are melted down into one race alloy, when there are no more Irish or Germans, Negroes and English, but only Americans, belonging to one defined American race."[12] It was because it was well understood that races were made and not given that philosophies of history built around the fact of racial mixing, usually after conquest, could be developed. Joseph-Arthur Comte de Gobineau's *Essai sur l'inégalité des races humaines* is built around the acknowledgment of such events in history. To believe, as Houston Stewart Chamberlain put it, that "race is not an originary phenomenon, it is produced," is to recognize that races are constructed by social practices like race mixing, as well as by the decisions of lawmakers.[13]

Fourth, the idea that race is at root a biological concept and therefore one about whose legitimacy biologists have a right to decide is an idea that came into its own only in the aftermath of the Second World War when the Western powers were desperately attempting to divorce their racist practices from those of the Nazis. Following the UNESCO Statement on Race of 1950, formulated largely by Ashley Montagu, the dominant way of combating racism has been, first, to assign race to the body and thus to biology and then to insist that because the biologists deny race, there is no basis for racism. Although the strategy was designed to combat racial ideologies, it also led to nonscientists being advised not to use the word "race."[14] One consequence of the UNESCO strategy is that it makes racism not so much a moral failing or a political tool as an epistemological error. Whereas the Nazis were properly demonized for their racism in the 1930s and 1940s, in the 1950s, when racism came to be associated more frequently with colonialism and segregation, a more forgiving approach was taken, and indeed one that tended to ignore or downplay systemic or structural racism.[15]

Finally, although it is sometimes claimed that the introduction of a mixed-race category can disrupt or serve to overturn the racial system because of its resistance to the dominant racial binary of Black and White, it is hard to find any historical support for this view.[16] Historically the racial system in the United States easily accommodated official use of the term "mulatto" in spite of difficulties in applying it for lack of information.[17] And in South Africa the category "coloured" (usually understood at the time to mean "brown hybrid") was used to produce a racial system different from that in the United States, but one that was no less racist.[18] Although the racial binary has played a significant role in distorting history and although it was a tool of oppression, for example, in the treatment of Mexicans, the racial system is not reliant on a binary. What is true is that any system of oppression tends to bifurcation by virtue of the oppositional antagonism that maintains it. This is why more inclusive descriptions of differences, including various forms of mixed race, are of themselves incapable of overturning the system.[19] Once again, racism is not an epistemological error to be resolved conceptually. Attempts to think of race as a relational concept have the advantage of making the valid point that no race understands itself or can be understood in isolation from the other races with which it has dealings, but such attempts can suffer from the defect of minimizing the divisiveness of race. For this reason, I prefer to employ in this context Sartre's concept of "reciprocity," especially insofar as it accommodates what he called "reciprocal antagonism."[20]

With these five pointers in mind and building on some of my earlier research in this area, I will now consider how race might be understood as a border concept, focusing especially on the way that the fear of race mixing has tended to dominate the history of thinking even as race mixing blurs the perceived borders between races and causes those borders to shift. This is what I understand by the racial borderlands.[21] In making this idea concrete I will focus mainly on U.S. history, not least because, by virtue of a certain ideological imperialism that I will also document in part, the U.S. racial code has become dominant even in parts of the world with radically different histories. This is especially evident in the attempts of the U.S. government to impose its racial code on lands it occupied. To be sure, to focus exclusively on this code even for critical purposes risks maintaining its dominance, but it is likely to remain dominant until we better understand the source of its resilience, which lies in its fluidity across time, even though at various moments in time it was enforced with uncompromising rigidity and stringency. In the next section I will show how the fluidity of the system of racial divisions is reflected in the porosity of the borders that define the various races. Immigrants to the United States are familiar with the fact that the American system of racialization is full of incoherences, contradictions, and paradoxes that came

108   CRITICAL PHILOSOPHY OF RACE

about as a result of a complex history and that are impossible to make sense of without reference to that history. Some immigrants come to recognize that that system is in large part sustained by the self-evidence many Americans attribute to it through their ignorance of much of that history.

Shifting Identities

One can call race a border concept in a mundane topographical sense because of the relation of race to geography. The divisions between the races frequently coincided with geographical borders, which themselves were often marked by geological barriers. That race as a concept has always been about constructing borders in this sense is already clear from the text that is conventionally considered the site of the first use of the word "race" in one of its modern senses, where race is understood to refer to a relatively small number of types of humanity based largely on differences in appearance. In 1684, François Bernier published anonymously an essay entitled "A New Division of the Earth, According to the Different Species or Races of Men Who Inhabit It, Sent by a Famous Traveller to Mons. [...]."[22] Bernier's idea was that whereas previously geographers had divided the earth according to the natural boundaries that separated regions, one could also conveniently divide it into four or five different parts according to the distribution of people across the earth, judging especially by the way they looked. The proposal was based on the observation that travelers were rarely mistaken in identifying the nation to which a person belongs. Bernier knew this firsthand: he had travelled extensively himself, including spending some eight years in India. Skin color was less important to Bernier than it would become to subsequent generations and not simply because he recognized that the climate could have an artificial effect on skin color. He was more focused on such characteristics as the shape of the head.[23] However, not long after Bernier introduced his proposal, migration and above all the forced migration of the slave trade meant that different bodily types were geographically dispersed, breaking up the relative uniformity of types in any given location that his account presupposed.

Borders marking both geographical and geopolitical divisions are crossed in the course of such population movements, but these changes led to another form of crossing to which the name "cross" or "cross-breed" is sometimes given. It was in the context of laws regulating sex that, at least

CROSSED LINES IN THE RACIALIZATION PROCESS   109

in North America, race first became a factor, even before slavery became fully racialized.[24] In Virginia on September 17, 1630, it was determined that Hugh Davis was to be "soundly whipped, before an assembly of Negroes and others for abusing himself to the dishonor of God and shame of Christians, by defiling his body in lying with a negro."[25] From the beginning the law assumed that one knew who was Black, who was White, and who was Indian. What would become the borderline cases—Asian Indians or North Africans, for example—were not yet in play in the New World. The question was how to treat someone of mixed heritage.

Marriage between an "English or other white man or woman" and a "negroe, mulatto or Indian man or woman bond or free" was to be punished.[26] But the definition of a mulatto employed by the law was so broad that only a relatively small fraction of Black ancestry for the time excluded a person from being considered White in Virginia. According to a Virginia law from 1705, "the child of an Indian and the child, grand-child, or great grand-child, of a Negro shall be deemed accounted, held and taken to be a mulatto."[27] Given the fact that the first Africans arrived in Virginia in 1619, one would anticipate there being few mulattos, if any, with one-eighth African ancestry and thus, at that moment, little chance of the son or daughter of a free mulatto couple being considered legally White. But, of course, as the years passed the fraction became much easier to attain. Indeed, a change in the law in 1785 such that the proportion of Negro ancestry needed to count as a mulatto was increased so that it would now have to be one-quarter or more suggests that a workable system of stratification rather than an obsession with racial purity governed racial identities at that time.[28]

The focus on race mixing as the primary site of contestation around which racial identities were shaped and reshaped led to paradoxes. Kant, who was the first to define race in scientific terms and who in many ways established the basic parameters of future thinking on the topic, was against race mixing.[29] But at the same time he believed that it took a highly artificial perspective—which he called "natural history"—to see "race" as he understood the term. What one observes, in the sense of what is accessible to what he called "natural description," is only human varieties, people grouped according to certain visible characteristics. Race, for Kant, as indeed for most people after him, was about permanent inheritable characteristics, but he was more insistent than others that in order to see someone's race one not only has to discount the impact of the environment, one also has to know something about how that person's children looked. Only those characteristics that were

110   CRITICAL PHILOSOPHY OF RACE

shared equally by any offspring in cases of race mixing were strictly racial characteristics. As a result, Kant seems to have believed that one cannot *see* race in the tropics or at the poles, because the impact of the environment is too strong in such places. Race is clearly visible only after generations and in a temperate climate and only after race mixing.[30] According to Kant, one could be sure that the parents were of different races only if the child shared equally in the racial characteristics of both parents. Skin color was his preferred example. This gives rise to the paradox that insofar as the races are identified only through race mixing, then the very imperative that seeks to maintain racial purity had to be transgressed so that one could know if a transgression was about to occur. To map the racial borders, the borders must be crossed. This establishes a further sense in which race from its first conceptualization is about transgression, especially sexual transgression.[31]

The systems of racial classification divided the races, but these were not merely divisions to be observed. They were to be enforced or policed, and the main context within which this took place from the very beginning was the context trying to limit and often prohibit race mixing. It was to control sex across the color line that so many of the other restrictions, known collectively under the title "segregation," were introduced after 1890.[32] At times the focus seems to have been more on the sex act itself, but at other times, more on the occasions when it resulted in a child and on the question of how that child was to be classified within the racial order.[33] The dominant class knew that the existence of large numbers of mixed-race children had the potential of changing the racial landscape. Race mixing expanded the racial borderlands to the extent that it was no longer as obvious, as it once had been, what race someone belonged to. But it was the redrawing of the racial lines by legislators to protect what at any given time counted as White purity that enlarged the zone of indeterminacy around the racial borderlands.

One can see the consequent confusion at work in a dramatic way in the fate of the children of Thomas Jefferson and Sally Hemings. Jefferson explained the laws of Virginia defining race in a letter to Francis Gray, who was from Massachusetts and who was clearly having difficulty understanding the Southern way of looking at race. In the letter Jefferson corrected a mistake he had apparently made when trying to explain Virginia's rules on racial identification to Gray on his visit to Monticello, which suggests that he had not previously given the matter as much thought as he might have done. In any event, even though he called the matter "a trifle," he employed a series of algebraic formulae to show that a slave who was less than one-quarter Black would, if freed, be legally White in Virginia.[34] This is indeed what happened with Eston Hemings, who was freed on Jefferson's death. Eston not only was considered White and listed as such in the 1830 census; he was White according to the laws of the day. However, another son, James Madison Hemings, although legally White like his brother, was considered "colored" by the 1830 census. To be White, it seems, it was not enough to meet the legal definition; one had to look White, which was not necessarily the same thing. From most people's perspective today, James Madison Hemings was Black, but according to the laws of the day he was White.[35]

It is tempting to conclude from this that slavery at that time was not yet fully racialized. Jefferson insisted that a slave was not free as a consequence of being White: being White did not "re-establish freedom, which depends on the condition of the mother" following civil law.[36] And yet Jefferson could not bring himself to think of a slave as White, even though the status of his own children by Sally Hemings was at stake. His careful formulation suggests that he preferred to think of slaves as accruing whiteness on gaining their freedom. He wrote that if someone who is one-eighth Negro blood (that is to say, after three crossings) "be emancipated, he becomes a free white man, and a citizen of the United States to all intents and purposes."[37]

In spite of the impression sometimes given by proslavery literature in the 1850s that ignored the existence of free Blacks, one was not a slave because one was Black, but either because one had recently been brought as a slave from elsewhere or because, as Jefferson said, one's mother was a slave. Both someone's status as a slave and their racial designation were hereditary, but the two were out of kilter. The disconnect between the legal definition of race and physical appearance was even more serious. As Jefferson's letter reluctantly shows, being legally or phenomenally Black was not only not a sufficient condition of being a slave; it was also not even a necessary condition. Already in the eighteenth century, visitors to Monticello saw slaves that they regarded as having no visible trace of African ancestry.[38] One needs to take into account that looking White in 1795 might not count as looking White two hundred years later, given the changes in the way the races were redefined in the intervening period, but this is because race itself, while serving as the largely unnamed organizing principle, was undertheorized. One is tempted to say it was the unthought in what was thought and done.

To be sure, what we today cannot but think of as race came to the fore already in 1669 when John Locke as secretary to the Lord Proprietors of Carolina recorded their agreement that "Every Freeman of Carolina shall

112   CRITICAL PHILOSOPHY OF RACE

have absolute Power and Authority over his Negro Slaves or what Opinion or Religion soever."[39] That marked a clear shift away from conceiving religion as the major factor determining who can and who cannot legitimately be enslaved. The convention was that Christians would not enslave their fellow Christians, but this article announced that from that time an exception would be made in the case of "Negroes."[40] What would come to be called "race" already trumped religion. But because race as such was undertheorized and would remain so until Kant, what I am calling the racial borderlands expanded. Put simply, a racial system that was indeterminate and beset with incoherences and contradictions was found to be adequate to the purpose, because nobody in power inquired too closely into it. Indeed, only when it was decided that the governing divisions were "racial determinations" did it became possible to ask what race was and thereby make the system's lack of foundation apparent. While the philosophers and scientists sought to explain race, the courts and politicians had to construct the rules that would address individual cases.

Was it appearance, genealogy, or behavior that revealed someone's race? In 1835 in South Carolina, a certain Judge Harper suggested that in some cases neither appearance nor genealogy was sufficient without reference to someone's reputation: "it may be . . . proper, that a man or worth . . . should have the rank of a white man, while a vagabond of the same degree should be confined to the inferior caste."[41] In Louisiana in the twentieth century, a system of "social validation" operated.[42] Even more remarkable are the "White Negroes" of Mississippi. At the beginning of the twentieth century, Whites who cohabited with African Americans were sometimes classified as Black by census enumerators and, more generally, Whites who socialized with Blacks were also so regarded, but as a result, when subsequently the state of Mississippi tried to enforce school segregation using the legal definitions, the law was found to be in conflict with the way people were regarded by their neighbors.[43]

Nevertheless, there was over time a hardening of the attitude that had led Jefferson to state so cautiously what was staring him in the face. The same Judge Harper who argued for reputation to have a role in determining a person's race added that "it is hardly necessary to say that a slave cannot be a white man."[44] He was saying that the idea of a White slave was so intolerable to people of that time that even if genealogy and appearance led one to conclude that a slave was White, it had to be ruled impossible. The whitening of the slave population over time, most often as a result of masters raping their slaves, had led to the point where slaves were sometimes whiter than their owners.[45] According to George Stroud in his *Sketch of the Laws Relating to Slavery* in 1827, "a person whose complexion is European could be legally retained as a slave."[46] In the second edition of 1856, he introduced a story dating from 1834 of how the people of Pike, Mississippi, had appealed to the law courts to free a ten-year-old slave from whom "all the physiological marks and distinctions which characterize the African descent have disappeared." When that failed, they tried to club together to purchase his freedom.[47] This shows that by this time many people of European descent were uncomfortable with the fact that people whose skin color matched their own were living in their midst as slaves, even though they did not always show the same discomfort about the fact that their own slaves looked like them because they were their own children.

At the end of the eighteenth century, there was still a general sense that if all aspects of someone's purported race were invisible, then they no longer had any tie to that race. Jefferson's understanding based on his knowledge of animal husbandry was that, just as a Merino ram on its fourth cross "gives an issue equivalent for all sensible purposes to the original blood," "negro blood" is cleared after "two crosses with the pure white and a third with any mixture, however small."[48] But in the middle of the nineteenth century, Josiah Nott created a stir with his paper "The Mulatto a Hybrid—Probable Extermination of the Two Races If the Whites and Blacks Are Allowed to Intermarry," which created a new source of anxiety about the consequences to health and fertility of racial crossing.[49] By the beginning of the twentieth century, the science had changed again. There was some talk of identifying someone on the basis of "a drop of colored blood in their veins" even before the Mendelian laws of heredity gave the idea scientific legitimacy.[50] But it was only following the dissemination of the ideas of Gregor Mendel that the one-drop idea became law, which began in 1910 with Tennessee and was decisively sealed, at least for Virginia, when in 1924 that state passed "An Act to Preserve Racial Integrity."[51] The reason for the resistance to such a law before then is clear from the South Carolina Constitutional Convention of 1895, when George Tillman opposed a proposal that the phrase a "one eighth or more" of Negro blood be changed from the draft of an anti-miscegenation law to read "any" Negro blood. His argument was that if the proposal was adopted there would not have been a single pure-blooded Caucasian participating in the Convention.[52]

114   CRITICAL PHILOSOPHY OF RACE

The aim of the one-drop rule, as the man mainly responsible for administering it in Virginia, Walter A. Plecker, state registrar at the Bureau of Vital Statistics in Richmond, Virginia, explained was to "postpone the evil day when this is no longer a white man's country."[53] He was obsessed with race mixing as he believed that it would eliminate "the higher type." Segregation was the attempt to transfer the conceptual borders between the races into legislation, and it is no accident that the Massenburg Bill passed in 1926 and in place until 1963 gave Virginia the most restrictive measures governing social interaction of any state.[54] To address the problem of race mixing on which "the life or death of our civilization depended," he believed it necessary to restrict all race mixing so far as it was possible, even though it meant reducing at a stroke the number of people who counted as White. But although he supported the redefinition of a White person as someone with "no trace whatsoever of blood other than Caucasian" on the grounds that it would reduce incidents of "passing,"[55] it inevitably made it easier for people to pass. Otherwise said, the more people who appeared on the face of it to be White were counted as Black as a result of such changes in the laws, the more those in the racial borderlands could flout the law by passing. So, in addition to all those who had their racial identity changed by the law, others chose to go against the law and change their racial designations for themselves. The point is that the legislation was aimed not at those who were in no doubt that they were African American, but at those in the borderlands. In fact, some of the people who were most impacted by the legislation were people who claimed some Native American lineage. They were supposed to be addressed by the so-called Pocahontas exception, but Plecker in his administration of the law was convinced that all Virginia Indians were tainted with some Black heritage and so were covered by the one-drop rule.[56] People in the United States were familiar with the fact that one's racial designation might change as one crossed state lines. One should not be surprised at people's readiness to do this, given that an estimated twenty-five hundred to twenty-five thousand persons a year changed their racial designation from Negro to White.[57]

Concerns about passing transform racism from being directed against a highly visible and thus easily identifiable Other onto those within one's circle. The number of legally White people who passed as Negro was for obvious reasons much smaller, but it was also much easier and not only because there was less suspicion. As Gunnar Myrdal explained, "To cross the caste line from the white side would be a comparatively easy matter, since in America a Negro is not necessarily supposed to have any Negro features at all."[58] And

CROSSED LINES IN THE RACIALIZATION PROCESS   115

there was also the possibility that one was "passing" without knowing it. Under Mendelian laws of heredity as understood at that time, everyone had to be suspicious of themselves to the extent that they did not know all the details of their own heritage.

Problems of Racial Identification

The previous section has demonstrated that for much of the history of the United States the production of race was governed by the drawing and redrawing of racial boundaries. The historical facts presented there are included in this chapter to make concrete the abstract idea of race as a border concept. They show that the racial assignments society supplied to each child at birth were for all those in the racial borderlands open to change as a result of new laws, new linguistic usage, changes in physical appearance through interaction with the environment, a change in status or reputation, or a change of place. The evidence also suggest that the meanings attached to racial assignments were also at least in principle open to change: this is especially clear in the case of the term "colored." Although race was for much of this period understood in terms of permanent inheritable characteristics, there was nothing permanent about the way the lines were drawn.

A new sense of race could also be imposed on people as a result of conquest, as when after 1848 the United States sought to use its own terms to racialize Mexicans. That was the date of the Treaty of Guadalupe Hidalgo, which transferred over half of Mexico to the United States in exchange for a money payment, with the result that some eighty thousand Mexicans who had woken up in Mexico discovered by the end of the day that they were in the United States and with a few exceptions were no longer welcome in their home country. It emerged that the protections the Treaty allegedly guaranteed them were restricted to those among them who were considered White, that is to say, to those who were considered representatives of "the Spanish race" as opposed to the darker skinned people of "the Mexican race."[59] The latter were, as a result of a change in the border, left in a kind of no-man's land, neither Black nor White, within a system dominated by the racial binary. On occasion the courts treated Mexicans as White without acknowledging them as White, which meant, among other things, that when Mexicans and Blacks married each other, they might be taken to court on the grounds of race mixing.[60]

116   CRITICAL PHILOSOPHY OF RACE

Similar problems arose after Spain ceded Puerto Rico to the United States in 1898. The rigid system of racial classification operating in the United States had now to be introduced from the outside. This was brazenly stated when in 1930 the Brookings Institution issued a lengthy report that included this observation:

> Racial statistics in Puerto Rico are only approximations to the truth, as the population is extremely intermixed and there are not only two colors, but an infinity of shades. It is next to impossible, in many cases, to determine whether a person is white or slightly colored. In such cases, of which there are thousands, the strictness or tolerance of the census agent determines how the person is to be classed.[61]

Having conceded that Puerto Ricans were "extremely intermixed," the authors nevertheless called upon census agents to impose the racial binary. The observers from the Brookings Institution saw what they no doubt anticipated seeing: the lack of a color line in Puerto Rico, as in much of Latin America. Another study from the same period agreed that the fusion of Spanish, Indian, and Negro was so complete "that it is impossible to say in just what proportion these various bloods are represented."[62] What these American observers seemed not to recognize is that there were major cities in the United States where similar mixtures of "bloods" or a spectrum of skin colors was present. The difference was that people in the United States were familiar with the process of having a racial identity assigned to them at birth. They grew up with people who knew their place within the system or knew at very least that they were supposed to have a place within the system. It only appeared more arbitrary in Puerto Rico because the system had yet to become sedimented.[63]

Every time an attempt was made to bring greater coherence and rigor to a system that was full of anomalies and arbitrariness, it seemed only to add to the confusion. One major reason for this was the fact that, as we have seen, the criteria were often conflicting between physical appearance, lineage, behavior, and social acceptance; but another reason was that the information needed to determine someone's lineage, which would normally be considered relevant, if not decisive, in determining that person's race, was not adequate to the purpose. It was often either lacking or was imprecise because different categories had been used or they had been used with a different purpose in mind. Difficulties of this kind had already arisen in Spain at the end

CROSSED LINES IN THE RACIALIZATION PROCESS   117

of the fifteenth century when it was a question of applying the purity of blood statutes. These statutes are often referred to as the birth of modern racism, but they also saw the birth of the *linajudo*, a group of people whose main task was to prepare family trees to assess whether a person had any *conversos* ancestry which, if found, would disqualify them for official offices and honors.[64]

A similar problem of racial identification also arose within apartheid South Africa. A fact paper from 1958 of the South African Institute of Race Relations tells a series of harrowing tales of people reclassified and having their lives turned around as a result of bureaucratic decisions. Part of the problem arose because sometimes the laws in South Africa conflicted about how someone should be classified. For example, "A person who appears to be White but is generally accepted as Coloured might be classified as Coloured under the Population Registration Act; but under the Group Areas Act he could be classified as White, unless an allegation is made, which he cannot disprove, that he is really Coloured."[65] At the same time South African law was continually being forced to rely on such formulations as the following, which is drawn from the 1950 Population Registration Act: "A 'White' person means a person who in appearance obviously is, or who is generally accepted as, a White person, but does not include a person who, although in appearance obviously a White person, is generally accepted as a Coloured person."[66] What this did was to throw the problem onto bureaucrats without giving them much guidance beyond their capacity to appeal to historical categories which had never been applied, nor were intended to be applied, with such rigor.[67]

In Virginia, Plecker faced another version of the same problem as he sought to administer the "Act to Preserve Racial Integrity." We have seen that, because the one-drop rule increased possibilities for passing, the Act's intentions could only be successfully fulfilled if it was rigorously enforced, but that was difficult even for a man like Plecker, because the records that would tell someone's racial heritage with that degree of precision did not exist. His main recourse was lists of the registrations of marriages from the previous century, but the categories used in those lists were much vaguer than would have been necessary for the law to be applied accurately.[68] The rigor introduced by the "Act to Preserve Racial Integrity" was illusory because it had no firm foundation on which to build and, as the name of the act shows, it was in large part designed to conceal the fact that whatever Earnest Sevier Cox meant by "White America" it was more mixed than he dare admit.

118 CRITICAL PHILOSOPHY OF RACE

Because so much is at stake with race, attempts are constantly being made to control the words used to identify races: White, Black, Negro, African American, Mongol, Indian, Native American, Anglo-Saxon, Celtic, German, Prussian, Jewish, and, more recently, Hispanic, Latinx, Chicano. There have always been attempts to control these terms, but the definitions are constantly shifting. And yet frequently a person's fate has depended on the success with which these words are controlled and construed: whether one was free or slave, citizen or illegal immigrant, welcome or unwelcome as an immigrant, and, more recently whether one qualifies as a beneficiary of affirmative action. One's fate could also depend on ever-shifting definitions of who one could marry, where one could live, whether one could legally enter into a country, and whether one could eat, sleep, or use the restroom. A change in how one was classified or in how one's identity was read could impact one's status. And because the different states in the United States very often defined those races differently—not only who was White, who was Indian, and who was Black, but in some cases also, for example, who was Mexican and what that meant—a difference of a few miles, a border crossing, changed one's status radically, just as today African Americans find themselves racialized in different ways as soon as they leave the country, particularly if they go, for example, to Brazil or to central Africa. It is always a question of where these ambiguous and contested lines are drawn, how rigidly they are defined, and, of course, especially who draws them.

Race as Facticity

Rather than seeing race in the United States as a rigid system whose boundaries were protected by laws,[69] we should see it as a fluid system that never succeeded in maintaining the borders it tried to establish, but whose resilience came from the capacity of the dominant class within the system to turn a blind eye to their inability to police those boundaries effectively. Thinking of race as a border concept serves as an invitation to break through the self-evidence of our everyday racial assignments by employing a hermeneutics of racialization to examine the unique connotations of the constantly shifting artificial categories used to determine racial identity in any given context. To say that they are artificial is not to say they are arbitrary. They are the product of material forces and reciprocal antagonism. Like much else that can be called socially constructed, race is not experienced as socially constructed, but as a facticity.[70] We are all born into a world already racialized and even though there is for some people today the opportunity to self-identify, not everyone experiences that as an option.

Even the small part of the history of racialization in the United States that I have been able to relate here threatens the self-evidence which many White Americans attribute to race and should lead us to rethink what we mean when we say, "we see race." An understanding of what it means to see race must include not only a knowledge of the history of racial oppression, and how people have suffered in the name of race, but also a knowledge of the history of racialization which has left this category that was constructed on the basis of its alleged visibility unable to rely simply on appearances. To focus on the borders that give shape to racial identities is not to deny that for many people, if not most people, in any given context there will be little ambiguity about how they are racialized. But to be racialized is to be located within a group alongside others and, even for those whose racial identity is unambiguous, the meaning of that identity cannot be separated from those at its borders. That is also part of what it means to say that race is a border concept, a dynamic concept whose core lies not at its center but at its edges and whose logic is constantly being reworked as the borders shift. The idea of race congeals around these borders so that it is more present in their transgression than in any essentiality that is attributed to an alleged racial core. But, as I have indicated, whereas in the past racialization has in large measure been driven by the law and by science so that how ordinary people thought about race was to a large extent guided by these forces, this is less true today. Neither the law, nor science, directs us how to classify people into races. Today self-identification is nominally the rule. To that extent we racialize ourselves, but we do not do so in isolation from the rest of society. Racialization as a social process is still conducted largely with reference to that history that is sedimented into society's conceptual framework. This is why an improved knowledge of that history is indispensable to a better understanding of why we see others and ourselves in the ways we do.

III.
BLACK PHILOSOPHERS
SPEAK OUT

7

Ottobah Cugoano's Place in the History of Political Philosophy

Slavery and the Philosophical Canon

The Silence of the Philosophers, Then and Now

At a time when there are calls from around the world for decolonizing the canon, there is an urgent need to clarify both the facts about what the thinkers who are served up to students in philosophy classes had to say on the enslavement of Africans and how their positions on that issue related to their philosophies more generally. Although much of this chapter is devoted to offering examples of the failures of seventeenth- and eighteenth-century canonical philosophers to use their authority to speak out on this issue, the thrust of my discussion is to highlight the widespread failure of philosophers today to engage this issue. Even when a canonical philosopher's support of slavery is well known, as in the case of John Locke and Immanuel Kant, until very recently there seems to have been little appetite on the part of specialists on these philosophers to mount a sustained investigation of what this means for our understanding of them, as if there were no possibility that the enslavement and murder of millions of Africans had any philosophical relevance.

Irrespective of its immense historical importance, the rejection at the end of the eighteenth century by Europeans within Europe of the traditional justifications for slavery would seem worthy of philosophical study in order to understand better how changes in morality take place. It is a striking fact that popular revulsion in England against the slave trade and against slavery did not await, in Robin Blackburn's phrase, "the approval of philosophers," but was generated by a small number of former slaves working with, mainly, clergymen.[1] To be sure, the political task of emancipating the slaves held by European colonists proved an inordinately slow process, but the moral transformation at the popular level, once it began, took place in Europe with astonishing speed. One gets an early indication of this by comparing the first

Critical Philosophy of Race. Robert Bernasconi, Oxford University Press. © Oxford University Press 2023.
DOI: 10.1093/oso/9780197587966.003.0008

124   CRITICAL PHILOSOPHY OF RACE

and second editions of William Paley's *Moral and Political Philosophy.* In February 1785, Paley observed in his chapter on slavery that "The great revolution which seems preparing in the Western world, may probably conduce, and who knows, but that it is designed to accelerate the fall of this abominable tyranny."[2] A year later this sentence was revised to read: "The great revolution which has taken place in the Western world, may probably conduce, and who knows, but that it is designed to accelerate the fall of this abominable tyranny."[3] But Paley was an exception. The most eminent philosophers of the time seem to have missed this seismic event and, perhaps for no better reason than this, philosophers today fail to study it. The canonical philosophers, who still today provide the models for how we think of moral and political philosophy, turned their backs on the sufferings of Black slaves, and many of the scholars who dedicate themselves to studying those canonical philosophers repeat the same avoidance mechanisms.

It is not anachronistic to complain about the way eighteenth-century philosophers approached the issue of slavery. When Condorcet published his *Réflexions sur l'esclavage des Nègres* in 1781, he attacked the moralists for remaining silent on the crime of reducing human beings to slaves, albeit he did so under a pseudonym thereby compromising the strength of his criticism.[4] A few years earlier, in 1773, Jacques-Henri Bernardin de Saint-Pierre completed his description of the way slaves were treated in Mauritius by complaining that he was "annoyed that philosophers who fight abuse so courageously mention the slavery of blacks only to make a joke of it."[5] He was probably thinking of David Hume's notorious remark, made in the context of a discussion of Negro slaves and subsequently recycled by Kant, that a Negro might be admired "for slender accomplishments, like a parrot who speaks a few words plainly."[6] What makes Bernardin de St. Pierre's observation especially significant for my purposes is that he also offered a diagnosis of why so many philosophers failed to criticize the horrors of the African slave trade at a time when others were doing so. He said that they "avoid the problem by looking to the past." If, as seems likely, he meant to highlight the way that philosophers frequently allow their attention to be drawn to past arguments directed to conditions that no longer pertain, thereby overlooking the contemporary conditions that are staring them in the face, then, as I will show in the second section, that was very much the case with writings on slavery by a number of prominent philosophers in the seventeenth and eighteenth centuries.

If one relied solely on textbooks of political philosophy, one would have no idea that the debate on the abolition of both the slave trade and the institution of slavery itself was one of the most prominent and contentious philosophical topics in Europe in the second half of the eighteenth century. The study of that debate has been handed over to the historians and, with the notable exception of Glen Doris, they usually ignore the role of canonical philosophers in those debates, although Montesquieu sometimes gets a mention.[7] The resulting silence about how canonical philosophers viewed slavery might lead one to conclude that they had little to say about it, but this is far from the case. It was a standard philosophical topic throughout the seventeenth and eighteenth centuries, and often took the form of commentary on previous studies. This seems to have given the philosophical discussion of slavery an inherently conservative tendency with the result that it was slow to adapt to changes in sentiment.

With my quick survey in the second section of the failure of canonical philosophers in the modern period as important background, in the third section I turn to Ottobah Cugoano's *Thoughts and Sentiments on the Evil and Wicked Traffic of the Slavery and Commerce of the Human Species*, first published in 1787.[8] Cugoano, who wrote explicitly as "a Native of Africa," knew what he was talking about at firsthand. By his own account, he was captured when he was about thirteen years old in what is now Ghana, taken to the West Indies in 1770 as a slave, and after two years brought to England. That was at the time of the Somerset decision delivered by Lord Mansfield, who ruled that a slave owner could not in England exercise dominion over his slaves according to American laws. Two years later, at the age of about eighteen, Cugoano was freed. One contemporary observer, Scipioni Piattoli, claimed that Cugoano's book caused a great sensation.[9] However, there is otherwise little record of its impact beyond Henri Grégoire's complaint that the book was both unmethodical and repetitious.[10] Grégoire also complained that Cugoano had too good an opinion of Europeans, a fact that added to their shame,[11] but what he and many others since failed to see was the striking originality of some of the philosophical arguments found there. My aim here is not to offer an assessment of the place Cugoano's *Thoughts and Sentiments* should be given within the historical debate on abolition. Others have sought to do this, and it is generally agreed that it was the most radical of all the abolitionist tracts.[12] My concern is to identify among the arguments that he introduced those that have a special resonance today.

126   CRITICAL PHILOSOPHY OF RACE

Philosophers on Slavery during the Enlightenment

The framework of modern political philosophy was established in the seventeenth century by such figures as Grotius, Hobbes, Pufendorf, and, of course, Locke, but none of them opposed the slave trade, let alone slavery, on principle. This has to be placed in historical context. I am not aware of any published seventeenth-century text, philosophical or not, that specifically attacked the enslavement of Africans without ambiguity. The English Puritan Richard Baxter insisted that anyone who bought "negroes or other slaves of such as we have just cause to believe did steal them by piracy, or buy them of those that have no power to sell them" had committed a "heinous sin": "by right the man is his own, and therefore no man else can have just title to him."[13] Nevertheless, Baxter seems to have been more tolerant of those slave owners whose intention was to baptize their slaves. Perhaps the most impressive attack on the enslavement of Africans from this period was that by Epifanio de Moirans, but his text, written in 1682, remained unpublished for three hundred years. Even so, his argument was not that the traditional justifications of slavery were wrong, but that they did not apply to the Africans who were being enslaved at that time.[14] Principled opposition to the institution of slavery was rare even at the beginning of the eighteenth century.[15]

The lack in the seventeenth century of a principled opposition to the institution of slavery is striking because there was some momentum against slavery in the previous century. Pope Paul III's 1537 bull, *Sublimis Deus*, is sometimes cited in this regard. It condemned the slavery of "Indians and other peoples," but it was soon forgotten and, in any event, was perhaps intended only as a local condemnation that was not meant to apply universally or perhaps even to Africans at all.[16] Jean Bodin's argument that the introduction of slavery had been very pernicious, as was its persistence into his own time, is a great deal more significant. But it is telling that with few exceptions Bodin's contribution receives even today little recognition from philosophers.[17] It is also telling that Bodin's rejection of slavery was already dismissed in his own time both because he lacked the support of Aristotle, whom he had explicitly criticized, and because he did not even countenance slavery among those of different religions.[18] Bernardin de St. Pierre said that his contemporaries were looking to the past as a way of avoiding the problem of slavery, and it seems that Bodin's contemporaries were already doing the same. A remarkable exception was Pierre Charron, who, somewhat under

Bodin's influence, rejected all the traditional justifications of slavery; it was for him "a monstrous custom, and highly reproachful to Human Nature."[19]

The twin temptations of Christianizing pagans while at the same time making money from them seems to have proved irresistible to Northern Europeans in the seventeenth century, and this tendency was already in evidence in sixteenth-century Spain in the *disputatio* between Bartolomé de Las Casas and Juan Ginés Sepúlveda held in Valladolid in 1550. It is the closest thing we have in the whole of the modern period to a genuine debate about slavery among philosophers where the participants were at the cutting edge of discussion of the issue. Earlier in the same year, Emperor Charles V even halted all conquests in the Indies, presumably while awaiting the outcome of the debate, although there was in the end no resolution, albeit after the debate Las Casas was allowed to continue to publish, whereas Sepúlveda's publications were restricted. Las Casas is clearly the more attractive figure. Nevertheless, he exoticized at least some of the Indians to the point where he could imagine them as being untouched by original sin.[20] To protect them from enslavement, he on a number of occasions proposed the use of African slaves in their place, and although he subsequently regretted this,[21] it tarnished his reputation for centuries afterward, and he seems never to have expressed the same deep concern for Africans that he did for the Indians. Las Casas did not argue that slavery was wrong, but that it was an obstacle to Christianizing the Indians and that one could never be certain that any of them had been captured unjustly.[22] In 1519, he rejected Aristotle's idea of slaves by nature,[23] but it was later promoted by Sepúlveda as the slavery of the philosophers. Even so, Sepúlveda did not consider the dullness and stupidity that he attributed to the Indians as permanent characteristics. He believed that through their subjection they would come to discard their savagery and be brought "to a more human life, milder customs, and the cultivation of virtue."[24] The Indians may have been short on what the Renaissance humanists called *humanitas*, a quality that he alleged the Spaniards displayed, but that did not mean they were not human: they were lesser humans with the potential to develop further (*homunculi*).[25] Sepúlveda also looked to arguments drawn from natural law, and this gave rise to what he called the slavery of the lawyers: the Indians were prisoners captured in a just war, and the war against them was just in his view because he believed they practiced human sacrifice.[26] At roughly the same time Francisco de Vitoria, while, on the one hand, restricting the right to enslave Indians if they persisted in their efforts to destroy the Spaniards, was also, on the other hand, willing to

128   CRITICAL PHILOSOPHY OF RACE

countenance war against the Indians if they did not allow the preaching of the gospel or if they forbade baptisms.[27]

The dominant way of justifying slavery throughout the seventeenth century and well into the eighteenth century was not by reference to permanent racial differences, although it is clear that the increasing focus in the second half of the eighteenth century on racial differences made it easy for observers to ignore the clear evidence that the other justifications being used were illegitimate. During this time period, appeals to Aristotle's conception of slaves by nature became increasingly rarer, although they can be found.[28] To be sure, the biblical argument in terms of the curse of Ham had long been in circulation alongside it.[29] But if one understands the racial argument in favor of slavery as an argument that appealed to the science of race where race is a category of natural history (as a precursor of biology), then, taking the United States as the example, it was only in the middle of the nineteenth century that racial justification of slavery became dominant. Nevertheless, there were precursors. One already finds the racial argument in its fully developed form in the late eighteenth century when Christoph Meiners, professor of philosophy or *Weltweisheit* at the University of Göttingen, translated various assertions from contemporary travel literature into the language of natural history.[30]

Kant can also be found translating proslavery literature into the language of natural history, but on close examination it can be seen that he did so more to justify race as a category within natural history than to use natural history to justify slavery. Nevertheless, he thereby helped to plant the seeds of the racial argument that would strengthen slavery as an institution, and he was doing so at a time when his contemporaries in Europe were turning against it. In his 1788 essay "On the Use of Teleological Principles in Philosophy," Kant made the claim that Negroes lacked the immediate drive to sustained activity that one calls industry. For him this was one of their permanent racial characteristics, but the evidence that he cited in support of the claim was the observation "that among the many thousand freed Negroes which one encounters in America and England" there was no example of one "engaged in a business which one could properly call *labor*."[31] The source of this claim was James Tobin's *Cursory Remarks upon the Reverend Mr. Ramsay's Essay on the Treatment and Conversion of African Slaves in the Sugar Colonies*,[32] But Tobin, albeit in a passage not available to Kant, was so far from espousing the racial justifications of later times that he explicitly denied that anyone had ever "pretended, that the slaves either of the Jews, Greeks, or Romans

OTTOBAH CUGOANO'S PLACE 129

of old, or the European and African slaves of modern times, were, or are, in way *inferior* to their masters, except in strength, policy, or good fortune."[33] To be sure, during the course of the seventeenth and eighteenth centuries, a link was increasingly being established in the minds of White people, both in Europe and the Americas, between slavery and Africans.[34] From early on, critics, like Thomas Tryon, of the way Africans were increasingly being singled out for slavery tried to break the connection between the two ideas, but it is telling that, until Meiners and Kant, any knowledge we have of what looks like racial arguments for enslaving Africans are known mainly from those who attacked those arguments.[35] Nor should we forget that in the seventeenth century what we think of as racial differences were not readily separated from religious differences. This can be seen in the strong convention among both Christians and Muslims that one did not enslave anyone with whom one shared a religion.

The main justification for the enslavement of Africans in the seventeenth and eighteenth centuries was the traditional argument that prisoners captured in war could be enslaved instead of being killed during hostilities. The argument was rehearsed by Hugo Grotius in his *The Rights of War and Peace*, which was first published in 1625 and repeatedly revised and commented upon. It contained extensive discussions of slavery that included a detailed presentation of the *ius gentium*, the law of the peoples, which offered the practices of the Greeks and Romans as a kind of justification, albeit one that lacked the authority of the *ius naturae*, the law of nature. This essentially backward-looking approach set the parameters for later discussions insofar as Grotius, together with Samuel Pufendorf, who in 1672 responded to him, were widely discussed inside and outside the universities in the eighteenth century. As often as not, the focus was on the practices of the Greeks and Romans, frequently accompanied by a declaration that political slavery was worse than domestic slavery. For example, we read in the manuscript of Adam Ferguson that "The Courtiers of Tiberius or Nero even the Senators of Neros [sic] time were debased to a degree far beyond that of the Slave to an Ordinary Master."[36]

Grotius and Pufendorf both allowed for different kinds of slavery, including slavery by contract, which subsequently came to be known as a form of indentured servitude. By adopting a narrower definition of slavery, according to which one could not sell oneself into slavery, Locke in his *Two Treatises of Government* was able to justify a harsher treatment of slaves, because it did not have to accommodate relations that one would never accept

130   CRITICAL PHILOSOPHY OF RACE

under the terms of a contract. Grotius was clear that the law of nations authorized the victors to dispose of prisoners captured in war as they saw fit. The options included enslaving or killing them, but he also insisted that there was in fact no right to kill someone once hostilities were over and that this established clear limits on the treatment of slaves. "No Masters, (if we judge by the Rules of Full and complete Justice, or before the Tribunal of Conscience) have the Power of Life and Death over their Slaves."[37] Locke explicitly rejected any such restriction, and this is what separates him from those who can be understood to belong to the mainstream: on slavery Locke was an outlier. Drawing on the "strange Doctrine" that "in the State of Nature, everyone has the Executive Power of the Law of Nature," he judged it legitimate to enslave anyone who had in the state of nature committed "some Act that deserves Death."[38] Locke excluded slavery between those who were party to the social contract, but to be outside of civil society, as Africans and Native Americans were thought to be, was to be in a state of war, and they could legitimately be punished by enslavement if they had gone against the law of nature, for example, by engaging in an unjust war.[39] Slavery was simply a continuation of the state of war. An anonymous reviewer of *Two Treatises of Government* in Jean Leclerc's *Bibliothèque Universelle*, perhaps Locke's friend Leclerc himself, understood very well what Locke meant by his claim that one can destroy anyone who makes war upon the innocent just as one kills wolves and lions, when he suggested that it could be applied to "the commerce which Europeans can have with barbarous peoples" who have neither magistrates nor laws.[40]

Locke had thereby found a philosophical justification for one of the provisions of "The Fundamental Constitutions of Carolina" with which he, as secretary to the Lord Proprietors, had been involved in 1669 and which he helped to revise in 1682 at the same time as he was writing relevant parts of the *Two Treatises of Government*. We read in "The Fundamental Constitutions of Carolina" that "Every freeman of Carolina shall have absolute power and authority over his *Negro slaves*, of what Opinion or Religion soever."[41] Baptism did not change their status. This provision claimed for the freemen of Carolina the right, against Grotius, of killing specifically Negro slaves, albeit by 1698 Locke had apparently departed from this position in instructions for Governor Nicholson that he drafted that punished by death "the willful killing of Indians and Negroes."[42] Nevertheless, the doctrine of *Two Treatises* was that slavery simply postponed execution of the death sentence that could therefore be reimposed at any time. This gave to the master

"Absolute, Arbitrary Power of another" in the sense that in relation to his slave the master could "take away his Life, when he pleases."[43] Slavery was not an alternative to passing a death sentence. Death as a punishment was only suspended, and it could be reimposed at any time. This formulation amounted to what we cannot see as anything other than an early step in the racialization of slavery, even if we must be cautious in trying to understand what people at that time understood by labels like "White" and "Negro." It is a crucial moment in the separation of race from religion.[44] To be sure, for the slaves themselves what would have mattered more was the adoption of the distinction between slaves and indentured servants, a racializing distinction, not readily made in Latin, that can be seen coming into focus in Richard Ligon's *A True & Exact History of the Island of Barbadoes*.[45]

It is hard to explain the presence of a justification for such an extreme form of slavery in *Two Treatises of Government*, a political discourse whose chief purpose was to defend the English from being treated by their own monarchs as "slaves" in some much broader sense, unless one acknowledges that Locke had Carolina on his mind as he was writing that part of the book. However, throughout the following century when university philosophers addressed slavery, they for the most part seemed to do everything they could to keep their students or their readers from thinking of the Atlantic slave trade. One clear exception was Gershom Carmichael of the University of Glasgow, who in 1724, in the course in of commenting on Pufendorf's discussion of slavery, explained that he had addressed the topic at length because "this usurped right of *owning* slaves like cattle, as it existed among the ancients, is exercised today by men who profess to be Christians, to the great shame of that holy name, with greater tyranny perhaps than it was by the ancient pagans."[46] By calling this form of slavery that was being practiced by Christians outside of Christian Europe "*a sure sign of the death of sociability*," he made it clear that he thought it the antithesis of everything Pufendorf stood for, although Jean Barbeyrac was not convinced, as can be seen from his commentary on Pufendorf.[47]

Nevertheless, Carmichael's immediate successor in the chair of moral philosophy at the University of Glasgow, Francis Hutcheson, did not take matters much further, even though he is sometimes credited with being the one who originated the modern attitude on slavery.[48] Hutcheson acknowledged Carmichael's commentary on Pufendorf in his discussion of slavery in his own textbook on moral philosophy.[49] He also cited Locke as an authority when denying that slavery was hereditary, albeit he failed to mention that he

132   CRITICAL PHILOSOPHY OF RACE

was going against Locke when he sided with Grotius in insisting that captives could not legitimately be put to death and in placing the burden on the purchaser of slaves to be sure that they were justly enslaved.[50] However, the central point is that Hutcheson remained silent in his *A Short Introduction to Moral Philosophy*, both about his contemporaries' reliance on slavery and the debates that were already beginning to take place around him. A much longer discussion of slavery appears in a manuscript that it is usually agreed he completed before the publication of *Short Introduction*, even though it was only published posthumously by his son in 1755. In a discussion of the duties and rights of masters and servants, he included a critique of the seventeenth-century practice of appealing to the law of nations: "As to the notions of slavery which obtained among the Grecians and Romans, and other nations of old, they are horribly unjust."[51] Even more strikingly, in an earlier chapter he dismissed as specious the argument that a merchant who bought captives in "barbarous nations" where they would otherwise be murdered, subsequently possessed the right to sell them as slaves elsewhere. He commented: "Strange, that in any nation where a sense of liberty prevails, where the Christian religion is professed, custom and high prospects of gain can so stupefy the consciences of men, and all sense of natural justice, that they can hear such computations made about the value of their fellowmen and their liberty, without abhorrence and indignation!"[52] This is not so different from what Carmichael had already said, but it is disturbing that Hutcheson chose not to publish in his lifetime his explanation of how general criticisms of slavery could be applied to the enslavement of Africans that was going on around him.

Hutcheson was not alone in his reluctance to court political controversy by speaking out directly against the slave trade, even though he had at his disposal the resources to do so. One of the clearest examples of a university philosopher whom we know to have been actively opposed to slavery was James Beattie. As early as 1764, Beattie was attacking contemporary slavery as unlawful in his lectures on moral philosophy, but his arguments did not appear in print until 1793 in *Elements of Moral Science*.[53] Even though in 1784 he openly attacked Hume's presentation of Negroes as inferior,[54] he never published his 1778 manuscript "On the Lawfulness and Expediency of Slavery, Particularly That of the Negroes" in spite of pleas for him to do so.[55] Although he was perfectly capable of exposing the frigidity and languor of intellectuals, he refused to publish his tract on slavery because, as he told Mrs. Montagu in 1779 somewhat defensively, "it would rather create enemies

OTTOBAH CUGOANO'S PLACE   133

to the author, than promote justice and benevolence."[56] Even Montesquieu in *The Spirit of the Laws* went no further than to say that "slavery is against nature" while at the same time appealing to his theory that the human varieties are determined by climate, in an effort to offer an explanation of why Blacks made such good slaves and why "natural slavery must be limited to certain particular countries of the world."[57] The result was that his discussion was so ambiguous and so marked by irony that he was appealed to by both opponents of slavery and its defenders.[58] To be sure, when in his unpublished *Pensées* he addressed slavery, albeit without mentioning the enslavement of Africans explicitly, he was a little more direct. He wrote "slavery is contrary to natural right," but although much of the discussion there found its way into *The Spirit of the Laws*, that clarifying sentence did not.[59] One has to assume that this omission was again motivated by a reluctance to speak out unambiguously against the strong vested interests that sought to perpetuate slavery.

But it was not only the cowardice of philosophers and their nostalgia for the Athenian polis that seems to have led philosophers to hold back from taking a principled stand against it. The fact that Christianity had for so long tolerated slavery presented an obstacle to some philosophers to come out against slavery in principle. William Paley, who was a clear opponent of the slave trade, on becoming Archdeacon of Carlisle in 1785 published his lectures at the University of Cambridge under the title *The Principles of Moral and Political Philosophy* with the clear hope that his book would be adopted as a textbook. In this he was extraordinarily successful because it did indeed become one of the standard textbooks for the teaching of ethics in both Britain and the United States until the mid-1830s, but it is striking that in his brief chapter on slavery, he did not rule out slavery as illegitimate and he spent more than a third of the chapter outlining his explanation of why Christians had not already abolished slavery, a question that clearly troubled him. He took the long-term view, and in keeping with it, he insisted that emancipation should be gradual. When in 1792 he gave a speech against the slave trade as "incompatible with the natural rights of man, contrary to the principles of religion and morality, founded in extreme injustice, and the cause of many cruelties," he expressly excluded proposing emancipation: "we do not aim at the emancipation of the slaves, in the British West-Indies, but only that the future importation of them, from Africa, may be prohibited."[60]

Paley's significance lies in the fact that he chose to address directly and at length the use of African slaves in the Americas in a philosophical context.

134　CRITICAL PHILOSOPHY OF RACE

His procedure was to examine the three circumstances—crime, captivity, and debt—under which traditionally slavery, understood as the obligation to labor for the benefit of one's master without contract or consent, was considered consistent with the law of nature. That is to say, he looked to past arguments to find a starting point on which there might be consensus and then proceeded, as Moirans had done a century earlier, to show that the African slave trade did not meet those conditions. By contrast, most philosophers of the time considered slavery only at an abstract level. Paley himself drew attention to this difference when in the Preface to his book he launched an attack on Adam Ferguson's *Institutes of Moral Philosophy*, which was then going into its third edition and which was a rival candidate for textbook use in the universities. Paley believed that philosophers like Ferguson chose to argue in a "sententious, apothegmatizing style" that concealed from their readers the implications of their arguments.[61] To illustrate his point, Paley cited three sentences from Ferguson found at the end of a section entitled "Of the Right to Command, or Service." They read: "No one is born a slave; because everyone is born with all his original rights. No one can become a slave; because no one from being a person can, in the language of the Roman law, become a thing, or subject of property. The supposed property of the master in the slave, therefore, is a matter of usurpation, not of right."[62] These statements have contributed to Ferguson's reputation as an advocate of abolition, but Paley was hearing nothing of this. His commentary is striking: "It may be possible to deduce from these few adages such a theory of the primitive rights of human nature, as will evince the illegality of slavery; but surely an author requires too much of his reader, when he expects him to make these deductions for himself; or to supply, perhaps from some remote chapter of the same treatise, the several proofs and explanations, which are necessary to render the meaning and truth of these assertions intelligible."[63] One might find Paley's verdict on Ferguson unduly harsh. If students at the University of Edinburgh could not conclude from these three sentences an opposition to slavery, this does not speak well of them. And yet if Paley's point was that the philosophy of the Enlightenment combined strong statements of principle with a widespread failure to draw the practical conclusions that would seem to follow from them, then he had a point.

Thomas Gisborne cast himself as a rival of Paley, insofar as he published in 1789 *The Principles of Moral Philosophy* in the hope that it would serve as the textbook at Cambridge University in place of Paley's *The Principles of Moral and Political Philosophy*. Like Paley, Gisborne presented himself as an abolitionist, but in this book he still allowed for slavery in cases of indemnification and as a punishment for crimes.[64] His argument was about the limits on the rights of masters and their corresponding duties. One could read the chapter on slavery and imagine that the enslavement of Africans was far from his mind, but, earlier in the book, he had addressed the argument that one should not emancipate "the West-Indian negroes, though in general reduced to slavery by unjust means" because there was a danger that they would massacre the planters.[65] Gisborne rejected that argument on the grounds that there was insufficient evidence that that would happen. Three years later he issued a pamphlet in which he argued that because the purchasers of African slaves were not taking any care to establish that the Africans were being enslaved according to the principles that he had set out in *The Principles of Moral Philosophy*, the slave trade "ought *instantly* and universally to be abandoned."[66] He also rejected racial justifications of slavery, but he was clear that he was arguing for the abolition of the trade in slaves, not their emancipation.[67] This pamphlet was, with some minor changes, incorporated into subsequent editions of *The Principles of Moral Philosophy*, but his only concession there to the cause of emancipation was to say that the inquiry about whether it would result in violence against the planters was one that should be examined at regular intervals and that, in the meantime, one could take preliminary steps toward emancipation.[68] Against this backdrop, it is relatively easy to demonstrate Cugoano's radicality and his importance for a rewriting of the history of political philosophy.

Cugoano and Responsibility

Cugoano published *Thoughts and Sentiments* in 1787, and it appeared in a French translation within a year, at a time when the campaign against the slave trade was gathering momentum. It was only in the previous year that Thomas Clarkson had published *An Essay on the Slavery and Commerce of the Human Species, Particularly the African*, an expanded English version of his prize-winning Latin essay submitted at the University of Cambridge in 1785.[69] The year 1787 also saw the foundation of both the Committee for Effecting the Abolition of the Slave Trade and the Sons of Africa, of which Cugoano was a founding member. Although among Africans writing against slavery in England at that time, Ignatius Sancho and Olaudah Equiano are now better known than Cugoano, his book is more conventionally

136 CRITICAL PHILOSOPHY OF RACE

philosophical in the sense of being more directly theoretical, whereas their writings are more literary and autobiographical. *Thoughts and Sentiments* belongs to the same genre as the abolitionist writings of Granville Sharp and Thomas Clarkson,[70] to which it is indebted, but I want to highlight three arguments that Cugoano introduced in his book that make it stand out in direct contrast with the writings of his contemporaries and that still merit the attention of philosophers today.

First, Cugoano rejected the gradualism of his contemporaries. Whereas other abolitionists focused on abolishing the traffic in slaves on the assumption that it would be better to work by increments in an effort to get the widest support possible, Cugoano argued for "an immediate end and stop" to this "base traffic," while also rejecting any delay before the "universal emancipation of slaves, and the enfranchisement of all the Black People employed in the culture of the Colonies."[71] He even set out the process by which this would happen, including mitigating "the labour of their slaves to that of a lawful servitude" until after seven years, having attained a "competent degree of knowledge of the Christian religion," they would be freed.[72] Gradualism was a strategy not only of White abolitionists like Paley,[73] but also of the proslavery faction because it delayed what was increasingly being seen as inevitable. It enabled even Tobin, a slave owner with plantations in Nevis, to claim that he should not be "ranked among the advocates of slavery," a claim readily dismissed by Cugoano.[74] Cugoano argued for a quick and sweeping resolution of the problem, not only of the slave trade but also of slavery itself, and this was at the forefront of his early embrace of so-called immediatism.[75]

In addition to refusing the compromises that were being promoted among his fellow abolitionists, Cugoano, secondly, insisted that nobody, even if they were not directly involved in the slave trade, could be considered innocent unless they spoke out against it. He wrote: "But while ever such a horrible business as the slavery and oppression of the Africans is carried on, there is not one man in all Great Britain and her colonies that knoweth anything of it, can be innocent and safe, unless he speedily riseth up with abhorrence of it in his own judgment, and, to avert evil declare himself against it, and all such notorious wickedness."[76] Cugoano here presented an idea of responsibility that is familiar in our time: the idea that there are no innocent bystanders and that moral responsibility extends further than those actions for which we can be held directly accountable according to legal standards. This sense of responsibility was less common in a period where people generally felt less empowered, but it was reflected to some degree in the petitions that the ordinary people of Britain were presenting to Parliament beginning in 1783 and culminating in the unprecedented campaigns of 1788 and 1792.[77]

Cugoano was among the first to frame a broad notion of responsibility, and his choice of the word is especially worth considering. Although the adjective "responsible" is much older, the noun "responsibility" and its French and German equivalents are a product of the 1780s. *The Oxford English Dictionary*, citing the *Federalist Papers*, gives 1787 as the first year in which the word "responsibility" was used in the English language, probably by James Madison.[78] Remarkably that was the same year in which it was used by Cugoano to highlight both "the guilty responsibility" of "the great men and the kings of Europe" for this "awful iniquity" and "the greatest eminence of responsibility" that belongs to the enslavers themselves.[79] More important than this linguistic innovation is Cugoano's broad application of the idea: "every man, as a rational creature, is responsible for his actions, and he becomes not only guilty in doing evil himself, but in letting others rob and oppress their fellow creatures with impunity, or in not delivering the oppressed when he has it in his power to help them."[80] It is an argument he also applied to other nations standing by "when it beholds another nation or people carrying on persecution, oppression and slavery."[81] Extending responsibility to all those bystanders who, whether individuals or nations, "saw others robbing the Africans, and carrying them into captivity and slavery," and who "neither helped them or opposed their oppressors in the least" was not characteristic of the anti-slavery literature up to this time.[82] It has a particular resonance in the light of Francis Wayland's *The Limitations of Human Responsibility*, where, some fifty years later the president of Brown University exonerated all citizens of Northern states from any responsibility for slavery.[83]

But Cugoano did not only challenge the innocence of bystanders, he also suggested, somewhat threateningly, that they might not be safe. This third aspect of his discussion that I have chosen to highlight has a number of different dimensions. Cugoano threatened with divine vengeance those who chose to ignore the issue of slavery. In this he followed Granville Sharp's *The Law of Retribution; or, a Serious Warning to Great Britain and Her Colonies, Founded on Unquestionable Examples of God's Temporal Vengeance against Tyrants, Slave-holders, and Oppressors*. But when Sharp listed the various ways in which the slave trade leads to deaths and included, alongside disease, "the Rising of the Negroes in Slave Ships," he was not thinking of them as instruments of divine vengeance.[84] By contrast, the threat can be clearly

138 CRITICAL PHILOSOPHY OF RACE

heard in Cugoano's final paragraph when he wrote that "the voice of our complaint implies a vengeance because of the great iniquity that you have done, and because of the cruel injustice done unto us Africans."[85] Historians have followed C. L. R. James in highlighting the role of slave revolts in bringing an end to slavery, but although rebellion might represent a principled opposition to all forms of slavery, it does not necessarily do so.[86] The revolts needed their spokespersons. One thinks, for example, of the speech attributed to Moses Bon Sàam in 1735. This former slave, in addition to attacking the morality of the slave trade and the grounds on which they were held, especially as hereditary slaves, threatened revolt.[87] Cugoano belongs in this lineage and he took it to the next level.

Cugoano brought a new perspective to the idea. It emerges in stages beginning, somewhat surprisingly until the argument as a whole is revealed, with Cugoano seeming to allow for the possibility that some forms of slavery might be legitimate. More specifically, he argued that "the greatest transgressors of the laws of civilization" are "the only species of men that others have a right to enslave."[88] His first example of such a transgression was the forging of money, but it soon emerged that the example he was aiming at was the biblical idea that if anyone should steal another human being they should die.[89] In other words, if one enslaves someone unjustly, then one should oneself be enslaved. The most widespread justification of slavery in the seventeenth and eighteenth centuries referenced prisoners captured in a just war, and this theory was regularly applied to the African slave trade. However, as I showed earlier, John Locke in his *Two Treatises of Government* gave this argument a rigor that was not usually attached to it, and with this rigor came an unprecedented harshness. We do not know if Cugoano had read Locke, but Cugoano's rejection of the application of this theory to Africans successfully turned Locke's argument on its head. Just in case his readers missed the point, Cugoano announced that the slaveholders had by virtue of transgressing the golden rule committed a greater violation than if the slaves were to have reversed the current order and enslaved their masters.[90] Abolitionists had previously attempted to influence the defenders of slavery by putting into their heads the thought of Africans enslaving them and their kin.[91] Cugoano went beyond this by suggesting that such a reversal would be legitimate. Furthermore, to the extent that exercising the executive power of the law of nature was a duty and not just a right, then there was perhaps even a duty to enslave the slavers, a possibility made even more relevant in the context of Locke's justification for slavery, given his unusual insistence on the executive power of the law of nature and on the fact that slavery was legitimate only in cases where the war was "unjust and unlawful."[92]

Cugoano acknowledged that his words—his thoughts and his sentiments—were "harsh" and it seems that they may have been too harsh for his contemporaries, even if they were less harsh than Locke's prescriptions.[93] In 1791, four years after the original publication, a second shorter edition was published. Scholars have speculated about the relation of these two versions, but it should be recognized that all three of the arguments I have just outlined were omitted from the second edition and that they were central to the harshness of the text. In other words, it seems that the second edition was designed to make the text more palatable. That means that it would be more palatable not least to White people, including White abolitionists, but it should be noted that whereas the first edition was, according to its title, "humbly submitted to the Inhabitants of Great Britain," the second edition was, again in the title, "Addressed to the Sons of Africa." This suggests that one should avoid the temptation of dismissing the religious and more conventional arguments that reappeared in the second edition as unimportant to Cugoano. Even though I have not dealt with them here, they have all been well summarized elsewhere.[94]

The three arguments I have isolated from Cugoano's text have to be seen in context. The argument against gradualism not only establishes a kind of rigorism that brooks no compromise, but it also highlights the hypocrisy of those who want to see an end to slavery but not yet. The second argument issues a warning against all those who attempt to justify their inactivity and refusal to speak out against slavery on the basis that they did not own slaves and so were not directly implicated in its operation. Those who did not own slaves could claim they could not be held legally accountable for the way the slaves were treated, but they remained responsible by virtue of belonging to a society whose prosperity derived from slavery. Finally, Cugoano took the doctrine that an unjust system can legitimately be overthrown by actions proportionate to the wrong being done, and applied it to the extreme case of slavery, which opened the door very wide indeed.

In a world that continues to be rife with racial inequality, all three arguments have a current relevance so that examining them does not amount simply to looking to the past. It is a reminder of an ongoing struggle to correct the wrongs that created the modern world and redistribute the wealth created by those wrongs. Cugoano's early evocation of the responsibility of bystanders not only recalls to mind Martin Luther King's critique of

140   CRITICAL PHILOSOPHY OF RACE

the White church but also points toward ideas of collective responsibility, as well as the hyperbolic responsibility announced by Sartre and Levinas when they said everyone is responsible for everything as opposed to being held accountable for specific acts of omissions.[95] Finally, Cugoano's text raises the question of the necessity of violence in bringing about the transformation necessary to liberate the oppressed, thereby placing him in the lineage of Frantz Fanon and Malcolm X. All too often the oppressed are silenced or ignored even in campaigns against oppression. This seems to have been true of Cugoano in his own time, and it remains true in the history of political thought. In Cugoano's *Thoughts and Sentiments* we can hear an anger commensurate to the evil under discussion. It was too radical for the eighteenth century, but perhaps the time has finally come when it can be heard.

Decolonizing the Philosophical Canon

In the late eighteenth century, the insight into the evil of slavery was a challenge to Christians like Paley; they needed an explanation as to why Christians had up until then failed to see what was becoming increasingly clear to them. Historians of philosophy today have a similar problem: why were so many of the philosophers that we still teach to our students for their ethical insights so reluctant to speak out against slavery or, even worse, why were they on the wrong side of ongoing debates? There is a tendency for these same historians to rush to the excuse that the philosophers in question were children of their time.[96] In this essay, I have made an initial attempt to show how contextualizing their contributions with reference to the debates that were going on around them helps to force the issue.

The rejection of slavery in all its forms is an ongoing process that is still incomplete. Given the importance of slavery within the Greek and Roman societies, a fact that philosophers have traditionally looked to for understanding the history of their discipline, understanding the steps by which slavery came increasingly under attack should be an important component of the study of the history of ethics. Cugoano's *Thoughts and Sentiments* is a challenge to the kind of complacency that ignores that process. We must not only investigate the failures of past philosophers but also question why academic philosophy is pursued today in such a fashion that it is considered acceptable to ignore the failure of the discipline, both past and present, in the face of slavery. No wonder many despair of academic philosophy and turn their backs on it. That philosophers look to the past does not need to be a defect of the discipline, if it is done with honesty. But until the discussion of slavery is given a more prominent place in studies of the history of moral and political philosophy, it is hard not to conclude that it is a dishonest history, a one-sidedly White supremacist history, a history that has been doctored to make it more palatable.

Decolonizing the philosophical canon has a much broader aim and more far-reaching consequences than anything that emerges simply from an examination of the eighteenth-century debate about slavery, but the fact that the canonical philosophers of that period do not have a place in the history of abolition is in and of itself a reason to reexamine both the canon of moral and political philosophy and the interests of those who once determined what belonged to it and of those who now sustain it. When the philosophical canon was being established around 1800, the treatment of slaves was not an important issue within the universities, especially as slavery as a form of property had helped Europe amass its wealth and power.[97] But this does not explain why today so many specialists appear to be indifferent to the question of what the philosophers on whom they focus had to say on the issue, as if their contributions to this debate should be entirely irrelevant to any assessment of their philosophies. But in addition to examining the failures of canonical philosophers, it is important to show that there were other original thinkers who can be an inspiration to future generations of students. It is my contention that Cugoano is such a thinker. When the debate over the legitimacy of slavery finally finds its rightful place in courses on political philosophy, Cugoano should be front and center.

8

A Haitian in Paris

Anténor Firmin as a Philosopher against Racism

Imagine the scene. This is Paris. It is July 17, 1884, and Anténor Firmin, a Black man newly arrived from Haiti, only thirty-three years old but already qualified as a lawyer, is elected to membership of the Société d'Anthropologie de Paris, the most important anthropological society anywhere in the world. He is not the first Black member. Indeed, his fellow countryman Louis-Joseph Janvier is one of the three members of the Société that propose him for membership, as the rules of the society require.[1]

After a year Firmin publishes a book of over 650 pages, inspired by a need to intervene in the debates he heard at the meetings of the Société. The book, *The Equality of Human Races*,[2] is announced, as is the custom in the Société, on October 1, 1885, at the first meeting after the summer recess, but this seems to have been almost the only notice taken of it.[3] It was virtually ignored in Europe and in the United States, until the publication in 2000 of an English translation. In the Preface he apologizes for the signs of haste in the book; these are indeed clearly visible at various points.[4] However, it is obvious today that it is a major statement in favor of the equality of races. The book includes a rich account of the intellectual life of Haiti in the nineteenth century, but my focus here will not be on Firmin as a forerunner of pan-Africanism, negritude, or postcolonial theory.[5] Instead, I will concentrate on what he can tell us about the science of race at the end of the nineteenth century.

The aim of this chapter is to read Firmin's book in relation to the science of his day. Because Firmin was a vigorous and insightful, if largely unheard, opponent of many of his most illustrious contemporaries, a study of his books not only helps to clarify what eminent scientists thought at that time, but it also indicates other options that were open to them; he indicates what they could have thought, but did not think, and so saves us from anachronism in our judgments of them.[6]

Critical Philosophy of Race. Robert Bernasconi, Oxford University Press. © Oxford University Press 2023.
DOI: 10.1093/oso/9780197587966.003.0009

The French Debate between Monogenesis and Polygenesis

What was the Société d'Anthropologie de Paris? It had been founded in 1859, the year of Charles Darwin's *The Origin of Species*. Before long, Darwin would be a point of contention between the members of the Société. However, the circumstances surrounding the foundation of the Société had nothing to do with Darwin. The Société d'Anthropologie arose from the growing resurgence of polygenesis, the theory that at least two human species were created separately. In May 1858, Paul Broca had presented to the Société de Biologie evidence that the offspring of a female rabbit and a male hare had been prolific over successive generations. He argued that this animal represented a challenge to Buffon's rule of species identification, according to which only animals of the same species could be fertile. Broca also saw that this represented a challenge to monogenesis, understood as the theory that the human species had a single origin. For this reason, the founding president of the Société de Biologie, Pierre Rayer, persuaded Broca to withdraw his article from the publication of the proceedings of the Société and to agree not to present such ideas in the future.[7]

Nevertheless, Broca, who was only thirty-four at that time, could not be silenced. He immediately began publication of his views on heredity in the *Journal de la Physiologie*.[8] He also organized a small gathering of polygenists. This was the start of the Société d'Anthropologie de Paris, and it soon began to expand its numbers and intellectual orientation. Among those who accepted the invitation to join in the second year of its existence was Jean Louis Armand de Quatrefages, the foremost monogenist in France at that time. The French debate between monogenesis and polygenesis was thus conducted within the confines of the Société itself, albeit the majority of its members were sympathetic to polygenesis.

The debate between monogenesis and polygenesis had been at the heart of the scientific discourse about race since Immanuel Kant provided the first definition of race in 1775, in response to the polygenetic theories of Voltaire and Henry Home, Lord Kames. Kant defined race in terms of inheritable characteristics that derived equally from both parents, with skin color his preferred example. His defense of monogenesis drew on the fact that because all varieties of human beings could interbreed, they satisfied Buffon's rule of species identification.[9] However, Kant and all monogenists who came after him were left with the problem of having to explain the

144   CRITICAL PHILOSOPHY OF RACE

permanence of racial characteristics. Primarily, it was a question of why Whites did not become Black if they moved to sub-Saharan Africa and why Blacks did not become White in northern Europe. As late as 1766, Buffon still believed that these transformations would occur, albeit over a number of generations.[10] Kant's solution, which later generations had difficulty accepting, involved positing the existence of four seeds or germs in the original human being, one of which was actualized to varying degrees at the expense of the other germs, as a result of the climate and other environmental factors.

However, in the late 1840s, monogenesis was threatened by a challenge more serious than its difficulty of explaining how permanent differences could arise from a common origin. The so-called American school of polygenesis, led by Josiah Nott, changed the terms of the debate, by arguing that Buffon's rule of species identification applied even where sterility was only gradual, or indeed was manifested only in disease or in a shorter life expectancy.[11] When Broca wrote his essay on hybridity, he referred to Nott's early discussions of hybridity, as did other polygenists like Georges Pouchet.[12] However, as Firmin himself noted, Broca and other French anthropologists were drawn to polygenesis on account of their anticlericalism, whereas Nott and George Gliddon advocated it in an effort to support slavery.[13]

After Broca died in 1880, a former student, Paul Topinard, was elected to succeed him as secretary-general of the Société d'Anthropologie. He was still the secretary-general when in 1884 Firmin was elected to membership, but during 1886 he was ousted by Charles Letourneau, who had presided over the meeting at which Firmin was elected. It was a victory of the scientific materialists over the positivists.[14] In that way, as in many others, Firmin, as a positivist himself, was swimming against the tide. The late nineteenth century saw an intensification of racism, motivated by the demands of imperialism and justified by social Darwinism. This no doubt helps to explain why Firmin's book was stillborn from the press.

The *Bulletins de la Société d'Anthropologie* gives a record of the discussions that took place at the meetings of the Société, and on that basis it seems that Firmin never made an intervention of any kind until much later. This happened only after he returned to Paris in 1892, following the failure of his political ambitions in Haiti, including a brief period as minister of finance, commerce and foreign relations in Florval Hyppolite's government. During meetings in April 1892, Firmin twice intervened to put in question the tendency to characterize certain races as irrevocably inferior without reference to environmental conditions.[15] Nevertheless, even in 1884, he was far from overawed by the famous scientists who attended these meetings. The book he decided to write soon after joining was critical to the point of outright hostility toward many of the luminaries of the Société d'Anthropologie. For example, he said of Broca, its founder and the teacher and sponsor of many of its current members, that "the eminent professor, the great anthropologist, who spent all his life measuring crania and discoursing on the human types, was more often than not totally ignorant about what he was talking about with the self-assurance of an expert."[16]

In his book Firmin recalls a debate that took place during the meeting at which he was elected.[17] An examination of the record of this session offers some clues as to what led Firmin to write his book. De Quatrefages, by then, at seventy-four, the grand old man of French anthropology, discussed some observations Paul Lévy had made on the impact that the American environment had made on the European races. The report was more amateurish than scientific: it included such gems as the idea that the sweat of a pure Negro had a different smell from that of a creole.[18] Janvier, Firmin's compatriot, and himself the author of a pamphlet with the title *The Equality of Races*,[19] responded at some length, arguing that to understand the creolization of the Black race, one would do well to look to Haiti. His intervention can be understood as an attempt to make the point that, with Janvier and now Firmin present at their meetings, one hardly needed to rely on reports of the testimony of Paul Lévy to find out about creolization in the Caribbean. However, if that was Janvier's point, it seems that it was lost on his audience. Nevertheless, it may well have framed Firmin's reaction to the exchange that took place between André Sanson and de Quatrefages immediately after Janvier's intervention and that Firmin subsequently recalled in his book. Firmin remarked on how both men saw the question of species in terms of monogenesis and polygenesis: "It is curious to see how passionate and vehement these usually calm men become whenever these issues are broached."[20] De Quatrefages believed that Sanson was confusing race, a matter of hereditary descent, with species, which is a matter of origin. In response, Sanson rehearsed the familiar puzzle with which the polygenists loved to taunt the monogenists: a White person cannot become Black, so how can the races all be said to have the same origin?[21]

146   CRITICAL PHILOSOPHY OF RACE

Firmin the Philosopher

To be sure, by 1884 many members of the Société would have considered the debate between monogenesis and polygenesis a dead issue. For example, Topinard had written in his *Anthropology* in 1876 that the debate no longer had any interest.[22] Darwinism had changed the intellectual context. Firmin seems to have been equally convinced that the debate between monogenesis and polygenesis was an irrelevancy, but he suspected that the passions that it aroused were a consequence of the underlying agendas of each camp. And, so far as he was concerned, this passionate response was evidence that they were not true scientists. Firmin was provoked when de Quatrefages, in *The Human Species*, had quoted approvingly Jean de Thévenot's remark, "The mulatto can do all that the white man can do; his intelligence is equal to ours," while nevertheless continuing to uphold the idea of the inequality of the races.[23] De Quatrefages was forced to argue that the mulatto inherits his or her intelligence solely from his or her White parent, while sharing equally in the physiological characteristics of both parents. Firmin suggested that the evidence pointed rather to the idea that race mixing concerned physiological characteristics alone and that the source of intelligence of the child was unpredictable.[24]

In this regard, Firmin clearly saw himself upholding true positivism against both the scientific materialists and the false representatives of positivism in the Société, like Topinard. Firmin presented himself as a positivist in anthropology.[25] He even subtitled his book "Positivist Anthropology" (*Anthropologie Positive*). But it would be a mistake to think that this makes Firmin an upholder of scientific facts at the expense of philosophy. In the opening chapter of his book, Firmin made clear his belief in the significance of philosophy. According to him, changes in scientific theories that eventually transform prevailing currents of thought are brought about by philosophical innovation.[26] This led him to begin his account of anthropology by considering Kant, whom he clearly appreciated, and Hegel, whose works he regarded as somewhat confused albeit sometimes brilliant.[27] However, it is clear that Firmin's philosophical sympathies lay with the positivism of Auguste Comte,[28] which he understood as opposed to "the metaphysical doctrines that have too long subjugated the human mind, from Plato to Hegel."[29] Comtean positivism is not only explicit in Firmin's endorsement of the idea that "the fetishistic stage is more conducive to the development of positivist philosophy than the theological stage,"[30] but it is also implicit in Firmin's frequent appeals to progress, perfectibility, and humanity.

A HAITIAN IN PARIS   147

For Firmin, positivism is not only a method but also a philosophy. He understood Comtean positivism to culminate in "a healthy philosophy [which] consists in following the laws of nature as we contribute intelligently to reinforcing the harmony of all elements, human beings and planets, on the immense expanse of our planet." He continued: "This need for harmony underlies the altruistic sentiments which make of humanity a concrete entity whose interdependent parts act, work, and progress toward a common destiny."[31] Firmin was so persuaded by this broad positivism that he called the doctrine of the inequality of the races not only anti-scientific, but also anti-philosophical.[32] One can see that conviction at work in his response to Georges Pouchet's claim that scientists must set aside "those infinitely honorable sentiments of equality and brotherhood which a noble heart must feel toward all human beings regardless of their origin and their color."[33] Firmin simply dismissed Pouchet's statement on the grounds that it exhibited "a regrettable absence of any philosophical thought."[34] Indeed, Firmin rejected all theories that contradicted progress and justice.[35] So far as he was concerned, the harmony of science and progress was so firmly established by Comte that a theory that was not "consistent with humanity's highest aspirations" could readily be rejected as false.[36]

The title of Firmin's book might lead one to believe that it was written as a refutation of Gobineau's idea of a racial hierarchy, as set out in his *The Inequality of Human Races*, but Gobineau was not Firmin's primary target. This was because Gobineau was not at that time as influential as he would later become. It is true that at one point Firmin wondered whether "anthropologists have found in Gobineau's fantastic notions and equivocal paradoxes such a bright light source that they take his conclusions for Gospel truth," but he has to admit that if they do so, it is without actually saying so.[37] In fact, I have found little evidence of anthropologists of that time having a deep commitment to Gobineau, although he was certainly read.[38] Gobineau's racial theories began to be genuinely popular at the end of the nineteenth century, although even then they were eclipsed by writers such as Houston Stewart Chamberlain.[39] Gobineau's importance was only fully established in the 1920s and 1930s. It would be a serious mistake to be convinced by Firmin to overestimate the significance of Gobineau's essay in the 1880s. Indeed, Gobineau, who died in 1882, had been forced four years earlier to give up his plan to publish an expanded edition of his work that took into account Darwin's theories, for lack of a willing publisher. Nevertheless, a virtually unchanged edition of the *Essai* appeared in France in 1884, the same year

148   CRITICAL PHILOSOPHY OF RACE

that Firmin began preparing his own book, and this was the edition Firmin used. However, its publication had only been possible by a subvention from Bayreuth, where Richard Wagner's circle continued their master's idiosyncratic enthusiasm for Gobineau's works.[40] Firmin's focus on Gobineau was more an accident of timing than a reflection of the book's reputation among scientists.

Even so, it is still worth trying to be clear about Gobineau's argument. Although the title of Gobineau's book, *Essai sur l'inégalité des races humaines*, might lead one to suppose it was a book primarily rehearsing familiar claims concerning the hierarchy of the races, it was in fact a novel attempt to write a philosophy of history organized around the relatively new obsession about race mixing as posing a biological threat to a people or nation. What was so distinctive about Gobineau's classic work was not his belief in the inequality of races, which was widespread, but his belief that civilization arose only through a process of racial intermixing that would eventually lead to the decline of humanity as a whole. According to Gobineau, although all civilizations derive from the "white race," clear advantages for civilization came from mixing with other races. Thus, artistic genius arises only from the mixing of Whites and Blacks.[41] This theory is very different from that of the French anthropologists who were Firmin's intended audience and main target. It also shows that Firmin was telling only half the story when he attributed to Gobineau the thesis that "the human races degenerate through certain [racial] crossings."[42]

Royer's Darwin

Whereas Gobineau would not become a central reference point in French discussions of race until the twentieth century, there is no doubt that Darwin's theory of evolution was, particularly as the result of speculation about the application of this theory to the human races. This debate had begun almost as soon as *The Origin of Species* was published in 1859. The book's full title—*On the Origin of Species by Means of Natural Selection, or the Preservation of Favoured Races in the Struggle for Life*—already suggested its application to human races. Darwin did not address these issues specifically until the publication of *The Descent of Man* in 1871, but Firmin dismissed the latter book in a couple of sentences on the grounds that the focus there fell more on developing the theory of sexual selection than on an in-depth ethnological study.[43] He was more interested in the efforts Darwin's contemporaries had made to speculate about the application of his theories to the human races. Even though Darwin had decided to omit any such discussion from the work, his readers wasted no time in trying to work out its implications. In Britain, Alfred Russel Wallace and Thomas Henry Huxley were the most prominent to take up the topic; in Germany, Ernst Haeckel did so; in France, Darwin's first translator, Clémence Royer, already prefaced her translation of *The Origin of Species* with a long introduction, part of which addressed the possible application of Darwinism to racial questions.

The growing reputation of Darwin in France and Clémence Royer's role as the translator and main spokesperson of Darwinism meant that Firmin had no choice but to confront Royer's work. Just as Huxley was Darwin's bulldog in England, Royer was Darwin's bulldog in France.[44] Nevertheless, Darwin had complained about her successive translations of the various editions of *The Origin of Species*, and particularly the prefaces and notes which she added. Darwin's dissatisfaction might not have been common knowledge, but there was no mistaking the fact that he arranged for a new translation to appear in 1873. Firmin was not alone in preferring the old edition.[45] Nevertheless, even though Firmin was faced with a distinguished author who had come to conclusions about racial equality and race mixing that were markedly different from his own, he recognized that they both drew on Darwin and Comtean positivism.[46] That was why Royer was a necessary as well as a convenient target for Firmin.

Royer became a member of the Société d'Anthropologie de Paris in 1870. Although her election was controversial both because she was a woman and someone strongly identified with Darwin's theories, she had the support of de Quatrefages, the Society's strongest critic of Darwinism.[47] However, the *Bulletins* of the Society show that she was an extraordinarily active member. Indeed, in December 1885 she was elected an honorary member, making her only the seventh person to be recognized in this way.[48] This was a singular honor, especially given the fact that she had a record of distorting the Society's positions and being openly critical of the Society in general.[49]

In her Introduction to her translation of Darwin's *The Origin of Species*, Royer presented it as a work dedicated to the idea of racial inequality. She believed that Darwin's theory of natural selection left no doubt that the superior races would progressively supplant the inferior races. The equality of human beings was to her a dangerous, impossible idea.[50] The passage in which Royer made these claims was cited at length by Firmin, and, given that

150   CRITICAL PHILOSOPHY OF RACE

they ran entirely counter to the thesis of his book, it is no surprise to find that he directed some of his usual invective toward her. Nevertheless, the precise character of the tirade is extraordinary. Here are some extracts:

> Clémence Royer is a scholar and a scientist, but she is a woman. There are problems of such complexity that they can be properly studied only by men, for only men, because of their education and their temperament as males, can see them from every angle. . . . Despite the high esteem in which I hold Darwin's translator, I cannot help but point out that she remains a woman.[51]

The depth of these misogynistic sentiments is extraordinary. Even if Firmin had been persuaded about the inequality of women by the scientific discourse that he must surely have encountered, one might have expected him to grant that Royer was an exception, just as scientific proponents of racial inequality were often willing to acknowledge exceptions, which might well have been how Firmin was regarded within the Société d'Anthropologie de Paris. One is therefore left wondering whether Firmin and the outspoken Royer had not had words with each other at one point or another. Even so, it is still hard to understand why Firmin devoted so much of his criticism of her, not at her main book, nor her Introduction to Darwin's *The Origin of Species*, but to some improvised remarks about race mixing she made at the *Congrès International des Sciences Ethnographiques* in 1878.[52] It was not because these remarks were any more controversial than her considered writings. Had Firmin cited Royer's book he could have addressed her claim that race mixing between inferior and superior races is immoral.[53]

Nevertheless, it has to be admitted that there is nothing in Darwin's text to support Firmin's claim that Darwin's theory of natural selection authorized a belief in the equality of races. On a couple of occasions Firmin actually conceded this, so that it seems that his goal was to subtract the more vicious aspects of social Darwinism from the theory of evolution. The European view of so-called inferior races was, according to Firmin, as follows: "These races were thought then to be ignorant and stupid, and so they are still and will be until the day they disappear from the earth, as Darwin's law decrees they must."[54] One can see those consequences clearly in a remarkable passage from Herbert Spencer that is quoted in part by Firmin:

> If it be said that as the Hebrews thought themselves warranted in seizing the lands God promised to them, and in some cases exterminating the

inhabitants, so we, to fulfil the "manifest intention of Providence," dispossess inferior races whenever we want their territories; it may be replied that we do not kill many more than seems needful, and tolerate the existence of those who submit.[55]

Were it not for these two passages, it might be tempting to suppose that Firmin did not recognize the vicious role of natural selection in Darwinian accounts of racial progress.

Ideas of Evolution

Firmin's account of Darwin's theory highlighted climate and environment as the primary causes of evolution, at the expense of natural selection. Firmin's neglect of natural selection is apparent when he writes that Darwin's theory showed that reference to environment and heredity is sufficient to explain "the difference in development of each ethnic group in the relatively short historical evolution of the entire species."[56] Perhaps he was not modifying Darwin's general presentation so much as observing that the brevity of the life of humanity as a whole would not need, nor perhaps even allow, reference to natural selection as the decisive factor, as it was in natural evolution in general. Firmin was interested in Darwin because he wanted to find a basis for asserting the influence of environment over both the physical features of the human races[57] and the intellectual qualities of the races[58] in such a way that allowed for the equality of the races.[59]

We saw earlier that monogenists were left with the question of why, given the apparent fixity or permanence of the races, the environmental forces that had led to the development of racial differences were not still operative: if they were still in effect it would seem that Whites in Africa might turn Black and that an Englishman who emigrated to the United States might take on the morphological features of a Native American. But within the longer chronology of natural evolution, the idea that racial characteristics were continuing to change could not be discounted. The decisive point was that if the races were still changing, one could not say definitively that one was naturally superior to another. Further changes could not be ruled out. This was the insight underlying Firmin's vision. It explains why he interpreted Darwin in terms of Lamarck's disavowal of the theory of the fixity of species.[60] This was a fairly widespread tendency at that time, but nobody used it to draw

152   CRITICAL PHILOSOPHY OF RACE

more radical conclusions for the theory of the equality of the races than did Firmin.

The impact of Firmin's application of natural evolution to the human races can be seen in his rejection of the argument that the skulls of ancient Egyptians were significantly larger than those of Negroes of his own day and therefore evidence that they were different races. One cannot underestimate the importance of this debate for the upholders of Negro inferiority, as they themselves were the first to point out. If the civilization of the ancient Egyptians was a Negro, or more broadly, a Black, civilization, then some of the more simplistic theories of racial hierarchy would collapse.[61] This explains why the debate over the racial identity of the ancient Egyptians was fought with such virulence.

In his chapter on Egypt, Firmin repeated his suspicions of craniometric studies. In particular, he targeted Samuel Morton, whom Firmin correctly identified as "the first to transform into a scientific doctrine the mistaken opinion that the ancient populations of Egypt had belonged to the White race."[62] However, Firmin also appealed to Darwinism in an effort to reconcile the results of those studies with the thesis that the ancient Egyptians were Negroes. Because the former were more civilized than uneducated Blacks in contemporary Africa, they could be expected to have had larger skulls and, as surviving representations showed, would be more handsome. This was a case of both material and moral "regressive transformations."[63] Firmin's argument about ancient Egypt was that the part of the Negro race that had created it had since declined, and this was reflected in their physical appearance. However, this story of decline did not compromise Firmin's belief in progress. He assumed that there was one single path for humanity to follow and that all the races were simply at different stages on the same trajectory.[64] Although he granted to the polygenists their belief that the human species arose in different parts of the world, they were wrong to use that as a basis for denying the unity of the human species.[65] They believed that not all races were endowed with the same evolutionary potential as the other neighboring groups,[66] but they lacked an explanation of why this might be the case.

Firmin's idea of human evolution was that each racial group developed its potential only under the appropriate circumstances. He picked up on the fact that the monogenists believed that, although the races consisted of unchangeable types, they could undergo some modification under the influence of civilization.[67] Had he had direct acquaintance with the work of James Cowles Prichard, the foremost race theorist of the first half of the nineteenth century, he would have had a powerful precedent for his ideas. Already in 1813, Prichard argued that civilization transformed both the physical features and intellectual features of a race. It was on this basis that Prichard defended the view, unusual for its time, that it was probable that "the fairest races of white people in Europe, are descended from, or have an affinity with Negroes."[68] Firmin knew Herbert Spencer's *Essais sur le progrès* and he would have read there that during the course of civilization, there are also changes in appearance.[69] He also appealed to the fact that the polygenist Broca, although initially an opponent of the idea that racial types change as an effect of civilization, had subsequently come round to it.[70] Climate and environment were, for Firmin, neither the only nor the decisive influence. For example, skin color was a function of climate and living environment, but the shape of the face was a function of the degree or level of civilization.[71] This meant that cranial measurements of the kind employed by Broca did not identify the different races but instead indicated the stage that they had reached on the path of human progress.[72]

Firmin appealed to the theories of evolution and sexual selection formulated by Spencer and Darwin to support his claim that there was a constant correlation between intellectual development and physical beauty.[73] However, at this point in the argument, Firmin's adoption of Comte's belief in progress was decisive: civilization leads men and women to "become equal and achieve the same qualities."[74] This applied to beauty of form[75] as well as to intellectual qualities. Firmin thus insisted on the perfectibility of the whole human species,[76] which was the point that he emphasized in *De l'égalité des races humaines* when he returned to it twenty years later.[77] This "unity of plan"[78] directly echoes Comte's belief that the "entire harmony of the Great Being" would "call out into intimate cooperation with each other the three great races," the Black (Affective), White (Speculative), and Yellow (Active).[79]

Royer had written at the end of her Preface to *The Origin of Species*: "For me, my choice is made: I believe in progress."[80] Firmin scoffed at these lines as confirmation that "women have a natural tendency to embrace current ideas and to perpetuate accepted notions."[81] However, his real objection must have been that she did not recognize that progress meant full equality for all. Nevertheless, he gave to "equality" a special meaning. By "equality" Firmin did not understand moral or legal equality, let alone actual physical or intellectual equality. He meant equal potential. Here is his own explanation of what he meant by the equality of the races: "they are all capable of

154   CRITICAL PHILOSOPHY OF RACE

rising to the most noble virtues, of reaching the highest intellectual development; they are equally capable of falling into a state of total degeneration."[82] That Firmin expressed his belief in the equality of races as a belief in human equality alongside his sexist characterizations of Royer as a woman is unfortunately one more instance of a philosopher being unable to put consistency above prejudice.

The Influence of Comte

It was this Comtean belief in progress toward human equality that led Firmin to his denial of the dominant views of race in his time. At the beginning of a long chapter on the classification of the races, Firmin summarized the definition of race found in zoology and botany: races are "the varieties of a given species when these varieties have been fixed through reproduction, with particularities which are at first imprecise or idiosyncratic, but which later become constant and transmissible through heredity without violating the general laws of the species."[83] Firmin challenged that conception, and he insisted that the science of anthropology as practiced by the French school would be utterly ruined on the day that it was proved that the human races have no essentially fixed characteristics other than color, which is a complex result of climate, food, and inheritance.[84] This led Firmin to claim in his Conclusion: "There will be no question of race, for the word implies a biological and natural fatality which has no correlation with the degree of ability observable among the different human communities spread around the globe."[85] Firmin wanted to replace the idea of racial hierarchy with a distinction between superior or civilized and inferior or savage peoples. He had no doubt that there would always be advanced and backward nations and that each nation's level of sociological development could be measured against "a certain ideal of the civilized state."[86] Such were the limits of progress and perfectibility. But he insisted: "Race has nothing to do with it."[87] Firmin's insistence that race was not as important as widely thought, and his conviction that it would become less so, can also be found already in Comte, who wrote that "the Progress of mankind in the mass, is gradually undermining the consequences of Race differences."[88] Firmin was thus entirely justified in identifying his anthropology as philosophically positivist in Comte's sense, but the detailed arguments he brought to bear were for the most part uniquely his own.

On one highly significant point Firmin diverged from Comte. Comte gave the leadership of humanity to Whites and he believed that the study of history should limit itself to their contribution. He was especially critical of the attention given to India and China by historians.[89] By contrast, Firmin took a broader view of history: "Nations and races interact in the stage of history, exit and return in different roles. In the larger scheme of human destiny, none of these roles is insignificant. Equally imbued with dignity, each actor takes a turn at the main role."[90] This also brought him into conflict with Hegel's racial view of history in his *Lectures on the Philosophy of World History*, even if one can still hear certain echoes of Hegel's conviction that different peoples take the central role at different times. Firmin's expansion of the *dramatis personae* of history, so as to include the Black race, which Hegel had explicitly excluded, would subsequently be echoed by W. E. B. Du Bois in his "Conservation of Races."[91] Like Du Bois, Firmin posited at the end of this process a transformation: "So they will continue to be until the day when the actors in the stage can comfortably exchange roles, and support and complement one another, effortlessly and without friction, in the larger enterprise which is to carry the intellectual torch."[92] Firmin even asserted a "right to partake in humanity's common patrimony, that is, to being elevated and to progress."[93] He believed that backward peoples needed contact with more advanced peoples to progress and that their progress has nothing to do with ethnic characteristics.[94] However, unlike Du Bois, who felt the force of Herder's idea that all cultures contribute to humanity, Firmin took up the idea of "civilization" as "common destiny." For Firmin, "civilization" is "the highest level of physical, moral, and intellectual achievement of the species."[95]

In the end Firmin believed that all races are equal, except for the Black race which is more equal than others insofar as it is more resistant to depression.[96] He also believed that because the Negro race has suffered so much, it is more prepared to understand and exercise justice. Its generosity will be the main contribution of the Black race to progress in striking contrast with the indifferent and heartless races that had arisen in Europe.[97]

Let me close by returning to Firmin's entry into that room in Paris on July 11, 1884, where the meeting of the Société d'Anthropologie de Paris was being held. It seems that Firmin at one and the same time recognized the emptiness and bias of the claims of its most prominent members and decided to confront them on their own terms by studying their works in what must have been a frenzy of activity on his part. Nevertheless, the tone he adopted

156 CRITICAL PHILOSOPHY OF RACE

suggests that his aim was not to persuade them to change their minds. It is as if in his eyes they were less a jury to be persuaded than criminals to be convicted. One can juxtapose this scene with another that took place in the same room on April 21, 1892. Firmin had just intervened to point out to a speaker that Black Africans live under difficult conditions and so are largely unable to show their great qualities, at which point Professor Bordier, president of the Society, intervened to ask him if he had any White ancestors. The implication of the question was clear: the assumption behind the question was that his intelligence could be explained only in this way. Certainly Firmin answered Bordier as if this was what he was asking, and it showed how in an instant Firmin's colleagues could switch from considering him a participant in their debates to treating him as an object of anthropological study.[98]

9

"Our Duty to Conserve"

W. E. B. Du Bois's Philosophy of History in Context

The Historical Context

W. E. B. Du Bois's "The Conservation of Races" is considered one of the founding classics of the critical philosophy of race, but the recent philosophical appropriation of this brief text has tended to distort its meaning by imposing an alien question on it. It has been read in terms of the question of the legitimacy of the concept of race as if Du Bois was asking if the language of race should be conserved. The idea of dropping the term *race* was advocated by Kwame Anthony Appiah specifically in the context of a reading of Du Bois's essay, but the debate his contribution spawned threw more light on the conditions under which one might legitimately employ the concept of race today than on what Du Bois was attempting in his lecture.[1] My aim in this paper is to determine what Du Bois meant by the conservation of races and to speculate on what he had in mind when he juxtaposed it with the threat of its self-obliteration. To help me do so, I will restore his lecture to its historical context, the inaugural meeting of the American Negro Academy held on March 5, 1897, less than one year after the U.S. Supreme Court handed down its decision in *Plessy v. Ferguson*.

However, the term *conservation* had another connotation, which derived from the prevalence of social Darwinism. Although, as has often been argued, the basic framework of Du Bois's lecture borrows extensively from the philosophies of history of both Johann Gottfried Herder and Wilhelm Friedrich Hegel, social Darwinism provided its immediate context. I will show that certain social Darwinists had recently pressed the issue of the survival of the Negro race in North America, and it was against them, as well as Frederick Douglass's pursuit of assimilation through amalgamation, that Du Bois wrote his paper.

The question to which "The Conservation of Races" was the answer was stated by Du Bois as follows: "Have we in America a distinct mission as a

Critical Philosophy of Race. Robert Bernasconi, Oxford University Press. © Oxford University Press 2023.
DOI: 10.1093/oso/9780197587966.003.0010

158   CRITICAL PHILOSOPHY OF RACE

race—a distinct sphere of action and an opportunity for race development, or is self-obliteration the highest end to which Negro blood dare aspire?"[2] It is with reference to this dichotomy, either a distinct mission or self-obliteration, that Du Bois framed his address. This means that Du Bois was concerned in this essay not with conserving the language of race, but with conserving African Americans as a race at a time when they were made to feel under threat by the White population and particularly by the science it promoted.

The historical context in which Du Bois addressed the founding members of the American Negro Academy and, more specifically, the political situation, is crucial to an understanding of his argument. The choice between, on the one hand, affirming race identity in terms of a "distinct mission" and, on the other hand, acquiescing in the "self-obliteration" of the race, should not be confused with the choice between separatism and assimilation that the preceding generation of African Americans, such as Douglass, had been faced with or at least thought they had been. The door leading to racial integration had been slammed shut in the faces of African Americans. Those leaders who had already committed themselves to it were now forced, like others of their race, to ride Jim Crow in Georgia. By the same token, the possibility of the self-obliteration of the race no longer primarily meant the abandonment of race consciousness as a result of a growing sense of human brotherhood, as it had meant in Douglass's day, but the threat of "self-obliteration" meant extinction as a result of race mixing. African Americans saw themselves in a struggle for existence. Hence Du Bois was drawn to the idea of a duty to conserve the Negro race, as it was called, and he sought to promote victory in the struggle not just by proposing the measures set out in the Creed that he proposed for the American Negro Academy, but by supplying a philosophy of hope.

Du Bois's Dynamic Conception of Race

There are good reasons to believe that Du Bois did not intend his lecture to be heard as a contribution to a debate on the viability of the concept of race. It is true that at the same time Du Bois was preparing his lecture, some scientists were beginning to question the utility of the concept of race within the science of natural history, but this was not leading them to call for its disappearance from everyday life, as some people do today. In the late nineteenth century the complaint was simply that the concept was too vague for scientific purposes without further refinement: Rudolf Virchow, for example, began his essay "Rassenbildung und Erblichkeit" by declaring that the concept of race, which had always been indeterminate, had in recent times become uncertain in the highest degree.[3] Recalling the context in which he wrote "The Conservation of Races," Du Bois in *Dusk of Dawn*, in 1940, acknowledged that in the nineteenth century race and race problems were spoken of "as a matter of course without explanation or definition."[4]

Although in *Dusk of Dawn* he seems to suggest that his recognition that the "scientific definition of race is impossible"[5] was a subsequent discovery, he had already been quite specific in "The Conservation of Races" that race probably transcended scientific definition: ". . . they [the races] perhaps transcend scientific definition, nevertheless, are clearly defined to the eye of the Historian and the Sociologist."[6] This means that even though in 1897 he had renounced the possibility of giving a rigorous scientific definition, it was nevertheless sufficiently clear that historians and sociologists were capable of recognizing race when they saw it. In 1897, Du Bois was not attempting to defend the use of the concept of race in ordinary life, because it was not being seriously contested, but he was not offering a radically new definition of it either.

In his later work, Du Bois was quite explicit that he had a dynamic conception of race.[7] In fact, this was already true of "The Conservation of Races." Du Bois reminded his readers that, with the formation of cities, purity of blood was replaced by the requirement of domicile as the decisive factor in establishing group identity.[8] He claimed there that the two or perhaps three great families of human beings the scientists agreed upon—"the whites and Negroes, possibly the yellow race"[9]—had given way in the course of history to eight main races: the Slavs, the Teutons, the English, the Romance nations, the Negroes, the Semites, the Hindoos, and the Mongolians.[10] Nevertheless, most European nations conceived themselves as having arisen through an amalgam of races.[11] Racial purity was associated with vigor and health, but racial purity was not so much inherited as it was a goal to be achieved through breeding out variety. It was primarily in the United States that existing races were defined by their purity. This was because what would have been defined in Europe as an amalgam of different European races was here identified racially as White, because what was important in North America was the exclusion of a significant Black component.[12] That Du Bois did not highlight the three racial families, but the eight main races, more than one of

160   CRITICAL PHILOSOPHY OF RACE

which was "intermingling" to forge the White race of the United States, is an indication of his dynamic conception of race, but it was not as unusual at that time as some people might imagine it was. Although he presented the idea of a state of "human brotherhood" that would make current race distinctions less important,[13] one cannot say for sure whether or not Du Bois would have excluded the possibility of a new American race forged from *all* the races already present in the United States. Nevertheless, it seems unlikely that Du Bois imagined that to be the future path of the United States, as the political context in which he wrote the essay was marked by the introduction of laws restricting the opportunities for social interaction between Blacks and Whites, where the White race alone was defined by racial purity, and at least in some parts of the United States, Blacks were bound together by requirements of domicile, whether of pure or mixed race.

Du Bois's so-called definition of race ran counter to many scientific conceptions of race at the time, but it did not diverge greatly from how the term was used by contemporaries engaged in writing philosophical histories:

> It [race] is a vast family of human beings, generally of common blood and language, always of common history, traditions and impulses, who are both voluntarily and involuntarily striving together for the accomplishment of certain more or less vividly conceived ideals of life.[14]

Du Bois did not exclude physical terms from the account, but he insisted that spiritual or psychical differences, although based on the physical differences, infinitely transcend them.[15] It is in part because the spiritual differences transcend the physical differences that race, as a concept employed by historians and sociologists, transcends scientific definition.

When, in the context of his account of the transition from two or three great families to eight main races, Du Bois acknowledged both the integration of physical differences and "the differentiation of spiritual and mental differences,"[16] by the latter phrase he meant not "spiritual and mental inequalities" but the distinct ideals that characterize each of the races. Similarly, on the one occasion when he used the term "conserve" in the main body of the essay, he referenced not only physical powers but also intellectual endowments and spiritual ideals. To conserve a race was to conserve all three together. He wrote:

it is our duty to conserve our physical powers, our intellectual endowments, our spiritual ideals; as a race we must strive by race organization, by race solidarity, by race unity to the realization of that broader humanity which freely recognizes differences in men, but sternly deprecates inequality in their opportunities of development.[17]

By physical powers Du Bois meant above all the virility necessary to perpetuate the race; by intellectual endowments he meant the gifts that a race inherits; and by referring to spiritual ideals he meant to open the race to hope in a possible future, the thought of which would sustain it in unpropitious times. It was especially by focusing on "ideals of life" as the primary agents of history that he sought to draw attention away from the conviction that racial purity was the main power in history, as had been maintained, for example, in Count Gobineau's philosophy of history.[18]

The duty to conserve race was not for all time. This was clearly stated in the second paragraph of his proposed Creed for the newly formed American Negro Academy:

2. We believe in the duty of the Americans of Negro descent, as a body, to maintain their race identity until this mission of the Negro people is accomplished, and the ideal of human brotherhood has become a practical possibility.[19]

Maintaining their race identity was imposed on African Americans primarily because of the need to organize in the face of racism and oppression. But it was also attached to the Herderian idea that each people has a mission to fulfill for the sake of humanity as a whole. This was Du Bois's answer to those who minimized race distinctions as if "human brotherhood . . . were the possibility of an already dawning to-morrow."[20] Du Bois recognized that maintaining race identity was, for the time being, a requirement, if human brotherhood was ever to be attained.[21] Race could be minimized or it could be emphasized. Du Bois argued for the need to emphasize it because, until they had fulfilled their mission as a race, African Americans would be unable to assert their equality from a position of strength.

The conception of racial identity that Du Bois argued for conserving was not primarily based on biology but on the racial ideals one might exemplify or promote. It did not look backward but—at least for the Negro race, whose time, on Du Bois's account, lay before it—was directed to the future. It is

162   CRITICAL PHILOSOPHY OF RACE

precisely because these ideals belonged to the future that Du Bois was unable to specify them. He was able to say that the English nation stood for constitutional liberty and commercial freedom, that the German nation stood for science and philosophy, and that the Romance nations stood for literature and art.[22] But that was because their time was past. Tomorrow would be Black,[23] and it was not for Du Bois to say what those ideals would be, even though he gave clear indications both in "The Conservation of Races" and in "The Souls of Black Folk" that he expected the ideals to arise in the process of working together to improve the races and that the contribution was likely to come in the area of music or spirituality.[24]

Du Bois's hope was that "Negroes inspired by one vast ideal, could work out in its fullness the great message we have for humanity."[25] This future is opened not by the dissolution of African Americans in America, but by the conservation of the Negro race. As he wrote of the American Negro in "The Souls of Black Folk," "He would not bleach his Negro soul in a flood of White Americanism, for he knows that Negro blood has a message for the world."[26] The argument employs the framework of the philosophy of history of the nineteenth century, while at the same time subverting the racist purposes to which it had previously been used. When Du Bois clarified the motivation behind "The Conservation of Races" in his chapter "The Concept of Race" in *Dusk of Dawn*, he complained about the scientific race dogma that he encountered at Harvard, above all in its social Darwinist form of the "Survival of the Fittest."[27] He also explained how in graduate school at Harvard and in Germany he encountered the cultural historical view of race:

> The history of the world was paraded before the observation of students. Which was the superior race? Manifestly that which had a history, the white race; there was some mention of Asiatic culture, but no course in Chinese or Indian history or culture was offered at Harvard, and quite unanimously in America and Germany, Africa was left without culture and without history.[28]

This was evidence of the influence of Hegel, who had asserted that Africa is not a historical part of the world.[29]

"The Conservation of Races" should be read as Du Bois's challenge not so much to the omission of Africa as to the consequences that had been drawn from its exclusion. Du Bois did not argue in this essay, as he would later, for giving more attention to Egypt or the other great cultures of Africa's past.

"OUR DUTY TO CONSERVE" 163

Indeed, he insisted that Egyptian civilization cannot be understood as "the full, complete Negro message of the whole Negro race."[30] Although it has been widely noted that there are strong echoes of both Herder and Hegel in Du Bois's philosophy of history, more attention still needs to be given to the fact that Herder and Hegel represent two rival tendencies within the philosophy of history, specifically with respect to notions of race and culture.[31] Herder rejected the notion of race, but, nevertheless, his conception of nations or peoples each with their own cultural unities, whose strength lies in their diversity from one another, seems to lie behind Du Bois's belief, as reflected in the first article of the Academy Creed, that each race has a unique contribution to make to civilization and humanity.[32] There is also a distant debt to Hegel's idea that different races and nations have a time in which to play their role in world history.[33] This is why Du Bois did not concede that Africa had already had its turn with Egypt.[34]

Crummell and the Negro Academy

When Du Bois was invited to address the American Negro Academy, he was assigned the topic, "The Duty of Cherishing and Fostering the Intellect of the Race."[35] The topic says a great deal about how he was seen, and with his idea of the talented tenth Du Bois did it justice. But by locating this duty within the broader duty of conserving identity he adopted a theme dear both to Alexander Crummell, spiritual leader of the American Negro Academy, and to his friend, Edward Blyden. For example, in "Study and Race," a lecture from 1893, Blyden had written of a similar duty:

> But the duty of every man, of every race is to contend for its individuality— to keep and develop it. Never mind the teachings of those who tell you to abandon that which you cannot abandon. If their theory were carried out, it would with all the reckless cruelty of mere theory, blot all the varieties of mankind, destroy all the differences, sacrifice nationalities, and reduce the human Race to the formless protoplasm from which we are told we came.[36]

Similar ideas can be found in Crummell's "The Destined Superiority of the Negro," a Thanksgiving Discourse from 1877. Crummell had sketched a theology in which God destroyed certain populations when the sins of a people had reached "a state of hateful maturity."[37] He found examples both in

164 CRITICAL PHILOSOPHY OF RACE

ancient history with reference to the people of Egypt, Assyria, Babylon, Tyre, and Persia, and also in the contemporary world with relation to American Indians and the aboriginal population of New Zealand. Indeed, Crummell posed a question in this address that was not unlike what Du Bois asked when he offered the dichotomy: either the Negro has a distinct mission or must face self-obliteration. Crummell asked of the Negro race: "Is this a race doomed to destruction? Or is it one possessed of those qualities, and so morally disciplined by trial, as to augur a vital destiny, and high moral uses, in the future?"[38] Crummell drew hope from "the great truth, that when God does not destroy a people, but, on the contrary, trains and disciplines it, it is an indication that He intends to make something of them, and to do something for them."[39] He called this "a Divine and merciful preservation of a people—for future uses" and argued that it called for the cultivation of definite moral qualities.[40]

The similarity of some of Du Bois's ideas with views already promulgated by Crummell helps to account for the latter's perception of Du Bois's lecture. According to Crummell, Du Bois presented "in a most lucid and original method, and in a condensed form, the long-settled conclusions of Ethnologists and Anthropologists upon the question of Race."[41] If Crummell identified Du Bois's distinctive contribution in "The Conservation of Races" as his original use of established conclusions of ethnology and anthropology, it is perhaps in part because he recognized the leading idea of Du Bois's lecture—the duty to preserve a race in the face of its possible destruction—as his own idea. Crummell seems not to have recognized that in integrating this idea with contemporary ethnology and anthropology, or, more precisely, the philosophy of history that had become an integral part of those studies, Du Bois transformed both in a radical way.[42] For Blyden and Crummell, the preservation of race was primarily a theological issue. For example, Blyden wrote: "Therefore, honour and love your Race. Be yourselves, as God intended you to be or he would not have made you thus."[43] Du Bois translated the arguments of Blyden and Crummell into the language of the philosophy of history.

Part of the novelty of Du Bois's account was the way he turned the conventional appeal to the foresight of Providence to the advantage of the Negro race. In his review of Herder's *Ideas on the Philosophy of the History of Mankind*, Kant had raised, but left unresolved, the question of why the people of Tahiti existed.[44] Du Bois had an answer to the question of why Blacks existed, or, more precisely, why they should conserve their race. He argued that the continued existence of the Negro race was evidence that there was a role awaiting them in history.

This is not to say that the theological dimension was totally absent from Du Bois's lecture, as, for example, when in quoting Tennyson he referred to the perfection of human life as that "one far off Divine event."[45] In four separate passages Du Bois referred to God,[46] and his argument relied heavily on a notion of Providence. One can try to ignore this, as Appiah does,[47] but it leads to a radical distortion of Du Bois's argument. The idea of Providence in one form or another was vital to the leading representatives of the philosophy of history in the late eighteenth century and throughout the nineteenth century. To omit it from one's understanding of Du Bois undercuts his position as readily as it would undercut Kant, Herder, or Hegel if it were subtracted from their accounts.

By translating Crummell's ideas from the deeply theological language in which they had originally been couched into the semi-religious language of the philosophy of history of his day, Du Bois opened those ideas to transformation. One example of this transformation of Crummell's ideas can be found in Du Bois's greater focus on novelty. Crummell identified imitation as "the grand preservative of the Negro": "One can clearly see that this quality of imitation, allied to the receptivity of the race, gives promise of great fitness for Christian training, and for the higher processes of civilization."[48] Crummell claimed to have observed "a strong assimilative tendency" by which Blacks became like those they are among, while yet retaining their own peculiarities.[49] Du Bois agreed with him that Blacks would not be absorbed, but, altering the emphasis, he insisted that the destiny of Blacks was "not a servile imitation of Anglo-Saxon culture, but a stalwart originality which shall unswervingly follow Negro ideals."[50] Freed from the blueprint imposed by Christianity on its followers, Du Bois could argue that Blacks could bring something radically new to the world. Crummell, by contrast, had offered an account in which Blacks retained something of their own, while receiving their religious training from Europe.

An even clearer illustration of Du Bois's translation of Crummell's ideas into the language of the philosophy of history lies in his use of the term "conservation," whereas Crummell had spoken only of preservation. This seems to have been in response to the contemporary fascination with applying the law of the conservation of force to the philosophy of history. There had been a number of attempts in the second half of the nineteenth century to apply physical principles to history and politics. Herbert Spencer was perhaps the

166 CRITICAL PHILOSOPHY OF RACE

most prominent of those to employ the idea, although he refused the phrase, preferring to write instead of "Persistence of Force."[51] Du Bois sought to limit the scope of applying the idea of the conservation of force to society, in an unpublished manuscript from 1905, "Sociology Hesitant." He sought to "give scope to Historian as well as Biologist" by leaving a place for the free human will alongside natural law in the sense of manifestations of force and the laws of nature.[52] This is also the perspective that dominates "The Conservation of Races," and it is announced early in the essay when Du Bois writes: "For it is certain that all human striving must recognize the hard limits of natural law, and that any striving, no matter how intense and earnest, which is against the constitution of the world, is vain."[53] Heeding the duty to conserve their race was the way in which African Americans might cooperate with that law, but by focusing on the idea of conservation with its connotation of force, rather than preservation, Du Bois offered a more dynamic conception than Crummell had done. This contributed to a more forward-looking approach. It also seems that Du Bois was suggesting with Hegel that as one race declines another must rise to take its place. However, looking beyond the White race that dominated Hegel's presentation, Du Bois promised to Blacks the turn at the center of history, the turn that Hegel had denied them.[54]

Du Bois's presentation was not merely the subversion of a Eurocentric philosophy of history. It was rooted in the existential struggle of living the American dilemma. This becomes apparent if one recalls the terms in which Douglass had expressed his strong opposition to race pride and isolation, as well as his advocacy of "one American nation." For example, in 1889, in "The Nation's Problem," he responded to the accusation that he lacked race pride by denying any need for it. He asked rhetorically, "What race?" and went on to explain that "a large percentage of the colored race are related in some degree to more than one race."[55] In an earlier essay Douglass had explicitly identified race mixing as the way forward:

My strongest conviction as to the future of the negro therefore is, that he will not be expatriated nor annihilated, nor will he forever remain a separate and distinct race from the people around him, but that he will be absorbed, assimilated, and will only appear finally, as the Phoenicians now appear on the shores of the Shannon, in the features of a blended race.[56]

Douglass denied that he was advocating race mixing. He insisted that he was not a propagandist, but a prophet, indicating what would happen.[57] Nevertheless, he was clearly among those that Du Bois alluded to in his opening paragraph of "The Conservation of Races" when he wrote critically of those of his race who had been led to deprecate and minimize race distinctions.[58]

Du Bois's address to the American Negro Academy was therefore in large measure a response to Frederick Douglass, who had died two years earlier. One member of Du Bois's audience, Walter B. Hayson, greeted Du Bois's lecture by proclaiming that "the day for the work of Mr. Douglass has passed."[59] There were people in Du Bois's audience ready to argue that on the American continent there had been a conglomeration of the world's races and that as a result there had been an erasing of those distinctions,[60] but Du Bois knew that an attack on Douglass would be welcome at the American Negro Academy. Crummell, the intellectual leader of the Academy, had consistently argued for Blacks retaining their separate organizations.[61] With the White backlash to Reconstruction already clearly signaled by *Plessy v. Ferguson*, Du Bois joined Crummell as a strong opponent of the minimizing of race distinctions. Indeed, in "The Race-Problem in America" from 1888, Crummell had already attacked the proposal that the solution to America's race problem lay in amalgamation, saying that "the principle of race" is persistent in the human constitution: "it is one of those structural facts in our nature which abides with a fixed, vital, and reproductive power."[62] He was thereby alluding to the idea that racial purity was associated with health and race mixing associated with sterility after some generations. Du Bois did not endorse such claims, which is why, in *The Health and Physique of the Negro American*, in 1906, he made the point that in regard to "mixed bloods" there was "much friction and prejudice" to be cleared away.[63] Nevertheless, in *The Philadelphia Negro*, published only two years after "The Conservation of Races," he warned, without specifying the danger precisely, that "mingling" between the two races would at this point of time be "disastrous to both races," even though he could take consolation in the fact that at that time there was "no danger of it taking place."[64]

Douglass not only foresaw a future for the United States in which race mixing prospered; he also favored dividing those Blacks who were racially pure from those who were mixed, so as to think of them as a separate identity. In his view it was only "prejudice against the Negro" that led those of

168   CRITICAL PHILOSOPHY OF RACE

mixed blood to be classified as Negroes, but he explained that it also arose from a desire to "degrade those of mixed blood."[65] However, in the context of a reading of "The Conservation of Races," the most important aspect of Douglass's reflections was his insistence on questioning those "men of mixed blood who apply the name '*negro*' to themselves, not because it is a correct ethnological description, but to seem especially devoted to the black side of their parentage."[66] It is no surprise that at least one member of Du Bois's audience, T. Thomas Fortune, suspected him of pandering to Crummell by resisting Douglass on this point and refusing to think of the mulatto as belonging to a separate clan.[67] Du Bois, who would later describe himself as having "a flood of Negro blood, a strain of French, a bit of Dutch, but, thank God! no 'Anglo-Saxon,' "[68] seems not on the occasion of his lecture to have objected to being heard in this way. The tension between so-called mulattos and racially pure Negroes was acute at this time. Crummell was well known as a critic of the pretensions and claims to superiority of the mulatto.[69] My argument is that Du Bois in part wrote "The Conservation of Races" in an effort to transcend the physical differences between mixed race and pure race Negroes by having them both rally round the same ideals and, more decisively, by having them recognize the similarity of their experiences in a society that lumped them together simply as Negroes.

The Existential Question of Race

Du Bois's response to those who saw a solution to America's race problem in "our being able to lose our race identity in the commingled blood of the nation"[70] was the following seven questions. With them he posed the existential dilemma underlying his presentation:

> What, after all, am I? Am I an American or am I a Negro? Can I be both? Or is it my duty to cease to be a Negro as soon as possible and be an American? If I strive as a Negro, am I not perpetuating the very cleft that separates Black and White America? Is not my only possible practical aim the subduction of all that is Negro in me to the American? Does my black blood place upon me any more obligation to assert my nationality than German, or Irish or Italian blood would?[71]

"OUR DUTY TO CONSERVE" 169

Douglass had adopted the simple formula "We are Americans," but Du Bois succeeded in problematizing it by exhibiting its limits.[72]

> We are Americans, not only by birth and by citizenship, but by our political ideals, our language, our religion. Farther than that, our Americanism does not go. At that point, we are Negroes, members of a vast historic race that from the very dawn of creation has slept, but half awakening in the dark forests of its African fatherland.[73]

Du Bois did not offer a clear resolution of the dilemma: either an American or a Negro. He readily acknowledged, even while he waited for Negroes to fulfill their—as yet unknown—destiny, that there are political ideals that are specifically American. But what is of special interest here is how Du Bois, by recognizing the existential dilemma that faced *every* Negro, used it to displace the question of race mixing as a means of assimilation. Mulattos were not here considered as being at the forefront of a transition to a new race forged by race mixing. Nor was it important that those few of them who could "pass" as White were faced with a choice as to how to present themselves within the restrictive framework of the time. Du Bois emphasized that all Blacks in the United States, including mulattos, were faced with a choice. All of them were dual identity, whether they were of mixed race or not, because they all shared the existential dilemma that was forced on them: "Am I an American or am I a Negro?" Du Bois insisted that this dilemma was what united African Americans, and it allowed him to oppose a too hasty embracing of the individualistic philosophy of the Declaration of Independence.[74]

By 1935, Du Bois reverted to seeing the alternatives facing African Americans in terms similar to those that Douglass had used fifty years earlier: "either amalgamation will take place gradually and quietly by mutual consent, or by equally peaceful methods the groups will seek separate careers or even separate dwelling places, either in the same or different lands."[75] However, Du Bois stressed more than Douglass that there was a strong possibility that "separate racial growth over a considerable time would achieve better results than a quick amalgamation."[76] However, there is nothing here about the fulfillment of a distant mission as a precondition of human brotherhood or about self-obliteration.

The final task is to decide precisely what Du Bois had in mind when he asked if "self-obliteration" was "the highest end to which Negro blood dare

170 CRITICAL PHILOSOPHY OF RACE

aspire."[77] Assimilation was Douglass's way to dissolve race, but it was no longer a viable option by 1897. Du Bois could have meant, but almost certainly did not mean, extermination, even though it had indeed placed Native Americans in jeopardy since the end of the eighteenth century. However, even before the advent of social Darwinism, an intellectual climate had developed in which the idea of the extinction of a race could be met with relative equanimity as nature's way of progressing.[78] At the end of "The Souls of Black Folk," Du Bois referenced this conception when he described "the silently growing assumption" that "the probation of races is past, and that the backward races of to-day are of proven inefficiency and not worth the saving."[79] He knew that there were Whites who saw that as the likely fate of Blacks, but Du Bois would not see that as *self*-obliteration without further qualification. It seems more likely, and indeed in keeping with the language of the day, that with the term "self-obliteration" Du Bois had in mind the impact of race mixing on the Black population. One sees similar concerns, expressed at a more popular level, in *Anthropology Applied to the American Negro and White Man*, a book by the African American writer Robert Gilbert Wells, which is mainly written as a dialogue between Sam, an African American, and Mr. Jones, a White man. Over twenty years after the event, Sam criticizes Frederick Douglass for marrying a White woman, calls for tough laws protecting Black women against White men, and, agreeing with Mr. Jones's warning that marriages between Blacks and Whites would likely take place between the worst elements of both races, adds the following warning of his own:

> I call upon the good coloreds who have the welfare of the race at heart, to raise their voices against this intermarriage. Well, of course, it is said that it will have a tendency of solving the race problem. Now, sir, are you going to cure the sick man by giving him a medicine that will kill the entire family. Do you intend to solve the race problem by doing away with the Negro. I say not.[80]

This is a clear case of a Black writer thinking of race mixing as leading to the self-obliteration of the Black race: the ongoing process of lightening the Black population had already reached the point where a few of those who, according to the laws of the land, were considered Black were phenotypically indistinguishable from the White population and so able to pass as White.

Responding to Social Darwinism

There was another sense in which race mixing could be thought at that time to lead to obliteration. Since 1842 the theory had circulated in scientific circles that mulattos had a lower life expectancy because they were more prone to disease and their progeny were prone to sterility. This theory was expounded by Josiah Nott, a doctor from Mobile, Alabama, who, in an attempt to defend what was euphemistically called the Southern way of life, speculated about the extermination of both races as an effort of race mixing.[81] These ideas quickly found an audience among some of the leading scientists in Europe.[82] It seems that Du Bois, having recognized that if it came to be believed in the Black community that to be mixed race was to be the bearer of the seeds of the biological decline of the race, then a wedge could easily be driven between mulattos and racially pure Negroes. Crummell was already inclined to give that distinction more significance than even Douglass, albeit for different reasons. Du Bois responded by developing a vision that would allow the Black race, reunited behind its ideals, to hope for the future.

Although Nott's idea had largely fallen out of favor by the 1880s, they resurfaced in a new form in August 1896 with the publication of Frederick Hoffman's *Race Traits and Tendencies of the American Negro*.[83] A statistician from Germany, Hoffman argued that the population of African Americans was declining and that they would soon face extinction or obliteration unless the race became more independent.[84] Even before reading Hoffman, Du Bois was familiar with the argument that people of mixed race were inferior to those who were racially pure. Heinrich von Treitschke had insisted on it in classes that Du Bois attended at the University of Berlin.[85] However, Hoffman's book had the authority of statistics behind it. Its scientific pretensions made it a matter of deep concern to the members of the American Negro Academy. This is apparent from the fact that Kelly Miller attacked its arguments directly at their inaugural meeting immediately after Du Bois's paper, and that Miller's paper, not Du Bois's more grandiose vision, was chosen to be the Academy's first publication.[86] Although Du Bois's most detailed response to Hoffman's book came in 1904 in "The Future of the Negro Race in America,"[87] he had already published his own highly critical review of Hoffman's book in the same year in the prestigious *Annals of the American Academy of Political Science*, early in 1897. This suggests that Hoffman's book would have been on his mind as he wrote "The Conservation of Races."[88] That Hoffman's arguments were of particular concern to Du Bois

172   CRITICAL PHILOSOPHY OF RACE

is apparent from the fact that, as late as 1928, Du Bois still referred to "the distortion and malevolence of F. L. Hoffman, the Negro-hating Statistician of the Prudential Life Insurance Company."[89]

Placing himself firmly in the context of social Darwinism, Hoffman maintained "the powerful influence of *race* in the struggle for life."[90] He claimed to have shown that people of mixed race, or, more specifically, of both Black and White ancestry, had less vitality than people of either pure Black or pure White ancestry. The urgency of Hoffman's warnings was further enhanced by his conviction that there were few Blacks left who were not of mixed blood. Miller's response to Hoffman included disputing his data, his inductions from it, and his failure to recognize the upheaval of emancipation, but Miller also felt compelled to counsel his fellow Blacks not to despair.

> To the Negro I would say, let him not be discouraged at the ugly facts which confront him. . . . The Negro should accept the facts with becoming humility, and strive to live in closer conformity with the requirements of human and divine law.[91]

Du Bois agreed wholeheartedly and said so explicitly in "The Future of the Negro Race in America," wherein the main argument was that the representatives of the race in the United States would survive if they maintained their hope.[92] This is why it should be no surprise to find that the first two publications of the American Negro Academy were responses to Hoffman. Miller had set the scene for Du Bois to specify what conforming to human and divine law entailed. Indeed, Du Bois's focus on the future and specifically a "Black to-morrow"[93] can be seen as in part a direct response to those, like Hoffman, who characterized Blacks as living largely in and for the present.[94]

To Hoffman's suggestion that prolonged contact with Whites provided the best hope for civilizing Blacks, so that keeping the races entirely separate in an effort to avoid the physical consequences of race mixing was not a viable option, Miller responded as follows:

> It is undoubtedly true that the Negro has not the initiative power of civilization. What race has? Civilization is not an original process with any race or notion known to history. The torch has been passed from race to race and from age to age. Where else can the Negro go? The white race at present has the light. This concession is no reproach to the Negro race, nor is it due to any peculiar race trait or tendency.[95]

"OUR DUTY TO CONSERVE" 173

Du Bois was less circumspect. He argued that if there was any statistical evidence suggesting the possible extinction of the Negro in America, then it was because of the policies being directed against them. This led him to claim that it was not a question of the survival of the fittest but of "plain murder."[96] Hoffman had not proved anything about the stamina and capabilities of the race as a whole, and if African Americans faced obliteration, it would not be through the self-obliteration that followed the ill effects of race mixing, but rather as a result of the direct hostility of the White population that kept them in poverty.

Instead of attacking social Darwinism, Du Bois, who was not beyond appealing to the idea of the survival of the fittest himself,[97] argued that its true meaning had been misunderstood in the popular imagination. In "The Future of the Negro Race in America," Du Bois denied that "the theories of Darwin and Spencer, properly interpreted, support any crude views of justice and right and the spread of civilization as those current today."[98] He challenged the claim that the culture of his day was incomparably superior to previous civilizations, but he accepted that the triumph of modern culture was represented by "the diffusion of its benefits among the lower strata of society."[99] This was, he asserted, in flat contradiction to the theory of the natural aristocracy of races. He conceded that he had no answer to the question of why the European races were leading civilization, while most African races were, as he put it, in barbarism, but he insisted that the ancient Greeks could have put a similar question to the ancestors of those same Europeans, just as in an even earlier time the Egyptians could have put the question to the ancestors of the Greeks.[100] So far as he was concerned, the fact that nobody had a satisfactory answer to the question of why civilizations arose at certain times and places in history was not to be taken as a reason for denying "the great light thrown upon race development by the theories of evolution and by sociological research."[101]

Du Bois was even more outspoken on this issue in "The Evolution of the Race Problem," a lecture delivered to the National Negro Conference in 1909. His argument was again not against "the splendid scientific work of Darwin, Weissman, Galton," but against the misinterpretation and misapplication of social Darwinism, according to which "civilization is a struggle for existence whereby the weaker nations and individuals will gradually succumb and the strong will inherit the earth."[102] Above all, he complained that this conception of social Darwinism was accompanied by "the silent assumption that the white European stock represents the strong surviving peoples and that

174 CRITICAL PHILOSOPHY OF RACE

the swarthy, yellow and black peoples are the ones rightly doomed to eventual extinction."[103] He maintained that even if one were to grant that "there are certain stocks of human beings whose elimination the best welfare of the world demands," they had not yet been identified with reasonable certainty.[104] When in this regard he asked if "the worst stocks of Whitechapel, the East Side and Montmartre" were "in all cases and under all circumstances the superior of any colored group, no matter what its ability or culture,"[105] he seemed to go further in accepting the language and relative judgments proposed by social Darwinism than he needed to. The same seems to be true of his treatment of the question of eugenics in the sense of what was called racial hygiene. Just as the absolution of class distinction did not mean the universal intermarriage of stocks but through personal and social selection a "survival of the fittest," so racial contact did not necessarily mean "contamination of blood and lowering of ability and culture" so long as it was supported by training to "breed intelligently."[106] Du Bois advocated "a civilized human selection of husbands and wives" as the best means to secure "the survival of the fittest," as opposed to the prevailing assumption that "unwise marriage can be stopped by the degradation of the blacks, the classing of their women with prostitutes, . . . and by burning public offenders at the stake."[107] This means that Du Bois was being somewhat disingenuous when in *Dusk of Dawn* he claimed that he had always recognized in the idea of the survival of the fittest "a scientific race dogma."[108]

Du Bois did not write "The Conservation of Races" as a response to a questioning of the idea of race, except insofar as he challenged those, like Douglass, who saw race mixing as a way in which race was already becoming less salient. Nor did Du Bois write it as a contribution to the debate about whether to promote assimilation or separation. Du Bois could see that events had made assimilation impossible, except for those Blacks light-skinned enough to pass as White. Rather, he wrote the essay to give hope to Blacks at a time when scientists were questioning their future on the basis of suspicions about the impact of race mixing on their capacity to survive the struggle for existence. This means that although Du Bois's essay can legitimately be understood as a contribution to the philosophy of history, more important than the implicit references to Herder and Hegel was the confrontation with social Darwinism and Du Bois's attempt to move the intellectual debate within the African American intellectual elite beyond the options offered by Douglass, Crummell, and Blyden in response to new political challenges. For Du Bois the conservation of race was not about preserving or promoting racial purity, as it was still for most Whites and even some Blacks, like Crummell and Blyden, but about disregarding past racial mixing that might divide African Americans, so as to unite them in hope for the future as they faced the existential dilemma provoked by their being continually oppressed within their own country.

10

Frantz Fanon and Psychopathology

The Progressive Infrastructure of *Black Skin, White Masks*

Frantz Fanon's writings, like his life, were a call to action, a call that still resonates today, but the arguments that he used to promote action—or *praxis* as he preferred to call it in key moments of *The Wretched of the Earth*[1]—are not always understood in all their complexity. I largely confine myself here to clarifying the overall argument of his first book, *Black Skin, White Masks*. I will focus on the book's sixth chapter, "The Negro and Psychopathology," as I believe it is the crucial chapter. The book's original title, before Francis Jeanson proposed a change, was "Essay on the Disalienation of the Black Man."[2] In keeping with the original title, Fanon described *Black Skin, White Masks* as "a mirror with a progressive infrastructure where the black man can find the path to disalienation."[3] That is to say, the reader—and for reasons I will explain, particularly the Black man as reader—is invited to follow a progressive path. This gives the book its *dialectical* structure (to employ a term Fanon himself made use of on several occasions), but one consequence of this is that one must always be aware of the point within the overall argument in which any one of Fanon's dramatic and eminently quotable lines on which commentators like to rely is to be found. As I proceed, I will give some examples of claims that Fanon makes at one point and that some of his commentators have treated as if they were his final view when in fact they are modified or even reversed by him later in the book.

Fanon published *Black Skin, White Masks* when he was only twenty-seven years old. In the previous year he had submitted his dissertation at the medical school at the University of Lyon under the title "Mental Alterations, Character Modifications, Psychic Disorders and Intellectual Deficit in Spinocerebellar Heredodegeneration."[4] The dissertation helps our reading of *Black Skin, White Masks* insofar as it shows his preoccupation with unpicking the links between hereditary neurological disturbance and the psychiatric symptoms to which it gave rise under specific social and cultural conditions.

Critical Philosophy of Race. Robert Bernasconi, Oxford University Press. © Oxford University Press 2023.
DOI: 10.1093/oso/9780197587966.003.0011

Much of *Black Skin, White Masks* is a continuation of this polemic. It takes the form of an attack on the way many psychological accounts emphasize biology and heredity at the expense of the social dimension of existence.[5]

I am not going to address the vexed question of the role of women, and especially Black women, in Fanon's account because it is a subject of its own and by no means an easy one to negotiate. The strategy of concealing the problem by assuming that whenever he says *le Noir* he means both men and women will not work in every case, and I will avoid doing so here. When Fanon used the term *le Noir*, I will usually translate it as "the Black man," even though it is only in some cases that one can be sure that he meant specifically to exclude women from the descriptions that follow and so in other cases the translation is overdetermined. But there is another translation issue that is at least equally offensive to our ears, if not more so. He frequently used the term *le Nègre*, which I will translate as the Negro, because on certain occasions the distinction between *le Noir* and *le Nègre* is important. Fanon frequently, although not always, uses *le Nègre* with all its negative connotations, not as a synonym, but to highlight how Blacks are seen by Whites in a racist context. On this, as on many points, neither the Markmann translation nor the Philcox translation is remotely adequate.[6]

Restructuring the World

Fanon's starting point was that one must never lose sight of the role of society, not just culturally but also economically.[7] Contrary to the exaggerated focus on the individual that he associated with Freud, Fanon's own position was that "the alienation of the black man is not an individual question." He believed that genuine disalienation would occur only when "*in the most materialist sense*" things had resumed their rightful place.[8] In other words, one cannot address the psychological problems facing Blacks by relying only on psychology to the neglect of the other sciences.[9] He explained at the end of chapter 3: "We shall see that another solution is possible. It implies restructuring the world."[10]

This solution was predicated on the conviction that psychological problems were not hereditary but were caused by the environment. For that reason, significant portions of the book were devoted to combating the way in which, in much of the psychological literature, problems that were caused by the environment and its culture were being misattributed both explicitly

178   CRITICAL PHILOSOPHY OF RACE

and implicitly to the patient's constitution. That was the theme of chapter 2 of *Black Skin, White Masks*, where he posed the question of "whether the *basic personality* is a constant or a variable."[11] At the same time Fanon sought to show the inapplicability of standard theories to Blacks. One would never guess from the secondary literature that the primary purpose of his discussion of Mayotte Capécia's novels, a discussion that has caused heated debate, was largely directed to showing that the withdrawal of the ego, which Anna Freud described as "a normal stage" in the development of the ego, is impossible for Blacks because they seek White approval.[12] Turning to Abdoulaye Sadji's novel *Nini*, which in its first, incomplete, version was published in installments in *Présence Africaine*, Fanon highlighted how its heroine, Dédée, gained White approval through marriage.[13] Fanon called this particular form of abnormal behavior which supported Dédée "affective erethism," with the implication again that this was "a cultural phenomenon" and not something constitutive.[14]

Similarly, when in the third chapter Fanon gave a reading of *Un homme pareil aux autres* (A Man Like the Others), René Maran's semi-autobiographical novel, it was primarily the occasion for him to demonstrate that, even if a problem with a patient persists after a change of environment, that does not prove the environment was not the main cause.[15] Maran's hero, Jean Veneuse, wonders whether he has not been betrayed by everyone around him, both by the Whites who deny him recognition as one of their own and by the Blacks who repudiate him.[16] But by reading the novel through the lens supplied by Germain Guex's *The Abandonment Neurosis*, Fanon showed that Veneuse's sense of betrayal is nothing other than the classic symptoms of the negative-aggressive type.[17] On this basis Fanon sought to demonstrate that the changes Veneuse prescribed for himself were intended only to corroborate his externalizing neurosis.[18] Fanon described Veneuse as someone who is "accidentally Black" but who is a neurotic who needs to be released from his infantile fantasies.[19] In other words, the novels of Capécia, Sadji, and Maran were not Fanon's real subjects; their books were merely the backdrop of an engagement with the psychological literature in service of the larger issue of improving understanding between Blacks, as well as between Blacks and Whites.

The most egregious example of an error in the psychological literature that Fanon wanted to expose in the book's early chapters was represented by Octave Mannoni's *Prospero and Caliban*, which he explored in chapter 4. Mannoni, drawing on the theories of Alfred Adler, placed responsibility for the colonization of the Malagasy not so much on the colonizers as on the dependency complex that he attributed to the Malagasy themselves.[20] Fanon returned to this critique in chapter 7, where he suggested that an Adlerian would conclude from a reading of Mannoni that the Malagasy should accept their place in society and not strive for anything else.[21] Fanon believed that the error arose from an insistence on locating psychological problems in the individual, whereas "in some circumstances the *socius* is more important than the individual."[22] In support of this conclusion, Fanon cited Pierre Naville's critique of Freud, which asserted that the real conditions in which the individual's sexuality is expressed are explained by the economic and social conditions of the class struggle.[23] Hence, Fanon's judgment in the context of his reading of Mannoni that "Freud's discoveries are of no use to us whatsoever."[24] This is one of the basic themes of the book, and Fanon made a similar critique when, in the context of his reading of Lacan's account of the mirror stage, he announced that he had already demonstrated that for the Black man, as compared with the White man, one must take into account historical and economic realities.[25] Echoing what he had written at the end of chapter 3, the main conclusion of chapter 4 was that the source of the conflict lay not in the dependency complex but in the social structure, and the solution therefore was to change it.[26]

The Progressive Structure of *Black Skin, White Masks*

Chapter 5, "The Lived Experience of the Black," is the most accessible and best-known chapter in Fanon's book. It was originally published as a stand-alone essay,[27] but when read in isolation it is misleading for three reasons. First, it exaggerates Fanon's distance from Sartre, as I have explained elsewhere.[28] Second, it ends with the words "I began to weep," thereby giving a false impression of where Fanon ended up;[29] this is especially clear if one compares it with the calls for action as well as the more hopeful tone adopted at the end of the book, where he asks the reader to feel the open dimension of every consciousness.[30] Above all, third, the fifth chapter highlights the lived experience of the individual at the expense of the individual's social and economic context, and so, when read in isolation, runs counter to the main thrust of *Black Skin, White Masks*.

The fifth chapter is not my main topic here, but for the sake of my theme of the progressive structure of the book, it is important to make one observation.

180 CRITICAL PHILOSOPHY OF RACE

In "Black Orpheus," a Preface written for Léopold Sédar Senghor's *Anthologie de la nouvelle poésie nègre et malgache de langue française*, Sartre, taking his cue from some of the Marxist poets anthologized there, applied the dialectic, conceived in a somewhat elementary and vulgar form, to make the point that Blacks were called upon to sacrifice their negritude in favor of "the realization of the human in a raceless society."[31] Every reader of *Black Skin, White Masks* seems to remember that this led Fanon to say that "Jean-Paul Sartre has destroyed black enthusiasm,"[32] but, in part because of the poor translations, few English-speaking readers realize that Fanon himself had already in the Preface warned against enthusiasm.[33] These same commentators often also tend not even to comment on the fact that what Sartre had destroyed was described by Fanon himself an illusion, an "unthinking position."[34] Certainly there is a criticism of Sartre here, but it largely derives from Fanon's view that because Sartre was White he could forget that "the Negro suffers in his body differently than the White."[35] In other words, in Fanon's view, Sartre was in no place to make the comment.[36] Most commentators assume that Fanon was saying that Sartre should not have applied the dialectic so as to look beyond the present to a time when negritude had given way to a society without race. They ignore Fanon's statement in chapter 6, where he says very clearly in the context of a reading of Aimé Césaire, "we can understand why Sartre sees in the black poets' Marxist stand the logical end to negritude."[37] The point is that Fanon's dramatic rejection of "Black Orpheus" is only one stage on the reader's journey, one that he explicitly reevaluated later.

Another aspect of the book's progressive structure is revealed when one compares the judgment at the end of the second chapter that both Freud and Adler would "help us understand the black man's notion of the world,"[38] but when at the beginning of chapter 6 he posed the question of the extent to which the psychoanalytic findings of Freud and Adler could be applied "in an attempt to explain the vision of the world of the man of color,"[39] he seemed to correct his earlier judgment and give a negative answer. So in chapter 6 he highlighted the incongruity between the psychoanalytic schema and the reality of the Black man,[40] just as in chapter 7, when he eventually turned to Adler, he explained his opposition to any application of Adler's theory to the Black man again because of its concentration on the individual to the neglect of society: "If there is a flaw, it lies not in the 'soul' of the individual, but in his environment."[41] What Fanon did not appear to deny was that Freud and Adler could help understand Whites, and this meant that they could contribute to what Blacks had to deal with in negotiating the White world. Indeed, the majority of the chapter is devoted to Whites rather than to Blacks.

The broader perspective that Fanon argued for in *Black Skin, White Masks* was not simply a theoretical concern but was at the heart of the approach he developed in his own psychiatric practice as an intern at Saint-Alban under the direction of François Tosquelles, the founder of "social psychotherapy" (later known as "institutional psychotherapy"). Subsequently Fanon adopted it in his own right at the psychiatric hospital in Blida in Algeria. There is some uncertainty about when Fanon actually completed *Black Skin, White Masks* and thus some uncertainty about whether the manuscript was already complete by the time Fanon came under Tosquelles's direction. Certainly there was a synergy between the two men. Félix Guattari, who also collaborated with Tosquelles, wrote a description of "institutional psychotherapy" in terms of its determination, first, never to isolate the study of mental illness from its social and institutional context, and, second, always to analyze institutions in terms of the real, symbolic and imaginary effects of society on individuals.[42] This is Fanon's approach in a nutshell, and nobody before him seems to have thought to apply it to the investigation of the effects of racism as rigorously as he did.

The sixth chapter of *Black Skin, White Masks* already shows Fanon moving in the direction of social psychotherapy. The immediate contrast with which the chapter begins is that between the environment of the Antillean and the very different environment that psychoanalysis takes for granted. Against Jacques Lacan's claim that "the psychic object and circumstance" is the family,[43] Fanon responded that the model of the family among Europeans is very different from that in the Antilles. In other words, universal structures had been presupposed where what was called for is "a concrete understanding."[44] He extended this observation to include the fact that there is a proportionality between the White family and the social milieu that is lacking for the Black family as a result of the racist context.[45] The traumatism that Black children suffer when confronted with images of themselves in magazines and nursery rhymes means that "a normal Black child, having grown up with a normal family, will become abnormal at the slightest contact with the white world."[46] Fanon turned to the French translation of Sigmund Freud's 1909 *Five Lectures on Psycho-Analysis* to show that he believed that the origins of psychic traumas are repressed in the unconscious.[47] In response, Fanon argue that this was simply not the case for the Black man for whom everything takes place at the level of existence: "he exists his drama."[48]

182   CRITICAL PHILOSOPHY OF RACE

This difference—Fanon calls it at this point a "dialectical substitution"—is even more apparent if the Black man leaves Antilles for Europe, as Fanon did, thereby indicating how the discussion in chapter 5 fits into chapter 6 as a kind of evidence, but now presented in the form of a testimony that initially did not fully understand itself for the reasons given earlier.

The Place of Psychoanalysis

The inapplicability of Freudianism to a discussion of the man of color, like the inapplicability of Adlerism later, should not be read as a total dismissal of psychoanalysis. It is necessary to remember Fanon's statement from the Introduction: "only a psychoanalytic interpretation of the black problem can reveal the affective disorders responsible for this network of complexes."[49] But what did he have in mind? This remark was made in the context of his announcement that the book was aiming at the lysis of the morbid universe, a reference to Angelo Hesnard's book *L'univers morbide de la faute* (The Morbid Universe of Transgression).[50] When he returned to that book in chapter 6, it was to make the point that both Jews and Blacks are scapegoats for a society that is suffering from collective guilt.[51] Psychoanalysis helps us understand how White guilt cannot be separated from White supremacy and so is very much part of the problem that creates the Black world. This shows how this book, so often read as if it was written almost exclusively about Blacks, hinges on the account of Whites given in this chapter, which is concerned with "the deep-rooted myth" concerning the Black man as he exists in the White unconscious.[52] This myth impacts both Blacks and Whites and contributes to the alienation of both of them.

In chapter 6, Fanon also explored two prevalent myths about the Black man that contributed to how he was seen and thus to how he came to see himself under oppressive conditions. According to the first, the Black man is genital and here Fanon again referred to Freudianism, albeit the word *imago*, which he used to describe the mechanism at work here, is more properly associated with Jung and Lacan.[53] According to the second myth, the Black man is evil, and this led Fanon to initiate a critique of Jung's account of the collective unconscious in this context. Initially he called the collective unconscious indispensable to an account of a racist society,[54] but subsequently he introduced serious qualifications on the grounds that Jung confused instincts, which are invariable, with habits, which are acquired.[55] Once that distinction is made, it becomes clear that the figure of the bad Negro is not an archetype in Jung's sense.[56] In an effort to dispel that confusion, Fanon replaced the role of collective unconscious in Jung with a mechanism to which he gave the name "cultural imposition."[57]

In addition to identifying these two myths, Fanon in chapter 6 highlighted what he called two "errors of analysis."[58] What is important about these two errors is that they represent positions that are readily attributed to Fanon himself if one takes some of his remarks out of the context of the dialectical presentation of the argument in which they are embedded. The first error he identified was that of insisting that there is "only one type of negro."[59] The refutation of this error turns out to be more complex than it might seem at first. In chapter 5, in the context of a discussion of Sartre's "Black Orpheus," he already wrote: "The negro experience is ambiguous, for there is not *one* negro—there are *many* negroes."[60] In keeping with this criticism, in the following chapter, he quoted, seemingly approvingly, Gabriel d'Arboussier's critical remarks on Sartre's "Black Orpheus." The long quotation from d'Arboussier begins: "This anthology that puts Antilleans, Guyanese, Senegalese, and Malagasies on the same footing creates a regrettable confusion. It thus poses the cultural problem of overseas territories by detaching the cultural issue from the historical and social reality of each country as well as the national characteristics and different conditions imposed on each of them by imperialist exploitation and oppression."[61] Fanon commented: "The objection is valid. It concerns us too. At the start, we wanted to confine ourselves to the Antilles."[62] This is a reference to his comment in the Introduction that "our observations and conclusions are valid only for the French Antilles."[63] But Fanon had in his own account failed to abide by this restriction that he had placed on himself at the beginning of the book.

Although Fanon conceded that d'Arboussier's objection could be used against him just as it could be used against Sartre, that was not for him the last word. He began chapter 6 by focusing on the Antilles, but after conceding the validity of d'Arboussier's point, he tried to explain to d'Arboussier, "dialectics, whatever the cost, got the upper hand and we have been forced to *see* that the Antillean is above all a black (*Noir*)."[64] Fanon acknowledged that "the universal situation of the negro is ambiguous," which is not exactly the same as what he said earlier when he acknowledged the ambiguity of the Negro's experience. In any event the ambiguity was resolved in "concrete existence": "In order to counter the alleged obstacles above, we shall resort to the obvious fact that *wherever he goes, a negro remains a negro*."[65] As the

184   CRITICAL PHILOSOPHY OF RACE

concluding chapter showed, Fanon was not insensitive to the different forms of alienation suffered by a physician from Guadeloupe and an African construction worker,[66] but he recognized that in concrete existence both of them were subject to the same inferiorizing gaze from Whites. Indeed, both were not only treated as Negroes by Whites, but they themselves had a culture imposed on them that makes them see themselves as Negroes, that is to say, see themselves as Whites see them, thereby compromising the diversity of Black experience. In spite of his admission that d'Arboussier's objection was valid, Fanon refused to concede the point because he recognized that in spite of local variations these two myths concerning the Negro were sufficiently widespread as a result of colonialism that they operated across all societies characterized by anti-Black racism. In short, the restriction of the analysis to the Antilles was overcome in the course of the book.

I quoted Fanon as saying that "the universal situation of the negro is ambiguous, but this is resolved in his concrete existence." He followed that comment with the sentence: "This in a way puts him alongside the Jew."[67] This takes us to what for him was the second error of analysis, which is said to be that of "equating anti-Semitism with negrophobia."[68] Certainly Fanon throughout *Black Skin, White Masks* drew parallels between these two forms of racism, mainly by way of Sartre's *Anti-Semite and Jew*, albeit already in chapter 5 he made the point that, as opposed to the Jew, as described by Sartre, the Black man is overdetermined from the outside.[69] In chapter 6 it was Joachim Marcus who exhibited the error, as illustrated by a long quotation in a footnote where it is said of anti-Semitism that the attitude finds the content.[70] But Fanon's point was that, whatever the formal similarities, one must take into account the concrete differences that can be traced back to the myths: "No anti-Semite, for example, would ever think of castrating a Jew. The Jew is killed or sterilized. The negro, however, is castrated."[71] To that extent, there is not racism as such: there are racisms.

Fanon's question about whether psychoanalysis can take account of the man of color gave way to two questions that are related to each other: "Can the White man behave in a sane manner toward the Black man and can the Black man behave in a sane manner toward the White man?"[72] He was least hopeful about Whites. To make the point the chapter ends with an extended discussion of a White woman who had a fear of imaginary Negroes. Fanon had observed the woman in 1951 during his time at the Saint-Ylié psychiatric hospital in Dôle.[73] Fanon's conclusion was that even if one were, contrary to his own beliefs, to attribute part of her problem to her "constitution," her "alienation" was aggravated by predetermined circumstances and until those circumstances had been addressed, any improvement in her illness was going to be limited.[74] The conclusion is clear: White people also need a change in the structures of the world if they are ever to become sane, or, as he also put it, if they are ever to achieve their ambition to become human.[75] Fanon did not exclude disalienation for either group: "Disalienation will be for those Negroes and Whites who have refused to let themselves be locked in the substantialized 'Tower of the Past.' "[76] He understood that the cause of the problems lay in the past and so a knowledge of history was requisite for assessing the situation. But he highlighted an additional option for those Negroes who refused to treat their actuality as definitive.

More precisely, Fanon offered clear indications of what would constitute a solution for Blacks. Indeed, he used the word *solution* twice at the end of chapter 6 in conjunction with a discussion of Césaire.[77] The solution turns on the earlier diagnosis that the Black man suffers from a collapsed ego that renders him reactional in the sense that his actions are dependent on the "Other" as the source of valorization.[78] For Fanon the answer lay in action: "to induce man to be actional."[79] He had already said it in chapter 4: the Black man must choose action with regard to the true conflictual source, which is the social structure of society.[80] By the time the reader reaches chapter 6, Fanon was able to explain himself more clearly. The Black man must, once he has discovered the White man in himself, kill him.[81] This is the heart of *Black Skin, White Masks*, and it does not necessitate literal violence, although it does appear to entail risking one's life in the fight for freedom.[82] Chapter 5 may end in tears, but, as chapter 6 shows, the path to disalienation is ultimately by way of action directed toward a transformation of the very structures of society. This would be different depending on the situation, the context. The question of what kinds of action that necessitates in the various contexts in which he found himself exercised him in his subsequent works until his death in 1961 at the age of only thirty-six.

11

Frantz Fanon's Engagement with Phenomenology

Unlocking the Temporal Architecture of *Black Skin, White Masks*

Frantz Fanon's *Black Skin, White Masks* operates on many different levels, and the various arguments fall into place only when readers are attentive to what Fanon meant when he wrote, "the architecture of the present work is situated in temporality."[1] In Chapter 10, I examined the book's organizational structure by focusing on the role of Fanon's sixth chapter, "The Negro and Psychopathology," in the context of the book as a whole: my argument there was an attempt to challenge the widespread assumption that the book's center of gravity belongs in Fanon's fifth chapter, "The Lived Experience of the Black."[2] It is the most accessible part of the book and the most frequently cited. It includes the narrative about the objectifying impact of the child's cry, "Look, a Negro!," the discussion of the body image, the debate about the meaning of negritude in Senghor and Césaire, and the shattering of his unreflected and enthusiastic endorsement of negritude when he read Sartre's "Black Orpheus." It is here, too, that Fanon developed his account of the way society refused to embrace him on his own terms but only as a Negro, so that he was locked in a vicious or infernal circle from which there seemed to be no escape.[3] This is why the chapter ends with the lament: "I began to weep."[4] But the book as a whole closes not in tears, but with a prayer addressed to his body: "O my body, make of me a man who questions!"[5] I will explore what happens in the intervening pages and the role of phenomenology in that shift in mood. Of course, highlighting Fanon's relation to the phenomenologists of his generation offers only a partial portrait of the various debates in which he was participating in *Black Skin, White Masks*, but comprehending the achievements of any major philosopher is incomplete until one understands how that philosopher relates to what he or she read most closely. I understood this current chapter as both a contribution to that process and an exercise in

Critical Philosophy of Race. Robert Bernasconi, Oxford University Press. © Oxford University Press 2023.
DOI: 10.1093/oso/9780197587966.003.0012

the reexamination of the path that existential phenomenology took during the 1950s through its participation in the struggle against colonialism.[6]

To be sure, Fanon referred to "The Lived Experience of the Black" as "the chapter devoted to phenomenological description," but it would be a mistake to rely solely on those pages in order to gauge Fanon's relation to phenomenology.[7] In the first section, I explain the nature of the mistake by locating "The Lived Experience of the Black" within the structure of the book as a whole as it is set out in the Introduction. In the second section, I integrate what Fanon called his "regressive" analyses with his understanding of "the progressive infrastructure" of the book and relate that to his attempt to enrich phenomenology.[8] In the third section, I examine the status he accorded to phenomenology in the book's final pages where, making good on his description in the Introduction of the book's temporal architecture, he presented his account of temporality in conversation with both Sartre and Merleau-Ponty. In the fourth and final section, I introduce a brief discussion of what Fanon identified as the various "levels" of his account in order to establish the limits he placed around his new understanding of the potential contribution of phenomenology.

Black Lived Experience

There is a widespread tendency in academic circles in North America and Europe to understand phenomenology in the narrow technical sense that it had for Edmund Husserl, but in postwar France it was embraced more broadly as a way of leaving behind academic abstractions and approaching the concrete in its fullness. This in no small measure is what drew Fanon to phenomenology: it assisted him in the task of arriving at "a concrete and ever new understanding of man."[9] Fanon's personal library was well stocked with texts by the French philosophers most closely associated with the phenomenological movement and the journals in which they published.[10] And, when in the fifth chapter of *Black Skin, White Masks*, he questioned some of the descriptions supplied by Sartre and Merleau-Ponty, in the first instance it was on the phenomenological basis that these White phenomenologists treated White experience as normative. This was at the heart of his rejection of Sartre's account of the relation to others on the grounds that its application to a Black consciousness "proves fallacious": "Jean-Paul Sartre had forgotten that the Negro suffers in his body quite differently from the white man."[11]

188 CRITICAL PHILOSOPHY OF RACE

Fanon's critique earlier in the chapter of Jean Lhermitte's idea of the corporeal schema points in the same direction. Fanon insisted that Black people experience their bodies differently from Whites because, unbeknownst to White philosophers, there is a historico-racial schema operating below the corporeal schema.[12] Although Merleau-Ponty is not mentioned at this point, Fanon would have known that the critique also applied to him. A similar critique governs the opening pages of the sixth chapter, now directed against the leading figures of psychopathology. He concluded that the schema developed in the service of a psychoanalysis focused on Whites did not apply to Blacks.[13]

The failings of White philosophers and White psychiatrists arose because in a racist society their whiteness pervaded their work but nevertheless remained invisible to them.[14] This was only one aspect of a larger problem that Fanon had already set out succinctly in the Introduction: "The black man wants to be white. The white man strives to realize the condition of being human."[15] According to Fanon's diagnosis, White society and its norms are sick to the core, and yet Black people, especially Black intellectuals, often aspired to be accepted by it on its own terms.[16] He placed this critique in the service of a positive goal. At the very moment that he described the fifth chapter as devoted to a phenomenological description, he added the coda: "but let us remember that our purpose is to make possible a healthy encounter between Black and White."[17] The fifth chapter demonstrates how the phenomenology that takes its starting point in the description of lived experience contributes to a diagnosis of the problem, but does it have any further role in proposing a solution?

The primary point of the sixth chapter was not to expose the differences between the formation of Whites and Blacks that led to the abnormalization of Black lived experience, nor to highlight the specific pathology of both Whites and Blacks, although the chapter does all of that. Rather, these analyses were a prelude to showing how, with few exceptions, every neurosis or abnormal manifestation among Antilleans was the product of their cultural situation, a situation brought about and perpetuated by Whites through what Fanon called "cultural imposition."[18] "Cultural imposition" names the way in which White society imposes its norms and its racist stereotypes on Black people, leading to the effect Fanon already described in the Introduction when he wrote, "White civilization and European culture have *imposed* an existential deviation on the Black."[19] This means that the sixth chapter goes beyond the account of lived experience found in the fifth chapter to address the "unreflected" mechanisms that lay behind the experiences of individuals described there.[20] Accounts of the lived experience of Blacks is indispensable to an understanding of the impact of a racist society, but, however genuine these accounts may be, they are incomplete to the extent that they do not investigate the mechanism of the system that produced those experiences.

Fanon even extended his critique of this widespread failure to include Aimé Césaire, the author of *Discourse on Colonialism*. In *Cahier d'un retour au pays natal* Césaire had described an incident that took place during his stay in France. While traveling on a streetcar, he observed "a black man as huge as a great ape" and, when the women on the bus laughed at this man troubled by poverty, Césaire was complicit with them and gave them a big smile. Fanon quoted the line from the poem where Césaire wrote that in that moment he had rediscovered his "cowardice."[21] But, although Fanon insisted that Césaire should have "nihilated" the situation, his main complaint at this point was not about the description, nor the complicity, nor the cowardice. His complaint was that Césaire nowhere explored the mechanism of this cowardice, which, according to Fanon, could only be accounted for in terms of cultural imposition.[22] In other words, Césaire's account of this racist incident remained at the level of the symptoms, just as the chapter "The Lived Experience of the Black" had done.

Fanon identified a similar problem with Sartre's account of the gaze in *Anti-Semite and Jew*, even though he described those pages as among the finest he had read because of their affective quality.[23] Sartre had recognized that assimilation was impossible for Jews and that an authentic being Jewish was impossible until there was a socialist revolution.[24] To that extent, Fanon's response to the problem of anti-Black racism was not so very different: he argued for a solution that involved "restructuring the world."[25] But Fanon's edge over Sartre at this point was that he was already going beyond an acknowledgment of the need to shake the edifice of the system that underlay individual experiences of racism by exposing the mechanisms that sustained it. It was not until the publication of *Critique of Dialectical Reason* that Sartre met that same challenge in a sustained way, a fact that helps to explain why Fanon so admired that book.[26]

Fanon had already prepared for the introduction of his insight into cultural imposition when in the fifth chapter he insisted that "the historico-racial schema" arose because "the white man" had "woven me out of a thousand details, anecdotes, stories."[27] At that point he thought that his

190   CRITICAL PHILOSOPHY OF RACE

best recourse was to construct a physiological self and a certain equilibrium. He explained that he "already knew that there were legends, stories, history, and above all *historicity*, which I had learned about from Jaspers."[28] This passing mention of Jaspers's concept of historicity has not been mined, but it is crucial as it is another moment when Fanon reminded his readers that his aim was to make possible a healthy encounter between Blacks and Whites. Given that Fanon did not read German, the most likely source for his understanding of what Jaspers understood by historicity was the study of Jaspers by Mikel Dufrenne and Paul Ricoeur.[29] As they explained, historicity for Jaspers meant being bound to situations and restrictions while taking them up and adopting them, so that they are constantly in question and subject to revocable decisions.[30] Historicity is not a being held captive; it is not destiny. It is the sense of possibility that arises from an understanding of historical reality: "Historicity signifies the fight for the peace of Transcendence."[31] In other words, referencing Jaspers at this point in the so-called phenomenological chapter served Fanon as a way to indicate that phenomenology provided not only some resources with which to state the problem but also a framework within which to address it.

The importance of Jaspers to understanding Fanon's *Black Skin, White Masks* is still not sufficiently appreciated.[32] His discussion of Jaspers's small volume on "metaphysical guilt" is impossible to miss, and it is now known that Fanon read Jaspers on Nietzsche.[33] But Jaspers's *General Psychopathology* is even more important, not least because it brought phenomenology and psychopathology together. Fanon did not abandon phenomenology in favor of psychopathology when he moved from "The Lived Experience of the Black" to "The Negro and Psychopathology." A number of the other authors on whom Fanon drew, both in *Black Skin, White Masks* and in his dissertation, also embraced phenomenology: Henri Ey, Jacques Lacan, Eugène Minkowski, and, although his relation to phenomenology is sometimes forgotten, Charles Odier.[34] Furthermore, although in 1952 Angelo Hesnard, whose idea of the morbid universe was adopted by Fanon, had not yet aligned himself with phenomenology, he would soon do so.[35] And François Tosquelles, with whom Fanon worked, belongs within this same heritage that united phenomenology with institutional psychotherapy.[36] In brief, the opposition sometimes drawn by Fanon's readers between phenomenology and psychopathology is imposed from the outside.

Fanon's Regressive Analysis

Many of the difficulties readers have had reconciling the fifth chapter with what is said elsewhere in the book, especially the final chapter, arise from a failure to appreciate the progressive structure of the book, its temporal architecture. When Fanon wrote, "The architecture of the present work is situated in the temporal," he was signaling that one aim of the book was to bring about a transformation from an inauthentic relation to time to an authentic one.[37] Anticipating an argument that he developed against Léopold Sédar Senghor in the fifth chapter, he already in the Introduction rejected those who "renounce the present and the future in the name of a mystical past."[38] In the Conclusion he expanded the argument: "I will not make myself the man of any past."[39] He extended it even to the point where he would refuse to make himself "a slave of the Slavery that dehumanized my ancestors."[40] That did not mean that Blacks could leave behind all memory of slavery. Or that anyone should. Any suggestion that Black people should do so would be as absurd as neglecting the ways in which Blacks suffer in their bodies differently from Whites. Nevertheless, Fanon proposed an approach that was forward-looking, and the reader, Black or White, who recognized themselves in the book had taken a step in the right direction.[41] He expressed this most clearly when he wrote: "My book is, I hope, a mirror with a progressive infrastructure where the black man can find the path toward disalienation."[42] The importance of this sentence cannot be exaggerated, given that the original title Fanon gave the book, before Francis Jeanson intervened, was "Essay on the Disalienation of the Black."[43]

The progressive infrastructure of the book was set in motion in the first instance by a series of analyses that Fanon called "regressive." Because of the way he combined these two approaches, one can legitimately say that he anticipated the "progressive-regressive method" embraced a few years later by Sartre in *Search for a Method*. As Sartre explained with reference to Henri Lefebvre's programmatic account of rural sociology: "We believe that this method, with its phase of phenomenological description, and its double movement of regression followed by progress, is valid . . . in all the domains of anthropology."[44] In any event, in the Introduction to *Black Skin, White Masks*, Fanon stipulated that the fourth and the fifth chapters were on "an essentially different level" from the rest of the book, which was "regressive."[45] In describing the remaining five chapters of the book as engaged in a regressive analysis, he was to a certain extent leaning on the Freudian approach of

192   CRITICAL PHILOSOPHY OF RACE

destructuring by accessing childhood experiences to which subsequent psychic dispositions could be attributed, but without using the term in its technical Freudian sense, as one can see when Fanon referenced the regression on the intellectual level of the White man who bases his perception of Blacks on comic books.[46] Fanon was, like Jaspers, skeptical of the value of Freud's idea of regression in clinical practice. Nevertheless, Jaspers did acknowledge some form of regression at work in his account of how some people want to escape individuation and do so in the form of "a regressive urge for childhood feelings."[47] This would seem to be the sense in which Fanon used the word when in retrospect he recognized one of the stages he had passed through in the fifth chapter as an embrace of irrationality, a moment of regression.[48]

However, the actual term "regressive analysis" was most likely borrowed from Sartre, who used it to describe the series of reflections that lead back to "the original relationship that the for-itself chooses with its facticity and with the world."[49] But, as Sartre insisted, this approach ignores the dimension of the future. It starts from the present and moves to the past and so it must be brought together with an understanding that moves in the opposite direction "through a synthetic progression" where "we come back down to the envisaged act and we grasp the integration within the total figure."[50] What unites the first three chapters of *Black Skin, White Masks* as regressive analyses is their focus on those Black people who seek an exit or escape from being locked into their racial identity by embracing the White world and seeking acceptance by it. That is how they choose to live their racial facticity. To be sure, in each of these chapters Fanon went beyond that diagnosis. In the first chapter he already warned that it is not enough to say that someone is the product of a psychological-economic system.[51] Across the second and third chapters, beyond arguing that someone's "basic personality" is not a given, a constant, or even something hereditary, as some racist psychologists believed, but something variable, he warned against the assumption that the alternative was to imagine a straightforward interaction between the individual and the milieu.[52] In the fourth chapter, in a break from regressive analysis, he addressed Octave Mannoni's account of the colonial situation. There he continued his attack on the belief in hereditary racial characteristics and also highlighted the limits of Mannoni's phenomenological account of the situation: it was too narrow. Whereas Mannoni blamed petty officials, for Fanon it was European civilization itself that was responsible for colonial racism.[53] Finally, where in the sixth chapter he returned to a regressive analysis, it was to reveal that the abnormalization of Blacks did not wait on the encounter with Whites in the gaze, as described in the fifth chapter, but in many cases already took place prior to direct contact with Whites as a function of society through cultural imposition.

This was the backdrop to Fanon's integration of the regressive analysis into the progressive infrastructure, the task of which was to explore the possibility of a healthy relation between Blacks and Whites, a theme he returned to at the end of a paragraph devoted to developing Jaspers's conception of how phenomenology could be put to use within the clinical context. This reference to Jaspers seems simple enough, until one recognizes that Fanon used the clinical context to support what amounted to a radical revision of phenomenology according to which positive change is implicit in the very project of description. In *General Psychopathology* Jaspers explained the ways in which a phenomenological approach valued "*concrete* description of the psychic state which patients actually experience," presenting it for observation.[54] Fanon was drawn to Jaspers's insistence that for the phenomenologist what is important is an intuitive and deep grasp of a few individual cases from which one can extrapolate by arriving at their meaning.[55] This served as a prelude to his examination of a single case at the end of the chapter. But he also postulated that the real task when faced with multiple individual cases was to disclose the underlying "mechanism." For the cases Fanon was exploring in *Black Skin, White Masks*, that mechanism was cultural imposition. The clinician approaches the patient already equipped with an implicit understanding that the patient is not healthy, so that the passage from diagnosis to a possible cure is already immanent within the task. Fanon made this point repeatedly. In the very first chapter he had paraphrased Marx's famous eleventh thesis that the point is to change the world.[56] Subsequently he insisted: "Every critique of the existent implies a solution."[57] In the context of the discussion of Jaspers on phenomenology, he wrote: "the decision to describe seems naturally to imply a critical approach and therefore an urgent surpassing toward some solution."[58] Phenomenological description, properly practiced, is already critical, whether we choose to call it critical phenomenology or not, and critical phenomenology is empty if it does not aim at solutions. Description, critique, and response are all of a piece. Later in the same chapter the idea of a "solution" to the larger problem of cultural imposition within a racist society is again broached, and with the aid of Césaire it is identified: one must kill the white man in oneself.[59] That is to say, one must be freed from "the desire to be White."[60] But that does not simply mean changing one's goals or ambitions. It can only be accomplished, Fanon explained in the seventh chapter in the

194 CRITICAL PHILOSOPHY OF RACE

context of reading Hegel, by, after having "reflected," becoming "actional" in a fight for freedom in which one is willing to accept death.[61]

The Concluding Pages of *Black Skin, White Masks*

The final pages of *Black Skin, White Masks* rely heavily on the reader's memory of what went before for their coherence. Their dominant theme is the need to transform one's temporality from being locked in "the substantialized tower of the past" to one that is actional and as such open to an open future.[62] Hence, after the lengthy epigraph from Marx's *The Eighteenth Brumaire*, where it is said that "the social revolution cannot draw its poetry from the past, but only from the future," Fanon invoked Negro workers. These workers are victims of a system of racial exploitation. They cannot conceive of their existence otherwise than in the form of a battle against exploitation, misery, and hunger.[63] They know that disalienation does not come through assimilation. They already know the conclusions of the previous two chapters: "there is only one solution: to fight."[64]

In the remainder of the Conclusion Fanon took a series of further steps that call for a line-by-line commentary. In the present context I confine myself to four of those steps, each of which is marked by a reference to the works of a phenomenologist.

Fanon's first invocation of phenomenology in the Conclusion takes the form of an enigmatic quotation from Merleau-Ponty. Fanon had attended Merleau-Ponty's lectures in Lyons, but this quotation is the only direct mention of him in the book and, although there has been growing interest on the part of some commentators in the themes that they share, this reference has been almost totally ignored. Indeed, in every edition and translation of *Black Skin, White Masks* of which I am aware, beginning with the first edition in 1952, the quotation has been ascribed to *Phenomenology of Perception*, whereas it is actually taken from the final chapter of *The Structure of Behavior*. The quotation reads: "For a being who has acquired the consciousness of self and his body, who has reached the dialectic of subject and object, the body is no longer the cause of the structure of consciousness; it has become the object of consciousness."[65] The immediate context in which Fanon cited this passage was his rehearsal of one of the ongoing themes of the book: the way Blacks and Whites in contemporary society are locked into their identities. He had insisted in the Introduction that "the White is locked in his

FANON'S ENGAGEMENT WITH PHENOMENOLOGY   195

whiteness."[66] He had followed that with the observation that "the Black is locked in his blackness," but at this moment in the conclusion, it is curtailed to read simply "there are times when the Black is locked into his body."[67] The context shows that Fanon wanted his Black readers in particular to take a dialectical approach to their bodies. But what did he mean by that?

In *The Structure of Behavior*, Merleau-Ponty opposed causal explanations of the relation of body and soul in favor of dialectical approaches in which each partial action is determined by its significance for the whole.[68] To mark that difference, he rejected an analysis of matter, life, and mind as three orders of reality or three kinds of being in favor of an account of "three levels (*plans*) of signification or three forms of unity."[69] He then passed to a discussion of the claim that, because El Greco's paintings of elongated bodies were somehow the result of a visual disorder, one could say that the artist had exercised his freedom by justifying his alleged astigmatism by infusing it with a metaphysical meaning. But Merleau-Ponty objected that this would not amount to true freedom: the apparent unity that the artist had thereby engendered could only be maintained in a chosen milieu; it would not be able to withstand an unexpected experience. In a sentence that must have caught Fanon's attention for its use of the word "slavery" in an extended sense, Merleau-Ponty explained: "Unity does not furnish an adequate criterion of the freedom which has been won, since a man dominated by a complex, for example, and subject to the same psychological mechanism in all his undertakings, realizes unity in slavery."[70] Merleau-Ponty, who, unlike Sartre, allowed for degrees of freedom, insisted that, if one knows the infirmity as such, instead of simply obeying by living the infirmity as slavery, it could be "the occasion of a greater freedom" if one "makes use of it as an instrument."[71] Not to know the infirmity as such is to live at the biological level and for such a being the infirmity is, Merleau-Ponty wrote, a fatality.[72] It is at this point that he introduced the enigmatic statement quoted by Fanon according to which someone who has acquired a consciousness of self and body no longer accepts the fatalism according to which the body is the cause of the structure of consciousness.

Fanon recognized in that sentence a partial parallel: Antilleans, so long as they stay within the Antilles, have been exposed to a cultural imposition that enslaves them, but they still live in a form of unity until such time as they go to France and are confronted by the White gaze, at which point the equilibrium collapses. The encounter shatters the false equilibrium they had established. But the parallel does not go beyond that. If this process fully mirrored

196   CRITICAL PHILOSOPHY OF RACE

Merleau-Ponty's account, the awareness that followed would bring a greater freedom. And yet this is not what happens when Blacks meet the White gaze, as was already clear from the account of the consciousness of the body that disrupts the bodily schema in "The Lived Experience of the Black."[73] The encounter with the child who cried out "Look, a Negro!" acted as a trigger. It served as what Jaspers called "a limit situation," although Fanon did not use that phrase.[74] But the escape from biological fatalism to reflection did not happen at that point. This is because the body of the narrator was not the object of his own consciousness, but the object of the child's consciousness. That is to say, the parallel between the case Merleau-Ponty described and the one that Fanon placed alongside it broke down, and in this case, as in the earlier account in the fifth chapter, the historico-racial schema intervened: in a racist society Black people experience their bodies differently from Whites.

To be locked into one's body is to be locked into the past in a perpetuation of slavery. As the very next sentence following the quotation from Merleau-Ponty explained: "The Black, however sincere, is a slave to the past."[75] The priority of the past is imposed on Blacks by Whites in a variety of ways. Fanon gave the example of an incident from his student days. He was confronted by an article which presented jazz as "an irruption of cannibalism in the modern world." Fanon's response to this memory was to reference "a German philosopher" who described the mechanism by which "some men want to fill the world with their presence" as "the pathology of freedom."[76] The philosopher in question was Günther Stern, now better known as Günther Anders, who studied with both Husserl and Heidegger in the 1920s. Fanon cited Anders in the first instance to make the point that "the defender of European purity" was trying to make Blacks take ownership of cannibalism, as if Whites were free of savagery. But the reason Anders is cited here is to make a larger point. One can be "the historical man," the one who, according to Anders, "already *is not* all" and so "must *have* it all."[77] Or one can belong to that group of people who Anders described as being themselves only in wanting to escape or exit from themselves.[78] That was the reactional path that would make them sacrifice their freedom to those who have an interest in putting them in their place.[79] Fanon wanted to join with Anders in rejecting both possibilities, and indeed all attempts to answer directly questions about what someone is and who they are authentically. Such questions are wrongly posed; they aim at being, whereas "*acting is not being*."[80] It was in this same spirit that Fanon took another step: he declared his solidarity with anyone who had said no to any attempt to enslave his fellow human beings.[81] He offered as his example his solidarity, not with a Negro past, but with the Vietnamese who were fighting at that very moment against the French in the Indo-China War. The solution does not come from recognizing the dynamics described in the fifth chapter but in becoming actional in relation to the dynamics of cultural imposition, as he explored in the sixth and seventh chapters.

The reference to Merleau-Ponty was an occasion to highlight the particular sense in which Blacks are locked into their bodies, which was explored with the reference to Anders as being locked into the past. For his third direct reference to phenomenology in the Conclusion, Fanon turned to Sartre's *Being and Nothingness* as a context in which to contrast this way of relating to the past to another form of temporality. Fanon wrote: "Sartre has shown that, in keeping with an inauthentic attitude, the past 'takes' *en masse*, and when solidly constructed, *informs* the individual."[82] Fanon was referring to Sartre's description of the way one is one's past: even if I try to deny my solidarity with my past by disassociating myself from it on one point or another, I am affirming it for the whole of my life.[83] The surpassed in itself remains in the form of original contingency. To illustrate the point, Sartre quoted André Malraux's famous saying that death transforms life into destiny.[84] Fanon perhaps alluded to this when in the next paragraph he returned to a formulation he had already invoked in the Introduction, where he had written, "For the black man there is only one destiny. And it is white."[85] In the Conclusion it is preceded by the sentence: "The black man wants to be like the white man." That is to say, in many cases this destiny is not simply imposed from the outside but can also be taken up. For Sartre the past is for the most part a facticity, as indeed race is for both Sartre and Fanon when we are locked in it.[86] But the central point that Sartre was making and that seems to have drawn Fanon's attention was that "it is in so far as I *am* my past that I am able to not be it."[87] This signals a possible passage from facticity to historicity.

Sartre allowed for the possibility of changing the meaning of the past and thus escaping the destiny that Fanon had theorized through his references to Merleau-Ponty and Anders.[88] Fanon took up this other possibility when he wrote that I can "revise my past, valorize it or condemn it through my successive choices."[89] In taking up this possibility, neither Sartre nor Fanon was thinking about how one can willfully change one's interpretation of the past. They were both addressing something more fundamental: the choice of oneself that is brought about through the nihilating power of consciousness. It is through this choice that the meaning of the past can be changed. That is why Fanon immediately returned to his diagnosis according to which

198   CRITICAL PHILOSOPHY OF RACE

many Blacks choose to be like a White person. Because Fanon had gone to such lengths to show that this choice to be White is imposed on Blacks by the racist culture, one might imagine that he was arguing against Sartre at this point. If Fanon was not talking about freedom in this original sense that Sartre develops, then one might be forced to respond that freedom is precisely what a racist society denies Black people. But as one reads the remainder of the Conclusion, their proximity on some key points becomes clear. Fanon insisted that his one duty is not to renounce his freedom through his choices; and, following a succession of claims in which he challenged the conception of history as destiny, he announced that it was in surpassing the historical that he could initiate the cycle of his freedom.[90] He even embraced Sartre's claim that "I am my own foundation."[91] And, as with Sartre, Fanon understood that this conception came with clear ethical and political implications.

Nevertheless, Fanon did not underestimate the obstacles. That is why when in the Introduction he referenced "a zone of non-being" where "an authentic upsurge" (*surgissement*) can be born, he warned that "*in most cases, the black man lacks the advantage of being able to accomplish this descent into a real hell*."[92] Nevertheless, Fanon twice explicitly attributed this capacity for descent to the rebel in Césaire's "And the Dogs Were Silent" in reference to what Fanon understood as the rebel's decision to kill the White man in himself.[93] Similarly, if Fanon was not talking about freedom in this original sense, then one might easily imagine that freedom is the preserve of White people. But freedom, as Fanon understood the term, is "what is most human in man."[94] One must never forget when one is reading Fanon, and especially not in regard to this point, that Whites are not yet human. They are locked in their whiteness and inhumanity. Indeed, Fanon is far less clear, and possibly more sanguine, about how Whites might win their freedom and humanity than he is about Blacks. Even so, for Fanon as for Sartre, one is not free except to the degree that one is pursuing the freedom of all, and freedom is not a state or a condition but a permanent tension associated with a recovery of the self and a divestment of one's skin, a *dépouillement*.[95]

All of this makes it clear, too, that, although Fanon's language of non-being, of authenticity, and of upsurge is developed in dialogue with Sartre, he was taking it to a place to which Sartre had not gone. So, for example, there is notoriously only one mention of authenticity in *Being and Nothingness*, and that is when Sartre simply says that "its description does not belong here."[96] Fanon embraced the term more readily, albeit not in the sense that it was questioned by Anders. Fanon rejected Sartre's characterization of love as doomed to bad

FANON'S ENGAGEMENT WITH PHENOMENOLOGY   199

faith and inauthenticity; he believed in the possibility of authentic love, although he seemed to grant that it would be unattainable for someone with
a feeling of inferiority; it awaited a restructuring of the world.[97] Similarly,
as an effect of childhood, that is to say, of cultural imposition, everybody is
drowning in contingency and only "an authentic grasp of the reality of the
negro" can break through it.[98] This is a call for nihilating the situation that
Césaire failed to enact when he made fun of the African on the bus, but, by
contrast, it is precisely what we see in the descent that Césaire's rebel enacted
in which he kills a part of himself. This happens within an analytic regression that leads to a nihilation practiced in the midst of immanence. Sartre
described it as follows: "To be able to question anything, man must be able
to be his own nothingness, which means he can be at the origin of *non-being*
within being only if his own being is shot through, in itself and by itself, by
nothingness."[99] This provides a decisive clue for understanding Fanon's final
prayer: "O my body, make of me a man who questions!"[100] The implicit contrast is between, on the one hand, an inauthentic attitude in which Fanon's
body is locked into its facticity by the White gaze and, on the other, a body
that through its willingness to be its own nothingness, to accept death for
the creation of a better world, attains "an authentic grasp of the reality of the
Negro." It is only in the latter case that "cultural crystallization" is put in question.[101] Because it is in bodily experience that Blacks are locked into their
bodies, it is through an alternative bodily experience that the break becomes
possible.

The final quotation from a phenomenological text is not immediately
visible. It occurs when Fanon cited Pascal's word "embarked" from his famous discussion of the wager.[102] The word "embarked" appears after Fanon
embraced the conception of transcendence by insisting that one's solidarity
with Being is in the measure that one surpasses it and that this is profiled
in the problem of action. He asked: "Placed in this world, in a situation,
'embarked,' as Pascal would have it, am I going to gather weapons?"[103] Fanon
most likely took up Pascal's word in a critique that René Étiemble leveled
against Sartre's Introduction to the first issue of *Les Temps Modernes* and
which Sartre then quoted from in *What Is Literature?* as a prelude to developing further his own account of the commitment of the writer.[104] A writer
is committed when he tries to achieve the most lucid and the most complete
consciousness of being embarked. This happens "when he causes the commitment of immediate spontaneity to advance, for himself and others, to the
reflective. The writer is, *par excellence*, a mediator and his commitment is to

200 CRITICAL PHILOSOPHY OF RACE

mediation."[105] This not only links with Fanon's discussion of choice a couple of pages earlier, but more especially with the passage from the sixth chapter, cited earlier and explicitly with reference to *What Is Literature?*, where he had announced the book's progressive infrastructure as his answer to the question of what he wanted from his book. But between the question and the answer he inserted these lines: "Ever since Sartre's decisive essay, *What Is Literature?*, originally in *Situations II*, literature has been committed more and more to its sole really contemporary task, which is to persuade the group to press to reflection and mediation."[106]

The reference is to another passage in *What Is Literature?*, one in which Sartre explored what he called a kind of dialectic of the idea of literature in its transition from the state of unreflective mediation to that of reflective mediation on its way to a concrete and liberated literature.[107] Fanon was here pointing to the way that the fifth chapter was written from an unreflected position until it was shattered by Sartre in "Black Orpheus" before being submitted to reflective mediation in the sixth chapter. The reflection arises when one brings to consciousness "the unreflected imposition of a culture" and from there is led to break the vicious circle and "restore to the other, through mediation and recognition, his human reality."[108] The mediation takes place in action as is apparent from the last sentence of the seventh chapter: "To educate man to be *actional*, preserving in all his relations his respect for the basic values that constitute a human world, is the prime task of him who, having reflected, prepares to act."[109]

Nine years later in *The Wretched of the Earth* the language has changed and the account has become more refined, but Fanon's point is still fundamentally the same: the way forward lies in action, in praxis, and it is indeed only in praxis and for praxis that the critical description, the diagnosis, is secured: "The colonized discover the real and transforms it through his praxis, his deployment of violence and his project for liberation."[110] What has changed is the clarity with which violence is endorsed. Violence, and not just action, is "the royal mediation," and it illuminates the agent because it "indicates to him both the means and the end."[111]

Fanon's Levels and the Limits of Phenomenology

The focus of this essay has been on the temporal architecture of *Black Skin, White Masks* and in particular the role of phenomenology within it.

Relatively little has been written about the book's temporal architecture and even less about the different levels (*plans*) on which the book operates, even though Fanon explicitly drew attention to the latter on some forty occasions. The language of levels was widespread within phenomenology at this time, but, because Fanon identified "a phenomenological level," it is especially important to this attempt to clarify the status of phenomenology in this text that the question of levels be addressed, even if it is possible to do so only briefly here.[112]

I mentioned earlier how in *The Structure of Behavior* Merleau-Ponty expressly renounced reference to orders of reality or kinds of being in favor of levels of signification or forms of unity as part of his rejection of causal explanations in favor of a dialectical approach that aims at the concrete where partial levels come together in a whole. He argued that the need to surpass created structures—whether economic, social, or cultural—so as to produce new structures could only be fulfilled by cultivating the ability to see the same thing under a plurality of aspects.[113] In Fanon this strategy was put in the service of disalienation when he advocated that Blacks engage the struggle on both the societal and the individual level, the objective and the subjective level.[114] To combat cultural imposition as a mechanism that degrades human beings and reduces them to a mechanism, he drew on whatever resources would illuminate it and challenge it.[115] Indeed, he explained in *Black Skin, White Masks* that his work in psychology had led him to take up a variety of positions and draw on other sciences.[116] Regressive analysis situated a large part of the book at one level. It led him in the sixth chapter to the biological, instinctual, and sometimes genital, level, all of which could be addressed at the psychoanalytical level. This was contrasted with the philosophical level, the level of ideas and knowledge, which is the universal level of the intellect or reason. But Fanon found this level inadequate to his lived experience at the phenomenological level. This, the concrete level, has a certain privilege over the abstract level. It leads to infinite perspectives, but it is only one of a number of levels.

When Fanon addressed the possibility of authentic love, he explicitly drew attention to the limits of both phenomenology and psychoanalysis.[117] But to go beyond those limits he turned to an account of temporality that drew on the resources of existential phenomenology with its account of freedom and surpassing. For Fanon the present cannot be taken as definitive; it is something to be surpassed.[118] This is because what is given to description is never simply given; it is in large part imposed through the culture. And yet

202 CRITICAL PHILOSOPHY OF RACE

one cannot dismiss the past as simply in the past. The past extends into the present and threatens to lock us into becoming prisoners of the past. Fanon found the solution to the problem by recognizing that this problem with the past can be addressed when the present is seen as opening onto the future in action. It is for this reason that he gave a place to a phenomenology that is both interdisciplinary and inventive by being both critical and actional. It is in bodily experience that the impulse to critical questioning begins, opening the path to a phenomenology dedicated to disalienation or, we might say today, decolonization, in which the norms of Whiteness are challenged through the project of becoming human under the maxim "freedom for all."

IV.

THE CONSTRUCTION OF THE CONCEPT OF RACISM

12

Nature, Culture, and Race

The UNESCO Strategy

Since 1950 the bulk of the academic community has built its fight against racism largely on the back of the distinction between nature and culture. The strategy took as its starting point a definition of racism as discrimination based on a belief in the correlation between, on the one hand, certain unwelcome behavioral patterns, deficient intellectual aptitudes, or immoral inclinations and, on the other hand, a certain genetic heritage which may or may not be reflected in inherited visible bodily attributes, but which are sufficiently permanent and consistent within a population as to justify calling them "races." Racism of this kind was vulnerable to the argument that, even if a correlation could be established between the behavioral patterns and the genetic heritage, it might not be the result of predetermined inheritance but of environmental or other contingent factors. The argument was reinforced by highlighting the radical difference between the two spheres across which the alleged correlation had been established: nature and culture. One way in which this was done was to insist that they belonged to distinct disciplines with very different methodologies: biology and anthropology. It should be noted that, so far as it goes, this argument still allows for the existence of races even if the identification of these races is no longer referred to by such features as skin color but by population genetics.

However, a further step is sometimes introduced: race cannot belong to anthropology because the word "race" is understood to refer to permanent characteristics, whereas anthropology is confined to the shifting sands of culture. But because biology, it is maintained, no longer has any use for the concept of race, that concept is now said to lack scientific warrant and so can be abandoned. This supplementary argument is sometimes taken a step further in the philosophical literature. Insofar as racism is defined as discrimination against someone on account of their race, racism is immediately exposed not only as ethically wrong, which is taken for granted, but also

Critical Philosophy of Race. Robert Bernasconi, Oxford University Press. © Oxford University Press 2023.
DOI: 10.1093/oso/9780197587966.003.0013

206   CRITICAL PHILOSOPHY OF RACE

as an epistemological error: it cannot be legitimate to discriminate against someone on the basis of what does not exist.

Everybody is familiar with these arguments and everybody knows the now standard response that even though by effectively outlawing the word "race" the champions of the fight against racism had robbed the racists of the one tool they needed to express themselves, they had also at the same time denied the targets of racism the means by which to express their solidarity. It was somewhat like trying to resolve the class struggle simply by outlawing the word "class." In other words, this solution had the effect, in spite of the intention, of shrouding the problem to be addressed beneath a cloak of invisibility.

The enthusiastic support that this approach to racism attracted has much to do with the need felt by intellectuals throughout the West to guard the academy from accusations of promoting racism after the evil deeds committed by the Nazis were out in the open. The Allied Powers at the end of the Second World War presented their success as a victory for justice, sacrifice for others, and a belief in humanity. But the new attention being given to racism, which first became an object of serious study in opposition to the rise of the Nazis,[1] meant that the Allied Powers could no longer conceal the fact that their power and wealth, which derived from a sordid racist history that embraced the Atlantic slave trade and colonial genocides, had survived the Second World War in the form of racial segregation in the United States and European imperialism. In this context, which was the period of the Cold War, there was a clear advantage to be gained if racism were defined in such a way that it could be isolated and expunged while everything else remained intact, including the conviction that the Western philosophical tradition was superior to all others. This was accomplished by conceiving racism, not as a structural or systemic problem, but as a false belief. On this basis it was possible to pretend that the existence at that time of segregation laws in the United States and apartheid in South Africa was not sustained by self-interest or evil intent, but was merely a consequence of muddled thinking, which could be corrected by education at virtually no cost to anyone. Racism was simply an unwarranted inference made possible by the failure to distinguish culture from nature. Now that the epistemological error had been exposed, the Western academy could be counted upon to herald the way into a new era of enlightenment, thereby restoring its own sense of moral as well as cultural superiority.

All of this is crucial for understanding why the first UNESCO statement on race from 1950, although highly controversial at the time, gave rise to a new

NATURE, CULTURE, AND RACE   207

dogmatism.[2] The dogmatism is not to be found in the original Statement, but derived from it because of a widespread longing to be done with race and the evils that had been done in its name.[3] UNESCO became involved in the fight against racism in response to a declaration of the United Nations Social and Economic Council in 1948 calling for the "dissemination of scientific facts designed to bring about the disappearance of that which is commonly called race prejudice."[4] Nevertheless the committee of eight international experts who met to draft the statement on race were mainly anthropologists and sociologists. It included E. Franklin Frazier from the United States, Morris Ginsberg from Britain, Claude Lévi-Strauss from France, Humayan Kabir from India, and Luiz A. Costa Pinto from Brazil, the country that UNESCO seemed to think was already beyond race.[5] However, the dominant figure in the committee was Ashley Montagu of Rutgers University, who as a physical anthropologist knew more about the biological science than the others. As the author of *Man's Most Dangerous Myth: The Fallacy of Race* in 1942, which had presented race as the product of a false deduction in which "a culturally produced difference" had mistakenly been given a biological significance, he had already announced the strategy he would propose to UNESCO for its 1950 statement.[6]

Montagu's role as the main author of this document was so well known that it was sometimes referred to at the time as the Ashley Montagu Statement.[7] And yet his failure to persuade committee colleagues to adopt all aspects of his position is reflected in the caution evident in paragraph 6 of the 1950 UNESCO declaration, which read in part that national, religious, geographic, linguistic, and cultural groups have "no demonstrated genetic connection with racial traits."[8] This is an indication that although he personally believed that the concept of race should be abandoned, he was not able to convince his colleagues to embrace this position fully. The Statement allowed that scientists could legitimately use the term "race." It was only the popular usage of the word that should be dropped altogether: the phrase "ethnic groups" was supposed to be used in its place.[9] However, already in 1942 Montagu's position was that the popular usage—"the cultural reference"—should be dropped altogether in favor of the term "caste." He wanted the phrase "ethnic group" to be employed in the context of biology.[10]

The UNESCO statement provoked a huge controversy that was played out in *Man: The Journal of the Royal Anthropological Institute of Great Britain and Ireland*. Partly as a result, in November 1952, a group largely composed of geneticists and physical anthropologists, including Ashley Montagu, rewrote

208 CRITICAL PHILOSOPHY OF RACE

the initial declaration on the grounds that "the scientific facts"[11] with which the first group had begun their statement had not been fairly represented. This did not stop the Second Statement from remaining less well known than the first. The phrase "ethnic groups" was noticeably absent, but just as anthropologists had spoken for the scientists, now scientists spoke for the anthropologists, as when they cited historical and sociological studies in support of the view that "genetic differences are of little significance in determining the social and cultural differences between different groups of men."[12] Again the distinction between nature and culture was in the background doing much of the work and perhaps on this occasion more than before, because these scientists were more cautious than the anthropologists had been in declaring what the evidence showed. They limited themselves to the skeptical conclusion that "the scientific material available to us at present does not justify the conclusion that inherited genetic differences are a major factor in producing the differences between the culture and cultural achievements of different peoples or groups."[13] The Second Statement went further than the First Statement in defining the legitimate meaning of the term "race": "groups of mankind possessing well-developed and primarily heritable physical differences from other groups."[14] A preamble written by L. C. Dunn, a geneticist from Columbia University, also acknowledged race as a biological category.[15]

These two committees addressed sensitive and serious issues in a responsible way, given their terms of reference, but it is striking that the tools that UNESCO selected for the fight against racism—principally the lack of scientific evidence for permanent racial inequality and the nature-culture distinction—do not appear to have been chosen on the basis of a thoroughgoing study of racism, even though these were beginning to become available.[16] The UNESCO statements were fundamentally directed only at scientific racism, such as a belief in an essentialist hierarchy of biologically defined races rooted in biology or a belief that race mixing led to physical degeneracy and mental disharmony.[17] The rejection of these forms of racism should indeed be celebrated, but the impact of doing so should not be exaggerated. Even if nobody any longer believed in these propositions and so in that sense there were no more racists, this would still leave intact a world structured by past racisms that cannot be located at the level of thought because they are now—and probably were always—primarily located within practices sustained not so much by individuals, but by institutions, both local and global.[18] The main task of this essay is to examine from a philosophical perspective the limits of the post–Second World War reliance on the distinction between nature and culture as the dominant way to combat racism.

Problematizing the Distinction between Nature and Culture

The distinction between nature and culture is regarded as self-evident in some intellectual circles, but since the beginning of the twentieth century phenomenologists have argued that abstracting mutually exclusive concepts of nature and culture from what is given in experience is of limited value. They see this reflected in the artificiality of the process by which both biology and anthropology identify their respective subject matters, a fact clearly indicated by the history of these two disciplines. To say this does not invalidate the sciences in question, but it argues that scientific claims must be approached with caution when they are taken out of their own sphere. Phenomenology teaches that because the natural sciences have to begin with an abstraction from the sociocultural world, the natural sciences are not fundamental. This has long been the point of phenomenological criticism of the sciences in general,[19] but it is particularly germane to the distinction between nature and culture, because critical scrutiny of this distinction has played a prominent role in the history of phenomenology from Husserl through Heidegger and Sartre to Merleau-Ponty.[20] As Merleau-Ponty expressed it decisively, "the distinction between two planes (natural and cultural) is abstract: everything is cultural in us (our *Lebenswelt* is "subjective") (our perception is cultural-historical) and everything is natural in us (even the cultural rests on the polymorphism of the wild Being)."[21] The phenomenologist finds that taking one's starting point from the distinction between nature and culture, as if these terms were fundamental, serves to distort the attempt to think concretely. From the phenomenological perspective race is thought of in terms of facticity, which belongs exclusively neither to nature nor to culture.[22]

The phenomenologist's sensitivity to questions of access means that she or he must always attend to the history of the terms used to preserve and convey lived experience. What seems intuitively clear often turns out to be merely the result of a complex history that calls for further investigation. In other words, if phenomenology is to satisfy its critical spirit, it must develop a hermeneutical understanding of the central concepts that initially serve to organize any field within which it is operating, and in the case of the distinction between

210   CRITICAL PHILOSOPHY OF RACE

nature and culture, we quickly find that the distinction is far from obvious. This is indicated by the fact that it is only relatively recently that the term "culture" has taken on a meaning that could place it in opposition to "nature." Before then, art, morals, customs, and nurture had all been placed opposed to nature. What happens when the term "culture" stands in their place?

Not so long ago it was widely believed that the nature-culture distinction was universal in the sense of being transcultural. It was as if culture was the most natural thing in the world. It was also thought to be one of the founding distinctions of Western thought. Certainly the ancient Greeks recognized a distinction between *phusis* and *nomos*,[23] but one should be cautious about assimilating this distinction into that between nature and culture. For the Greeks, when laws were not simply mere conventions, it was because they conformed to nature, which was in this context normative.[24] A similar perspective is reflected in Aristotle's idea that habits could attain the status of a kind of "second nature."[25] The continuity of this tradition within European thought is suggested by the fact that Hegel used the term "second nature" in the *Philosophy of Right* to give the impression that spirit was superior to or higher than nature. So he declared the system of right to be the realm of actualized freedom, which he equated with "the world of spirit produced from within itself as a second nature."[26] But we must understand this speculatively: the distinction is being problematized. Pascal had already used the term "second nature" to question the very idea of a distinction between nature and habit or custom, because of the capacity of custom to become natural. He wrote: "Habit (*Le coutume*) is a second nature that destroys the first. But what is nature? Why is habit not natural? I am very much afraid that nature itself is only a first habit, just as habit is a second nature."[27] Pascal and Hegel would have agreed that nature and custom blend into one another and that they cannot easily be separated.

In the *Discourse on the Origin of Inequality among Men*, Rousseau similarly questioned the rigor with which the distinction between nature and the morals or mores of society could be drawn. In this text he addressed the question posed by the Academy of Dijon as twofold: what was the origin of inequality, and was inequality authorized by natural law? In his answer Rousseau explored the difference between the Greek idea of nature, according to which the Law of Nature is one that nature imposes on itself, and the modern idea of nature, such that nature only offers a prescription.[28] This makes it imperative to know what nature decrees, but insofar as history is understood as a departure from nature, then it immediately gives rise to the problem of explaining how anything could arise that did not ultimately derive from nature. Any departure from nature must have already been inscribed in nature to have been possible at all. He expressed this concern, which arises from a radically distinct notion of nature in his statement, "it is no light undertaking to separate what is original from what is artificial in the present Nature of man, and to know correctly a state which no longer exists, which perhaps never existed, which probably never will exist, and about which it is nevertheless necessary to have precise Notions in order to judge our present state correctly."[29] Under these circumstances it is hard to know whether anything can be more artificial, less natural, than this alleged state of nature. This new conceptual framework has more general implications for the distinction between the natural and the moral, or indeed any parallel distinction. It is no accident that one of the founding works of deconstruction, Jacques Derrida's *Of Grammatology*, makes a similar point, not only in its reading of Rousseau but also of Lévi-Strauss.[30]

These examples show that the Western philosophical tradition was by no means universally blind to the way that whenever nature is considered primary it becomes hard to differentiate it from its other. Seen from a theological perspective, nature is secondary to the supernatural or divine, presenting a theoretical problem when humans depart from nature, but this problem can be addressed using the tools of theology. It was within the very different lexical context of secular thought that the term "culture" took on a new prominence. The word "culture" is not recent. It is Roman in origin, deriving from *colere*, "to cultivate." This sense survives in the term "agriculture," a word which underlines the deep connection between nature and culture.[31] When one cultivates a field, what results remains subject to nature: it does not cease to be natural. Cicero is usually the one credited with taking the word "culture" and applying it to the life of the mind. He wrote of philosophy as the cultivation of the soul, a *cultura animi*.[32] Cicero's understanding of culture as a process of culturation survived as the dominant sense until the very end of the eighteenth century, and it was only then that "culture" gained anything like its modern meaning.[33]

This is confirmed by Kroeber and Kluckhohn in their classic 1952 study, in which after exhaustive research they presented 164 different definitions of culture. They showed with reference to Johann Christoph Adelung's famous German dictionary of 1793 that the sense of culture as ennoblement (*Veredlung*) was still uppermost at that time.[34] Culture is there defined as "the ennoblement or refinement of the total mental and bodily forms of a human

212   CRITICAL PHILOSOPHY OF RACE

being or a people; so that the word includes not only the enlightenment, the ennoblement of the understanding through liberation from prejudices, but also the polishing [*Politur*] and refinement of customs [*Sitten*]."[35] But Kroeber and Kluckhohn also point out that as early as 1782, one can find in Adelung's *Versuch einer Geschichte der Cultur des menschlichen Geschlechts* a shift in the direction of the modern sense of culture as the product of cultivation and not just the act of cultivating. Adelung understood very well that he was naming something relatively new, and he explained that he borrowed the word from Latin and French after having rejected all German terms that came to mind, such as those for refinement, enlightenment, and development of abilities (*Verfeinerung, Aufklärung, Entwicklung der Fähigkeiten*).[36]

For Kroeber and Kluckhohn, what is important is that Adelung was thinking of culture as a sum. This can be seen, for example when he locates culture "on the one hand in a sum of clear concepts and on the other in an amelioration and refinement of the body and of customs (*Sitten*) brought about in a mass of people (*Volksmenge*) in a limited space."[37] It was by making the act of refinement an object of comparative study that Adelung came to see culture as a product rather than a process. It is studied in a process of differentiation: differences across time or across space, albeit there is not yet here any talk of cultures in the plural, which represents another stage in the transformation of the term. When we focus on cultures in the plural, we are no longer distinguishing between what is inherited and what is acquired, but investigating differences between societies, something that is almost always done relative to some normative perspective.

During the nineteenth century, the period in which the concept of race was most indispensable, Lamarckianism and the idea of the inheritance of acquired characteristics was dominant. This meant that anthropology at its inception could not be organized in terms of the nature-culture distinction.[38] Nevertheless, the thinker who comes closest to anticipating something like the notion of nature as permanent inherited characteristics was Immanuel Kant, who arrived at it in the course of elucidating his concept of race. What enabled him to do so was his attempt, unusual for the time, to isolate the workings of heredity within the study of generation.[39] On Kant's account race was the result of acquired but preformed characteristics becoming permanent. Indeed, he intimated that racial characteristics—particularly skin color—were the only characteristics that conformed to this description. At its very root in Kant, the science of race was constituted at the point where certain acquired characteristics came to be considered natural and it was ruled that no further changes were possible. This attempt to fix nature, to see it as unchanging, played a decisive role in the rise of a racial essentialism in which the hierarchy of races would be perpetuated. However, he was forced by his critics to concede that these permanent characteristics were not directly visible insofar as artifice, either in the form of the effects of climate or some form of human behavior such as dyeing one's skin, meant that only experiments with inheritance conducted in a moderate climate would reveal what was hereditary and thus attributable to nature and what was artificial and in that sense contingent. This led him to question whether anyone could ever know the true skin color of a human being unless that person had been born in a temperate climate, such as France.[40] It is not surprising that Georg Forster, who had been around the world with Captain James Cook, had difficulty understanding how Europe was supposed, in effect, to be free of climate.[41]

Nevertheless Kant was still very far from anticipating the mid-twentieth-century notion of culture. As the first to propose a scientific definition of race, which identified as natural what was inherited—as opposed to what was the product of so-called "accidental circumstances," such as climate, and diet—he put in place an account of how the hierarchy of the races arose and was perpetuated through inheritance.[42] The differences between the races were not mere differences. Climate and diet had initially formed the seeds or germs (*Keime*) into those racial characteristics that had on Kant's account subsequently become permanent and could no longer be undone by a change of climate. That is to say, race was not original but accidental, and yet racial characteristics subsequently formed a kind of essentialism. In this way Kant assigned race to a hidden nature, but he still lacked Adelung's notion of culture as product. For Kant culture meant "aptitude for ends" or purposes.[43] He did not assign different races to different cultures. Rather, he identified certain races as devoid of culture, in the sense that they could be trained but not educated.[44]

Lévi-Strauss and UNESCO

Contrary to what is often thought, the separation of nature and culture in the operative sense did not begin with Franz Boas, who, in keeping with the nineteenth-century practice of locating human biology within anthropology, still continued to think of cultural and physical anthropology as part of one

214   CRITICAL PHILOSOPHY OF RACE

unified discipline.[45] In fact, it should be attributed to Robert H. Lowie, who had been a student of Franz Boas, but who subsequently broke with him. In an essay "Culture and Race" in his book *Culture and Ethnology* from 1917, Lowie argued for "a complete disassociation of the concept of race from the concept of culture."[46] Lowie's own *History of Ethnological Theory*, written a full twenty years later, gives us an opportunity to clarify the genealogy of this distinction, which made possible the claim that culture is "that part of anthropology . . . which is not primarily concerned with races as biological differences of *Homo sapiens*."[47] Lowie highlighted Tylor's famous definition of culture from 1871, which is widely referenced as the first use in English of what became the dominant social scientific sense.[48] Tylor wrote: "Culture or civilization, taken in its wide ethnographic sense, is that complex whole which includes knowledge, belief, art, morals, law, custom, and any other capabilities and habits acquired by man as a member of society."[49] Lowie's own definition of "culture" drew on Tylor's definition. Lowie understood culture as "the sum total of what an individual acquired from his society—these beliefs, customs, artistic norms, food-habits and crafts which come to him not by his own creative activity but as a legacy from the past, conveyed by formal or informal education."[50] It is striking that the definition emphasizes that culture is understood as inherited in the sense of being acquired from the past, just as racial differences had been said to be. This means that one's culture was still being seen as a kind of destiny rather than the site of change and transformation, which is how it tends to be seen today: cultures are adopted; they adapt; and they can be discarded like old clothes.

The 1948 edition of A. L. Kroeber's *Anthropology* provides another example of what is new in the separation of anthropology from biology. Culture is explained there as "all those things about man, that are more than just biological or organic, and are also more than merely psychological."[51] But we do not find a parallel definition in the original 1923 edition of the same book.[52] He could not have given the 1948 definition of culture in 1923 because the word had not yet taken on that meaning. Furthermore, it is no accident that it appears in a four-page section on "Society and Culture" that was introduced into the new edition only after he had drawn a distinction between physical and cultural anthropology, a distinction that was crucial for sustaining the separation between race and culture.[53] In another edition Kroeber explained that although race, defined as "a group united by heredity," is a valid biological concept and therefore a concern of physical anthropology, "it is not a valid sociocultural concept; the term 'race' is usually ambiguous, and is best not used in cultural situations."[54] He concluded the chapter in both editions with the same appeal:

> Biology has secured for its processes the exclusive use of the term "heredity"; and biologists employ the term "race" only with reference to a hereditary subdivision of a species. It is equally important that the word be used with the same exact denotation in anthropology, else all discussion of race degenerates irretrievably into illogical sliding in and out between organic and social factors.[55]

But whereas in 1923 that meant that the concept "race," used properly, supplied a solid scientific foundation for anthropology, in 1948 the same pair of sentences meant that there was no place for the term "race" in anthropology. Anthropology at the extreme effectively renounced having any say in monitoring the word "race." It was a word that could be used only as biologists proclaimed it should be used and only to the extent that they did so.

The key figure who had intervened between the two editions of Kroeber's book was Ashley Montagu, a student of both Boas and Ruth Benedict, who herself in 1940 had adopted in a radicalized form Lowie's distinction between nature and culture by holding culture as constant while employing race as the variable, instead of the other way around.[56] It was an insight produced within a world for which migration, followed by assimilation, had become commonplace. In 1942, Montagu used this same distinction to argue that the concept of race was a fallacy, the product of a false deduction: culturally produced differences were mistakenly being given a biological significance. This was the perspective Montagu brought to his role on the international committee charged with formulating UNESCO's fight against racism. By examining briefly Lévi-Strauss's relation to the UNESCO statement, which, as a member of Montagu's committee he also helped to draft, one gains some insight both into the process by which the statement was arrived at and the intellectual shortcomings of the UNESCO approach.

In 1952, Lévi-Strauss was invited to write an essay in support of the 1950 UNESCO declaration, and he complied with "Race and History," in which he supported the distinction between nature and culture. He wrote, for example, that "the original sin of anthropology" consisted in confusing "the idea of race in the purely biological sense (assuming that there is any factual basis for the idea, even in this limited field—which is disputed by modern genetics), with the sociological and psychological products of human civilizations."[57]

216   CRITICAL PHILOSOPHY OF RACE

However, twenty years later in celebration of the Year of Action to Combat Racism and Racial Discrimination, UNESCO called on Lévi-Strauss to repeat the success of his earlier lecture. This lecture, called "Race and Culture," caused a furor because Lévi-Strauss challenged the UNESCO "catechism," as he put it, and in the 1983 preface to a reprinting of his essay in *The View from Afar* he explained that it was not because he had changed his mind but because, at the age of sixty-three, he had reached an age when felt he could be honest. As he put it, "in order to serve the international institutions, which I felt I had to support more than I do today, I had somewhat overstated my point in the conclusion to 'Race and History.'"[58]

Doubtless what upset the people at UNESCO the most was the question he posed about the effectiveness of their efforts: "are we so sure that the racist form of intolerance results chiefly from the wrong ideas of this or that group of people about the dependence of cultural evolution on organic evolution?"[59] Lévi-Strauss's claim was that what UNESCO had isolated and attacked as racism was merely "ideological camouflage for more concrete oppositions based on a desire to subjugate other groups and maintain a position of power."[60]

Lévi-Strauss in this essay no longer called for renouncing the concept of race, although he was cautious about its use. His main claim here was that rather than race determining culture, as had been largely thought to be the case in the first half of the twentieth century, he wrote: "we now realize that the reverse situation exists: the cultural forms adopted . . . determine to a very great extent the rhythm of their biological evolution and its direction." In other words, "race—or what is generally meant by this term—is one function among others of culture."[61] Superficially this sounds like Montagu's claim from 1942, but, unlike Montagu, Lévi-Strauss was not prepared to give biology the authority to determine what did and did not exist. This meant that the claims were very different.

Alain Locke's 1924 essay "The Concept of Race as Applied to Social Culture" provides a useful point of comparison. In Locke's own words, "instead of the race explaining the cultural condition, the cultural conditions must explain the race traits."[62] Both Locke and Lévi-Strauss call this a reversal. Locke proposed "a reversal of emphasis,"[63] and Lévi-Strauss used the dramatic verb *bouleverser* and a phrase that can be literally translated as "things take place in the other direction."[64] But when culture displaces the primacy of nature in this way, even if the context is scrupulously delineated in advance, the displacement is no longer a simple reversal and everything depends on how fully the theorist recognizes that it destabilizes the meaning of the words, thereby opening the way to a deconstruction of the opposition. This seems to be the case in Locke.[65] And one can add that at the very least the nature-culture distinction is far less simple in the case of Lévi-Strauss than at first appears.

In 1961 in *The Savage Mind*, Lévi-Strauss wrote: "The opposition between nature and culture to which I attached much importance at one time . . . now seems to be of primarily methodological importance."[66] The admission was based on the recognition, readily familiar to phenomenologists, that "No empirical analysis (*analyse réelle*) . . . can determine the point of transition between natural and cultural facts, nor how they are connected."[67] What made this admission strange was that Lévi-Strauss referenced *The Elementary Structures of Kinship* from twelve years earlier as the place where he had first exaggerated the value of the distinction, even though when one turns to this book one finds that he openly acknowledged there that the distinction was indeed only a methodological instrument and that it lacked historical significance. In other words, albeit without his saying it and perhaps even without his recognizing it, it was his appeal to the distinction in support of UNESCO's fight against racism that had given it an undue significance.

Lévi-Strauss's departure from the UNESCO statement did not end there. The conjunction of his narrow view of racism, similar to UNESCO's, and his belief that people had by human nature "a desire to subjugate" meant that Lévi-Strauss was questioning not only the centrality of the idea of race but also, more problematically, the centrality of racism.[68] He was quite explicit that even if one could rid the world of racism it would not be a better world because the partiality one has for one's own values would still express itself as hostility to other cultures. He highlighted contemporary attitudes toward hippies and asked: "Are the feelings of repulsion and even hostility that they have inspired in most people substantially different from racial hatred?"[69] One can only conclude that Lévi-Strauss had not read Frantz Fanon's account of the lived experience of race or his critique of Octave Mannoni for failing to understand racism as a structure that permeates a whole society.[70] Nor can Lévi-Strauss have thought deeply about how racisms based on genetic inheritance provided a rationale for genocide that is lacking in standard cases of hostility.

Even in the Preface to *The View from Afar*, where "Race and Culture" was republished, Lévi-Strauss accepted a narrow definition of racism similar to the one UNESCO worked with: "Racism is a doctrine that claims to

218   CRITICAL PHILOSOPHY OF RACE

see the mental and moral characteristics of a group of individuals (however the group may be defined) as the necessary effect of a common genetic heritage."[71] To be sure, there is no explicit mention of race here, and that is no accident. Ideas of "race" seemed, as we have seen, to be less and less important to Lévi-Strauss's analysis of the partiality one culture might direct against another. For Lévi-Strauss the difficulty lay not in charting racism but in determining when normal and appropriate partiality turned into an excessive hatred. What occasioned such a transformation in his view involved the experience of inequality and a lack of physical distance.[72] Strangely, even though in the final chapter of *The Savage Mind* Lévi-Strauss had studied and indeed attacked Sartre's *Critique of Dialectical Reason*, he failed to see its account of the practico-inert as one of the richest accounts of racism as a system embedded in institutions.

Montagu and Lévi-Strauss represented two different traditions, indeed, to recall a phrase that would become famous in the debate between Lévi-Strauss and Sartre, "two sorts of reason."[73] Montagu's approach was plainly in sight in the title of his book *Man's Most Dangerous Myth: The Fallacy of Race*. He appealed to science but only as a forerunner to locating errors in logic. Once the myth had been exposed by analytic reason, there was an end to the matter. Montagu became increasingly vociferous in his opposition to the word. This culminated in the following remarks in the Introduction to the sixth and final edition: "The purpose of the present, sixth edition is to make use of the scientifically established facts to show that the term 'race' is a socially constructed artifact—that there is no such thing in reality as 'race,' that the very word is racist."[74] Whereas for Montagu to identify the myth of race was enough for it to be dismissed, for Lévi-Strauss this was merely a beginning, as myths should be explored on their own terms.

My argument has been that the radical distinction between nature and culture was and remains inadequate to the tasks both of mounting a defense against racism in its myriad forms and of illuminating the history of racism. The attempt to displace talk of races into talk of ethnic groups, defined not by their biology but by their culture, appears at first sight to liberate us from racial essentialism to the degree that we think of culture as hybrid and fluid, which, of course, has not always been the case. But as long as some cultures are seen as uniquely equipped to embody the characteristics that represent social development, then this opens the door to a certain form of cultural racism, one that is sponsored by bodies like UNESCO and the United Nations.[75] This is only one example. There is nothing inherent in the distinction between nature and culture that sets it against any but the most narrowly conceived and relatively recent scientific racism. A critical philosophy of race that limits itself to attacking this target leaves worlds of racisms intact. An existential phenomenology informed by hermeneutics is not tempted by this route because it knows the artificiality of the opposition between nature and culture, a distinction which is not given in experience but which is produced by an artificial division of labor between disciplines. But phenomenology with its capacity to describe the lived experience of racism has, when combined with a knowledge of history, the resources to pursue the investigation of racism in its myriad forms and thus to take up the task which the UNESCO statement on race from 1950 addressed only partially.

13

A Most Dangerous Error

The Boasian Myth of a Knock-Down Argument against Racism

Race and *Racism*

In the middle of the nineteenth century, the word *race* appeared to be one of the most powerful words in the English language. In a novel first published in 1847, Benjamin Disraeli wrote: "All is race; there is no other truth."[1] In 1850, Robert Knox echoed him: "Race is everything: literature, science, art, in a word, civilization, depend on it."[2] These statements reflect a widespread belief in Europe at that time that drew its understanding of race primarily from history, albeit with the growing conviction that nature herself favored racial purity and thereby shaped how race mixing was seen. At this time, appealing to race understood in terms of historical destiny was widely thought to provide sufficient justification for colonialism and chattel slavery in spite of the misery associated with them.[3] Soon after the beginning of the twentieth century, when fears about race mixing became more acute, in part as a result of the widespread acceptance of Mendelian laws of heredity, the belief in biological race as destiny came to be used as a basis for justifying segregation in the United States and apartheid in South Africa, as well as genocide. Such was the ideological power of *race*.

Beginning in the late 1930s, a new word came into the English language, and in this chapter I explore how it acquired its own political power: the word *racism*. The French word *raciste* was introduced at the end of the nineteenth century, and what it named was not always thought of negatively, as is reflected in the fact that one of its earliest uses was in the formulation: "I myself am also a racist."[4] Although the word *racisme* was initially used in the context of promoting a specifically French identity or in some cases an even more exclusive Gallic understanding of what it was to be French, in the 1920s the French increasingly used the word *raciste* to translate the German word *völkisch*, highlighting the German refusal of the kind of universalism with

Critical Philosophy of Race. Robert Bernasconi, Oxford University Press. © Oxford University Press 2023.
DOI: 10.1093/oso/9780197587966.003.0014

which the French identified.[5] The rise of National Socialism strengthened these negative connotations, and during the Second World War the term *racism* was virtually synonymous with National Socialism.[6] That is to say, the English word *racism* was not formed with Africans and people of African descent in mind.[7]

The English language was already well equipped with phrases like *race prejudice, racial discrimination, race hatred, White chauvinism, xenophobia,* and even *racialism.* There was nothing inevitable about the way the word *racism* came to displace these other terms in prominence. In the next section I will argue that the strategies developed specifically to counter racism, as distinct from those directed against more general ideas of racial prejudice and discrimination, were dependent on the very narrowness of what was understood by the term, and that the term proved problematic when it was extended to include other groups without considering the limited context that had determined its initial formulation. To make this case, I will focus largely on the contributions of Franz Boas to this change in vocabulary. I will show that he used the term in an effort to establish as broad an agreement as possible on what people could readily reject about Nazi attitudes toward the Jews without sacrificing their prejudices against other groups.

After demonstrating that in the English-speaking world the most prominent theorists of racism were anthropologists concerned with isolating certain singular aspects of select Nazi racial theories that they believed they could refute, I turn in the third section to show how their approach continued to take anti-Black racism almost for granted, thereby rendering it invisible. I will contrast this with the accounts of systemic racism that have predominantly been given by thinkers of African descent who have shown that the dominant theorization of racism was inadequate to the situation faced by Black people, whether in the colonial context or elsewhere. These thinkers recognized that to bring to light the pervasive character of anti-Black racism would call for other ways of thinking than those promoted from the metropole. Unfortunately, their efforts went largely unheard in the mainstream discussion. In the final section, I offer an account for the political power that the word *racism* has attained. I will argue that part of its appeal lies in the capacity of the word to deflect attention from the real issues. My concern here is less with what the word *racism* serves to bring into focus and more with what the word conceals: the system that produced what is conventionally called racism.

222   CRITICAL PHILOSOPHY OF RACE

Racism as Anti-Semitism

Franz Boas, an immigrant from Germany who lived in the United States for fifty-five years before his death in 1942, tends to have a prominent place in triumphant narratives about the defeat of racism. Thomas Gossett's assessment that "it is possible that no man did more to combat race prejudice than any other person in history" still survives in some departments of anthropology.[8] But whereas there is no question that he was a vocal opponent of some of the most ignominious American racial theorists of his generation— such as Madison Grant, Lothrop Stoddard, and Harry Laughlin—and that he made positive contributions to debates about immigration at a time when there was a campaign to restrict it drastically, the limitations of his approach should not be forgotten and they are distilled into his promotion of the word *racism* at the end of his career.[9]

Boas's main contribution was his advocacy of a hard distinction between inherited factors, which were considered permanent, and environmental factors, which were the causes of variation. He insisted that the environment was of much greater significance than had previously been thought. In 1911, on behalf of the Immigration Commission of the United States, he argued for the instability of human types on the basis of data amassed from almost eighteen thousand immigrants, predominantly east European Jews and southern Italians: he explained the fact that the bodily form of the descendants of immigrants was markedly different from that of their parents by reference to "the influence of [the] American environment."[10] Having correlated the distinction between heredity and environment with that between nature and culture, the Boasians assigned race to nature and thus to physical anthropology or biology.[11] Meanwhile, outside the Boasian school the tendency at that time was still to see race as embracing both physical and mental characteristics. The distinction between nature and culture also framed the way racial prejudice itself came to be seen by the Boasians. Whereas at the beginning of the twentieth century the phrase *race prejudice* was widely thought to refer to something largely natural, Boas insisted that race antagonism "was not by any means a universal trait of mankind."[12]

Early in his career Boas's focus in this area tended to be on immigration and on the oppression of Black people in the United States. One sees this, for example, in the final chapter of the 1911 edition of *The Mind of Primitive Man*, which was called "Race Problems in the United States," albeit his prescriptions therein were scandalous, by the standard of both his day and

A MOST DANGEROUS ERROR   223

our own. What he said there was in line with remarks made in the previous year, when he had looked to race mixing to bring about "the disappearance of the most distinctive type of Negro" as a way "to alleviate the acuteness of race feeling."[13] Furthermore, the conclusion of his 1921 essay "The Negro in America" read: "Thus it would seem that man being what he is, the Negro problem will not disappear in America until the Negro blood has been so much diluted that it will no longer be recognized just as anti-Semitism will not disappear until the last vestige of the Jew as a Jew has disappeared."[14] But although Boas on occasion continued to draw parallels between African Americans and Jews, he believed that there is a Black race but no German or Jewish races.[15] Boas's focus changed as a result of the rise of National Socialism: this can be illustrated by the major changes the chapter on "Race Problems in the United States" underwent when in 1938 he rewrote it for the revised version of *The Mind of Primitive Man* under the title "The Race Problem in Modern Society."

He now no longer looked to the virtual disappearance of Jews as Jews as a way out of anti-Semitism. It was sufficient to acknowledge the *possibility* of their disappearance into the general population. Boas did not deny the racial differences between Blacks and Whites,[16] but because race was not a factor in the difference between Jews and Germans, any alleged difference between the culture of the Jews and that of the Germans could be referred simply to historical and social conditions. In short, he had come to focus on a strategy that was intended to be effective against certain forms of Nazi anti-Semitism and its North American sympathizers on the basis that the Jews were not a race, but in the face of anti-Black racism he could do no more than point to the lack of sufficient evidence to justify inferences from the physical to the mental at the level of race.

This approach came to be distilled into the term *racism* as can be seen in *Science Condemns Racism*, a 1939 pamphlet coauthored by Boas and issued by the American Committee for Democracy. The immediate target of the pamphlet was Harry Laughlin, the superintendent of the Eugenics Record Office and the proud recipient in 1936 of an honorary degree from the University of Heidelberg, in part because of his promotion of sterilization. In *Conquest by Immigration*, Laughlin insisted that the immigration policy of the United States should be governed by racial considerations, and among his complaints was the way disproportionate numbers of Jews were entering the United States because the policy was regulated by place of origin rather than race.[17] The objections of the authors of *Science Condemns Racism*

224   CRITICAL PHILOSOPHY OF RACE

were largely confined to identifying those of Laughlin's scientific claims they thought of as false, as distinguished from those they considered unproven. Science could condemn racism because what was meant by racism was the narrow band of racial prejudice that purported to be scientific. The argument was that there was no scientific basis for race bias as yet, without ruling out the possibility of evidence emerging later. Elsewhere Boas announced that it was "easy to show that racism has no scientific standing" because "according to its claims the hostile groups are biologically determined, and therefore permanent, while all the other groupings change with the change in cultural pattern."[18] To be sure, that form of racism went against his thesis about the instability of human types, but it is worth remembering that his strongest evidence against permanent biological difference was drawn from his 1911 study of different White populations and that he allowed that Africans constituted a race. And not all racism assumes the permanence of races.

The tendency to use anti-Semitism as the paradigm for racism, with racism defined narrowly in terms of bad science, continued after the Second World War. It was the approach adopted by the United Nations Educational, Scientific and Cultural Organization (UNESCO) when it issued its 1950 Statement on Race, which was prepared under the chairmanship of Ashley Montagu, a former student of Franz Boas and the author in 1942 of *Man's Most Dangerous Myth: The Fallacy of Race*. The 1950 Statement insisted that what people normally understood by "race" was no more than a social myth, but it accepted, as Boas himself had, a dynamic differentiation between the Mongoloid, the Negroid, and the Caucasoid divisions.[19] This view placed limits on the Declaration as a resource for anti-Black racism. One way in which the document addressed anti-Black racism was by claiming that nonscientists simply did not understand what biologists meant by race and for that reason nonscientists should use the phrase "ethnic group" instead.[20] This was in fact a proposal that had already been made in 1935 by Julian Huxley and Alfred C. Haddon in their book *We Europeans*, but their motivation in proposing that race talk be abandoned in favor of the even vaguer idea of ethnic groups was directed against the growth of nationalism within Europe.[21] That is to say, in rejecting talk of race, they had in mind the European tendency, going back to the nineteenth century, to think of each European nation in terms of the various races that inhabited it, as the French had done when they were promoting racism. Nevertheless, this focus on European unity had serious side effects. As one commentator explained, "the title of the work, *We Europeans*, speaks to the imagined community of a unified Europe made possible by the scientific evidence that erases all racial dividing lines, at least those separating Europeans from each other."[22] The book might as well have been called *We Whites*, thereby showing its inappropriateness as a resource for anti-Black racism. And the fact that this approach was still thought relevant after the defeat of the Nazis is reflected in the fact that *We Europeans* appeared in French translation in 1947, when Huxley was living in Paris as the director general of UNESCO.[23]

In fact, Boas's approach, although presented as a way of combatting National Socialism, would not have been especially effective in undermining its treatment of the Jews: the kinds of racial theories that Boas and his students were able to demolish, while prominent in some academic circles in Nazi Germany, played a much less significant role in persuading ordinary Germans to embrace the nationalism of that period than, for example, *Volkskunde*.[24] Whereas Boas and his students chose to attribute to the Nazis a biologism that still to this day is often thought to have been the foundation of Nazi anti-Semitism, Huxley and Haddon knew better. They acknowledged in 1935 that Hitler's racial characterizations in *Mein Kampf* were "based not on any biological concept of physical descent ... but almost entirely on social and cultural elements."[25]

Boas explicitly targeted such Nazi race theorists as Eugen Fischer and Hans Günther, and another Nazi, Fritz Lenz, who, along with Fischer, was one of the authors of *Menschliche Erblichkeitslehre und Rassenhygiene*, among the books that Hitler was supposed to have read while in prison. In that volume, Lenz, a long-standing opponent of Boas, referenced *Kultur und Rasse*, the 1914 slightly reworked German edition of Boas's *The Mind of Primitive Man*, as an example of a text falsely denying racial mental differences. He also attacked Boas for his Lamarckian tendency of giving a major role to the environment.[26] Lenz believed that Jews, of whom Boas was one, were attracted to Lamarckianism because it enabled them to believe that assimilation was a genuine possibility. Lenz argued against Lamarck and in favor of Kant: "The Nordic thinker Kant, to whom the modern 'idealists' especially appeal, was himself careful to avoid over-estimating the importance of environmental influences."[27]

Lenz himself lends support to the claim that the UNESCO strategy was fundamentally directed against anti-Semitism rather than anti-Black racism.[28] The 1950 statement proved controversial: physical anthropologists and geneticists challenged some of its claims. It was decided to produce a second document, and in preparation for doing so, some ninety-six experts were

226   CRITICAL PHILOSOPHY OF RACE

invited to respond. Among the seventy who did so were, somewhat remarkably, Fischer and Lenz. Lenz had supported the legislation of the National Socialist state, but in his response he observed that the 1951 statement, like its predecessor in 1950, "was intended to counteract anti-Semitism" and that this was only one aspect of racism.[29] He recognized that the word *racism* was molded in such a way as to combat anti-Semitism but that it was ill suited to address the specific forms of oppression directed against Blacks. This might not have been an accident. To gain support from Europeans at this time, one had to accommodate ideas of both European unity and colonialism, and to gain support from southerners in the United States one had to accommodate segregation. Even some White South Africans in the process of forging the apartheid regime found that they could accommodate the UNESCO Statement on Race.[30]

A narrowly constructed definition of racism was necessary in order to form a broad political consensus, even if that meant leaving the status quo largely untouched. To establish this consensus, it was also helpful that questions of morality were put to one side: racism was an epistemological error that could be refuted or overcome by scientific education.[31] The idea was that the racists were not morally at fault; they were simply ignorant, having fallen victim to an improper use of the term *race*. The campaign against racism not only distorted the problem; it also in some ways contributed to it by distracting attention away from the real task. Having argued in 1911 that "the undesirable traits that are at present undoubtedly found in our negro population" lay largely in "social surroundings for which we are responsible,"[32] Boas did not promote a social program that took responsibility for those conditions.

In retrospect it looks like an elaborate two-step: first, the biologists claimed to be the only ones knowledgeable enough to use the word *race* legitimately, and then, by denying that they themselves had any use for the term, they were able to outlaw the word altogether. If racism is discrimination against someone on account of their race, then society can be cured of its racism by being persuaded there are no races. Problem solved. It was a strategy that was subsequently adopted by Anthony Appiah.[33] But it is worth noting that the wholesale denial of race altogether did not come until the 1960s. In fact, it was not until the fourth edition of *Man's Most Dangerous Myth* in 1964 that Montagu decided to extend the strategy that had been deployed against anti-Semitism and deny the existence of biological races altogether,[34] at which point the biologists began to police the use of the word *race* as if it were itself as vicious as a racial slur. When in the first edition of 1942 he addressed the social problems facing "Negroes" and Jews in the social context of the United States, it was to make the point that this was an issue of caste, not of race. Race was a biological term and so "there can be no cultural 'races'; there can only be cultural castes."[35] Whereas Montagu had not lost sight of the condition of African Americans,[36] he still recognized that they were a race as the Jews were not. In fact, when in 1960 *The UNESCO Courier* devoted a whole issue to racism under that title, the main thrust of the lead article was to establish the difference between "Anti-Semitism and colour prejudice" by denying that "the distinction between Jew and Gentile is of the same nature as that between Negroid and Caucasoid and Mongoloid."[37] That is to say, in spite of the insistence on the irrelevance of race, it seemed important to the adherents of the UNESCO strategy to insist that there was a Negroid race but not a Jewish race.

The Invisibility of Anti-Black Racism

The 1950 and 1951 UNESCO Statements on Race of 1950 did not mention racism by name, although there is no doubt that was the intended target, so that when the Declaration was published, the headline of the *UNESCO Courier* for July–August 1950 read "Fallacies of Racism Exposed." One possible explanation of why the Declaration failed to mention racism as such was because it continued the Boasian approach of trying to solve a problem without a proper prior investigation of what the problem was, for fear that it might break the consensus surrounding the proposals.

The lack of an adequate diagnosis of the problem to be addressed was widespread. One might easily imagine that the Swedish sociologist Gunnar Myrdal, who was one of the experts consulted before the 1950 UNESCO Statement was released but by no means a follower of Boas,[38] might have done so in his two-volume collaborative sociological study, *An American Dilemma*. But Myrdal focused on "discrimination"[39] and thereby situated the problem in the heads and hearts of White people as individuals rather than on the system that produced them.

One sees the same failure in Ruth Benedict's *Race: Science and Politics* (published in England in 1942 as *Race and Racism*). Benedict, who was another student of Boas, included a lengthy chapter that must be the earliest history of racism as such in the English language. The history of racism became a crucial site of contestation in the attempt to establish the new concept of

228   CRITICAL PHILOSOPHY OF RACE

racism. If racism was dependent on the biological concept of race as had been claimed, then the advent of racism had to await the introduction of the science of race in the late eighteenth century. In spite of the fact that the Boasian approach has remained wedded to this idea, Boas himself knew better: "Even when the Declaration of Independence was signed there was race prejudice, and this because there were Negro slaves. . . . In George Washington's time, there was no adequate scientific basis for the discussion of race."[40] Benedict tried a different approach by retaining the Boasian distinction between race and culture,[41] while giving the term *racism* a different meaning. Whereas for Boas and Montagu racism amounted to a false scientific claim that could be combatted by demonstrating the falsity of the notion of race on which it relied, Benedict, by contrast, separated racism from science altogether. On her account, race was not a modern superstition but a fact, whereas racism was the superstition.[42]

But what is so shocking about Benedict's history of racism, which can again best be explained by the need to establish a consensus in the United States against Nazi racism, was her insistence that, properly speaking, it was an almost exclusively European phenomenon that came to dominance only at the very end of the nineteenth century with such figures as Houston Stewart Chamberlain. In spite of her acknowledgment of the persistence of slave-owner attitudes in the southern United States, she believed that what one found in North America was not the new European racism but the old "doctrine of the innate superiority of a class."[43] She was so committed to the task of separating North American racism from German racism that, in spite of the clear evidence that, as James Q. Whitman has shown, Nazi authors often leaned heavily on North American authors, she issued the disingenuous claim that "the racist literature of the United States deals hardly at all with our great national racial problem, the Negro."[44] One need only think, for example, of Madison Grant who in his *The Conquest of a Continent* mourned the fact that one could no longer rely upon natural selection "to solve the problem by a gradual elimination of the Negro in America."[45] Even so, when Benedict in *The Races of Mankind*, a pamphlet coauthored with Gene Weltfish, offered a mild suggestion that the United States should "clean its own house" if it was to "stand unashamed before the Nazis and condemn, without confusion, their doctrines of a Master Race,"[46] it provoked a major controversy.[47]

This strange blindness to anti-Black racism can also be found in Boas. It is present even in relation to his signature contribution, the separation of race and culture. In 1938, he wrote that the idea, prevalent in Germany in relation to Jews, that race determined culture or "mental status" gained wide support only in the twentieth century: "Until the first decade of our century the opinion that race determines culture had been, in Europe at least, rather a subject of speculation of amateur historians and sociologists than a foundation of public policy. Since that time it has spread among the masses."[48] But he then added, almost as an afterthought, that what was happening there was "quite analogous to the status assigned to the Negro at an earlier period." In other words, he knew that the error he was presenting as an illicit inference was not in fact as new as he had just suggested, but was rather an extension of what had long been the case if one thought of racism not in terms of anti-Jewish sentiment but anti-Black sentiment.

Furthermore, this blindness to North American anti-Black racism goes far beyond the Boasian school because it seems to have been ingrained in the psyche of White Americans that the racism that shaped the country from the arrival of the Europeans was natural, like the institutions that they deployed to impose their rule. What seems to have eventually opened the eyes of some White Americans to their own racism was seeing a parallel between the racial discrimination practiced by the Nazis, especially against the Jews, and their own practices. It is striking that this seems first to have occurred to White Americans not in respect of the imposition of segregation and laws against interracial marriage, but in respect of their treatment of the Japanese after Pearl Harbor. When Justice Frank Murphy in 1944 introduced the word *racism* for the first time into Supreme Court opinions, it was in the case of *Korematsu v. United States of America* in regard to the detention of American citizens of Japanese descent. In his published opinion, he reiterated the mantra that "Distinctions based on color and ancestry are utterly inconsistent with our traditions and ideals." But he went on to say, "Today is the first time, so far as I am aware, that we have sustained a substantial restriction of the personal liberty of citizens of the United States based on the accident of race or ancestry." Such a brazen denial of the way African Americans had been treated in the United States once they received citizenship through the Fourteenth Amendment is remarkable enough. Even more astonishing was the fact that in a draft of his opinion he had questioned himself: "is this so [?] How about laws in most states on marriages with Ethiopians?" The example is an odd one because as stated it refers to restrictions on White citizens to marry African Americans, but it is clear that Justice Murphy knew in advance that the claim made in his published opinion was false.[49] Legal

230 CRITICAL PHILOSOPHY OF RACE

measures against African Americans were well known to him, but he had so normalized these restrictions that he somehow discounted them.

Although these examples might seem to suggest that the main problem lay in the way anti-Black racism had been rendered invisible because the vast majority of White people took it for granted, in the same way that they had earlier come to take slavery for granted, the deeper problem lay with how anti-Black racism had been theorized on the basis of anti-Semitism without Blacks in mind. Systemic issues were ignored even though they had long been a part of how Blacks understood their oppression, going back at least to the Haitian mulatto Pompée Valentin de Vastey, who at the beginning of the nineteenth century appropriated Pierre Malouet's account of colonialism as a system in order to denounce it.[50] In the context of the theorization of racism as such, the failure was already highlighted by Oliver Cromwell Cox, the Trinidadian-American sociologist. In 1948, in *Caste, Class, and Race*, he objected to the way that "the substance of modern race antagonism" was being seen in terms of racial ideology when what was needed was "the study of social facts and situations."[51] He specifically challenged Benedict's use of the term *racism* for taking attention away "from the real impersonal causes of race prejudice."[52] Even earlier, in an essay published in *The Journal of Negro Education* in 1944, Cox dismissed the idea of attacking race prejudice as false, when it is in fact "only a symptom of a materialistic social fact."[53] He concluded: "The white man's ideas about his racial superiority are rooted deeply in the social system; and it can be corrected only by overthrowing the system itself."[54]

Frantz Fanon came to a similar conclusion. For him racism was "only one element of a vaster whole: that of the systematized oppression of a people."[55] On the way to that conclusion Fanon exposed the vacuity of the UNESCO approach that focused exclusively on the racism that aspired to be "rational, individual, genotypically and phenotypically determined."[56] He saw that this merely displaced racism into what he called "cultural racism," and he seems to have been the first to use that phrase. It was an idea that would have made no sense to Montagu, but it represented an essential insight into the operation of racism in an oppressive society that had, at least nominally, rejected the simpler biological forms of racism but had kept much else intact.

The invisibility of systemic racism to White people was explored further by Stokely Carmichael and Charles V. Hamilton in 1967 in *Black Power*, where they introduced the phrase "institutional racism" to describe "acts by the total white community against the black community."[57] To be sure, since then the term has been domesticated by White people to the extent that some of them have embraced it to refer only to the culture of certain specific institutions. So in England, Sir William Macpherson in his report on the racially motivated murder in 1993 of Stephen Lawrence, a young Black man who was simply waiting for a bus, defined institutional racism as "the collective failure of an organisation to provide an appropriate and professional service to people because of their colour, culture, or ethnic origin."[58] Even in this version, the term is still often rejected in the United States.[59] There are multiple reasons why this is so, but a reading of Jean-Paul Sartre's *Critique of Dialectical Reason* would suggest that it lies in the dominance there of an analytically based abstract individualism. Sartre summarized how a focus on racism as a material system is distinct from the Boasian approach: "the essence of racism, in effect, is that it is not a system of thought, which might be false or pernicious. . . . *It is not a thought at all*. It cannot even be formulated."[60] He understood that part of the attraction of racist ideas lay in their very stupidity in the sense that they attempt to fix thought, to bring it to a standstill and give it the solidity of a stone, whereas there is nothing static about the various ways in which racism happens. But, more importantly, he highlighted how ideas of race that were often presented as a justification of racism, like those that appeared in the middle of the nineteenth century, arose only after the system was in place. They were not the cause of the system, although they might have helped to direct its development. They were a consequence, which is a point Fanon had already made.[61]

What the Word *Racism* Conceals

In judging what is racist and what is not, White people in particular, for the most part lacking the experience of being the target of racism, rely heavily on their intuitions as they are set by the genealogy of the word, a part of which I have set out here. The word *racism*, like the word *sexism*, which was modeled on it,[62] succeeded in focusing attention on certain beliefs, attitudes, and behaviors, but at the same time it drew attention away from the conditions that helped to sustain those beliefs, attitudes, and behaviors. We can speculate as to why efforts to revise the concept have not taken hold as successfully as one might have anticipated. In addition to the vested interests that are threatened by it, one must give some weight to the dominance of liberal individualism and the fact that the dominant forms of reasoning in operation today

232   CRITICAL PHILOSOPHY OF RACE

are heavily analytical, able to break things apart but blind to the big picture, which is why, against this tendency, many African and African American theorists from C. L. R. James to Fanon and Biko, embraced dialectical reason.

Through its lack of a serious account of racism as a material system, the UNESCO strategy has been complicit with maintaining the status quo, notwithstanding its success in changing the way people think about the scientific standing of race as a concept. But the greater problem lay in its promotion of an analysis of racism that isolates it from the society that sustains and produces it. By reducing racism to something definable, as if it were a dead thought, a sitting target that could easily be held in one's sights, the campaign against racism itself became something clunky, trotted out on every occasion but with any effectiveness it might once have had now a thing of the past. One might ask the extent to which the formulae in which these legitimations were expressed when they were taken up by the general population actually did much more than serve as a bond among those with a shared interest in perpetuating the system. Racist expressions, whether in the form of slurs and name-calling or more elaborate rationales, serve to let the hearer know they are among people who identify as being against a certain group, like a secret handshake. It is in this sense that racism is not a thought and that racist speech is best understood as a symptom of a materialist social fact.

Beyond the argument that a wholesale rejection of the term *race* deprives the opponents of anti-Black racism of the means to highlight racism, there is the issue of what the term *racism* itself conceals. So long as racism is narrowly construed, it diverts attention from the deeply embedded societal racism that sustains White privilege as a product of White supremacy and that is in evidence in national and global rates of, for example, poverty, unemployment, incarceration, and infant mortality. If one takes into account the ways in which resistance on the part of many Whites to the idea of institutional racism has its source in the notion of racism itself, it seems that we have inherited this term, *racism*, that still successfully accommodates systemic racism. To that extent my argument mirrors, although it is significantly broader in its application, that of Stephen Steinberg, who has argued that the rhetorical function of the term "race relations" was to "normalize and naturalize racial oppression, to pretend that it is consensual, and to conceal its violent underpinnings and periodic atrocities."[63]

The early Boasian campaigns against racism in the United States, such as that found in *Science Condemns Racism*, began the tendency to rely on an ideology of individualism in the conviction that if one focused on the individual, then one would somehow bypass racism.[64] But this same ideology also served White American racists by rendering institutional racism less apparent to them, thereby concealing from them the structural dimensions of White privilege. The idea that one overcomes racism by seeing the individual and not their race was matched by the idea that racists, too, should be seen as individuals and in that way divorced from the historical conditions that produced the inequalities at issue, as when the inheritors of the benefits produced by slavery and colonialism try to deny any link with those systems. The focus on individualism gave the racists themselves a basis on which they could cast themselves as the victims. They are even more ideological than the racists who were simply misinformed by false ideas, rather than morally corrupt.

When I wrote at the beginning of this chapter that *racism* is one of the most powerful words in the English language, I was not thinking of its power to condemn others on the basis of a presumed general consensus against racism. Still less was I thinking of the power of the phrase "I am not a racist but . . . ," however hackneyed it has now become and however revealing it is of the Boasian approach that placed racism in the mind of the racist. I was thinking rather of the fact that to condemn someone else's racism is a way of saying that I am not myself a racist. One denies racism in oneself by denouncing it in others, giving the word *racism* the force that at one time belonged to the word *race*. *Race* once had the power to condemn the other unreservedly as a matter of destiny. Now the word *racist* can be used by White people to exonerate themselves: because I condemn racism, I am no longer complicit with it. Even though one of the first occurrences of the term *raciste* in French was in the phrase "I myself am also a racist," in English, since the introduction of the word, it has almost always been the other who is the racist: Nazis, Afrikaners, poor Whites, and so on. That belonged to the logic of the word in 1940, when its function was to isolate features of Nazi racial ideology that the people using the term did not recognize in themselves. Indeed, it did not matter at that time to the people using it that the word did not accurately record the core ideology of National Socialism, still less the actions, of the Nazis, which is why they made very little effort to show that it did. What mattered was that it was a term around which one could rally in opposition. This is still true today in its own way. The word *racism* has been cathartic for White people. It is the word through which people of European descent could say what they are not. Its power was the power to disown and so to purify the past. Histories of racism, by focusing on extreme cases, allow

234   CRITICAL PHILOSOPHY OF RACE

it to be seen as an anomaly. It is in this way the word *racism* frequently serves to perpetuate what it purports to denounce.

In conclusion, the basic outlines of the concept of racism were set some eighty years ago in very different circumstances with very different issues in mind, and I have given some reasons why the efforts to revise it, largely by authors of African descent, have not taken hold. I have not argued that we should abandon the word *racism*. To do so would be to mimic the process by which the Boasians sought to outlaw the word *race*, and their failure should serve as a cautionary note. If the Boasian strategy had been the appropriate one, the rejection of the term *race* would itself have contributed to the fight against racism, but we are all now familiar with the counterargument that only so long as society persists with using racial terms in its self-examination can structural racism be tracked. Jacques Barzun argued already in 1940 that there was a complicity between the words *race* and *racism*: he understood that the introduction of the word *racism* gave a new lease on life to the word *race*.[65] The UNESCO strategy failed because of the lack of an adequate diagnosis of the character of racism, and one should equally be cautious about proposals to abandon the word *racism* for some other word without an adequate study of the problem, a study which if Fanon and Sartre are our guides, would seem to be predicated on a transformation of our forms of reasoning. The problem is not a problem of language but of the modes of thinking that conceal the material system; and, until we learn to think otherwise, changing the words will not change the way the world appears to us. But in the meanwhile we have every reason to be suspicious of the term *racism* and what it conceals.

14

Making Nietzsche's Thought Groan

The History of Racisms and Foucault's Genealogy of Nietzschean Genealogy in *"Society Must Be Defended"*

Praising Racism?

On January 28, 1976, Foucault began the fourth lecture of the course subsequently published as *"Society Must Be Defended"* in a strange way. He said: "You might have thought, last time, that I was trying to both trace the history of racist discourse and praise it."[1] It is strange, first, because the lecture of the previous week does not read like a praise of racism, although later during that same January 28 lecture he said, "Racism was a revolutionary discourse," which might indeed look like a praise of racism.[2] It is strange, second, because Foucault did not say to his students that some of them had thought this and brought it to his attention. This is what he did say the following week when referencing some oral and written questions that had been addressed directly to him, but here, instead of saying what some students had told him, he speculated about what some *might* have thought.[3] It was as if he was trying to put the idea into their heads. This leads to the question of why he might have wanted to raise the specter of racism about his own lecture. To say, "You might have thought, last time, that I was trying to both trace the history of racist discourse and praise it," even if only to disavow it, comes a little too close to the formulation "I am not a racist but . . ." Why did he introduce the idea if there were not something to it? In any case, once entertained it is a difficult idea to forget.

As one reads further into Foucault's attempt to deny the charge of racism that he himself introduced, things become curious. He continued: "And you would not have been entirely wrong, except in one respect. It was not exactly racist discourse whose history I was tracing and that I was praising: it was the discourse of race war or race struggle." Instead of taking the option of saying he was only tracing a history, he admitted that he was praising this history. He relied instead on a somewhat tenuous distinction between racist

---

Critical Philosophy of Race. Robert Bernasconi, Oxford University Press. © Oxford University Press 2023.
DOI: 10.1093/oso/9780197587966.003.0015

236   CRITICAL PHILOSOPHY OF RACE

discourse and a discourse of race war or race struggle. What stops the discourse of race war from being racist? The answer he gave to this question was in terms of historical periodization: "I think we should reserve the expression 'racism' or 'racist discourse' for something that was basically no more than a particular and localized episode in the great discourse of race war or race struggle. Racist discourse was really no more than an episode, a phase, the reversal, or at least the reworking, at the end of the nineteenth century, of the discourse of race war."[4] But does this strategy work?

There is certainly a difference between the old discourse of a race war that arose in the seventeenth and eighteenth century and the kind of racist discourse that was associated with what Foucault later in the lecture course would call "biopolitics" and which already in the fourth lecture he called "State racism."[5] This "biological and centralized racism" emerged only in the second half of the nineteenth century with the introduction of biopower, which modified it. Foucault was not alone in trying to restrict the term "racism" to this period even if his characterization of the racism was different from what one finds in Hannah Arendt and Ruth Benedict, who similarly sought to restrict racism to the same limited historical period.[6] It is a strategy for which commentators have criticized Foucault because it leads, for example, to the counterintuitive claim that racialized slavery and the discourse used to justify it in the seventeenth and eighteenth centuries was not, strictly speaking, racist.[7] And yet before the end of the lecture course he had withdrawn the claim. With reference to the advent of biopower in the nineteenth century, he concluded: "I am certainly not saying that racism was invented at this time. It had already been in existence for a very long time."[8] He distinguished the new "racism of the evolutionist kind, biological racism" from "the ordinary racism that takes the form of mutual contempt or hatred between races," which he also called "ethnic racism" both here and elsewhere.[9] This pluralization of racisms opened the door to the accusation that he had illegitimately used an unduly narrow definition of racism to deflect the objection that he had praised racism, and would seem to amount to an admission that his defense against the gratuitous objection he himself had introduced in the fourth lecture had to be abandoned, leaving one less clear than ever why it was introduced in the first place. Indeed, he was already aware of the problem at the beginning of the fifth lecture when some students raised the question of why he appeared to be ignoring religious racism in the Middle Ages, especially religious anti-Semitism, even if his answer at that point was evasive.[10]

At the end of this paper I will offer an explanation for the opening sentences of the January 28 lecture, according to which he already knew from the outset that the defense he introduced, borrowed as it were from elsewhere, and then withdrawn, was as specious as the initial offense. I will suggest that the reason he decided to play these elaborate mind games with his auditors on such a serious topic was an attempt to get them to question the way in which it was possible for racism to be normalized in philosophical discourse. To make that case, I must first investigate the way in which Foucault developed the theme of racism throughout the lecture course.

At first sight, racism is only a peripheral theme of *"Society Must Be Defended."* Indeed, in the course summary that Foucault subsequently published, race is referenced only once.[11] The topic of racism slips in and out of focus during the lecture course as if Foucault was uncertain about whether he wanted to go where his thought was leading him. At the end of the first lecture Foucault presented his plan to examine Nietzsche's claim that war is a historical principle behind the workings of power in the context of "the race problem" because it was in terms of racial binaries that the West was led for the first time to analyze political power as war.[12] This was confirmed in the third lecture when he said that he would trace "the full development of a biologic-social racism," but by the fifth lecture he seemed to draw back from this plan: he insisted that he was not concerned with racism as such but with the emergence in the West of a critical, historical, political analysis of the state, with its institutions and power mechanisms, where the war between the two groups is waged in apparently peaceful ways.[13] Nevertheless, on March 17, 1976, in the final lecture of the course, he did return to the topic of racism and confirmed there that it was a central topic of the lecture course when he said that he was trying to "get back to the problem I was trying to raise."[14]

Furthermore, in order to make sense of Foucault's strategies in *"Society Must Be Defended,"* I will show that the lecture course is an extended and rigorous confrontation with the portrait of Nietzsche he had drawn in "Nietzsche, Genealogy, History," his 1971 contribution to a Festschrift for Jean Hyppolite, which is still often cited as if it were his definitive statement on the topic of Nietzsche's genealogical account of history.[15] The case that Nietzsche is very much at stake in *"Society Must Be Defended"* is at first sight tenuous, given that he is named in only two of the lectures, where one of them is a passing and seemingly inconsequential reference to him in connection with Boullainvillier's portrait of the barbarian.[16] The other reference

238   CRITICAL PHILOSOPHY OF RACE

has already been mentioned. It was his announcement in the first lecture of *"Society Must Be Defended"* that he was about to undertake a genealogical examination of what he called "Nietzsche's hypothesis," which is the claim that "the basis of the power relation lies in a warlike clash between forces."[17] He was clear that this hypothesis, like Wilhelm Reich's repression hypothesis, had guided his own work for some years, but whereas the latter hypothesis was one from which he had already distanced himself, he believed it was now time to interrogate Nietzsche's hypothesis. He had in fact relied on it as recently as the previous year: *Discipline and Punish* ends with Foucault inviting his readers to hear in "the effect and instrument of complex power relations, bodies and forces subjected by multiple mechanisms of 'incarceration,'" what he called "the distant roar of battle."[18] Whereas numerous commentators readily acknowledge the shift in Foucault's thinking that was taking place at this time, they largely seem to neglect what it meant for his relation to Nietzsche, still less how a transformation in his understanding of Nietzsche might have helped to motivate this shift. Nevertheless, in June 1975, a mere six months before he began the lectures that would become the book *"Society Must Be Defended,"* Foucault openly declared a change in his relation to Nietzsche. In the context of the remark that if he wanted to be pretentious he would call his current work a "genealogy of morals," he explained that he no longer talked about Nietzsche as he once did. "The only valid tribute to thought such as Nietzsche's is precisely to use it, to deform it, to make it groan and protest. And if commentators then say that I am being faithful or unfaithful to Nietzsche, that is of absolutely no interest."[19]

The fact that Foucault presented *"Society Must Be Defended"* as a genealogy already suggests another way in which his relation to Nietzsche might be at stake there. To be sure, Foucault's relation to the idea of genealogy was never simple. In the 1968 meeting organized by the Cercle d'épistémologie de l'École normale supérieure specifically on the Genealogy of the Sciences, Foucault did not even mention the word *genealogy* but insisted on talking about archaeology, which was his preferred term for what he was doing in much of his early work.[20] When he did introduce the term *genealogy* to describe his own work, it was always introduced as an addition to archaeology, a supplement to it.[21] In his lecture course of 1972–1973, he wrote: "After an archaeological type of analysis, it is a matter of undertaking a dynastic, genealogical type of analysis, focusing on filiations on the basis of power relations."[22] There is a similar formulation in *"Society Must Be Defended"*: "Archaeology is the method specific to the analysis of local discursivities, and genealogy is the tactic which, once it has described these local discursivities, brings into play the desubjugated knowledges that have been released from them."[23] Foucault was still drawing a distinction between archaeology and genealogy in 1978 when he announced that archaeology is the analysis of a theoretical field by trying to discover its guiding principles, the rules of the formation of concepts, and its theoretical elements, whereas genealogy concerns technologies of power.[24] However, in the same year in an interview he came close to reappropriating some of his earlier works, written before his adoption of the word *genealogy* for that style of his thinking: "In writing *Madness and Civilization* and *The Birth of the Clinic* I meant to do a genealogical history of knowledge. But the real guiding thread was this problem of power."[25] And indeed in 1967, referring to *The Order of Things*, Foucault explained in an interview: "If I had to begin again this book that I finished two years ago, I would try not to give Nietzsche this ambiguous status, absolutely privileged and metahistorical, that I gave him out of weakness. It is due to the fact no doubt my archeology owes more to the Nietzschean genealogy than to structuralism properly called."[26]

How much does Foucauldian genealogy owe to Nietzschean genealogy? The question of the genealogy of Foucauldian genealogy seems to invite the answer given to it by Michael Mahon that it is Nietzschean, but such a claim would be both un-Nietzschean and un-Foucauldian.[27] As Foucault explained in *The Archaeology of Knowledge*, one must not reduce Nietzsche's genealogy to a search for origins.[28] This means that one cannot answer the question of the genealogy of genealogy with a proper name. It would amount to giving what Foucault called a "false paternity."[29] Furthermore, genealogies should be multiple.[30] I support John Marks's thesis that Foucault constructed a genealogy of his own genealogical perspective in *"Society Must Be Defended,"* and especially his observation that Foucault went out of his way to present Boulainvilliers as a precursor of Nietzsche, but I will attempt in the remainder of this essay to show that much more is happening in *"Society Must Be Defended"* in terms of Foucault's relation to Nietzsche.[31] Indeed, I read these lectures as a sustained genealogical critique of his own earlier essay on Nietzsche's genealogy, as well as a profound, albeit largely concealed, meditation on the role of race in Nietzsche's philosophy.

240 CRITICAL PHILOSOPHY OF RACE

Foucault, Genealogy, History

In the third section of this chapter, I will show that Foucault organized his presentation of the historical figures discussed in the central lectures of *"Society Must Be Defended"* according to a schema that derives from Nietzsche's 1874 essay "On the Uses and Disadvantages of History for Life." In order to prepare for my demonstration of that claim, I will in the present section offer a brief reading of "Nietzsche, Genealogy, History." In the fourth and final section, I will explore the way in which in *"Society Must Be Defended"* Foucault presented a genealogy of racisms in such a way as to locate Nietzsche implicitly within that genealogy, thereby offering a new perspective on Nietzsche that is Foucauldian in inspiration but only implied by him and not presented thematically.

Even though in 1971 Foucault had not yet with any consistency adopted the word *genealogy* to describe his own work, there is not the slightest doubt that from the very beginning of the essay he wrote it with a view to his own work and as an attack on his contemporaries rather than as an attempt to describe accurately what Nietzsche understood by genealogy. The opening sentence—"Genealogy is gray, meticulous, and patiently documentary"[32]—taken as a whole, better describes Foucault's way of working than Nietzsche's.[33] Furthermore, Foucault in this essay relies on a distinction between *Ursprung* and *Herkunft* which, if it is Nietzschean at all, is certainly not employed by him with any consistency. The most important part of "Nietzsche, Genealogy, History" for the purpose of understanding *"Society Must Be Defended"* is the last section where Foucault highlighted the way that the distinction between monumental, antiquarian, and critical history, which Nietzsche's introduced in his 1874 essay "On the Uses and Disadvantages of History for Life," could be understood as transformed in Nietzsche's subsequent genealogical writings. According to Nietzsche, the function of monumental history is to teach that "the greatness that once existed" might again be possible, albeit in responding to this demand it sparks off the most terrible struggle.[34] The aim of the antiquarian historian is "to preserve for those who will emerge after him the conditions under which he himself has come into existence." It gives a sense of identity allowing the transitory individual existence to feel part of "the spirit of his house, his lineage, and his city."[35] Finally, critical history has the task of bringing the past before a tribunal and being prepared to condemn it.[36] Nietzsche's point was that all three modalities of history needed to be "in the service of life," but that they tended to be used to inhibit it.[37] Monumental history enables the dead to bury the living; antiquarian history mummifies life; and critical history needs to learn that it is not always possible to free oneself of the aberrations and errors of the past.[38] To live and to be unjust are the same. "At best we arrive at an antagonism between our inherited, ancestral nature and our knowledge, or perhaps even at the struggle of a new, stricter discipline against what was long ago inborn and inbred. We cultivate a new habit, a new instinct, a second nature, so that the first nature withers away."[39]

In "Nietzsche, Genealogy, History," Foucault took these three modalities of history and showed how Nietzsche's approach to them became transformed in his subsequent writings. Monumental history became parody directed against reality; antiquarian history became a systematic dissociation of identity; and, most radically, critical history, based on the insight that all knowledge rests upon injustice, pursued "the destruction of the man who maintains knowledge [*connaissance*] by the injustice proper to the will to knowledge [*savoir*]."[40]

However, there is another aspect of "Nietzsche, Genealogy, History" that needs to be considered in this context and it is one that, so far as I know, has received little attention, if any. It is the fact that Nietzsche's ideas about race play a prominent role in Foucault's 1971 essay, but without their receiving any critical attention from him. For example, having identified *Herkunft* ("provenance" or "descent") and *Entstehung* ("emergence") as the two key components of genealogy, the two concepts that displace the ordinary notion of *Ursprung*, or origin, Foucault drew on Nietzsche's accounts of race to illustrate and further determine these notions. Indeed, Foucault expressly acknowledged that "the analysis of *Herkunft* often involves a consideration of race or social type."[41] To support this connection of *Herkunft* with race, Foucault first referenced a passage from Nietzsche's *Gay Science* about the Jews and the "Jewification" that took place through Christianity.[42] The other citations are to *Beyond Good and Evil* sections 202, 242, and 246, and to the fifth paragraph of the first treatise of *On the Genealogy of Morals*, and their dominant focus is on race mixing and therefore on the multiplicity of origins.[43] This suggests that the function of these references is to prepare for his observation that, when the Germans (or any other racialized group) sought to account for their complexity by positing a dual origin that produced a double soul, they were reductively domesticating a multiplicity that challenged any idea of coherent identity.[44] That is to say, it was in the context of his examination of descent that, according to Foucault at least,

242 CRITICAL PHILOSOPHY OF RACE

Nietzsche developed his insight into the "dissociation of the Me"[45] that was fundamental to his portrayal of Nietzsche's contribution. Furthermore, when Foucault turned to the discussion of emergence (*Entstehung*), he referenced one of Nietzsche's most powerful discussions of breeding.[46] To be sure, the points that Foucault was making do not in any strict sense rely on the racial references, but that makes it all the more striking that, unlike his French contemporaries, he drew attention to the racial dimension of Nietzsche's work, albeit without the kind of critical commentary that seems to be called for. Whatever his motivation for doing so at the time, it set up the discussion of racism in *"Society Must Be Defended."*

Boulainvilliers and Nietzsche

Foucault wrote during a period when it was rare for canonical philosophers to be criticized for their racism. After the Second World War, there was a brief moment when even some mainstream philosophers, such as Hannah Arendt and Karl Popper, could be found at least raising the question of the extent to which the tradition of Western philosophy had contributed to the thinking that led to the Holocaust. But until recently—by a combination of diminishing the importance of philosophy by withdrawing it from the world and by treating as exceptions some of the thinkers who offended most egregiously, such as Fichte and Heidegger—the question of Western philosophy's broader complicity with racism, colonialism, and genocide remained the preserve of a few who were themselves on the margins, such as Aimé Cesaire and Frantz Fanon.[47] I am arguing here that in *"Society Must Be Defended"* Foucault, albeit only implicitly, entertained the question of Nietzsche's complicity, a complicity that could then be extended to those of his readers who approach him without sensitivity to these issues.

Foucault's genealogical investigation of the historico-political discourses on society, which promoted the idea of the power relation as a warlike clash between forces, was conducted under the assumption that among the merits of this idea was its capacity to provide "a concrete analysis of the multiplicity of power relations."[48] Unlike the philosophico-juridical discourse of thinkers like Hobbes and Rousseau, these historico-political discourses were less interested in passing judgments than in rediscovering beneath the forms of justice "the blood that has dried in the codes."[49] This formulation was clearly intended by Foucault to invoke not only Nietzsche's genealogy but also his own genealogy in *Discipline and Punish* that would have been familiar to most of his auditors. Foucault's genealogy of Nietzsche's hypothesis took the form of tracing the historico-political discourses that entertained this idea back to some of its earliest antecedents, focusing primarily, but by no means exclusively, on the work of Henri de Boulainvilliers. However, the role of Nietzsche in Foucault's account was by no means limited to an evocation of Nietzsche's critical questioning of the law. I will show here that when Foucault presented the ritualistic histories to which these historico-political discourses responded as counterhistories, it was in terms of the three modalities of history that Nietzsche had deployed early in his essay "On the Uses and Disadvantages of History for Life." Once one becomes aware that the genealogy of the Nietzschean hypothesis was investigated by Foucault in terms derived from Nietzsche himself, the degree to which *"Society Must Be Defended"* is a sustained reexamination of his own earlier study of Nietzsche becomes apparent.

What Foucault called "ritualistic history" dominated from the time of the Roman annalists all the way to the later Middle Ages. Its overall function was to serve as "an intensifier of power" by establishing "a juridical link" between the sovereigns of the present and "the mighty sovereigns" of the past.[50] Foucault called the first axis along which it performed this function the "genealogical" axis.[51] Its task was to demonstrate the uninterrupted nature of the right of the sovereign as the source of its ineradicable force on the grounds that "the greatness of the events or men of the past could guarantee the value of the present, and transform its pettiness and mundanity into something equally heroic and equally legitimate."[52] It thus corresponded directly to what Nietzsche called monumental history, which teaches that "the greatness that once existed . . . will probably be possible once again."[53] In his exposition this was followed, second, by the memorialization axis. Making the deeds of the sovereign memorable renders them permanent, thereby showing that what sovereigns do is never pointless, futile, or petty. Memorializing history corresponds to Nietzsche's antiquarian history, which had the function of preserving and revering. Foucault left the third axis of the historical discourse of the later Middle Ages unnamed but, given that its function was to put examples into circulation so as to make it possible to judge the present, it clearly corresponded to what Nietzsche called critical history.[54]

In the next few meetings of the 1976 lecture course Foucault identified how, beginning in late sixteenth-century England, the historico-political discourses that developed the account of power in terms of war could be

244 CRITICAL PHILOSOPHY OF RACE

seen as variations on ritualistic history according to this same grid with its three axes. Whereas the genealogical axis operated within ritualistic history to establish continuities that gave luster to the inheritors of power, these counterhistories recorded the emergence of the nation that would eventually replace the monarch as the subject of history and generate ideas of peoples, races, and classes.[55] There was no appeal to continuity on the part of those who do not have behind them "the great and glorious genealogy in which the law and power flaunt themselves."[56] As a result, "Europe becomes populated by memories and ancestors whose genealogy it had never before written."[57] Second, in place of the attempt to enhance the luster of power and the law through the memorialization axis of ritualistic history, the new counterhistories sought to decipher how the laws were "born of the contingency and injustice of battles."[58] And, third, the critical function of judging the present from the past was replaced by a discourse that attacked the jurisprudence of a power that retained rights across history by demanding rights that had not been recognized.[59] As a potent example of how the sovereign, no longer binding the people into a unity through their implicit identification with the monarch, divided them by enslaving them through the abusive power of the law, Foucault referenced John Warr, who in 1669 wrote in his *The Corruption and Deficiency of the Laws of England Soberly Discovered*: "many times the very law is the badge of our oppression, its proper intent being to enslave the people."[60] In sum, where ritualistic history emphasized a continuity that glorifies and leads to reverence, this counterhistory introduced invention on behalf of those who have no glory.[61]

Although Foucault repeatedly insisted that Boulainvilliers was not an isolated figure, insofar as much of what he had to say could also be found in other authors, he is unquestionably the central figure in Foucault's presentation. This is reflected in the way that the grid of intelligibility supplied by Nietzsche and exemplified in ritualistic history determined the schematic way Foucault introduced him. Whereas ritualistic history sought to demonstrate the uninterrupted nature of the right of the sovereign, the introduction in Boulainvilliers of the nobility as a new, hitherto unknown, subject of history breaks the genealogical axis.[62] The memorialization axis of ritualistic history came to be seen as a mystification of history. A new tracing of the sources of historical knowledge and memory restored to the nobility a memory it had lost and a knowledge it had always neglected.[63] Finally, the critical axis was replaced by a discourse that shattered the praise heaped on Rome in the preexisting discourse.[64] Criticism directed against the present from the point of view of the past was replaced by a criticism of the past from the present.

Foucault's schematic portrait of Boulainvilliers in terms derived from Nietzsche's essay on history operates on the surface of the lecture course and locates within a genealogy the claim that Boulainvilliers defined the principle of "the relational character of power."[65] By identifying a generalized war that permeated the whole social body, Boulainvilliers made it possible to determine the force relationship that underpinned the relation to right.[66] Indeed, in what seems to have been an unguarded moment, given genealogy's suspicion of the notion of origin, Foucault located in Boulainvilliers "the origin of the idea that war is basically historical discourse's truth matrix."[67] As Boulainvilliers expressed it on the very first page of his *Essais sur la noblesse de France*, "Violence had introduced the distinctions between liberty and slavery and between nobility and commonality, but although this origin is vicious, the usage has been established in the world for so long that it has acquired the force of a natural law."[68] Foucault could have called the hypothesis he attributed to Nietzsche "Boulainvilliers's hypothesis." It was in the context of Boulainvilliers's account of the barbarian that Foucault introduced the reference to Nietzsche's discussion of the blond beast.[69] When Foucault presented Boulainvilliers as arguing that the nobles did not know themselves, he was offering a description that could easily be tied to Nietzsche's claim that Europeans did not know themselves.[70] When Foucault attributed to Boulainvilliers the idea of a battle being fought not with weapons but with knowledge, we cannot help but be reminded of the discussion of knowledge at the end of "Nietzsche, Genealogy, History."[71] Finally, when Foucault attributed to Boulainvilliers the claim "the first criterion that defines freedom is the ability to deprive others of their freedom," this can be read as an anticipation of Nietzsche's claim, cited by Foucault himself in "Nietzsche, Genealogy, History," that "class domination generates the idea of liberty."[72] According to Foucault, this insight that liberty as "an invention of the ruling classes" need not be seen as "fundamental to man's nature or at the root of his attachment to being and truth" was a product of genealogical analysis.[73] We should not be surprised therefore to find that in 1976 Foucault described Boulainvilliers as giving "a sort of genealogy of the struggles that go in all the various conflicts recorded by history."[74] It was a genealogy more in the vein of Nietzsche than of ritualistic history. But to the question of why in *"Society Must Be Defended"* so much effort went into making Boulainvilliers sound like Nietzsche, we must answer that it was not only to show that many of the

246   CRITICAL PHILOSOPHY OF RACE

claims to originality often attributed to Nietzsche can be challenged but also to allow Foucault to take some distance from his presentation of Nietzschean genealogy of five years earlier.[75] It was an exhibition of the self-reflexivity characteristic of his genealogical approach.[76]

However, before exploring the implications of this gesture, it is necessary to continue the trajectory of the lectures. More specifically, it is necessary to show that Foucault persisted with his application of Nietzsche's schema of three modalities of history when he passed from the discussion of Boulainvilliers onto an examination of the historic-political discourses of the nineteenth century, most notably, that of Augustin Thierry.[77] The genealogical axis of ritualistic history, as Foucault had described it earlier, whereby "the greatness of the events or men of the past could guarantee the value of the present," is reversed as the present is now seen as the moment of greatest intensity.[78] Whereas at the time of Boulainvilliers the present is "the moment of a profound forgetfulness," with Augustin Thierry there is an inversion of the value of the present: one "begins with the present . . . to reveal the elements and processes of the past."[79]

The late nineteenth century saw further innovations and it was in this context that Foucault introduced into his lexicon—and ours—the terms "biopower" and "biopolitics." To investigate the transformation that these terms describe, it is necessary, as Foucault himself found, to place the issue of racism front and center, which is why it is so prominent in the final lecture of the course.

From a Historico-Political Concept of Race to Biopolitics

There is a strange drama at the end of *"Society Must Be Defended"* about whether or not the hypothesis that understood war as a permanent social relationship had come to an end in the nineteenth century. Early in the lecture course Foucault had announced that it survived into the late nineteenth century when it was adopted by "racist biologists and eugenicists."[80] However, as the lecture course developed, it increasingly seemed that Foucault was moving closer to the claim that Nietzsche's hypothesis had lost its usefulness and indeed was already on the way out by Nietzsche's time. That seemed to be suggested when at the beginning of the penultimate lecture of the course Foucault announced that the element of war was "from the revolution onward gradually, if not eliminated from the discourse of history, at least reduced, restricted, colonized, settled, scattered, civilized if you like, and up to a point pacified."[81] The penultimate lecture ended with a similar message: in the context of his reading of Augustin Thierry, Foucault announced that war's function as "an analyzer of historical processes" had been strictly curtailed. He wrote: "War is now no more than an ephemeral and instrumental aspect of confrontations which are not of a warlike nature."[82] He summarized this train of thought at the beginning of the final lecture of the course as follows: "the very notion of war was eventually eliminated from historical analysis by the principle of national universality."[83] What survived, Foucault announced, was the theme of race.

This means that only in the final lecture did it emerge with full clarity that Foucault's focus on Boulainvilliers and Augustin Thierry as the central figures in his genealogy of Nietzsche's hypothesis was largely to highlight the role of race in the historico-political discourse, which it effectively did insofar as a French audience would have been well aware that both men helped to shape the ethnic concept of race.[84]

But, on Foucault's account, it was not *their* historical concept of race that was operative in the late nineteenth century into the twentieth century, but what he called the biological concept of race. That is one measure of the transformation that took place at that time. With it came a new racism, state racism, but, and this is decisive for an understanding of the status of Nietzsche's hypothesis, at the end of the nineteenth century this new racism was "modeled on war."[85] Biopower wages war as Foucault indicated when he wrote that "a biopower that wished to wage war had to articulate the will to destroy the adversary with the risk that it might kill those whose lives it had, by definition, to protect, manage, and multiply."[86] Almost casually Foucault returned to the original claim that what he had called Nietzsche's hypothesis persisted in the discourse of unnamed racial biologists and eugenicists of the late nineteenth century. The crucial question thus becomes: Where, on Foucault's account, did Nietzsche himself stand in relation to these contemporaneous discourses that embodied what from the beginning of the course he had called "Nietzsche's hypothesis"?

The best way to answer this question is to return to "Nietzsche, Genealogy, History" and in particular its concluding section, where Foucault offered his account of how Nietzsche himself transformed the three modalities of history that he had listed in "On the Uses and Disadvantages of History for Life." On Foucault's reconstruction of Nietzsche, monumental history became a parody offering the European who "no longer knows himself or what name

248 CRITICAL PHILOSOPHY OF RACE

he should adopt, the possibility of alternative identities."[87] In place of antiquarian history with its focus on identity, Foucault attributed to Nietzsche a history committed to dissipation and dissociation.[88] Finally, in place of critical history, Foucault posited the sacrificial, directed against truth. On the one hand, these transformations constitute precisely what is most radical in Nietzsche and what indeed contributes to setting him apart. On the other hand, the fact that, as Foucault emphasized, all this was accomplished in the name of life seems to attach Nietzsche to biopolitics, and this made him a representative of what was most characteristic of the period and most demanding of critical inquiry.

Seen through the grid of intelligibility associated with the counterhistories of Boulainvilliers and Augustin Thierry, there are clear signs of a continuity across the discontinuity that separates them from Nietzsche and, as Foucault himself noted, the discourse on race struggle has "a great aptitude for metamorphosis."[89] I have already highlighted the connection Foucault built between Boulainvilliers and Nietzsche on the question of the alternative identities that arise from a certain not-knowing, but one striking difference is the way in which Foucault presented a certain dissociation of identity that took place in Thierry in the form of a simple doubling: the nation, which had become the subject of history, was a "national duality" in the sense of a "racial duality."[90] This might seem to bring Thierry and Nietzsche even closer together in their joint celebration of certain forms of race mixing, until we recall Foucault's observation that accounting for complexity simply by positing a dual origin is insufficient to challenge the idea of a coherent identity.[91] To be sure, the specific racial references Foucault cited in "Nietzsche, Genealogy, History" mean that Nietzsche did not himself always meet this criterion, but this serves to emphasize the degree to which, from the perspective of "Society Must Be Defended," Nietzsche is a transitional figure.[92]

Some of the same terms that Foucault in "Nietzsche, Genealogy, History" had highlighted as characteristic of Nietzsche were said in "Society Must Be Defended" to belong to the framework that was surpassed by biopolitics. For example, in 1971 Foucault highlighted the central role of the body in Nietzsche as the surface of the inscription of events, as the focus of the dissociation of the one, and as a volume in perpetual disintegration.[93] By contrast, according to "Society Must Be Defended," with the advent of biopolitics the body is displaced by the idea of population, and the technologies of discipline, formerly directed to the body, are now addressed to man as a species, which is also under the sway of technologies of regulation.[94] In this way in

MAKING NIETZSCHE'S THOUGHT GROAN   249

the process of restoring Nietzsche's hypothesis to its context, Foucault deprived it of some of its originality. Aspects of Nietzschean genealogy that had seemed radical or transgressive in 1971 also came to appear less novel when viewed not from the philosophico-juridical discourse that was and is still largely dominant in philosophy, but from the perspective of the historico-political discourse into which Foucault implicitly placed it. But what makes Nietzsche a transitional figure within the genealogy into which Foucault placed him was also what remains most problematic for any celebration of his work: his promotion of a racialized biopolitics. Nietzsche's refusal of the new forms of anti-Semitism that were emerging in his time must be noted, but his discussions of race in general departed from mainstream views largely in the context of his early exaggerated emphasis on what Francis Galton would call "eugenics."[95] And this is precisely where Nietzsche's discourse passed from the historico-political discourse of the early nineteenth century into biopolitics. It began to do so in effect at the point when in 1874 Nietzsche scrutinized the three modalities of history in terms of their use for life, even if what that meant became clear only when, under the name *Züchtung*, he showed a commitment to racialized breeding and he combined it with a celebration of certain forms of human extinction, thereby showing how easily the theme of evolutionism could turn into a justification for eugenics and genocide.[96]

The culmination of *"Society Must Be Defended"* is not the demonstration that biopower was at work both in Nazi Germany and Stalinist Russia, but Foucault's observation about socialism's lack of a "critique of the theme of biopower."[97] Insofar as genealogy was introduced early in the lecture course in terms of the use of an historical knowledge in contemporary tactics, then this lack, as a question posed to his contemporaries, lies at the heart of what he had to say.[98] It came to the fore when he denounced as racist those forms of socialism that "stress the problem of the struggle."[99] The question Foucault posed about his own racism early in the course must be seen in this light. In the 1971 essay, he had referred, without offering any criticism, to some of the texts in which Nietzsche had demonstrated a clear racism. To the extent that Foucault knew from the outset where his tracing of the discourse of a certain form of racism would lead him in *"Society Must Be Defended,"* he must have suspected that some of his more perspicuous students would have been able to see its implications for his 1971 essay and his subsequent deployment of Nietzsche's hypothesis. That is to say, Foucault had perhaps come to ask himself whether praising Nietzsche amounted to praising racism. Hence he

250   CRITICAL PHILOSOPHY OF RACE

raised the question of racism in order to encourage his audience to think how easily *in the absence of critique* a discourse, and especially a philosophical discourse, finds itself complicit with racism simply because racism in one or other of its forms permeates the discourse of the Western philosophical tradition. Because self-reflexivity is characteristic of Foucauldian genealogy, he could not have raised the question of Nietzsche's biopolitical racism and socialism's lack of a critique of a racialized biopower without entertaining the possibility of his own racism and encouraging his auditors to reflect on that possibility. That is why he began the lecture of January 28 as he did. To be sure, Foucault remained loyal to Nietzsche. In the so-called final interview in which he revealed himself to be a closet Heideggerian, he also said "I am simply a Nietzschean."[100] It represents a strange epitaph for someone who had earlier said that he would make Nietzsche's thought groan and protest without caring whether or not in the process of doing so he was being faithful to Nietzsche, but that perhaps makes it all the more important to cherish that moment when Foucault in a moment of self-reflexivity invited those who were listening to raise the question of how easy it is to pass from tracing a history to praising it. It is something we must all learn to practice.

15

Existentialism against Colonialism

Sartre, Fanon, and the Place of Lived Experience

Fanon against Sartre, Fanon with Sartre

The global impact of Frantz Fanon's *The Wretched of the Earth* extends far beyond academia, and it has served as a Bible to numerous anti-colonial movements. One thinks especially of its importance to the Black Panther Party in the United States and the Black Consciousness movement in South Africa. Indeed, there is still today no shortage of passionate readers of *The Wretched of the Earth* in South Africa up to and including proponents of the Rhodes Must Fall movement.[1] I have argued elsewhere that *The Wretched of the Earth* should be read in conjunction with Jean-Paul Sartre's *Critique of Dialectical Reason*.[2] Fanon himself left this in no doubt. He had read it with enthusiasm, and when he arranged for a third party to approach Sartre requesting that he write a preface to *The Wretched of the Earth*, he asked that Sartre be told: "each time I sit down at my desk, I think of him."[3] Nevertheless, one tendency in recent literature on Fanon has been to try to separate him from Sartre, whereas, as I will demonstrate here, reading them in tandem illuminates both of them.

That Frantz Fanon's first book, *Black Skin, White Masks*, is a major existentialist text should not be in doubt. Recently the focus of major commentators has been more on his understanding of psychopathology than on his understanding of Sartre, but this is mainly because the publication of his dissertation and other psychiatric writings has shown the extent of his reading in that area and in so doing has opened up new and highly productive lines of research.[4] Current research on Fanon's relation to Sartre is less robust. Just as some scholars of Simone de Beauvoir have thought that to enhance her reputation it was necessary to create a gulf between her and Sartre, some promoters of Black existentialism have been anxious to distance him from Sartre, as if the connection diminished his work. Such efforts strike me as misguided not only because neither Beauvoir nor Fanon sought to minimize

Critical Philosophy of Race. Robert Bernasconi, Oxford University Press. © Oxford University Press 2023.
DOI: 10.1093/oso/9780197587966.003.0016

252   CRITICAL PHILOSOPHY OF RACE

their debt to Sartre, but also because their own contributions are sufficiently incisive not to need such help. But this tendency has had an unfortunate effect on studies of the relation of Fanon to Sartre. The focus has largely fallen on Fanon's critical remarks on Sartre's account of the negritude movement in "Black Orpheus," in the fifth chapter of Fanon's *Black Skin, White Masks*, entitled "The Lived Experience of the Black," which is often treated in isolation from the rest of the book.[5]

The context of Sartre's "Black Orpheus" should not be forgotten. This was not a gratuitous intervention into a discussion where he had no place. He was not an uninvited guest. He had been asked to write a Preface to an anthology of poetry by Black Francophone writers who identified with the negritude movement.[6] Instead of a brief introduction he wrote a major interpretive essay in which many of his more problematic claims derived directly from the material he was discussing, such as a tendency toward a kind of racial essentialism, as when he wrote of "the black soul."[7] In the course of bringing together the different strands of that movement, he reduced them to two dominant tendencies. In so doing, he privileged the dialectical account offered by Aimé Césaire over the backward-looking perspective of Léopold Sédar Senghor. To that extent his perspective was not so different from Fanon's own in *Black Skin, White Masks*.[8] That is what allowed Fanon to say in the following chapter that "we can understand why Sartre sees in the black poets' Marxist stand the logical end to negritude."[9] Furthermore, Fanon praised *Anti-Semite and Jew*: "Certain pages of *Anti-Semite and Jew* are some of the finest we have ever read."[10] His striking, albeit deeply problematic, claim there was that the anti-Semite makes the Jew.[11] Fanon took this up and applied it to anti-Black racism: "it is the racist who creates the inferiorized."[12] He did so without in any way minimizing the different kinds of experiences that separate Blacks from Jews.[13] But just as Jews questioned Sartre's account of what it is to be a Jew, so Fanon questioned his account of what it is to be Black: "Jean-Paul Sartre forgets that the black man suffers in his body differently from the white man."[14] As Fanon explained in a footnote, Sartre's account of relations to the other in *Being and Nothingness* was "correct" as far as it went, but it could not be applied to a Black consciousness for whom the other is "the master, whether real or imaginary."[15] This is what Sartre at this point of his life did not appreciate and where he overstepped.

According to Fanon, Sartre's early intervention was deficient not only because he lacked the lived experience of being Black, but also because he paid insufficient attention to the power differential between Blacks and Whites and how it gave rise to certain oppressive mechanisms. As soon as one understands this difference, which derives from what is sometimes called an author's subject position, the importance of Fanon's voice becomes clear. The difference lay in the lived experience from which he wrote and in what that lived experience allowed him to write. Sartre could never *know* firsthand how Blacks suffer differently in their bodies from Whites. He knew there was a difference, but his awareness that there was this difference was one that he could easily put to one side.

"The Lived Experience of the Black" has given rise to a whole subfield within critical philosophy of race.[16] Multiple scholars have written auto-biographical studies of their experiences of racism and in so doing have forced many White readers to face their ignorance of the lived experience of being racialized as Black, Native American, Latin American, and so on. Through this single chapter, existentialism has left its mark on how race is thought of within academia in the United States. But Fanon's chapter is often read in isolation. It is not only cut off from Sartre, who in *Being and Nothingness* had provided a brief account of race in terms of the body's facticity that was then taken up by Fanon.[17] It is also, and more importantly, cut off from the historical context of the anti-colonial wars that Fanon references in praising the Vietnamese who, in their colonial struggle, "accept death for the sake of the present and the future."[18] And above all, it is cut off from the rest of *Black Skin, White Masks*. Indeed, it is not even in this chapter that Fanon marked his most significant advance on Sartre. In the sixth chapter, "The Negro and Psychopathology," Fanon demonstrated that racism cannot be adequately approached in terms of the individual situations that dominated the discussion in the previous chapters. Fanon's point is that one has to go beyond the looks and actions of individual racists to investigate the societal mechanisms, such as "cultural imposition," through which Black people were inferiorized.[19] In 1952, Fanon had a richer understanding of the operation of structural racism than Sartre, but the book was not only a diagnosis. It was also a call to action in which the oppressed, by risking their lives, could find the means to overcome the inferiority complex that society had produced. In *The Wretched of the Earth*, actions of this kind would be described as disintoxicating violence (*la violence désintoxique*): they could address a person's inferiority complex at the individual level.[20] But to transform society these actions needed to lead to a restructuring of the world.[21]

Systemic Racism

In *Anti-Semite and Jew*, Sartre had already recognized that, although he had begun with the individual anti-Semite, only a transformation of society could bring about the eradication of anti-Semitism: "it could not exist in a classless society."[22] But it seems that at this point he lacked the resources to take the diagnosis further. He would soon be inducted into a different racial politics by his visits to the United States in 1947 and 1948.[23] Within a few years, in the context of the Algerian War of Independence, Sartre took a major step in his theorization of this struggle, when in 1956 he gave a talk under the title "Colonialism Is a System."[24] In the following year, in a review of Albert Memmi's *The Colonizer and the Colonized*, he claimed that Memmi saw only a situation, whereas he himself saw a system.[25] It was an objection that Sartre should have acknowledged could equally have been leveled against his own *Anti-Semite and Jew*, not least because it was most likely from that book that Memmi took the notion of situation.

Sartre's adoption of the term *system* might seem to challenge a standard conception of existentialism, but he was not attempting to readjudicate Kierkegaard's protest on behalf of the individual against the Hegelian system. For both Sartre in *Critique of Dialectical Reason* and Fanon in *The Wretched of the Earth*, what was at issue was a racist material system, not, as with Hegel, a system of thought. Sartre, in *Search for a Method*, in preparation for publishing *Critique of Dialectical Reason*, offered a detailed discussion of the role of existentialism in his work at that time.

Existentialism aims at the concrete. Indeed, according to Sartre, it is "the only concrete approach to reality."[26] He also wrote of the *Critique of Dialectical Reason* that the concrete was "the hidden conclusion of the entire investigation."[27] By contrast, to begin with individual experience and stay with it is ultimately to remain in the abstract. Both Sartre and Fanon acknowledge that to focus exclusively on individual acts of racism, as still so often happens, is to abstract from the real problem, which is colonialism as a racist material system. The racialized individual is racialized less by the gaze than by cultural imposition. This insight takes one beyond *Anti-Semite and Jew*, and the account of cultural imposition in *Black Skin, White Masks* only goes part of the way.

Fanon had himself already taken a further step on the way to the concrete in 1956 in "Racism and Culture" when he described racism as "one element of a vaster whole: that of the systematized oppression of a people."[28]

Subsequently, at the very beginning of *The Wretched of the Earth*, he accomplished the integration of the individualist dimension of his account with the broader systemic perspective that makes sense of it: "It is the colonist who *fabricated* and *continues to fabricate* the colonized subject. The colonist derives his truth, i.e., his wealth, from the colonial system."[29] In these two sentences, first, Fanon adapted Sartre's famous formulation that the anti-Semite makes the Jew to the colonial context and then, second, he located that experience within the colonial system that sustains it.

Sartre in *Critique of Dialectical Reason* made a similar point when he revisited his earlier account of the gaze. He took as his example the workers' gaze toward their employers, who in turn realize themselves concretely as objects of hatred in the form of "a common individual."[30] Sartre had already, earlier in the book, modified the account of how one is made this or that by lodging it in an account of the passive syntheses of materiality.[31] Whereas in *Being and Nothingness* and *Anti-Semite and Jew* it is the direct gaze that determines relations with others, in *Critique of Dialectical Reason* our relations to others are mediated both by materiality and our relations to others across other others. The dominant understanding of racism that locates it primarily in the idea or sentiments of the individual is thereby overturned: "racism is a passive constitution in things before being an ideology."[32] This does not mean that theories play no part in racism, but rather that racism is lived before it is thought: "racism is the colonial interest lived as a link of all the colonialists of the colony through the serial flight of alterity."[33] More precisely, it is "a *praxis* illuminated by a theory ('biological', 'social', or empirical racism, it does not matter which) aiming to keep the masses in a state of molecular aggregation, and to use every possible means to increase the 'sub-humanity' of the natives."[34]

When racism is reduced to a thought or a sentiment, attention is being diverted to what is only a symptom of racism as a material system. The tendency to limit racism to the individual experience of it serves to perpetuate it by concealing and distorting the all-pervasive character of systemic racism. Racism, like everything, is not inside, but, to employ a phrase Sartre had deployed much earlier in another context, "outside, in the world, among others."[35] It is not lodged in the deep recesses of hearts and minds, but within the system, as the account of colonialism in *Critique of Dialectical Reason* demonstrates.[36] It is in the same spirit that Fanon in *The Wretched of the Earth* equated existential problems with objective problems.[37] Existentialism is not reducible to the subjective as some of its critics want to maintain.

256   CRITICAL PHILOSOPHY OF RACE

Dialectics

Sartre's *Critique of Dialectical Reason* and Fanon's *The Wretched of the Earth* are preoccupied with the same two questions. First, how does the existentialist render the material system visible? Second, once that has been done, where does that leave the accounts of lived experience on which existentialists have frequently relied? The first of these questions is explicitly formulated in *Search for a Method*, wherein Sartre explored how it is possible to "conceive of the appearance of systematic processes such as capitalism or colonialism."[38] His immediate response was not only that standard form of thought, what he sometimes called analytic reason, was incapable of doing so. The same accusation could also be leveled against the Marxists of his day. Indeed, Engels had already blocked this possibility.[39] What the Marxism of Sartre's day allegedly lacked was "the existential project," that is to say, "the project which throws him toward the social possible in terms of a defined situation."[40] So while it might seem at first sight that existentialism, as normally conceived, lacks a conception of the system and might even be thought to be inimical to it, in fact it is on Sartre's account indispensable for its role in producing the path to a dialectical conception of the system.

To be sure, the existential account itself needs the help of a revivified Marxism. From the very first pages of *Search for a Method*, Sartre indicated that existentialism needs Marxism to free it from the inherited abstract forms of thought that limit our conceptions of class (and race) and thereby promote a form of theoretical isolationism that he calls "atomization."[41] A one-sided focus on the abstract individual removed from the concrete conditions of his or her existence is characteristic of contemporary society and deprives that society of the resources it needs in order to identity and stay focused on the problems created by systemic racism. Without these resources problems that are endemic to the institutions themselves can easily be presented as occasional abuses.[42] This happened, for example, when slavery and colonialism were presented as in and of themselves neutral, or even positive, so that the abuses associated with them could be explained in terms of the selfish goals of evil individuals. Something similar still happens when police violence against racial minorities is treated as a problem of serial cases of rogue cops who are characterized as no more than bad apples. Hence the importance of Sartre's conclusion at the end of *Critique of Dialectical Reason* that dialectics can establish the conditions for such things as classes, whereas analytical reason, through its atomization of society and denial of material reciprocity, is "an oppressive praxis for dissolving them."[43] Those are the two options that, according to Sartre, face the theorist.

Sartre presented dialectics "as the practical consciousness of an oppressed class struggling against its oppressor."[44] That is to say, it is not something rarefied, possessed only by a few who have studied closely the writings of Hegel and Marx.[45] It belongs to the oppressed and they share in it insofar as they engage in praxis.[46] What is understood by praxis here? Sartre in the *Critique of Dialectical Reason* defines it as "an organising project which transcends material conditions towards an end and inscribes itself, through labour, in inorganic matter as a rearrangement of the practical field and a reunification of means in the light of the end."[47] However, beyond this generalized sense of the term, praxis in Sartre has a definite sense: "Concrete thought must be born from *praxis* and must turn back upon it in order to clarify it."[48]

It is even more clear that in *The Wretched of the Earth* it is not lived experience as such that reveals the operation of the colonial system, but revolutionary praxis understood dialectically. The masses themselves have "a voracious taste for the concrete" that they receive from the praxis and that throws them into a desperate struggle.[49] It is through praxis, the deployment of violence, and "the project of liberation" that "the colonized subject discovers reality and transforms it."[50] "Praxis enlightens the agent" because it shows the agent the means and the end.[51] That is to say, there is an understanding that belongs to concrete praxis. Whereas praxis helps to reveal the situation, the project locates it within a larger totalizing frame, and when the praxis takes the form of revolutionary praxis aimed at undermining the material system, then it is the system itself that comes to light. The relation of praxis to dialectical reason is crucial here where new meanings arise from this action. He wrote: "The nationalist militant who fled the town, revolted by the demagogic and reformist maneuvers of the leaders, and disillusioned by 'politics,' discovers in concrete praxis a new politics which in no way resembles the old."[52] Similar considerations had led Sartre to conclude that the dialectic cannot experience itself "except in and through the *praxis of struggle*."[53]

But if it is through praxis, rather than in lived experience, that systemic racism is revealed, where does that leave Fanon's appeal to the lived experience of the Black in *Black Skin, White Masks*? It is an important question given the prominence of lived experience in contemporary work in critical philosophy of race, which takes its inspiration from him. The organization of the book suggests that the evidence of lived experience on its own was

258   CRITICAL PHILOSOPHY OF RACE

already in question there. The fifth chapter ends in tears: "Not responsible for my acts, at the crossroads between Nothingness and Infinity, I began to weep."[54] By contrast, the book ends on a very different note, with Fanon asking the reader to feel the open dimension of every consciousness to which is added a final prayer, "O my body, always make me a man who questions!"[55] It seems that one cannot rely on the evidence of lived experience. It does not know itself. Hence, in the evolution of Fanon's thought, lived experience, as described in chapter 5 of *Black Skin, White Masks*, gives way later in the book to action, and that, in turn, points to what in *The Wretched of the Earth* is described as the experience of revolutionary praxis.

In *Search for a Method*, Sartre provides the theoretical basis for such a trajectory when he gives a revised account of what he calls "the method of the existentialist approach," but what is most remarkable is how he provides here for the first time an account of the place of lived experience.[56] He describes this method as "a regressive-progressive and analytic-synthetic method." By "progressive" he understands movement toward the objective result, and by "regressive," a going back toward the original conditions.[57] He explains that this is nothing other than the "dialectical movement which explains the act by its terminal signification in terms of its starting conditions."[58] In other words, the existential method and the dialectical method fold into one another. It remains only to understand how that happens.

To appreciate Sartre's attempt to place existential phenomenology at the service of a dialectical Marxism, it is helpful to look at a footnote in *Search for a Method* which he devoted to Henri Lefebvre's 1953 essay "Perspectives on Rural Sociology."[59] Lefebvre presented an account of how sociology and history can be integrated into a materialist dialectic. He identified three phases of the inquiry: descriptive, analytico-regressive, and historico-genetic.[60] In recounting them, Sartre changed Lefebvre's meaning by recharacterizing the first phase in terms of "phenomenological description."[61] He seemed to understand by that a description of the situation that does not yet attain to the level of the system as such.

Sartre's existential-dialectical method can be illustrated by a brief reference to his account of colonization as developing history in *Critique*, where he distinguishes three levels of intelligibility that correspond to Lefebvre's account. Sartre writes: "The play of flat appearances which can be studied by economic Reason has no intelligibility except in relation to the anti-dialectical system of super-exploitation. And this in turn is not intelligible unless one begins by seeing it as a product of human labour which created it and continues to control it."[62] The description of appearances has no meaning unless related to an account of power that is accessible only to the analytico-regressive movement, but this meaning gives rise to understanding only when seen through a historical dialectics. Analytical reason is indispensable but in and of itself inadequate to the task of investigating "oppression as a historical *praxis* realizing itself, determining itself and controlling itself in the milieu of passive activity."[63] If phenomenological description is to be placed in the service of political action, it must be seen dialectically, which means referring it back to the meanings sedimented in past praxis.

The Depth of Lived Experience

In *Search for a Method*, Sartre wrote of "the profundity of the lived (*la profondeur du vécu*)."[64] This gives to lived experience a significance that one is surprised to discover that it lacked in his earlier thought. It was not from the early Sartre but, most likely, from Merleau-Ponty's *Phenomenology of Perception* that Fanon took the idea of lived experience. Lived experience can be described phenomenologically, but its depth and intelligibility are given only when it is located within an analysis of power relations. This, using the terms Fanon deploys in *The Wretched of the Earth*, would mean evoking the reciprocal exclusion of colonizer and colonized governed "by a purely Aristotelian logic."[65] This corresponds to the way in which in *Search for a Method* the lived is said to be revealed through the regressive moment of the investigation where one begins from the absolute concrete and descends to its most abstract conditioning, in the sense of the material conditions as they are lived by abstract subjects.[66] But, as Sartre warned, this offers at most only an outline of the dialectical movement, which only fully emerges when the progressive moment of the investigation is fueled when the impasse is broken by the new meanings arising from historical praxis.

Long before Sartre formalized the approach in this way, Fanon had enacted it. In the sixth chapter of *Black Skin, White Masks*, he introduced an objection made against Sartre's "Black Orpheus" by Gabriel d'Arboussier. D'Arboussier argued that by describing the negritude poets as a movement, Sartre had ignored the historical and social realities of the different countries from which they came and that had the effect of separating them.[67] Fanon defended Sartre and at the same time acknowledged that the objection, if valid, would apply to him, too. Fanon began *Black Skin, White Masks* by recalling his own

260 CRITICAL PHILOSOPHY OF RACE

subject position: "As those of an Antillean, our observations and conclusions are valid only for the French Antilles."[68] However, in response to d'Arboussier he acknowledges that in pursuing his account he had had no choice but to lift the restriction: "At the start, we wanted to confine ourselves to the Antilles. But dialectics, at all cost, got the upper hand and we have been forced to *see* that the Antillean is above all a black man."[69] Fanon conceded that the Negro race is dispersed and no longer unified, that insofar as one operates simply by way of descriptions located at the phenomenal level, one simply opens the door to an infinite number of perspectives. But Fanon insists that at the concrete level the problem is resolved: "The universal situation of the black man is ambiguous, but this is resolved in his concrete existence."[70] He presented as evidence the fact that "wherever he goes the negro remains a negro."[71] Dialectics is vindicated but only to the extent that it attains the concrete by passing through the account of lived experience.

The importance Sartre in his late work gave to what he called "the depth of lived experience" is indicated in *Search for a Method* in the last part of the text and further demonstrated throughout the multivolume study of Flaubert where it is constantly in play.[72] It is explained further when in an interview from 1969 entitled "Itinerary of a Thought" Sartre marked the place he then gave to lived experience. He acknowledged that it was absent from his early thought and that its introduction marked the major change in his late work from the thinking of *Being and Nothingness*. "My early work was a rationalist philosophy of consciousness" that in the end "becomes an irrationalism, because it cannot account rationally for those processes which are 'below' consciousness and which are also rational, but lived as irrational."[73] This is at first sight surprising. One might imagine that the turn to history was the major shift, as he indicated at another point.[74] Or one might highlight his turn to dialectical reason as the major innovation of his late thought because it allowed him, for example, to think of colonialism as a system. But for Sartre the notion of lived experience changes everything because it was for him a dialectical concept when seen through the lens of the regressive-progressive method. He indicated this explicitly: "What I call *le vécu*—lived experience— is precisely the ensemble of the dialectical process of psychic life, in so far as this process is obscure to itself because it is a constant totalization, thus necessarily a totalization which cannot be conscious of what it is."[75]

Sartre explained that lived experience does not know itself: "It is the terrain in which the individual is perpetually overflowed by himself and his riches and consciousness plays the trick of determining itself by forgetfulness."[76]

That is to say, lived experience is "so opaque and blind before itself that it is also an absence from itself."[77] Fanon knew all that implicitly, and this is reflected by the way he described the lived experience of the Black in terms of inferiority in the fifth chapter of *Black Skin, White Masks*. But "lived experience" is given a different meaning when in the following chapter he combined an account of how cultural imposition produces that experience with an account of the action or praxis that promises to free Blacks from the sense of inferiority opposed on them. To that extent one can say that the existential method Fanon deployed in *Black Skin, White Masks* and refined in *The Wretched of the Earth* finds its formal exposition in *Search for a Method*.

It was their intent to address the colonial system as such and their shared commitment to the Algerian War of Independence in particular that led Sartre and Fanon to retool existentialism. The later Sartre and Fanon not only did not leave existentialism behind, they also showed why an existentialism that remains locked into the paradigm of the gaze risks bypassing the historical context by its neglect of material structures. The global reception of *The Wretched of the Earth* suggests that, even though theoreticians may dismiss his conception of an existentialist dialectics, Fanon found a language that resonates with the oppressed and their understanding, informed by praxis, of colonialism as a racist material system.

Notes

Introduction

1. I primarily have in mind narratives that assume that race and racial identities were seen in the seventeenth century much as they were in the late nineteenth century. However, another narrative that is gaining traction suggests that Black people were not seen as human. There is some evidence for this, but cases of this are not as widespread as sometimes believed. If the claim is that they were not treated as human beings should be treated, it is incontestable. Furthermore, there were believed to be degrees of humanity. But the crime was that human beings, people who, for example, could be baptized, were treated inhumanely. To suggest that most slave owners genuinely did not think of their slaves as humans gives those slave owners a strange alibi: they were not so much evil, as they were ignorant. Or, more precisely, the charge against them is being reduced to cruelty to animals. As Jean-Paul Sartre would say (but in order to capture the comment in all its richness it is necessary to restore it to its context), in order to treat human beings as dogs, you must first recognize them as human beings. See Sartre, *Critique de la raison dialectique*, 190 and 206; trans. *Critique of Dialectical Reason*, 110–11 and 130. I believe the weight of evidence shows that this was the standard case and that exceptions to it are rare. For further complications, see my discussion of Francis Brokesby in Chapter 3 at note 12.
2. The term "White supremacy" goes back at least to Henry Bevan's *Thirty Years in India*, where the author advocates that Europeans in their dealings with "the Hindoos" should "abandon, or at least conceal, those notions of White supremacy, which are frequently absurd, and always offensive" (299). However, it gains traction in the immediate aftermath of the Civil War, when John Van Evrie of New York, who had earlier issued an attack on race mixing under the name *Subgenation*, republished an earlier book on slavery with only minor additions under the new title, *White Supremacy and Negro Subordination*.
3. Georg Forster, "Noch etwas über die Menschenrassen: An Herrn Dr. Biester," 163; trans. "Something More about the Human Races," 165.
4. Charles Mills, "Critical Philosophy of Race."
5. Robert Bernasconi, "Islamophobia as a Racism."
6. I have presented this argument in more detail elsewhere. Some of the essays that do so will soon be collected under the tentative title *Race and Racism in Kant and Hegel*. That volume will also serve to complicate the oversimplified opposition between a Kantian biological racism and a Hegelian historical racism that can be found in the

264 NOTES

present volume: in particular, Kant at the very least foreshadowed the racism that gave the White race a privileged role in history.

7. William Waller Hening, *The Statutes at Large*, vol. 3, 86–88. I have at times throughout this book used jarring words like "negro." I do so because, in the course of studying history, it is important to know which words were used and the connotations they conveyed.

8. Du Bois, "Conservation of Races," in *DuBois: Writings*, 817.

9. See Robert Bernasconi, "The Assumption of Negritude."

10. Frantz Fanon, "Peau noir, masques blancs," in *Frantz Fanon: Oeuvres*, 174–75; trans. Charles Lam Markmann, *Black Skin, White Masks*, 138.

11. In the case of South Africa, this is reflected in apartheid-era discussions of the Nazi racial policies. See Shirli Gilbert, "Nazism and Racism in South African Textbooks."

12. Frantz Fanon, "Pour la revolution africaine: *Écrits politiques*," in *Frantz Fanon: Oeuvres*, 683–878, at 716; trans. *Toward the African Revolution*, 32.

13. Sartre, *Critique de la raison dialectique*, 692; trans. *Critique of Dialectical Reason*, 739.

14. Frantz Fanon, "Les damnés de la terre," in *Frantz Fanon: Oeuvres*, 419–681, at 572; trans. *The Wretched of the Earth*, 129.

Chapter 1

1. Kimberlé Crenshaw, "Introduction," in Crenshaw et al., eds., *Critical Race Theory: The Key Writings That Formed the Movement*.

2. Anténor Firmin, *De l'égalité des races humaines*, 203; trans. *The Equality of the Human Races*, 140.

3. W. E. B. Du Bois, *Writings*, 821.

4. Lewis R. Gordon, *Fanon and the Crisis of European Man: An Essay on Philosophy and the Human Sciences*, 14–18, and "Existential Dynamics of Theorizing Black Invisibility," 70.

5. Du Bois, *Writings*, 817; Kwame Anthony Appiah, *In My Father's House: Africa in the Philosophy of Culture*, 28–46.

6. Appiah, "Race, Culture, Identity: Misunderstood Connections," 78–79.

7. Edmund Husserl, *Ideen zu einer reinen Phänomenologie und Phänomenologischen Philosophie*, Book 2, 378; trans. *Ideas Pertaining to a Pure Phenomenology and to a Phenomenological Philosophy*, Book 2, 388.

8. Husserl, *Ideen*, 183; trans. *Ideas*, 192–93.

9. See Robert Bernasconi, "Ludwig Ferdinand Clauss and Racialization."

10. Ludwig Ferdinand Clauss, *Von Seele und Antlitz der Rassen und Völker: eine Einführung in die vergleichende Ausdrucksforschung*, 96.

11. Clauss, *Rasse und Seele*, 27; see Husserl, *Ideas Pertaining to a Pure Phenomenology*, 110.

12. Clauss, *Die Nordische Seele*, 9.

13. Eric Voegelin, *Rasse und Staat*, 12; trans. *Race and State*, 12.

NOTES 265

14. Edith Stein, "Eine Untersuchung über den Staat," 87–88; trans. *An Investigation Concerning the State*, 133.

15. Max Scheler, *Probleme einer Soziologie des Wissens*, 17–51; trans. *Problems of a Sociology of Knowledge*, 33–63. Alfred Schutz, "Equality and the Meaning Structure of the Social World," 249.

16. Schutz, "Equality and the Meaning Structure," 272.

17. Jean-Paul Sartre, *L'être et le néant*, 393, 410; trans. *Being and Nothingness*, 440, 459. Frantz Fanon, *Peau noire, masques blancs*, in *Oeuvres*, 93; trans. Richard Philcox, *Black Skin, White Masks*, 27.

18. Bernasconi, "Can Race Be Thought in Terms of Facticity? A Reconsideration of Sartre's and Fanon's Existential Theories of Race," 207.

19. Donna-Dale Marcano, "Sartre and the Social Construction of Race," in Bernasconi, ed., *Race and Racism in Continental Philosophy*, 214–26, at 225.

20. Sartre, *Critique de la raison dialectique*, 240; trans. *Critique of Dialectical Reason*, 171.

21. Linda Martín Alcoff, *Visible Identities: Race, Gender, and the Self*, 194.

22. Paulette Nardal, "Éveil de la conscience de Race," 29; trans. T. Denean Sharpley-Whiting, "The Awakening of Race Consciousness," in Bernasconi, ed., *Race*, 107–11, at 109.

23. Du Bois, *Writings*, 364; Paul Taylor, "W. E. B. Du Bois," 904–15, at 913.

24. Alice Cherki, *Frantz Fanon: A Portrait*, 15–16.

25. Sartre, *Réflexions sur la question juive*, 89; trans. *Anti-Semite and Jew*, 69.

26. Jonathan Judaken, *Jean-Paul Sartre and the Jewish Question: Anti-antisemitism and the Politics of the French Intellectual*, 241–44. Fanon, *Peau noire, masques blancs*, in *Oeuvres*, 137; trans. Philcox, *Black Skin, White Masks*, 73.

27. Thomas F. Slaughter Jr., "Epidermalizing the World: A Basic Mode of Being-Black," 283–87, at 284–85; George Yancy, *Black Bodies, White Gazes: The Continuing Significance of Race*, 70–75.

28. Penelope Deutscher, *The Philosophy of Simone de Beauvoir: Ambiguity, Conversion, Resistance*, 74–78; Robert E. Birt, "The Bad Faith of Whiteness"; Gordon, *Bad Faith and Antiblack Racism*, 6.

29. Jeremy Weate, "Fanon, Merleau-Ponty and the Difference of Phenomenology," in Bernasconi, ed., *Race*, 169–83; Charles Johnson, "A Phenomenology of the Black Body," 602; Emily S. Lee, "Towards a Lived Understanding of Race and Sex."

30. Fanon, *Peau noire, masques blancs*, in *Oeuvres*, 174–75; trans. Philcox, *Black Skin, White Masks*, 117.

31. Judaken, "Sartre on Racism: From Existential Phenomenology to Globalization and 'the New Racism,'" 23–54.

32. Richard Wright, *White Man, Listen!* See Bernasconi, "Richard Wright as Educator: The Progressive Structure of Simone de Beauvoir's Account of Racial Hatred in the United States."

33. Schutz, "Equality and the Meaning Structure," 250–69; Michael D. Barber, *The Participating Citizen: A Biography of Alfred Schutz*, 181–95.

34. Mariana Ortega, "Being Lovingly, Knowingly Ignorant: White Feminism and Women of Color."

266 NOTES

35. Fanon, *Peau noire, masques blancs*, in *Oeuvres*, 142; trans. Philcox, *Black Skin, White Masks*, 80.
36. Albert Memmi, *Portrait du colonisé précédé du Portrait du colonisateur*, 77; trans. *The Colonizer and the Colonized*, 56.
37. Sartre, *Colonialisme et néo-colonialisme*, 25–48; trans. *Colonialism and Neocolonialism*, 48–64.
38. Sartre, *Critique de la raison dialectique*, 692; trans. *Critique of Dialectical Reason*, 739.
39. Fanon, *Les damnés de la terre*, in *Oeuvres*, 452; trans. Philcox, *The Wretched of the Earth*, 2.
40. Fanon, *Les damnés de la terre*, in *Oeuvres*, 532; trans. *The Wretched of the Earth*, 89. Sartre, "Orphée noir," xiv, xl; trans. MacCombie, "Black Orpheus," in Bernasconi, ed., *Race*, 115–42, at 118, 137.
41. Sartre, *Critique de la raison dialectique*, 318; trans. *Critique of Dialectical Reason*, 268.
42. Fanon, *Les damnés de la terre*, in *Oeuvres*, 489; trans. *Wretched*, 44.
43. Bernasconi, "The Great White Error and the Great Black Mirage," 88–89.
44. Lucius T. Outlaw Jr., *Critical Social Theory in the Interests of Black Folks*, 111–16.
45. Sartre, *Cahiers pour une morale*, 579–82; trans. *Notebooks for an Ethics*, 561–63.
46. Hannah Arendt, *The Origins of Totalitarianism*, 192.
47. Kathryn Gines, "Race Thinking and Racism in Hannah Arendt's *The Origins of Totalitarianism*," in Richard H. King and Dan Stone, eds., *Hannah Arendt and the Uses of History*, 38–53, at 49–50.
48. Arendt, *Origins of Totalitarianism*, 206.
49. Bernasconi, "When the Real Crime Began: Hannah Arendt's *The Origins of Totalitarianism* and the Dignity of the Western Philosophical Tradition," in King and Stone, eds., *Hannah Arendt and the Uses of History*, 54–67, at 61–62.
50. Bernasconi, "Race and Earth in Heidegger's Thinking During the Late 1930s," 57–58.
51. Falguni A. Sheth, *Toward a Political Philosophy of Race*, 21–39.
52. Houston Stewart Chamberlain, *Die Grundlagen des neunzehnten Jahrhunderts*, vol. 2, 343; trans. *The Foundations of the Nineteenth Century*, vol. 1, 354.
53. Oskar Becker, "Para-Existenz: Menschliches Dasein und Dawesen"; Wolfram Hogrebe, "Die Selbstverstrickung des Philosophen Oskar Becker."
54. Bernasconi, "Sartre and Levinas: Philosophers against Racism and Antisemitism."

Chapter 2

1. See Chapter 12 in this volume.
2. Staffan Müller-Wille and Hans-Jörg Rheinberger, "Heredity—The Formation of an Epistemic Space," in Müller-Wille and Rheinberger, eds., *Heredity Produced: At the Crossroads of Biology, Politics, and Culture, 1500–1870*, 13–23.
3. Thomas Blake, *The Birth Priviledge, or, Covenant-Holinesse of Beleevers and Their Issue in the Time of Gospel Together with the Right of Infants to Baptisme*, 5–6.

NOTES 267

4. María Elena Martínez, *Genealogical Fictions: Limpieza de Sangre, Religion, and Gender in Colonial Mexico*, 53.

5. Samuel Purchas, *Purchas His Pilgrimage, or Relations of the World and the Religions Observed in All Ages*, 27.

6. Nicolas-Sylvestre Bergier, *Encyclopédie Méthodique: Théologie*, vol. 3, 339–47.

7. Bergier, *Encyclopédie Méthodique*, vol. 3, 347–49.

8. Immanuel Kant, "Zum ewigen Frieden," in *Kants Werke*, Akademie Textausgabe, vol. 8, 367n; trans. "Toward Perpetual Peace," 336n.

9. Kant, *Die Religion innerhalb der Grenzen der blossen Vernunft*, in *Kants Werke* Akademie Textausgabe, vol. 6, 109; trans. "Religion within the Boundaries of Mere Reason," 142.

10. Kant, "Zum ewigen Frieden," in *Kants Werke*, Akademie Textausgabe, vol. 8, 341–86, at 367n; trans. "Toward Perpetual Peace," 336n.

11. Richard Hooker, *Of the Lawes of Ecclesiastical Politie*, 186.

12. Joan-Pau Rubiés, *Travel and Ethnology in the Renaissance: South India through European Eyes, 1250–1625*, 173.

13. Surekha Davies, *Renaissance Ethnography and the Invention of the Human: New Worlds, Maps and Monsters*, 217.

14. Jean Bodin, *Method for the Easy Comprehension of History*, 110.

15. Edward Herbert, *De religione gentilium*, 1–2.

16. Kant, "Von den verschiedenen Racen der Menschen," in *Kants Werke*, Akademie Textausgabe, vol. 2, 427–44, at 432; trans. "Of the Different Races of Human Beings," in Kant, *Anthropology, History, and Education*, 84–97, at 87.

17. Pierre de Charron, *De la sagesse*, 378; trans. *Of Wisdom: Three Books*, 722–23.

18. David Hume, *A Dissertation on the Passions: The Natural History of Religions*, 33.

19. Charles Blount, *Great Is Diana of the Ephesians, or, The Original of Idolatry: Together with the Politick Institutions of the Gentile Sacrifices*, 3.

20. To the extent that they did so, they brought their usage more in line with the general shift in the theoretical understanding of the term "religion," meticulously documented by Ernst Feil, whereby after the middle of the seventeenth century, religion increasingly came to be understood not in terms of practices but in terms of feelings. Religion ceased to be visible but was locked within the inner dimension of the human person; Feil, *Religio*, vol. 3, 481. The new concept of religion is already indicated by Thomas Hobbes when he wrote: "Seeing there are no signes, nor fruit of *Religion*, but in Man onely"; Hobbes, *Leviathan, or, The matter, forme, & power of a common-wealth ecclesiasticall and civill*, 52.

21. Pope Pius XII, *Plane Compertum Est*, published in 1940 in *Acta Apostolicae Sedis*, the official journal of the Vatican.

22. For Couplet's role, see Thierry Meynard, *Confucius Sinarum Philosophus (1687): The First Translation of the Confucian Classics*, 12–18.

23. Meynard, *Confucius Sinarum Philosophus*, 195.

24. Meynard, *Confucius Sinarum Philosophus*, 60–64.

25. Feil, *Religio*, vol. 4, 68–88.

268 NOTES

26. Christian Wolff, *Oratio de sinarum philosophia practica*, 120n30; trans. "The Practical Philosophy of the Chinese," 156n24.

27. Wolff, *Oratio de sinarum philosophia practica*, 132n41; trans. "Discourse on the Practical Philosophy of the Chinese," 159n32.

28. Daniel Purdy, "Chinese Ethics within the Radical Enlightenment: Christian Wolff," 126–30.

29. White Kennet, *The Lets and Impediments in Planting and Propagating the Gospel of Christ*, 16.

30. Matthew Tindal, *Christianity as Old as the Creation: Or, The Gospel, A Republication of the Religion of Nature*, 1.

31. Tindal, *Christianity as Old as the Creation*, 133.

32. Tindal, *Christianity as Old as the Creation*, 166–67.

33. Bartholomäus Ziegenbalg, *An Account of the Religion, Manners, and Learning of the People of Malabar in the East Indies*, 8.

34. Ziegenbalg, *Thirty Four Conferences between the Danish Missionaries and the Malabarian Bramans (or Heathen Priests) in the East Indies*, 16.

35. Ziegenbalg, *Thirty Four Conferences*, 137.

36. Brijraj Singh, *The First Protestant Missionary to India: Bartholomaeus Ziegenbalg, 1683–1719*, 140.

37. Ziegenbalg, *Account of the Religion, Manners, and Religion*, 34.

38. Will Sweetman, *Mapping Hinduism: "Hinduism" and the Study of Indian Religions, 1600–1776*, 125–26.

39. Ziegenbalg, "Genealogie der malabarischen Götter," 37; trans. "The Genealogy of the South Indian Deities," 48.

40. François Bernier, "Lettre à Monsieur Chapelain," 79–80; trans. *Travels in the Mogul Empire*, 328.

41. Kant, "Anthropologiekolleg vom Winter 1791/92," 277–78.

42. Meynard, *The Jesuit Reading of Confucius: The First Complete Translation of the Lunyu (1687) Published in the West*, 607.

43. Peter Harrison, *The Territories of Science and Religion*, 101–2.

44. S. N. Balagangadhara, *"The Heathen in His Blindness": Asia, the West and the Dynamic of Religion*, 102–3.

45. Johannes De Laet, *De imperio magni mogolis, sive India vera commentaries*, 115.

46. Bernier, "Lettre à Monsieur Chapelain," 17; trans. *Travels in the Mogul Empire*, 306.

47. Alexander Ross, *Pansebeia, or, a View of All Religions in the World: With the Several Church-Governments, from the Creation, to These Times*, 95.

48. Ross, *Pansebeia*, ix.

49. Thomas Broughton, *Bibliotheca Historico-sacra*, 172–74.

50. Broughton, *Bibliotheca Historico-sacra*, 179–80.

51. Broughton, *Bibliotheca Historico-sacra*, i.

52. Hannah Adams, *A Dictionary of All Religions and Religious Denominations: Jewish, Heathen, Mahometan, and Christian, Ancient and Modern*, 107, 110.

53. Adams, *Dictionary of All Religions*, 46 and 49.

NOTES 269

54. Tomoko Masuzawa, *The Invention of World Religions: Or, How European Universalism Was Preserved in the Language of Pluralism*, 61.

55. Paola von Wyss-Giacosa, *Religionsbilder der frühen Aufklärung*.

56. Jean-Frédéric Bernard, *Ceremonies et Coutumes religieuses de tous les peuples du monde*, 1–2; my translation.

57. Bernard, *Ceremonies et Coutumes*, 8; my translation.

58. Lynn Hunt et al., *The Book That Changed Europe: Picart and Bernard's "Religious Ceremonies of the World,"* 307–8.

59. Bernard, *The Ceremonies and Religious Customs of the Various Nations of the Known World*, 217.

60. John Toland, *Letters to Serena*, 127.

61. Johann Christian Edelmann, *Unschuldige Wahrheiten: Gesprächs-weise abgehandelt zwischen Doxophilo und Philaletho*, 63.

62. Richard H. Popkin, *Isaac La Peyrère (1596–1676): His Life, Work and Influence*, 11.

63. Isaac de La Peyrère, *Praeadamitae sive exercitatio*, 29; trans. *Men before Adam*, 22.

64. Morgan Godwyn, *The Negro's & Indians Advocate, Suing for Their Admission into the Church*, 15–18.

65. Edward Long, *The History of Jamaica Or, General Survey of the Antient and Modern State of That Island*, vol. 2, 356.

66. Anthony, Earl of Shaftesbury, *Characteristicks of Men, Manners, Opinions, Times*, vol. 3, 45–46.

67. Charles-Louis de Secondat Montesquieu, *De l'esprit des loix*, 312; trans. *The Spirit of the Laws*, 236.

68. Georges-Louis Leclerc de Buffon, *Histoire naturelle, générale et particulière*, vol. 3, 523–24.

69. Buffon, *Histoire naturelle*, vol. 3, 385. The self-evidence, and thus primacy, that is sometimes accorded to the supposed visibility of race is easily disturbed by the history of what was reported. In the seventeenth and much of the eighteenth century, the Chinese were seen as "white like us in Europe" (Alvarez Semedo, *The History of That Great and Renowned Monarchy of China*, 22), an observation that Buffon, while acknowledging some difference in the reports, depending on location and exposure to the sun, supported (Buffon, *Histoire naturelle*, vol. 3, 385). It was not until later that the Chinese came to be seen as yellow (Walter Demel, "How the Chinese Became Yellow: A Contribution to the Early History of Race Theories," 31).

70. Buffon, *Histoire naturelle*, vol. 3, 375.

71. Buffon, *Histoire naturelle*, vol. 4, 471–72.

72. Buffon, *Histoire naturelle*, vol. 3, 529–30.

73. Kant, "Von den verschiedenen Racen der Menschen," in *Kants Werke*, Akademie Textausgabe, vol. 2, 427–44, at 430; trans. "Of the Different Races of Human Beings," in Kant, *Anthropology, History, and Education*, 85.

74. Bernasconi, "Who Invented the Concept of Race? Kant's Role in the Enlightenment Construction of Race."

75. François Bernier, "Nouvelle division de la terre, par les differentes Especes ou Races d'hommes qui l'habitent, envoyée par un fameux Voyageur à M. [. . .]."; trans. "A new

270 NOTES

division of the earth, according to the different species or races of men who inhabit it, sent by a famous traveller to Mons. [. . .]."

76. Thomas Browne, *Religio Medici*, 1.

77. Alberico Gentili, *De jure belli libri tres*, vol. 2, 328–32.

78. Richard Ligon, *A True & Exact History of the Island of Barbadoes*, 50.

79. Richard Baxter, *A Christian Directory: Or, a Sum of Practical Divinity*, 74.

80. Mattie Erma Parker, "The Fundamental Constitutions of Carolina," 164.

81. Katharine Gerbner, *Christian Slavery: Conversion and Race in the Protestant Atlantic World*, 84, 89.

82. William Waller Hening, *The Statutes at Large; Being a Collection of all the Laws of Virginia*, vol. 2, 170.

83. Hening, *Statutes at Large*, vol. 2, 447–48

84. Hening, *Statutes at Large*, vol. 2, 449–50.

85. Hening, *Statutes at Large*, vol. 2, 459.

86. Rebecca Anne Goetz, *The Baptism of Early Virginia: How Christianity Created Race*, 6.

87. Goetz, *Baptism of Early Virginia*, 83.

88. Albert A. Sicroff, *Les controversies des statuts de "pureté de sang" en Espagne du XVe au XVIIe siècle.*

89. Yosef Hayim Yerushalmi, *Assimilation and Racial Anti-Semitism: The Iberian and the German Models*, 12.

90. Francisco de Torrejoncillo, *Centinela contra Judíos*, 214. François Soyer, *Popularizing Anti-Semitism in Early Modern Spain and Its Empire: Francisco de Torrejoncillo and the* Centinela contra Judíos *(1674)*, 34–38.

91. Ildephonsi Perez de Lara Toletani, *De anniversariis et capellaniis, libri duo*, 214, 281–83.

92. Juan Escobar del Corro, *Tractatus bipartitus de puritate et nobilitate probanda*, 9.

93. Juan de Solórzano Pereira, *Politica Indiana*, 214.

94. Maria Elena Martínez, *Genealogical Fictions: Limpieza de Sangre, Religion, and Gender in Colonial Mexico*, 201–6.

95. Ann Twinam, "Racial Passing: Informal and Official 'Whiteness' in Colonial Spanish America," 253–54.

96. Twinam, "Racial Passing," 249–50.

97. John Tate Lanning, "Legitimacy and *Limpieza de Sangre* in the Practice of Medicine in the Spanish Empire," 47–48.

98. Martínez, *Genealogical Fictions*, 245–57.

Chapter 3

1. Benjamin Disraeli, *Lord George Bentinck: A Political Biography*, 331.

2. Robert Knox, *The Races of Men: A Fragment*, v.

3. Johann Gottfried Herder, *Ideen zur Philosophie der Geschichte der Menschheit*, 80; trans. *Outlines of a Philosophy of the History of Man*, 166.

NOTES 271

4. John Mitchell, "An Essay upon the Causes of the different Colours of People in different Climates," 148.

5. Robert Bernasconi, "Who Invented the Concept of Race? Kant's Role in the Enlightenment Construction of Race."

6. Immanuel Kant, "Von den verschiedenen Racen der Menschen," in *Kants Werke*, Akademie Textausgabe, vol. 2, 427–44, at 430; trans. "Of the Different Races of Human Beings," in Kant, *Anthropology, History, and Education*, 84–97, at 85.

7. Kant, "Bestimmung des Begriffs einer Menschenrace," in *Kants Werke*, Akademie Textausgabe, vol. 8, 89–106, at 100; trans. "Determination of the Concept of a Human Race," in Kant, *Anthropology, History, and Education*, 143–59, at 154.

8. Isaac de La Peyrère, *Systema Theologicum, ex Praeadamitarum hypothesi*, 148–54; trans. *A Theological Systeme upon That Presupposition, That Men Were before Adam*, 164–70.

9. La Peyrère, *Systema Theologicum*, 105–16; trans. *Theological Systeme*, 118–28.

10. La Peyrère, *Systema Theologicum*, 82; trans. *Theological Systeme*, 90.

11. Morgan Godwyn, *The Negro's & Indians Advocate: Suing for Their Admission into the Church*, 14.

12. Francis Brokesby, *Some Proposal Towards Propagating the Gospel*, 3. Henry Dodwell, *An Epistolary Discourse*.

13. Georges-Louis Leclerc de Buffon, *Histoire naturelle, générale et particulière*, vol. 15, 314.

14. Henry Home, *Sketches of the History of Man*, vol. 1, 38–39; vol. 2, 70–75. Voltaire, *Essai sur les moeurs*, vol. 1, 6; trans. *The Philosophy of History*, 5.

15. Kant, "Von den verschiedenen Racen der Menschen," in *Kants Werke*, Akademie Textausgabe, vol. 2, 427–44, at 432, 441; trans. "Of the Different Races of Human Beings," in Kant, *Anthropology, History, and Education*, 84–97, at 87, 95.

16. Kant, "Von den verschiedenen Racen der Menschen," in *Kants Werke*, Akademie Textausgabe, vol. 2, 427–44, at 442; trans. "Of the Different Races of Human Beings," in Kant, *Anthropology, History, and Education*, 84–97, at 96.

17. Kant, "Über den Gebrauch teleologischer Principien in der Philosophie," in *Kants Werke*, Akademie Textausgabe, vol. 8, 157–84, at 180n; trans. "On the Use of Teleological Principles in Philosophy," in Kant, *Anthropology, History, and Education*, ed. Günter Zöller and Robert B. Louden, 192–218, at 214n. Kant, "Kritik der Urtheilskraft," in *Kants Werke*, Akademie Textausgabe, vol. 5, 165–485, at 414; trans. *Critique of the Power of Judgment*, 292.

18. Johann Friedrich Blumenbach, *De generis humani varietate nativa*, 285–86; trans. "On the Natural Variety of Mankind," in *The Anthropological Treatises of Johann Friedrich Blumenbach*, 264.

19. Norbert Klatt, "Einleitung," xxiii–xxiv.

20. Bernasconi, "Kant and Blumenbach's Polyps: A Neglected Chapter in the History of the Concept of Race," in Sara Eigen and Mark Larrimore, eds., *The German Invention of Race*, 73–90, at 84–85.

21. Blumenbach, *De generis humani varietate nativa*, 115; trans. *Anthropological Treatises*, 207.

272 NOTES

22. Theodor Waitz, *Anthropologie der Naturvölker*, vol. 1; trans. *Introduction to Anthropology*.

23. Mitchell, "Causes of the different Colours of People," 148; Samuel Stanhope Smith, *An Essay on the Causes of the Variety of Complexion and Figure in the Human Species* [...] (1787), 52–88.

24. Smith, *An Essay on the Causes of the Variety of Complexion and Figure in the Human Species* [...] (1810).

25. James Cowles Prichard, *Researches into the Physical History of Mankind*, 2nd ed., vol. 2, 544; Hannah F. Augstein, *James Cowles Prichard's Anthropology: Remaking the Science of Man in Early Nineteenth Century Britain*, 113.

26. Prichard, *Researches into the Physical History of Mankind*, 1st ed., 239.

27. Christoph Girtanner, *Über das Kantische Prinzip für die Naturgeschichte*. Friedrich Schelling, *Einleitung Entwurf eines Systems der Naturphilosophie*, 53–56; trans. *First Outline of a System of the Philosophy of Nature*, 44–46.

28. Schelling, *Einleitung in die Philosophie der Mythologie*, 98; trans. *Historical-critical Introduction to the Philosophy of Mythology*, 71–72.

29. Georges Cuvier, *Discours sur les révolutions du globe*. Samuel George Morton, *Crania Americana*; Schelling, *Einleitung in die Philosophie der Mythologie*, 498–504.

30. Schelling, *Philosophie der Mythologie*, 513.

31. Prichard, *Researches into the Physical History of Mankind*, 3rd ed., vol. 1, 109.

32. Alfred Russel Wallace, "The Origin of Human Races and the Antiquity of Man deduced from the theory of 'Natural Selection,'" clxvi.

33. G. W. F. Hegel, *Schriften und Entwürfe I (1817–1825)*, 225; trans. M. J. Petry, *Philosophy of Subjective Spirit*, vol. 1, 113.

34. Hegel, *Vorlesungen über die Philosophie des Subjektiven Geistes*, vol. 25.1, 231–39, and *Vorlesungen über die Philosophie des Subjektiven Geistes*, vol. 25.2, 605–12.

35. Hegel, *Vorlesungen über die Philosophie des Subjektiven Geistes*, vol. 25.1, 232, and *Vorlesungen über die Philosophie des Subjektiven Geistes*, vol. 25.2, 610.

36. I am here referencing *Vorlesungen über die Philosophie der Weltgeschichte*, the newly available German text that allows us for the first time to contrast Hegel's lectures on the philosophy of history from the years 1822/23, 1824/25, 1826/27, 1830/31, and the most recent English translation, *Lectures on the Philosophy of History* (2011), of Karl Hegel's 1840 edition, which drew on student notes from a number of different years. See *Philosophie der Weltgeschichte*, 1290, and trans. *Philosophy of History*, 156. See also Bernasconi, "With What Must the Philosophy of World History Begin? On the Racial Basis of Hegel's Eurocentrism."

37. Hegel, *Philosophie der Weltgeschichte*, 1230; trans. *Philosophy of History*, 92.

38. Bernasconi, "Hegel at the Court of the Ashanti."

39. Hegel, *Philosophie der Geschichte*, 253; trans. *Philosophy of History*, 188.

40. Bernasconi, "The Return of Africa: Hegel and the Question of the Racial Identity of the Egyptians."

41. Hegel, *Philosophie der Weltgeschichte*, 1458 and 1537; trans. *Philosophy of History*, 317 and 379.

42. Friedrich L. Jahn, *Deutsches Volksthum*, 25. My translation.

NOTES 273

43. Kant, "Recensionen von J. G. Herders Ideen zur Philosophie der Geschichte der Menschheit," in *Kants Werke*, Akademie Textausgabe, vol. 8, 43–66, at 65; trans. "Review of J. G. Herder's *Ideas on the Philosophy of the History of Humanity, Parts 1 and 2*," in Kant, *Anthropology, History, and Education*, 124–42, at 142.

44. Bernasconi, "Why Do the Happy Inhabitants of Tahiti Bother to Exist at All?"

45. William Frédéric Edwards, *Des caractères physiologiques des races humaines considérés dans leurs rapports avec l'histoire: Lettre à M. Amédée Thierry*, 22–29.

46. Victor Courtet de l'Isle, *La science politique fondée sur la science de l'homme: Ou etude des races humaines sous le rapport philosophique, historique et social*, 389–91; Gustave d'Eichthal and Ismayl Urbain, *Lettres sur la race noire et la race blanche*, 18–19 and 62–69.

47. Wolfgang Menzel, *Geist der Geschichte*, 160, 84–85.

48. Gustave Klemm, *Allgemeine Cultur-Geschichte der Menschheit*, 204.

49. Prichard, *Physical History of Man*, 3rd ed., vol. 1, 146.

50. Claude Blanckaert, "Of Monstrous Métis? Hybridity, Fear of Miscegenation, and Patriotism from Buffon to Paul Broca," in Sue Peabody and Tyler Stovall, eds., *The Color of Liberty: Histories of Race in France*, 42–70, at 49.

51. Josiah C. Nott, "The Mulatto a Hybrid: Probable Extermination of the Two Races If the Whites and Blacks Are Allowed to Intermarry."

52. Johann Peter Frank, *System einer vollständigen medicinischen Polizey*; 404–11. Sara Eigen, "Policing the *Menschen = Racen*," in Eigen and Mark Larrimore, eds., *The German Invention of Race*, 185–202, at 194.

53. Nott and George R. Gliddon, *Types of Mankind*.

54. Georges Pouchet, *De la pluralité des races humaines*, 10; trans. *The Plurality of the Human Race*, 7.

55. John Lynch, *Simón Bolivar: A Life*, 284.

56. G. Reginald Daniel, *Race and Multiraciality in Brazil and the United States: Converging Paths?* 37.

57. Arthur de Gobineau, *Essai sur l'inegalité des races humaines*, vol. 1, vi; trans. *The Inequality of Human Races*, xiv.

58. Gobineau, *L'inegalité des races humaines*, vol. 1, 218; trans. *Inequality of Human Races*, 208.

59. Gobineau, *L'inegalité des races humaines*, vol. 2, 563; trans. "Conclusion," in *Gobineau: Selected Political Writings*, 162–76 at 175.

60. Gobineau, *L'inegalité des races humaines*, vol. 1, 29; trans. *Inequality of Human Races*, 30.

61. Gobineau, *The Moral and Intellectual Diversity of Races, with Particular Reference to Their Respective Influence in the Civil and Political History of Mankind*, 157–58.

62. Knox, *Races of Men*, 16–17, 266.

63. Houston Stewart Chamberlain, *Immanuel Kant: Die Persönlichkeit als Einführung in das Werk*, 715; trans. *Immanuel Kant: A Study and a Comparison with Goethe, Leonardo Da Vinci, Bruno, Plato and Descartes*, vol. 2, 332.

64. Chamberlain, *Immanuel Kant*, 701; trans. *Immanuel Kant*, vol. 2, 339.

274 NOTES

65. Chamberlain, *Die Grundlagen des neunzehnten Jahrhunderts*, vol. 1, 269n4; trans. *Foundations of the Nineteenth Century*, vol. 1, 266n.

66. Chamberlain, *Neunzehnten Jahrhunderts*, vol. 2, 343; trans. *Nineteenth Century*, vol. 1, 354.

67. Disraeli, *Coningsby; or, the New Generation*, vol. 2, 138. Chamberlain, *Neunzehnten Jahrhunderts*, vol. 1, 273–74; trans. *Nineteenth Century*, vol. 1, 271.

68. Richard Popkin, "The Philosophical Basis of Modern Racism," 79.

69. María Elena Martinez, "The Black Blood of New Spain: Limpieza de Sangre, Racial Violence, and Gendered Power in Early Colonial Mexico."

70. Jakob Friedrich Fries, *Über die Gefährdung der Wohlstandes und Charakters der Deutschen durch die Juden*, 12.

71. Ernest Renan, *De l'origine du langage: Histoire générale et système comparé des langues sémitiques*, 577. Michael R. Marrus, *The Politics of Assimilation: A Study of the French Jewish Community at the Time of the Dreyfus Affair*, 11–15.

72. Moses Hess, *Rom und Jerusalem: Die Letzte Nationalitatenfräge*, 26; trans. Meyer Waxman, *Rome and Jerusalem*, 59. Paul Lawrence Rose, *German Question/Jewish Question: Revolutionary Antisemitism from Kant to Wagner*, 321.

73. Hermann Cohen, *Ein Bekenntnis in der Judenfrage*, 15.

74. Rose, *German Question/Jewish Question*, 273–74.

75. Bruno Bauer, *Russland und das Germanenthum*, 9.

76. Eugen Dühring, *Die Judenfrage als Racen-, Sitten- und Culturfrage*, 144. My translation.

77. Frederick L. Hoffman, *Race Traits and Tendencies of the American Negro*, 310–11 and 328–29.

78. Kelly Miller, "A Review of Hoffman's Race Traits and Tendencies of the American Negro."

79. Kwame Anthony Appiah, *In My Father's House*, 28–46.

80. Douglass, "The Future of the Colored Race," 438.

81. W. E. B. Du Bois, *DuBois: Writings*, 821.

82. Du Bois, *Writings*, 821.

83. Edward Wilmot Blyden, *Black Spokesman: Selected Published Writings*, 201; Alexander Crummell, *Destiny and Race*, 195.

84. Du Bois, *Writings*, 825.

85. Kant, "Ideen zu einer allgemeinen Geschichte in weltbürgerlicher Absicht," in In *Kants Werke*, Akademie Textausgabe, vol. 8, 15–31, at 29; trans. "Idea for a Universal History with a Cosmopolitan Aim," in Kant, *Anthropology, History, and Education*, 107–20, at 119. Herder, *Geschichte der Menschheit*, vol. 2, 206; trans. *Philosophy of the History of Man*, 224.

86. Hegel, *Philosophie der Weltgeschichte*, 1222–30; trans. *Philosophy of History*, 84–92. See Bernasconi, "Hegel's Racism: A Reply to McCarney," 36.

87. Du Bois, *Writings*, 818.

88. Buffon, *Histoire naturelle, générale et particulière*, vol. 12, 223.

NOTES 275

89. Jean-Baptiste Lamarck, *Philosophie zoologique, ou, exposition des considerations relatives à l'histoire naturelle des Animaux*, vol. 1, 64; trans. Hugh Elliot, *Zoological Philosophy: An Exposition with Regard to the Natural History of Animals*, 39.

90. Lamarck, *Philosophie zoologique*, vol. 1, 349–57; trans. *Zoological Philosophy*, 169–77.

91. Lamarck, *Philosophie zoologique*, vol. 1, 235; trans. *Zoological Philosophy*, 113.

92. Marvin Harris, *The Rise of Anthropological Theory: A History of Theories of Culture*, 83–84.

93. Georgios Varouxakis, "Empire, Race, Euro-centrism: John Stuart Mill and His Critics," 139.

94. Carl Gustav Carus, *Denkschrift zum Hundertjährigen Geburtsfeste Goethe's*.

95. John Stuart Mill, *Collected Works of John Stuart Mill*, vol. 21, *Essays on Equality, Law and Education*, 93.

96. Thomas Carlyle, "Occasional Discourse on the Negro Question," 676–77; Mill, *Equality, Law and Education*, 92.

97. Mill, *Collected Works*, vol. 21, *Equality, Law and Education*, 93.

98. E.g., Hoffman, *Race Traits and Tendencies*, 310.

99. Mill, *Collected Works*, vol. 20, *Essays on French History and Historians*, 235–36; Mill, *Collected Works*, vols. 14–17, *The Later Letters of John Stuart Mill*, 691, 1093, 1563.

100. Mill, *Collected Works*, vols. 14–17, 1972, *Later Letters*, 691.

101. Mill, *Collected Works*, vols. 12–13, *The Earlier Letters of John Stuart Mill*, 329.

102. Mill, *Collected Works*, vols. 12–13, *Earlier Letters*, 404 and 456.

103. Mill, *Collected Works*, vol. 21, *Equality, Law and Education*, 309–10.

104. Mill, *Collected Works*, vols. 18–19, *Essays on Politics and Society*, 224.

105. Mill, *Collected Works*, vol. 14–17, *Later Letters*, 1563.

106. Charles Wentworth Dilke, *Greater Britain*, vol. 1, 308.

107. Mill, *Collected Works*, vols. 22–25, *Newspaper Writings*, 236.

108. Bart Schultz, "Mill and Sedgwick, Imperialism and Racism," 123–30.

109. Henry Sidgwick, *The Elements of Politics*, 313–14.

110. Carl Peters, *Willenswelt und Weltwille: Studien und Ideen zu einer Weltanschauung*.

111. Herbert Spencer, "Personal Beauty," 423, 427.

112. Spencer, "Personal Beauty," 425.

113. Fritz Schultze, *Kant und Darwin: Ein Beitrag zur Geschichte der Entwicklungslehre*. Johannes Unold, *Die Ethnologischen und anthropogeographischen Anschauungen bei I. Kant und J. Reinh. Forster*.

114. Ernst Haeckel, *Natürliche Schöpfungsgeschichte* (1868), 80–85; *Natürliche Schöpfungsgeschichte* (1874), 89–94; *Natürliche Schöpfungs-Geschichte* (1902), vol. 1, 89–95.

115. Pouchet, *De la pluralité des races humaines*, 197; trans. Victor Masson, *The Plurality of the Human Race*, 133.

116. Pouchet, *La biologie Aristotélique*.

117. Clémence Royer, "Préface de la première edition," in *De l'origine des espèces par Charles Darwin*, lvii.

276 NOTES

118. Auguste Comte, *Système de politique de positive*, vol. 2, 462; trans. *System of Positive Polity*, vol. 2, 378.
119. Firmin, *De l'égalité des races humaines*, 124; trans. *The Equality of the Human Races*, 83.
120. Wallace, "Origin of Human Races," clxiv–clxv.
121. Wallace, "Origin of Human Races," clxix.
122. Firmin, *De l'égalité des races humaines*, 661–62; trans. *Equality of the Human Races*, 450.
123. Firmin, *De l'égalité des races humaines*, 660–61; trans. *Equality of the Human Races*, 449.
124. Firmin, *De l'égalité des races humaines*, 582–99; trans. *Equality of the Human Races*, 393–404.
125. Francis Galton, *Inquiries into Human Faculty and Its Development*, 24–25n.
126. Galton, *English Men of Science: Their Nature and Nurture*, 12.
127. R. S. Cowan, "Nature and Nurture: The Interplay of Biology and Politics in the Work of Francis Galton," 176–77.
128. Bernasconi, "Ethnic Race: Revisiting Alain Locke's Neglected Proposal," 128–30.
129. Gregory Moore, *Nietzsche, Biology and Metaphor*, 134–35, 145–46, 160–63.
130. Gerd Schank, *"Rasse" und "Züchtung" bei Nietzsche*. See Bernasconi, "Nietzsche as a Philosopher of Racialized Breeding."
131. Friedrich Nietzsche, *Sämtliche Werke*, vol. 5, *Jenseits von Gut und Böse*, 194; trans. *Beyond Good and Evil/On the Genealogy of Morality*, in *The Complete Works of Friedrich Nietzsche*, 156–57.
132. Nietzsche, *Sämtliche Werke*, vol. 5, 184; trans. *Beyond Good and Evil*, in *Complete Works*, 149.
133. Nietzsche, *Sämtliche Werke*, vol. 5, 263; trans. *Beyond Good and Evil*, in *Complete Works*, 222. Rudolf Virchow, *Gesamtbericht über die von der deutschen anthropologischen Gesellschaft veranlassten Erhebungen über die Farbe der Haut, der Haare und der Augen der Schulkinder in Deutschland*.
134. Nietzsche, *Sämtliche Werke*, vol. 2, *Der Wanderer und sein Schatten*. 309–10; trans. *Human, All Too Human I*, in *The Complete Works of Friedrich Nietzsche*, 257–58.
135. Nietzsche, *Sämtliche Werke*, vol. 5, 194; trans. *Beyond Good and Evil*, in *Complete Works*, 157.
136. Moritz Busch, *Graf Bismarck und seine Leute während des Kriegs mit Frankreich*, vol. 2, 218.
137. Nietzsche, *Sämtliche Werke*, vol. 5, 219; trans. *Beyond Good and Evil*, in *Complete Works*, 179.
138. Nietzsche, *Sämtliche Werke*, vol. 5, 303; trans. *Beyond Good and Evil*, in *Complete Works*, 256 and 320.
139. Nietzsche, *Sämtliche Werke*, vol. 5, 138; trans. *Beyond Good and Evil*, in *Complete Works*, 109.
140. Nietzsche, *Sämtliche Werke*, vol. 3, *Die fröhliche Wissenschaft*. 213; trans. *Dawn: Thoughts on the Presumption of Morality*, in *The Complete Works of Friedrich Nietzsche*, 180.

NOTES 277

141. Nietzsche, *Sämtliche Werke*, vol. 5, 289; trans. *On the Genealogy of Morality*, 245.
142. Nietzsche, *Sämtliche Werke*, vol. 6, *Götzen-Dämmerung*, 134; trans. Carol Diethe, *Twilight of the Idols*, 108.
143. Moore, *Nietzsche, Biology and Metaphor*, 46–55.
144. Schultz, "Mill and Sedgwick," 120, 129. Kathy J. Cooke, "The Limits of Heredity: Nature and Nurture in American Eugenics before 1915," 267–68.
145. Galton, *Inquiries into Human Faculty*, 308–17.
146. Alain Locke, *The Philosophy of Alain Locke: Harlem Renaissance and Beyond*, 192; Bernasconi, "Ethnic Race," 131.
147. William Bateson, "Heredity in the Physiology of Nations: A Review of *The Principles of Heredity* by G. Archdall Reid" 456, 459.

Chapter 4

1. Georges Pouchet, *De la pluralité des races humaines* (1864), 10; trans. *The Plurality of the Human Race*, 7.
2. Pouchet, *De la pluralité des races humaines* (1858), 9.
3. Reginald Horsman, *Race and Manifest Destiny: The Origins of American Racial Anglo-Saxonism*, 145–47; Anon., "Natural History of Man," 328.
4. For example, Theodor Waitz, *Anthropologie der Naturvölker*, vol. 1, 430; trans. *Introduction to Anthropology*, 351.
5. Samuel Stanhope Smith, *An Essay on the Causes of the Variety of Complexion and Figure in the Human Species* [. . .]. (1810), 210.
6. Anténor Firmin, *De l'égalité des races humaines*, 51; trans. *The Equality of the Human Races*, 38.
7. William Stanton, *The Leopard's Spots: Scientific Attitudes toward Race in America, 1815–1859*, 223n4.
8. Julien-Joseph Virey, *Histoire naturelle du genre humaine* [History of Mankind], 65–83; J. H. Guenebault, *Natural History of the Negro Race*, 120–27.
9. Thomas Jefferson, *Notes on the State of Virginia*, 229.
10. Frederick Douglass, "The Claims of the Negro, Ethnologically Considered," in *The Frederick Douglass Papers*, series 1, vol. 2, 497–525, at 524.
11. J. L. Cabell, *The Testimony of Modern Science to the Unity of Mankind*, 267n.
12. John Mitchell, "An Essay upon the Causes of the Different Colours of People in Different Climates," 146.
13. William Charles Wells, "An Account of a Female of the White Race of Mankind, Part of Whose Skin Resembles That of a Negro," 432–39.
14. Henry Home, *Sketches of the History of Man*, vol. 1, 11.
15. Robert Knox, *The Races of Men: A Fragment*, 75–99.
16. Smith, *An Essay on the Causes of the Variety of Complexion and Figure in the Human Species* [. . .]. (1787), 6.
17. Smith, *Causes of the Variety* (1787), 59–60n.

278 NOTES

18. Smith, *Causes of the Variety* (1787), 57–58.
19. Smith, *Causes of the Variety* (1810), 255n.
20. Firmin, *De l'égalité des races*, 404–25; trans. *Equality of the Human Races*, 274–86.
21. Douglass, "The Future of the Colored Race," 438.
22. Charles Caldwell, *Thoughts on the Original Unity of the Human Race*, 27.
23. James Cowles Prichard, *Researches into the Physical History of Mankind* (1826), 2 and 584–95; Caldwell, *Thoughts on the Original Unity*, 17–50.
24. Samuel George Morton, *Crania Americana*, 88.
25. Stanton, *The Leopard's Spots*, 149–54.
26. Morton, "Hybridity in Animals, Considered in Reference to the Question of the Unity of the Human Species," 212.
27. Morton, "Hybridity in Animals," 40n.
28. Louis Agassiz, "Sketch of the Natural Provinces of the Animal World and Their Relation to the Different Types of Man," in J. C. Nott and George R. Gliddon, eds., *Types of Mankind*, lviii–lxxvi, at lxxvi.
29. Josiah C. Nott, *Two Lectures on the Natural History of the Caucasian and Negro Races*, 8.
30. Nott and George R. Gliddon, eds., *Types of Mankind or Ethnological Researches*, 373.
31. Nott and Gliddon, *Types of Mankind*, 405.
32. John Bachman, *The Doctrine of the Unity of the Human Race*, 106.
33. Prichard, *Researches into the Physical History of Mankind* (1836), vol. 1, 148–49.
34. Nott, "The Mulatto a Hybrid—Probable Extermination of the Two Races If the Whites and Blacks Are Allowed to Intermarry," 253.
35. Elizabeth Cary Agassiz, ed., *Louis Agassiz: His Life and Correspondence*, vol. 2, 608.
36. Agassiz, *Louis Agassiz*, vol. 2, 598–600.
37. Agassiz, *Louis Agassiz*, vol. 2, 597.
38. Count Oscar Reichenbach, "On the Vitality of the Black Race, or the Coloured People in the United States, According to the Census."
39. Franz Broca, "Des phénomènes d'hybridité dans le genre humaine" (1860), 400–401; trans. *On the Phenomena of Hybridity in the Genus Homo*, 33. Jean Boudin, *Traité de géographie et de statistique médicales et des maladies*, vol. 2, 220.
40. Broca, "Des phenomenes d'hybridité dans le genre humaine" (1859), 602; trans. *On the Phenomena of Hybridity*, 2.
41. Prichard, *Researches into the Physical History of Mankind* (1826), vol. 1, 97–98.
42. Caldwell, *Thoughts on the Original Unity*, 39–40.
43. Morton, "Hybridity in Animals," 211.
44. Morton, "Hybridity in Animals," 210.
45. Arthur de Gobineau, *Essai sur l'inégalité des races humaines*, 28–29; trans. *The Inequality of Human Races*, 29–30. Robert C. Young, *Colonial Desire: Hybridity in Theory, Culture and Race*, 107.
46. Gobineau, *Essai sur l'inégalité*, 175 and 217–19; trans. *The Inequality of Human Races*, 170 and 208–10.
47. J. H. Guenebault, *Natural History of the Negro Race*, 88.

NOTES 279

48. Gobineau, *The Moral and Intellectual Diversity of Races with Particular Reference to Their Respective Influence in the Civil and Political History of Mankind*.
49. W. W. Wright, "Amalgamation," 3 and 13.
50. Wright, "Amalgamation," 13.
51. Louisa S. McCord, "Diversity of the Races: Its Bearing upon Negro Slavery," 414.
52. Thomas Smyth, "The Unity of the Human Races," 345.
53. R. W. Haskins, *History and Progress of Phrenology*, 111.
54. Nott, *Two Lectures on the Natural History of the Caucasian and Negro Races*, 38.
55. S. Kneeland, "Introduction," in *The Natural History of the Human Species*, 92.
56. Nott and Gliddon, *Types of Mankind*, 69.
57. Lewis Henry Morgan, *League of the Ho-dé-no-sau-nee, Or Iroquois*, 33 and 143.
58. James Sullivan, *The History of the District of Maine*, 139.
59. George W. Stocking Jr., *Race, Culture, and Evolution: Essays in the History of Anthropology*, 42–68.
60. Nott and Gliddon, *Types of Mankind*, 50.
61. Herbert Spencer, *The Data of Ethics*, 240.
62. Joseph C. G. Kennedy, *Population of the United States in 1860*, xii.
63. Frederick Hoffman, "Vital Statistics of the Negro," 531.
64. W. E. B. Du Bois, *The Conservation of Races*; see also Chapter 8 in this volume.
65. Lois Wood Burkhalter, *Gideon Lincecum, 1793–1874: A Biography*, 96.
66. Mark Largent, *Breeding Contempt: The History of Coerced Sterilization in the United States*, 25–27.
67. Francis Galton, *Inquiries into Human Faculty and Its Development*, 63; Spencer, *The Man versus the State*, 69n.
68. Robert Dugdale, *"The Jukes": A Study in Crime, Pauperism, Disease and Heredity*, 65.
69. Eugen Fischer, *Die Rehobother Bastards und das Bastardierungsproblem beim Menschen*, 305–6.

Chapter 5

1. Sometimes very different discourses were employed away from North America and northern Europe, and a study of them would uncover different kinds of racism that had different kinds of effects. But the unprecedented racial violence of European nations in the twentieth century provides justification enough for my focus, especially given the fact that the link between racisms in North America and northern Europe, although recognized in some of the historical literature, still needs further examination. See Stefan Kühl, *The Nazi Connection*, and James Q. Whitman, *Hitler's American Model*.
2. Ann Laura Stoler, the first person in English to take seriously Foucault's discussion of race, already drew attention to his failure to address race-based slavery, colonialism, and imperialism in all but the most perfunctory terms. See Stohler, *Race and the Education of Desire* and *Carnal Knowledge and Imperial Power*. It is possible

280 NOTES

that at one point Foucault intended to make good this lack, insofar as the original plan for *The History of Sexuality*, the sixth and final volume, was to have been called "Population and Races." See Arnold Davidson, "Ethics as Ascetics," 117. See also Ladelle McWhorter, *Racism and Sexual Oppression in Anglo-America*.

3. Dan Stone, *History, Memory and Mass Atrocity*, 217.

4. I prefer the term "medicalizing" because, although I agree with Foucault that the dominant discourse on race in both Europe and North America in the middle of the nineteenth century was a historical, rather than a biological, discourse, what was new about the racial discourse of the late nineteenth century was not its recognition of biological heredity, which can already be found in the late eighteenth century, especially in Kant, but its sense that by selective breeding once could manipulate or make races: they were no longer simply given. See Chapter 3 in this volume.

5. Michel Foucault, *Histoire de la sexualité*, vol. 1, 188–91; trans. *The History of Sexuality*, vol. 1, 143–45.

6. Foucault, *"Il faut défendre la société,"* 53; trans. *"Society Must Be Defended,"* 61.

7. Foucault, *Histoire de la sexualité*, vol. 1, 197; trans. *History of Sexuality*, vol. 1, 149.

8. Foucault, *"Il faut défendre la société,"* 75; trans. *"Society Must Be Defended,"* 87.

9. Foucault, *Les anormaux*, 294; trans. Graham Burchell, *Abnormal*, 316.

10. Foucault, *"Il faut défendre la société,"* 70; trans. *"Society Must Be Defended,"* 80. See Chapter 14 of this volume.

11. Foucault, *Les anormaux*, 311; trans. *Abnormal*, 328.

12. Foucault, *Histoire de la sexualité*, vol. 1, 197; trans. *History of Sexuality*, vol. 1, 149.

13. Foucault, *"Il faut défendre la société,"* 57; trans. *"Society Must Be Defended,"* 65.

14. Foucault, *"Il faut défendre la société,"* 229; trans. *"Society Must Be Defended,"* 257.

15. Foucault, *Histoire de la sexualité*, vol. 1, 181; trans. *History of Sexuality*, vol. 1, 138. Foucault, *"Il faut défendre la société,"* 214–21; trans. *"Society Must Be Defended,"* 241–48.

16. Foucault, *"Il faut défendre la société,"* 228; trans. *"Society Must Be Defended,"* 256.

17. Patrick Brantlinger, "'Dying Races': Rationalizing Genocide in the Nineteenth Century," 51.

18. Foucault, *Histoire de la sexualité*, vol. 1, 178; trans. *History of Sexuality*, vol. 1, 135.

19. Hugo Grotius, *De jure belli ac pacis*, xxx; trans. *The Rights of War and Peace*, 1495. Samuel Pufendorf, *De officio hominis et civis: Juxta legem naturalem*, 113; trans. *On the Duty of Man and Citizen According to Natural Law*, 129.

20. Morgan Godwyn, *The Negro's and Indians Advocate: Suing for Their Admission into the Church*, 14–19.

21. Thomas Jefferson "To Francis C. Gray, 4 March 1815," in *The Papers of Thomas Jefferson*, 311.

22. Godwyn, *Negro's and Indians Advocate*, 41–42.

23. See Mattie Erma Parker, ed., *North Carolina Charters and Constitutions, 1578–1648*, 164.

24. Grotius, *De jure belli ac pacis*, xxx; trans. *The Rights of War and Peace*, 558. *De officio hominis et civis*, 114; trans. *On the Duty of Man and Citizen*, 130.

NOTES 281

25. John Locke, *Two Treatises of Government*, 302. See also Robert Bernasconi, "Proto-Racism: Carolina in Locke's Mind," 76–77.

26. Foucault, *"Il faut défendre la société,"* 51; trans. *"Society Must Be Defended,"* 60.

27. Foucault, *Histoire de la sexualité*, vol. 1, 37; trans. *History of Sexuality*, vol. 1, 26.

28. Foucault, *Histoire de la sexualité*, vol. 1, 35; trans. *History of Sexuality*, vol. 1, 24–25.

29. Foucault, "La politique de la santé au xviiie siècle," in *Dits et écrits*. vol. 3, 13–27, at 18; trans. "The Politics of Health in the Eighteenth Century," in James D. Faubion, ed., *Power*, 90–105, at 95. See also "La naissance de la médecine sociale," in *Dits et écrits*, vol. 3, 207–28, at 212; trans. "The Birth of Social Medicine," in James D. Faubion, ed., *Power*, 134–56, at 140. And *Histoire de la sexualité*, vol. 1, 35; trans. *History of Sexuality*, vol. 1, 25.

30. Sara Eigen Figal, *Heredity, Race, and the Birth of the Modern*, 98–127.

31. Johann Peter Frank, *System einer vollständigen medicinischen Polizey*, 2n; trans. *A System of Complete Medical Police*, 12n.

32. Frank, *System einer vollständigen medicinischen Polizey*, 340–41; trans. *Complete Medical Police*, 51.

33. Frank, *System einer vollständigen medicinischen Polizey*, 405n.

34. Bernasconi, "Who Invented the Concept of Race? Kant's Role in the Enlightenment Construction of Race," 21–24.

35. Immanuel Kant, "Von den verschiedenen Racen der Menschen," in *Kants Werke*, Akademie Textausgabe, vol. 2, 427–44, at 429–31; trans. "Of the Different Races of Human Beings," in Kant, *Anthropology, History, and Education*, 82–97, at 84–87.

36. Kant "Anthropologie in pragmatischer Hinsicht," in *Kants Werke*, Akademie Textausgabe, vol. 7, 117–333, at 320–21; trans. "Anthropology from a Pragmatic Standpoint," in Kant, *Anthropology, History, and Education*, 227–429, 415–16.

37. Augustin Thierry, *Dix ans d'études historiques*, 633.

38. William Frédéric Edwards, *Des caractères physiologiques des races humaines considérés dans leurs rapports avec l'histoire: Lettre à M. Amédée Thierry*, 22–29.

39. Victor Courtet follows Kant's thinking of the children of parents of different races as being midway between the two, in *La science politique fondée sur la science de l'homme*, 83–84. See also Jean Boissel, *Victor Courtet (1813–1867): premier théoricien de la hiérarchie des races*, 143–70, and Loïc Rignol and Philippe Régnier, "Races et politique dans l'Histoire de France chez Victor Courtet de l'Isle (1813–1867)," in Philippe Régnier, ed., *Études saint-simoniennes*, 127–52. See also Sandrine Lemaire, "Gustave d'Eichtal ou les ambiguïtiés d'une ethnologie saint-simonienne," in Régnier, ed., *Études saint-simoniennes*.

40. James Cowles Prichard, *Researches into the Physical History of Mankind*, 148–49.

41. Félix von Azara, *Reise nach Sud-Amerika von Don Felix von Zara in den Jahren 1781 bis 1801*, 367.

42. Bernasconi, "Kant as an Unfamiliar Source of Racism," 156–58.

43. María Elena Martínez, "The Black Blood of New Spain," 483–86.

44. Bernasconi, "Kant as an Unfamiliar Source of Racism," 76–77.

45. Friedrich L. Jahn, *Deutsches Volksthum*, 25.

282 NOTES

46. Claude Blanckaert "Of Monstrous Métis? Hybridity, Fear of Miscegenation, and Patriotism from Buffon to Paul Broca," in Sue Peabody and Tyler Stovall, ed., *The Color of Liberty: Histories of Race in France*, 42–70, at 48–53.

47. Robert Knox, *The Races of Men: A Fragment*, 7. See also 10, 13, 14, and 90.

48. Arthur de Gobineau, *Essai sur l'inégalité des races humaines*, vol. 1, vi; trans. *The Inequality of Human Races*, xiv.

49. Gobineau, *Essai sur l'inégalité des races humaines*, vol. 1, 217–18; trans. *Inequality of Human Races*, 208–9.

50. Gobineau, *Essai sur l'inégalité des races humaines*, vol. 2, 563.

51. David Goodman Croly and George Wakeman, *Miscegenation: The Theory of the Blending of the Races, Applied to the American White Man and Negro*.

52. Samuel Cartwright "The Diseases of Negroes," 335.

53. Georges Pouchet, *De la pluralité des races humaines*, 10; trans. *The Plurality of the Human Race*, 7.

54. Foucault, *Les anormaux*, 110; trans. *Abnormal*, 119.

55. Bénédict A. Morel, *Traité des dégénérescences physiques, intellectuelles et morales de l'espèce humaine*, 73. Philippe Buchez wrote: "No one [until Morel] had affirmed that certain diseases, certain forms of poisoning, certain habits of the parents, have the power to create, in the children, a truly consecutive state, indefinitely transmissible, unto the extinction of the stock—unless some intervention arrests it." Cited in Ruth Friedlander, "Bénédict-Augustin Morel and the Development of the Theory of Degenerescence." See also Daniel Pick, *Faces of Degeneration*, 50–67.

56. Morel, *Traité des dégénérescences physiques*, 385–86.

57. Morel, *Traité des dégénérescences physiques*, 45–46.

58. Anon., "On Degenerations in Man," 456.

59. Morel, *Traité des dégénérescences physiques*, 5–6.

60. Morel, *Traité des dégénérescences physiques*, 5.

61. Morel, *Traité des dégénérescences physiques*, 356 and 661.

62. Foucault, *"Il faut défendre la société,"* 70–71; trans. *"Society Must Be Defended,"* 81.

63. See Foucault, *"Il faut défendre la société,"* 230; trans. *"Society Must Be Defended,"* 258.

64. Josiah Nott, "Negro Population of the South with Reference to Life Statistics," 292–99; 292–301.

65. Frederick L. Hoffman, *Race Traits and Tendencies of the American Negro*, 328.

66. Frederick Douglass, "The Future of the Colored Race," 439.

67. W. W. Wright, "Amalgamation," 13.

68. Gobineau, *The Moral and Intellectual Diversity of Races*; see Bernasconi, "The Logic of Whiteness," 83.

69. Georg Forster, "Noch etwas über die Menschenrassen: An Herrn Dr. Biester," 82–83.

70. Foucault, *Les anormaux*, 124; trans. *Abnormal*, 133.

71. Samuel C. Williams, *Annotated Code of Tennessee*, 307.

72. Walter A. Plecker, *Eugenics in Relation to the New Family and the Law on Racial Integrity*, 31.

73. Eugen Fischer *Die Rehobother Bastards und das Bastardierungsproblem beim Menschen*, 101.

NOTES 283

74. See Bernasconi, "After the German Invention of Race: Conceptions of Race Mixing from Kant to Fischer and Hitler," 96–99.
75. Foucault, *"Il faut défendre la société,"* 53; trans. *"Society Must Be Defended,"* 62.
76. Al Carthill, *The Lost Dominion: The Story of England's Abdication in India*, 158. Adolf Hitler, *Mein Kampf*, 442; trans. *Mein Kampf*, 400.
77. William Bateson, "Heredity in the Physiology of Nations," 456–59, at 456.
78. Bateson, "Heredity in the Physiology of Nations," 458–59.
79. Quoted by Benno Müller-Hill, *Tödliche Wissenschaft*, 13–14; trans. *Murderous Science*, 10.

Chapter 6

1. Linda Martín Alcoff, "Toward a Phenomenology of Racial Embodiment," in Robert Bernasconi, ed., *Race*.
2. Ann Laura Stoler, *Carnal Knowledge and Imperial Power: Race and the Intimate in Colonial Rule*, 144. See also Stoler, "Racial Histories and Their Regimes of Truth."
3. Ariela J. Gross, *What Blood Won't Tell: A History of Race on Trial in America*, 11.
4. Gross, *What Blood Won't Tell*, 11.
5. For example, Michelle Brattain, "Miscegenation and Competing Definitions of Race in Twentieth-Century Louisiana," 648.
6. Audrey Smedley, *Race in North America: Origin and Evolution of a Worldview* (1993), 109 and 264–65. See also Audrey and Brian D. Smedley, *Race in North America: Origin and Evolution of a Worldview* (2012), 118 and 262.
7. The main works of the American polygenist school have been reprinted in Robert Bernasconi, ed., *American Theories of Polygenesis: Types of Mankind*.
8. Johann Friedrich Blumenbach, *De generis humani varietate nativa*, 285; trans. "On the Natural Variety of Mankind," 264.
9. Johann Friedrich Blumenbach, *Handbuch der Naturgeschichte*, 54.
10. Mark S. Weiner, *Americans without Law: The Racial Boundaries of Citizenship*, 100–102.
11. Jean-Baptiste Lamarck, *Philosophie zoologique*, vol. 1, 235; trans. *Zoological Philosophy: An Exposition with Regard to the Natural History of Animals*, 113.
12. Clarence King, "Style and the Monument," 443–44. On King, see Martha A. Sandweiss, *Passing Strange: A Gilded Age Tale of Love and Deception across the Color Line*. See also Frederick Douglass, "The Future of the Colored Race," 437–40.
13. Houston Stewart Chamberlain, *Die Grundlagen des neunzehnten Jahrhunderts*, vol. 2, 343; trans. John Lees, *Foundations of the Nineteenth Century*, 354.
14. See Jean Hiernaux and Michael Banton, "Statement of Race, Paris, July 1950," 31.
15. On structural racism, see, for example, Angela Y. Davis, "Race and Criminalization: Black Americans and the Punishment Industry," 265 and 270–71. See also Robert Bernasconi, "Racism Is a System: How Existentialism Became Dialectical in Fanon and Sartre."

284   NOTES

16. Naomi Zack has argued that today the mixed-race category could play the role of disrupting the Black-White racial dichotomy; *Race and Mixed Race*, 169. Similar claims have been made on the part of the concept of hybridity because it allegedly "breaks down the symmetry and duality of self/other, inside/outside"; Homi K. Bhabha, *The Location of Culture*, 116. Hybridity theory has been criticized on the grounds that its attempt at anti-essentialism cannot escape its own essentialism, but I would argue that a historical perspective that recognizes the error of tying racism too tightly to essentialism sees the problem differently. The exploration of that different perspective is one main aim of the present chapter.

17. "Mulatto" was a category in the official census from 1850 to 1920, and in 1890 it was briefly joined by "quadroon" and "octoroon"; Martha Hodes, "Fractions and Fictions in the United States Census of 1890," 241. See also Jennifer L. Hochschild and Brenna M. Powell, "Racial Reorganization and the United States Census 1850–1930," 59–96.

18. "Brown hybrid" was the preferred phrase of the "coloured" author C. Ziervogel in *Brown South Africa*, 19. For a discussion which also clarifies how members of the "coloured" community conceive their identity today, see Mohamed Adhikari, *Not White Enough, Not Black Enough*, 41–45.

19. See Lauren L. Basson, *White Enough to Be American? Race Mixing, Indigenous People, and the Boundaries of State and Nation*, 6.

20. On the concept of reciprocity, see Jean-Paul Sartre, *Critique de la raison dialectique*, 814–15; trans. Alan Sheridan-Smith, *Critique of Dialectical Reason*, 688–89.

21. I am not using the term "borderlands" as Gloria Anzaldúa does, although there is evidently some overlap. She employs the notion of borderlands to describe not just contact between cultures, races, and classes, but the space where two individuals share intimacy; *Borderlands/La Frontera: The New Mestiza*, 19. In my usage, the primary focus is on racial categories as the fluid, divisive site where race is continually being produced and recreated.

22. François Bernier, "Nouvelle division de la Terre, par les différentes espèces ou races d'hommes qui l'habitent, envoyée par un fameux Voyageur à M. [. . .]."

23. On Bernier, see Pierre H. Boulle, "François Bernier and the Origins of the Modern Concept of Race," in Sue Peabody and Tyler Stovall, ed., *The Color of Liberty: Histories of Race in France*, 11–27.

24. See Bernasconi, "Proto-Racism: Carolina in Locke's Mind." The question of whether and to what degree a term like "Negro" is already what we would understand as a racial term prior to any clear understanding of race is too complex to be considered here.

25. William Waller Hening, ed., *The Statutes at Large; Being a Collection of All the Laws of Virginia, from the First Session of the Legislature in the Year 1619*, vol. 1, 146.

26. Hening, *Statutes at Large*, vol. 3, 87. At the same time, in 1691, fines were composed on "any English woman "having a bastard child by any negro or mulatto."

27. "An Act declaring who shall not bear office in this country," in Hening, *Statutes at Large*, vol. 3, 252.

28. Hening, *Statutes at Large*, vol. 2, 184.

NOTES 285

29. Bernasconi, "Kant as an Unfamiliar Source of Racism," in *Philosophers on Race: Critical Essays*, 152–60.

30. See Bernasconi, "True Colors: Kant's Distinction between Nature and Artifice in Context."

31. On Kant's role in the history of the conceptualization of race, see Bernasconi, "Who Invented the Concept of Race? Kant's Role in the Enlightenment Concept of Race."

32. Paul Finkelman, "The Crime of Color." For the later period, see Chapter 5 in this volume.

33. See Werner Sollors, "Prohibitions of Interracial Marriage and Cohabitation."

34. Thomas Jefferson, "To Francis C. Gray, 4 March [1915]," in *The Papers of Thomas Jefferson*, 310–12.

35. Annette Gordon-Reed, *Thomas Jefferson and Sally Hemings: An American Controversy*, 7–58. See also Frank W. Sweet, *Legal History of the Color Line*, 153–56. Some contributions to the literature suggest that James Madison Hemings must have looked light enough to pass for White, but this is far from clear: E. M. Halliday, *Understanding Thomas Jefferson*, 178.

36. Jefferson, *Papers*, 311.

37. Jefferson, *Papers*, 311.

38. Fawn Brodie, *Thomas Jefferson: An Intimate History*, 287. Quoted in Annette Gordon-Reed, *Thomas Jefferson and Sally Hemings: An American Controversy*, 53–54.

39. Mattie Erma Parker, "The Fundamental Constitutions of Carolina, Version of 21 July 1669," 164.

40. A similar law had been passed in 1667 in Virginia in the sense that it was enacted that "the conferring of baptisme doth not alter the condition of the person as to his bondage or freedom"; Hening, *Statutes at Large*, vol. 2, 260. However, no racial or ethnic terms were specified.

41. Helen Tunnicliff Catterall, *Judicial Cases Concerning American Slavery and the Negro*, 269.

42. Brattain, "Miscegenation," 650.

43. Victoria E. Bynum, " 'White Negroes' in Segregated Mississippi: Miscegenation, Racial Identity, and the Law," 247–76.

44. Catterall, *Judicial Cases*, 264.

45. See Bernasconi, "The Logic of Whiteness: Hybridity and the Philosophy of Racial Segregation in the Nineteenth Century," 88n23.

46. George M. Stroud, *A Sketch of the Laws Relating to Slavery in the Several States of the United States of America* (1827) 12n.

47. Stroud, *A Sketch of the Laws Relating to Slavery in the Several States of the United States of America* (1856) 19–20n.

48. Stroud, *Sketch of the Laws* (1856) 270.

49. Josiah Clark Nott, "The Mulatto a Hybrid: Probable Extermination of the Two Races if the Whites and Blacks Are Allowed to Intermarry," *American Journal of the Medical Sciences* 6, 252; reprinted in vol. 1 of *Race, Hybridity, and Miscegenation*, 6.

50. For example, Sandweiss, *Passing Strange*, 187.

286   NOTES

51. The act is reprinted and discussed in an appendix to Earnest Sevier Cox, *White America*, 323–25. Cox was one of its chief supporters. On the role of Mendel, see Walter A. Plecker, "Virginia's Attempt to Adjust the Color Problem," 114. See also Gregory Michael Dorr, *Segregation's Science: Eugenics and Society in Virginia*, 1–10. Nevertheless, there were countervoices that maintained that even while Mendelian inheritance applied in some cases, there could be "no reversion to the Negro type in the offspring of mixed parents"; Earnest A. Hooton, in Caroline Bond Day, *A Study of Some Negro-White Families in the United States*, 107. See also Louis Wirth and Herbert Goldhamer, "The Hybrid and the Problem of Miscegenation, 329.

52. George B. Tindall, "The Question of Race in the South Carolina Constitutional Convention of 1895," 299.

53. Plecker, "Virginia's Attempt," 116.

54. J. Douglas Smith, "The Campaign for Racial Purity and the Erosion of Paternalism in Virginia 1922–1930," 95.

55. Plecker, "Virginia's Attempt," 114–15.

56. Smith, "Campaign for Racial Purity," 85–87.

57. John H. Burma, "The Measurement of Negro 'Passing,'" 20–21. The figure of twenty-five thousand was supplied by Hornell N. Hart in 1921, in *Selective Migration as a Factor in Child Welfare in the United States, with Special Reference to Iowa*, and referred to the 1890s. The lower figures were the more recent figures.

58. Gunnar Myrdal, *An American Dilemma: The Negro Problem and Modern Democracy*, 683. For a remarkable case, where a White man lived a double life as a Black husband, see Sandweiss, *Passing Strange*.

59. The 1930 census tried to institute a Mexican race, or at least include these in "people of other races," but this idea was dropped by 1940 following pressure from the League of United Latin American Citizens; Ariela J. Gross, *What Blood Won't Tell: A History of Race on Trial in America*, 217, 257, and 267.

60. Gross, *Blood Won't Tell*, 259 and 262. On the task of a conception of whiteness among some Mexicans, see 263.

61. Victor S. Clark et al., *Porto Rico and Its Problems*, 546. Laura Briggs, in *Reproducing Empire: Race, Sex, Science and U.S. Imperialism in Puerto Rico*, 88, cites the passage but mistakenly gives the page number as 576.

62. Bailey W. Diffie and Justine Whitfield Diffie, *Porto Rico: A Broken Pledge*, 8.

63. On boundary shifting in Puerto Rico, see Mara Loveman and Jeronimo O. Muniz, "How Puerto Rico Became White: Boundary Dynamics and Intercensus Racial Reclassification," 915–39.

64. See Ruth Pike, *Linajudos and Conversos in Seville: Greed and Prejudice in Sixteenth- and Seventeenth-Century Spain*. On the place of the purity of blood statutes in the history of racism, see Richard Popkin, "The Philosophical Basis of Modern Racism," 79–80.

65. Muriel Horrell, *Race Classification in South Africa: Its Effects on Human Beings*, 9.

66. Horrell, *Race Classification*, 6–7.

67. For an American example of the chaos created in the courts by the appeal to experts and nonexperts for their attempt to determine race on the basis of appearance, see the

report on the 1939 trial of Marie Antoinette Monks in Peggy Pascoe, "Miscegenation Law, Court Cases, and Ideologies of 'Race' in Twentieth-Century America," 56–57. Immigration authorities in the early twentieth century decided that while distinctions between the major races could be made on the basis of appearances, the people so categorized could best be approached reliably by immigration authorities only on the basis of language. This decision was explained in this way by the Immigration Commission under the chairmanship of Senator William Dillingham, in *Dictionary of Races or Peoples*, 4.

68. See J. Douglas Smith, *Managing White Supremacy: Race, Politics, and Citizenship in Jim Crow Virginia*, 89–106. There were similar problems in Louisiana where the term "colored" became synonymous with "Negro" only in the post–Civil War era, notably in the case of *Sunseri v. Cassagne*, 191 La. at 214, cited by Brattain in "Miscegenation," 646.

69. Basson, *White Enough*, 177.

70. Bernasconi, "Can Race Be Thought in Terms of Facticity? A Reconsideration of Sartre's and Fanon's Existential Theories of Race," 195–213.

Chapter 7

1. Robin Blackburn, *The Overthrow of Colonial Slavery, 1776–1848*, 36.
2. William Paley, *The Principles of Moral and Political Philosophy* (1785), 197.
3. Paley, *The Principles of Moral and Political Philosophy* (1786), 197.
4. Joachim Schwartz, "Réflexions sur l'esclavage des Nègres," 318.
5. Jacques-Henri Bernardin de Saint-Pierre, *Voyage à l'Isle de France, à l'Isle de Bourbon, au Cap de Bonne-Espérance, &c*, vol. 1, 204; trans. *Journey to Mauritius*, 132–33.
6. David Hume, "Of National Characters," 208n. Immanuel Kant, "Beobachtungen über das Gefühl des Schönen und Erhaben," in *Kants Werke*, Akademie Textausgabe, vol. 2, 205–56, at 253; trans. "Observations on the Feeling of the Beautiful and Sublime," in Kant, *Anthropology, History, and Education*, 23–62, at 59.
7. Glen Doris, "The Scottish Enlightenment and the Politics of Abolition."
8. In this chapter, I refer to the 1999 edition, *Thoughts and Sentiments on the Evil of Slavery*.
9. Ottabah Cugoano, *Réflexions sur la traite et l'esclavage des nègres*, 22. See Gregory Pierrot, "Insights on 'Lord Hoth' and Ottobah Cugoano."
10. Henri Grégoire, *De la littérature des Nègres, ou Recherches sur leur facultés intellectuelles, leurs qualités morales et leur littératures*, 218; trans. *On the Cultural Achievements of Negroes*, 91–92.
11. Grégoire, *De la littérature des Nègres*, 223; trans. *Cultural Achievements of Negroes*, 94.
12. Anthony Bogues, *Black Heretics, Black Prophets: Radical Political Intellectuals*, 32–46. On Cugoano and in addition to the works cited in the main body of the text, and in Vincent Carretta's introduction to Cugoano's *Thoughts and Sentiments*, see Julie K. Ward, "'The Master's Tools': Abolitionist Arguments of Equiano and Cugoano";

288   NOTES

Helena Woodard, *African-British Writings in the Eighteenth Century*; Roxann Wheeler, "'Betrayed by Some of My Own Complexion': Cugoano, Abolition, and the Contemporary Language of Racialism"; Paget Henry, "Between Hume and Cugoano: Race, Ethnicity and Philosophical Entrapment"; and Stefan M. Wheelock, *Barbaric Culture and Black Critique*. Cugoano's originality and literary competence has been challenged by S. E. Ogude et al., in *Genius in Bondage: A Study of the Origins of African Literature in English*, 120–30. For a response, see Jeffrey Gunn, "Creating a Paradox: Quobna Ottobah Cugoano and the Slave Trade's Violation of the Principles of Christianity, Reason, and Property Ownership." The most powerful case for Cugoano's originality at a general level is made by Bogues in *Black Heretics, Black Prophets*, 32–46. What I do here is focus on specific arguments. I am grateful to Chike Jeffers for sharing with me his as-yet-unpublished essay "Slavery, Freedom, and Equality: Cugoano and Locke on Natural Rights."

13. Richard Baxter, *A Christian Directory: Or, a Sum of Practical Divinity*, 73.

14. Epifanio de Moirans, *A Just Defense of the Natural Freedom of Slaves: All Slaves Should Be Free*, 177.

15. Russell Parsons Jameson, *Montesquieu et l'esclavage*, 185–87.

16. Joel S. Panzer, *The Popes and Slavery*, 81; Pius Onyemechi Adiele, *The Popes, the Catholic Church and the Transatlantic Enslavement of Black Africans, 1418–1839*, 370–74.

17. Jean Bodin, *Les Six Livres de la République: Livre premier*, 309. See Henry Heller, "Bodin on Slavery and Primitive Accumulation," 61–64.

18. Alberico Gentili, *De jure belli libri tres*, trans. vol. 1, 541; vol. 2, 331. See Harold E. Braun, "Making the Canon? The Early Reception of the *République* in Castilian Political Thought," 286–87.

19. Pierre de Charron, *De la sagesse: Trois livres*, 163; trans. *Of Wisdom: Three Books*, 498.

20. Bartolomé Las Casas, *Obras completas, Historia de las Indias*, vol. 2, 1467.

21. Las Casas, *Obras completas, Historia de las Indias*, vol. 3, 2324.

22. Las Casas, *Tratados de 1532*, 239–54; trans. Francis Patrick Sullivan, *Indian Freedom: The Cause of Bartolomé de las Casas, 1484–1566*, 255–69.

23. Las Casas, *Obras completas, Historia de las Indias*, vol. 3, 2412.

24. Juan Ginés Sepúlveda, *Obras completas*, vol. 3, *Demócrates Segundo*, 56.

25. Sepúlveda, *Demócrates Segundo*, 65–66.

26. Sepúlveda, *Demócrates Segundo*, 68.

27. Francisco de Vitoria, *Relectio de Indis; o, Libertad de los indios*, 84–86 and 89; trans. "On the American Indians," in *Vitoria: Political Writings*, 282–83 and 285.

28. E.g., Algernon Sidney, *Discourses concerning Government*, 4.

29. E.g., Sidney, *Discourses concerning Government*, 239.

30. Christoph Meiners, "Fortgesetzte Betrachtungen über den *Sclavenhandel*, und die Freylassung der Neger," 22–25.

31. Kant, "Über den Gebrauch teleologischer Principien in der Philosophie," in *Kants Werke*, Akademie Textausgabe, vol. 8, 157–84, at 174; trans. "On the Use of Teleological Principles in Philosophy," in Kant, *Anthropology, History, and Education*, 192–218, at 209.

32. James Tobin, *Cursory Remarks upon the Reverend Mr. Ramsay's Essay on the Treatment and Conversion of African Slaves in the Sugar Colonies,* 117; trans., "Anmerkungen über Ramsays Schrift von der Behandlung der Negersklaven in den Westindischen Zuckerinseln," 287. See Robert Bernasconi. "Kant as an Unfamiliar Source of Racism," 149–52.
33. Tobin, *Cursory Remarks,* 141.
34. Nell Irvin Painter, *The History of White People,* xi, 42. Andrew S. Curran, *The Anatomy of Blackness: Science and Slavery in the Age of Englightenment,* 9–10, 53.
35. Thomas Tryon, *Friendly Advice to the Gentlemen-Planters of the East and West Indies,* 114–17; Peter Kitson, *Romantic Literature, Race, and Colonial Encounter,* 114–21.
36. Vincenzo Merolle, ed., *The Manuscripts of Adam Ferguson,* 145.
37. Hugo Grotius, *De jure belli ac pacis,* 196; trans. *The Rights of War and Peace,* 558.
38. John Locke, *Two Treatises of Government,* 275.
39. Locke, *Two Treatises of Government,* 284–85.
40. Anon., "Review of An Essay Concerning the True Original, Extent and End of Civil Government," 577; Locke, *Two Treatises of Government,* 278–79.
41. Mattie Erma Parker, "The Fundamental Constitutions of Carolina, Version of 21 July 1669," 164, 204–5. See Bernasconi, "Proto-Racism: Carolina in Locke's Mind."
42. James Farr, "'So Vile and Miserable an Estate': The Problem of Slavery in Locke's Political Thought," 269.
43. Locke, *Two Treatises of Government,* 284.
44. For a more nuanced treatment of this point, see Chapter 2 of this volume.
45. Richard Ligon, *A True & Exact History of the Island of Barbadoes,* 43, 54, 107.
46. Gershom Carmichael, *S. Puffendorfii: De officio hominis et civis, juxta legim naturalem,* 360; trans., "Supplements and Observations upon the Two Books of Samuel Pufendorf's *On the Duty of Man and Citizen,*" 144.
47. Samuel Pufendorf, *Les devoirs de l'homme, et du citoein,* 286–87.
48. Wylie Sypher, "Hutcheson and the 'Classical' Theory of Slavery," 280.
49. Francis Hutcheson, *Philosophiae Moralis Institutio Compendiaria,* 282n; trans., *A Short Introduction to Moral Philosophy,* 275n.
50. Hutcheson, *Philosophiae Moralis,* 285; trans. *Short Introduction to Moral Philosophy,* 277.
51. Hutcheson, *A System of Moral Philosophy,* 202.
52. Hutcheson, *A System of Moral Philosophy,* 85.
53. James Beattie, *Elements of Moral Science,* 153–87.
54. Beattie, *An Essay on the Nature and Immutability of Truth, in Opposition to Sophistry and Scepticism,* 463–68.
55. Beattie, *Miscellaneous Items.* See Doris, "An Abolitionist Too Late? James Beattie and the Scottish Enlightenment's Lost Chance to Influence the Slave Trade Debate."
56. Roger Robinson, *The Correspondence of James Beattie,* vol. 3, 115.
57. Charles-Louis de Secondat Montesquieu, *De l'esprit des loix,* 332–33; trans. Anne M. Cohler, *The Spirit of the Laws,* 252.

290 NOTES

58. George Wallace, *A System of the Principles of the Law of Scotland*, 888–98; Gordon Turnbull, *An Apology for Negro Slavery: or the West-India Planters Vindicated from the Charge of Inhumanity*, 3.
59. Montesquieu, *Pensées: Le spicilège*, 227; trans. *My Thoughts*, 58.
60. Paley, *Recollections of a Speech, upon the Slave Trade; Delivered in Carlisle, on Thursday the 9th of February, 1792*, 12.
61. Paley, *Principles of Moral and Political Philosophy* (1785), vi.
62. Adam Ferguson, *Institutes of Moral Philosophy for the Use of Students in the College of Edinburgh*, 222.
63. Paley, *Principles of Moral and Political Philosophy* (1785), 197.
64. Thomas Gisborne, *The Principles of Moral Philosophy: Investigated, and Briefly Applied to the Constitution of Civil Society* (1789), 95.
65. Gisborne, *Principles of Moral Philosophy: Investigated* (1789), 70–71.
66. Gisborne, *On Slavery and the Slave Trade*, 15.
67. Gisborne, *On Slavery and the Slave Trade*, 23.
68. Gisborne, *The Principles of Moral Philosophy: Investigated, and Briefly Applied to the Constitution of Civil Society* (1798), 141.
69. Thomas Clarkson, *An Essay on the Slavery and Commerce of the Human Species, Particularly the African*.
70. Granville Sharp, *The Law of Retribution; or, a Serious Warning to Great Britain and Her Colonies* [. . .].; Clarkson, *Slavery and Commerce*.
71. Cugoano, *Thoughts and Sentiments on the Evil of Slavery*, 75 and 91.
72. Cugoano, *Thoughts and Sentiments*, 99.
73. Paley, *Recollections of a Speech, upon the Slave Trade*, 15.
74. Tobin, *Cursory Remarks upon the Reverend Mr. Ramsay's Essay*, 15; Cugoano, *Thoughts and Sentiments*, 1999, 15.
75. David Brion Davis, "The Emergence of Immediatism in British and American Antislavery Thought."
76. Cugoano, *Thoughts and Sentiments*, 79.
77. A number of philosophers signed these petitions, including Thomas Reid. See Knud Haakonssen and Paul Wood, eds., *Thomas Reid on Society and Politics*, xxxiii. Nevertheless, Reid's comments on slavery in his lectures at the University of Glasgow, published in Haakonssen, ed., *Thomas Reid on Practical Ethics* (132–35), still do not live up to the promise of his predecessor, Carmichael.
78. Alexander Hamilton et al., *The Federalist or The New Constitution*, 422.
79. Cugoano, *Thoughts and Sentiments*, 81 and 83.
80. Cugoano, *Thoughts and Sentiments*, 87.
81. Cugoano, *Thoughts and Sentiments*, 87.
82. Cugoano, *Thoughts and Sentiments*, 88.
83. Francis Wayland, *The Limitations of Human Responsibility*, 161–88.
84. Sharp, *The Law of Retribution*, 148–49.
85. Cugoano, *Thoughts and Sentiments*, 111.
86. C. L. R. James, *A History of Negro Revolt*, 16.

NOTES 291

87. Moses Bon Sàam, "The Speech of Moses Bon Sàam, a Free Negro, to the Revolted Slaves in One of the Most Considerable Colonies of the West Indies," 21–23; Léon-François Hoffmann, "An Eighteenth Century Exponent of Black Power: Moses Bon Sàam."
88. Cugoano, *Thoughts and Sentiments*, 58.
89. Adapted from Deuteronomy 24:7.
90. Cugoano, *Thoughts and Sentiments*, 59.
91. John Wesley, *Political Writings of John Wesley*, 104.
92. Locke, *Two Treatises of Government*, 383.
93. Cugoano, *Thoughts and Sentiments*, 110.
94. Keith A. Sandiford, *Measuring the Moment: Strategies of Protest in Eighteenth-Century Afro-English Writing*, 93–117.
95. Martin Luther King, "Letter from Birmingham City Jail," 298; Bernasconi, "Before Whom and for What? Accountability and the Invention of Ministerial, Hyperbolic, and Infinite Responsibility."
96. Bernasconi, "Silencing the Hottentots: Kolb's Pre-Racial Encounter with the Hottentots and Its Impact on Buffon, Kant, and Rousseau," 108.
97. Peter J. Park, *Africa, Asia, and the History of Philosophy: Racism in the Formation of the Philosophical Canon, 1780–1830*.

Chapter 8

1. Janvier had been elected in December 1882. Another Haitian, J. B. Dehoux, who had been director of the medical school in Port-au-Prince, was elected a member on June 21, 1883. *Bulletins de la Société d'Anthropologie de Paris*, series 3, vol. 6 (1883), 599.
2. Anténor Firmin, *De l'égalité des races humaines* (1885); trans. *The Equality of the Human Races* (2000). A photomechanical reprint of the original edition was published in 1993 as the eighth of nine volumes of *Race and Anthropology*, ed. Robert Bernasconi.
3. *Bulletins de la Société d'Anthropologie de Paris*, series 3, vol. 8 (1885), 599. Firmin may or may not have been present at the meeting. In any event he did not take the opportunity that some authors did of introducing the work in detail. See also the review by Léonce Manouvrier in *Revue Philosophique de la France et de l'Étranger*, January 1886. The review is discussed by Géloin in her informative introduction to *De l'égalité des races humaines*, cited on xii, n1.
4. Some are obvious. A well-known passage from Kant's *Observations on the Beautiful and the Sublime* is attributed to the *Critique of Pure Reason* (Firmin, *L'égalité des races humaines*, 471; trans. *Equality of the Human Races*, 325); a book by Bowdich is attributed to Bosman, who lived a century earlier (*L'égalité des races humaines*, 355n2; trans. *Equality of the Human Races*, 253n28); and so on. Unfortunately matters are no better in the English translation, which, so far as I can see, corrects none of Firmin's errors but introduces a number of new ones, which were not corrected when it was reprinted

292 NOTES

by the University of Illinois Press in 2002. However, the fact that the work is in translation at all is to be celebrated.

5. For Firmin as an early advocate of pan-Africanism, see Carolyn Fluehr-Lobban, "Anténor Firmin: Haitian Pioneer of Anthropology."

6. Consider the comment by Francis Schiller, "We must not expect a Broca, a Lincoln, indeed any enlightened minds, to have believed in racial equality," in *Paul Broca: Founder of French Anthropology, Explorer of the Brain*, 137. Reading Firmin makes such easy excuses more difficult to sustain.

7. See Paul Broca, "Introduction aux mémoires sur l'hybridité" (1877).

8. Broca, "Mémoire sur l'hybridité en général, sur la distinction des especes animals" (1858) and "Des phénomènes d'hybridité dans le genre humain" (1859).

9. Immanuel Kant, "Von den verschiedenen Racen der Menschen," in *Kants Werke*, Akademie Textausgabe, vol. 2, 427–44; trans. "Of the Different Races of Human Beings," in Kant, *Anthropology, History, and Education*, 84–97. See Bernasconi, "Who Invented the Concept of Race? Kant's Role in the Enlightenment Construction of Race."

10. George-Louis Leclerc, Comte de Buffon, *Histoire Naturelle* (1766), 314.

11. For a selection of Josiah Nott's writings and other related documents, see the first two volumes of *Race, Hybridity, and Miscegenation*, ed. Bernasconi and Kristie Dotson.

12. Broca, *Recherches sur l'hybridité animale en général et sur l'hybridité humaine en particulier*, 626–27 (1860). Georges Pouchet, *De la pluralité des races humaines* (1858), 138.

13. Firmin, *L'égalité des races humaines*, 48–51; trans. *Equality of the Human Races*, 36–38. Firmin's observation is supported by scholars today. See, for example, Claude Blanckaert, "L'esclavage des Noirs et l'ethnographie américaine: Le point de vue de Paul Broca en 1858," and Luc Forest, "De l'abolitionnisme à l'esclavagisme? Les implications des anthropologues dans le débat sur l'esclavage des Noirs aux États-Unis (1840–1870)."

14. See Joy Harvey, "Evolutionism Transformed: Positivists and Materialists in the *Société d'Anthropologie de Paris* from Second Empire to Third Republic." Harvey identifies the scientific materialists by their insistence on "physical explanation in terms of matter imbued with force" (291), and she highlights their indebtedness to Carl Vogt, but more still needs to be done to clarify the differences between the two groups.

15. *Bulletins de la Société d'Anthropologie de Paris*, series 4, vol. 3 (1892), 236 and 329.

16. Firmin, *L'égalité des races humaines*, 58; trans. *Equality of the Human Races*, 42. Translation modified.

17. Firmin, *L'égalité des races humaines*, 47n1; trans. *Equality of the Human Races*, 48n1.

18. Armand de Quatrefages, "Observations à propos d'un passage d'une lettre de Paul Lévy," *Bulletins de la Société d'Anthropologie de Paris*, series 3, vol. 7, 580.

19. Louis-Joseph Janvier, *L'égalité des races*, published in 1884.

20. Firmin, *L'égalité des races humaines*, 47n; trans. *Equality of the Human Races*, 84n.

21. Quatrefages, "Observations à propos d'un passage d'une lettre de Paul Lévy," in *Bulletins de la Société d'Anthropologie de Paris*, series 3, vol. 7 (1884), 583–87.

22. Paul Topinard, *L'anthropologie* (1877), 546; trans. *Anthropology* (1878) 561.

NOTES 293

23. Quatrefages, *L'espèce humaines* (1877), 211; trans. *The Human Species* (1879), 283. Cited at *L'égalité des races humaines*, 303–4; *Equality of the Human Races*, 204.

24. Firmin, *L'égalité des races humaines*, 308; *Equality of the Human Races*, 207.

25. Firmin, *L'égalité des races humaines*, ix; *Equality of the Human Races*, liv.

26. Firmin, *L'égalité des races humaines*, 14; *Equality of the Human Races*, 9.

27. Firmin, *L'égalité des races humaines*, 6; *Equality of the Human Races*, 5.

28. Firmin, *L'égalité des races humaines*, 248; *Equality of the Human Races*, 166.

29. Firmin, *L'égalité des races humaines*, 254; *Equality of the Human Races*, 171.

30. Firmin, *L'égalité des races humaines*, 504; *Equality of the Human Races*, 343. See Auguste Comte, *Système de politique positive*, vol. 4, 42–43 and 517–518; trans. *System of Positive Polity*, vol. 4, 39–40 and 450–51.

31. Firmin, *L'égalité des races humaines*, 167; *Equality of the Human Races*, 167.

32. Firmin, *L'égalité des races humaines*, 204; *Equality of the Human Races*, 140.

33. I have not found this precise quotation in Pouchet, but he expresses similar sentiments in *De la pluralité des races humaines* at 203–4. However, it is noteworthy that even after having liberated anthropology from all humanitarian tendencies, Pouchet insists that whatever is true is good.

34. Firmin, *L'égalité des races humaines*, 65; *Equality of the Human Races*, 46.

35. Firmin, *L'égalité des races humaines*, 644; *Equality of the Human Races*, 437–38.

36. Firmin, *L'égalité des races humaines*, 444; *Equality of the Human Races*, 438.

37. Firmin, *L'égalité des races humaines*, 213; *Equality of the Human Races*, 145. It should be noted that Gobineau is fully aware that his theories appear paradoxical. Arthur de Gobineau, *Essai sur l'inégalité des races humaines*, vol. 1, 18; trans. *The Inequality of Human Races* (1915), 19.

38. Broca in 1859 had already begun that portion of his long study of hybridity in man with a rejection of Gobineau. Broca, "Des phénomènes d'hybridité dans le genre humain," *Journal de la physiologie de l'homme et des animaux*, vol. 2 (1859), 601–2; trans. C. Carter Blake, *On the Phenomena of Hybridity in the Genus Homo* (1864), 1.

39. Paul Fortier, "Gobineau and German Racism," 344–46.

40. Since 1876, when Gobineau first made the acquaintance of Richard Wagner, the latter had shown an interest in his racial theories, and by the early 1880s essays by and about Gobineau appeared in the *Bayreuther Blätter*. Michael D. Biddiss, *Father of Racist Ideology: The Social and Political Thought of Count Gobineau*, 246–47 and 255–56.

41. Gobineau, *Essai sur l'inégalité des races humaines*, vol. 1, 217–23; trans. *The Inequality of Human Races* (1915) 208–11.

42. Firmin, *L'égalité des races humaines*, 303; *Equality of the Human Races*, 204. Translation modified.

43. Firmin, *L'égalité des races humaines*, 398; *Equality of the Human Races*, 270. Firmin was not saying that Darwin was not interested in the question of the philosophical study of the development of the human races. Indeed, he quoted a sentence from *The Origin of Species* to show that, from the time of the first publication of the book, Darwin was interested in the issue. Unfortunately, the sentence he chose was first introduced only in the sixth edition in 1872.

294 NOTES

44. The phrase "Darwin's bulldog" was apparently Huxley's own self-description. It was recalled by Henry Fairfield Osborn after Huxley's death: "A Student's Reminiscences of Huxley" in *Biological Lectures Delivered at the Marine Biological Laboratory of Wood's Holl in the Summer Session of 1895* (1896), 32. For more on the history of this phrase, see John van Wyhe, "Why There Was No 'Darwin's Bulldog'": Thomas Henry Huxley's Famous Nickname."

45. Linda L. Clark, *Social Darwinism in France*, 15–16. Joy Harvey, *"Almost a Man of Genius": Clémence Royer, Feminism, and Nineteenth-Century Science*, 100–101.

46. She may not have been a self-confessed follower of Auguste Comte, but her thinking at various points owes a great deal to his method and to his formulations.

47. Harvey, "*Almost a Man of Genius*," 105.

48. *Bulletins de la Société d'Anthropologie de Paris*, series 3, vol. 6 (1883), xvii and 702.

49. Harvey, "*Almost a Man of Genius*," 79. See also her comments cited by Firmin at *L'égalité des races humaines*, 17; *Equality of the Human Races*, 12: *Congrès International des Sciences Ethnographiques tenu à Paris du 15 au 17 juillet 1878* (1881), 438.

50. Clémence Royer, "Préface de la première édition," in Charles Darwin, *De l'origine des espèces*, 3rd ed., lxix. Firmin cites the 4th ed. at *L'égalité des races humaines*, 399; *Equality of the Human Races*, 271.

51. Firmin, *L'égalité des races humaines*, 400; *Equality of the Human Races*, 271.

52. Firmin, *L'égalité des races humaines*, 305; *Equality of the Human Races*, 205.

53. Royer, *Origine de l'homme et des sociétés* (1870), 532.

54. Firmin, *L'égalité des races humaines*, 395; *Equality of the Human Races*, 267.

55. Herbert Spencer, *The Data of Ethics*, 240. Quoted by Firmin in *L'égalité des races humaines*, 571–72; *Equality of the Human Races*, 385, from the French translation, *Les bases de la morale évolutionniste* (1880), 206.

56. Firmin, *L'égalité des races humaines*, 401; *Equality of the Human Races*, 272.

57. Firmin, *L'égalité des races humaines*, 411; *Equality of the Human Races*, 278.

58. Firmin, *L'égalité des races humaines*, 414; *Equality of the Human Races*, 280.

59. Firmin, *L'égalité des races humaines*, 403; *Equality of the Human Races*, 273.

60. Firmin, *L'égalité des races humaines*, 396; *Equality of the Human Races*, 269.

61. "I must show that the Caucasian or white, and the Negro races were distinct at a very remote date, and *that the Egyptians were Caucasians*. Unless this point can be established the contest must be abandoned." Josiah Nott, *Two Lectures on the Natural History of the Caucasian and Negro Races* (1844), 8. Italics in original.

62. Firmin, *L'égalité des races humaines*, 339; *Equality of the Human Races*, 229. Firmin twice refers to Morton's *Crania Ethnica* but he almost certainly means *Crania Aegyptica* (1844) (*L'égalité des races humaines*, 21 and 339; *Equality of the Human Races*, 25 and 229). See further Bernasconi, "Black Skin, White Skulls: The Nineteenth Century Debate over the Racial Identity of the Ancient Egyptians."

63. Firmin, *L'égalité des races humaines*, 429; *Equality of the Human Races*, 288. Translation modified.

64. Firmin, *L'égalité des races humaines*, 404–5; *Equality of the Human Races*, 274. This might seem to be contradicted by Firmin's claim that "for our species civilization does not evolve in a linear pattern" (*L'égalité des races humaines*, 580; *Equality of the Human*

NOTES 295

Races, 390). But this is a mistranslation, perhaps inspired by a desire to make Firmin fit a multicultural agenda. In fact, Firmin is merely stating that the work of civilizing the human species is continuous: "Ils sont appelés à savoir qu'il n'ya pas de solution de continuité dans l'oeuvre de la civilisation de notre espèce." This error in translation is perhaps what encourages Gérarde Magloire-Danton to say that Firmin's evolutionary perspective is "not rigidly linear." She is also misled when she says, in support of her interpretation, that "most evolutionists" disregard "historical and sociological discontinuities." "Anténor Firmin and Jean Price-Mars: Revolution, Memory, Humanism," 160. See, for example, Clémence Royer, *Origine de l'homme et des Sociétés*, 274.

65. Firmin, *L'égalité des races humaines*, 123; *Equality of the Human Races*, 82.

66. Firmin, *L'égalité des races humaines*, 408; *Equality of the Human Races*, 277.

67. Firmin, *L'égalité des races humaines*, 420; *Equality of the Human Races*, 283.

68. James Cowles Prichard, *Researches into the Physical History of Man*, 1st ed., 239. Not surprisingly Prichard's views on the effects of civilization were challenged by Josiah C. Nott: "History affords no evidence that cultivation, or any known causes but physical amalgamation, can alter a primitive conformation in the slightest degree." Nott, "Hybridity of Animals, Viewed in Connection with the Natural History of Mankind," in J. C. Nott and George R. Gliddon, eds., *Types of Mankind*, 372–410, at 404.

69. Herbert Spencer, "Personal Beauty," *Essays: Scientific, Political, and Speculative* (1858); trans. M. A. Burdeau, "La Beauté dans *la personne humaine*" in *Essais de morale de science et d'esthétique. I. Essais sur le progrès* (1877).

70. Firmin, *L'égalité des races humaines*, 420–21; *Equality of the Human Races*, 283–84. Firmin cites "Les Sélections," Broca's long review of French translations of Darwin's *The Descent of Man* and of Alfred Russel Wallace's *Contributions to the Theory of Natural Selection*. The review was reprinted in *Mémoires d'anthropologie*, vol. 3 (1877).

71. Firmin, *L'égalité des races humaines*, 168; *Equality of the Human Races*, 115.

72. Firmin, *L'égalité des races humaines*, 407–8; *Equality of the Human Races*, 276.

73. Firmin, *L'égalité des races humaines*, 287–88; *Equality of the Human Races*, 193.

74. Firmin, *L'égalité des races humaines*, 291; *Equality of the Human Races*, 195.

75. Firmin, *L'égalité des races humaines*, 282; *Equality of the Human Races*, 190.

76. Firmin, *L'égalité des races humaines*, 411; *Equality of the Human Races*, 278.

77. Firmin, *M. Roosevelt Président des États-Unis et la République d'Haiti* (1905), 231.

78. Firmin, *L'égalité des races humaines*, 116; *Equality of the Human Races*, 78.

79. Comte, *Système de politique positive*, vol. 2, 462; trans. Richard Congreve, *System of Positive Polity*, vol. 2, 378.

80. Clémence Royer, "Préface de la première édition," lxxi.

81. Firmin, *L'égalité des races humaines*, 400; *Equality of the Human Races*, 271.

82. Firmin, *L'égalité des races humaines*, 462; *Equality of the Human Races*, 450.

83. Firmin, *L'égalité des races humaines*, 126; *Equality of the Human Races*, 87.

84. Firmin, *L'égalité des races humaines*, 282; *Equality of the Human Races*, 190.

85. Firmin, *L'égalité des races humaines*, 660–61; *Equality of the Human Races*, 449.

86. Firmin, *L'égalité des races humaines*, 660; *Equality of the Human Races*, 449.

87. Firmin, *L'égalité des races humaines*, 424; *Equality of the Human Races*, 285.

296 NOTES

88. Auguste Comte, *Système de politique de positive*, vol. 2, 461; trans. *System of Positive Polity*, vol. 2, 377.
89. Léon Poliakov, *The Aryan Myth: A History of Racist and Nationalist Ideas in Europe*, 361.
90. Firmin, *L'égalité des races humaines*, 653; *Equality of the Human Races*, 445.
91. For example, G. W. F. Hegel, *Philosophie der Weltgeschichte*, 1230; trans. Ruben Alvarado, *Philosophy of History*, 92. W. E. B. Du Bois, "The Conservation of Races," in Nathan Huggins, ed., *DuBois: Writings*, 815–26, at 819–20.
92. Firmin, *L'égalité des races humaines*, 653; *Equality of the Human Races*, 445.
93. Firmin, *L'égalité des races humaines*, 425; *Equality of the Human Races*, 286. Translation modified.
94. Firmin, *L'égalité des races humaines*, 437–38; *Equality of the Human Races*, 296.
95. Firmin, *L'égalité des races humaines*, 124; *Equality of the Human Races*, 83.
96. Firmin, *L'égalité des races humaines*, 559; *Equality of the Human Races*, 377.
97. Firmin, *L'égalité des races humaines*, 654–55; *Equality of the Human Races*, 446.
98. *Bulletins de la Société d'Anthropologie de Paris*, series 4, vol. 3 (1892), 329.

Chapter 9

1. Kwame Anthony Appiah, *In My Father's House*, 28–46. Since the first publication of this essay, Appiah has returned to Du Bois's essay and approached it in a more historical manner, most notably in *Lines of Descent: W. E. B. Du Bois and the Emergence of Identity*. The most important early responses to Appiah are those by Tommy L. Lott, "Du Bois on the Invention of Race"; Lucius Outlaw, " 'Conserve' Races? In Defense of W. E. B. Du Bois," and Robert Gooding-Williams, "Outlaw, Appiah, and Du Bois's 'The Conservation of Races,' " both in Bernard W. Bell et al., eds., *W. E. B. Du Bois on Race and Culture: Philosophy, Politics, and Poetics*, 15–37 and 39–56, respectively; and Paul Taylor, "Appiah's Uncompleted Argument: Du Bois and the Reality of Race."
2. Du Bois, "The Conservation of Races," in *Du Bois: Writings*, 815–26, at 821.
3. Rudolf Virchow, "Rassenbildung und Erblichkeit," 1. See also A. H. Keane, *Ethnology*, 4–5.
4. Du Bois, "Dusk of Dawn: An Essay Toward an Autobiography of a Race Concept," in *Du Bois: Writings*, 549–802, at 627.
5. Du Bois, "Dusk of Dawn," in *Du Bois: Writings*, 654.
6. Du Bois, "The Conservation of Races," in *Du Bois: Writings*, 817. When Appiah says that the scientific notion "is not fully transcended" (*My Father's House*, 31), he assumes that this was what Du Bois was attempting. Appiah could argue that this is a generous reading of Du Bois insofar as Appiah believes that there is no basis for a scientific notion of race. But Outlaw is correct to say that Du Bois was trying to unite both the biological and the socio-historical; " 'Conserve' Races?" 23. Tommy Lott has explained the question of Du Bois's apparent distortion in 1940 of his earlier position; see Lott, "Du Bois's Anthropological Notion of Race," in Robert Bernasconi, ed., *Race*,

59–83, at 59. For Du Bois's subsequent treatment of race, see, for example, *Black Folk Then and Now*, 1, and *The Negro*, 13.

7. Du Bois, *Black Folk Then and Now*, 11, and *The Negro*, 16.
8. Du Bois, "Conservation of Races," in *Du Bois: Writings*, 819.
9. Du Bois, "Conservation of Races," in *Du Bois: Writings*, 816.
10. Du Bois, "Conservation of Races," in *Du Bois: Writings*, 817–18.
11. Most of the time this recognition was readily acknowledged; however, in the 1870s, in the aftermath of the German attack on France, it had become a source of major political controversy. See Armand de Quatrefages, *La race prussienne*. Rudolf Virchow responded and subsequently came to emphasize "the theory of 'mixed races.'" See his "Anthropology in the Last Twenty Years," 557–58.
12. See Robert Bernasconi, "The Logic of Whiteness: Hybridity and the Philosophy of Racial Segregation in the Nineteenth Century."
13. Du Bois, "Conservation of Races," in *Du Bois: Writings*, 825.
14. Du Bois, "Conservation of Races," in *Du Bois: Writings*, 817.
15. Du Bois, "Conservation of Races," in *Du Bois: Writings*, 818.
16. Du Bois, "Conservation of Races," in *Du Bois: Writings*, 818–19.
17. Du Bois, "Conservation of Races," in *Du Bois: Writings*, 822.
18. Joseph Arthur de Gobineau, *Essai sur l'inégalité des races humaines*. The first of the four books was translated into English as *The Moral and Intellectual Diversity of Races*.
19. Du Bois, "Conservation of Races," in *Du Bois: Writings*, 825.
20. Du Bois, "Conservation of Races," in *Du Bois: Writings*, 815.
21. Du Bois, "Conservation of Races," in *Du Bois: Writings*, 825.
22. Du Bois, "Conservation of Races," in *Du Bois: Writings*, 819.
23. Du Bois, "Conservation of Races," in *Du Bois: Writings*, 822.
24. Du Bois, "Conservation of Races," in *Du Bois: Writings*, 822. Although Du Bois was insistent that the American Negro Academy should be representative in character in the sense of being inclusive of the best (823), it should not be forgotten that he identified the Negro people in the United States as "the advance guard" of the race (820) and among them, he looked to the talented tenth. See Joseph P. DeMarco, "The Concept of Race in the Social Thought of W. E. B. Du Bois," 231. It should also be noted that he addressed only men at the American Negro Academy; no women were invited.
25. Du Bois, "Conservation of Races," in *Du Bois: Writings*, 820.
26. Du Bois, "The Souls of Black Folk," in *Du Bois: Writings*, 357–547, at 365.
27. Du Bois, "Dusk of Dawn," in *Du Bois: Writings*, 625.
28. Du Bois, "Dusk of Dawn," in *Du Bois: Writings*, 626.
29. G. W. F. Hegel, *Vorlesungen über die Philosophie der Geschichte* (1840), 123; trans. *Lectures on the Philosophy of History* (1884), 103. This is not now considered the best edition, but it was the one available to Du Bois.
30. Du Bois, "Conservation of Races," in *Du Bois: Writings*, 820.
31. A number of authors have noted Du Bois's debt to both Herder and Hegel; for example, Sieglinde Lemke, "Berlin and Boundaries: *sollen* versus *geschehen*." On Du Bois's knowledge of Herder, see Ingeborg Solger, "Herder and the 'Harlem Renaissance' of Black Culture in America: The Case of the 'Neger-Idyllen,'" 402–3.

298 NOTES

32. Du Bois, "Conservation of Races," in *Du Bois: Writings*, 825. See Bernasconi, "'Ich mag in keinen Himmel, wo Weisse sind': Herder's Critique of Eurocentrism."

33. G. W. F. Hegel, *Vorlesungen über die Philosophie der Geschichte* (1840), 113–23; trans. *Lectures on the Philosophy of History* (1884), 95–104.

34. To be sure, it is far from clear that Du Bois expects what he calls the "minor race groups"—American Indians, Eskimos, and South Sea Islanders, for example ("Conservation of Races," in *Du Bois: Writings*, 818)—now to fulfill their destiny, if they have not already done so. This would mean at very least that there is no necessity attached to the idea that each race will take its turn or perhaps even has a turn.

35. Alfred A. Moss, Jr., *The American Negro Academy*, 31. Du Bois was the only one of the four speakers initially invited to this meeting who accepted; Moss, *The American Negro Academy*, 33. The titles offered to the other speakers also tended to confirm the Academy's mission to address the educated.

36. Edward Wilmot Blyden, "Study and Race," in *Black Spokesman: Selected Published Writings of Edward Wilmot Blyden*, 201.

37. Alexander Crummell, *Destiny and Race*, 195.

38. Crummell, *Destiny and Race*, 199.

39. Crummell, *Destiny and Race*, 204.

40. Crummell, *Destiny and Race*, 202.

41. Crummell, *Destiny and Race*, 299.

42. Wilson Jeremiah Moses has established the proximity of "The Conservation of Races" to the views of Crummell, but Moses, perhaps like Crummell himself, did not see the extent to which Du Bois separated himself from Crummell; Moses, *The Golden Age of Black Nationalism, 1850–1925*, 134.

43. Blyden, "Study and Race," in *Black Spokesman*, 201.

44. Immanuel Kant, "Recensionen von J. G. Herder's *Ideen zur Philosophie der Geschichte der Menschheit*," in *Kants Werke*, Akademie Textausgabe, vol. 8, 43–66, at 65; trans. "Review of J. G. Herder's Ideas on the Philosophy of the History of Mankind," in Kant, *Anthropology, History, and Education*, 124–42, at 142.

45. Alfred Tennyson, "In Memoriam," 403. Quoted by Du Bois, "Conservation of Races," in *Du Bois: Writings*, 819.

46. Du Bois, "Conservation of Races," in *Du Bois: Writings*, 815, 822–23, 825, and 826.

47. Appiah, *My Father's House*, 30.

48. Crummell, *Destiny and Race*, 202.

49. Crummell, *Destiny and Race*, 201.

50. Du Bois, "Conservation of Races," in *Du Bois: Writings*, 820.

51. David Duncan, *Life and Letters of Herbert Spencer*, vol. 1, 232. For his explication of the persistence of force, see Herbert Spencer, *First Principles*, 251–58 and 438–39. For Spencer's application of the principle of the persistence of force to race, see *The Principles of Biology*, 289–91. See also J. D. Y. Peel, *Herbert Spencer: The Evolution of a Sociologist*, 142–46. Among those who explicitly distanced himself from the application of the conservation of force to history was Walter Bagehot, *Physics and Politics*, 10.

52. Du Bois, "Sociology Hesitant," 44.

NOTES 299

53. Du Bois, "Conservation of Races," in *Du Bois: Writings*, 815.
54. See Bernasconi, "With What Must the Philosophy of World History Begin? On the Racial Basis of Hegel's Eurocentrism," 171–201.
55. Frederick Douglass, "The Nation's Problem," In *The Frederick Douglass Papers*, series 1, vol. 5, 413.
56. Douglass, "The Future of the Colored Race," 438.
57. Douglass, "The Future of the Colored Race," 439.
58. Du Bois, "Conservation of Races," in *Du Bois: Writings*, 815.
59. This statement is recorded in the typescript verbatim account of stenographer Edward J. Beckham, in "Organization of the Academy for the Promotion of Intellectual Enterprise among American Negroes," 19, as quoted by Moses in "W. E. B. Du Bois's 'The Conservation of Races' and Its Context: Idealism, Conservation and Hero Worship," 282n27.
60. Moses, "W. E. B. Du Bois's 'The Conservation of Races,'" 285.
61. Crummell, *Destiny and Race*, 201.
62. Crummell, *Africa and America: Addresses and Discourses*, 46.
63. Du Bois, *The Health and Physique of the Negro American: A Social Study Made under the Direction of Atlanta University by the Eleventh Atlanta Conference*, 36.
64. Du Bois, *The Philadelphia Negro: A Social Study*, 394.
65. Douglass, "Future of the Colored Race," 439–40.
66. Douglass, "Future of the Colored Race," 439–40.
67. Moses, *Alexander Crummell: A Study of Civilization and Discontent*, 265.
68. Du Bois, *Darkwater: Voices from within the Veil*, 9.
69. On Du Bois's identity as seen from the perspective of Blyden (and Crummell), see Michael J. C. Echeruo, "Edward W. Blyden, W. E. B. Du Bois, and the 'Color Complex,'" 678.
70. Du Bois, "Conservation of Races," in *Du Bois: Writings*, 821.
71. Du Bois, "Conservation of Races," in *Du Bois: Writings*, 821.
72. Douglass, "The Nation's Problem," in *The Frederick Douglass Papers*, series 1, vol. 5, 412–15.
73. Du Bois, "Conservation of Races," in *Du Bois: Writings*, 822.
74. Du Bois, "Conservation of Races," in *Du Bois: Writings*, 817.
75. Du Bois, "Miscegenation," 100.
76. Du Bois, "Miscegenation," 100.
77. Du Bois, "Conservation of Races," in *Du Bois: Writings*, 821.
78. See Robert E. Bieder, *Science Encounters the Indian, 1820–1880: The Early Years of American Ethnology*, 82, 99.
79. Du Bois, "The Souls of Black Folk," in *Du Bois: Writings*, 544.
80. Robert Gilbert Wells, *Anthropology Applied to the American White Man and Negro*, 69.
81. Josiah C. Nott, "The Mulatto a Hybrid—Probable Extermination of the Two Races If the Whites and Blacks Are Allowed to Intermarry." For this essay and further documents illustrating the nineteenth-century debate about race mixing, see Robert Bernasconi and Kristie Dotson, eds., *Race, Hybridity, and Miscegenation*.

300 NOTES

82. Paul Broca, *Recherches sur l'hybridité animale en général et sur l'hybridité humaine en particulier*, 626–27; trans. *On the Phenomena of Hybridity in the Genus Homo*, 33–34. Georges Pouchet, *De la pluralité des races humaines*, 138.

83. Frederick L. Hoffman, *Race Traits and Tendencies of the American Negro*. Hoffman explicitly confirms Nott's claims about the inferiority of mulattos to Blacks and their lack of vital force; *Race Traits*, 182. For some of the background to this work, see John S. Haller, "Race, Mortality and Life Insurance: Negro Vital Statistics in the Late Nineteenth Century." On Hoffman himself, see F. J. Sypher, ed., *Frederick L. Hoffman: His Life and Works*.

84. Hoffman, *Race Traits*, 329.

85. Du Bois, "Dusk of Dawn," in *Du Bois: Writings*, 626.

86. Kelly Miller, "A Review of Hoffman's *Race Traits and Tendencies of the American Negro*."

87. Du Bois, "The Future of the Negro Race in America."

88. Du Bois, "Review of *Race Traits and Tendencies of the American Negro* by Frederick Hoffman."

89. Herbert Aptheker, ed., *Book Reviews by W. E. B. Du Bois*, 117. Du Bois had still not let go of Hoffman in 1940. See "Dusk of Dawn," in *Du Bois: Writings*, 626.

90. Hoffman, *Race Traits*, 310.

91. Miller, "Review of Hoffman," 36.

92. Du Bois, "Future of the Negro Race," 192.

93. Du Bois, "Conservation of Races," in *Du Bois: Writings*, 822.

94. Hoffman, *Race Traits*, 143. Hoffman was drawing on Philip A. Bruce, *The Plantation Negro as a Freeman*, 151 and 158.

95. Miller, "Review of Hoffman," 9–10.

96. Du Bois, "Future of the Negro Race," 191.

97. For example, Du Bois, "The Evolution of the Race Problem," 207.

98. Du Bois, "Future of the Negro Race," 190. Reference to this essay is sufficient to refute DeMarco's assertion that social Darwinism "never occupied a strong role in his [Du Bois's] thought"; DeMarco, *The Social Thought of W. E. B. Du Bois*, 69. See the comments by Adolph L. Reed Jr., *W. E. B. Du Bois and American Political Thought*, 203n23.

99. Du Bois, "Future of the Negro Race," 190.

100. Cf. Du Bois, "Souls of Black Folk," in *Du Bois: Writings*, 544.

101. Du Bois, *Future of Negro Race*, 191.

102. Du Bois, "The Evolution of the Race Problem (June 1, 1909)," 202.

103. Du Bois, "Evolution of Race Problem," 203.

104. Du Bois, "Evolution of Race Problem," 204.

105. Du Bois, "Evolution of Race Problem," 205.

106. Du Bois, "Evolution of Race Problem," 207–8.

107. Du Bois, "Evolution of Race Problem," 208–9.

108. Du Bois, "Dusk of Dawn," in *Du Bois: Writings*, 625.

NOTES 301

Chapter 10

1. Frantz Fanon, *Les damnés de la terre*, in *Frantz Fanon: Oeuvres*, 419–681, at 543; trans. *The Wretched of the Earth*, 97–98.
2. Alice Cherki, *Frantz Fanon: A Portrait*, 24, 277n41.
3. Fanon, *Peau noire, masques blancs*, in *Frantz Fanon: Oeuvres*, 45–257, at 211; trans. Richard Philcox, *Black Skin, White Masks*, 161. In this chapter, unless otherwise noted, references to *Black Skin, White Masks* are to the Philcox translation (2008) as the most readily available.
4. Fanon, *Écrits sur l'aliénation et la liberté*, 168–232; trans. *Alienation and Freedom*, 203–75.
5. Jean Khalfa, *Poetics of the Antilles*, 209–35.
6. Fanon, *Black Skin, White Masks*; trans. Charles Lam Markmann, 1967; trans. Richard Philcox, 2008.
7. Fanon, *Peau noire, masques blancs*, in *Oeuvres*, 66; *Black Skin, White Masks*, xv.
8. Fanon, *Peau noire, masques blancs*, in *Oeuvres*, 66; *Black Skin, White Masks*, xv. My italics.
9. Fanon, *Peau noire, masques blancs*, in *Oeuvres*, 96; *Black Skin, White Masks*, 31.
10. Fanon, *Peau noire, masques blancs*, in *Oeuvres*, 125; *Black Skin, White Masks*, 63.
11. Fanon, *Peau noire, masques blancs*, in *Oeuvres*, 97; *Black Skin, White Masks*, 31. Italicized phrase in English in the original.
12. Anna Freud, *Das Ich und die Abwehrmechanismen*, 120; trans. *The Ego and the Mechanisms of Defense*, 102–3. Fanon, *Peau noire, masques blancs*, in *Oeuvres*, 99; *Black Skin, White Masks*, 34.
13. Abdoulaye Sadji, "Nini," 498.
14. Fanon, *Peau noire, masques blancs*, in *Oeuvres*, 105, 187; *Black Skin, White Masks*, 41, 130–31.
15. Fanon, *Peau noire, masques blancs*, in *Oeuvres*, 124; *Black Skin, White Masks*, 62.
16. René Maran, *Un homme pareil aux autres*, 36. Cited Fanon, *Oeuvres*, 119; *Black Skin, White Masks*, 55.
17. Germaine Guex, *La névrose d'abandon*, 28; trans. *The Abandonment Neurosis*, 18. Cited Fanon, *Peau noire, masques blancs*, in *Oeuvres*, 119; *Black Skin, White Masks*, 55.
18. Fanon, *Peau noire, masques blancs*, in *Oeuvres*, 124; *Black Skin, White Masks*, 62.
19. Fanon, *Peau noire, masques blancs*, in *Oeuvres*, 123; *Black Skin, White Masks*, 61.
20. Octave Mannoni, *Psychologie de la colonisation*, 71n; *Prospero and Caliban*, 70n.
21. Fanon, *Peau noire, masques blancs*, in *Oeuvres*, 237; *Black Skin, White Masks*, 190–91.
22. Fanon, *Peau noire, masques blancs*, in *Oeuvres*, 146; *Black Skin, White Masks*, 86.
23. Pierre Naville, *Psychologie, Marxisme, Matérialisme*, 151.
24. Fanon, *Peau noire, masques blancs*, in *Oeuvres*, 145; *Black Skin, White Masks*, 84.
25. Jacques Lacan, "Le complexe, facteur concret de la psychologie familiale," 5. Cited Fanon, *Oeuvres*, 194n; *Black Skin, White Masks*, 139n.
26. Fanon, *Peau noire, masques blancs*, in *Oeuvres*, 142; *Black Skin, White Masks*, 80.
27. Fanon, "L'expérience vécue du Noir"; trans. Valentine Moulard, "The Lived Experience of the Black," in Robert Bernasconi, ed., *Race*, 184–201.

302 NOTES

28. Bernasconi, "On Needing Not to Know and Forgetting What One Never Knew: The Epistemology of Ignorance in Fanon's Critique of Sartre."

29. Fanon, *Peau noire, masques blancs*, in *Oeuvres*, 176; *Black Skin, White Masks*, 119.

30. Fanon, *Peau noire, masques blancs*, in *Oeuvres*, 251; *Black Skin, White Masks*, 206.

31. Jean-Paul Sartre, "Orphée Noir" xli; trans. "Black Orpheus," in Bernasconi, ed., *Race*, 115–42, at 137. Quoted Fanon, *Peau noire, masques blancs*, in *Oeuvres*, 171; *Black Skin, White Masks*, 112.

32. Fanon, *Peau noire, masques blancs*, in *Oeuvres*, 172; *Black Skin, White Masks*, 113. Translation modified.

33. Fanon, *Peau noire, masques blancs*, in *Oeuvres*, 64; *Black Skin, White Masks*, xviii. Translation modified.

34. Fanon, *Peau noire, masques blancs*, in *Oeuvres*, 175, 173; *Black Skin, White Masks*, 116, 114. Translation modified.

35. Fanon, *Peau noire, masques blancs*, in *Oeuvres*, 175; *Black Skin, White Masks*, 117. Translation modified.

36. Bernasconi, "The European Knows and Does Not Know: Fanon's Response to Sartre," 107.

37. Fanon, *Peau noire, masques blancs*, in *Oeuvres*, 221; *Black Skin, White Masks*, 174. Bernasconi, "The Assumption of Negritude: Aimé Césaire, Frantz Fanon, and the Vicious Circle of Racial Politics."

38. Fanon, *Peau noire, masques blancs*, in *Oeuvres*, 107; *Black Skin, White Masks*, 43.

39. Fanon, *Peau noire, masques blancs*, in *Oeuvres*, 179; *Black Skin, White Masks*, 120. Translation corrected.

40. Fanon, *Peau noire, masques blancs*, in *Oeuvres*, 186; *Black Skin, White Masks*, 129

41. Fanon, *Peau noire, masques blancs*, in *Oeuvres*, 235; *Black Skin, White Masks*, 188.

42. Félix Guattari, "L'étudiant, les fou et les Katangais," 104.

43. Lacan, "Le complexe, facteur concret," 5. Cited Fanon, *Peau noire, masques blancs*, in *Oeuvres*, 179; *Black Skin, White Masks*, 120.

44. Fanon, *Peau noire, masques blancs*, in *Oeuvres*, 75; *Black Skin, White Masks*, 6. Translation corrected.

45. Fanon, *Peau noire, masques blancs*, in *Oeuvres*, 180; *Black Skin, White Masks*, 121.

46. Fanon, *Peau noire, masques blancs*, in *Oeuvres*, 181; *Black Skin, White Masks*, 122.

47. Sigmund Freud, *Psychologie collective et analyse du moi: suivi de cinq leçons de la psychanalyse*, 140; *Two Short Accounts of Psycho-Analysis: Five Lectures on Psycho-Analysis, the Question of Lay Analysis*, 52.

48. Fanon, *Peau noire, masques blancs*, in *Oeuvres*, 186; *Black Skin, White Masks*, 129. Translation modified.

49. Fanon, *Peau noire, masques blancs*, in *Oeuvres*, 65; *Black Skin, White Masks*, xiv.

50. Angelo Hesnard, *L'univers morbide de la faute*.

51. Fanon, *Peau noire, masques blancs*, in *Oeuvres*, 218; *Black Skin, White Masks*, 170. See also Fanon, *Peau noire, masques blancs*, in *Oeuvres*, 210; *Black Skin, White Masks*, 160.

52. Fanon, *Peau noire, masques blancs*, in *Oeuvres*, 185, 222; *Black Skin, White Masks*, 128, 175.

53. Fanon, *Peau noire, masques blancs*, in *Oeuvres*, 199; *Black Skin, White Masks*, 146.

NOTES   303

54. Fanon, *Peau noire, masques blancs*, in *Oeuvres*, 136, 181; *Black Skin, White Masks*, 72, 123.
55. Fanon, *Peau noire, masques blancs*, in *Oeuvres*, 214; *Black Skin, White Masks*, 165.
56. Fanon, *Peau noire, masques blancs*, in *Oeuvres*, 214; *Black Skin, White Masks*, 164.
57. Fanon, *Peau noire, masques blancs*, in *Oeuvres*, 216–19; *Black Skin, White Masks*, 167–71.
58. Fanon, *Peau noire, masques blancs*, in *Oeuvres*, 210; *Black Skin, White Masks*, 160–61.
59. Fanon, *Peau noire, masques blancs*, in *Oeuvres*, 210; *Black Skin, White Masks*, 160. Translation modified.
60. Fanon, *Peau noire, masques blancs*, in *Oeuvres*, 173; *Black Skin, White Masks*, 115. Translation corrected.
61. Gabriel d'Arboussier, "Une dangereuse mystification: la théorie de la négritude," 38–39.
62. Fanon, *Peau noire, masques blancs*, in *Oeuvres*, 202; *Black Skin, White Masks*, 150.
63. Fanon, *Peau noire, masques blancs*, in *Oeuvres*, 70; *Black Skin, White Masks*, xviii.
64. Fanon, *Peau noire, masques blancs*, in *Oeuvres*, 202; *Black Skin, White Masks*, 150. Translation modified.
65. Fanon, *Peau noire, masques blancs*, in *Oeuvres*, 202; *Black Skin, White Masks*, 150. Translation corrected.
66. Fanon, *Peau noire, masques blancs*, in *Oeuvres*, 245; *Black Skin, White Masks*, 198
67. Fanon, *Peau noire, masques blancs*, in *Oeuvres*, 202; *Black Skin, White Masks*, 150.
68. Fanon, *Peau noire, masques blancs*, in *Oeuvres*, 210; *Black Skin, White Masks*, 160.
69. Sartre, *Réflexions sur la question juive*, 102; *Anti-Semite and Jew*, 95. Fanon, *Peau noire, masques blancs*, in *Oeuvres*, 158; *Black Skin, White Masks*, 95.
70. Joachim Marcus, "Structures familiales et comportements politiques," 282. Cited Fanon, *Peau noire, masques blancs*, in *Oeuvres*, 191–29; *Black Skin, White Masks*, 136.
71. Fanon, *Peau noire, masques blancs*, in *Oeuvres*, 194; *Black Skin, White Masks*, 140. Translation corrected.
72. Fanon, *Peau noire, masques blancs*, in *Oeuvres*, 199; *Black Skin, White Masks*, 146.
73. David Macey, *Frantz Fanon: A Biography*, 133–34.
74. Fanon, *Peau noire, masques blancs*, in *Oeuvres*, 229; *Black Skin, White Masks*, 184. Translation corrected.
75. Fanon, *Peau noire, masques blancs*, in *Oeuvres*, 65; *Black Skin, White Masks*, xviii.
76. Fanon, *Peau noire, masques blancs*, in *Oeuvres*, 247; *Black Skin, White Masks*, 201. Translation modified.
77. Fanon, *Peau noire, masques blancs*, in *Oeuvres*, 219, 221; *Black Skin, White Masks*, 171, 174.
78. Fanon, *Peau noire, masques blancs*, in *Oeuvres*, 189, 235; *Black Skin, White Masks*, 132, 187.
79. Fanon, *Peau noire, masques blancs*, in *Oeuvres*, 243; *Black Skin, White Masks*, 197.
80. Fanon, *Peau noire, masques blancs*, in *Oeuvres*, 142; *Black Skin, White Masks*, 80.
81. Fanon, *Peau noire, masques blancs*, in *Oeuvres*, 222; *Black Skin, White Masks*, 175.
82. Fanon, *Peau noire, masques blancs*, in *Oeuvres*, 240; *Black Skin, White Masks*, 194.

304 NOTES

Chapter 11

1. Frantz Fanon, *Peau noire, masques blancs*, in *Oeuvres*, 67; trans. Charles Lam Markmann, *Black Skin, White Masks* (1967), 14. Translation modified. Throughout I have also consulted the translation by Richard Philcox (2008). Neither of these translations is sensitive to the fact that the language of existentialism pervades the book. The dominance of male terms in Fanon's book is grating to readers today, but I have reluctantly maintained it so as not to conceal an underlying problem with his account. Thus, when Fanon used the term *le Noir*, I will sometimes retain the translation of it as "the Black man" because we can never be sure when he meant it to be inclusive. Where I think that phrase can be avoided, I will often use the term "Blacks," which, like all racial designations, also has problems. Fanon frequently used the term *le Nègre*, which I will translate as the Negro, but he meant that term to be grating; it is often, although not always, used by him to emphasize how Whites see Blacks and how Blacks experience being seen by Whites in a racist society.

2. See Chapter 10 in this volume.

3. Fanon, *Peau noire, masques blancs*, in *Oeuvres*, 158, 176; trans. *Black Skin, White Masks* (1967), 116, 140. In this chapter all references to *Black Skin, White Masks* are to the Markman translation (1967) as marginally more sensitive to the language of phenomenology.

4. Fanon, *Peau noire, masques blancs*, in *Oeuvres*, 176; trans. *Black Skin, White Masks*, 140.

5. Fanon, *Peau noire, masques blancs*, in *Oeuvres*, 80, 251; trans. *Black Skin, White Masks*, 29, 232. On this sentence, see Jean Khalfa, *Poetics of the Antilles*, 183–84.

6. For a broader view, see Robert Bernasconi, "Dialectical Praxis and the Decolonial Struggle: Sartre and Fanon's Contributions to Political Phenomenology."

7. Fanon, *Peau noire, masques blancs*, in *Oeuvres*, 124; trans. *Black Skin, White Masks*, 80.

8. Fanon, *Peau noire, masques blancs*, in *Oeuvres*, 68, 211; trans. *Black Skin, White Masks*, 15, 184.

9. Fanon, *Peau noire, masques blancs*, in *Oeuvres*, 75; trans. *Black Skin, White Masks*, 6. Translation modified.

10. Fanon's library included works not only by Sartre and Merleau-Ponty but also by Gaston Bachelard, Simone de Beauvoir, Gabriel Marcel, Emmanuel Levinas, and Jean Wahl. He also owned some issues of the journal *Recherches philosophiques*, which published some of the most original French phenomenological works of the 1930s. See Jean Khalfa, "La bibliothèque de Frantz Fanon," in Fanon, *Écrits sur l'aliénation et la liberté*, 585–655; trans. "Frantz Fanon's Library," in Jean Khalfa and Robert J. C. Young, eds., *Alienation and Freedom*, 719–78.

11. Fanon, *Peau noire, masques blancs*, in *Oeuvres*, 175; trans. *Black Skin, White Masks*, 138. See further, Bernasconi, "'The European Knows and Does Not Know': Fanon's Response to Sartre," 107.

12. Fanon, *Peau noire, masques blancs*, in *Oeuvres*, 154; trans. *Black Skin, White Masks*, 111. Although in the secondary literature this passage tends to be immediately linked with Merleau-Ponty, Fanon's own reference was to Jean Lhermitte, who, along with

most notably Paul Schilder, was among Merleau-Ponty's sources for the corporeal schema.

13. Fanon, *Peau noire, masques blancs*, in *Oeuvres*, 186; trans. *Black Skin, White Masks*, 150–51.

14. Sara Ahmed, "A Phenomenology of Whiteness," 157.

15. Fanon, *Peau noire, masques blancs*, in *Oeuvres*, 65; trans. *Black Skin, White Masks*, 10. Translation modified.

16. Fanon, *Peau noire, masques blancs*, in *Oeuvres*, 245; trans. *Black Skin, White Masks*, 223–24.

17. Fanon, *Peau noire, masques blancs*, in *Oeuvres*, 124; trans. *Black Skin, White Masks*, 80.

18. Fanon, *Peau noire, masques blancs*, in *Oeuvres*, 187; trans. *Black Skin, White Masks*, 152. For "cultural imposition," see *Peau noire, masques blancs*, in *Oeuvres*, 216–19; trans. *Black Skin, White Masks*, 191–95. Fanon also uses the term "cultural crystallization"; it is a term that has come to be associated with Jaspers's writings on history, but I have so far been unable to make any direct connection between those texts and Fanon; *Peau noire, masques blancs*, in *Oeuvres*, 225; trans. *Black Skin, White Masks*, 203.

19. Fanon, *Peau noire, masques blancs*, in *Oeuvres*, 68; trans. *Black Skin, White Masks*, 16. Translation modified. My italics.

20. Fanon, *Peau noire, masques blancs*, in *Oeuvres*, 216–17; trans. *Black Skin, White Masks*, 167–68.

21. Fanon, *Peau noire, masques blancs*, in *Oeuvres*, 217–18; trans. *Black Skin, White Masks*, 193. Citing Aimé Césaire, *Cahier d'un retour au pays natal*, 118.

22. Fanon, *Peau noire, masques blancs*, in *Oeuvres*, 217–18; trans. *Black Skin, White Masks*, 193. Translation modified.

23. Fanon, *Peau noire, masques blancs*, in *Oeuvres*, 209; trans. *Black Skin, White Masks*, 181.

24. Jean-Paul Sartre, *Réflexions sur la question juive*, 195; trans. *Anti-Semite and Jew*, 150.

25. Fanon, *Peau noire, masques blancs*, in *Oeuvres*, 185; trans. *Black Skin, White Masks*, 82.

26. See Bernasconi, "Fanon's *The Wretched of the Earth* as the Fulfillment of Sartre's Critique of Dialectical Reason."

27. Fanon, *Peau noire, masques blancs*, in *Oeuvres*, 193; trans. *Black Skin, White Masks*, 111.

28. Fanon, *Peau noire, masques blancs*, in *Oeuvres*, 193; trans. *Black Skin, White Masks*, 112.

29. Karl Jaspers, *Psychopathologie Générale*. Sartre had helped with the preparation of the translation. See Mikel Dufrenne and Paul Ricoeur, *Karl Jaspers et la philosophie de l'existence*, 180–84. See also Joseph de Tonquédoc, *L'existence d'après Karl Jaspers*, 37–39, 44–50. Fanon owned both of these books.

30. Dufrenne and Ricoeur, *Karl Jaspers et la philosophie de l'existence*, 182.

31. Dufrenne and Ricoeur, *Karl Jaspers et la philosophie de l'existence*, 302.

32. Jaspers is also a crucial figure in Fanon's dissertation: *Écrits sur l'aliénation et la liberté*, 221–23; trans. *Alienation and Freedom*, 264–66.

306　NOTES

33. Fanon, *Peau noire, masques blancs*, in *Oeuvres*, 133; trans. *Black Skin, White Masks*, 89. Jaspers, *Nietzsche et le christianisme*.

34. Charles Odier presented himself as doing phenomenology: *L'angoisse et la pensée magique*, 58; trans. *Anxiety and Magic Thinking*, 68. Mannoni also spoke of phenomenology, but Fanon criticized his lack of commitment to it: *Peau noire, masques blancs*, in *Oeuvres*, 133; trans. *Black Skin, White Masks*, 88.

35. Angelo Hesnard, *L'univers morbide de la faute*. Fanon, *Oeuvres*, 65; trans. *Black Skin, White Masks*, 12.

36. Jean Naudin and Tudi Goze, "Psychothérapie institutionnelle et phénoménologie."

37. Fanon, *Peau noire, masques blancs*, in *Oeuvres*, 67; trans. *Black Skin, White Masks*, 14. Translation modified.

38. Fanon, *Peau noire, masques blancs*, in *Oeuvres*, 68, 167–68; trans. *Black Skin, White Masks*, 16, 129.

39. Fanon, *Peau noire, masques blancs*, in *Oeuvres*, 247; trans. *Black Skin, White Masks*, 226.

40. Fanon, *Peau noire, masques blancs*, in *Oeuvres*, 68, 250; trans. *Black Skin, White Masks*, 15, 230.

41. Fanon, *Peau noire, masques blancs*, in *Oeuvres*, 66; trans. *Black Skin, White Masks*, 14.

42. Fanon, *Peau noire, masques blancs*, in *Oeuvres*, 211; trans. *Black Skin, White Masks*, 184. Translation modified.

43. Alice Cherki, *Frantz Fanon: A Portrait*, 277n41.

44. Sartre, *Critique de la raison dialectique*, 43; trans. *Search for a Method*, 52. Henri Lefebvre, "Perspectives de Sociologie Rurale," 73–74; trans. "Perspectives on Rural Sociology," 117. See Chapter 15 in this volume.

45. Fanon, *Peau noire, masques blancs*, in *Oeuvres*, 67; trans. *Black Skin, White Masks*, 13. Translation modified.

46. Fanon, *Peau noire, masques blancs*, in *Oeuvres*, 206; trans. *Black Skin, White Masks*, 177. Jaspers was also skeptical of the value of Freud's idea of regression in the clinical setting: *Allgemeine Psychopathologie*, 242–43; trans. *Psychopathologie Générale*, 336.

47. Jaspers, *Allgemeine Psychopathologie*, 590; trans. *General Psychopathology*, 702. Fanon would not have known this passage as it was added by Jaspers to the 4th edition.

48. Fanon, *Peau noire, masques blancs*, in *Oeuvres*, 163; trans. *Black Skin, White Masks*, 123.

49. Jean-Paul Sartre, *L'être et le néant*, 534; trans. *Being and Nothingness*, 598.

50. Sartre, *L'être et le néant*, 534–36; trans. *Being and Nothingness*, 600–2.

51. Fanon, *Peau noire, masques blancs*, in *Oeuvres*, 84; trans. *Black Skin, White Masks*, 35.

52. Fanon, *Peau noire, masques blancs*, in *Oeuvres*, 97, 124; trans. *Black Skin, White Masks*, 49, 81.

53. Fanon, *Peau noire, masques blancs*, in *Oeuvres*, 134; trans. *Black Skin, White Masks*, 90.

54. Jaspers, *Allgemeine Psychopathologie*, 35; trans. *Psychopathologie Générale*, 47; trans. *General Psychopathology*, 55. The word "concrete," italicized in the French and English editions, does not appear in the original German text.

55. Jaspers, *Allgemeine Psychopathologie*, 36; trans. *Psychopathologie Générale*, 49; trans. *General Psychopathology*, 56.

NOTES 307

56. Karl Marx, "Marx über Feuerbach," 72.

57. Fanon, *Peau noire, masques blancs*, in *Oeuvres*, 107; trans. *Black Skin, White Masks*, 62. Translation modified.

58. Fanon, *Peau noire, masques blancs*, in *Oeuvres*, 199; trans. *Black Skin, White Masks*, 168. Translation modified.

59. Fanon, *Peau noire, masques blancs*, in *Oeuvres*, 219–22; trans. *Black Skin, White Masks*, 195–98.

60. Fanon, *Peau noire, masques blancs*, in *Oeuvres*, 68; trans. *Black Skin, White Masks*, 16.

61. Fanon, *Peau noire, masques blancs*, in *Oeuvres*, 242, 239–40; trans. *Black Skin, White Masks*, 222, 218–19. See further, Bernasconi, "Fanon's French Hegel," xiii–xxiii.

62. Fanon, *Peau noire, masques blancs*, in *Oeuvres*, 247; trans. *Black Skin, White Masks*, 226. For an alternative reading of these pages, see David Marriott, *Whither Fanon?*, 198–209.

63. Karl Marx, *The Eighteenth Brumaire*, 106. Fanon was probably thinking of the poetry of Césaire and the novels of Richard Wright.

64. Fanon, *Peau noire, masques blancs*, in *Oeuvres*, 245; trans. *Black Skin, White Masks*, 223–24. Translation modified.

65. Maurice Merleau-Ponty, *La structure du comportement*, 277; trans. *The Structure of Behavior*, 204.

66. Fanon, *Peau noire, masques blancs*, in *Oeuvres*, 65; trans. *Black Skin, White Masks*, 11. Translation modified.

67. Fanon, *Peau noire, masques blancs*, in *Oeuvres*, 246; trans. *Black Skin, White Masks*, 225. Translation modified. But recall the context in which he had just said "the white man struggles with himself to realize/achieve a human condition." Both are locked; neither is human. But Fanon can indicate a way to unlock the Black man. It is not clear that the White man will be unlocked, but if it is possible it will happen through the actions of Blacks.

68. Merleau-Ponty, *La structure du comportement*, 274; trans. *The Structure of Behavior*, 202.

69. Merleau-Ponty, *La structure du comportement*, 274; trans. *The Structure of Behavior*, 201. Translation modified.

70. Merleau-Ponty, *La structure du comportement*, 276; trans. *The Structure of Behavior*, 203. Translation modified.

71. Merleau-Ponty, *La structure du comportement*, 277; trans. *The Structure of Behavior*, 204.

72. Merleau-Ponty, *La structure du comportement*, 277; trans. *The Structure of Behavior*, 204.

73. Fanon, *Peau noire, masques blancs*, in *Oeuvres*, 154; trans. *Black Skin, White Masks*, 110.

74. Jaspers, *Einführung in die Philosophie*, 20–24; trans. *Introduction à la philosophie*, 19–24. Dufrenne and Ricoeur, *Karl Jaspers et la philosophie de l'existence* 173–78. See also Marriott, *Whither Fanon?* 86–88.

75. Fanon, *Peau noire, masques blancs*, in *Oeuvres*, 246; trans. *Black Skin, White Masks*, 225.

308 NOTES

76. Fanon, *Peau noire, masques blancs*, in *Oeuvres*, 247; trans. *Black Skin, White Masks*, 226.

77. Günther Stern [Günther Anders], "Pathologie de la liberté. Essai sur la non-identification," 52, 38; trans. "The Pathology of Freedom: An Essay on Non-Identification," 166, 157.

78. Stern, "Pathologie de la liberté," 43; trans. "The Pathology of Freedom," 160.

79. Stern, "Pathologie de la liberté," 54; trans. "The Pathology of Freedom," 168.

80. Stern, "Pathologie de la liberté," 52; trans. "The Pathology of Freedom," 166.

81. Fanon, *Peau noire, masques blancs*, in *Oeuvres*, 247; trans. *Black Skin, White Masks*, 226.

82. Fanon, *Peau noire, masques blancs*, in *Oeuvres*, 248; trans. *Black Skin, White Masks*, 228. Translation modified. Fanon's emphasis.

83. Sartre. *L'être et le néant*, 158; trans. *Being and Nothingness*, 173.

84. Sartre. *L'être et le néant*, 156, 158; trans. *Being and Nothingness*, 170, 174.

85. Fanon, *Peau noire, masques blancs*, in *Oeuvres*, 249; trans. *Black Skin, White Masks*, 228. See also *Oeuvres*, 66; trans. *Black Skin, White Masks*, 12.

86. Sartre, *L'être et le néant*, xx; trans. *Being and Nothingness*, 1xx. On the concept of facticity in Fanon, see Bernasconi, "Can Race Be Thought in Terms of Facticity? A Reconsideration of Sartre's and Fanon's Existential Theories of Race," 195–213.

87. Sartre, *L'être et le néant*, 161; trans. *Being and Nothingness*, 177.

88. Sartre, *L'être et le néant*, 160; trans. *Being and Nothingness*, 175.

89. Fanon, *Peau noire, masques blancs*, in *Oeuvres*, 248; trans. *Black Skin, White Masks*, 228.

90. Fanon, *Peau noire, masques blancs*, in *Oeuvres*, 249–50; trans. *Black Skin, White Masks*, 229–31.

91. Fanon, *Peau noire, masques blancs*, in *Oeuvres*, 250; trans. *Black Skin, White Masks*, 231. Sartre, *L'être et le néant*, 162; trans. *Being and Nothingness*, 178. Because my understanding of Sartre, like my understanding of Fanon, at times goes against conventional wisdom, I refer the reader to my essay, "None Is Free until All Are Free: Sartre's Ontology of Freedom and His Politics." See also Nigel C. Gibson, *Fanon: The Postcolonial Imagination*, 27.

92. Fanon, *Peau noire, masques blancs*, in *Oeuvres*, 64; trans. *Black Skin, White Masks*, 10. Translation modified. Emphasis added. For non-being (*non-être*) in the context of Sartre's discussion of temporality, see *L'être et le néant*, 161; trans. *Being and Nothingness*, 176.

93. Fanon, *Peau noire, masques blancs*, in *Oeuvres*, 219, 221; trans. *Black Skin, White Masks*, 195, 198. Matthieu Renault, *Frantz Fanon: De l'anticolonialisme à la critique postcoloniale*, 75–76.

94. Fanon, *Peau noire, masques blancs*, in *Oeuvres*, 243; trans. *Black Skin, White Masks*, 222.

95. Fanon, *Peau noire, masques blancs*, in *Oeuvres*, 251; trans. *Black Skin, White Masks*, 231. *The Wretched of the Earth* ends with a similar image: one must cast the slough (*il faut faire peau neuve*): *Les damnés de la terre*, in *Oeuvres*, 676; trans. *The Wretched of the Earth*, 239. Translation modified. See Bernasconi, "Casting the Slough: Fanon's New Humanism for a New Humanity."

NOTES 309

96. Sartre, *L'être et le néant*, 111n; trans. *Being and Nothingness*, 117n.

97. Fanon, *Peau noire, masques blancs*, in *Oeuvres*, 93, 125; trans. *Black Skin, White Masks*, 41–42, 82. See Sartre, *L'être et le néant*, 478; trans. *Being and Nothingness*, 537.

98. Fanon, *Peau noire, masques blancs*, in *Oeuvres*, 251, 225; trans. *Black Skin, White Masks*, 231, 203. Translation modified.

99. Sartre, *L'être et le néant*, 83–84; trans. *Being and Nothingness*, 86. Emphasis added.

100. Fanon, *Peau noire, masques blancs*, in *Oeuvres*, 251; trans. *Black Skin, White Masks*, 232.

101. Fanon, *Peau noire, masques blancs*, in *Oeuvres*, 239, 225; trans. *Black Skin, White Masks*, 218, 203.

102. Fragment 418. Blaise Pascal, *Pensées*, 176; trans. *Pensées*, 150.

103. Fanon, *Peau noire, masques blancs*, in *Oeuvres*, 250; trans. *Black Skin, White Masks*, 229–30. Translation modified. This is the first of a series of four questions, and given that Fanon's answer to the subsequent three questions is clearly in the negative, it seems reasonable to assume that the answer to this first question is in the negative, too. This is surprising given both his earlier endorsement of the Negro workers, as well as the Vietnamese, and the way in which those endorsements point to his later work. But as the other three questions point to rejecting a focus on the past, it is perhaps in that sense that the apparent rejection of the possibility outlined in the first one should also be understood.

104. Jean-Paul Sartre, *Situations, II: Qu'est-ce que la littérature?* 123; trans. *"What Is Literature?" and Other Essays*, 76.

105. Sartre, *Situations, II*, 124; trans. *"What Is Literature?"* 77.

106. Fanon, *Peau noire, masques blancs*, in *Oeuvres*, 210–11; trans. *Black Skin, White Masks*, 183–84.

107. Sartre, *Situations, II*, 190–91; trans. *"What Is Literature?"* 134–35.

108. Fanon, *Peau noire, masques blancs*, in *Oeuvres*, 216, 238; trans. *Black Skin, White Masks*, 191, 217.

109. Fanon, *Peau noire, masques blancs*, in *Oeuvres*, 242; trans. *Black Skin, White Masks*, 222.

110. Fanon, *Peau noire, masques blancs*, in *Oeuvres*, 468; trans. *The Wretched of the Earth*, 21.

111. Fanon, *Peau noire, masques blancs*, in *Oeuvres*, 489; trans. *The Wretched of the Earth*, 44. Translation modified.

112. Fanon, *Peau noire, masques blancs*, in *Oeuvres*, 191; trans. *Black Skin, White Masks*, 157.

113. Merleau-Ponty, *La structure du comportement*, 237; trans. *The Structure of Behavior*, 175.

114. Fanon, *Peau noire, masques blancs*, in *Oeuvres*, 66; trans. *Black Skin, White Masks*, 13.

115. Fanon, *Peau noire, masques blancs*, in *Oeuvres*, 75; trans. *Black Skin, White Masks*, 23.

116. Fanon, *Peau noire, masques blancs*, in *Oeuvres*, 96; trans. *Black Skin, White Masks*, 48.

117. Fanon, *Peau noire, masques blancs*, in *Oeuvres*, 91; trans. *Black Skin, White Masks*, 41.

118. Fanon, *Peau noire, masques blancs*, in *Oeuvres*, 247, 67; trans. *Black Skin, White Masks*, 226, 15.

310 NOTES

Chapter 12

1. Magnus Hirschfeld, *Racism.*
2. All four statements are reprinted with commentary by Ashley Montagu in his *Statement on Race.* There were three more statements before 1967.
3. For a good but not definitive account of the misreading of the first UNESCO Statement, see Jenny Reardon, *Race to the Finish: Identity and Governance in an Age of Genomics*, 17–45.
4. For the background to the statement, see Elazar Barkan, "The Politics of the Science of Race: Ashley Montagu and UNESCO's Anti-Racist Declarations," 96–105.
5. This assessment of Brazilian race relations was challenged in 1965 by his fellow countryman Florestan Fernandes in work sponsored by UNESCO. See Edward E. Teller, *Race in Another America: The Significance of Skin Color in Brazil*, 42–43.
6. Montagu, *Man's Most Dangerous Myth* (1942), 21–22.
7. *Man* 51 (January 1951): 17.
8. UNESCO, "Statement of 1950," in *Race, Science, and Society*, 343–47, at 344.
9. The proposal that "ethnic groups" be used in place of "race" can be traced back to Julian S. Huxley et al., *We Europeans: A Survey of "Racial" Problems*, 108.
10. Montagu, *Man's Most Dangerous Myth*, 74.
11. UNESCO, "Statement of 1950," 343.
12. UNESCO, "Statement on the Nature of Race and Race Differences—June 1951," 353.
13. UNESCO, "Statement June 1951," 352.
14. UNESCO, "Statement June 1951," 350.
15. L. C. Dunn, "Reformulation of the Statement on the Concept of Race," 82.
16. Most notably Gunnar Myrdal, *An American Dilemma: The Negro Problem and Modern Democracy.*
17. See Chapter 5 in this volume.
18. I have discussed this broader idea of racism in a number of places. See, for example, Robert Bernasconi, "Racism Is a System: How Existentialism Became Dialectical in Fanon and Sartre," 342–60; see also Chapter 13 in this volume.
19. See, for example, Martin Heidegger, *Sein und Zeit*, 45–50; trans. *Being and Time* (1996), 47–48.
20. Even though Husserl liked to start from "mere nature," in the sense of sensuous objects, to which he opposed "the spirit as alien to it," he recognized in the same place that this rested on an abstraction and rendered problematic any subsequent investigation of what is posited as alien to one in that way. Edmund Husserl, *Ideen zu einer reinen Phänomenologie und phänomenologischen Philosophie*, Book 2, 378–79; trans. *Ideas Pertaining to a Pure Phenomenology and to a Phenomenological Philosophy*, Book 2, 388–89.
21. Maurice Merleau-Ponty, *Le visible et l'invisible*, 306–7; trans. Alphonso Lingis, *The Visible and the Invisible*, 253.
22. See Bernasconi, "Can Race Be Thought in Terms of Facticity? A Reconsideration of Sartre's and Fanon's Existential Theories of Race" 195–213.
23. For example, Aristotle, *Nicomachean Ethics* 1.3.1094b30.

NOTES 311

24. Aristotle, *Nicomachean Ethics* 5.7.1135a5.
25. Nevertheless, it seems that the phrase was introduced by Democritus in opposition to Aristotle's doctrine of the ruler by nature. See Peter Wade, *Race, Nature and Culture*, 118.
26. G. W. F. Hegel, *Grundlinien der Philosophie des Rechts*, 34; trans. *Elements of the Philosophy of Right*, trans. H. B. Nisbet, section 4, 35.
27. Blaise Pascal, *Pensées*, 1976, Fragment 159, 85; 1962, 126.
28. Jean-Jacques Rousseau, *Discours sur l'origine et les fondements de l'inégalité*, 124–25; trans. *Discourse on the Origins of Inequality*, 14.
29. Rousseau, *Discours sur l'origine et les fondements de l'inégalité*, 123; trans. *Discourse on the Origins of Inequality*, 13.
30. Jacques Derrida, *De la grammatologie*, 152–54; trans. *Of Grammatology*, 103–5. For an indication of the underlying reading of Rousseau, see Bernasconi, "No More Stories, Good or Bad: De Man's Criticisms of Derrida on Rousseau," 137–66.
31. Hannah Arendt, *Between Past and Future*, 212.
32. Cicero, *Tusculan Disputations* 2.5.13.
33. Joseph Niedermann, *Kultur: Werden und Wandlungen des Begriffs und seiner Ersatzbigriffe von Cicero bis Herder*.
34. Alfred L. Kroeber and Clyde Kluckhohn, *Culture: A Critical Review of Concepts and Definitions*, 21.
35. Johann Christoph Adelung, *Grammatisch-kritisches Wörterbuch der hochdeutschen Mundart*, 1352–53.
36. Adelung, *Versuch einer Geschichte der Cultur des menschlichen Geschlechts*, ix (unnumbered). Moses Mendelssohn confirms the novelty of the word in his "What Is Enlightenment?" but said the same of "enlightenment" and "education." See also Michael C. Carhart, *The Science of Culture in Enlightenment Germany*, 1–23.
37. Adelung, *Versuch einer Geschichte*, x (unnumbered).
38. See Chapter 3 in this volume.
39. Peter McLaughlin, "Kant on Heredity and Adaptation," in Staffan Müller-Wille and Hans-Jörg Rheinberger, eds., *Heredity Produced: At the Crossroads of Biology, Politics, and Culture, 1500–1870*, 277–91.
40. Immanuel Kant, "Bestimmung des Begriffs einer Menschenrace," in *Kants Werke*, Akademie Textausgabe, vol. 8, 89–106, at 92; trans. "Determination of the Concept of a Human Race," in Kant, *Anthropology, History, and Education*, 143–59, at 146.
41. Georg Forster, "Noch etwas über die Menschenrassen: An Herrn Dr. Biester"; trans. Jon M. Mikkelsen, "Something More about the Human Races," 152–54. On the way in which Kant in response to Forster in some ways anticipates the nature-culture distinction, see Bernasconi, "True Colors: Kant's Distinction between Nature and Artifice in Context."
42. Bernasconi, "Who Invented the Concept of Race? Kant's Role in the Enlightenment Construction of Race."
43. Kant, "Kritik der Urteilskraft," in *Kants Werke*, Akademie Textausgabe, vol. 5, 165–485, at 431; trans. *Critique of the Power of Judgment*, 299.

312 NOTES

44. Kant, "Über den Gebrauch teleologischer Principien in der Philosophie," in *Kants Werke*, Akademie Textausgabe, vol. 8, 157–84, at 175–76; trans. "On the Use of Teleogical Principles in Philosophy," in Kant, *Anthropology, History, and Education*, 192–218, at 211.

45. Historians of the concept of race contributed greatly to the narrative that the distinction between nature and culture was crucial in overcoming the nineteenth-century concept of race. Foremost among these was George W. Stocking, who highlighted the contribution of Franz Boas, even while conceding that he was not solely responsible for the process or always conscious of it: *Race, Culture, and Evolution*, 264–65. For an important challenge to the preeminence according to Boas to which I am much indebted, see Kamala Visweswaran, "Race and the Culture of Anthropology."

46. Robert Lowie, *Culture and Ethnology*, 17. However, even Lowie did not exclude some influence on culture of hereditary traits.

47. Lowie, *The History of Ethnological Theory*, 3.

48. For example, Kroeber, "The Concept of Culture in Science," 183.

49. Edward Burnett Tylor, *Primitive Culture*, vol. 1, 1. Lowie refers to this distinction in *The History of Ethnological Theory*, 12 and 200.

50. Lowie, *History of Ethnological Theory*, 3.

51. Kroeber, *Anthropology* (1948), 8.

52. Kroeber, *Anthropology* (1923).

53. Kroeber, *Anthropology* (1948), 7–10.

54. Kroeber, *Anthropology* (1948), 124.

55. Kroeber, *Anthropology* (1923), 57, and Kroeber, *Anthropology* (1948), 176.

56. Ruth Benedict, *Race: Science, and Politics*, 19.

57. Claude Lévi-Strauss, "Race et Histoire," 242; trans. "Race and History," 1956, 124. See Christopher Johnson, *Claude Lévi-Strauss. The Formative Years*, 109–20.

58. Lévi-Strauss, *Le regard éloigné*, 13; trans. *The View from Afar*, xiii. See also his conversations with Didier Eribon, *De prés et de loin*, 204–11; trans. *Conversations with Claude Lévi-Strauss*, 147–52. See also Kamala Visweswaran, "The Interventions of Culture: Claude Lévi-Strauss, Race and the Critique of Historical Time," in Bernasconi, *Race and Racism in Continental Philosophy*, 227–48.

59. Lévi-Strauss, *Le regard éloigne*, 43; trans. *The View from Afar*, 20.

60. Lévi-Strauss, *Le regard éloigne*, 43; trans. *The View from Afar*, 20.

61. Lévi-Strauss, *Le regard éloigme*, 35–36; trans. *The View from Afar*, 14–15.

62. Alain Locke, "The Concept of Race as Applied to Social Culture," 194.

63. Locke, "The Concept of Race," 194.

64. Lévi-Strauss, *Le regard éloigne*, 35–36; trans. *The View from Afar*, 14.

65. See Bernasconi, "Ethnic Race: Revisiting Alain Locke's Neglected Proposal."

66. Lévi-Strauss, *Les structures élémentaires de la parenté*, 1; trans. James Hale Bell, John Richard von Sturmer, and Rodney Needham, *The Elementary Structures of Kinship*, 3. Lévi-Strauss, *La pensée sauvage*, 327; trans. anon, *The Savage Mind*, 247n.

67. Lévi-Strauss, *Les structures élémentaires*, 9; trans. *The Elementary Structures of Kinship*, 8.

68. Lévi-Strauss, *Le regard éloigne*, 43; trans. *The View from Afar*, 20.

NOTES 313

69. Lévi-Strauss, *Le regard éloigne*, 44; trans. *The View from Afar*, 21.

70. Frantz Fanon, *Peau noire, masques blancs*, in Fanon, *Ouevres*, 45–251, at 74; trans. Richard Philcox, *Black Skin, White Masks*, 72.

71. Lévi-Strauss, *Le regard éloigne*, 15; trans. *The View from Afar*, xiv.

72. Lévi-Strauss, *Le regard éloigne*, 44; trans. *The View from Afar*, 21.

73. See Robert J. C. Young, *White Mythologies*, 76–77. The reference is to Claude Lévi-Strauss, *La pensée sauvage*, 325; trans. *The Savage Mind*, 246.

74. Montagu, *Man's Most Dangerous Myth: The Fallacy of Race* (Walnut Creek, CA: Altamira Press, 1997), 31.

75. See Bernasconi, "The Limits of the European Idea of Development."

Chapter 13

1. Benjamin Disraeli, *Tancred: Or the New Crusade*, 303.

2. Robert Knox, *The Races of Men: A Fragment*, 7.

3. D. G. Ritchie, "The Rationality of History," 142–43.

4. Pierre-André Taguieff, *La force du préjugé*, 123–38; trans. *The Force of Prejudice on Racism and Its Doubles*, 86.

5. Taguieff, *Force of Prejudice*, 82–96.

6. Elazar Barkan, *The Retreat of Scientific Racism*, 334.

7. For more on the history of the word *racism*, see Robert Bernasconi, "Where Is Xenophobia in the Fight against Racism?" and "Racism."

8. Thomas Gossett, *Race: The History of an Idea in America: Political Essays*, 418.

9. For problems in Boas's early attempts to address the prejudices leveled against African Americans, see Vernon J. Williams, Jr., *Rethinking Race: Franz Boas and His Contemporaries*, 4–36. This book also includes a useful survey of some earlier controversies surrounding Boas and racism: 104–7.

10. Franz Boas, *Changes in Bodily Form of Descendants of Immigrants*, 7.

11. See Chapter 12 in this volume.

12. Boas, "What Is a Race?" 89.

13. Boas, "The Real Race Problem," 25.

14. Boas, *Race and Democratic Society*, 81.

15. Boas, "Aryans and Non-Aryans," 221.

16. Boas, *The Mind of Primitive Man* (1938), 238–39.

17. Harry Laughlin, *Conquest by Immigration*, 20–21.

18. Boas, "Racial Purity," 231.

19. UNESCO, "Statement of 1950," in *Race, Science, and Society*, 343–47, at 344.

20. UNESCO, "Statement of 1950," in *Race, Science, and Society*, 344.

21. Julian Huxley and Alfred C. Haddon, *We Europeans*, 282, 287.

22. Richard W. Rees, *Shades of Difference: A History of Ethnicity in America*, 94.

23. Huxley and Haddon, *Nous Européens*.

314   NOTES

24. Christopher M. Hutton, *Race and the Third Reich: Linguistics, Racial Anthropology and Genetics in the Dialectic of* "Volk," 15.

25. Huxley and Haddon, *We Europeans*, 38.

26. Fritz Lenz, "Die Erblichkeit der geistigen Begabung," 575; trans. "The Inheritance of Intellectual Gifts," 689–90.

27. Lenz, "Die Erblichkeit," 583; trans. "Inheritance," 699.

28. See Barnor Hesse, "Im/Plausible Deniability: Racism's Conceptual Double Bind," 14.

29. Lenz, cited in UNESCO, *The Race Concept: Results of an Inquiry*, 30–31.

30. Saul Dubow, *Scientific Racism in Modern South Africa*, 277.

31. Boas, *Race and Democratic Society*, 81.

32. Boas, *Mind of Primitive Man*, 271.

33. Kwame Anthony Appiah, "The Uncompleted Argument: Du Bois and the Illusion of Race," 35.

34. Ashley Montagu, *Man's Most Dangerous Myth: The Fallacy of Race* (1964), 25.

35. Montagu, *Man's Most Dangerous Myth: The Fallacy of Race* (1942), 71–72

36. Anthony Hazard, "Ashley Montagu, the 'Most Dangerous Myth,' and the 'Negro Question' during World War II," 296–99.

37. Cyril Bibby, "Race Prejudice and Education," 7.

38. Lee Baker, *From Savage to Negro*, 181.

39. Gunnar Myrdal, *An American Dilemma: The Negro Problem and Modern Democracy*, 1065–70.

40. Boas, *Race and Democratic Society*, 5–6.

41. Tracy Teslow, *Constructing Race: The Science of Bodies and Cultures in American Anthropology*, 242.

42. Ruth Benedict, *Race: Science and Politics*, 152–53. See also Kamala Visweswaran, "Race and the Culture of Anthropology," 73–74.

43. Benedict, *Race: Science and Politics*, 191.

44. Benedict, *Race: Science and Politics*, 198.

45. Madison Grant, *The Conquest of the Continent; or, The Expansion of Races in America*, 285–86.

46. Ruth Benedict and Gene Weltfish, *The Races of Mankind*, 31.

47. Teslow, *Constructing Race*, 246–65.

48. Boas, *The Mind of Primitive Man* (1938), 253.

49. J. Woodford Howard, *Mr. Justice Murphy: A Political Biography*, 305.

50. Pompée Valentin de Vastey, *The Colonial System Unveiled*, 107.

51. Oliver Cromwell Cox, *Caste, Class, and Race: A Study in Social Dynamics*, 482.

52. Cox, *Caste, Class, and Race*, 480.

53. Cox, "The Racial Theories of Robert E. Park and Ruth Benedict," 452.

54. Cox, "Racial Theories," 452.

55. Frantz Fanon, *Pour la révolution africaine. Écrits politiques*, in *Oeuvres*, 683–878, at 717; trans. *Toward the African Revolution: Political Essays*, 33.

56. Fanon, *Pour la révolution africaine*, 716; trans. *Toward the African Revolution*, 32.

57. Stokely Carmichael and Charles V. Hamilton, *Black Power: The Politics of Liberation in America*, 4.

NOTES   315

58. William Macpherson, *The Stephen Lawrence Inquiry*, 22.
59. Katherine Krueger, "Mike Pence Denies 'Implicit Bias' and 'Institutional Racism' in Policing at VP Debate."
60. Jean-Paul Sartre, *Critique de la raison dialectique*, 344; trans. *Critique of Dialectical Reason*, 300.
61. Fanon, *Pour la révolution africaine*, 723; trans. *Toward the African Revolution*, 40.
62. Fred R. Shapiro. "Historical Notes on the Vocabulary of the Women's Movement," 7.
63. Stephen Steinberg, *Race Relations: A Critique*, 43–44.
64. American Committee for Democracy and Intellectual Freedom, *Science Condemns Racism*, 6.
65. Jacques Barzun, "Race and Racism," 372.

Chapter 14

1. Michel Foucault, *"Il faut défendre la société,"* 57; trans. David Macey, *"Society Must Be Defended,"* 65.
2. Foucault, *"Il faut défendre la société,"* 71; trans. *"Society Must Be Defended,"* 81.
3. Foucault, *"Il faut défendre la société,"* 75; trans. *"Society Must Be Defended,"* 87.
4. Foucault, *"Il faut défendre la société,"* 75; trans. *"Society Must Be Defended,"* 87.
5. Foucault, *"Il faut défendre la société,"* 71 and 216; trans. *"Society Must Be Defended,"* 82 and 243.
6. See Ruth Benedict, *Race: Science and Politics*, 191, and Hannah Arendt, *The Origins of Totalitarianism*, 158–84.
7. See Ann Laura Stoler's early critique in *Race and the Education of Desire: Foucault's History of Sexuality and the Colonial Order of Things*, 60. For a more sympathetic approach, see Richard Groulx, *Michel Foucault, la politique comme guerre continuée: De la guerre des races au racisme d'État*, 155–64. Nevertheless, it should be added that Foucault's idea of biopower has helped illuminate what is new in late nineteenth-century racism: see Chapter 5 in this volume. See also Brad Elliott Stone, "Power, Politics, Racism," in Christopher Falzon et al., eds., *A Companion to Foucault*, 353–67.
8. Foucault, *"Il faut défendre la société,"* 227; trans. *"Society Must Be Defended,"* 254. Foucault later in the same year returned to this issue, this time in print and complicated it somewhat by placing more emphasis on continuity. He identified a type of racism manifested in the eighteenth century by the nobility for preservative ends and said of this "dynamic racism, a racism of expansion" that "even if it was still in a budding state, [it was] awaiting the second half of the nineteenth century to bear the fruits that we have tasted." Foucault, *Histoire de la sexualité*, vol. 1, 166; trans. *The History of Sexuality*, vol. 1, 125.
9. Foucault, *"Il faut défendre la société,"* 230 and 233; trans. *"Society Must Be Defended,"* 258 and 261. See also Foucault, *Les Anormaux*, 229; trans. *Abnormal*, 316; and the entry by François Ewald on Foucault in *Dictionnaire historique et critique du racism*, 692–96.

316 NOTES

10. Foucault, *"Il faut défendre la société,"* 75–78; trans. *"Society Must Be Defended,"* 87–89. David Nirenberg made fun of what he took to be Foucault's evasiveness in "Was There Race before Modernity? The Example of 'Jewish' Blood in Late Medieval Spain," 236–39.

11. Foucault, *"Il faut défendre la société,"* 244; trans. *"Society Must Be Defended,"* 272.

12. Foucault, *"Il faut défendre la société,"* 19; trans. *"Society Must Be Defended,"* 18–19.

13. Foucault, *"Il faut défendre la société,"* 52 and 75–76; trans. *"Society Must Be Defended,"* 61 and 88.

14. Foucault, *"Il faut défendre la société,"* 226; trans. *"Society Must Be Defended,"* 254.

15. Foucault, "Nietzsche, la généalogie, l'histoire," 145–72 (cited from *Dits et écrits 1954–1988*, vol. 2, 145–72, at 136–56); trans. "Nietzsche, Genealogy, History." Although first published in 1971, it dates back to a conference in 1969; see Daniel Defert, "Chronology," in Christopher Falzon et al., eds., *A Companion to Foucault*, 11–83, at 41.

16. Foucault, *"Il faut défendre la société,"* 132; trans. *"Society Must Be Defended,"* 149.

17. Foucault, *"Il faut défendre la société,"* 17; trans. *"Society Must Be Defended,"* 16.

18. Foucault, *Surveiller et punir*, 315: trans. *Discipline and Punish*, 308.

19. Foucault, "Entretien sur la prison: le livre et sa méthode," in Foucault, *Dits et écrits 1954–1988*, vol. 2, 740–53, at 753; trans. Colin Gordon, "Prison Talk," 53–54.

20. Foucault, "Réponse au Cercle d'épistémologie."

21. In his inaugural lecture at the Collège de France delivered in December 1970 under the title *L'ordre du discours*, Foucault already introduced a genealogical component to his work, describing it as concerned with "the effective formation of discourse," but its role at that time was unclear and seemingly somewhat marginal: Foucault, *L'ordre du discours*, 67; trans. "The Discourse on Language," 233.

22. Foucault, *La société punitive*, 86; trans. *The Punitive Society*, 84. It is striking that, as Bernard E. Harcourt observed, Foucault initially took up the word *dynastics* as if to try to avoid the word *genealogy*; see his comment at *La société punitive*, 95–96: trans. *The Punitive Society*, 93–94.

23. Foucault, *"Il faut défendre la société,"* 11–12; trans. *"Society Must Be Defended,"* 10–11.

24. Foucault, *Sécurité, Territoire, Population*, 38; trans. Graham Burchell, *Security, Territory, Population*, 36.

25. Foucault, "Entretien avec Michel Foucault," in Foucault, *Dits et écrits 1954–1988*, vol. 4, 41–95, at 82; trans. "Interview with Michel Foucault," in Foucault, *Power*, 239–97, at 283.

26. Foucault, "Sur les façons d'écrire l'histoire (entretien avec R. Bellour)," in Foucault, *Dits et écrits, 1954–1988*, vol. 1, 585–600, at 599; trans. "The Discourse of History," 31. See Béatrice Han, *Foucault's Critical Project*, 76–77.

27. Michael Mahon, *Foucault's Nietzschean Genealogy: Truth, Power, and the Subject*.

28. Foucault, *L'archéologie du savoir*, 23; trans. *The Archaeology of Knowledge*, 13. See also Foucault, "Nietzsche, la généalogie, l'histoire," 137; trans. "Nietzsche, Genealogy, History," 370.

29. Foucault, *"Il faut défendre la société,"* 51 and 243; trans. *"Society Must Be Defended,"* 59 and 270.

NOTES 317

30. Foucault, *"Il faut défendre la société,"* 9; trans. *"Society Must Be Defended,"* 8. See also *Sécurité, Territoire, Population,* 123n; trans. *Security, Territory, Population,* 119n.

31. John Marks, in his essay, "Foucault, Franks, Gauls: *'Il faut défender la société,'*" 133. In a subsequent essay Marks slightly modifies this claim, calling the lectures "the genealogy of an important component of his own method"; Marks, "Michel Foucault: Biopolitics and Biology," 88. Marks raises questions about race in the former essay but does not pursue them in the latter.

32. Foucault, "Nietzsche, la généalogie, l'histoire," 136; trans. "Nietzsche, Genealogy, History," 369.

33. Friedrich Nietzsche, of course, himself described genealogy as "gray," in *Sämtliche Werke,* vol. 5, *Jenseits von Gut und Böse,* 254; trans. *The Complete Works of Friedrich Nietzsche,* vol. 8, *Beyond Good and Evil / On the Genealogy of Morality,* 210.

34. Nietzsche, *Sämtliche Werke,* vol. 1, "Vom Nutzen und Nachteil der Historie für das Leben," in *Die Geburt der Tragödie / Unzeitgemässe Betrachtungen,* 243–334, at 260; trans. "On the Uses and Disadvantages of History for Life," in *The Complete Works of Friedrich Nietzsche,* vol. 2, *Unfashionable Observations* 83–167, at 98.

35. Nietzsche, "Vom Nutzen und Nachteil," 265; trans. "On the Uses and Disadvantages of History for Life," 102–3.

36. Nietzsche, "Vom Nutzen und Nachteil," 269; trans. "On the Uses and Disadvantages of History for Life," 106.

37. Nietzsche, "Vom Nutzen und Nachteil," 269; trans. "On the Uses and Disadvantages of History for Life," 106.

38. Nietzsche, "Vom Nutzen und Nachteil," 264, 267–68, and 269–70; trans. "On the Uses and Disadvantages of History for Life," 102, 105, and 106–7.

39. Nietzsche, "Vom Nutzen und Nachteil," 270; trans. "On the Uses and Disadvantages of History for Life," 107.

40. Foucault, "Nietzsche, la généalogie, l'histoire," 152–56; trans. "Nietzsche, Genealogy, History," 385–89. On the distinction between *connaissance* and *savoir,* see Foucault, "Entretien avec Michel Foucault," in *Dits et écrits 1954–1988,* vol. 4, 41–95, at 57; trans. "Interview with Michel Foucault," in *Power,* 239–97, at 256.

41. Foucault, "Nietzsche, la généalogie, l'histoire," 140; trans. "Nietzsche, Genealogy, History," 373. Translation corrected because it treats *race* and *social type* as equivalent terms, while Foucault himself clearly separates them by offering different references to support each term. Foucault references, first, Nietzsche's *The Gay Science,* section 135. The most thorough attempt to minimize the importance of race in Nietzsche is Gerd Schank's *"Rasse" und "Züchtung" bei Nietzsche.* For an alternative view, see Robert Bernasconi, "Nietzsche as a Philosopher of Racialized Breeding."

42. Nietzsche, *Sämtliche Werke,* vol. 3, *Die fröhliche Wissenschaft,* 486–87; trans. Josefine Nauckhoff, *The Gay Science,* 124–25. The paragraph, which attributes the invention of sin to Judaism, writes of the goodwill of *Geschlechter.* Foucault reads *Geschlecht* here as race, whereas the English translation takes the option of translating it as "generation." The term *Rasse* is not used here.

43. Nietzsche, *Sämtliche Werke,* vol. 5, *Jenseits von Gut und Böse,* 120–21 and 182–83, 184–86, and 262–64. Section 242 is the anomalous text on this list not only because

318 NOTES

the term used is *Heraufkunft*, not *Herkunft*, but because this is a text in which Nietzsche highlighted the physiological process by which "the developing European became detached from its origins."

44. Foucault, "Nietzsche, la généalogie, l'histoire," 141; trans. "Nietzsche, Genealogy, History," 374.

45. Foucault, "Nietzsche, la généalogie, l'histoire," 141; trans. "Nietzsche, Genealogy, History," 374.

46. Nietzsche, *Sämtliche Werke*, vol. 5, *Jenseits von Gut und Böse*, section 262, 214–17; trans. *The Complete Works of Friedrich Nietzsche*, vol. 8, *Beyond Good and Evil*, 175–77. Cited at Foucault, "Nietzsche, la généalogie, l'histoire," 143–44; trans. "Nietzsche, Genealogy, History," 376–77.

47. Bernasconi, "When the Real Crime Began: Hannah Arendt's *The Origins of Totalitarianism* and the Dignity of the Western Philosophical Tradition," in Richard H. King and Dan Stone, eds., *Hannah Arendt and the Uses of History*, 54–67.

48. Foucault, "*Il faut défendre la société*," 37; trans. "*Society Must Be Defended*," 43.

49. Foucault, "*Il faut défendre la société*," 48; trans. "*Society Must Be Defended*," 56.

50. Foucault, "*Il faut défendre la société*," 58; trans. "*Society Must Be Defended*," 66.

51. In February 1971, Foucault already referenced "the recital of the genealogy, of the exploits of ancestors and the king himself" as constituting "a new beginning on the basis of the beginning" that amounted to a "revivifying epic of royal power." *Leçons sur la volonté de savoir*, 106; trans. *Lectures on the Will to Know*, 111.

52. Foucault, "*Il faut défendre la société*," 58; trans. "*Society Must Be Defended*," 66.

53. Nietzsche, "Vom Nutzen und Nachteil," 260; trans. "On the Uses and Disadvantages of History for Life," 98.

54. Foucault, "*Il faut défendre la société*," 59; trans. "*Society Must Be Defended*," 67.

55. Foucault, "*Il faut défendre la société*," 125–26 and 149; trans. "*Society Must Be Defended*," 142 and 168.

56. Foucault, "*Il faut défendre la société*," 62; trans. "*Society Must Be Defended*," 70.

57. Foucault, "*Il faut défendre la société*," 66; trans. "*Society Must Be Defended*," 76.

58. Foucault, "*Il faut défendre la société*," 63; trans. "*Society Must Be Defended*," 72.

59. Foucault, "*Il faut défendre la société*," 64; trans. "*Society Must Be Defended*," 73.

60. John Warr, "The Corruption and Deficiency of the Laws of England Soberly Discovered," 102. Foucault, "*Il faut défendre la société*," 93; trans. "*Society Must Be Defended*," 107.

61. Foucault, "*Il faut défendre la société*," 61; trans. "*Society Must Be Defended*," 70.

62. Foucault, "*Il faut défendre la société*," 116; trans. "*Society Must Be Defended*," 133.

63. Foucault, "*Il faut défendre la société*," 137 and 152; trans. "*Society Must Be Defended*," 155 and 171.

64. Foucault, "*Il faut défendre la société*," 125; trans. "*Society Must Be Defended*," 141.

65. Foucault, "*Il faut défendre la société*," 150; trans. "*Society Must Be Defended*," 168.

66. Foucault, "*Il faut défendre la société*," 144; trans. "*Society Must Be Defended*," 162–63.

67. Foucault, "*Il faut défendre la société*," 146; trans. "*Society Must Be Defended*," 64–65.

68. Henri de Boulainvilliers, *Essais sur la noblesse de France, contenant une dissertation sur son origine et abaissement*, 1. My translation.

NOTES 319

69. Foucault, *"Il faut défendre la société,"* 132; trans. *"Society Must Be Defended,"* 149. See Boulainvilliers, *Essais sur la noblesse de France,* 17–18. André Devyer already drew a connection between Boullainvilliers and Nietzsche on this point, in *Le sang épuré: Les préjugés de race chez les gentilhommes français de l'Ancien Regime (1560–1720),* 359.

70. Foucault, "Nietzsche, la généalogie, l'histoire," 152; trans. "Nietzsche, Genealogy, History," 384.

71. Foucault, *"Il faut défendre la société,"* 137; trans. *"Society Must Be Defended,"* 155; Foucault, "Nietzsche, la généalogie, l'histoire," 154–56; trans. "Nietzsche, Genealogy, History," 387–89.

72. Foucault, *"Il faut défendre la société,"* 139; trans. *"Society Must Be Defended,"* 157. Nietzsche, *Sämtliche Werke,* vol. 2, *Der Wanderer und sein Schatten,* 545; trans. *The Complete Works of Friedrich Nietzsche,* vol. 4, *Human, All Too Human II,* 156. Foucault, "Nietzsche, la généalogie, l'histoire," 145; trans. "Nietzsche, Genealogy, History," 377.

73. Foucault, "Nietzsche, la généalogie, l'histoire," 138; trans. "Nietzsche, Genealogy, History," 371.

74. Foucault, *"Il faut défendre la société,"* 170; trans. *"Society Must Be Defended,"* 191.

75. There is now a growing literature on Foucault and Boulainvilliers, and as one studies it, one wonders to what extent Foucault distorted Boulainvilliers for the purpose, such as constructing a Boulainvilliers that anticipates Nietzsche as Foucault saw him. See Diego Venturino, "A la politique comme à la guerre? A propos des cours de Michel Foucault au Collège de France," and "Race et histoire: Le paradigme nobiliaire de la distinction sociale au début du XVIIIe siècle"; Ian Wood, *The Modern Origins of the Early Middle Ages,* 19–28; Bernasconi, "Henri de Boulainvilliers," 577–79.

76. See Han, *Foucault's Critical Project,* 105.

77. One aspect of this genealogy that Foucault does not tell but which helps show its broader relevance is how Thierry gained much of his inspiration from Sir Walter Scott's *Ivanhoe* and how the idea of a race war between Normans and Saxons not only goes back to the seventeenth century but also filtered through Scott to the understanding of race in the southern United States in the middle half of the nineteenth century. See Ritchie Devon Watson, Jr., *Normans and Saxons: Southern Race Mythology and the Intellectual History of the American Civil War,* 47–71.

78. Foucault, *"Il faut défendre la société,"* 58 and 208; trans. *"Society Must Be Defended,"* 66 and 233.

79. Foucault, *"Il faut défendre la société,"* 208; trans. *"Society Must Be Defended,"* 233.

80. Foucault, *"Il faut défendre la société,"* 43; trans. *"Society Must Be Defended,"* 50.

81. Foucault, *"Il faut défendre la société,"* 193; trans. *"Society Must Be Defended,"* 215. See also 201–2, 211, and 213; trans. 225, 236, and 239.

82. Foucault, *"Il faut défendre la société,"* 211; trans. *"Society Must Be Defended,"* 236.

83. Foucault, *"Il faut défendre la société,"* 213; trans. *"Society Must Be Defended,"* 239.

84. The focus on Boulainvilliers and Augustin Thierry in the construction of the modern discourse of race can be seen especially among those who gave a central

320 NOTES

role to Gobineau. See Ernest Seillière, "Introduction," *Le Comte de Gobineau et l'aryanisme historique*, i–xxxiv; and Théophile Simar, *Étude critique sur la formation de la doctrine des races au XVIIIe siècle*, 20–35 and 73–75. Both these works appear to have helped to guide Foucault. Boulainvilliers is also prominent in Arendt's account in *The Origins of Totalitarianism*, 162–64: she also seems to have relied heavily on Seillière and Simar. On Thierry's racial thinking, see Kieran Joseph Carroll, *Some Aspects of the Historical Thought of Augustin Thierry, 1795–1856*, 32–50.

85. Foucault, *"Il faut défendre la société,"* 230; trans. *"Society Must Be Defended,"* 258.

86. Foucault, *"Il faut défendre la société,"* 230; trans. *"Society Must Be Defended,"* 258.

87. Foucault, "Nietzsche, la généalogie, l'histoire," 153; trans. "Nietzsche, Genealogy, History," 385.

88. Foucault, "Nietzsche, la généalogie, l'histoire," 152–54; trans. "Nietzsche, Genealogy, History," 385–87.

89. Foucault, *"Il faut défendre la société,"* 67; trans. *"Society Must Be Defended,"* 76.

90. Foucault, *"Il faut défendre la société,"* 103 and 110–11; trans. *"Society Must Be Defended,"* 117 and 126.

91. Foucault, "Nietzsche, la généalogie, l'histoire," 141; trans. "Nietzsche, Genealogy, History," 374.

92. Seen from the perspective of *"Society Must Be Defended,"* Nietzsche did not represent what in "Nietzsche, Genealogy, History" he had called a "solid identity." "Nietzsche, la généalogie, l'histoire," 153; trans. "Nietzsche, Genealogy, History," 386. Nietzsche equally could be said to have belonged to, or at least straddled, two grids of intelligibility, which is not extraordinary given that the same was said of the historical discourse of Augustin Thierry; *"Il faut défendre la société,"* 202–8; trans. *"Society Must Be Defended,"* 226–33.

93. Foucault, "Nietzsche, la généalogie, l'histoire," 143; trans. "Nietzsche, Genealogy, History," 375.

94. Foucault, *"Il faut défendre la société,"* 216 and 225; trans. *"Society Must Be Defended,"* 242 and 253.

95. Francis Galton, *Inquiries into Human Faculty and Its Development*.

96. See Foucault, *"Il faut défendre la société,"* 229; trans. *"Society Must Be Defended,"* 257. I will not rehearse here the textual evidence for Nietzsche's form of racism, having done so recently in Bernasconi, "Nietzsche as a Philosopher of Racialized Breeding," 57–60. Of course, one should also note here how Nietzsche's refusal to place any value on racial purity, which separated him from certain of his contemporaries, would also distance him from other aspects of biopolitics as Foucault understood it. See Foucault, *"Il faut défendre la société,"* 70–71; trans. *"Society Must Be Defended,"* 81.

97. Foucault, *"Il faut défendre la société,"* 233; trans. *"Society Must Be Defended,"* 261.

98. Foucault, *"Il faut défendre la société,"* 9–10; trans. *"Society Must Be Defended,"* 8. See also Foucault, "Le souci de a verité," in *Dits et écrits 1954–1988*, vol. 4, 668–78, at 674; trans. "The Concern for Truth," 262.

99. Foucault, *"Il faut défendre la société,"* 234; trans. *"Society Must Be Defended,"* 262.

100. Foucault, "Le retour de la morale," in Michel Foucault, *Dits et écrits*, vol. 4, 704; trans. "The Return of Morality," 471.

NOTES 321

Chapter 15

1. See, for example, James Yaki Sayles, *Meditations on Frantz Fanon's Wretched of the Earth: New Afrikan Revolutionary Writings*; Thomas K. Ramuga, "Frantz Fanon and Back Consciousness in Azania (South Africa)"; and Mabogo Percy More, "Locating Frantz Fanon in Post-Apartheid South Africa."

2. Robert Bernasconi, "Fanon's *The Wretched of the Earth* as the Fulfillment of Sartre's *Critique of Dialectical Reason*," and "Dialectical Praxis and the Decolonial Struggle: Sartre and Fanon's Contributions to Political Phenomenology."

3. Quoted by Annie Cohen-Solal, *Sartre 1905–1980*, 555; trans. *Sartre: A Life*, 433.

4. Frantz Fanon, "Altérations mentales, modifications caractérielles, troubles psychiques et déficit intellectual dans l'hérédo-dégénération spino-cérébelleuse," in Fanon, *Écrits sur l'aliénation et la liberté*, 168–232; trans. "Mental Alterations, Character Modifications, Psychic Disorders and Intellectual Deficit in Spinocerebellar Heredodegeneration," in Fanon, *Alienation and Freedom*, ed. Jean Khalfa and Robert J. C. Young, 203–75.

5. Fanon, *Peau noire, masques blancs*, in *Oeuvres*, 170–75; trans. Richard Philcox, *Black Skin, White Masks* (2008), 111–17. Neither the Philcox translation nor the earlier Charles Lam Markmann translation of *Black Skin, White Masks* (1967) is sensitive to the language of existentialism that pervades the book. I have given references here to the Philcox translation because it is more readily available. On some of the inadequacies of Philcox's translation of *The Wretched of the Earth*, see Ben Etherington, "An Answer to the Question: What Is Decolonization?" On this debate, see Bernasconi, "On Needing Not to Know and Forgetting What One Never Knew: The Epistemology of Ignorance in Fanon's Critique of Sartre."

6. Ch.-André Julien, "Avant-Propos."

7. Jean-Paul Sartre, "Orphée noir," xv; trans. "Black Orpheus," in Bernasconi, ed., *Race*, 119.

8. See Bernasconi, "The Assumption of Negritude: Aimé Césaire, Frantz Fanon, and the Vicious Circle of Racial Politics."

9. Fanon, *Peau noire, masques blancs*, in *Oeuvres*, 45–251, at 221; *Black Skin, White Masks*, 174.

10. Fanon, *Peau noire, masques blancs*, in *Oeuvres*, 209; *Black Skin, White Masks*, 158.

11. Sartre, *Réflexions sur la question juive*, 89; trans. George J. Becker, *Anti-Semite and Jew*, 69. For the history of the criticisms this claim elicited, see Jonathan Judaken, *Jean-Paul Sartre and the Jewish Question*.

12. Fanon, *Peau noire, masques blancs*, in *Oeuvres*, 137; *Black Skin, White Masks*, 73.

13. Fanon, *Peau noire, masques blancs*, in *Oeuvres*, 202; *Black Skin, White Masks*, 150.

14. Fanon, *Peau noire, masques blancs*, in *Oeuvres*, 175; *Black Skin, White Masks*, 117. Fanon repeatedly uses the term *man* to refer to both men and women in a way that, quite properly, is not acceptable today. He also uses it in its narrower sense. Often it is undecidable in which sense he is using it. I am retaining the word both in quoting and paraphrasing him, as this is not the place to try to decide in each case which sense is to be understood.

322 NOTES

15. Fanon, *Peau noire, masques blancs*, in *Oeuvres*, 175n; *Black Skin, White Masks*, 117n24.

16. Fanon's "The Lived Experience of the Black" was first published as a stand-alone essay in 1951: "L'expérience vécue du Noir"; trans. "The Lived Experience of the Black," in Bernasconi, ed., *Race* (2001), 184–201. There were only relatively minor changes before its republication in 1952 as the fifth chapter of *Black Skin, White Masks*.

17. Sartre, *L'être et le néant*, 393; trans. *Being and Nothingness*, 440. See Bernasconi, "Can Race Be Thought in Terms of Facticity? A Reconsideration of Sartre's and Fanon's Existential Theories of Race."

18. Fanon, *Peau noire, masques blancs*, in *Oeuvres*, 248; *Black Skin, White Masks*, 202.

19. Fanon, *Peau noire, masques blancs*, in *Oeuvres*, 216; *Black Skin, White Masks*, 167.

20. Fanon, *Les damnés de la terre*, in *Oeuvres*, 496; *The Wretched of the Earth*, 51.

21. Fanon, *Peau noire, masques blancs*, in *Oeuvres*, 125; *Black Skin, White Masks*, 63.

22. Sartre, *Réflexions sur la question juive*, 193–194; trans. *Anti-Semite and Jew*, 149.

23. Cohen-Solal, *Sartre*, 318; trans. *Sartre*, 241. See also Bernasconi, "Sartre's Gaze Returned: The Transformation of the Phenomenology of Racism," 201–2.

24. Sartre, *Colonialisme et néo-colonialisme*, 25–38; trans. "Colonialism Is a System," in *Colonialism and Neocolonialism*, 30–47. On the role of *Les Temps Modernes* during the Algerian War of Independence, see Michel-Antoine Burnier, *Les existentialistes et la politique*, 108–18, 123–24, and 131–45; trans. *Choice of Action: The French Existentialists in Politics*, 99–107, 114–15, and 121–35.

25. Sartre, "Review of Albert Memmi, *Portrait du colonisé précédé du portrait du colonisateur*," 291. The review was reprinted as an Introduction to the English translation of Memmi's book and then added as a Preface to a new French edition. See Sartre, "Préface," in Memmi, *Portrait du colonisé précédé du portrait du colonisateur*, 26n; trans. Lawrence Hoey, "Introduction," in Memmi, *The Colonizer and the Colonized*, xxv.

26. Sartre, *Critique de la raison dialectique*, 24; trans. *Search for a Method*, 21.

27. Sartre, *Critique de la raison dialectique*, 519; *Critique of Dialectical Reason*, 521.

28. Fanon, *Pour la révolution africaine*, in *Oeuvres*, 717; trans. "Racism and Culture," in Fanon, *Toward the African Revolution*, 31–34, at 33.

29. Fanon, *Les damnés de la terre*, in *Oeuvres*, 452; *The Wretched of the Earth*, 2. Translation modified.

30. Sartre, *Critique de la raison dialectique*, 706; *Critique of Dialectical Reason*, 757. Sartre had already reversed the gaze at the beginning of "Black Orpheus" when he wrote in the famous opening lines of "Black Orpheus": "When you removed the gag that was keeping these black mouths shut, what were you hoping for? That they would sing your praises?" Sartre, "Orphée noir," ix; trans. "Black Orpheus," in Bernasconi, ed., *Race*, 115–42, at 115.

31. Sartre, *Critique de la raison dialectique*, 289; *Critique of Dialectical Reason*, 231–32.

32. Sartre, *Critique de la raison dialectique*, 134; *Critique of Dialectical Reason*, 39.

33. Sartre, *Critique de la raison dialectique*, 300n; *Critique of Dialectical Reason*, 300n. By "serial alterity" Sartre understands the way all colonialists act in each of them, so that when a colonialist beats a native, each does so through the beatings given to other

NOTES 323

natives by other colonialists: they each act in this way "because this is *what one does*" (*Critique de la raison dialectique*, 685n; *Critique of Dialectical Reason*, 731n).

34. Sartre, *Critique de la raison dialectique*, 677; *Critique of Dialectical Reason*, 721.

35. Sartre, "Une idée fondamentale de la 'phénoménologie' de Husserl, l'intentionalité," 132; trans. Chris Turner, "A Fundamental Idea of Husserl's Phenomenology: Intentionality," 45.

36. See especially Sartre, *Critique de la raison dialectique*, 673–88; *Critique of Dialectical Reason*, 716–34. See also Paige Arthur, *Unfinished Projects: Decolonization and the Philosophy of Jean-Paul Sartre*, 77–94.

37. Fanon, *Les damnés de la terre*, in *Oeuvres*, 596; *The Wretched of the Earth*, 153.

38. Sartre, *Critique de la raison dialectique*, 68n; *Search for a Method*, 100n.

39. Sartre, *Critique de la raison dialectique*, 68n; *Search for a Method*, 100n.

40. Sartre, *Critique de la raison dialectique*, 111; *Search for a Method*, 181.

41. Sartre, *Critique de la raison dialectique*, 16; *Search for a Method*, 5–6.

42. In a lecture course from 1822 to 1823, Hegel developed this argument in a discussion of the corruption of the Church prior to the Reformation: *Vorlesungen über die Philosophie der Weltgeschichte*, 496; trans. Robert F. Brown and Peter C. Hodgson, *Lectures on the Philosophy of World History*, vol. 1, 501. It was taken up by C. L. R. James in "Dialectical Materialism and the Fate of Humanity," 76.

43. Sartre, *Critique de la raison dialectique*, 743; *Critique of Dialectical Reason*, 804.

44. Sartre, *Critique de la raison dialectique*, 742; *Critique of Dialectical Reason*, 803.

45. Fanon insists on the same point: *Les damnés de la terre*, in *Oeuvres*, 582; *The Wretched of the Earth*, 141.

46. Sartre, *Critique de la raison dialectique*, 106; *Search for a Method*, 172.

47. Sartre, *Critique de la raison dialectique*, 687; *Critique of Dialectical Reason*, 734.

48. Sartre, *Critique de la raison dialectique*, 25; *Search for a Method*, 22.

49. Fanon, *Les damnés de la terre*, in *Oeuvres*, 496; *The Wretched of the Earth*, 52. Translation modified.

50. Fanon, *Les damnés de la terre*, in *Oeuvres*, 468; *The Wretched of the Earth*, 21.

51. Fanon, *Les damnés de la terre*, in *Oeuvres*, 489; *The Wretched of the Earth*, 44.

52. Fanon, *Les damnés de la terre*, in *Oeuvres*, 538; *The Wretched of the Earth*, 95. Translation modified. Philcox seems to have an allergy to translating the French word *concret* as "concrete." Of at least six occurrences in *The Wretched of the Earth*, he takes this route only once.

53. Sartre, *Critique de la raison dialectique*, 744; *Critique of Dialectical Reason*, 804.

54. Fanon, *Peau noire, masques blancs*, in *Oeuvres*, 176; *Black Skin, White Masks*, 119.

55. Fanon, *Peau noire, masques blancs*, in *Oeuvres*, 251; *Black Skin, White Masks*, 206.

56. Sartre, *Critique de la raison dialectique*, 94; *Search for a Method*, 148.

57. Sartre, *Critique de la raison dialectique*, 97; *Search for a Method*, 154.

58. Sartre, *Critique de la raison dialectique*, 96; *Search for a Method*, 153.

59. Sartre, *Critique de la raison dialectique*, 42n; *Search for a Method*, 51n.

60. Henri Lefebvre, "Perspectives de sociologie rurale," *Cahiers internationaux de sociologie*, 134–35; trans. Stuart Elden, "Perspectives on Rural Sociology," 117.

61. Sartre, *Critique de la raison dialectique*, 42n; *Search for a Method*, 52n.

324 NOTES

62. Sartre, *Critique de la raison dialectique*, 683; *Critique of Dialectical Reason*, 729.

63. Sartre, *Critique de la raison dialectique*, 683–84; *Critique of Dialectical Reason*, 729.

64. Sartre, *Critique de la raison dialectique*, 92; *Search for a Method*, 145.

65. Fanon, *Les damnés de la terre*, in *Oeuvres*, 454; *The Wretched of the Earth*, 4.

66. Sartre, *Critique de la raison dialectique*, 92; *Search for a Method*, 145.

67. Gabriel d'Arboussier, "Une dangereuse mystification: La théorie de la négritude," 38–39. For some of the context, see Ian Birchall, *Sartre against Stalinism*, 81–82.

68. Fanon, *Peau noire, masques blancs*, in *Oeuvres*, 68; *Black Skin, White Masks*, xviii.

69. Fanon, *Peau noire, masques blancs*, in *Oeuvres*, 202; *Black Skin, White Masks*, 150.

70. Fanon, *Peau noire, masques blancs*, in *Oeuvres*, 202; *Black Skin, White Masks*, 150. Translation modified.

71. Fanon, *Peau noire, masques blancs*, in *Oeuvres*, 202; *Black Skin, White Masks*, 150. Translation modified.

72. Sartre, *Critique de la raison dialectique*, 92; *Search for a Method*, 145.

73. Sartre, "Sartre par Sartre," 112; trans. "Itinerary of a Thought: Interview with Jean-Paul Sartre," 50.

74. Cohen-Solal, *Sartre*, 531; trans. *Sartre*, 412. See *Critique de la raison dialectique*, 673–674; *Critique of Dialectical Reason*, 716.

75. Sartre, "Sartre par Sartre," 111; "Itinerary of a Thought," 49.

76. Sartre, "Sartre par Sartre," 108; "Itinerary of a Thought," 48.

77. Sartre, "Sartre par Sartre," 112; "Itinerary of a Thought," 50.

Bibliography

Adams, Hannah. *A Dictionary of All Religions and Religious Denominations*. New York: James Eastburn, 1817.

Adelung, Johann Christoph. *Grammatisch-kritisches Wörterbuch der hochdeutschen Mundart*. Vol. 1. 2nd ed. Leipzig: Johann Gottlob Immanuel Breitkopf, 1793.

[Adelung, Johann Christoph]. *Versuch einer Geschichte der Cultur des menschlichen Geschlechts*. Leipzig: Christian Gottlieb Hertel, 1782.

Adhikari, Mohamed. *Not White Enough, Not Black Enough: Racial Identity in the South African Coloured Community*. Athens: Ohio University Press, 2005.

Adiele, Pius Onyemechi. *The Popes, the Catholic Church and the Transatlantic Enslavement of Black Africans, 1418–1839*. Hildesheim: Georg Olms, 2017.

Agassiz, Elizabeth Cary, ed. *Louis Agassiz: His Life and Correspondence*. 2 vols. Boston: Houghton Mifflin, 1885.

Ahmed, Sara. "A Phenomenology of Whiteness." *Feminist Theory* 8, no. 2 (2007): 149–68.

Alcoff, Linda Martín. *Visible Identities: Race, Gender, and the Self*. Oxford: Oxford University Press, 2006.

American Committee for Democracy and Intellectual Freedom. *Science Condemns Racism*. New York: ACDIF, 1939.

Anonymous. "Natural History of Man." *The United States Magazine and Democratic Review* 26 (1850): 327–45.

Anonymous. "On Degenerations in Man": Review of Morel, *Traité des* dégénerescences. *British Quarterly Review* 78 (April 1864): 425–59.

Anonymous. "Review of an Essay Concerning the True Original, Extent and End of Civil Government." In vol. 19 of *Bibliothèque Universelle et Historique de l'Année*, 573–91. Amsterdam: Chez les Héritiers d'Antoine Schelte, 1699.

Anonymous. "Vital Statistics of Negroes and Mulattoes." *Boston Medical and Surgical Journal* 27, no. 10 (1842): 168–70.

Anzaldúa, Gloria. *Borderlands/La Frontera: The New Mestiza*. 3rd ed. San Francisco: Aunt Lute Books, 2007.

Appiah, Kwame Anthony. *In My Father's House: Africa in the Philosophy of Culture*. Oxford: Oxford University Press, 1992.

Appiah, Kwame Anthony. *Lines of Descent: W. E. B. Du Bois and the Emergence of Identity*. Cambridge, MA: Harvard University Press, 2014.

Appiah, Kwame Anthony. "The Uncompleted Argument: Du Bois and the Illusion of Race." In *"Race," Writing, and Difference*, edited by Henry Louis Gates, 21–37. Chicago: University of Chicago Press, 1986.

Appiah, K. Anthony. "Race, Culture, Identity: Misunderstood Connections." In *Color Conscious: The Political Morality of Race*, edited by K. Anthony Appiah and Amy Gutmann, 30–105. Princeton, NJ: Princeton University Press, 1996.

Aptheker, Herbert, ed. *Book Reviews by W. E. B. Du Bois*. Millwood, NY: KTO Press, 1977.

326 BIBLIOGRAPHY

Arendt, Hannah. *Between Past and Future: Six Exercises in Political Thought.* London: Faber, 1961.

Arendt, Hannah. *The Origins of Totalitarianism.* London: George Allen and Unwin, 1967.

Arthur, Paige. *Unfinished Projects: Decolonization and the Philosophy of Jean-Paul Sartre.* London: Verso, 2010.

Augstein, Hannah F. *James Cowles Prichard's Anthropology: Remaking the Science of Man in Early Nineteenth Century Britain.* Amsterdam: Rodopi, 1999.

Azara, Félix von. *Reise nach Süd-Amerika von Don Felix de Azara in den Jahren 1781 bis 1801.* Translated from the French by C. Weyland. Berlin: Voss, 1810.

Bachman, John. *The Doctrine of the Unity of the Human Race.* Charleston, SC: C. Canning, 1850.

Bagehot, Walter. *Physics and Politics; or, Thoughts on the Application of the Principles of "Natural Selection" and "Inheritance" to Political Society.* New York: D. Appleton, 1873.

Baker, Lee. *From Savage to Negro: Anthropology and the Construction of Race, 1896–1954.* Berkeley: University of California Press, 1998.

Balagangadhara, S. N. *"The Heathen in His Blindness": Asia, the West and the Dynamic of Religion.* New Delhi: Manohar, 2005.

Barber, Michael D. *The Participating Citizen: A Biography of Alfred Schutz.* Albany: SUNY Press, 2004.

Barkan, Elazar. "The Politics of the Science of Race: Ashley Montagu and UNESCO's Anti-racist Declarations." In *Race and Other Misadventures: Essays in Honor of Ashley Montagu in His Ninetieth Year,* edited by Larry T. Reynolds and Leonard Lieberman, 96–105. New York: General Hall, 1996.

Barkan, Elazar. *The Retreat of Scientific Racism: Changing Concepts of Race in Britain and the United States between the World Wars.* Cambridge: Cambridge University Press, 1992.

Barzun, Jacques. "Race and Racism." Review of *Race: Science and Politics* by Ruth Benedict." *The Nation* 151, no. 16 (1940): 372.

Basson, Lauren L. *White Enough to Be American? Race Mixing, Indigenous People, and the Boundaries of State and Nation.* Chapel Hill: University of North Carolina Press, 2008.

Bateson, William. "Heredity in the Physiology of Nations: A Review of *The Principles of Heredity* by G. Archdall Reid." In *William Bateson, F.R.S., Naturalist: His Essays and Addresses together with a Short Account of His Life,* edited by Beatrice Bateson, 456–59. Cambridge: Cambridge University Press, 1928.

Bauer, Bruno. *Russland und das Germanenthum.* Charlottenburg: Egbert Bauer, 1853.

Baxter, Richard. *A Christian Directory: Or, a Sum of Practical Divinity. The Second Part: viz. Christian Oeconomicks.* London: Nevill Simmons, 1677.

Beattie, James. *Elements of Moral Science.* Vol. 2. Edinburgh: William Creech, 1793.

Beattie, James. *An Essay on the Nature and Immutability of Truth, in Opposition to Sophistry and Scepticism.* London: Dilly, 1774.

Beattie, James. *Miscellaneous Items.* Bristol: Thoemmes Continuum, 1999.

Becker, Oskar. "Para-Existenz: Menschliches Dasein und Dawesen." *Blätter für deutsche Philosophie* 17 (1943–1944): 62–95.

Bell, Bernard, Emily R. Grosholz, and James B. Stewart, eds. *W. E. B. Du Bois on Race and Culture: Philosophy, Politics, and Poetics.* London: Routledge, 1996.

Benedict, Ruth. *Race: Science and Politics.* New York: Modern Age Books, 1940.

Benedict, Ruth, and Gene Weltfish. *The Races of Mankind.* New York: Public Affairs Committee, 1943.

BIBLIOGRAPHY 327

Bergier, [Nicolas-Sylvestre] M. L'Abbé. *Encyclopédie Méthodique*. Vol. 3. Paris: Panckoucke, 1790.

[Bernard, Jean-Frédéric]. *The Ceremonies and Religious Customs of the Various Nations of the Known World*, illustrated by Bernard Picart. Vol. 6, part 1. London: William Jackson and Claude Dubosc, 1737.

[Bernard, Jean-Frédéric]. *Ceremonies et Coutumes religieuses de tous les peuples du monde*, illustrated by Bernard Picart. Vol. 1. Amsterdam: J. F. Bernard, 1739.

Bernardin de Saint-Pierre, Jacques-Henri. *Journey to Mauritius*. Translated by Jason Wilson. New York: Interlink, 2003.

[Bernardin de Saint-Pierre, Jacques-Henri]. *Voyage à l'Isle de France, à l'Isle de Bourbon, au Cap de Bonne-Espérance*, &c. Vol. 1. Amsterdam: Merlin, 1773.

Bernasconi, Robert. "After the German Invention of Race: Conceptions of Race Mixing from Kant to Fischer and Hitler." In *Remapping Black German: New Perspectives on Afro-German History, Politics, and Culture*, edited by Sara Lennox, 91–104. Amherst: University of Massachusetts Press, 2017.

Bernasconi, Robert. *American Theories of Polygenesis: Types of Mankind*. 7 vols. Bristol: Thoemmes Press, 2002.

Bernasconi, Robert. "The Assumption of Negritude: Aimé Césaire, Frantz Fanon, and the Vicious Circle of Racial Politics." *Parallax* 8, no. 2 (April–June 2002): 69–83.

Bernasconi, Robert. "Before Whom and for What? Accountability and the Invention of Ministerial, Hyperbolic, and Infinite Responsibility." In *Difficulties of Ethical Life*, edited by Shannon Sullivan and Dennis J. Schmidt, 131–146. New York: Fordham University Press, 2008.

Bernasconi, Robert. "Black Skin, White Skulls: The Nineteenth Century Debate over the Racial Identity of the Ancient Egyptians." *Parallax* 13, no. 2 (April 2007): 6–20.

Bernasconi, Robert. "Can Race Be Thought in Terms of Facticity? A Reconsideration of Sartre's and Fanon's Existential Theories of Race." In *Rethinking Facticity*, edited by François Raffoul and Eric Nelson, 195–213. Albany: SUNY Press, 2008.

Bernasconi, Robert. "Casting the Slough: Fanon's New Humanism for a New Humanity." In *Fanon: A Critical Reader*, edited by Lewis R. Gordon, T. Denean Sharpley-Whiting, and Renée T. White, 113–121. Oxford: Blackwell, 1996.

Bernasconi, Robert. "Dialectical Praxis and the Decolonial Struggle: Sartre and Fanon's Contributions to Political Phenomenology." In *Political Phenomenology: Experience, Ontology, Episteme*, edited by Thomas Bedorf and Steffen Herrmann, 17–31. New York: Routledge, 2019.

Bernasconi, Robert. "Ethnic Race: Revisiting Alain Locke's Neglected Proposal." In *Race or Ethnicity? On Black and Latino Identity*, edited by Jorge J. E. Gracia, 123–36. Ithaca, NY: Cornell University Press, 2007.

Bernasconi, Robert. "'The European Knows and Does Not Know': Fanon's Response to Sartre." In *Frantz Fanon's "Black Skin, White Masks": New Interdisciplinary Essays*, edited by Max Silverman, 100–111. Manchester: Manchester University Press, 2005.

Bernasconi, Robert. "Fanon's French Hegel." In *Violence, Slavery and Freedom between Hegel and Fanon*, edited by Ulrike Kistner and Philippe Van Haute, xiii–xxiii. Johannesburg: Wits University Press, 2020.

Bernasconi, Robert. "Fanon's *The Wretched of the Earth* as the Fulfillment of Sartre's Critique of Dialectical Reason." *Sartre Studies International* 16, no. 2 (2010): 36–46.

328   BIBLIOGRAPHY

Bernasconi, Robert. "The Great White Error and the Great Black Mirage." In *Living Fanon: Global Perspectives*, edited by Nigel Gibson, 85–92. New York: Palgrave Macmillan, 2011.

Bernasconi, Robert. "Hegel at the Court of the Ashanti." In *Hegel after Derrida*, edited by Stuart Barnett, 41–63. London: Routledge, 1998.

Bernasconi, Robert. "Hegel's Racism: A Reply to McCarney." *Radical Philosophy* 119 (May/June 2003): 35–37.

Bernasconi, Robert. "Henri de Boulainvilliers (1658–1722)." In *The Cambridge Foucault Lexicon*, edited by Leonard Lawlor and John Nale, 577–79. Cambridge: Cambridge University Press, 2014.

Bernasconi, Robert. "'Ich mag in keinen Himmel, wo Weisse sind': Herder's Critique of Eurocentrism." *Acta Institutionis Philosophiae et Aestheticae* 13 (1995): 69–81.

Bernasconi, Robert. "Kant as an Unfamiliar Source of Racism." In *Philosophers on Race: Critical Essays*, edited by Julie K. Ward and Tommy L. Lott, 145–66. Oxford: Blackwell, 2002.

Bernasconi, Robert. "The Limits of the European Idea of Development." In *Social Development: Between Intervention and Integration*, edited by Jacob Rendtorff, Adam Diderichsen, and Peter Kemp, 185–203. Copenhagen: Rhodos, 1997.

Bernasconi, Robert. "The Logic of Whiteness: Hybridity and the Philosophy of Racial Segregation in the Nineteenth Century." *Annals of Scholarship* 14, no. 1 (2000): 75–91.

Bernasconi, Robert. "Ludwig Ferdinand Clauss and Racialization." In *Husserl's Ideen*, edited by Lester Embree and Thomas Nenon, 55–70. Contributions to Phenomenology 66. Berlin: Springer, 2013.

Bernasconi, Robert. "Nietzsche as a Philosopher of Racialized Breeding." In *The Oxford Handbook of Philosophy and Race*, edited by Naomi Zack, 54–64. Oxford: Oxford University Press, 2017.

Bernasconi, Robert. "No More Stories, Good or Bad: De Man's Criticisms of Derrida on Rousseau." In *Derrida: A Critical Reader*, edited by David Wood, 137–66. Oxford: Blackwell, 1992.

Bernasconi, Robert. "None Is Free until All Are Free: Sartre's Ontology of Freedom and His Politics." In *The Modern Prince and the Modern Sage: Transforming Power and Freedom*, edited by Ananta Kumar Giri, 476–93. New Delhi: Sage, 2009.

Bernasconi, Robert. "On Needing Not to Know and Forgetting What One Never Knew: The Epistemology of Ignorance in Fanon's Critique of Sartre." In *Race and Epistemologies of Ignorance*, edited by Shannon Sullivan and Nancy Tuana, 231–39. Albany: SUNY Press, 2007.

Bernasconi, Robert. "Proto-Racism: Carolina in Locke's Mind." In *Racism and Modernity: Festschrift for Wulf D. Hund*, edited by Iris Wigger and Sabine Ritter, 68–82. Münster: LIT, 2011.

Bernasconi, Robert, ed. *Race*. Oxford: Blackwell, 2001.

Bernasconi, Robert, ed. *Race and Anthropology*. 9 vols. Bristol: Thoemmes Press, 2003.

Bernasconi, Robert. "Race and Earth in Heidegger's Thinking during the Late 1930s." *Southern Journal of Philosophy* 48, no. 1 (2010): 49–66.

Bernasconi, Robert. "Racism." In *Key Concepts in the Study of Antisemitism*, edited by Sol Goldberg, Scott Ury, and Kalman Weiser, 245–56. Cham, Switzerland: Palgrave Macmillan, 2021.

BIBLIOGRAPHY 329

Bernasconi, Robert. "Racism Is a System: How Existentialism Became Dialectical in Fanon and Sartre." In *The Cambridge Companion to Existentialism*, edited by Steven Crowell, 342–60. Cambridge: Cambridge University Press, 2012.

Bernasconi, Robert. "The Return of Africa: Hegel and the Question of the Racial Identity of the Egyptians." In *Identity and Difference*, edited by P. Grier, 201–16. Albany: SUNY Press, 2007.

Bernasconi, Robert. "Richard Wright as Educator: The Progressive Structure of Simone de Beauvoir's Account of Racial Hatred in the United States." *Yale French Studies* 135–36 (2019): 151–68.

Bernasconi, Robert. "Sartre and Levinas: Philosophers against Racism and Antisemitism." In *Race after Sartre: Antiracism, Africana Existentialism, Postcolonialism*, edited by Jonathan Judaken, 31–39. Albany: SUNY Press, 2008.

Bernasconi, Robert. "Sartre's Gaze Returned: The Transformation of the Phenomenology of Racism." *Graduate Faculty Philosophy Journal* 18, no. 2 (1995): 201–21.

Bernasconi, Robert. "Silencing the Hottentots: Kolb's Pre-Racial Encounter with the Hottentots and Its Impact on Buffon, Kant, and Rousseau." *Graduate Faculty Philosophy Journal* 35, nos. 1–2 (2014): 101–24.

Bernasconi, Robert. "True Colors: Kant's Distinction between Nature and Artifice in Context." In *Klopffechtereien—Missverständnisse—Widersprüche? Methodische und methodologische Perspektiven auf die Kant—Forster—Kontroverse*, edited by Rainer Godel and Gideon Stiening, 191–207. Munich: Wilhelm Fink, 2012.

Bernasconi, Robert. "Where Is Xenophobia in the Fight against Racism?" *Critical Philosophy of Race* 2, no. 1 (2014): 5–19.

Bernasconi, Robert. "Who Invented the Concept of Race? Kant's Role in the Enlightenment Construction of Race." In *Race*, edited by Bernasconi, 11–36. Oxford: Blackwell, 2001.

Bernasconi, Robert. "Why Do the Happy Inhabitants of Tahiti Bother to Exist at All?" In *Genocide and Human Rights: A Philosophical Guide*, edited by John K. Roth, 139–48. New York: Palgrave Macmillan, 2005.

Bernasconi, Robert. "With What Must the Philosophy of World History Begin? On the Racial Basis of Hegel's Eurocentrism." *Nineteenth-Century Contexts* 22, no. 2 (2000): 171–201.

Bernasconi, Robert, with Sybol Cook, eds. *Race and Racism in Continental Philosophy*. Bloomington: Indiana University Press, 2003.

Bernasconi, Robert, and Kristie Dotson, eds. *Race, Hybridity, and Miscegenation*. 3 vols. Bristol: Thoemmes Press, 2005.

[Bernier, François]. "Lettre a Monsieur Chapelain, October 4, 1667." In *Suite des Memoires du Sr Bernier, sur l'Empire du Grand Mogol*. Paris: Claude Barbin, 1671.

[Bernier, François]. "Nouvelle division de la Terre, par les différentes espèces ou races d'hommes qui l'habitent, envoyée par un fameux Voyageur à M. [. . .]." *Journal des Sçavans* 12 (April 14, 1684): 148–57.

Bernier, François. "A New Division of the Earth, According to the Different Species or Races of Men Who Inhabit It, Sent by a Famous Traveller to Mons. [. . .]," translated by T. Bendyshe. In *Memoirs Read Before the Anthropological Society of London*, vol. 1, 1863–1864, 360–64. London: Trübner and Co., 1865.

Bernier, François. *Travels in the Mogul Empire*. Translated by Archibald Constable. London: Humphrey Milford, 1914.

Bhabha, Homi K. *The Location of Culture*. London: Routledge, 1994.

330 BIBLIOGRAPHY

Bibby, Cyril. "Race Prejudice and Education." *The UNESCO Courier* 13, no. 10 (1960): 6–12.

Biddiss, Michael D. *Father of Racist Ideology: The Social and Political Thought of Count Gobineau*. London: Weidenfeld and Nicolson, 1970.

Bieder, Robert E. *Science Encounters the Indian, 1820–1880: The Early Years of American Ethnology*. Norman: University of Oklahoma Press, 1986.

Birchall, Ian H. *Sartre against Stalinism*. New York: Berghahn, 2004.

Birt, Robert E. "The Bad Faith of Whiteness." In *What White Looks Like: African-American Philosophers on the Whiteness Question*, edited by George Yancy, 55–64. New York: Routledge, 2004.

Blackburn, Robin. *The Overthrow of Colonial Slavery, 1776–1848*. London: Verso, 1998.

Blake, Thomas. *The Birth Priviledge, or, Covenant-Holinesse of Beleevers and Their Issue in the Time of Gospel Together with the Right of Infants to Baptisme*. London, 1644.

Blanckaert, Claude. "L'esclavage des noirs et l'ethnographie américaine: Le point de vue de Paul Broca en 1858." In *Nature, histoire, société: Essais en homage à Jacques Roger*, edited by Claude Blanckaert, Jean-Louis Fischer, and Roselyne Rey, 391–417. Paris: Klincksieck, 1995.

Blanckaert, Claude. *De la race à l'évolution: Paul Broca et l'anthropologie française (1850–1900)*. Paris: L'Harmattan, 2009.

[Blount, Charles]. *Great Is Diana of the Ephesians, or, The Original of Idolatry: Together with the Politick Institutions of the Gentile Sacrifices*. London, 1695.

Blumenbach, Johann Friedrich. *The Anthropological Treatises of Johann Friedrich Blumenbach*. Translated by Thomas Bendyshe. London: Longman, Green, Longman, Roberts, & Green, 1865.

Blumenbach, Johann Friedrich. *De generis humani varietate nativa*. 3rd ed. Göttingen: Vandenhoeck and Ruprecht, 1795.

Blumenbach, Johann Friedrich. *Handbuch der Naturgeschichte*. 4th ed. Göttingen: Johann Christian Dieterich, 1791. 5th ed. Göttingen: Johann Christian Dieterich, 1797.

Blumenbach, Johann Friedrich. "On the Natural Variety of Mankind." In *The Anthropological Treatises of Johann Friedrich Blumenbach*, translated by Thomas Bendyshe, 145–276. London: Longman, Green, Longman, Roberts, and Green, 1865.

Blyden, Edward Wilmot. *Black Spokesman: Selected Published Writings of Edward Wilmot Blyden*. Edited by Hollis R. Lynch. London: Frank Cass, 1971.

Blyden, Edward Wilmot. *Christianity, Islam and the Negro Race*. London: W. B. Whittingham, 1887.

Boas, Franz. "Aryans and Non-Aryans." *The American Mercury* 32, no. 16 (1934): 219–23.

Boas, Franz. *Changes in Bodily Form of Descendants of Immigrants*. Washington, DC: Government Printing Office, 1911.

Boas, Franz. *The Mind of Primitive Man*. New York: Macmillan, 1911; 2nd rev. ed. New York: Macmillan, 1938.

Boas, Franz. *Race and Democratic Society*. New York: J. J. Augustin, 1945.

Boas, Franz. "Race Prejudice from the Scientists' Angle." *Forum and Century* 98, no. 2 (1937): 90–94.

Boas, Franz. "Racial Purity." *Asia* 40, no. 5 (1940): 231–34.

Boas, Franz. "The Real Race Problem." *The Crisis: A Record of the Darker Races* 1, no. 2 (1910): 22–25.

Boas, Franz. "What Is a Race?" *The Nation* 120, no. 3108 (1925): 89–91.

BIBLIOGRAPHY 331

Bodin, Jean. *Les Six Livres de la République: Livre premier*. Bilingual critical edition. Edited by Mario Turchetti. Paris: Garnier, 2013.

Bodin, Jean. *Method for the Easy Comprehension of History*. Translated by Beatrice Reynolds. New York: Columbia University Press, 1945.

Bogues, Anthony. *Black Heretics, Black Prophets: Radical Political Intellectuals*. New York: Routledge, 2003.

Boissel, Jean. *Victor Courtet (1813–1867): Premier théoricien de la hiérarchie des races*. Paris: Presses Universitaires de France, 1972.

Boudin, Jean. *Traité de géographie et de statistique médicales et des maladies*. 2 vols. Paris: J. B. Baillière, 1857.

Boulainvilliers, Henri de. *Essais sur la noblesse de France, contenans une dissertation sur son origine et abaissement*. Amsterdam, 1732.

Brantlinger, Patrick. "'Dying Races': Rationalizing Genocide in the Nineteenth Century." In *The Decolonization of Imagination: Culture, Knowledge, and Power*, edited by Jan N. Pieterse and Bhikhu Parekh, 43–56. Oxford: Oxford University Press, 1997.

Brattain, Michelle. "Miscegenation and Competing Definitions of Race in Twentieth-Century Louisiana." *Journal of Southern History* 71, no. 3 (August 2005): 621–58.

Braun, Harald E. "Making the Canon? The Early Reception of the *République* in Castilian Political Thought." In *The Reception of Bodin*, edited by Howell A. Lloyd, 257–92. Leiden: Brill, 2013.

Briggs, Laura. *Reproducing Empire: Race, Sex, Science, and U.S. Imperialism in Puerto Rico*. Berkeley: University of California Press, 2002.

Broca, Paul. "Introduction aux mémoires sur l'hybridité." In *Mémoires d'anthropologie*, vol. 3, 321–25. Paris: Reinwald, 1877.

Broca, Paul. "Mémoire sur l'hybridité en général, sur la distinction des especes animals." *Journal de la Physiologie de l'homme et des animaux* 1 (1858): 433–71, 684–729; 2 (1859): 218–58, 345–96.

Broca, Paul. *On the Phenomena of Hybridity in the Genus Homo*. Translated and edited by C. Carter Blake. London: Longman, Green, Longman, and Roberts, 1864.

Broca, Paul. "Des phénomènes d'hybridité dans le genre humain." *Journal de la physiologie de l'homme et des animaux* 2 (1859): 601–25 and 3 (1860): 392–439.

Broca, Paul. *Recherches sur l'hybridité animale en général et sur l'hybridité humaine en particulier*. Paris: Claye, 1860.

Broca, Paul. "Les sélections." Review of French translations of Darwin's *The Descent of Man* and Alfred Russel Wallace's *Contributions to the Theory of Natural Selection*; reprinted in Paul Broca, "Les Sélections." Reprinted in vol. 3 of *Mémoires d'anthropologie*, 205–50. Paris: Reinwald, 1877.

Brodie, Fawn M. *Thomas Jefferson: An Intimate History*. New York: W.W. Norton, 1974.

Brokesby, Francis. *Some Proposals towards Propagating of the Gospel in Our American Plantations*. London: George Sawbridge, 1708.

Broughton, Thomas. *Bibliotheca Historico-Sacra; or, an Historical Library of the Principal Matters Relating to Religion, Ancient and Modern, Pagan, Jewish, Christian and Mohammedan*. 2 vols. London: R. Reily, 1737.

Browne, Thomas. *Religio Medici*. London: Andrew Crook, 1672.

Bruce, Philip A. *The Plantation Negro as a Freeman: Observations on His Character, Condition, and Prospects in Virginia*. New York: G. P. Putnam's, 1889.

[Buffon, Georges-Louis Leclerc de]. *Histoire naturelle, générale et particulière*. 36 vols. Paris: De l'imprimerie royale, 1749–1804.

332 BIBLIOGRAPHY

Burkhalter, Lois Wood. *Gideon Lincecum, 1793–1874: A Biography*. Austin: University of Texas Press, 1965.

Burma, John H. "The Measurement of Negro 'Passing.'" *American Journal of Sociology* 52, no. 1 (July 1946): 18–22.

Burnier, Michel-Antoine. *Choice of Action: The French Existentialists in Politics*. Translated by Bernard Murchland. New York: Random House, 1968.

Burnier, Michel-Antoine. *Les existentialistes et politique*. Paris: Gallimard, 1966.

Busch, Moritz. *Graf Bismarck und seine Leute während des Kriegs mit Frankreich*. 2 vols. Leipzig: Grunow, 1878.

Bynum, Victoria E. "'White Negroes' in Segregated Mississippi: Miscegenation, Racial Identity, and the Law." *Journal of Southern History* 64, no. 2 (May 1998) 247–76.

Cabell, J. L. *The Testimony of Modern Science to the Unity of Mankind*. New York: Robert Carter, 1859.

Caldwell, Charles. Review of "An Essay on the Causes of the Variety of Complexion and Figure in the Human Species," by Samuel Stanhope Smith. *The Port Folio* 4, Series 4 (1814): 8–33, 148–63, 252–71, 362–82, and 447–57.

Caldwell, Charles. *Thoughts on the Original Unity of the Human Race*. Cincinnati, OH: J. A. and U. P. James, 1852.

Carhart, Michael C. *The Science of Culture in Enlightenment Germany*. Cambridge, MA: Harvard University Press, 2007.

Carlyle, Thomas. "Occasional Discourse on the Negro Question." *Fraser's Magazine* 40 (1849): 670–79.

Carmichael, Gershom. *S. Puffendorfii: De officio hominis et civis, juxta legim naturalem*. Book 2. Edinburgh: Joannis Mosman, 1724.

Carmichael, Gershom. "Supplements and Observations upon the Two Books of Samuel Pufendorf's *On the Duty of Man and Citizen*." In *Natural Rights on the Threshold of the Scottish Enlightenment*, edited by James Moore and Michael Silverthorne, 3–217. Indianapolis, IN: Liberty Fund, 2002.

Carmichael, Stokely, and Charles V. Hamilton. *Black Power: The Politics of Liberation in America*. New York: Random House, 1967.

Carroll, Kieran Joseph. *Some Aspects of the Historical Thought of Augustin Thierry, 1795–1856*. Washington, DC: Catholic University of America, 1951.

Carthill, A. *The Lost Dominion: The Story of England's Abdication in India*. Edinburgh: Blackwood, 1924.

Cartwright, Samuel. "The Diseases of Negroes." *De Bow's Review* 11, New Series 4 (1851): 209–213 and 331–36.

Carus, Carl Gustav. *Denkschrift zum Hundertjährigen Geburtsfeste Goethe's*. Leipzig: F. A. Brockhaus, 1849.

Catterall, Helen Tunnicliff. *Judicial Cases Concerning American Slavery and the Negro*. Vol. 2. New York: Octagon Books, 1968.

Césaire, Aimé. *Cahier d'un retour au pays natal*. Bilingual edition. Translated by N. Gregson Davis. Durham, NC: Duke University Press, 2017.

Chamberlain, Houston Stewart. *Foundations of the Nineteenth Century*. 2 vols. Translated by John Lees. London: John Lane, 1913.

Chamberlain, Houston Stewart. *Die Grundlagen des neuzehnten Jahrhunderts*. 3 vols. Munich: F. Bruckmann, 1899.

Chamberlain, Houston Stewart. *Immanuel Kant: Die Persönlichkeit als Einführung in das Werk*. Munich: F. Bruckmann, 1905.

BIBLIOGRAPHY 333

Chamberlain, Houston Stewart. *Immanuel Kant: A Study and a Comparison with Goethe, Leonardo Da Vinci, Bruno, Plato and Descartes.* Translated by Lord Redesdale. 2 vols. London: John Lane, 1914.

[Charron, Pierre de]. *De la sagesse: Trois livres.* Paris: David Douceur, 1604.

Charron, Pierre de. *Of Wisdom: Three Books.* 3rd ed. Translated by George Stanhope. London: J. Tonson, J. Walthoe, et al., 1729.

Cherki, Alice. *Frantz Fanon: A Portrait.* Translated by Nadia Benabid. Ithaca, NY: Cornell University Press, 2006.

Clark, Linda L. *Social Darwinism in France.* Tuscaloosa: University of Alabama Press, 1984.

Clark, Victor S., et al. *Porto Rico and Its Problems.* Washington, DC: The Brookings Institution, 1930.

Clarkson, Thomas. *An Essay on the Slavery and Commerce of the Human Species Particularly the African.* London: J. Phillips, 1786.

Clauss, Ludwig Ferdinand. *Die Nordische Seele.* Munich: J. F. Lehmann, 1933.

Clauss, Ludwig Ferdinand. *Rasse und Seele.* Munich: J. F. Lehmann, 1926.

Clauss, Ludwig Ferdinand. *Von Seele und Antlitz der Rassen und Völker: eine Einführung in die vergleichende Ausdrucksforschung.* Munich: J. F. Lehmann, 1929.

Cohen, Hermann. *Ein Bekenntnis in der Judenfrage.* Berlin: Dümmler, 1880.

Cohen-Solal, Annie. *Sartre: 1905–1980.* Paris: Gallimard, 1985.

Cohen-Solal, Annie. *Sartre: A Life.* Translated by Anna Cancogni. London: Heinemann, 1987.

Comte, Auguste. *System of Positive Polity.* 4 vols. Translated by Richard Congreve. London: Longmans, Green, 1875 and 1877.

Comte, Auguste. *Système de politique de positive.* Vols. 2 and 4. Paris: Carilian-Goeury, 1852 and 1854.

Congrès international des Sciences ethnographiques tenu à Paris du 15 au 17 juillet 1878. Paris: Imprimerie Nationale, 1881.

Cooke, Kathy J. "The Limits of Heredity: Nature and Nurture in American Eugenics before 1915." *Journal of the History of Biology* 31, no. 2 (1998): 263–78.

Cooper, Anna Julia. *A Voice from the South.* Xenia, OH: Aldine, 1892.

Courtet de l'Isle, Victor. *La science politique fondée sur la science de l'homme: Ou etude des races humaines sous le rapport philosophique, historique et social.* Paris: Arthus Bertrand, 1838.

Cowan, R. S. "Nature and Nurture: The Interplay of Biology and Politics in the Work of Francis Galton." In *Studies in History of Biology*, vol. 1, edited by William Coleman and Camille Limoges, 133–208. Baltimore: Johns Hopkins University Press, 1977.

Cox, Earnest Sevier. *White America.* Congress Edition. Richmond, VA: White America Society, 1925.

Cox, Oliver Cromwell. *Caste, Class, and Race: A Study in Social Dynamics.* New York: Doubleday, 1948.

Cox, Oliver Cromwell. "The Racial Theories of Robert E. Park and Ruth Benedict." *The Journal of Negro Education* 13, no. 4 (1944): 452–63.

Crenshaw, Kimberlé, Neil Gotanda, et al., eds. *Critical Race Theory: The Key Writings That Formed the Movement.* New York: The New Press, 1995.

[Croly, David Goodman, and George Wakeman]. *Miscegenation: The Theory of the Blending of the Races, Applied to the American White Man and Negro.* New York: H. Dexter Hamilton, 1864.

334 BIBLIOGRAPHY

Crummell, Alexander. *Africa and America: Addresses and Discourses*. Springfield, MA: Willey, 1891.

Crummell, Alexander. *Destiny and Race*. Edited by Wilson Jeremiah Moses. Amherst: University of Massachusetts Press, 1992.

Cugoano, Ottobah. *Réflexions sur la traite et l'esclavage des nègres*. Paris: Éditions La Découverte, 2009.

Cugoano, Ottobah. *Thoughts and Sentiments on the Evil of Slavery*. Edited by Vincent Carretta. New York: Penguin, 1999.

Curran, Andrew S. *The Anatomy of Blackness: Science and Slavery in the Age of Enlightenment*. Baltimore: Johns Hopkins University Press, 2011.

Cuvier, Georges. *Discours sur les révolutions du globe*. Edited by Ferdinand Hoefer. Paris: Didot, 1850.

d'Arboussier, Gabriel. "Une dangereuse mystification: la théorie de la négritude." *La nouvelle critique: Revue du marxisme militant* 7 (June 1949): 34–47.

d'Eichthal, Gustave, and Ismay Urbain. *Lettres sur la race noire et la race blanche*. Paris: Paulin, 1839.

Daniel, G. Reginald. *Race and Multiraciality in Brazil and the United States: Converging Paths?* University Park: Pennsylvania State University Press, 2006.

Davidson, Arnold. "Ethics as Ascetics: Foucault, the History of Ethics, and Ancient Thought." In *The Cambridge Companion to Foucault*, edited by Gary Gutting, 115–40. Cambridge: Cambridge University Press, 1994.

Davies, Surekha. *Renaissance Ethnography and the Invention of the Human: New Worlds, Maps and Monsters*. Cambridge: Cambridge University Press, 2016.

Davis, Angela Y. "Race and Criminalization: Black Americans and the Punishment Industry." In *The House That Race Built: Original Essays by Toni Morrison, Angela Y. Davis, Cornel West, and Others on Black Americans*, edited by Wahneema Lubiano, 264–79. New York: Pantheon, 1997.

Davis, David Brion. "The Emergence of Immediatism in British and American Antislavery Thought." *The Mississippi Valley Historical Review* 49, no. 2 (1962): 209–30.

Day, Caroline Bond. *A Study of Some Negro-White Families in the United States*. In Varia Africana V., Harvard African Studies, vol. 10. Cambridge, MA: Peabody Museum of Harvard University, 1932.

[De Laet, Johannes]. *De imperio magni mogolis, sive India vera commentarius*. Leiden: Ex Officina Elzeviriana, 1631.

de Vastey, Pompée Valentin. *The Colonial System Unveiled*. Translated and edited by Chris Bongie. Liverpool: Liverpool University Press, 2014.

Delany, Martin R. *Principia of Ethnology: The Origins of Races and Color*. Philadelphia: Harper, 1879.

DeMarco, Joseph P. "The Concept of Race in the Social Thought of W. E. B. Du Bois." *Philosophical Forum* 3, no. 2 (Winter 1972): 227–42.

DeMarco, Joseph P. *The Social Thought of W. E. B. Du Bois*. Lanham, MD: University Press of America, 1983.

Demel, Walter. "How the Chinese Became Yellow: A Contribution to the Early History of Race Theories." In *China in the German Enlightenment*, edited by Bettina Brandt and Daniel Leonhard Purdy, 20–59. Toronto: University of Toronto Press, 2016.

Derrida, Jacques. *De la grammatologie*. Paris: Minuit, 1967.

Derrida, Jacques. *Of Grammatology*. Translated by Gayatri Spivak. Baltimore: Johns Hopkins University Press, 1976.

BIBLIOGRAPHY 335

Deutscher, Penelope. *The Philosophy of Simone de Beauvoir: Ambiguity, Conversion, Resistance*. Cambridge: Cambridge University Press, 2008.

Devyer, André. *Le sang épuré. Les préjugés de race chez les gentilhommes français de l'Ancien Regime (1560–1720)*. Brussels: Editions de l'Université de Bruxelles, 1973.

Diffie, Bailey W., and Justine Whitfield Diffie. *Porto Rico: A Broken Pledge*. New York: Vanguard Press, 1931.

Dilke, Charles Wentworth. *Greater Britain: A Record of Travel in English Speaking Countries during 1866 and 1867*. 2 vols. London: MacMillan, 1868.

Dillingham, William, et al. *Dictionary of Races or Peoples*. Reports of the Immigration Commission, vol. 5. Washington, DC: Government Printing Office, 1911.

Disraeli, Benjamin. *Coningsby; or, the New Generation*. 3 vols. London: Henry Colburn, 1844.

Disraeli, Benjamin. *Lord George Bentinck: A Political Biography*. London: Colburn & Co., 1852.

Disraeli, Benjamin. *Tancred: Or the New Crusade*. London: Henry Colburn, 1850.

Dodwell, Henry. *An Epistolary Discourse, Proving, from the Scriptures and the First Fathers, That the Soul Is a Principle Naturally Mortal; but Immortalized Actually by the Pleasure of God, to Punishment, or to Reward, by the Union with the Divine Baptismal Spirit*. London: R. Smith, 1706.

Doris, Glen. "An Abolitionist Too Late? James Beattie and the Scottish Enlightenment's Lost Chance to Influence the Slave Trade Debate." *Journal of Scottish Thought* 2, no. 1 (2011): 83–98.

Doris, Glen. "The Scottish Enlightenment and the Politics of Abolition." PhD Diss., University of Aberdeen, Aberdeen, Scotland, 2011.

Dorr, Gregory Michael. *Segregation's Science: Eugenics and Society in Virginia*. Charlottesville: University of Virginia Press, 2008.

Douglass, Frederick. *The Frederick Douglass Papers. Series 1: Speeches, Debates, and Interviews*. Edited by John W. Blassingame et al. 5 vols. New Haven, CT: Yale University Press, 1982.

Douglass, Frederick. "The Future of the Colored Race." *North American Review* 142, no. 354 (May 1886): 437–40.

Du Bois, W. E. B. *Black Folk Then and Now*. Millwood, NY: Kraus-Thomson, 1990.

Du Bois, W. E. B. *The Conservation of Races*. Washington, DC: American Negro Academy, 1897.

Du Bois, W. E. B. *Darkwater: Voices from within the Veil*. New York: Harcourt, Brace and Howe, 1920.

Du Bois, W. E. B. *Du Bois: Writings*. Edited by Nathan Huggins. New York: Library of America, 1986.

Du Bois, W. E. B. "The Evolution of the Race Problem (June 1, 1909)." In *W. E. B. Du Bois Speaks: Speeches and Addresses, 1890–1919*, edited by Philip S. Foner, 209–24. New York: Pathfinder, 1970.

Du Bois, W. E. B. "The Future of the Negro Race in America." In *Writings by W. E. B. Du Bois in Periodicals Edited by Others: Vol. 1, 1891–1909*, edited by Herbert Aptheker, 186–95. Millwood, NY: Kraus-Thomson, 1982.

Du Bois, W. E. B. *The Health and Physique of the Negro American: A Social Study Made under the Direction of Atlanta University by the Eleventh Atlanta Conference*. Atlanta University Publications no. 11. Atlanta, GA: Atlanta University Press, 1906.

336 BIBLIOGRAPHY

Du Bois, W. E. B. "Miscegenation." In *Against Racism: Unpublished Essays, Papers, Addresses, 1887–1961*, edited by Herbert Aptheker, 90–102. Amherst: University of Massachusetts Press, 1988.

Du Bois, W. E. B. *The Negro*. Millwood, NY: Kraus-Thomson, 1988.

Du Bois, W. E. B. *The Philadelphia Negro: A Social Study*. Millwood, NY: Kraus-Thomson, 1973.

Du Bois, W. E. B. "Review of *Race Traits and Tendencies of the American Negro* by Frederick Hoffman." *Annals of the American Academy of Political and Social Science* 9, no. 1 (January 1897): 127–33.

Du Bois, W. E. B. "Sociology Hesitant." *Boundary 2: An International Journal of Culture and Literature* 27, no. 3 (Fall 2000): 37–44.

Dubow, Saul. *Scientific Racism in Modern South Africa*. Cambridge: Cambridge University Press, 1995.

Dufrenne, Mikel, and Paul Ricoeur. *Karl Jaspers et la philosophie de l'existence*. Paris: Seuil, 1947.

Dugdale, Robert. *"The Jukes": A Study in Crime, Pauperism, Disease and Heredity*. New York: G. P. Putnam's, 1877.

Dühring, Eugen. *Die Judenfrage als Racen-, Sitten- und Culturfrage*. Karlsruhe: H. Reuther, 1881.

Duncan, David. *Life and Letters of Herbert Spencer*. Vol. 1. New York: D. Appleton, 1908.

Dunn, L. C. "Reformulation of the Statement on the Concept of Race." In *The Race Concept: Results of an Inquiry*, 82–91. Paris: UNESCO, 1953.

Echeruo, Michael J. C. "Edward W. Blyden, W. E. B. Du Bois, and the 'Color Complex.'" *Journal of Modern African Studies* 30, no. 4 (December 1992): 669–84.

Edelmann, Johann Christian. *Unschuldige Wahrheiten: Gesprächs-weise abgehandelt zwischen Doxophilo und Philaletho*. n. p., 1735.

Edwards, William Frédéric. *Des caractères physiologiques des races humaines considérés dans leurs rapports avec l'histoire: Lettre à M. Amédée Thierry*. Paris: Compère Jeune, 1829.

Eigen, Sara, and Mark Larrimore, eds. *The German Invention of Race*. Albany: SUNY Press, 2006.

Escobar del Corro, Juan. *Tractatus bipartitus de puritate et nobilitate probanda*. Lugduni [Lyon]: Rochi Deville and L. Chalmette, 1733.

Etherington, Ben. "An Answer to the Question: What Is Decolonization? Frantz Fanon's *The Wretched of the Earth* and Jean-Paul Sartre's *Critique of Dialectical Reason*." *Modern Intellectual History* 13, no. 1 (2016): 151–78.

Falzon, Christopher, Timothy O'Leary, and Jana Sawicki, eds. *A Companion to Foucault*. Oxford: Blackwell, 2013.

Fanon, Frantz. *Alienation and Freedom*. Translated by Steven Corcoran. Edited by Jean Khalfa and Robert J. C. Young. London: Bloomsbury, 2018.

Fanon, Frantz. *Black Skin, White Masks*. Translated by Charles Lam Markmann. New York: Grove Weidenfeld Press, 1967. Translated by Richard Philcox. New York: Grove Press, 2008.

Fanon, Frantz. *Les damnés de la terre*. In *Frantz Fanon: Oeuvres*, 419–681. Paris: La Découverte, 2011.

Fanon, Frantz. *Écrits sur l'aliénation et la liberté*. Paris: La Découverte, 2015.

Fanon, Frantz. "L'expérience vécue du Noir." *Esprit* 179 (May 1951): 657–79.

BIBLIOGRAPHY   337

Fanon, Frantz. *Peau noire, masques blancs*. In *Frantz Fanon: Oeuvres*, edited by Jean Khalfa and Robert Young, 45–257. Paris: La Découverte, 2011.

Fanon, Frantz. *Pour la revolution africaine*. In *Frantz Fanon: Oeuvres*, edited by Jean Khalfa and Robert Young, 683–878. Paris: La Découverte, 2011.

Fanon, Frantz. *Toward the African Revolution: Political Essays*. Translated by Haakon Chevalier. New York: Monthly Review Press, 1967.

Fanon, Frantz. *The Wretched of the Earth*. Translated by Richard Philcox. New York: Grove Press, 2004.

Farr, James. "'So Vile and Miserable an Estate': The Problem of Slavery in Locke's Political Thought." *Political Theory* 14, no. 2 (1986): 263–289.

Feil, Ernst. *Religio*. Vol. 3, *Die Geschichte eines neuzeitlichen Grundbegriffs im 17. und frühen 18. Jahrhundert*. Göttingen: Vandenhoeck & Ruprecht, 2001.

Feil, Ernst. *Religio*. Vol. 4, *Die Geschichte eines neuzeitlichen Grundbegriffs im 18. und frühen 19. Jahrhundert*. Göttingen: Vandenhoeck & Ruprecht, 2007.

Ferguson, Adam. *Institutes of Moral Philosophy for the Use of Students in the College of Edinburgh*. Edinburgh: A. Kincaid and J. Bell, 1769. 2nd ed., revised and corrected, 1773. 3rd ed., enlarged, 1785.

Figal, Sara Eigen. *Heredity, Race, and the Birth of the Modern*. New York: Routledge, 2008.

Finkelman, Paul. "The Crime of Color." *Tulane Law Review* 67, no. 6 (1993): 2081–86.

Firmin, Anténor. *De l'égalité des races humaines*. Paris: F. Pichon, 1885.

Firmin, Anténor. *The Equality of the Human Races*. Translated by Asselin Charles. New York: Garland, 2000.

Firmin, Anténor. *M. Roosevelt: Président des États-Unis et la République d'Haiti*. Paris: F. Pichon and Durand-Auzias, 1905.Fischer, Eugen. *Die Rehobother Bastards und das Bastardierungsproblem beim Menschen*. Jena: Gustav Fischer, 1913.

Fluehr-Lobban, Carolyn. "Anténor Firmin: Haitian Pioneer of Anthropology." *American Anthropologist* 102, no. 3 (2000): 449–66.

Forest, Luc. "De l'abolitionnisme à l'esclavagisme? Les implications des anthropologues dans le débat sur l'esclavage des Noirs aux États-Unis (1840–1870)." *Revue française d'histoire d'outre-mer* 85, no. 320 (1998): 85–102.

Forster, Georg. "Noch etwas über die Menschenrassen: An Herrn D. Biester." *Der teutsche Merkur* (October–November 1786): 57–86 and 150–66.

Forster, Georg. "Something More about the Human Races." In *Kant and the Concept of Race: Late Eighteenth-Century Writings*, translated and edited by Jon M. Mikkelsen, 143–68. Albany: SUNY Press, 2013.

Fortier, Paul A. "Gobineau and German Racism." *Comparative Literature* 19, no. 4 (1967): 341–50.

Foucault, Michel. *Abnormal*. Translated by Graham Burchell. New York: Picador, 2003.

Foucault, Michel. *Les anormaux*. Paris: Seuil/Gallimard, 1999.

Foucault, Michel. *The Archaeology of Knowledge*. Translated by A. M. Sheridan Smith. New York: Pantheon Books, 1972.

Foucault, Michel. *L'archéologie du savoir*. Paris: Gallimard, 1969.

Foucault, Michel. "The Concern for Truth." In *Politics, Philosophy, Culture: Interviews and Other Writings, 1977–1984*, translated by Alan Sheridan, edited by Lawrence D. Kritzman, 255–70. New York: Routledge, 1988.

Foucault, Michel. *Discipline and Punish*. Translated by Alan Sheridan. New York: Vintage, 1979.

338 BIBLIOGRAPHY

Foucault, Michel. "The Discourse of History." In *Foucault Live: Collected Interviews, 1961–1984*, translated by John Johnston, edited by Sylvère Lotringer, 19–32. New York: Semiotext(e), 1996.

Foucault, Michel. "The Discourse on Language." In *The Archaeology of Knowledge*, translated by A. M. Sheridan Smith, 215–37. New York: Pantheon Books, 1972.

Foucault, Michel. *Dits et écrits, 1954–1988*. 4 vols. Paris: Gallimard, 1994.

Foucault, Michel. *Essential Works of Foucault, 1954–1984*. 3 vols. Edited by James D. Faubion. New York: The New Press, 1998.

Foucault, Michel. *"Il faut défendre la société": Cours au Collège de France, 1975–1976*. Paris: Seuil/Gallimard, 1997.

Foucault, Michel. *Histoire de la sexualité*. Vol. 1, *La volonté de savoir*. Paris: Gallimard, 1976.

Foucault, Michel. *The History of Sexuality*. Vol. 1. Translated by Robert Hurley. New York: Vintage, 1990; New York: Vintage, 1978.

Foucault, Michel. *Leçons sur la volonté de savoir: Cours au Collège de France, 1970–1971, suivi de Le Savoir d'Œdipe*. Paris: Seuil/Gallimard, 2011.

Foucault, Michel. *Lectures on the Will to Know: Lectures at the College de France, 1970–1971, with Oedipal Knowledge*. Translated by Graham Burchell and edited by Daniel Defert. New York: Palgrave Macmillan, 2013.

Foucault, Michel. "Nietzsche, Genealogy, History," translated by Donald F. Brouchard and Sherry Simon. In *Aesthetics, Method, and Epistemology*, vol. 2 of *Essential Works of Foucault, 1954–1984*, edited by James D. Faubion, 369–91. New York: The New Press, 1998.

Foucault, Michel. "Nietzsche, la généalogie, l'histoire." In *Hommage à Jean Hyppolite*, edited by Suzanne Bachelard, 145–72. Paris: Presses Universitaires de France, 1971.

Foucault, Michel. *L'ordre du discours*. Paris: Gallimard, 1970.

Foucault, Michel. *Power*. Translated by Colin Gordon. Edited by James D. Faubion. New York: The New Press, 2000.

Foucault, Michel. "Prison Talk." In *Power/Knowledge: Selected Interviews and Other Writings 1972–1977*, translated and edited by Colin Gordon, 37–54. New York: Pantheon Books, 1980.

Foucault, Michel. *The Punitive Society: Lectures at the Collège de France, 1972–1973*. Translated by Graham Burchell. New York: Palgrave Macmillan, 2015.

Foucault, Michel. "Réponse au Cercle d'épistémologie." *Cahiers pour l'Analyse* 9: *Généalogie des sciences* (Summer 1968): 9–40.

Foucault, Michel. "The Return of Morality," *Foucault Live: Collected Interviews, 1961–1984*, translated by John Johnston and edited by Sylvère Lotringer, 465–73. New York: Semiotext(e), 1996.

Foucault, Michel. *La société punitive*. Paris: Seuil/Gallimard, 2013.

Foucault, Michel. *"Society Must Be Defended": Lectures at the Collège de France, 1975–1976*. Translated by David Macey and edited by Mauro Bertani. New York: Picador, 2003.

Foucault, Michel. *Sécurité, Territoire, Population*. Paris: Seuil/Gallimard, 2004.

Foucault, Michel. *Security, Territory, Population*. Translated by Graham Burchell. New York: Palgrave Macmillan, 2007.

Foucault, Michel. *Surveiller et punir*. Paris: Gallimard, 1975.

Frank, Johann Peter. *System einer vollständigen medicinischen Polizey*. 3rd ed. Vol. 1. Vienna: Johann Thomas Edler von Trattner, 1786.

Frank, Johann Peter. *A System of Complete Medical Police*. Translated by E. Vilim and edited by Erna Lesky. Baltimore: Johns Hopkins University Press, 1976.

BIBLIOGRAPHY   339

Freud, Anna. *The Ego and the Mechanisms of Defense.* Vol. 2: 1936, *The Writings of Anna Freud*, translated by Cecil Baines. New York: International Universities Press, 1973.

Freud, Anna. *Das Ich und die Abwehrmechanismen.* Vienna: Internationaler Psychoanalytischer Verlag, 1936.

Freud, Sigmund. *Psychologie collective et analyse du moi: suivi de cinq leçons de la psychanalyse.* Paris: Payot, 1950.

Freud, Sigmund. *Two Short Accounts of Psycho-analysis: Five Lectures on Psycho-Analysis, the Question of Lay Analysis.* Translated by James Strachey. Harmondsworth: Penguin, 1962.

Friedlander, Ruth. "Bénédict-Augustin Morel and the Development of the Theory of Degenerescence." PhD Diss., University of California, San Francisco, 1973.

Fries, Jakob Friedrich. *Über die Gefährdung der Wohlstandes und Charakters der Deutschen durch die Juden.* Heidelberg: Mohr and Winter, 1816.

Galton, Francis. *English Men of Science: Their Nature and Nurture.* London: Macmillan and Co., 1874.

Galton, Francis. *Inquiries into Human Faculty and Its Development.* London: Macmillan, 1883.

Garnet, Henry Highland. *The Past and the Present Condition, and the Destiny, of the Colored Race.* Troy, NY: J. C. Kneeland, 1848.

Géloin, Ghislaine. "Introduction." In Anténor Firmin, *De l'égalité des races humaines*, edited by Géloin, xi–xxvii. Paris: L' Harmattan, 1993.

Gentili, Alberico. *De jure belli libri tres.* 2 vols. Translated by John C. Rolfe. Oxford: Clarendon Press, 1933.

Gerbner, Katharine. *Christian Slavery: Conversion and Race in the Protestant Atlantic World.* Philadelphia: University of Pennsylvania Press, 2018.

Gibson, Nigel C. *Fanon: The Postcolonial Imagination.* Cambridge: Polity Press, 2003.

Girtanner, Christoph. *Über das Kantische Prinzip für die Naturgeschichte.* Göttingen: Vandenhoeck und Ruprecht, 1796.

Gisborne, Thomas. *On Slavery and the Slave Trade.* London: Stockdale, 1792.

Gisborne, Thomas. *The Principles of Moral Philosophy.* London: T. Bensley, 1789; 4th ed. London: T. Cadell, 1798.

Gobineau, Arthur de. *Essai sur l'inégalité des races humaines.* 2 vols. Paris: Firmin-Didot, 1853–1854; 2nd ed., 2 vols. Paris: Firmin-Didot, 1884.

Gobineau, Arthur de. *The Inequality of Human Races.* Translated by Adrian Collins. London: Heinemann, 1915.

Gobineau, Arthur de. *Gobineau: Selected Political Writings.* Edited by Michael D. Bidiss. New York: Harper and Row, 1970.

Gobineau, Arthur de. *The Moral and Intellectual Diversity of Races, with Particular Reference to Their Respective Influence in the Civil and Political History of Mankind.* Translated by H. Hotz and with additional notes by Josiah Nott. Philadelphia: Lippincott, 1856.

Godwyn, Morgan. *The Negro's & Indians Advocate: Suing for Their Admission into the Church.* London: J. D., 1680.

Goetz, Rebecca Anne. *The Baptism of Early Virginia: How Christianity Created Race.* Baltimore: Johns Hopkins University Press, 2012.

Gordon, Lewis R. *Bad Faith and Antiblack Racism.* Atlantic Highlands, NJ: Humanities Press, 1995.

Gordon, Lewis R. "Existential Dynamics of Theorizing Black Invisibility." In *Existence in Black*, edited by Lewis R. Gordon, 69–79. New York: Routledge, 1997.

340 BIBLIOGRAPHY

Gordon, Lewis R. *Fanon and the Crisis of European Man: An Essay on Philosophy and the Human Sciences*. New York: Routledge, 1995.

Gordon-Reed, Annette. *Thomas Jefferson and Sally Hemings: An American Controversy*. Charlottesville: University of Virginia Press, 1997.

Gossett, Thomas. *Race: The History of an Idea in America: Political Essays*. New York: Schocken, 1971.

Grant, Madison. *The Conquest of the Continent; or The Expansion of Races in America*. New York: Charles Scribner's Sons, 1933.

Grégoire, Henri. *De la littérature des Nègres, ou Recherches sur leur facultés intellectuelles, leurs qualités morales et leur littératures*. Paris: Maradan, 1808.

Grégoire, Henri. *On the Cultural Achievements of Negroes*. Translated by Thomas Cassirer and Jean-Françoise Brière. Amherst: University of Massachusetts Press, 1996.

Gross, Ariela J. *What Blood Won't Tell: A History of Race on Trial in America*. Cambridge, MA: Harvard University Press, 2008.

Grotius, Hugo. *De jure belli ac pacis*. Edited by P. C. Molhuysen. Leiden: A. W. Sitjoff, 1919; Clark, NJ: Lawbook Exchange, 2005.

Grotius, Hugo. *The Rights of War and Peace*. 3 vols. Translated by John Morrice and edited by Richard Tuck. Indianapolis, IN: Liberty Fund, 2005.

Groulx, Richard. *Michel Foucault, la politique comme guerre continuée: De la guerre des races au racisme d'État*. Paris: L'Harmattan, 2015.

Guattari, Félix. "L'étudiant, les fou et les Katangais." *Partisans* 46 (February–March 1969): 104–11.

Guenebault, J. H. *Natural History of the Negro Race*. Charleston, SC: D. J. Dowling, 1837.

Guex, Germaine. *The Abandonment Neurosis*. Translated by Peter D. Douglas. London: Karnac, 2015.

Guex, Germaine. *La névrose d'abandon*. Paris: Presses Universitaires de France, 1950.

Gumplowicz, Ludwig. "Über das Naturgesetz der Staatenbildung: Vortrag gehalten am 23. September 1875." In Ludwig Gumplowicz, *Der Rassenkampf: Soziologische Untersuchungen*, 394–401. Innsbruck: Wagner, 1909.

Gunn, Jeffrey. "Creating a Paradox: Quobna Ottobah Cugoano and the Slave Trade's Violation of the Principles of Christianity, Reason, and Property Ownership." *Journal of World History* 21, no. 4 (2010): 629–656.

Haakonssen, Knud, ed. *Thomas Reid on Practical Ethics*. Edinburgh: Edinburgh University Press, 2015.

Haakonssen, Knud, and Paul Wood, eds. *Thomas Reid on Society and Politics*. Edinburgh: Edinburgh University Press, 2015.

Haeckel, Ernst. *Natürliche Schöpfungsgeschichte*. Berlin: Georg Reimer, 1868; 5th ed. Berlin: Georg Reimer, 1874; 10th ed. Berlin: Georg Reimer, 1902.

Haller, John S. "Race, Mortality and Life Insurance: Negro Vital Statistics in the Late Nineteenth Century." *Journal of the History of Medicine and Allied Sciences* 25, no. 3 (July 1970): 247–61.

Halliday, E. M. *Understanding Thomas Jefferson*. New York: Harper Collins, 2001.

Hamilton, Alexander, James Madison, and John Jay. *The Federalist or The New Constitution*. New York: Heritage Press, 1945.

Han, Béatrice. *Foucault's Critical Project*. Translated by Edward Pile. Stanford, CA: Stanford University Press, 2002.

Harris, Marvin. *The Rise of Anthropological Theory: A History of Theories of Culture*. New York: Thomas Y. Crowell, 1968.

BIBLIOGRAPHY 341

Harrison, Peter. *The Territories of Science and Religion*. Chicago: University of Chicago Press, 2015.

Hart, Hornell N. *Selective Migration as a Factor in Child Welfare in the United States, with Special Reference to Iowa*. Iowa City: The University, 1921.

Harvey, Joy. *"Almost a Man of Genius"*: *Clémence Royer, Feminism, and Nineteenth-Century Science*. New Brunswick, NJ: Rutgers University Press, 1997.

Harvey, Joy. "Evolutionism Transformed: Positivists and Materialists in the *Société d'Anthropologie de Paris* from Second Empire to Third Republic." In *The Wider Domain of Evolutionary Thought*, edited by David Oldroyd and Ian Langhan, 289–310. Dordrecht: D. Reidel, 1983.

Haskins, R. W. *History and Progress of Phrenology*. Buffalo, NY: Steele and Peck, 1839.

Hazard, Anthony. "Ashley Montagu, the 'Most Dangerous Myth,' and the 'Negro Question' during World War II." *Journal of Anthropological Research* 72, no. 3 (2016): 289–310.

Hegel, G. W. F. *Elements of the Philosophy of Right*. Translated by H. B. Nisbet. Cambridge: Cambridge University Press, 1991.

Hegel, G. W. F. *Grundlinien der Philosophie des Rechts*. Edited by Eduard Gans. *Werke* 8. Berlin: Duncker und Humblot, 1833.

Hegel, G. W. F. *Lectures on the Philosophy of History*. Translated by J. Sibree. London: George Bell, 1884. Translated by Ruben Alvarado. Aaalten, the Netherlands: Wordbridge, 2011.

Hegel, G. W. F. *Lectures on the Philosophy of World History*. Vol. 1, *Manuscripts of the Introduction and the Lectures of 1822–1823*. Translated by Robert F. Brown and Peter C. Hodgson. Oxford: Oxford University Press, 2011.

Hegel, G. W. F. *Philosophy of Subjective Spirit*. 3 vols. Edited by Michael J. Petry. Dordrecht: Reidel, 1978.

Hegel, G. W. F. *Schriften und Entwürfe I (1817–1825)*. Edited by Friedrich Hogemann and Christoph Jamme. *Gesammelte Werke* 15. Hamburg: Felix Meiner, 1990.

Hegel, G. W. F. *Vorlesungen über die Philosophie der Geschichte*. Werke 9. 2nd ed. Edited by Karl Hegel. Berlin: Duncker und Humblot, 1840.

Hegel, G. W. F. *Vorlesungen über die Philosophie der Weltgeschichte*. Edited by Karl Heinz Ilting, Karl Brehmer, and Hoo Nam Seelman. *Vorlesungen* 12. Hamburg: Felix Meiner, 1966.

Hegel, G. W. F. *Vorlesungen über die Philosophie der Weltgeschichte*. Edited by Walter Jaeschke. *Gesammelte Werke* 27.4. Hamburg: Felix Meiner, 2020.

Hegel, G. W. F. *Vorlesungen über die Philosophie des Subjektiven Geistes*. Edited by Christoph Johannes Bauer. *Gesammelte Werke* 25.1–2. Hamburg: Felix Meiner, 2008–2011.

Heidegger, Martin. *Being and Time*. Translated by John Macquarrie and Edward Robinson. Oxford: Basil Blackwell, 1967. Translated by Joan Stambaugh. Albany, NY: SUNY Press, 1996.

Heidegger, Martin. "Overcoming Metaphysics." In *The End of Philosophy*. Translated by Joan Stambaugh, 84–110. New York: Harper & Row, 1973.

Heidegger, Martin. "The Question concerning Technology." In *The Question Concerning Technology and Other Essays*, translated by William Lovitt, 3–25. New York: Harper & Row, 1977.

Heidegger, Martin. *Sein und Zeit*. Tübingen: Niemeyer, 1949.

Heller, Henry. "Bodin on Slavery and Primitive Accumulation." *Sixteenth Century Journal* 25, no. 1 (1994): 53–65.

342 BIBLIOGRAPHY

Hening, William Waller, ed. *The Statutes at Large; Being a Collection of all the Laws of Virginia, from the First Session of the Legislature, in the Year 1619.* 13 vols. Vols. 1–2, New York: R. & W. & G. Bartow, 1823. Vol. 3, Philadelphia: Thomas Desilver, 1823.

Henry, Paget. "Between Hume and Cugoano: Race, Ethnicity and Philosophical Entrapment." *Journal of Speculative Philosophy* 18, no. 2 (2004): 129–148.

Herbert, Edward. *De religione gentilium.* Amsterdam: Typis Blaevorium, 1663.

Herder, Johann Gottfried. *Ideen zur Philosophie der Geschichte der Menschheit.* 4 vols. Riga: Johann Friedrich Hartnoch, 1784–1791.

Herder, Johann Gottfried. *Outlines of a Philosophy of the History of Man.* Translated by T. Churchill. London: J. Johnson, 1800.

Hesnard, Angelo. *L'univers morbide de la faute.* Paris: Presses Universitaires de France, 1949.

Hess, Moses. *Rome and Jerusalem: A Study in Jewish Nationalism.* Translated by Meyer Waxman. New York: Bloch, 1918.

Hess, Moses. *Rom und Jerusalem: Die Letzte Nationalitatenfräge.* Jerusalem: R. Löwit, 1935.

Hesse, Barnor. "Im/Plausible Deniability: Racism's Conceptual Double Bind." *Social Identities* 10, no. 1 (2004): 9–29.

Hiernaux, Jean, and Michael Banton. "Statement of Race. Paris, July 1950." In *Four Statements on the Race Question.* Paris: UNESCO, 1969.

Hirschfeld, Magnus. *Racism.* Translated and edited by Eden Paul and Cedar Paul. London: Victor Gollancz, 1938.

Hitler, Adolf. *Mein Kampf.* Munich: Eher, 1942.

Hitler, Adolf. *Mein Kampf.* Translated by Ralph Manheim. Boston: Houghton Mifflin, 1971.

Hobbes, Thomas. *Leviathan, or, The Matter, Forme, & Power of a Common-wealth Ecclesiasticall and Civill.* London: Andrew Crooke, 1651.

Hochschild, Jennifer L., and Brenna M. Powell. "Racial Reorganization and the United States Census 1850–1930: Mulattoes, Half-Breeds, Mixed Parentage, Hindoos, and the Mexican Race." *Studies in American Political Development* 22, no. 1 (Spring 2008): 59–96.

Hodes, Martha. "Fractions and Fictions in the United States Census of 1890." In *Haunted by Empire: Geographies of Intimacy in North American History,* edited by Ann Laura Stoler, 240–70. Durham, NC: Duke University Press, 2006.

Hoffman, Frederick L. *Race Traits and Tendencies of the American Negro.* Publications of the American Economic Association, vol. 11, nos. 1–3. New York: Macmillan, 1896.

Hoffman, Frederick L. "Vital Statistics of the Negro." *The Arena* 29 (April 1892): 529–42.

Hoffmann, Léon-François. "An Eighteenth Century Exponent of Black Power: Moses Bon Sàam," *Caribbean Studies* 15, no. 3 (1975): 149–61.

Hogrebe, Wolfram. "Die Selbstverstrickung des Philosophen Oskar Becker." In *Philosophie im Nationalsozialismus,* edited by Hans Jörg Sandkühler, 157–90. Hamburg: Meiner, 2009.

[Home, Henry]. *Sketches of the History of Man.* 2 vols. Edinburgh: W. Creech, 1774.

Hooker, Richard. *Of the Lawes of Ecclesiastical Politie.* London: Will Stansby, 1617.

Horrell, Muriel. *Race Classification in South Africa: Its Effect on Human Beings.* Fact Paper no. 2. Johannesburg, South Africa: S.A. Institute of Race Relations, 1958.

Horsman, Reginald. *Race and Manifest Destiny: The Origins of American Racial Anglo-Saxonism.* Cambridge, MA: Harvard University Press, 1981.

BIBLIOGRAPHY 343

Howard, Woodford J. *Mr. Justice Murphy: A Political Biography*. Princeton, NJ: Princeton University Press, 1968.

Hume, David. *A Dissertation on the Passions: The Natural History of Religions*. Edited by Tom L. Beauchamp. Oxford: Oxford University Press, 2007.

Hume, David. "Of National Characters." In *Essays: Moral, Political, and Literary*, edited by Eugene F. Miller, 244–57. Indianapolis, IN: Liberty Fund, 1987.

Hunt, Lynn, Margaret C. Jacob, and Wijnand Mijnhardt. *The Book That Changed Europe: Picart & Bernard's "Religious Ceremonies of the World."* Cambridge, MA: Harvard University Press, 2010.

Husserl, Edmund. *Ideas Pertaining to a Pure Phenomenology and to a Phenomenological Philosophy*. Book 2, *Studies in the Phenomenology of Constitution* Translated by Richard Rojcewicz and André Schuwer. Dordrecht: Kluwer, 1989.

Husserl, Edmund. *Ideen zu einer reinen Phänomenologie und phänomenologischen Philosophie*. Book 2, *Phänomenologische Untersuchungen zur Konstitution*. Husserliana 4. Hague: Martinus Nijhoff, 1952.

Hutcheson, Francis. *A Short Introduction to Moral Philosophy*. Glasgow: Robert Foulis, 1747.

Hutcheson, Francis. *Philosophiae Moralis Institutio Compendiaria*. Glasgow: Robert Foulis, 1745.

Hutcheson, Francis. *A System of Moral Philosophy*. Vol. 2. London: A. Millar, 1755.

Hutton, Christopher M. *Race and the Third Reich: Linguistics, Racial Anthropology and Genetics in the Dialectic of Volk*. Cambridge: Polity Press, 2005.

Huxley, Julian S. and Alfred C. Haddon, with A. M. Carr-Saunders. *Nous Européens*. Translated by Jules Castier. Paris: Minuit 1947.

Huxley, Julian S., and Alfred C. Haddon, with A. M. Carr-Saunders. *We Europeans: A Survey of "Racial" Problems*. London: Jonathan Cape, 1935.

Jahn, Friedrich L. *Deutsches Volksthum*. Lübeck: Niemann, 1810.

James, C. L. R. "Dialectical Materialism and the Fate of Humanity." In C. L. R. James, *Spheres of Existence: Selected Writings*, 70–105. Westport, CT: Lawrence Hill, 1980.

James, C. L. R. *A History of Negro Revolt*. London: Fact, 1938.

Jameson, Russell Parsons. *Montesquieu et l'esclavage*. New York: Lennox Hill, 1911.

Janvier, Louis-Joseph. *L'égalité des races*. Paris: G. Rougier, 1884.

Jaspers, Karl. *Allgemeine Psychopathologie*. Berlin: Julius Springer, 1923.

Jaspers, Karl. *Einführung in die Philosophie*. Munich: Piper, 1959.

Jaspers, Karl. *General Psychopathology*. Translated by J. Hoenig and Marian W. Hamilton. Manchester: Manchester University Press, 1963.

Jaspers, Karl. *Introduction à la philosophie*. Translated by Jeanne Hersch. Paris: Plon, 1951.

Jaspers, Karl. *Nietzsche et le christianisme*. Translated by Jeanne Hersch. Paris: Minuit, 1949.

Jaspers, Karl. *Psychopathologie Générale*. Translated by A. Kastler and J. Mendousse. Paris: Félix Alcan, 1933. Translated by J. Mendousse. Paris: Félix Alcan, 1933.

Jefferson, Thomas. *Notes on the State of Virginia*. London: John Stockdale, 1787.

Jefferson, Thomas. *The Papers of Thomas Jefferson*. Retirement Series, vol. 8, October 1814 to August 1815. Edited by J. Jefferson Looney. Princeton, NJ: Princeton University Press, 2012.

Johnson, Charles. "A Phenomenology of the Black Body." *Michigan Quarterly Review* 32, no. 4 (1993): 599–614.

Johnson, Christopher. *Claude Lévi-Strauss: The Formative Years*. Cambridge: Cambridge University Press, 2003.

344 BIBLIOGRAPHY

Judaken, Jonathan, ed. "Sartre on Racism: From Existential Phenomenology to Globalization and 'the New Racism.'" In *Race after Sartre: Antiracism, Africana Existentialism, Postcolonialism*, edited by Jonathan Judaken, 23–54. Albany: SUNY Press, 2008.

Judaken, Jonathan. *Jean-Paul Sartre and the Jewish Question: Anti-antisemitism and the Politics of the French Intellectual*. Lincoln: University of Nebraska Press, 2009.

Julien, Ch.-André. "Avant-Propos." In Léopold Sédar Senghor, *Anthologie de la nouvelle poésie nègre et malgache de langue française*, vii–viii. Paris: Presses Universitaires de France, 1948.

Kant, Immanuel. "Anthropologiekolleg vom Winter 1791/92." In *Königsberger Kantiana*, Kant-Forschungen, vol. 12, edited by Sabina Laetitia Kowalewski and Werner Stark, 183–454. Hamburg: Felix Meiner, 2000.

Kant, Immanuel. *Anthropology, History, and Education*. Translated by Mary Gregor et al. Edited by Günter Zöller and Robert B. Louden. Cambridge: Cambridge University Press, 2007.

Kant, Immanuel. *Critique of the Power of Judgment*. Translated by Paul Guyer and Eric Matthews. Cambridge: Cambridge University Press, 2000.

Kant, Immanuel. *Kants Werke*, Akademie Textausgabe. 11 vols. Berlin: Walter de Gruyter, 1968.

Kant, Immanuel. "Religion within the Boundaries of Mere Reason." In *Religion and Rational Theology*, translated and edited by Allen W. Wood and George di Giovanni, 39–215. Cambridge: Cambridge University Press, 1996.

Kant, Immanuel. "Toward Perpetual Peace." In *Practical Philosophy*, translated and edited by Mary J. Gregor, 315–51. Cambridge: Cambridge University Press, 1996.

Keane, A. H. *Ethnology*. Cambridge: Cambridge University Press, 1896.

Kennedy, Joseph C. G. *Population of the United States in 1860*. Washington, DC: Government Printing Office, 1864.

Kennet, White. *The Lets and Impediments in Planting and Propagating the Gospel of Christ*. London: John Downing, 1712.

Khalfa, Jean. *Poetics of the Antilles: Poetry, History and Philosophy in the Writings of Perse, Césaire, Fanon and Glissant*. Bern: Peter Lang, 2017.

[King, Clarence]. "Style and the Monument." *North American Review* 141 (November 1885): 443–53.

King, Martin Luther. "Letter from Birmingham City Jail." In *A Testament of Hope: The Essential Writings of Martin Luther King, Jr.*, edited by James M. Washington, 289–302. San Francisco: Harper & Row, 1986.

King, Richard H., and Dan Stone, eds. *Hannah Arendt and the Uses of History: Imperialism, Nation, Race, and Genocide*. New York: Berghahn Books, 2007.

Kitson, Peter J. *Romantic Literature, Race, and Colonial Encounter*. New York: Palgrave Macmillan, 2007.

Klatt, Norbert. "Einleitung." In *The Correspondence of Johann Friedrich Blumenbach*, Vol. 2, *1783–1785*, edited by F. W. P. Dougherty, viii–xxx. Göttingen: Klatt, 2007.

Klemm, Gustave. *Allgemeine Cultur-Geschichte der Menschheit*. Vol. 1. Leipzig: Teubner, 1843.

Kneeland, S. "Introduction." In Charles Hamilton Smith, *The Natural History of the Human Species*, 15–98. Boston: Gould & Lincoln, 1851.

Knox, Robert. *The Races of Men: A Fragment*. London: Henry Renshaw, 1850; London: Lea and Blanchard, 1850; Philadelphia: Lea and Blanchard, 1850.

Kroeber, Alfred L. *Anthropology*. New York: Harcourt, Brace and Company, 1923; New York: Harcourt, Brace and Company, 1948.

Kroeber, Alfred L. "The Concept of Culture in Science." *Journal of General Education* 3, no. 3 (April 1949): 182–96.

Kroeber, Alfred L., and Clyde Kluckhohn. *Culture: A Critical Review of Concepts and Definitions*. Papers of the Peabody Museum of American Archaeology and Ethnology, vol. 47, no. 1. Cambridge, MA: Peabody Museum, 1952.

Krueger, Katherine. "Mike Pence Denies 'Implicit Bias' and 'Institutional Racism' in Policing at VP Debate." *Splinter*, October 4, 2016. https://splinternews.com/mike-pence-denies-implicit-bias-and-institutional-rac-1793862465.

Kühl, Stefan. *The Nazi Connection: Eugenics, American Racism, and German National Socialism*. Oxford: Oxford University Press, 1994.

[La Peyrère, Isaac de]. *Men before Adam*. London, 1656.

[La Peyrère, Isaac de]. *Praeadamitae sive exercitatio super versibus* [. . .]. *Epistolae D. Pauli ad Romanos*. n. p., 1655.

La Peyrère, Isaac de. *Systema Theologicum, ex Praeadamitarum hypothesi*. n.p., 1655.

La Peyrère, Isaac de. *A Theological Systeme upon That Presupposition, That Men Were before Adam*. London, 1655.

Lacan, Jacques. "Le complexe, facteur concret de la psychologie familiale." *Encyclopédie française* 8, no. 40 (1938): 5–16.

Lamarck, Jean-Baptiste. *Philosophie zoologique ou exposition des considerations relatives à l'histoire naturelle des animaux*. Paris: Dentu, 1809; Paris: Schleicher Frères, 1907.

Lamarck, Jean-Baptiste. *Zoological Philosophy: An Exposition with Regard to the Natural History of Animals*. Translated by Hugh Elliot. Chicago: University of Chicago Press, 1984.

Lanning, John Tate. "Legitimacy and 'Limpieza de Sangre' in the Practice of Medicine in the Spanish Empire." In *Jahrbuch für Geschichte Lateinamerikas* 4, no. 1 (1967): 37–60.

Largent, Mark. *Breeding Contempt: The History of Coerced Sterilization in the United States*. New Brunswick, NJ: Rutgers University Press, 2008.

Las Casas, Bartolomé de. *Indian Freedom: The Cause of Bartolomé de las Casas, 1484–1566, A Reader*. Translated and edited by Francis Patrick Sullivan. Kansas City: Sheed and Ward, 1995.

Las Casas, Bartolomé de. *Obras completas*. Vols. 3–5, *Historia de las Indias, I–III*, edited by Isacio Pérez Fernández. Madrid: Alianza, 1994. Vol. 10, *Tratados de 1532*, edited by Ramón Hernández and Lorenzo Galmés. Madrid: Alianza, 1994.

Laughlin, Harry. *Conquest by Immigration*. New York: Chamber of Commerce of the State of New York, 1939.

Lee, Emily S. "Towards a Lived Understanding of Race and Sex." *Philosophy Today* 49, Issue Supplement (2005): 82–88.

Lefebvre, Henri. "Perspectives de sociologie rurale." *Cahiers internationaux de sociologie* 14 (1953): 122–40.

Lefebvre, Henri. "Perspectives on Rural Sociology." In *Henri Lefebvre: Key Writings*, edited by Stuart Elden, Elizabeth Lebas, and Eleonore Kofman, 111–20. New York: Continuum, 2003.

Lemke, Sieglinde. "Berlin and Boundaries: *sollen* versus *geschehen*." *Boundary 2: An International Journal of Culture and Literature* 27, no. 3 (Fall 2000): 45–78.

346   BIBLIOGRAPHY

Lenz, Fritz. "Die Erblichkeit der geistigen Begabung." In Erwin Baur, Eugen Fischer, and Fritz Lenz, *Menschliche Erblichkeitslehre*, vol. 2, 469–583. 3rd ed. Munich: J. F. Lehmanns, 1927.

Lenz, Fritz. "The Inheritance of Intellectual Gifts." In *Human Heredity*, translated by Eden Paul and Cedar Paul, 563–699. London: George Allen and Unwin, 1931.

Lévi-Strauss, Claude. *The Elementary Structures of Kinship*. Translated by James Harle Bell, John Richard von Sturmer, and Rodney Needham. Boston: Beacon, 1969.

Lévi-Strauss, Claude. *La pensée sauvage*. Paris: Plon 1962.

Lévi-Strauss, Claude. "Race and History." In *The Race Question in Modern Science*, 123–63. New York: UNESCO, 1956.

Lévi-Strauss, Claude. "Race et Histoire." In *Le Racisme devant la science*, 241–81. Paris: UNESCO, 1960.

Lévi-Strauss, Claude. *Le regard éloigné*. Paris: Plon, 1983.

Lévi-Strauss, Claude. *The Savage Mind*. Translated by Anon. London: Weidenfield and Nicholson, 1972.

Lévi-Strauss, Claude. *Les structures élémentaires de la parenté*. Paris: Presses Universitaires de France, 1949.

Lévi-Strauss, Claude. *The View from Afar*. Translated by Joachim Neugroschel and Phoebe Hoss. New York: Basic Books, 1985.

Lévi-Strauss, Claude, and Didier Eribon. *Conversations with Claude Lévi-Strauss*. Translated by Paula Wissing. Chicago: University of Chicago Press, 1991.

Lévi-Strauss, Claude, and Didier Eribon. *De près et de loin*. Paris: Odile Jacob, 1988.

Ligon, Richard. *A True & Exact History of the Island of Barbadoes*. London: Peter Parker, 1673.

Locke, Alain. "The Concept of Race as Applied to Social Culture." In *The Philosophy of Alain Locke: Harlem Renaissance and Beyond*, edited by Leonard Harris, 187–200. Philadelphia: Temple University Press, 1989.

Locke, Alain. *The Philosophy of Alain Locke: Harlem Renaissance and Beyond*. Edited by Leonard Harris. Philadelphia: Temple University Press, 1989.

Locke, John. *Two Treatises of Government*. Edited by Peter Laslett. Cambridge: Cambridge University Press, 1988.

Long, Edward. *The History of Jamaica. Or, General Survey of the Antient and Modern State of That Island*. 3 vols. London: T. Lowndes, 1774.

Lott, Tommy L. "Du Bois on the Invention of Race." *The Philosophical Forum* 24, nos. 1–3 (Fall/Spring 1992/1993): 166–87.

Loveman, Mara, and Jeronimo O. Muniz. "How Puerto Rico Became White: Boundary Dynamics and Intercensus Racial Reclassification." *American Sociological Review* 72, no. 6 (2007): 915–39.

Lowie, Robert H. *Culture and Ethnology*. New York: Douglas C. McMurtrie, 1917.

Lowie, Robert H. *The History of Ethnological Theory*. New York: Farrar and Rinehart, 1937.

Lukács, Georg. *The Destruction of Reason*. Translated by Peter Palmer. Atlantic Highlands, NJ: Humanities Press, 1981.

Lynch, John. *Simón Bolivar: A Life*. New Haven, CT: Yale University Press, 2006.

Macey, David. *Frantz Fanon: A Biography*. New York: Picador, 2001.

Macpherson, William. *The Stephen Lawrence Inquiry*. London: Stationery Office, 1999.

Magloire-Danton, Gérarde. "Anténor Firmin and Jean Price-Mars: Revolution, Memory, Humanism." *Small Axe* 9, no. 2 (2005): 150–70.

BIBLIOGRAPHY 347

Mahon, Michael. *Foucault's Nietzschean Genealogy: Truth, Power, and the Subject.* Albany: SUNY Press, 1992.

Mannoni, Octave. *Prospero and Caliban.* Translated by Pamela Powesland. New York: Frederick A. Praeger, 1956.

Mannoni, Octave. *Psychologie de la colonisation.* Paris: Seuil, 1950.

Manouvrier, Léonce. "Revue Philosophique de la France et de l'Étranger." *Revue Philosophique de la France et de l'Étranger* 21 (January 1886): 180–82.

Maran, René. *Un homme pareil aux autres.* Paris: Albin Michel, 1947.

Marcus, Joachim. "Structures familiales et comportements politiques." *Revue française de psychanalyse* 13, no. 2 (April–June 1949): 277–313.

Marks, John. "Foucault, Franks, Gauls: *Il faut défender la société:* The 1976 Lectures at the College de France." *Theory, Culture & Society* 17, no. 5 (2000): 127–47.

Marks, John. "Michel Foucault: Biopolitics and Biology." In *Foucault in an Age of Terror: Essays on Biopolitics and the Defence of Society,* edited by Stephen Morton and Stephen Bygrave, 88–105. New York: Palgrave Macmillan, 2008.

Marriott, David. *Whither Fanon? Studies in the Blackness of Being.* Stanford, CA: Stanford University Press, 2018.

Marrus, Michael R. *The Politics of Assimilation: A Study of the French Jewish Community at the Time of the Dreyfus Affair.* Oxford: Oxford University Press, 1971.

Martinez, María Elena. "The Black Blood of New Spain: Limpieza de Sangre, Racial Violence, and Gendered Power in Early Colonial Mexico." *William and Mary Quarterly* 61, no. 3 (July 2004): 479–519.

Martínez, María Elena. *Genealogical Fictions: Limpieza de Sangre, Religion, and Gender in Colonial Mexico.* Stanford, CA: Stanford University Press, 2008.

Marx, Karl. *The Eighteenth Brumaire* (1852). In *Collected Works 1851–1853,* vol. 11. London: Lawrence and Wishart, 1979.

Marx, Karl. "Marx über Feuerbach." In Friedrich Engels, *Ludwig Feuerbach und der Ausgang der klassischen Deutschen Philosophie,* 69–72. Stuttgart: Dietz, 1888.

Masuzawa, Tomoko. *The Invention of World Religions: Or, How European Universalism Was Preserved in the Language of Pluralism.* Chicago: University of Chicago Press, 2005.

McCord, Louisa S. "Diversity of the Races: Its Bearing upon Negro Slavery." *The Southern Quarterly Review* 3, no. 6 (April 1851): 392–419.

McWhorter, Ladelle. *Racism and Sexual Oppression in Anglo-America: A Genealogy.* Bloomington: Indiana University Press, 2009.

Meiners, Christoph. "Fortgesetzte Betrachtungen über den *Sclavenhandel,* und die Freylassung der Neger," *Neues Göttingisches historisches* 2, no. 1 (1793): 1–58.

Memmi, Albert. *The Colonizer and the Colonized.* Translated by Howard Greenfield. New York: Orion, 1965.

Memmi, Albert. *Portrait du colonisé précédé du Portrait du colonisateur.* Corrêa: Buchet/ Chastel, 1955.

Mendelssohn, Moses. "On the Question: What Is Enlightenment?" In *What Is Enlightenment? Eighteenth-Century Answers and Twentieth-Century Questions,* edited by James Schmidt, 53–57. Berkeley: University of California Press, 1996.

Menzel, Wolfgang. *Geist der Geschichte.* Stuttgart: Liesching, 1835.

Merleau-Ponty, Maurice. *La structure du comportement.* Paris: Presses Universitaires de France, 1942.

Merleau-Ponty, Maurice. *The Structure of Behavior.* Translated by Alden L. Fisher. London: Methuen, 1965.

348 BIBLIOGRAPHY

Merleau-Ponty, Maurice. *The Visible and the Invisible*. Translated by Alphonso Lingis. Evanston, IL: Northwestern University Press, 1968.

Merleau-Ponty, Maurice. *Le visible et l'invisible*. Paris: Gallimard, 1964.

Merolle, Vincenzo, ed. *The Manuscripts of Adam Ferguson*. London: Pickering & Chatto, 2006.

Meynard, Thierry, S. J., ed. *Confucius Sinarum Philosophus (1687): The First Translation of the Confucian Classics*. Rome: Institutum Historicum Societatis Jesu, 2011.

Meynard, Thierry, S. J. *The Jesuit Reading of Confucius: The First Complete Translation of the Lunyu (1687) Published in the West*. Leiden: Brill, 2015.

Mill, John Stuart. *Collected Works of John Stuart Mill*. 33 vols. Edited by John M. Robson. Toronto: University of Toronto Press, London: Routledge and Kegan Paul, 1963–1991.

Miller, Kelly. "A Review of Hoffman's Race Traits and Tendencies of the American Negro." The American Negro Academy, Occasional Papers, no. 1. Washington, DC: American Negro Academy, 1897.

Mitchell, John. "An Essay upon the Causes of the Different Colours of People in Different Climates." *Philosophical Transactions* 43 (1744–1745): 102–50.

Moirans, Epifanio de. *A Just Defense of the Natural Freedom of Slaves: All Slaves Should Be Free*. Translated and edited by Edward R. Sunshine. Lewiston, NY: Edwin Mellen Press, 2007. Original title of unpublished manuscript, "Servi liberi seu naturalis mancipiorum libertatis iusta defensio" (1682).

Montagu, Ashley. *Man's Most Dangerous Myth: The Fallacy of Race*. New York: Columbia University Press, 1942; Cleveland, OH: World Publishing Company, 1964; Walnut Creek, CA: Altamira Press, 1997.

Montagu, Ashley. *Statement on Race*. Oxford: Oxford University Press, 1972.

Montesquieu, Charles-Louis de Secondat. *My Thoughts*. Translated by Henry C. Clark. Indianapolis, IN: Liberty Fund, 2012.

Montesquieu, Charles-Louis de Secondat. *De l'esprit des loix. Oeuvres*, vol. 1. Amsterdam: Arkstée & Merkus, 1758.

Montesquieu, Charles-Louis de Secondat. *Pensées: Le spicilège*. Edited by Louis Desgraves. Paris: Robert Laffont, 1991.

Montesquieu, Charles-Louis de Secondat. *The Spirit of the Laws*. Translated and edited by Anne M. Cohler, Basia C. Miller, and Harold S. Stone. Cambridge: Cambridge University Press, 1989.

Moore, Gregory. *Nietzsche, Biology and Metaphor*. Cambridge: Cambridge University Press, 2002.

More, Mabogo Percy. "Locating Frantz Fanon in Post-Apartheid South Africa." *Journal of Asian and African Studies* 52, no. 2 (2017): 127–41.

Morel, Bénédict A. *Traité des dégénérescences physiques, intellectuelles et morales de l'espèce humaine. et des causes qui produisent des variétés maladives*. Paris: Baillière, 1857.

Morgan, Lewis Henry. *League of the Ho-dé-no-sau-nee, Or Iroquois*. Rochester, NY: Sage and Brother, 1851.

Morton, Samuel George. *Crania Aegyptica*. Philadelphia: John Pennington, 1844.

Morton, Samuel George. *Crania Americana*. Philadelphia: J. Dobson, 1839.

Morton, Samuel George. "Hybridity in Animals, Considered in Reference to the Question of the Unity of the Human Species." *American Journal of Science and Arts* 3 (1847): 39–50 and 203–12.

Moses, Wilson Jeremiah. *Alexander Crummell: A Study of Civilization and Discontent*. Amherst: University of Massachusetts Press, 1992.

BIBLIOGRAPHY 349

Moses, Wilson Jeremiah. *The Golden Age of Black Nationalism, 1850–1925*. Oxford: Oxford University Press, 1988.

Moses, Wilson Jeremiah. "W. E. B. Du Bois's 'The Conservation of Races' and Its Context: Idealism, Conservation, and Hero Worship." *The Massachusetts Review* 34, no. 2 (Summer 1993): 275–94.

Moss, Alfred A. Jr. *The American Negro Academy*. Baton Rouge: Louisiana State University Press, 1981.

Müller-Hill, Benno. *Murderous Science: Elimination by Scientific Selection of Jews, Gypsies, and Others, Germany 1933–1945*. Translated by George R. Fraser. Oxford: Oxford University Press, 1988.

Müller-Hill, Benno. *Tödliche Wissenschaft: Die Aussonderung von Juden, Zigeunern und Geisteskranken, 1933–1945*. Hamburg: Rowohlt, 1984.

Müller-Wille, Staffan, and Hans-Jörg Rheinberger, eds. *Heredity Produced: At the Crossroads of Biology, Politics, and Culture, 1500–1870*. Cambridge, MA: MIT Press, 2007.

Müller-Wille, Staffan, and Hans-Jörg Rheinberger, eds. *Heredity Produced: At the Crossroads of Biology, Politics, and Culture, 1500–1870*. Cambridge, MA: MIT Press, 2007.

Myrdal, Gunnar. *An American Dilemma: The Negro Problem and Modern Democracy*. 2 vols. New York: Harper and Brothers, 1944.

Nardal, Paulette. "Éveil de la conscience de race." *La Revue du Monde Noir* 6 (1932): 25–31.

Naudin, Jean, and Tudi Goze. "Psychothérapie institutionnelle et phénoménologie." *Sud/Nord* 26, no. 1 (2016): 33–42.

Naville, Pierre. *Psychologie, Marxisme, Matérialisme*. Essais Critiques, deuxième edition, revue et augmentée. Paris: Marcel Rivière et Cie, 1948.

Niedermann, Joseph. *Kultur: Werden und Wandlungen des Begriffs und seiner Ersatzbegriffe von Cicero bis Herder*. Florence: Bibliopolis, 1941.

Nietzsche, Friedrich. *The Complete Works of Friedrich Nietzsche*. 19 vols. Translated by Alan Schrift et al. Edited by Ernst Behler and Bernd Magnus. Stanford, CA: Stanford University Press, 1995–.

Nietzsche, Friedrich. *The Gay Science: With a Prelude of Rhymes and an Appendix of Songs*. Translated by Josefine Nauckhoff. Cambridge: Cambridge University Press, 2001.

Nietzsche, Friedrich. *Sämtliche Werke*. 15 vols. Edited by Giorgio Colli and Mazzino Montinari. Berlin: Walter de Gruyter, 1980.

Nirenberg, David. "Was There Race Before Modernity? The Example of 'Jewish' Blood in Late Medieval Spain." *The Origins of Racism in the West*, edited by Miriam Eliav-Feldon, Benjamin Isaac, and Joseph Ziegler, 232–64. Cambridge: Cambridge University Press, 2009.

Nott, Josiah C. "The Mulatto a Hybrid—Probable Extermination of the Two Races If the Whites and Blacks Are Allowed to Intermarry." *American Journal of the Medical Sciences*. New Series 6 (July 1843): 252–56.

Nott, Josiah C. "Negro Population of the South with Reference to Life Statistics." In *The Industrial Resources, Statistics, etc. of the United States and More Particularly of the Southern and Western States*. Vol. 2, edited by James D. B. De Bow, 292–301. New York: Appleton, 1854.

Nott, Josiah C. *Two Lectures on the Natural History of the Caucasian and Negro Races*. Mobile, AL: Dade and Thompson, 1844.

Nott, Josiah C., and George Robins Gliddon, eds. *Types of Mankind*. Philadelphia: Lippincott, Grambo, & Co., 1854.

350 BIBLIOGRAPHY

Odier, Charles. *Anxiety and Magic Thinking*. Translated by Marie-Louise Schoelly and Mary Jane Sherfey. New York: International Universities Press, 1956.

Odier, Charles. *L'angoisse et la pensée magique*. Paris: Delachaux et Niestle, 1947.

Ogude, S. E., et al. *Genius in Bondage: A Study of the Origins of African Literature in English*. Ile-Ife: University of Ife Press, 1983.

Ortega, Mariana. "Being Lovingly, Knowingly Ignorant: White Feminism and Women of Color." *Hypatia* 21, no. 3 (Summer 2006): 56–74.

Osborn, Henry Fairfield. "A Student's Reminiscences of Huxley." In *Biological Lectures Delivered at the Marine Biological Laboratory of Wood's Holl in the Summer Session of 1895*, 29–42. Boston: Ginn, 1896.

Outlaw, Lucius T., Jr. *Critical Social Theory in the Interests of Black Folks*. Lanham, MD: Rowman and Littlefield, 2005.

Painter, Nell Irvin. *The History of White People*. New York: W. W. Norton, 2010.

Paley, William. *The Principles of Moral and Political Philosophy*. London: R. Faulder, 1785.

Paley, William. *The Principles of Moral and Political Philosophy*. London: Faulder, 1786.

[Paley, William]. *Recollections of a Speech, upon the Slave Trade; Delivered in Carlisle, on Thursday the 9th of February, 1792*. Carlisle, UK: F. Jollie, 1792.

Panzer, Joel S. *The Popes and Slavery*. New York: Alba House, 1996.

Park, Peter J. *Africa, Asia, and the History of Philosophy: Racism in the Formation of the Philosophical Canon, 1780–1830*. Albany: SUNY Press, 2014.

Parker, Mattie Erma, ed. "The Fundamental Constitutions of Carolina, Version of 21 July 1669." In *North Carolina Charters and Constitutions, 1578–1698*, 132–52. Raleigh, NC: Carolina Charter Tercentenary Commission, 1963.

Parker, Mattie Erma, ed. *North Carolina Charters and Constitutions, 1578–1698*. Raleigh, NC: Carolina Charter Tercentenary Commission, 1963.

Pascal, Blaise. *Pensées*. Edited by Louis Lafuma. Paris: Seuil, 1962. Edited by Philippe Sellier. Paris: Mercure de France, 1976.

Pascal, Blaise. *Pensées*. Translated by A. J. Krailsheimer. Harmondsworth, England: Penguin, 1966.

Pascoe, Peggy. "Miscegenation Law, Court Cases, and Ideologies of 'Race' in Twentieth-century America." *Journal of American History* 83, no.1 (June 1996): 44–69.

Peabody, Sue, and Tyler Stovall, eds. *The Color of Liberty: Histories of Race in France*. Durham, NC: Duke University Press, 2003.

Peel, J. D. Y. *Herbert Spencer: The Evolution of a Sociologist*. New York: Basic Books, 1971.

Perez de Lara Toletani, Ildephonsi. *De anniversariis et capellaniis, libri duo*. Lugduni [Lyon]: Petrus Chevalier, 1739.

Peters, Carl. *Willenswelt und Weltwille: Studien und Ideen zu einer Weltanschauung*. Leipzig: Brockhaus, 1883.

Pick, Daniel. *Faces of Degeneration: A European Disorder, c.1848–c.1918*. Cambridge: Cambridge University Press, 1989.

Pierrot, Gregory. "Insights on 'Lord Hoth' and Ottobah Cugoano." *Notes and Queries* 59, no. 3 (2012): 367–69.

Pike, Ruth. *Linajudos and Conversos in Seville: Greed and Prejudice in Sixteenth- and Seventeenth-Century Spain*. New York: Peter Lang, 2000.

Pius XII, Pope. "Plane Compertum Est." In *Acta Apostolicae Sedis* 32, no. 2 (1940): 24–26.

Plecker, Walter A. *Eugenics in Relation to the New Family and the Law on Racial Integrity*. Richmond, VA: Davis Bottom, 1924.

BIBLIOGRAPHY 351

Plecker, Walter A. "Virginia's Attempt to Adjust the Color Problem." *American Journal of Public Health* 15, no. 2 (1925): 111–15.

Poliakov, Léon. *The Aryan Myth: A History of Racist and Nationalist Ideas in Europe.* Translated by Edmund Howard. New York: Barnes and Noble, 1974.

Popkin, Richard H. *Isaac la Peyrère (1596–1676): His Life, Work and Influence.* Leiden: Brill, 1987.

Popkin, Richard H. "The Philosophical Basis of Modern Racism." In *The High Road to Pyrrhonism*, edited by Richard A. Watson and James E. Force, 79–102. San Diego, CA: Austin Hill, 1980.

Pouchet, Georges. *La biologie Aristotélique.* Paris: Félix Alcan, 1885.

Pouchet, Georges. *De la pluralité des races humaines.* Paris: Baillière, 1858; 2nd ed., Paris: Victor Masson, 1864.

Pouchet, Georges. *The Plurality of the Human Race.* Translated and edited by Hugh J. C. Beavan. London: Longman, Green, Longman, and Roberts, 1864.

Prichard, James Cowles. *Researches into the Physical History of Man.* 1st ed. London: John and Arthur Arch, 1813; 2nd ed., 2 vols. London: John and Arthur Arch, 1826; 3rd ed., 5 vols. London: Sherwood, Gilbert, and Piper, 1836–1847.

Pufendorf, Samuel. *Les devoirs de l'homme, et du citoein.* Vol. 2. Translated by Jean Barbeyrac. Amsterdam: Coup and Kuyper, 1734.

Pufendorf, Samuel. *De officio hominis et civis: Juxta legem naturalem.* Cambridge: Hayes, 1682.

Pufendorf, Samuel. *On the Duty of Man and Citizen According to Natural Law.* Edited by James Tully. Translated by Michael Silverthorne. Cambridge: Cambridge University Press, 1991.

Purchas, Samuel. *Purchas His Pilgrimage, or Relations of the World and the Religions Observed in All Ages.* London: William Stansby, 1613.

Purdy, Daniel. "Chinese Ethics within the Radical Enlightenment: Christian Wolff." In *The Radical Enlightenment in Germany: A Cultural Perspective*, edited by Carl Niekerk, 112–30, Leiden: Brill, 2018.

Quatrefages, Armand de. *L'espèce humaines.* Paris: Germer Baillière, 1877.

Quatrefages, Armand de. *The Human Species.* New York: Appleton, 1879.

Quatrefages, Armand de. "Observations à propos d'un passage d'une lettre de Paul Lévy." In *Bulletins de la Société d'Anthropologie de Paris.* Series 3, vol. 7, edited by G. Masson, 579–87. Paris: G. Masson, 1884.

Quatrefages, Armand de. *La race prussienne.* Paris: Hachette, 1871.

Ramuga, Thomas K. "Frantz Fanon and Black Consciousness in Azania (South Africa)." *Phylon* 47, no. 3 (1986): 182–91.

Reardon, Jenny. *Race to the Finish: Identity and Governance in an Age of Genomics.* Princeton, NJ: Princeton University Press, 2005.

Reed, Adolph L. Jr. *W. E. B. Du Bois and American Political Thought: Fabianism and the Color Line.* Oxford: Oxford University Press, 1997.

Rees, Richard W. *Shades of Difference: A History of Ethnicity in America.* New York: Rowman and Littlefield, 2007.

Régnier, Philippe, ed. *Études saint-simoniennes.* Lyon: Presses Universitaires de Lyon, 2002.

Reichenbach, Count Oscar. "On the Vitality of the Black Race, or the Coloured People in the United States, According to the Census." *Journal of the Anthropological Society of London* 2 (1864): lxv–lxxiii.

352 BIBLIOGRAPHY

Renan, Ernest. *De l'origine du langage: Histoire générale et système comparé des langues sémitiques*. Vol. 8 of *Oeuvres complètes de Ernest Renan*, edited by Henriette Psichari. Paris: Calmann-Lévy, 1947.

Renault, Matthieu. *Frantz Fanon: De l'anticolonialisme à la critique postcoloniale*. Paris: Éditions Amsterdam, 2011.

Ritchie, D. G. "The Rationality of History." In *Essays in Philosophical Criticism*, edited by Andrew Seth and R. B. Haldane, 126–58. London: Longmans, 1883.

Robinson, Roger, ed. *The Correspondence of James Beattie*. Vols. 3–4. Bristol: Thoemmes Continuum, 2004.

Rose, Paul Lawrence. *German Question/Jewish Question: Revolutionary Antisemitism from Kant to Wagner*. Princeton, NJ: Princeton University Press, 1990.

Ross, Alexander. *Pansebeia, or, a View of All Religions in the World: With the Several Church-Governments, from the Creation, to These Times*. London: John Saywell, 1653.

Rousseau, Jean-Jacques. *Discours sur l'origine et les fondements de l'inégalité*. Edited by B. Gagnebin and M. Raymond. Vol. 3 of *Oeuvres complétes*. Paris: Gallimard, 1964.

Rousseau, Jean-Jacques. *Discourse on the Origins of Inequality (Second Discourse), Polemics, and Political Economy*. Vol. 3 of *The Collected Writings of Rousseau*. Edited by Roger D. Masters and Christopher Kelly, translated by Judith R. Bush, Roger D. Masters, Christopher Kelly, and Terence Marshall. Hanover, NH: University Press of New England, 1992.

Royer, Clémence. *Origine de l'homme et des Sociétés*. Paris: Guillaumin et Masson, 1870.

Royer, Clémence. "Avant-Propos." In Charles Darwin, *De l'origine des espèces par Charles Darwin*, translated by Clémence Royer, i–xiii. Paris: Victor Masson, 1866.

Royer, Clémence. "Préface de la troisième édition." In Charles Darwin, *De l'origine des espèces*, translated by Clémence Royer, v–xxvi. 3rd ed. Paris: Victor Masson, 1870.

Rubiés, Joan-Pau. *Travel and Ethnology in the Renaissance: South India through European Eyes, 1250–1625*. Cambridge: Cambridge University Press, 2000.

Sàam, Moses Bon. "The Speech of Moses Bon Sàam, a Free Negro, to the Revolted Slaves in One of the Most Considerable Colonies of the West Indies." *Gentleman's Magazine* 5 (January 1735): 21–23.

Sadji, Abdoulaye. "Nini." *Présence Africaine* 3 (1947–1948): 89–110, 276–98, 458–504, and 647–66.

Sandiford, Keith A. *Measuring the Moment: Strategies of Protest in Eighteenth-Century Afro-English Writing*. Selinsgrove, PA: Susquehanna University Press, 1988.

Sandweiss, Martha A. *Passing Strange: A Gilded Age Tale of Love and Deception across the Color Line*. New York: Penguin, 2009.

Sartre, Jean-Paul. *Anti-Semite and Jew: An Exploration of the Etiology of Hate*. Translated by George J. Becker. New York: Schocken, 1976.

Sartre, Jean-Paul. *Being and Nothingness*. Translated by Sarah Richmond. London: Routledge, 2018.

Sartre, Jean-Paul. *Cahiers pour une morale*. Paris: Gallimard, 1983.

Sartre, Jean-Paul. *Colonialism and Neocolonialism*. Translated by Azzedine Haddour, Steve Brewer, and Terry McWilliams. New York: Routledge, 2006.

Sartre, Jean-Paul. *Colonialisme et néo-colonialisme*. Situations V. Paris: Gallimard, 1964.

Sartre, Jean-Paul. *Critique de la raison dialectique*. Paris: Gallimard, 1960.

Sartre, Jean-Paul. *Critique of Dialectical Reason*. Translated by Alan Sheridan-Smith. Edited by Jonathan Rée. London: New Left Books, 1976.

Sartre, Jean-Paul. *L'être et le néant*. Paris: Gallimard, 1943.

BIBLIOGRAPHY 353

Sartre, Jean-Paul. "A Fundamental Idea of Husserl's Phenomenology: Intentionality," translated by Chris Turner. In Jean-Paul Sartre, *Critical Essays (Situations I)*, 40–46. New York: Seagull, 2010.

Sartre, Jean-Paul. "Une idée fondamentale de la 'phénoménologie' de Husserl: l'intentionalité." *La nouvelle revue Française* 27 no. 304 (1939): 129–32.

Sartre, Jean-Paul. "Introduction," translated by Lawrence Hoey. In Albert Memmi, *The Colonizer and the Colonized*, xxi–xxix. New York: Orion Press, 1965.

Sartre, Jean-Paul. "Itinerary of a Thought: Interview with Jean-Paul Sartre." *New Left Review* 58 (November–December 1969): 43–66.

Sartre, Jean-Paul. *Notebooks for an Ethics*. Translated by David Pellauer. Chicago: University of Chicago Press, 1992.

Sartre, Jean-Paul. "Orphée noir." In *Anthologie de la nouvelle poésie nègre et malgache de langue française*, edited by Léopold Sédar Senghor, ix–xliv. Paris: Presses Universitaires de France, 1948.

Sartre, Jean-Paul. "Préface." In Albert Memmi, *Portrait du colonisé précédé du portrait du colonisateur*, 23–29. Paris: Gallimard, 1966.

Sartre, Jean-Paul. *Réflexions sur la question juive*. Paris: Paul Morihien, 1946.

Sartre, Jean-Paul. "Review of Albert Memmi: *Portrait du colonisé précédé du portrait du colonisateur*." *Les Temps Modernes* 137–38 (July–August 1957): 289–93.

Sartre, Jean-Paul. "Sartre par Sartre." In Jean-Paul Sartre, *Situations IX: Melanges*, 99–134. Paris: Gallimard, 1972.

Sartre, Jean-Paul. *Search for a Method*. Translated by Hazel E. Barnes. New York: Alfred A. Knopf, 1963.

Sartre, Jean-Paul. *Situations, II: Qu'est-ce que la littérature?* Paris: Gallimard, 1948.

Sartre, Jean-Paul. *"What Is Literature?" and Other Essays*. Translated by Bernard Frechtman. Cambridge, MA: Harvard University Press, 1988.

Sayles, James Yaki. *Meditations on Frantz Fanon's* Wretched of the Earth: *New Afrikan Revolutionary Writings*. Montreal: Kersplebedeb, 2010.

Schank, Gerd. *"Rasse" und "Züchtung" bei Nietzsche*. Berlin: Walter de Gruyter, 2000.

Scheler, Max. *Probleme einer Soziologie des Wissens*. In *Die Wissensformen und die Gesellschaft*. Edited by Maria Scheler, 9–190. Bern: A. Franke, 1960.

Scheler, Max. *Problems of a Sociology of Knowledge*. Translated by Manfred S. Frings. London: Routledge, 1980.

Schelling, Friedrich. *Einleitung Entwurf eines Systems der Naturphilosophie*. Jena: Christian Ernst Gabler, 1799.

Schelling, Friedrich. *Einleitung in die Philosophie der Mythologie. Sämmtliche Werke* 3, 1. Edited by Karl Friedrich August Schelling. Stuttgart: J. G. Cotta, 1856.

Schelling, Friedrich. *First Outline of a System of the Philosophy of Nature*. Translated by Keith R. Peterson, Albany: SUNY Press, 2004.

Schelling, Friedrich. *Historical-Critical Introduction to the Philosophy of Mythology*. Translated by Mason Richey and Markus Zisselsberger. Albany: SUNY Press, 2007.

Schiller, Francis. *Paul Broca: Founder of French Anthropology, Explorer of the Brain*. Berkeley: University of California Press, 1979.

Schultz, Bart. "Mill and Sedgwick, Imperialism and Racism." *Utilitas* 19, no. 1 (2007): 104–30.

Schultze, Fritz. *Kant und Darwin: Ein Beitrag zur Geschichte der Entwicklungslehre*. Jena: Hermann Dufft, 1875.

354   BIBLIOGRAPHY

Schutz, Alfred. "Equality and the Meaning Structure of the Social World." In *Collected Papers II*, edited by Arvid Brodersen, 226–73. The Hague: Martinus Nijhoff, 1964.

Schwartz, Joachim. "Réflexions sur l'esclavage des Nègres." In Condorcet, *Esquisse d'un tableau historique des progrès de l'esprit humain; suivie de réflexions sur l'esclavage des nègres*. 317–400. Paris: Masson et Fils, 1822.

Seillière, Ernest. "Introduction." In Ernest Seillière, *Le Comte de Gobineau et l'aryanisme historique*, i–xli. Paris: Plon 1903.

Semedo, Alvarez. *The History of That Great and Renowned Monarchy of China*. London: E. Tyler, 1655.

Sepúlveda, Juan Ginés. *Obras completas*. Vol. 3, *Demócrates Segundo*, edited by A. Coroleu Lletget. Salamanca: Ayuntamiento de Pozoblanco, 1997.

Shaftesbury, Anthony, Earl of. *Characteristicks of Men, Manners, Opinions, Times*. 3 vols. London: John Darby, 1711.

Shapiro, Fred R. "Historical Notes on the Vocabulary of the Women's Movement." *American Speech* 60, no. 1 (1985) 3–16.

Sharp, Granville. *The Law of Retribution; or, a Serious Warning to Great Britain and her Colonies* [. . .]. London: Richardson, 1776.

Sheth, Falguni A. *Toward a Political Philosophy of Race*. Albany: SUNY Press, 2009.

Sicroff, Albert A. *Les controverses des statuts de "pureté de sang" en Espagne du XVe au XVIIe siècle*. Paris: Didier, 1960.

Sidgwick, Henry. *The Elements of Politics*. London: Macmillan, 1891.

Sidney, Algernon. *Discourses Concerning Government*. London: J. Darby, 1704.

Simar, Théophile. *Étude critique sur la formation de la doctrine des races au XVIIIe siècle et son expansion au XIXe siècle*. Brussels: Maurice Lamertin, 1922.

Singh, Brijraj. *The First Protestant Missionary to India: Bartholomaeus Ziegenbalg, 1683–1719*. Oxford: Oxford University Press, 1999.

Slaughter, Thomas F., Jr. "Epidermalizing the World: A Basic Mode of Being-Black." In *Philosophy Born of Struggle: Anthology of Afro-American Philosophy from 1917*, edited by Leonard Harris, 283–87. Dubuque, IA: Kendall/Hunt, 1983.

Smedley, Audrey. *Race in North America: Origin and Evolution of a Worldview*. 1st ed. Boulder, CO: Westview Press, 1993.

Smedley, Audrey, and Brian D. Smedley. *Race in North America: Origin and Evolution of a World View*. 2nd ed. Boulder, CO: Westview Press, 2012.

Smith, J. Douglas. "The Campaign for Racial Purity and the Erosion of Paternalism in Virginia, 1922–1930: 'Nominally White, Biologically Mixed, and Legally Negro.'" *Journal of Southern History* 68, no. 1 (February 2002): 65–106.

Smith, J. Douglas. *Managing White Supremacy: Race, Politics, and Citizenship in Jim Crow Virginia*. Chapel Hill: University of North Carolina Press, 2002.

Smith, Samuel Stanhope. *An Essay on the Causes of the Variety of Complexion and Figure in the Human Species* [. . .]. Philadelphia: Aitken, 1787; New Brunswick, NJ: J. Simpson, 1810.

Smyth, Thomas. "The Unity of the Human Races." In vol. 8 of *Complete Works of Rev. Thomas Smyth, D. D.*, edited by Rev. Prof. J. Wm. Flinn, D. D., 5–392. Columbia, SC: R. L. Bryan, 1910.

Solger, Ingeborg. "Herder and the 'Harlem Renaissance' of Black Culture in America: The Case of the 'Neger-Idyllen.'" In *Herder Today: Contributions from the International Herder Conference, Nov. 5–8, 1987, Stanford, California*, edited by Kurt Mueller-Vollmer, 402–14. Berlin: Walter de Gruyter, 1990.

BIBLIOGRAPHY   355

Sollors, Werner. "Prohibitions of Interracial Marriage and Cohabitation." In Sollors, *Neither Black nor White yet Both: Thematic Explorations of Interracial Literature*, 395–410. Oxford: Oxford University Press, 1997.

Solórzano Pereira, Juan de. *Politica Indiana*. Madrid: Gabrièl Ramirez, 1739.

Soyer, François. *Popularizing Anti-Semitism in Early Modern Spain and Its Empire: Francisco de Torrejoncillo and the "Centinela contra Judíos" (1674)*. Leiden: Brill, 2014.

Spencer, Herbert. "La Beauté dans la personne humaine," In *Essais de morale de science et d'esthétique*. Vol. 1, *Essais sur le progrès*, translated by M. A. Burdeau, 263–72. Paris: Germer Baillière, 1877.

Spencer, Herbert. "Personal Beauty." In *Essays: Scientific, Political, and Speculative*, 417–29. London: Longman, 1858.

Spencer, Herbert. *First Principles*. London: Williams and Norgate, 1862.

Spencer, Herbert. *Les bases de la morale évolutionniste*. Paris: Germer Baillière, 1880.

Spencer, Herbert. *The Data of Ethics*. London: Williams and Norgate, 1879.

Spencer, Herbert. *The Man versus the State*. London: Williams and Norgate, 1884.

Spencer, Herbert. *The Principles of Biology*. Vol. 1. London: Williams and Norgate, 1864.

Stanton, William. *The Leopard's Spots: Scientific Attitudes toward Race in America, 1815–1859*. Chicago: University of Chicago Press, 1960.

Stein, Edith. "Eine Untersuchung über den Staat." *Jahrbuch für Philosophie und phänomenologische Forschung* 7 (1925): 1–123.

Stein, Edith. *An Investigation Concerning the State*. Translated by Marianne M. Sawicki. Washington, DC: Institute of Carmelite Studies, 2006.

Steinberg, Stephen. *Race Relations: A Critique*. Stanford, CA: Stanford University Press, 2007.

Stern, Günther [Günther Anders]. "Pathologie de la liberté: Essai sur la non-identification." *Recherches philosophiques* 6 (1936–1937): 22–54.

Stern, Günther [Günther Anders]. "The Pathology of Freedom: An Essay on Non-Identification," translated by Katharine Wolfe. In *The Life and Work of Günther Anders: Émigré, Iconoclast, Philosopher, Man of Letters*, edited by Günther Bischof, Jason Dawsey, and Bernhard Fetz, 145–70. Innsbruck: Studien, 2014.

Stocking, George W. Jr. *Race, Culture, and Evolution: Essays in the History of Anthropology*. Chicago: University of Chicago Press, 1982.

Stoler, Ann Laura. *Carnal Knowledge and Imperial Power: Race and the Intimate in Colonial Rule*. Berkeley: University of California Press, 2002.

Stoler, Ann Laura. *Race and the Education of Desire: Foucault's* History of Sexuality *and the Colonial Order of Things*. Durham, NC: Duke University Press, 1995.

Stoler, Ann Laura. "Racial Histories and Their Regimes of Truth." In *Political Power and Social Theory*, vol. 11, edited by Diane E. Davis, 183–206. Bingley, UK: Emerald, 1997.

Stone, Dan. *History, Memory and Mass Atrocity: Essays on the Holocaust and Genocide*. London: Mitchell, 2006.

Stroud, George M. *A Sketch of the Laws Relating to Slavery in the Several States of the United States of America*. Philadelphia: Kimber and Sharpless, 1827; 2nd ed., Philadelphia: Henry Longstreth, 1856.

Sullivan, James. *The History of the District of Maine*. Boston: I. Thomas and E. T. Andrews, 1795.

Sweet, Frank W. *Legal History of the Color Line: The Rise and Triumph of the One-Drop Rule*. Palm Coast, FL: Backintyme, 2005.

356   BIBLIOGRAPHY

Sweetman, Will. *Mapping Hinduism: "Hinduism" and the Study of Indian Religions, 1600–1776*. Halle: Verlag der Franckeschen Stiftungen, 2003.

Sypher, F. J., ed. *Frederick L. Hoffman: His Life and Works*. Philadelphia: Xlibris, 2002.

Sypher, Wylie. "Hutcheson and the 'Classical' Theory of Slavery." *Journal of Negro History* 24, no. 3 (1939): 263–80.

Taguieff, Pierre-André. *La force du préjugé*. Paris: La Découverte, 1988.

Taguieff, Pierre-André. *The Force of Prejudice on Racism and Its Doubles*. Translated and edited by Hassan Melehy. Minneapolis: University of Minnesota Press, 2001.

Taylor, Paul C. "Appiah's Uncompleted Argument: Du Bois and the Reality of Race." *Social Theory and Practice* 26, no. 1 (Spring 2000): 103–28.

Taylor, Paul C. "W. E. B. Du Bois." *Philosophy Compass* 5, no. 11 (2010): 904–15.

Teller, Edward E. *Race in Another America: The Significance of Skin Color in Brazil*. Princeton, NJ: Princeton University Press, 2004.

Tennyson, Alfred. "In Memoriam." In *Poems of Tennyson*, edited by T. Herbert Warren, 316–403. Oxford: Oxford University Press, 1917.

Teslow, Tracy. *Constructing Race: The Science of Bodies and Cultures in American Anthropology*. Cambridge: Cambridge University Press, 2014.

Thierry, Augustin. *Dix ans d'études historiques*. Oeuvres, vol. 2. Paris: Hauman, 1839.

[Tindal, Matthew]. *Christianity as Old as the Creation: Or, The Gospel, A Republication of the Religion of Nature*. London, 1730.

Tindall, George B. "The Question of Race in the South Carolina Constitutional Convention of 1895." *Journal of Negro History* 37, no. 3 (July 1952): 277–303.

[Tobin, James]. "Anmerkungen über Ramsays Schrift von der Behandlung der Negersklaven in den Westindischen Zuckerinseln." In *Beiträge zur Völker und Länderkunde*, vol. 5, edited by Matthias C. Sprengel, 267–92. Leipzig: Weygand, 1786.

[Tobin, James]. *Cursory Remarks upon the Reverend Mr. Ramsay's Essay on the Treatment and Conversion of African Slaves in the Sugar Colonies*. London: G. and T. Wilkie, 1785.

Toland, John. *Letters to Serena*. London: Bernard Lintot, 1704.

Tonquédoc, Joseph de. *L'existence d'aprés Karl Jaspers*. Paris: Beauchesne, 1945.

Topinard, Paul. *L'anthropologie*. 2nd ed. Paris: Reinwald, 1877.

Topinard, Paul. *Anthropology*. Translated by Robert T. Bartley. London: Chapman and Hall, 1878.

Torrejoncillo, Francisco de. *Centinela contra Judios*. Barcelona: Joseph Girált, 1731.

Tryon, Thomas. *Friendly Advice to the Gentlemen-Planters of the East and West Indies*. London: Andrew Sowle, 1684.

Turnbull, Gordon. *An Apology for Negro Slavery: or the West-India Planters Vindicated from the Charge of Inhumanity*. London: J. Stevenson, 1786.

Twinam, Ann. "Racial Passing: Informal and Official 'Whiteness' in Colonial Spanish America." In *New World Orders: Violence, Sanction, and Authority in the Colonial Americas*, edited by John Smolenski and Thomas J. Humphrey, 249–72. Philadelphia: University of Pennsylvania Press, 2005.

Tylor, Edward Burnett. *Primitive Culture: Researches into the Development of Mythology, Philosophy, Religion, Art, and Custom*. 2 vols. London: John Murray, 1871.

UNESCO. *The Race Concept: Results of an Inquiry*. Paris: UNESCO, 1952.

UNESCO. "Statement of 1950." In *Race, Science, and Society*, edited by Leo Kuper, 343–47. New York: Columbia University Press, 1975.

BIBLIOGRAPHY 357

UNESCO. "Statement on the Nature of Race and Race Differences—June 1951." In *Race, Science and Society*, edited by Leo Kuper, 348–54. New York: Columbia University Press, 1975.

Unold, Johannes. *Die Ethnologischen und anthropogeographischen Anschauungen bei I. Kant und J. Reinh. Forster*. Leipzig: Dietz'sche Hofbuchdruckerei, 1886.

Van Amringe, William Frederick. *An Investigation of the Theories of the Natural History of Man, by Lawrence Prichard, and Others Founded upon Animal Analogies*. New York: Baker and Scribner, 1848.

Varouxakis, Georgios. "Empire, Race, Euro-centrism: John Stuart Mill and His Critics." In *Utilitarianism and Empire*, edited by Bart Schultz and Georgios Varouxakis, 137–54. Lanham, MD: Lexington, 2005.

Venturino, Diego. "A la politique comme à la guerre? A propos des cours de Michel Foucault au Collège de France." *Storia della Storiografia* 23 (1993):135–52.

Venturino, Diego. "Race et histoire: Le paradigme nobiliaire de la distinction sociale au début du XVIIIe siècle." In *L'idée de "race" dans les sciences humaines et la littérature (XVIIIe et XIXe siècles)*, edited by Sarga Moussa, 19–38. Paris: L'Harmattan, 2003.

Virchow, Rudolf. "Anthropology in the Last Twenty Years." In *Annual Report of the Board of Regents of the Smithsonian Institution, Showing the Operations, Expenditures, and Condition of the Institution to July, 1889*, 555–70. Washington, DC: Government Printing Office, 1890.

Virchow, Rudolf. "Rassenbildung und Erblichkeit." In *Festschrift für Adolf Bastian zu seinem 70. Geburstage*, 1–43. Berlin: D. Reimer, 1896.

Virchow, Rudolf. *Gesamtbericht über die von der deutschen anthropologischen Gesellschaft veranlassten Erhebungen über die Farbe der Haut, der Haare und der Augen der Schulkinder in Deutschland. Sämtliche Werke 3*, edited by Christian Andree, 275–475. Heidelberg: Georg Olms, 2009.

Virey, Julien-Joseph *Histoire naturelle du genre humaine*. Paris: Crochard, 1824.

Visweswaran, Kamala. "Race and the Culture of Anthropology." *American Anthropologist* 100, no. 1 (March 1998): 70–83.

Vitoria, Francisco de. "On the American Indians." In *Vitoria: Political Writings*, edited by Anthony Pagden and Jeremy Lawrance, 231–92. Cambridge: Cambridge University Press, 1991.

Vitoria, Francisco de. *Relectio de Indis; o, Libertad de los indios*. Edited by Luciano Pereña and J. M. Pérez-Prendes. Madrid: Consejo Superior de Investigaciones Científicas, 1967.

Voegelin, Eric. *The History of the Race Idea: From Ray to Carus*. Translated by Ruth Hein. Baton Rouge: Louisiana State University Press, 1998.

Voegelin, Eric. *Race and State*. Translated by Ruth Hein. Baton Rouge: Louisiana State University Press, 1997.

Voegelin, Eric. *Rasse und Staat*. Tübingen: J. C. B. Mohr, 1933.

Voltaire. *Essai sur les moeurs*. 2 vols. Paris: Garnier, 1963.

Voltaire. *The Philosophy of History*. New York: Philosophical Library, 1965.

Wade, Peter. *Race, Nature and Culture: An Anthropological Perspective*. London: Pluto, 2002.

Waitz, Theodor. *Anthropologie der Naturvölker*, vol. 1. Leipzig: Friedrich Fleischer, 1859.

Waitz, Theodor. *Introduction to Anthropology*. Translated and edited by J. Frederick Collingwood. London: Longman, Green, Longman, and Roberts, 1863.

358 BIBLIOGRAPHY

Wallace, Alfred Russel. "The Origin of Human Races and the Antiquity of Man Deduced from the Theory of 'Natural Selection.'" *Journal of the Anthropological Society of London* 2 (1864): clviii–clxxxvii.

Wallace, George. *A System of the Principles of the Law of Scotland*, vol. 1. Edinburgh: G. Hamilton and J. Balfour, 1760.

Ward, Julie K. "'The Master's Tools': Abolitionist Arguments of Equiano and Cugoano." In *Subjugation and Bondage: Critical Essays on Slavery and Social Philosophy*, edited by Tommy L. Lott, 79–98. Lanham, MD: Rowman and Litttlefield, 1998.

Warr, John. "The Corruption and Deficiency of the Laws of England Soberly Discovered." In *A Spark in the Ashes: The Pamphlets of John Warr*, edited by Stephen Sedley and Lawrence Kaplan, 89–110. London: Verso, 1992.

Watson, Ritchie Devon Jr. *Normans and Saxons: Southern Race Mythology and the Intellectual History of the American Civil War.* Baton Rouge: Louisiana State University Press, 2008.

Wayland, Francis. *The Limitations of Human Responsibility.* Boston: Gould, Kendall and Lincoln, 1838.

Weiner, Mark S. *Americans without Law: The Racial Boundaries of Citizenship.* New York: New York University Press, 2006.

Wells, Robert Gilbert. *Anthropology Applied to the American White Man and Negro.* Buxton, IA: Wells, 1905.

Wells, William Charles. "An Account of a Female of the White Race of Mankind, Part of Whose Skin Resembles That of a Negro." In William Charles Wells, *Two Essays: One upon Single Vision with Two Eyes; the Other on Dew*, 423–39. Edinburgh: Archibald Constable, 1818.

Wesley, John. *Political Writings of John Wesley.* Edited by Graham Maddox. Bristol: Thoemmes Press, 1998.

Wheeler, Roxann. "'Betrayed by Some of My Own Complexion': Cugoano, Abolition, and the Contemporary Language of Racialism." In *Genius in Bondage: Literature of the Early Black Atlantic*, edited by Vincent Carretta and Philip Gould, 17–38. Lexington: University Press of Kentucky, 2001.

Wheelock, Stefan M. *Barbaric Culture and Black Critique: Black Antislavery Writers, Religion, and the Slaveholding Atlantic.* Charlottesville: University of Virginia Press, 2016.

Whitman, James Q. *Hitler's American Model: The United States and the Making of Nazi Race Law.* Princeton, NJ: Princeton University Press, 2017.

Williams, Samuel C., ed. *Annotated Code of Tennessee.* Indianapolis, IN: Bobbs-Merrill, 1934.

Williams, Vernon J. Jr., *Rethinking Race: Franz Boas and His Contemporaries.* Lexington: University Press of Kentucky, 1966.

Wirth, Louis, and Herbert Goldhamer. "The Hybrid and the Problem of Miscegenation." In *Characteristics of the American Negro*, edited by Otto Klineberg, 250–369. New York: Harper and Brothers, 1944.

Wolff, Christian. "Discourse on the Practical Philosophy of the Chinese." In *Moral Enlightenment: Leibniz and Wolff on China*, edited by Julia Ching and Willard G. Oxtoby, 143–86. Nettetal: Styler, 1992.

Wolff, Christian. *Oratio de sinarum philosophia practica.* Edited by Michael Albrecht. Hamburg: Felix Meiner, 1985.

Wood, Ian. *The Modern Origins of the Early Middle Ages*. Oxford: Oxford University Press, 2013.

Woodard, Helena. *African-British Writings in the Eighteenth Century*. Westport, CT: Greenwood Press, 1999.

Wright, Richard. *White Man, Listen!* Boston: Doubleday, 1957.

Wright, W. W. "Amalgamation." *De Bow's Review* 29 (1860): 1–20.

Wyhe, John van. "Why There Was No 'Darwin's Bulldog': Thomas Henry Huxley's Famous Nickname." *The Linnean* 35, no. 1 (April 2019): 26–30.

Wyss-Giacosa, Paola von. *Religionsbilder der frühen Aufklärung: Bernard Picarts Tafeln für die "Cérémonies et Coutumes religieuses de tous les Peuples du Monde."* Wabern: Bebteli, 2006.

Yancy, George. *Black Bodies, White Gazes: The Continuing Significance of Race*. Lanham, MD: Rowman and Littlefield, 2008.

Yerushalmi, Yosef Hayim. *Assimilation and Racial Anti-Semitism: The Iberian and the German Models*. New York: Leo Baeck Institute, 1982.

Young, Robert J. C. *Colonial Desire: Hybridity in Theory, Culture and Race*. London: Routledge, 1995.

Young, Robert J. C. *White Mythologies: Writing History and the West*. 2nd ed. London: Routledge, 2004.

Zack, Naomi. *Race and Mixed Race*. Philadelphia: Temple University Press, 1993.

[Ziegenbalg, Bartholomaeus]. *An Account of the Religion, Manners, and Learning of the People of Malabar in the East-Indies*. Translated by Jenkin Philipps. London: W. Mears and J. Brown, 1717.

Ziegenbalg, Bartolomäus. "Genealogie der malabarischen Götter." In *Genealogie der malabarischen Götter. Edition der Originalfassung von 1713*, edited by Daniel Jeyaraj, 19–231. Halle: Franckesche Stiftungen, 2003.

Ziegenbalg, Bartholomaeus. "The Genealogy of the South Indian Deities." In *Genealogy of the South Indian Deities*, translated by Daniel Jeyaraj, 35–198. London: Routledge Curzon, 2005.

[Ziegenbalg, Bartholomäus]. *Thirty Four Conferences between the Danish Missionaries and the Malabarian Bramans (or Heathen Priests) in the East Indies*. Translated by Jenkin Philipps. London: H. Clements, 1719.

Ziervogel, C. *Brown South Africa*. Cape Town: Maskew Miller, [1938].

Index

For the benefit of digital users, indexed terms that span two pages (e.g., 52–53) may, on occasion, appear on only one of those pages.

Adams, Hannah, 42
Adelung, Johann Christoph, 211–12, 213
  *Versuch einer Geschichte der
    Cultur*, 211–12
Adler, Alfred, 178–79, 180–81
Agassiz, Louis, 60, 76, 77, 81–82, 95–96
Alcoff, Linda Martín, 25–26, 103–4
  "The Phenomenology of Racial
    Embodiment," 25–26
Algerian War of Independence, 254, 261
Allied Powers, 28, 206
amalgamation, 60–61, 68, 83–84, 98, 105–
  6, 157, 167, 169. *See also* interracial
  marriage; miscegenation; race
  mixing
American Committee for
  Democracy, 223–24
American Negro Academy, 14, 63–64,
  157, 158, 161, 163–68, 171–72,
  297n.24
Antilles, 181–82, 183–84, 188–89, 195–
  96, 259–60
anti-Semitism, 16–17, 26–28, 48–50, 72–
  73, 184, 189, 222–27, 230, 236, 248–
  49, 252, 254–55. *See also* Jews
Anzaldúa, Gloria, 284n.21
apartheid, 11–13, 16–17, 74–75, 87, 101–2,
  117, 206, 220, 225–26
Appiah, Kwame Anthony, 22–23, 157,
  165, 226–27
Arendt, Hannah, 28–29, 236, 242
  The Origins of Totalitarianism, 28–29,
    319–20n.84
Aristotle, 126–28, 210
  De generatione animalium, 69–70
Asian-Americans, 26
Asians, 28–29

assimilation, 39–40, 46–47, 62–63, 64,
  157, 158, 169–70, 174–75, 189, 194,
  215, 225
Azara, Félix von, 93

Bachman, John, 69, 77, 81–82
Bagehot, Walter, 64, 298n.51
Barbeyrac, Jean, 131
Barzun, Jacques, 234
Bateson, William, 75, 101
Bauer, Bruno, 63
Baxter, Richard, 47, 126
Beattie, James, 132–33
Beauvoir, Simone de, 26, 251–52
Becker, Oskar, 9, 30
Benedict, Ruth, 215, 230
  Race: Science and Politics, 227–28
  The Races of Mankind, 228, 236
Bergier, Nicolas-Sylvestre, 34–35
Bernard, Jean-Frédéric, on
    Catholicism, 42–43
  *Ceremonies and Religious
    Customs*, 42–43
Bernardin de Saint-Pierre, Jacques-Henri,
  124, 126–27
Bernier, François, 39–41, 44, 46, 53, 108
  "A new division of the earth," 46, 108
Bevölkerung (population), 92
Biko, Steve, 231–32
Bildungstrieb (formative drive), 55, 56–57
biopolitics, 10–11, 60, 84–86, 236, 246–50
biopower, 87–102, 236, 246, 247, 249–50
Birt, Robert, 26
Black consciousness, 187–88, 251, 252
Black Panther Party, 251
Blackburn, Robin, 123–24
Blake, Thomas, 33

362 INDEX

Blount, Charles, 36–37
Blumenbach, Johann Friedrich, 45, 55–57, 79, 105
    "On the Natural Variety of Mankind," 271n.18
Blyden, Edward William, 64–65, 164, 174–75
    Christianity, Islam and the Negro Race, 22
    "Study and Race," 163
Boas, Franz, 16–17, 86, 213–14, 220–34
    The Mind of Primitive Man, 222–23, 225
    "The Negro in America," 222–23
    "The Race Problem in Modern Society," 222–23
    "Race Problems in the United States," 222–23
    Science Condemns Racism, 223–24, 232–33
Bodin, Jean, 35–36, 126–27
Boers, 86
Bolivar, Simón, 60
Bonnet, Charles, 66
Boudin, Jean, 82
Boulainvilliers, Henri de, 91, 239, 242–46, 247, 248, 316n.25
    Essais sur la noblesse de France, 245–46
Broca, Paul, 60, 69, 82, 95–96, 143–45, 152–53, 293n.38
Brokesby, Francis, 53–54
    Some Proposal Towards Propagating the Gospel, 271n.12
Broughton, Thomas, 41–42
Brown v. Board of Education, 26–27
Browne, Peter A., 80–81
Browne, Thomas, 46
Buchez, Philippe, 96
Buddhism, 40–42
Buffon, Georges-Louis Leclerc de, 44–46, 54–55, 81, 82–83, 143–44
    Histoire naturelle, 44–46, 92–93, 271n.13

Cabell, James, 77, 78
Caldwell, Charles, 80–81, 82–83, 84
Capécia, Mayotte, 177–78
Carlyle, Thomas, 66–67

Carmichael, Gershom, 131–32
Carmichael, Stokely, *Black Power*, 16–17, 230–31
Cartwright, Samuel, 95
Césaire, Aimé, 14–15, 179–80, 185, 186–87, 189, 193–94, 198–99, 242, 252
    Cahier d'un retour au pays natal, 189
    Discourse on Colonialism, 189
    "And the Dogs Were Silent," 198
Chamberlain, Houston Stewart, 29–30, 61–62, 105–6, 147–48, 228
    Foundations of the Nineteenth Century, 61
    Immanuel Kant, 61
Charron, Pierre de, 36–37, 42–43, 126–27
Chinese Rites controversy, 35, 37–38
Cicero, 211
Clarkson, Thomas, 135–36
Clauss, Ludwig Ferdinand, 9, 23–25
Cohen, Hermann, 62–63
Cold War, 206
colonialism, 14–15, 16–18, 27, 49–50, 106, 183–84, 186–87, 189, 220, 225–26, 230, 232–33, 242, 251–61
coloured, use of term in South Africa, 106–7, 117
Committee for Effecting the Abolition of the Slave Trade and the Sons of Africa, 135–36
Comte, Auguste, 70, 146–47, 154–56, 294n.46
Condorcet, Nicolas de, 124
Confucianism, 37–38, 49–50
    Confucian school (*Schola Confuciana*), 40–41
Cook, Captain James, 55–56, 212–13
Cooper, Anna Julia, 21–22
Courtet de l'Isle, Victor, 59, 91, 93, 94
Cox, Ernest Sevier, 117, 286n.51
Cox, Oliver Cromwell, 16–17, 230
    Caste, Class, and Race, 230
Creole, 49–50, 145
critical philosophy of race, 1, 4–5, 7, 8–9, 14, 18, 21–30, 51, 63–64, 103–4, 157, 218–19, 257–58
critical race theory, 4–5, 21
cross-breed, meaning of term, 108–9

INDEX   363

Crummell, Alexander, 64–65, 163–68, 171, 174–75, 298n.42
  "The Destined Superiority of the Negro," 163
  "The Race-Problem in America," 167
Cugoano, Ottabah, 7–8, 13–14, 123–41
  Thoughts and Sentiments on the Evil of Slavery, 7–8, 125, 135–36, 139–41
cultural imposition, 14–15, 182–83, 188–90, 192–94, 195–97, 198–99, 201, 253, 254, 260–61
cultural racism, 14–15, 16–17, 218–19, 230
Cuvier, Georges, 56–57
  Discours sur les révolutions du globe, 56–57

d'Arboussier, Gabriel, 183–84, 259–60
d'Eichthal, Gustave, 61, 67–68, 93
Darwin, Charles, 10, 68, 69–74, 143, 148–52, 153, 173–74, 293n.43
  The Descent of Man, 69, 148–49
  The Origin of Species, 69, 70–71, 84–85, 143, 148–49, 150, 153–54
Darwinism, social, 64, 74–75, 101, 144, 150, 157, 162, 169–70, 171–75, 300n.98
Davenport, Charles, 86
De Bow, James, *The Industrial Resources, Statistics, etc. of the United States*, 97–98
De Bow's Review, 97–99
De Laet, Johannes, 40–41
de Vastey, Pompée Valentin, 230
Delany, Martin, 22
Derrida, Jacques, 210–11
dialectics, 8–9, 10, 256–60, 261
Dilke, Charles, 67–68
disalienation, 176, 177, 184–85, 191, 194, 201–2
Disraeli, Benjamin, 51, 62, 72, 220
Dodwell, Henry, 53–54
  An Epistolary Discourse, 271n.12
Doris, Glen, 125
Douglass, Frederick, 64, 70, 78, 80, 98, 157, 158, 166, 167, 169–70, 171, 174–75
  "The Claims of the Negro Ethnologically Considered," 22, 78
  "The Nation's Problem," 166

Du Bois, W. E. B., 14, 22–23, 63–65, 155, 157–75
  "The Concept of Race," 162
  "The Conservation of Races," 14, 22, 63–64, 70, 85, 97–98, 155, 157–60, 161–63, 164, 165–66, 167–68, 171–72, 174–75, 296–97n.6, 297n.24
  Dusk of Dawn, 158–59, 162, 173–74
  "The Future of the Negro Race in America," 171–72, 173
  The Health and Physique of the Negro American, 167
  The Philadelphia Negro, 167
  "The Souls of Black Folk," 26, 161–62, 169–70, 297n.24
Dufrenne, Mikel, 189–90
Dugdale, Robert, 85–86
Dühring, Eugen, 63
Dunn, L. C., 207–8
Dupont-White, Charles, 67–68

Edelmann, Johann Christian, 43
Edwards, William Frédéric, 59, 91, 93, 94
El Greco, 195
Engels, Friedrich, 256
environmentalism, 54, 65–69
Equiano, Olaudah, 135–36
Escobar del Corro, Juan, 49–50
Étiemble, René, 199–200
eugenics, 11–13, 29, 69–75, 84–86, 87, 89, 95, 98–99, 101–2, 173–74, 223–24, 248–49
existentialism, 65–69, 168–70, 251–61, 304n.1
Ey, Henri, 190

Fanon, Frantz, 9, 14–18, 103–4, 230–31, 234
  Black Skin, White Masks, 14–15, 22, 26, 176–85, 186–202, 251–53, 254, 257–58, 259–61
  lived experience and, 7–8, 14–15, 17–18, 26–27, 217, 251–61
  "The Lived Experience of the Black," 26, 179, 186–87, 189, 190, 195–96, 251–52, 253
  "Mental Alterations," 176–77

364 INDEX

Fanon, Frantz (*cont.*)
 "The Negro and Psychopathology," 176,
  186–87, 190, 253
 phenomenology and, 186–202
 psychopathology and, 14–15, 176–85
 "Racism and Culture," 254–55
 The Wretched of the Earth, 17–18, 27,
  176, 200, 251, 253, 254–56, 257–
  58, 259, 260–61
Feil, Ernst, *Religio*, 267n.20
Ferguson, Adam, 129, 133–34
 Institutes of Moral Philosophy, 133–34
Fichte, Johann Gottlieb, 242
Firmin, Anténor, 13–14, 70–71, 76,
  80, 142–56
 *The Equality of the Human
  aces*, 22, 70
Fischer, Eugen, 86, 100–1, 225–26
Forster, Georg, 7, 55–56, 98–99, 212–13
Foucault, Michel, 9, 10–11, 17, 28, 29, 60,
  87–90, 91–92, 94–95, 96, 97, 98–99,
  100–2, 235–50
 The Archaeology of Knowledge, 239
 The Birth of the Clinic, 238–39
 Discipline and Punish, 237–38,
  242–43
 The History of Sexuality, 88–89, 279–
  80n.2, 315n.7
 Madness and Civilization, 238–39
 "Nietzsche, Genealogy, History," 237–
  38, 240–42, 245–46, 247–49
 The Order of Things, 238–39, 315n.7
 "Society Must Be Defended," 17, 28, 88–
  89, 235–50
Fourteenth Amendment, 229–30
Frank, Johann Peter, 60, 91–92
Frankfurt school, 21
Freud, Anna, 177–78
Freud, Sigmund, 177–79, 180–83, 191–92
 *Five Lectures on Psycho-
  Analysis*, 181–82
Fries, Jakob, 62–63

Galton, Francis, 71–72, 74, 85–86, 100,
  173–74, 248–49
 *Inquiries into Human Faculty and Its
  Development*, 72
Garnet, Henry Highland, 22

genealogy, racism and, 4–5, 8–9, 10–11, 17,
  28–30, 35, 46–47, 75, 87–88, 112–13
 Foucault's and Nietzsche's, 235–50
genocide, 89, 206, 217, 220, 226–27,
  242, 248–49
Gentiles, 35–37, 40–41, 44, 49–50
Girtanner, Christoph, 56–57
Gisborne, Thomas, 134–35
Gliddon, George, 144
 The Types of Mankind, 60, 81
Gobineau, Arthur de, 13, 61, 83–84, 94–
  95, 98–99, 147–49, 161
 The Inequality of Human Races, 61, 97,
  105–6, 147–48
Godwyn, Morgan, 271n.11
Gooding-Williams, Robert, 296n.1
Gordon, Lewis, 26
Gossett, Thomas, 222
Grant, Madison, 222, 228
 The Conquest of a Continent, 228
Grégoire, Henri, 125
Gross, Ariela, 104–5
Grotius, Hugo, 90–91, 126, 129–32
 The Rights of War and Peace, 129
Guattari, Félix, 181
Guenebault, J. H., 77, 83–84
Guex, Germaine, 178
Gumplowicz, Ludwig, 95–96
Günther, Hans, 225

Haddon, Alfred C., 224–25
Haeckel, Ernst, 69–70, 148–49
 The History of Creation, 69–70
Hamilton, Charles V., 16–17, 230–31
Harper, Judge, 112–13
Haskins, Roswell, 84
Hayson, Walter B., 167
Hegel, G. W. F., 10, 57–58, 64–65, 146, 155,
  157, 162–63, 165–66, 174–75, 193–
  94, 210, 254, 257
 Philosophy of Right, 210
 Philosophy of World History, 155
Heidegger, Martin, 9, 28, 29, 30, 196–97,
  209, 242, 249–50
 Being and Time, 28
 "Overcoming Metaphysics," 29
 "The Question Concerning
  Technology," 29

INDEX 365

Hemings, Sally, 110–11
Herbert, Edward of Cherbury, 36
Herder, Johann Gottfried, 52, 64, 66, 157, 162–63, 165
  Ideas on the Philosophy of the History of Mankind, 164–65
Hesnard, Angelo, 182, 190
  L'univers morbide de la faute, 182
Hess, Moses, 62–63
Hindu, 36, 39, 40–42, 44, 54–55, 159–60
Hispanic, 93, 118
historicity, 189–90, 197
historico-political concept, 242–44, 246–50
historico-racial schema, 187–88, 189–90, 195–96
history, modalities of, 240–41, 242–43, 246, 247–49
Hobbes, Thomas, 126, 242–43
  Leviathan, 267n.20
Hoffman, Frederick, 63–64, 85, 97–98, 171–72, 173
  Race Traits and Tendencies of the American Negro, 63–64, 97–98, 171–72
Holocaust, 81–82, 86, 87, 242
Home, Henry (Lord Kames), 54, 56, 79, 143–44
  Sketches of the History of Man, 271n.14
Hottentots, 46, 86
Hume, David, 124, 132–33
  A Natural History of Religions, 36–37
Husserl, Edmund, 23, 25, 187–88, 209
  Ideas, 24
Hutcheson, Francis, 131–33
Huxley, Julian, *We Europeans*, 224–25
Huxley, Thomas Henry, 148–49
hybridity, 29–30, 284n.17
Hyppolite, Florvil, 144–45
Hyppolite, Jean, 237–38

Immigration Commission of the United States, 222
immigration, U.S., 82, 86, 105, 222–24, 286–87n.67
Indian, American. *See* Indigenous (Native) Americans
Indian, Asian, 39–40, 112–13

Indigenous (Native) Americans, 10–11, 44, 47–50, 53, 60, 62–63, 67–68, 77–79, 81–82, 84–86, 92, 97–98, 108–9, 114, 116, 118, 126–28, 130–31
infertility, mixed races and, 81–82, 83–84, 97
interracial marriage, 99–100, 109, 220–21. *See also* amalgamation; miscegenation; race mixing
intersectionality, 5, 21–22
Inzucht (in-breeding), 62
Islamophobia, 10

Jacquinot, Honoré, 60
Jahn, Friedrich Ludwig, *Deutsches Volksthum*, 58, 93–94
James, C. L. R., 137–38, 231–32
Janvier, Louis-Joseph, 142, 145
Japanese, 36–37, 42–43, 105
  Korematsu v. United States of America, 229–30
Jaspers, Karl, 189–90, 191–92, 193–94
  General Psychopathology, 190, 193–94
Jeanson, Francis, 176, 191
Jefferson, Thomas, 78, 89–90, 110–11, 112–13
Jews, 10–11, 27–28, 30, 33–34, 35–36, 41–43, 47–50, 53–54, 59, 60–63, 72–73, 81–82, 100–1, 118, 128–29, 182, 184, 221, 222, 223–27, 228–30, 241–42, 252. *See also* anti-Semitism
Jim Crow, 85–86, 158
Johnson, Charles, 26
Jung, Carl, 182–83

Kant, Immanuel, 7, 10, 13, 29–30, 34–35, 36, 39–40, 45–46, 51, 52, 53–56, 57–59, 60, 61–62, 64–66, 69, 75, 92–94, 100, 109–10, 111–12, 123, 124, 128–29, 143–44, 146, 164–65, 212–13, 225, 311n.41
  Critique of the Power of Judgment, 56–57, 69–70
  "Determination of the Concept of a Human Race," 271n.7
Kierkegaard, Søren, 254
King, Clarence, 105–6
King, Martin Luther Jr., 139–40

366 INDEX

Klemm, Gustav, 59
Kluckhohn, Clyde, 211–12
Knox, Robert, 51, 62, 79, 94–95, 220
  The Races of Men, 270n.2
Kroeber, A. L., 211–12
  Anthropology, 214–15

La Peyrère, Isaac de, 44, 53–54, 62–63
  Men before Adam, 271n.8
Lacan, Jacques, 178–79, 181–83, 190
Lamarck, Jean-Baptiste, 65–69, 225
Lamarckianism, 52, 65–69, 74, 105–6,
  212–13, 225
  Philosophie zoologique, 65–66
Las Casas, Bartolomé de, 38–39,
  127–28
Laughlin, Harry, 86, 222, 223–24
  Conquest by Immigration, 223–24
Lawrence, Stephen, 230–31
Leclerc, Jean, 129–30
Lee, Emily, 26
Lefebvre, Henri, 191–92, 258
  "Perspectives on Rural Sociology," 258
Lenz, Fritz, 23–24, 225–26
  *Menschliche Erblichkeitslehre und
    Rassenhygiene*, 225
Letourneau, Charles, 144
Levinas, Emmanuel, 30, 139–40
Lévi-Strauss, Claude, 206–7, 210–11
  *The Elementary Structures of
    Kinship*, 217
  "Race and Culture," 215–16, 217–18
  "Race and History," 215–16
  The Savage Mind, 217–18
  The View from Afar, 215–16, 217–18
  UNESCO and, 213–19
Lévy, Paul, 145
Ligon, Richard, 47, 130–31
Lincecum, Gideon, 85–86
lived experience, 5, 7–9, 14–15, 17–18,
  22, 25–27, 179, 186–90, 195–96, 201,
  209–10, 217, 218–19, 251–61
Locke, Alain, 13, 74, 90–91, 111–12, 123,
  126, 129–32, 138–39, 216–17
  "The Concept of Race as Applied to
    Social Culture," 216–17
  "The Fundamental Constitutions of
    Carolina," 47, 90–91, 130–31

Two Treatises of Government, 90–91,
  129–31, 138–39
Locke, John, "The Fundamental
  Constitutions of Carolina," 130–31
  Two Treatises of Government, 90–91,
    129–31, 138–39
Long, Edward, 44
Lott, Tommy L., 296n.1, 296–97n.6
Lowie, Robert H., 213–14, 215
  Culture and Ethnology, 213–14
  History of Ethnological Theory, 213–14
Lukács, Georg, 28

Macpherson, Sir William, 230–31
Magloire-Danton, Gérarde, 294–95n.64
Malcolm X, 139–40
Malouet, Pierre, colonialism and, 230
Malraux, André, 197
Man, Royal Anthropological Institute
  journal, 207–8
Mannoni, Octave, 192–93, 217
  Prospero and Caliban, 178–79
Maran, René, 178
Marcus, Joachim, 184
Markmann, Charles Lam, 177,
  304n.1, 321n.2
Marx, Karl, 58, 193–94, 257
Marxism, 256–57, 258
  The Eighteenth Brumaire, 194
Marxist poets, 63, 179–81, 252
McCord, Louisa S., 83–84
Meiners, Christoph, 128–29
Memmi, Albert, 27, 254
  The Colonizer and the Colonized, 254
Mendel, Gregor, 100, 113
Mendelian laws of inheritance, 11–13, 75,
  86, 99–100, 113, 114–15, 220
Mendelism, 75, 100–1
Menzel, Wolfgang, 59, 61
Merleau-Ponty, Maurice, 25–26, 187–
  88, 194–98, 201, 209
  Phenomenology of Perception, 194–
    95, 259
  The Structure of Behavior, 194–95, 201
mestizos, 99–100
Mexicans, 36–37, 106–7, 115, 118
Mexico, Treaty of Guadalupe
  Hidalgo, 115

INDEX 367

Mill, John Stuart, 66–68
"On Liberty," 67–68
"The Subjection of Women," 67–68
Miller, Kelly, 63–64, 171–72
"A Review of Hoffman," 300n.86
Mills, Charles, 9
Minkowski, Eugène, 190
miscegenation, 10–13, 16–17, 59–60, 69–75, 78–84, 94–95, 97, 113, 286n.57. *See also* amalgamation; interracial marriage; race mixing
missionaries, 35, 36–41, 46–47
Mitchell, John, 56, 78–79
Moirans, Epifanio de, 126, 133–34
monogenesis, 44–46, 52, 54, 56–58, 60, 76, 77, 80, 81, 82–83, 95–96, 143–45, 146
Montagu, Ashley, 86, 106, 206–8, 215, 216, 218, 224–25, 227–28, 230
Man's Most Dangerous Myth, 206–7, 218, 224–25, 226–27
Montaigne, 36–37
Montesquieu, Charles-Louis de Secondat, 44, 125, 132–33
Pensées, 132–33
The Spirit of the Laws, 44, 132–33
Morel, Bénédict A., 88–89, 96–97
Traité des dégénerescences, 88–89
Morgan, Henry, 84
Morton, Samuel George, 60, 76, 77, 80–83, 95–96, 105, 152
Crania Americana, 56–57, 105, 152
mulatto, 10–11, 47–48, 49–50, 83–84, 106–7, 109, 146, 167–68, 220–34. *See also* Nott, Josiah: "The Mulatto a Hybrid"
Murphy, Supreme Court Justice Frank, 229–30
Myrdal, Gunnar, 114–15, 227
An American Dilemma, 227

Nardal, Paulette, 26
National Negro Conference, 173–74
National Socialism, 16–17, 220–21, 222–23, 225–26. *See also* Nazi
nature-culture distinction, 65–66, 205–19
Naville, Pierre, 178–79
Nazi, 11–13, 16–17, 23–24, 28, 29–30, 72–73, 100–1, 106, 206, 221, 223, 224–25,

228, 229–30, 233–34, 249–50. *See also* National Socialism
negritude, 26, 142, 179–80, 186–252, 259–60
negrophobia, 184
Nietzsche, Friedrich, 17, 72–74, 190, 235–50
Beyond Good and Evil, 73–74, 241–42
Gay Science, 241–42
"On the Uses and Disadvantages of History," 240–41, 242–43
Twilight of the Idols, 73–74
Nott, Josiah, 10–13, 14, 60–61, 69, 76, 77, 81–85, 95–96, 97–99, 105, 113, 144, 171, 295n.68
"The Mulatto a Hybrid," 60, 81–82, 95, 113, 299n.81
The Types of Mankind, 60, 81–82, 95–96

Odier, Charles, 190
Oken, Lorenz, 51
one-drop rule, 75, 99–101, 113–14, 117
Outlaw, Lucius, 28, 296n.1, 296–97n.6
Ozawa, Takao, 105

Paley, William, 123–24, 133–35, 136, 140
Pan-Africanism, 142
Pascal, Blaise, 199–200, 210
Perez de Lara Toletani, Ildephonsi, 49–50
Peters, Carl, 68
phenomenology, 8–9, 17–18, 21–26, 28–29, 30, 103–4, 209–10, 218–19, 258, 259
Black Skin, White Masks and, 14–15, 186–202
Philcox, Richard, 177, 301n.3, 304n.1, 321n.5, 323n.52
philosophico-juridical discourses, 242–43, 248–49
philosophy of biology, 10
philosophy of history, 10, 51–52, 57–65, 94, 148, 157–75
Piattoli, Scipioni, 125
Picart, Bernard, 42–43
Ceremonies and Religious Customs illustrator, 42–43

368 INDEX

Pietists, 38–39
Plecker, Walter A., 99–100, 114, 117
Plessy v. Ferguson, 14, 157, 167
police violence, 2–4, 256–57
policing of race mixing, 10–11, 74, 87–102
Polizeiwissenschaft (police science), 4, 60 91–92
polygenesis, 13–14, 44, 45–46, 52–58, 60–61, 74–75, 76–77, 80, 81–85, 89–90, 95–96, 99–100, 105, 143–45, 146, 152
Pope Paul III, 126–27
Pope Pius XII, 37–38
Popper, Karl, 242
postracialism, 104–5
Pouchet, Georges, 60, 76, 144, 147
The Plurality of the Human Race, 69–70, 95–96
praxis, 17–18, 176, 200, 255, 256–59, 260–61
Prichard, James Cowles, 45, 56, 57, 59, 60–61, 80, 82–83, 93, 152–53
Researches into the Physical History of Mankind, 56
psychoanalysis, 180–85, 187–88, 201–2
psychopathology, 14–15, 176–85, 186–88, 190, 193–94, 251–52, 253
Puerto Rico, 116
Pufendorf, Samuel, 90–91, 126, 129–30, 131–32
Purchas, Samuel, 33–35
purity of blood statutes, 10–11, 46–47, 48–50, 62–63, 93–94, 117, 159–60

Quatrefages, Jean Louis Armand de, 143, 145–46, 149

race, mixed, 7, 10–11, 14, 29–30, 49–50, 60, 68–69, 72–73, 81–82, 94–95, 96, 97–98, 100–1, 106–7, 110, 159–60, 167–68
race mixing, 10–11, 52–75, 80–86, 87–102, 105–6, 107–8, 109–10, 114, 158, 166–75, 208–9, 220, 222–23, 241–42, 248. *See also* amalgamation; interracial marriage; miscegenation

racial essentialism, 10–11, 52, 66, 80, 84–85, 87, 101–2, 105, 212–13, 218–19, 252
racial hygiene, 89, 95, 173–74
racial identity, 11–13, 39, 99–100, 108–19, 152, 159–60, 161–62, 192–93
racial purity, 11–13, 29–30, 58–59, 60–61, 62, 64–65, 81–82, 85–86, 95–102, 109–10, 159–63, 167, 174–75, 220
racialization, 11–13, 25–26, 33–50, 62–63, 103–19
racism, anti-racist, 8–9, 16–17, 27
racism, institutional, 1, 2–4, 6–7, 230–31, 232–33
racism, meaning, 18, 205–6, 217–18, 225–26, 231–34
racism, medicalizing of, 10–13, 14, 60, 74–75, 87–102. *See also* biopower
racism, structural, 1, 2–4, 5–7, 10–11, 106, 206, 232–34, 253
racism, systemic, 1–9, 17–18, 87–88, 106–7, 206, 221, 230–32, 254–55, 256–58
Rayer, Pierre, 143
Reconstruction, 11–13, 167
Reich, Wilhelm, 237–38
Reichenbach, Count Oscar, 82
Renan, Ernest, 62–63
Rhodes Must Fall movement, 251
Ricci, Matteo, 37–38
Ricoeur, Paul, 189–90
Rolph, W. H., 73–74
Ross, Alexander, 41
Rousseau, Jean-Jacques, 210–11, 242–43
Discourse on the Origin of Inequality, 210–11
Royer, Clémence, 70, 148–51, 153–54

Sàam, Moses Bon, 137–38
Sadji, Abdoulaye, 177–78
"Nini," 177–78
Saint-Simonians, 59, 93
Saint-Ylié psychiatric hospital, 184–85
Sancho, Ignatius, 135–36
Sanson, André, 145
Sartre, Jean-Paul, 9, 14–15, 16–18, 22–23, 25, 26–27, 28, 103–4, 106–7, 139–40, 179–80, 183–84, 186–88, 189,

191–93, 195, 197–200, 209, 217–18,
230–31, 234, 251–61, 263n.1
Anti-Semite and Jew, 26–27, 184, 189,
252, 254, 255
Being and Nothingness, 25, 197, 198–99,
252, 253, 255, 260
"Black Orpheus," 26–27, 179–80, 183,
186–87, 200, 251–52, 259–60,
322n.30
"Colonialism Is a System," 254
Critique of Dialectical Reason, 16–17,
25, 189, 217–18, 230–31, 251, 254,
255–57, 258–59
Introduction to *Les Temps Modernes*,
199–200
"Itinerary of a Thought," 260
Search for a Method, 17–18, 191–92,
254, 256–57, 258, 259, 260–61
What Is Literature?, 199–200
Scheler, Max, 24–25
Schelling, Friedrich, 56–57
*First Outline of a System of the
Philosophy of Nature*, 56–57
Schiller, Francis, 292n.6
Schultze, Fritz, 69–70
Schutz, Alfred, 24–25, 26–27
Second World War II, 15–16, 22, 65–66,
106, 206, 208–9, 220–21, 224–25, 242
segregation, 2–3, 6–7, 10–11, 16–17, 51,
64, 68, 74–75, 87–88, 97–98, 101–2,
106, 110, 112, 114, 206, 220, 225–
26, 229–30
self-obliteration, racial, 14, 64, 157–58,
163–64, 169–70, 173
Semedo, Alvarez, *The History of That Great
and Renowned Monarchy of China*,
269n.69
Senghor, Léopold Sédar, 179–91, 252
Sepúlveda, Juan Ginés, 127–28
sexual repugnance between races, 78–
84, 98–99
Shaftesbury, Anthony, Earl of, 44
Sharp, Granville, 125, 135–36
The Law of Retribution, 137–38
Sheth, Falguni, 29
Sidgwick, Henry, 68
slavery, 5–8, 10–13, 28, 46–48, 50, 53,
56–57, 59, 61, 76–78, 79, 80, 83–84,

85, 88–91, 95, 97–98, 101–2, 105,
111–13, 118, 123–41, 144, 191, 195,
196–97, 206, 220, 228, 230, 232–33,
236, 245–46, 256–57, 263n.1
Smith, Samuel Stanhope, 56, 79–80
*An Essay on the Causes of the Variety of
Complexion*, 56
Société d'Anthropologie de Paris, 60, 70,
76, 82, 142, 143–46, 149, 150,
155–56
Société de Biologie, 143
Solórzano Pereira, Juan de, 49–50
South Africa, Group Areas Act of, 117
South Africa Population Registration Act
of 1950, 117
South African Institute of Race
Relations, 117
Spanish Inquisition, 49–50
Spencer, Herbert, 64, 68–69, 75, 84–86,
150, 153, 173, 298n.51
Essais sur le progrès, 152–53
"Personal Beauty," 68–69
Stalinist Russia, 249–50
Stein, Edith, 24–25
Steinberg, Stephen, 232
sterilization, forced, 75, 85–86, 87, 101–
2, 223–24
Stern, Günther [Anders], 196–99
Stoddard, Lothrop, 222
Stoler, Ann Laura, 104–5, 279–80n.2
Stroud, George, *Sketch of the Laws Relating
to Slavery*, 112–13

Taoism, 40–41
Taylor, Paul, 296n.1
Tennyson, Alfred, Lord, 165
Thévenot, Jean de, 146
Thierry, Amédie, 91
Thierry, Augustin, 91, 93, 246–47, 248
Tillman, George, 113
Tindal, Matthew, *Christianity as Old as the
Creation*, 38–39
Tobin, James, 128–29, 136
Toland, John, 43
Topinard, Paul, 144, 146
Tosquelles, François, 181, 190
Tryon, Thomas, 128–29
Tylor, Edward Burnett, 213–14

370 INDEX

UNESCO (United Nations Educational, Scientific and Cultural Organization), 16–17, 205–9, 230, 232, 234
  Lévi-Strauss and, Statements on Race of, 15–16, 22–23, 86, 106, 206–9, 213–19, 224–26, 227
UNESCO Courier, 226–27
United States Magazine and Democratic Review, 76
Unold, Johannes, 69–70

Van Amringe, W. F., 76
Virchow, Rudolf, 72, 158–59
  "Rassenbildung und Erblichkeit," 158–59
Virey, Julien-Joseph, 77, 83–84
  History of Mankind, 77
Virginia Act Concerning Servants and Slaves of 1705, 47–48
Virginia Act Declaring Who Shall Not Bear Office in This Country, 284n.27
Virginia Act Suppressing Outlying Slaves of 1691, 10–13

Virginia Act to Preserve Racial Integrity of 1924, 11–13, 99–100, 113, 117
Voegelin, Eric, 24
  The History of the Race Idea, 28
Voltaire, 54, 143–44

Waitz, Franz Theodor, 55–56
  Anthropologie der Naturvölker, 55–56
Wallace, Alfred Russel, 57, 71, 148–49
Warr, John, 243–44
Wayland, Francis, 137
Wells, Robert Gilbert, 169–70
Wells, William Charles, 78–79
Weltfish, Gene, *The Races of Mankind*, 228
White Negroes of Mississippi, 112
White privilege, 7–8, 232–33
White supremacy, 7, 182, 232
Whitman, James Q., 228
Wolff, Christian, 38–39
World War II. *See* Second World War
Wright, Richard, 26–27
Wright, W. W., 98–99

Ziegenbalg, Bartholomäus, 39